Pro Power BI Architecture

Development, Deployment, Sharing, and Security for Microsoft Power BI Solutions

Second Edition

Reza Rad

Apress®

Pro Power BI Architecture: Development, Deployment, Sharing, and Security for Microsoft Power BI Solutions

Reza Rad
Auckland, New Zealand

ISBN-13 (pbk): 978-1-4842-9537-3   ISBN-13 (electronic): 978-1-4842-9538-0
https://doi.org/10.1007/978-1-4842-9538-0

Managing Director, Apress Media LLC: Welmoed Spahr
Acquisitions Editor: Jonathan Gennick
Development Editor: Laura Berendson
Editorial Project Manager: Shaul Elson
Copy Editor: Kezia Endsley

Cover image by wal_172619 from Pixabay

Distributed to the book trade worldwide by Springer Science+Business Media New York, 1 New York Plaza, Suite 4600, New York, NY 10004-1562, USA. Phone 1-800-SPRINGER, fax (201) 348-4505, e-mail orders-ny@ springer-sbm.com, or visit www.springeronline.com. Apress Media, LLC is a California LLC and the sole member (owner) is Springer Science + Business Media Finance Inc (SSBM Finance Inc). SSBM Finance Inc is a **Delaware** corporation.

For information on translations, please e-mail booktranslations@springernature.com; for reprint, paperback, or audio rights, please e-mail bookpermissions@springernature.com.

Apress titles may be purchased in bulk for academic, corporate, or promotional use. eBook versions and licenses are also available for most titles. For more information, reference our Print and eBook Bulk Sales web page at at https://www.apress.com/bulk-sales.

Any source code or other supplementary material referenced by the author in this book is available to readers on GitHub via the book's product page, located at www.apress.com/. For more detailed information, please visit http://www.apress.com/source-code.

Printed on acid-free paper

To Leila

Who showed me how strong a human being can be

Table of Contents

About the Author

Reza Rad is a Microsoft regional director, a best-selling author, a Microsoft certified trainer, a consultant, and a noted international speaker featured at Microsoft Ignite, Microsoft Business Applications Summit, Data Insight Summit, and PASS Summit, among others. He has a BSc in computer engineering and more than 20 years of experience in data analysis, BI, databases, programming, and development, mostly related to Microsoft technologies. He has been a Microsoft Data Platform MVP for 13 years. A leader in his field, Reza leads the New Zealand Business Intelligence users group and is the co-founder and co-organizer of RADACAD, a training and consulting business focusing on Microsoft data analytics technologies, the Difinity conference in New Zealand, the Power BI Summit (the largest Power BI conference), and the Data Insight Summit (Chicago, USA). Reza has also been recognized as a Dynamic Communities Emerald award winner, a Power BI All-Star award winner, and a Microsoft Fast Track Recognized Solution Architect. Reza has also earned the MCP, MCSE, and MCITP for BI certifications.

An active blogger, Reza's articles on different aspects of technologies, especially on BI, can be found on his blog at radacad.com/blog. He was also an active member on online technical forums such as MSDN and Experts-Exchange, and was a moderator of MSDN SQL Server forums. Reza has written more than 12 books on BI, Power BI, and analytics, including the popular *Power BI: From Rookie to Rock Star* and *Power BI Pro Architecture,* both published by Apress.

When Reza is not doing data-related work, he enjoys playing fetch with his Akitas, Khersi and Lucy, rewatching the *Lord of the Rings* and *Star Wars,* strumming classical guitar, and working his way toward a helicopter flying license. You can connect with Reza on LinkedIn (www.linkedin.com/in/rezarad/), Twitter (twitter.com/Rad_Reza), and his blog (radacad.com/contact-us).

About the Technical Reviewers

Dr. Greg Low is a member of the Microsoft Regional Director program that Microsoft describes as "150 of the world's top technology visionaries chosen specifically for their proven cross-platform expertise, community leadership, and commitment to business results." He is the founder and principal consultant at SQL Down Under, a boutique data-related consultancy firm in Australia. Greg is a long-term data platform MVP, a well-known data community leader, and a public speaker at conferences worldwide. He is known for his pragmatic attitude to business transformation and to solving issues for businesses of all sizes.

Gilbert Quevauvilliers has been working in the data analytics space for the past 14 years, with experience in Azure and Power BI. Gilbert has also been recognized by Microsoft as a Microsoft MVP for the past six years. Gilbert works at FourMoo, consulting with clients to use their data as an asset. You can find Gilbert on Twitter @gilbertQue and at LinkedIn.

Eugene Meidinger works as an independent BI consultant and Pluralsight author, specializing in Power BI and the Azure Data Platform. He is a Microsoft MVP for the data platform. He has been working with data for over ten years and speaks regularly at user groups and conferences. He also helps run the GroupBy online conference.

Acknowledgments

Writing a book at this scale is a big project. There are many whom I want to thank for helping me complete this project. First, I want to thank my book's wonderful team of reviewers—Gilbert, Eugene, and Greg—for their wealth of expertise and knowledge of Power BI. They reviewed every chapter of this book, and they are the main reason for the high quality of the book's content. I must also thank Apress and my editor Shonmirin for helping with this project.

Big thanks go to the readers of my blog articles, my YouTube channel subscribers, and the students of my Power BI courses worldwide. They provided the most valuable feedback. They brought up discussion points so that I could challenge the solutions and develop new ways of doing things.

I'd also like to thank Microsoft's Power BI team for their outstanding work building a fantastic service and product, which is the core of this book. It is no wonder that Power BI has been at the forefront of all the analytical tools and services in the market these past few years: The team behind it is the greatest team I have seen building a Microsoft product.

Last but not least, I'd like to thank Leila for the lessons and the feedback, and for sharing her wealth of experience and support while I completed this project.

Introduction

Since 2018, when I wrote the first edition of this book, many features and significant updates have been added to the world of Power BI. Many of these features changed the architecture of Power BI solutions. To design the right architecture, you must understand all the features, services, tools, and components of Power BI and make informed decisions about using these components in the right situations.

The first edition, written in 2018, covered many aspects of architecture (which are still valid now), but this newer edition has many additions. When I was thinking about the second edition of this book, my initial thought was that it would require 50 percent new content, but in the end, I have to say about seventy percent of the content is new and updated from the first edition.

This book targets architects of Power BI solutions. This might be someone with the title of Power BI architect or data analytics architect, or a developer designing an architecture for a Power BI solution. Because architecture is the focus of this book, many features and components are explained throughout this book, but they are not discussed at a deep technical level. Architects must know what each component is, what it does, and how it works with other components, but they might not necessarily know how to implement them all. That is the job of development. Because of that, many aspects of Power BI development are not discussed in this book. This is not a book about creating a Power BI report or writing a DAX measure. However, this book includes chapters that explain best practices for some of these actions and many other important facts.

A good Power BI architecture leads to good Power BI adoption and an easy-to-maintain Power BI implementation that will last for years. Your entire organization can benefit from it.

This book is for Power BI developers, analysts, architects, and managers who want to look at the Power BI implementation holistically and consider all aspects. The book is split into parts for developing, deploying, and sharing Power BI solutions.

The development part of this book starts with looking at the different types of connections in the Power BI environment. It takes a detailed look at Import Data, DirectQuery, and Live Connection and explains the differences between these connection methods. It also expands the DirectQuery connection topic to include the Power BI datasets, composite mode, and the pros and cons of each.

The book then continues with a detailed look at dataflow, including its use cases, how it works with the shared dataset concept, and how the datamart plays a role in the architecture. This book explains the differences between dataflows, datasets, and datamarts, and how they work together to build a multi-layered Power BI architecture.

The book continues with aspects related to Power BI development, which are explained for specific cases such as paginated reports for printing or using Analyze in Excel and real-time streaming datasets for an IoT dashboard.

The development part wraps up with performance-tuning tips for big data projects, such as aggregations and incremental refresh, and includes general Power BI development best practices.

The deployment part of the book covers the Power BI service as the cloud-based hosting solution for Power BI and compares it with the Power BI Report Server, which is a fully-on-premises hosting option for Power BI. The role of the on-premises gateway is fully explained in this book. Some chapters explain the licensing of Power BI in detail.

The administration part of Power BI tenant, such as tenant settings and PowerShell cmdlets or REST API calls for admins, is explained throughout this book. Features such as the XMLA endpoint and its role in managing a Power BI solution are also discussed, with examples.

The book continues with a detailed look at all Power BI sharing methods. It starts from individual object sharing to the workspaces to sharing via Power BI apps. It also covers features such as Power BI Embedded, the embed code, and the differences between the Publish to Web option and options such as embedding in SharePoint Online. The book explains the differences between all these sharing methods and discusses their pros and cons.

The deployment part then continues with a look at how workspaces should be set up, how their roles and access levels need to be set, and the deployment pipeline needed to manage multiple environments. The book also covers some aspects of governance, such as content certification, and some aspects of security, such as row-level security.

I cover a lot of components in this book. Based on years of experience designing Power BI architecture, I find them all related to architecture design. The Power BI service and its features are a moving target when it comes to writing books. I encourage you to check out my blog at `radacad.com` for updates on new features added after this book's publish date. I hope you enjoy the book.

—Reza Rad

PART I

■ ■ ■

Getting Started

CHAPTER 1

■ ■ ■

Power BI Components

Power BI is more than just the Power BI Desktop. It is a combination of several components. Learning about these components and their roles is important before you go further. It is impossible to talk about architecture when you don't know about Power Query or Power BI. These components play an important role in the Power BI solution. This chapter covers the following components:

- Power BI
- The Power BI Desktop, a tool for report development
- Power Query, a tool for data transformation
- DAX and modeling, the analytical engine
- The Power BI Service, for hosting reports
- Power BI mobile apps
- The Power BI Report Server, an on-premises host for Power BI
- The Power BI Report Builder, for building paginated reports
- On-premises gateways
- Dataflows
- Datamarts
- Datasets
- Reports
- Paginated reports
- Dashboards
- Metrics and scorecards
- Deployment pipelines
- Workspaces
- Power BI apps
- Power BI Premium
- Power BI Embedded
- The Developer API

© Reza Rad 2023
R. Rad, *Pro Power BI Architecture*, https://doi.org/10.1007/978-1-4842-9538-0_1

What Is Power BI?

Power BI is a cloud-based technology from Microsoft for reporting and analyzing data. This reporting technology allows developers to create reports. Power BI is a simple, easy-to-use, and user-friendly environment for creating reports. It is based on several powerful components that help you create reports from complex scenarios.

Each component in Power BI is responsible for a specific part of the technology. There are components for building reports, connecting to data sources, performing analytics calculations, sharing reports, and so on. The following sections explain the applicable components. Other components are explained in detail in the future chapters of this book.

The Power BI Desktop

The Power BI Desktop is an important component of Power BI. This tool is the report development or report authoring editor for Power BI reports. It's free to download, install, and use. This tool is lightweight, about 450MB, and can be easily downloaded and installed. There is no configuration necessary when installing it. The Power BI Desktop supports installation only on Windows machines at the time of writing this chapter. There are some ways to install it on non-Windows machines—such as on Macs—using utility tools, but that topic is outside this chapter's scope.

Figure 1-1 shows the Power BI Desktop at the time of writing this chapter.

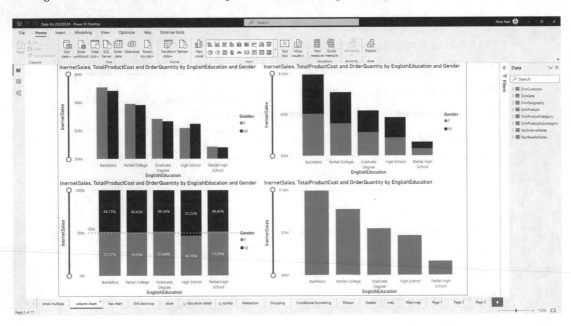

Figure 1-1. *The Power BI Desktop, a tool for authoring reports*

The Power BI Desktop is not a complex tool. Although most report development these days uses the Power BI Desktop, the Power BI team is currently enabling the Power BI Service's user interface to provide the same functionality. This means that without installing a tool and on any operating system, users will be able to build Power BI reports in the future.

Power Query for Data Transformation

A component of every reporting tool is connecting to data sources and preparing data (or data transformation). Power Query, also called Get Data and Transform, is used for that purpose. Power Query connects to different types of data sources, gets data from those sources, gives you the ability to apply transformations, and finally loads the data into your Power BI dataset.

Power Query comes in different shapes and sizes. It is not just available within the Power BI Desktop. You can even find it in Excel. This component is part of the Power BI Desktop. When you install the Power BI Desktop, Power Query (shown in Figure 1-2) is automatically installed. You can start working with it by choosing Get Data from Power BI.

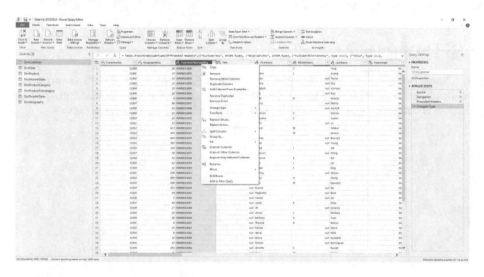

Figure 1-2. *Power Query, the data transformation engine*

There are many data sources you can access data from when using Power Query. You can even create connectors yourself.[1] Power Query has a window for development called the Power Query Editor. The Power Query Editor is where you apply all data transformations, and it prepares data to load into Power BI. This process usually happens before the data loads into Power BI.

Power Query uses a functional language called M,[2] as shown in Figure 1-3. M is the behind-the-scenes language for data transformation in Power BI.

---

[1] To learn more, visit radacad.com/power-bi-custom-connector-connect-to-any-data-sources-hello-world

[2] To learn more about M, visit radacad.com/basics-of-m-power-query-formula-language

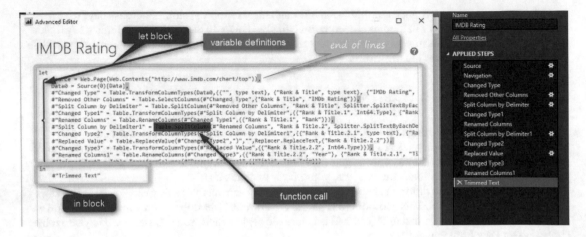

Figure 1-3. *The M scripting language for Power Query*

The Power BI Report

The Power BI Report (shown in Figure 1-4) is the visualization layout of Power BI. The Power BI Report is an interactive set of visualizations across multiple pages. This visualization allows the users to slice and dice the data. The Power BI Report is designed either in the Power BI Desktop or through the Power BI Service.

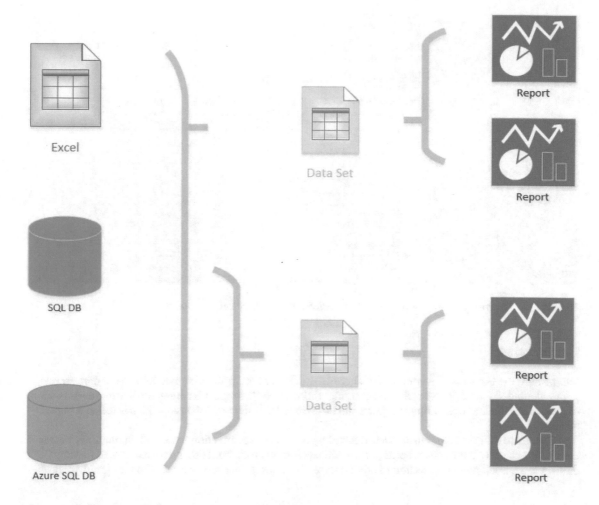

Figure 1-4. *The Power BI Report connected to Power BI datasets*

Analytical Engine (Tabular Engine)

This component is the analytical core and engine of the Power BI data model. The Tabular Engine installs as part of the Power BI Desktop, with no specific editor window. All modeling, calculations, and configurations are shown in the Power BI Desktop window. DAX and modeling are built into the Power BI Desktop in a way that most people consider a non-detachable part of the Power BI Desktop. However, the data model component of Power BI is a separate object, called a *dataset*.

The Power BI Analytical Engine is similar to the SQL Server Analysis Services Tabular or Azure Analysis Service, as shown in Figure 1-5. Depending on the Power BI license you use, there might be differences between those two services.

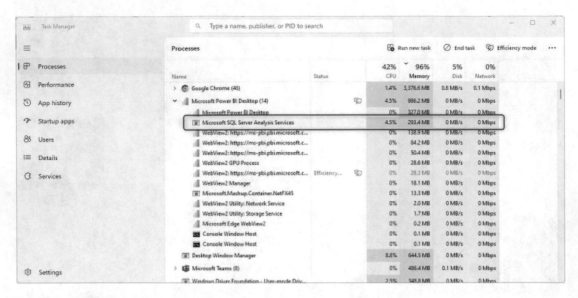

Figure 1-5. *The analytics engine of Power BI is called Analysis Services Tabular*

Datasets

A dataset in the Power BI environment is where all the data, relationships, connections to the data source, DAX calculations, and field- or table-level configurations live. The report is connected live to this dataset to produce visualizations. Multiple reports can be created from the same dataset, which is called a *shared dataset.*

There are different types of datasets depending on how the connection is created. Sometimes a dataset uses a DirectQuery connection. Sometimes, a dataset imports data from other data sources. Sometimes, a dataset is a DirectQuery connection to other datasets. A dataset can even be a real-time streaming dataset.

The Power BI Dashboard

Although the report is the core of visualization in the Power BI environment, the *dashboard* can sometimes be used to provide a holistic view across multiple reports. A dashboard in the Power BI environment is a visualization element that is not interactive (unlike the report). It provides a single view of multiple reports, as illustrated in Figure 1-6. It also comes with features such as data-driven alerts, real-time tiles, and auto-refresh.

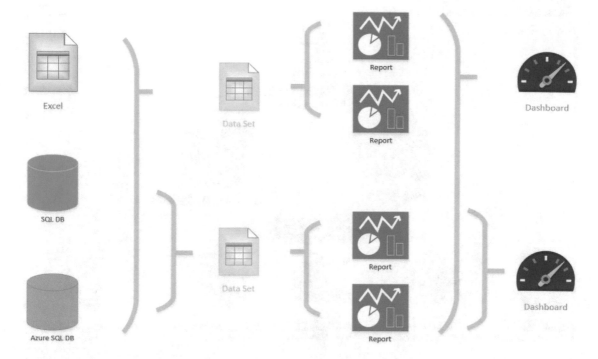

Figure 1-6. *The Power BI Dashboard can consolidate visualizations from multiple reports*

Dataflows

The data transformation layer of Power BI can be separated from the dataset so that it provides better storage capabilities. This enables multiple datasets to use the tables generated from Power Query. The component and engine that provide such a feature is called a *dataflow*. Dataflows exist in Power BI as service-only components. The data for the tables is stored in Azure Data Lake Storage, as shown in Figure 1-7 (other storage options will be available in the future, such as an Azure SQL database). Dataflows enable the Power BI developer to separate the data transformation layer of the Power BI implementation from the rest of the model and, as a result, have a reusable solution.

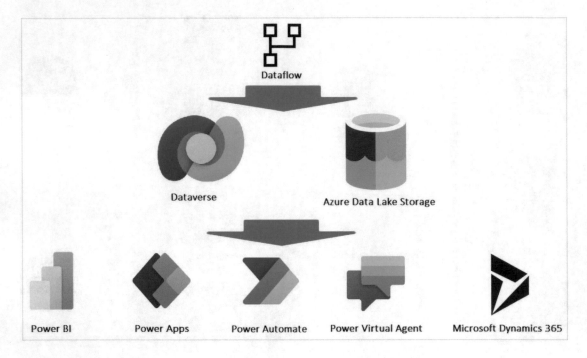

Figure 1-7. *Dataflow*

Datamarts

Datamarts simplify the creation of multiple Power BI components through one unified editor. Using a datamart, you can have the dataflow, a central repository of the data based on Azure SQL database, and the dataset through one object. Datamarts can be created through the Power BI Service. Datamarts are a recent addition to the Power BI components. Figure 1-8 shows what datamarts offer.

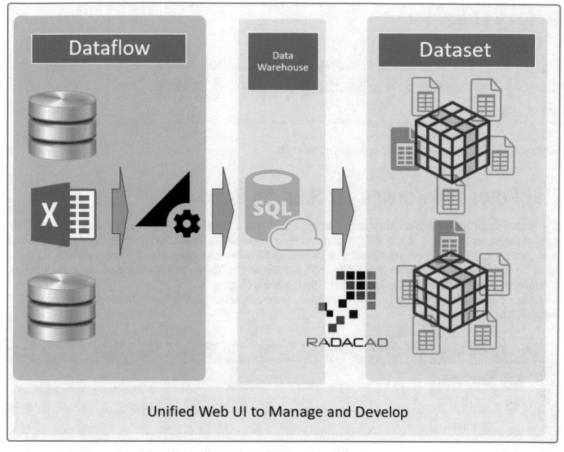

Power BI Datamart

Figure 1-8. *The Power BI datamart*

The DAX Language

DAX stands for Data Analysis Expression. It is a language you use to write calculations in Power BI. This language is very powerful and gives you analytical power over your model. DAX is not just part of Power BI. It is also part of Excel Power Pivot, SQL Server Analysis Services Tabular Model, and Azure Analysis Services. DAX has a steep and long learning curve. Some consider DAX the hardest part of learning about Power BI. However, the most important part of learning about Power BI is its data modeling services.

Figure 1-9 shows the process of writing a calculation in DAX. Don't worry if you don't understand what this DAX expression does at this time.

```
1 InernetSales YTD =
2 TOTALYTD(
3        SUM('FactInternetSales'[InernetSales]),
4        'DimDate'[FullDateAlternateKey].[Date]
5     )
```

Figure 1-9. *DAX is the analytical language in Power BI*

The Power BI Service for Hosting Reports

The Power BI Desktop, Power Query, and DAX are all components used to create and develop reports. After developing reports, you need to publish them and share them with others. The Power BI Service, previewed in Figure 1-10, is the online service hosted on the Power BI website for hosting and sharing reports. You must have a Power BI account to work with the Power BI Service. There are a few options when choosing an account; you learn about them in full detail in the licensing chapter.

After publishing your reports to the website, they are accessible via the Power BI Service (or website) through app.powerbi.com/.

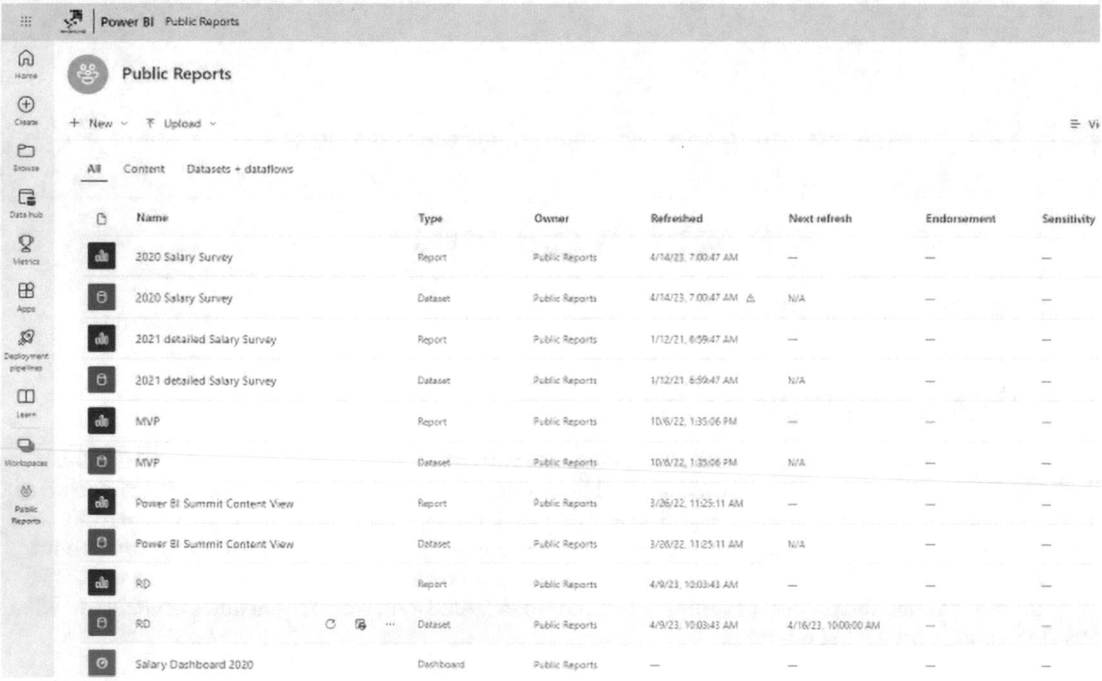

Figure 1-10. *The Power BI Service for hosting Power BI objects*

As shown in Figure 1-11, you can edit or author reports in the Power BI Service. However, not all the Power BI Desktop development functionality is available on the service.

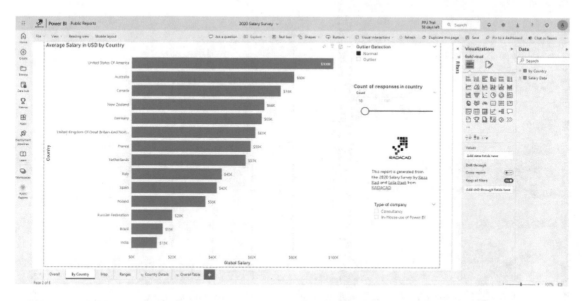

Figure 1-11. *Editing reports in the Power BI Service directly*

The Power BI Service can be accessed via different browsers if you use their recent versions. The Power BI Service works based on the HTML5 standard, which is supported in all new browsers—IE, Edge, Safari, Chrome, Firefox, and so on.

The Power BI Mobile App

Besides using browsers to connect to the Power BI Service and browse reports, there is another way to access reports interactively. The Power BI mobile app is available from the Microsoft Windows store, the Apple App Store, or the Google Play store. The app is free; you can easily download and install it. After logging in to the app, you can browse the Power BI reports from your mobile device. Mobile reports can be designed to be different from normal reports. Figure 1-12 shows a Power BI report opened on a mobile app.

Figure 1-12. *The Power BI mobile app*

Having the report on the mobile app gives you some specific features, such as annotation and sharing the annotation with others.

The Power BI Report Server

The Power BI Report Server is an on-premises hosting spot for Power BI. Many businesses still prefer to keep their solutions and data on-premises. Power BI is a cloud-based technology. However, it has a version that works on-premises. This edition of Power BI keeps the report, data, and everything on-premises. Power BI on-premises leverages a component called the Power BI Report Server.

The Power BI Report Server, shown in Figure 1-13, is a specific version of SQL Server Reporting Services developed for hosting Power BI reports. Reports are shared with other users through this environment. There are a lot of features in the Power BI Service that have not yet been implemented on the report server. However, this solution gives users an on-premises experience of Power BI reports. There is a chapter in this book that explains the Power BI Report Server in detail, where you learn about installing, configuring, and using it.

Figure 1-13. *The Power BI Report Server*

Paginated Reports

If you need to print your Power BI reports, it is better to design a different kind of report, called a Power BI Paginated Report (see Figure 1-14). Power BI Paginated Report has major differences from the normal Power BI Report; one of them is that the paginated report is not as interactive, as easy to use, or as easy to build as the Power BI Report. On the other hand, the paginated report can be designed for fine-printing details, whereas the normal Power BI report can't. Paginated reports cannot be developed by the Power BI Desktop. They have to be developed using a different tool, the Power BI Report Builder.

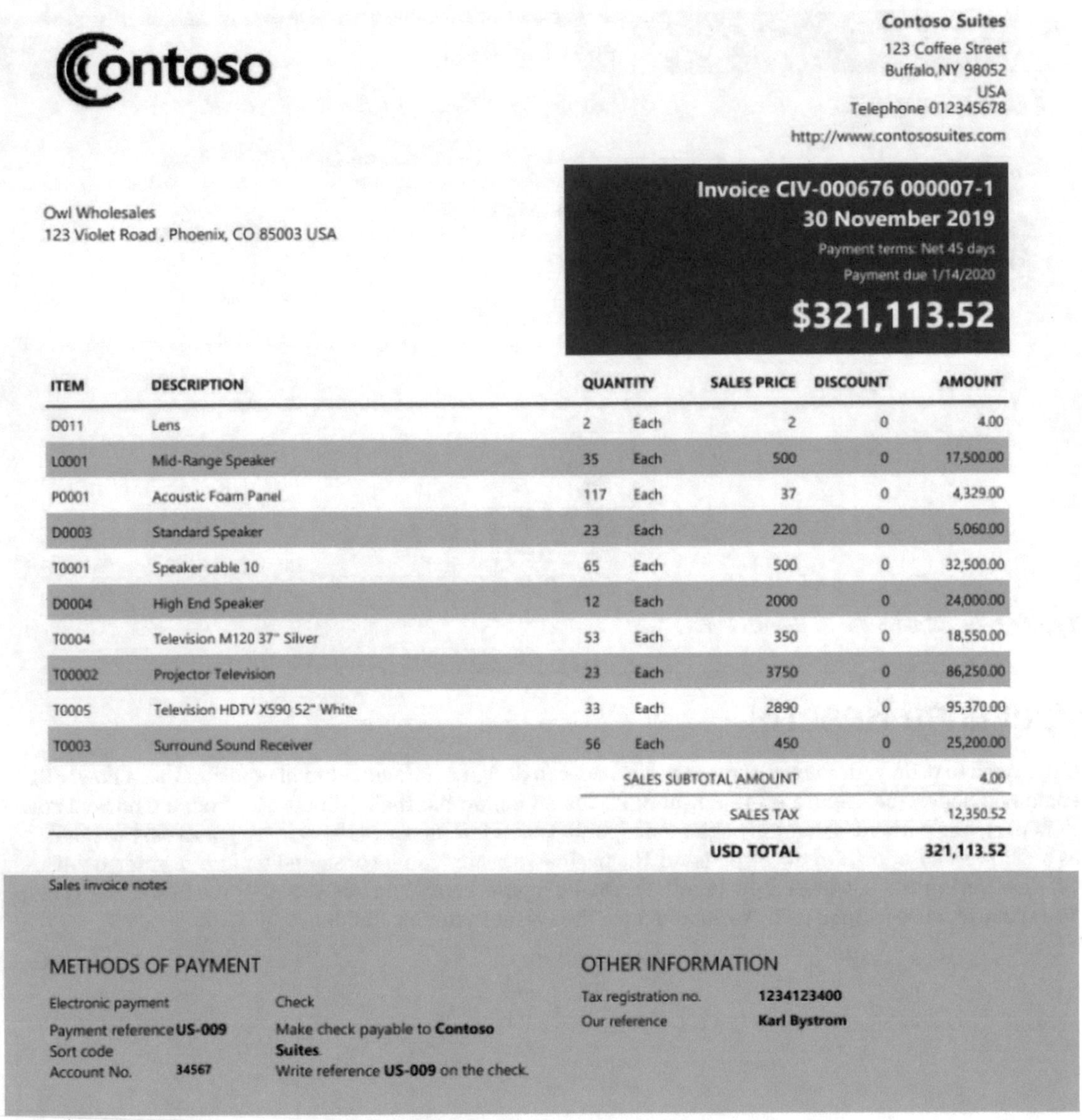

Contoso Suites
123 Coffee Street
Buffalo,NY 98052
USA
Telephone 012345678
http://www.contososuites.com

Owl Wholesales
123 Violet Road , Phoenix, CO 85003 USA

Invoice CIV-000676 000007-1
30 November 2019
Payment terms: Net 45 days
Payment due 1/14/2020
$321,113.52

ITEM	DESCRIPTION	QUANTITY		SALES PRICE	DISCOUNT	AMOUNT
D011	Lens	2	Each	2	0	4.00
L0001	Mid-Range Speaker	35	Each	500	0	17,500.00
P0001	Acoustic Foam Panel	117	Each	37	0	4,329.00
D0003	Standard Speaker	23	Each	220	0	5,060.00
T0001	Speaker cable 10	65	Each	500	0	32,500.00
D0004	High End Speaker	12	Each	2000	0	24,000.00
T0004	Television M120 37" Silver	53	Each	350	0	18,550.00
T00002	Projector Television	23	Each	3750	0	86,250.00
T0005	Television HDTV X590 52" White	33	Each	2890	0	95,370.00
T0003	Surround Sound Receiver	56	Each	450	0	25,200.00
				SALES SUBTOTAL AMOUNT		4.00
				SALES TAX		12,350.52
				USD TOTAL		321,113.52

Sales invoice notes

METHODS OF PAYMENT

Electronic payment
Payment reference US-009
Sort code
Account No. 34567

Check
Make check payable to Contoso Suites.
Write reference US-009 on the check.

OTHER INFORMATION

Tax registration no. 1234123400
Our reference Karl Bystrom

***Figure 1-14.** A Power BI Paginated Report for printing*

The Power BI Report Builder

The Power BI Report Builder, previewed in Figure 1-15, is the tool that creates paginated reports. This tool can be installed on a Windows machine. This tool was inherited from the SQL Server Reporting Services Report Builder. Power BI Paginated Reports are descendants of Reporting Services Reports and have an RDL extension.

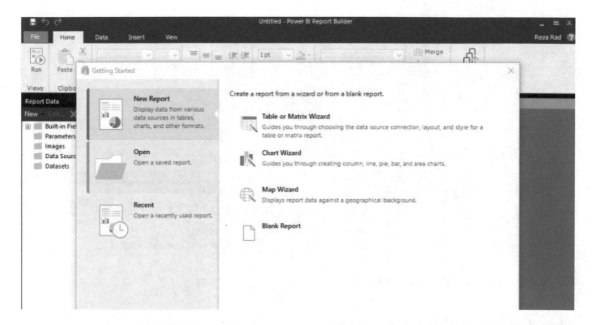

Figure 1-15. *The Power BI Report Builder*

Metrics and Scorecards

In every business, key performance indicators (KPIs) are measured often, and when compared to targets, you can tell if your business is on track or behind schedule. In the Power BI environment, the component used to create these KPIs is called *Metrics*. You can create Power BI Metrics with scorecards and get their values from a Power BI dataset. Rules and status identifiers can be defined on the scorecard to automatically track the KPI's current status, as demonstrated by Figure 1-16. Metrics and scorecards must be created in the Power BI Service, but they can be embedded into a Power BI Report using the Power BI Desktop. Power BI Metrics was previously called Power BI Goals.

Figure 1-16. *Power BI Metrics to track KPIs*

The On-Premises Gateway

The on-premises gateway is another component of Power BI used to create a connection between the Power BI Service (a cloud-based technology) and the on-premises data source. This component is installed on an on-premises server and manages the connection for the Power BI Reports. This gateway is unnecessary if the data source is cloud-based (such as an Azure SQL Database).

Gateway installation has some options and configurations that need careful consideration. A chapter later in this book explains the details of installing a gateway, configuring it, adding data sources to it, and scheduling datasets to be refreshed through a gateway connection.

Workspaces

In the Power BI Service, objects are placed inside *workspaces*. Workspaces can contain multiple Power BI objects (reports, paginated reports, dashboards, datasets, dataflows, datamarts, and so on). Workspaces are the core of deployment and sharing in the Power BI Service environment. The access level can be defined on the workspace itself. Users can consume the content of a workspace through Power BI Apps. Figure 1-17 offers a glimpse of a workspace landing page.

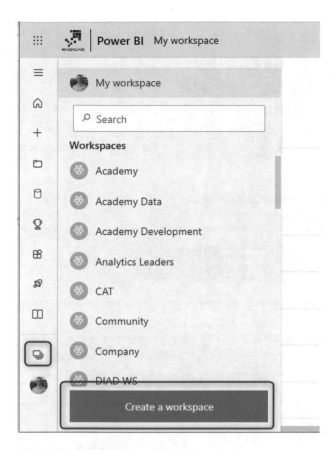

Figure 1-17. *Power BI workspaces*

Power BI App

Although the workspace's content can be shared directly with the users, creating a separate environment for the users is better. In the user environment, you can also have custom navigation to make it easier for the users to consume reports. Power BI has a component that offers these features, called *Power BI App*. Power BI App, depicted in Figure 1-18, differs from the Power BI mobile app. Power BI App shares content with the users.

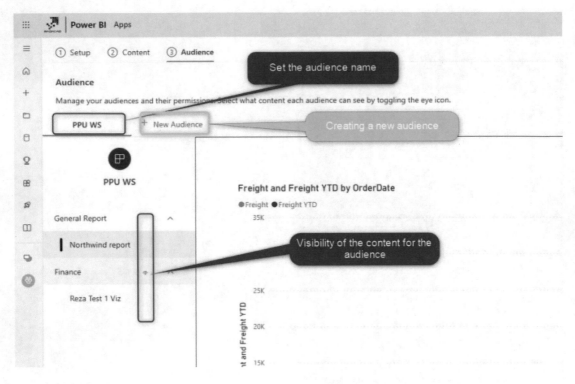

Figure 1-18. *Power BI App*

Power BI Premium

The Power BI licensing has a variety of options. The most comprehensive license for Power BI is called Power BI Premium. This license provides full functionality throughout all the components of Power BI. It also provides a dedicated capacity through the Power BI Service, which can be used to enhance the performance of reports and datasets. Power BI Premium comes in various nodes, each with different specifications for the dedicated capacity.

Power BI Embedded

If you need the Power BI Report to be embedded in a custom web application so the users of that custom application can use the Power BI Report, you can use Power BI Embedded. It allows you to embed Power BI reports inside a web application. Power BI Embedded works with a licensing plan. Web developers must embed the Power BI content inside the web application and manage the authentication and authorization processes.

Developer API or REST API

Power BI is not just a tool for report developers; it is also for application developers and programmers. There are few APIs in Power BI that developers can interact with. REST API is an API for .NET (C# or VB), and developers can use it through ASP.NET or mobile applications. This API lets you interact with the report in the Power BI Service. You can embed a report into an application (see Figure 1-19), refresh the dataset in the Power BI Service, change the gateway configuration, and more. You learn about the REST API of Power BI later in this book.

Figure 1-19. *Power BI Embedded*

There are also other SDKs that developers can work with, including an SDK for creating custom connectors in Visual Studio and another for creating custom visuals.

Summary

It is important to understand these Power BI components before developing solutions with Power BI. This chapter explained some of those concepts very briefly. There are still many terms that are not included here, and many of them are explained in future chapters. A Power BI architect, developer, and data analyst should be familiar with these components, so they can choose whether they need to use them.

CHAPTER 2

■ ■ ■

Tools and Preparation

This book discusses the features and components of Power BI. It is not a to-do book. However, there are examples throughout the book that you can follow if you have the tools you need. This chapter explains the tools you need to install and set up. The following topics are covered:

- Getting the Power BI Desktop

- Setting up multiple Power BI Service accounts

- Installing the Power BI mobile app

- Downloading dataset files

Using the Power BI Desktop

If you want to develop Power BI reports, you need the Power BI Desktop application. It comes in two ways—you can download it separately and install it on your Windows machine, or you can get it from Microsoft Store as an app. The question that I often get is, what is the difference and which one is better? This section addresses that question.

© Reza Rad 2023
R. Rad, *Pro Power BI Architecture*, https://doi.org/10.1007/978-1-4842-9538-0_2

The Power BI Desktop: Report Authoring Tool

The Power BI Desktop, previewed in Figure 2-1, is a tool that every Power BI developer needs to build Power BI reports. This tool is free.

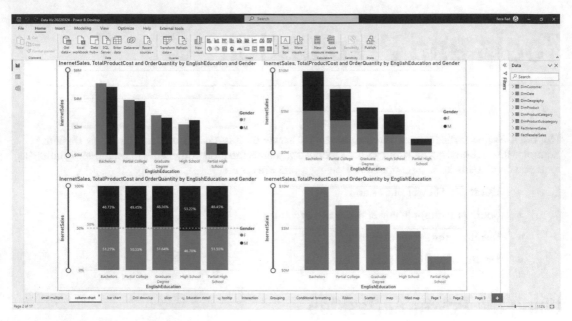

Figure 2-1. *Power BI in action*

When you open the Power BI Desktop the first time, a pop-up window asks you to log in, but that is not mandatory. You can use the Power BI Desktop without an account, a username, or login credentials.

The Power BI Desktop from the Microsoft Store

One of the ways to download the Power BI Desktop is to get it from the Microsoft Store. Again, that doesn't mean you need to pay for it. All you need is a Microsoft account (which can be live account) to access apps from the store. The Power BI Desktop app is free, as you can see in Figure 2-2.

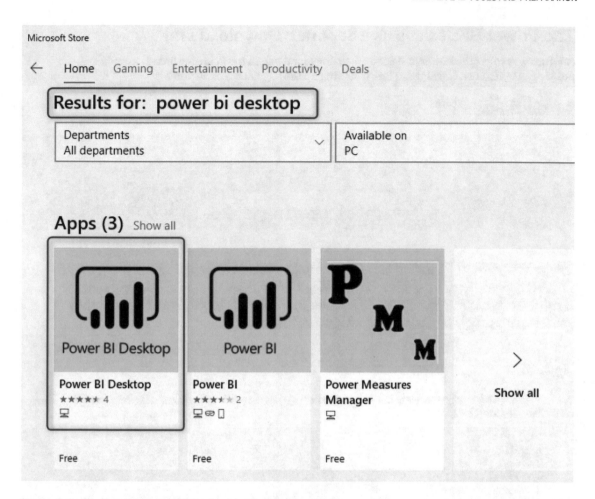

Figure 2-2. *Finding the Power BI Desktop in the app store*

The Power BI Desktop can be searched in the Microsoft Store and easily downloaded. You can use this option if you have the Windows operating system on your machine.

The Power BI Desktop as a Separate Download Link

Another way to get the Power BI Desktop is to download it from the following link: `aka.ms/pbiSingleInstaller`. Clicking this link will bring up the page shown in Figure 2-3.

Microsoft Power BI Desktop

Important! Selecting a language below will dynamically change the complete page content to that language.

Select Language: English   Download

Microsoft Power BI Desktop is built for the analyst. It combines state-of-the-art interactive visualizations, with industry-leading data query and modeling built-in. Create and publish your reports to Power BI. Power BI Desktop helps you empower others with timely critical insights, anytime, anywhere.

⊖ Details

Note: There are multiple files available for this download. Once you click on the "Download" button, you will be prompted to select the files you need.

Version:	Date Published:
2.116.622.0	4/11/2023
File Name:	**File Size:**
PBIDesktopSetup_x64.exe	463.7 MB
PBIDesktopSetup.exe	422.3 MB

Figure 2-3. *Downloading Power BI*

You can simply download the file and install it on your machine.

Auto-Update from the Microsoft Store App

Now that you are aware of the two methods to access Power BI Desktop, let's look at the differences. The first difference is that the Microsoft Store version of Power BI Desktop updates automatically. As soon as a new update is available from the Power BI Team, the application automatically updates itself to the latest version. You don't need to do anything to keep it up-to-date.

The Power BI Team updates the Power BI Desktop tool every month, and keeping that manually up to date is a big hassle. If you want to always be on the cutting edge of updates and enjoy the fascinating new features announced every month, consider getting the Power BI Desktop from the Microsoft Store.

Flexibility on Installation: The Download Link

One of the problems of the Microsoft Store version of Power BI Desktop is that it is not available for all versions of Windows. For some versions, you can only use the download link. Another scenario is that for some reason, someone might want to use an older version of Power BI Desktop for their report development work. Using the Microsoft Store app won't allow this, because it automatically updates the version. You have more flexibility on what you want to have installed and where using the download link.

Development Work

In terms of building the report, there is no difference between the two versions (if both versions are up to date). You can build the same report using either method. There is no difference in the Power BI file (*.PBIX file) that is created. You can use either version to open a file created with either of these, as long as they are both up to date. In the examples throughout this book, there aren't any differences between the two types of installs.

Setting Up Power BI Accounts

To go through the examples in this book, you may also need Power BI accounts. You need more than one account to test some of the functions, such as sharing and security. Power BI accounts can be free or Pro. The Free account does not support sharing (it should be part of paid subscription, which is Pro or Premium only).

To run the examples in this book, you can create a free account and apply for a trial Pro account. Trial Pro accounts last for 60 days and don't cost you anything. The process of creating a Power BI account is explained next.

Go to the Power BI website, `powerbi.microsoft.com`, and click Try Free, as shown in Figure 2-4. (Use this option if you don't already have a Power BI account. If you have an existing account, click Sign In.)

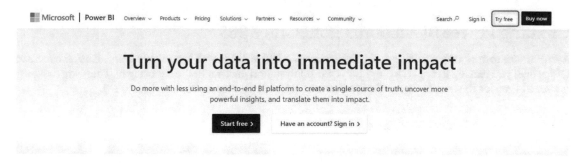

Figure 2-4. *Try Power BI for free*

In the next window, enter your email address, as shown in Figure 2-5.

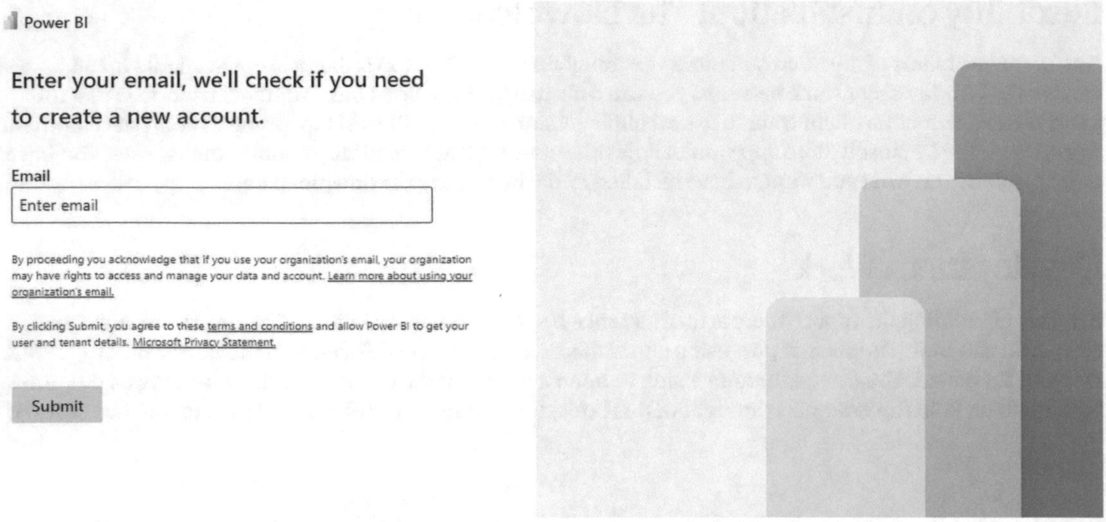

Figure 2-5. *Registering login information with Power BI*

The email used in this step should *not* be a public domain email address. You cannot use email domains such as Gmail, Yahoo, or Live. You can use your organization, company, or university account for this. After entering the email, click Sign Up.

After clicking Sign Up, you will receive an email from support@email.microsoftonline.com. Make sure that your company firewall doesn't block this email as a sender. This email will contain a verification code, which you need to enter in the next step.

After this step, you will get a message that your account has been set up correctly. You can then go to the Power BI service at `powerbi.microsoft.com` and log in.

Creating Power BI Accounts from Office 365

Another way to assign Power BI licensing is through the Office 365 Portal. If you have administrator access to Office 365, you can log in to `portal.office.com` and then find the user in the list of users. Then you assign Power BI Free for the user (or Power BI Pro if you want). This process is shown in Figure 2-6.

Figure 2-6. *Assigning Power BI licensing through the Office 365 Portal*

Is Your Account Pro, Free, or PPU?

One way to check your account designation—Pro, Free, or Premium Per User—is by using the Power BI Service and clicking the Profile icon, as shown in Figure 2-7.

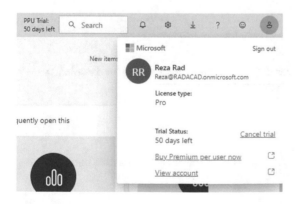

Figure 2-7. *Checking your account tier designation*

In the window, you can identify your account type—Free, Pro Trial, or Pro. If your account is free, you can choose to try Pro for free (the trial lasts 60 days) or upgrade it to Pro.

Installing Power BI Mobile App

Although you don't need Power BI Mobile App for this book, you may still want to install it. With Windows, Mac, and Android devices, you can simply search for the app and install it. After installing the app, you can log in using the same account you created in the previous step.

Power BI Report Server

You learn how to install the Power BI Report Server in a later chapter of this book.

On-Premises Gateway

You learn how to install an on-premises gateway in a later chapter of this book.

Microsoft SQL Server Database and Management Tools

To run through some of the examples in this book, you need to install Microsoft SQL Server and services such as SQL Server Analysis Services Tabular. However, they are only useful with a few chapters, such as the DirectQuery and Live Connection chapters. Explaining how to install SQL Server is outside this book's scope. I suggest that if you have it on your machine, use it; otherwise, skip that example.

The Power BI Helper

The last chapter of this book explains some of the useful features that you can use by installing Power BI Helper. Power BI Helper is a free tool that can be downloaded from `powerbihelper.org/` and installed through an installation wizard.

Downloading Dataset Files

All the sample files, including datasets and sample Power BI (`*.pbix`) files, are available for download at `https://github.com/Apress/pro-power-BI-architecture-2nd`.

Summary

This chapter explained the tools and setup you need to run some of the code examples in this book. In the next chapter, you learn about connection types in Power BI.

PART II

■ ■ ■

Development

CHAPTER 3

Import Data or Scheduled Refresh

Power BI supports more than one type of connection. Each connection type has its pros and cons. This chapter covers everything about the Import Data or Scheduled Refresh type of connection. You learn how Power BI stores data in the xVelocity in-memory engine, and the pros and cons of using this method.

The Connection Type Is Not the Data Source Type

The connection type doesn't refer to the data source type. Power BI supports more than 160 data source types. The connection type is the way that the data source reaches the connection. One data source can support multiple types of connections. For example, you can connect to a SQL Server database with Import Data or DirectQuery. It is the same data source, regardless of how to access it.

Every connection type has advantages and disadvantages. Some connection types are suitable for smaller datasets, others for bigger datasets, yet others provide better flexibility, and so on. You cannot change the connection type in the middle of your Power BI development cycle. You should decide on the connection type at the beginning of the process. Otherwise, you could end up with a lot of re-work.

This book covers the following connection types:

- – Import Data
- – DirectQuery
- – Live Connection
- – Composite Mode

Import Data or Scheduled Refresh

The Import Data connection type imports the entire dataset into memory. This is the memory of the machine that hosts the Power BI dataset. If you have a Power BI dataset opened on the Power BI Desktop, it will be the memory of the machine where Power BI Desktop is running. When you publish your Power BI file to the Power BI website, it will be the memory of that machine in the cloud.

Loading data into memory also means something more; data needs to be refreshed. You need to schedule data updates if you are using this method. Otherwise, the data will become obsolete. That is why this technique is called Import Data or Scheduled Refresh.

A Closer Look at Import Data

To take a closer look at import data, create a report with this type of connection. Open the Power BI Desktop and click Get Data. Select Excel, as shown in Figure 3-1.

© Reza Rad 2023

R. Rad, *Pro Power BI Architecture*, https://doi.org/10.1007/978-1-4842-9538-0_3

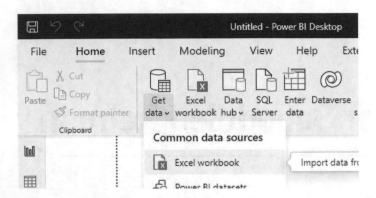

Figure 3-1. *Selecting Excel as the source for data import*

Get the data from the Excel workbook. Select the Excel file called `Pubs Descriptions.xlsx`, select all the tables from the list shown in the Navigator, and then click Load. See Figure 3-2.

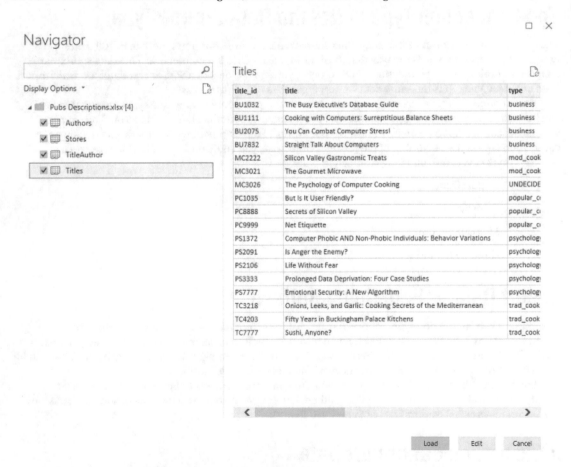

Figure 3-2. *The Navigator window*

Loading Data to the Model

You will see that Power BI loads the data into the model, as shown in Figure 3-3.

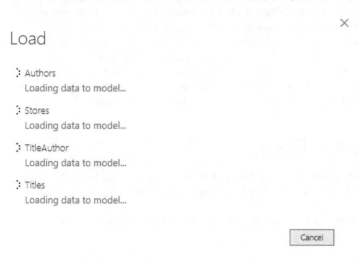

Figure 3-3. *Loading data to into the Power BI model*

As you probably guessed already, this is Import Data Connection Type. The Excel data source only supports the Import Data Connection type. If multiple connection types are supported, you can choose one when you connect to that source. For example, if you are connecting to SQL Server database, you will see, as in Figure 3-4, an option to choose Import Data.

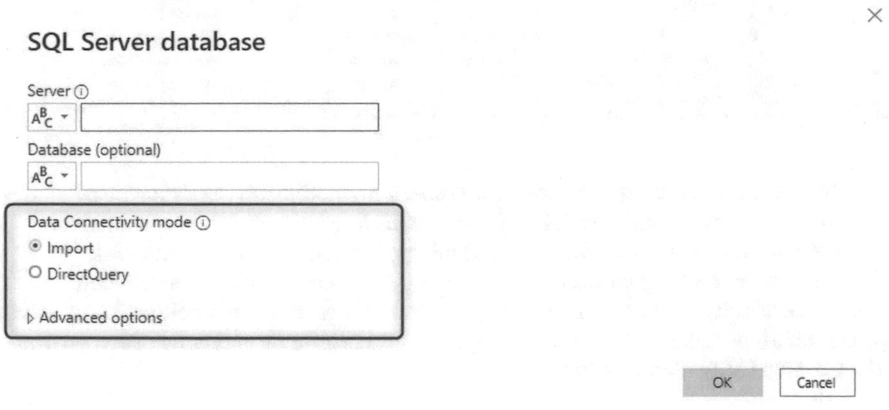

Figure 3-4. *Getting data from SQL Server database*

How Power BI Stores Data in Memory

The first question that might come to your mind is how big the memory needs to be. What if you have hundreds of millions of records? Or many gigabytes of data? How does Power BI store data in memory? To answer these questions, you need to first learn a little bit about the in-memory engine called *xVelocity*.

Power BI, SQL Server Analysis Services Tabular, and Power Pivot are three technologies that use the same engine for storing data—the in-memory engine called xVelocity. xVelocity stores data in memory. However, it applies a few compression steps to the data before storing it. The data stored in memory will not be the same size as your data source in the majority of the cases. Data is compressed significantly. However, the compression is not always at the same rate. Depending on many factors, it might behave differently.

How xVelocity Compresses Data

To really understand the concept of data compression in xVelocity, you would need to read an entire book. However, in this section, I'm going to briefly explain what happens when the xVelocity engine works on compressing the data.

Traditional database technologies stored data on disk because the dataset was too large. Consider Table 3-1.

Table 3-1. *Traditional Way of Storing Data*

4 bytes	4 bytes	4 bytes	8 bytes	3 bytes	16 bytes	16 bytes		Total each row: 100 bytes
Order ID	Quarter	Quantity	Sales Amount	Oder Date	uniqueidentifier	text	other columns	
1	1	5	43254	7/01/2017				
2	1	2	123423	8/01/2017				
3	1	67	234	9/01/2017				Number of rows: 100 Million
4	1	1	523	10/01/2017				
5	1	7	132	11/01/2017				Total space needed: 100M * 100bytes= 10GB
6	1	34	675	12/01/2017				
7	1	3	79678	13/01/2017				
8	2	8	90780	10/05/2017				
9	2	45	89	11/05/2017				
10	2	9	868	12/05/2017				

As you can see in Table 3-1, every column consumes some space depending on the data type of the column. The whole row ends up with 100 bytes. Then for 100 million rows in the table, you need ten gigabytes of space on the disk. That is why the traditional technologies stored their data on the disk.

xVelocity uses column-store technology combined with other performance-tuned compression algorithms. In simple words, xVelocity stores data column by column. It first sorts every column by its values. Then it creates a mapping table (see Table 3-2) for it with indexes at the beginning and end of each section (this is also run-length encoding [RLE] compression).

Table 3-2. *xVelocity Compression and Mapping Table*

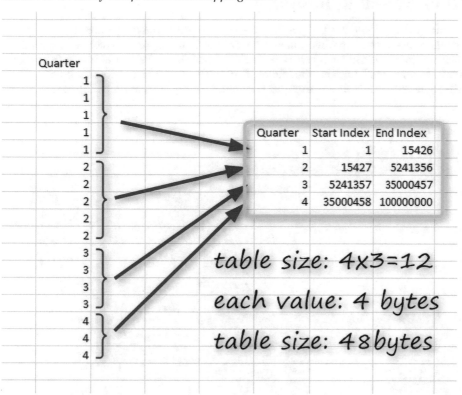

The whole point of this compression is that when you have a huge column, a lot of values are repetitive. For the Quarter column in Table 3-2, you can have only four unique values. So instead of storing that 100 million times, which takes about 400MB of space (4 bytes for every value, multiplied by 100 million rows), you can store unique values and their start and end indexes.

The mapping table shown in Table 3-2 image is a table of three columns and four rows mean 12 values. Even considering four bytes for each; this table would end up being 48 bytes. This is roughly how the compression engine works in xVelocity.

Compression has other levels as well, and it even compresses data more than this little bit. But this mapping table is the core of compression. The size of data is probably not the same as the data in your source database or file. You might have an Excel file that's 800MB, and when you load it into Power BI, your model becomes 8MB. The compression obviously depends on many things—cardinality of the data, number of unique values in each column, and so on.

■ **Important**   If you have a column with a lot of unique values, the compression engine of Power BI suffers, and Power BI memory consumption will be huge. Examples are ID of the fact tables (not ID of dimensions that used in the fact table as a foreign key), or some created or update DateTime columns that even sometimes have millisecond information.

Where Data Is Stored in Memory

Power BI models are always loaded into the Analysis Services engine. Even if you don't have Analysis Services installed, it will be in your system when you use Power BI with the Import Data connection type.

To check this feature, go to the Task Manager of the machine that has a Power BI Desktop with Import Data connection mode opened. You'll find that the Microsoft SQL Server Analysis Services engine is running, as shown in Figure 3-5. This is where your data is stored. Analysis Services keeps it in memory.

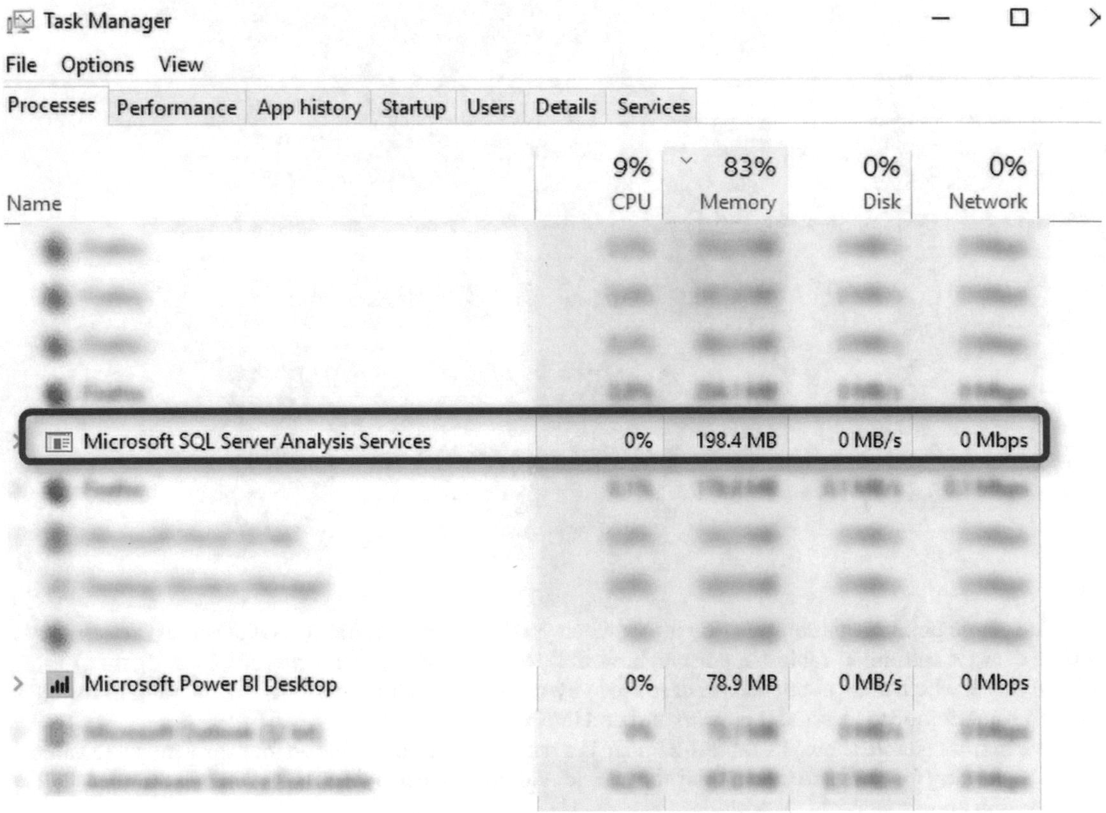

Figure 3-5. SQL Server Analysis Services stores the data into memory

When you save and close your Power BI file, that data will be persisted in a `*.pbix` file. The next time you open the file, data will be loaded again into Analysis Services' in-memory engine.

How About Power BI Service?

In the Power BI Service, you can also see how much memory every dataset consumes. Just click the Setting icon, and then choose Manage Personal Storage, as shown in Figure 3-6.

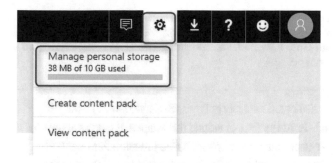

Figure 3-6. *Managing personal storage from the Power BI Service*

Figure 3-7 shows all the datasets and their sizes.

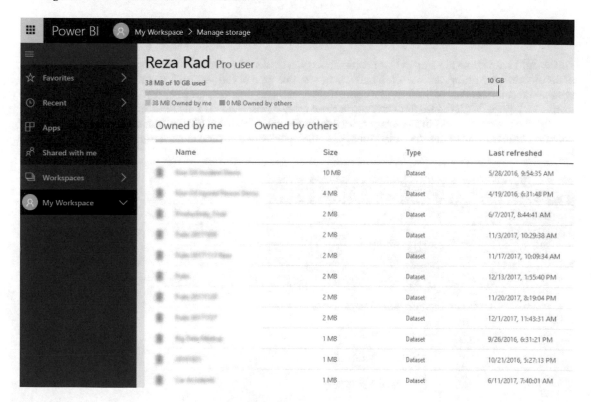

Figure 3-7. *Checking the dataset size in the Power BI Service*

Is There a Limitation on Size?

If you are developing Power BI files and then publishing them to the service, there is a limitation on the size of the files. Because the Power BI Service is a cloud-based shared hosting service for Power BI datasets, it needs to limit access so that everyone can use the service with a reasonable response time.

At the time of writing this chapter, the limit for Power BI's files is 1GB per model (or dataset in other words) if you use a Power BI Pro or Free account. You will have 10GB of space in your account, but every file cannot be more than 1GB. If you load your data into Power BI, and the file size ends up being more than 1GB, you need to think about another connection type.

■ **Important**   Power BI Premium licensing offers dedicated capacity in Power BI Service. With Power BI Premium, you can have much more extensive datasets. At the time of writing this chapter, the dataset max for Power BI Premium models is 400GB. There is a per-user option for premium called Premium Per User (PPU), which gives you the dataset size of 100GB. To learn more about the licensing options in Power BI, read the chapter related to that subject that appears later in this book.

Combining Data Sources; Power Query Unleashed

You should know how the Import Data connection type works. This section looks at scenarios that this type of connection is suitable for. One of the advantages of this type of connection is the ability to combine any type of data source. Part of the data can come from Excel, and another part from SQL Server database or from a web page. With the Import Data connection type, Power Query is fully functional.

To see how this works in an example, try this. In the same Power BI file that you used earlier (which contains data from the Pubs Descriptions.xlsx file), click Get Data and choose from Text/CSV, as shown in Figure 3-8.

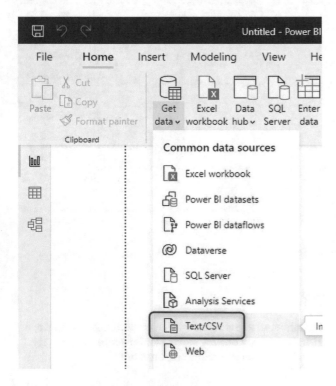

Figure 3-8. *Getting data from CSV*

Now select the Pubs Transactions.csv file and then click Load. Then click the Model tab. The Model tab is the bottom option on the left side panel. As shown in Figure 3-9, you will see that the tables from both data sources are connected to each other.

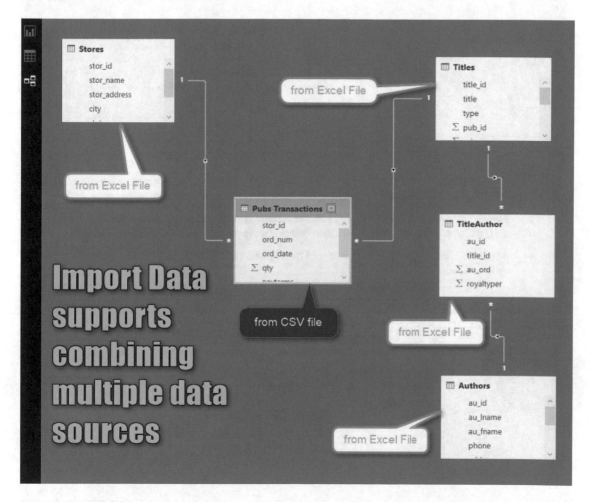

Figure 3-9. Model diagram; Import Data supports combining multiple data sources

One of the main benefits of Import Data is that you can bring in data from any data source and combine it with other sources. You can also leverage a fully functional Power Query with this connection type. You can do many data transformations and calculations with Power Query.

To see the Power Query transformations, click Transform Data, as shown in Figure 3-10.

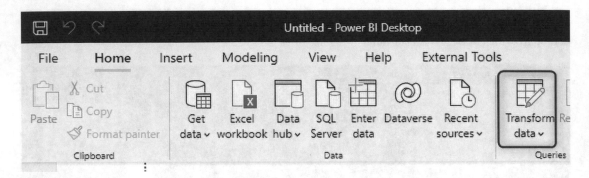

Figure 3-10. *Transforming data*

You can then see the Power Query Editor (see Figure 3-11) with many built-in transformations. To learn more about Power Query, I recommend checking out these two books that I wrote on this subject:

- *Getting started with Power Query in Power BI and Excel* (RADACAD, 2021); `www.amazon.com/Getting-started-Power-Query-Excel-ebook/dp/B09DSPNZJH`

- *Mastering Power Query in Power BI and Excel* (RADACAD, 2021); `www.amazon.com/gp/product/B09DTLC4S2`

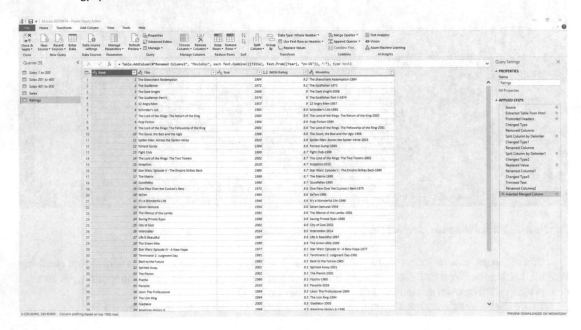

Figure 3-11. *Power Query Editor*

DAX: A Powerful Analytical Expression Language

Another powerful feature of Power BI that you have access to when using Import Data is DAX. DAX is the language that you can leverage to do analytical calculations. Calculations such as year to date, a rolling average of 12 months, and many others become super-efficient in DAX. DAX is supported by all xVelocity technologies of Microsoft (Power BI, Power Pivot, and SQL Server Analysis Services Tabular).

You can write DAX calculations in Import Data mode, such as quantity year to date, as shown in Figure 3-12.

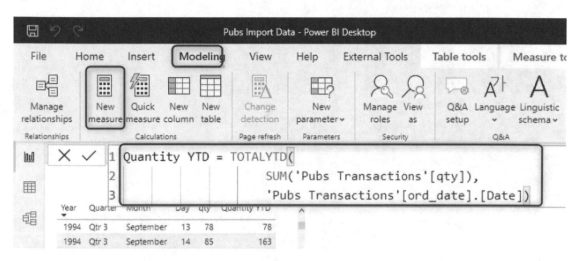

Figure 3-12. *DAX calculation for year-to-date quantity*

This calculation is defined in DAX with the following code:

```
Quantity YTD = TOTALYTD(
                SUM('Pubs Transactions'[qty]),
                'Pubs Transactions'[ord_date].[Date])
```

The result of that code calculates the year-to-date value of the quantity, as shown in Figure 3-13.

Year	Quarter	Month	Day	qty	Quantity YTD
1994	Qtr 3	September	13	78	78
1994	Qtr 3	September	14	85	163
1994	Qtr 3	September	15		163
1994	Qtr 3	September	16		163
1994	Qtr 3	September	17		163
1994	Qtr 3	September	18		163
1994	Qtr 3	September	19		163
1994	Qtr 3	September	20		163
1994	Qtr 3	September	21		163
1994	Qtr 3	September	22		163
1994	Qtr 3	September	23		163
1994	Qtr 3	September	24		163
1994	Qtr 3	September	25		163
1994	Qtr 3	September	26		163
1994	Qtr 3	September	27		163
1994	Qtr 3	September	28		163
1994	Qtr 3	September	29		163
Total				493	163

Figure 3-13. *Year-to-date calculation visualized in a table*

DAX is another powerful component of Power BI. It's fully functional in Import Data. DAX is a whole language to learn. I recommend reading *Power BI DAX Simplified* (Rad, 2021); `www.amazon.com/gp/product/B099SBN1XP`, which includes many DAX examples.

Publishing a Report

Publishing a report is the same regardless of the connection you use. You simply click Publish on the Home tab to publish the report to your workspace.

Gateway Configuration

For Import Data connection types that use on-premises data sources, you need to have a gateway. If your data sources are all cloud-based (such as Azure SQL database), you don't need a gateway.

Because you can easily combine multiple data sources with the Import Data connection type, it is very likely that your Power BI file will have more than one data source in it. You first need to check all the data sources in your Power BI Desktop and define them all under the gateway.

To find data sources in your Power BI Desktop, click the Home tab, and under Transform Data, select Data Source Settings, as shown in Figure 3-14.

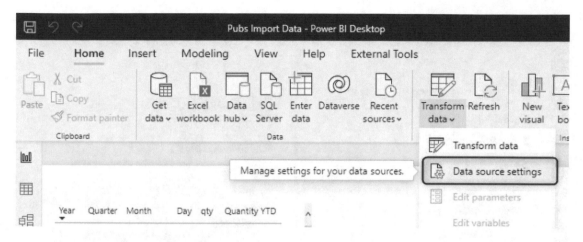

Figure 3-14. *Data source settings*

Figure 3-15 shows where you will find all the data sources.

Data source settings

Manage settings for data sources that you have connected to using Power BI Desktop.

⦿ Data sources in current file   ○ Global permissions

```
Search data source settings
```

🗋 c:\users\rezarad\dropbox (rada...05\code\pubs descriptions.xlsx

🗋 c:\users\rezarad\dropbox (rada... 05\code\pubs transactions.csv

Figure 3-15. *All the data sources in the current file*

In a later chapter, I explain how to add data sources to the gateway. You need to make sure that all data sources in the *.pbix file are defined under the same gateway, as shown in Figure 3-16. Otherwise, you won't be able to use that gateway for the dataset. To learn how to install a gateway or add data sources to it, read the gateway chapter in this book.

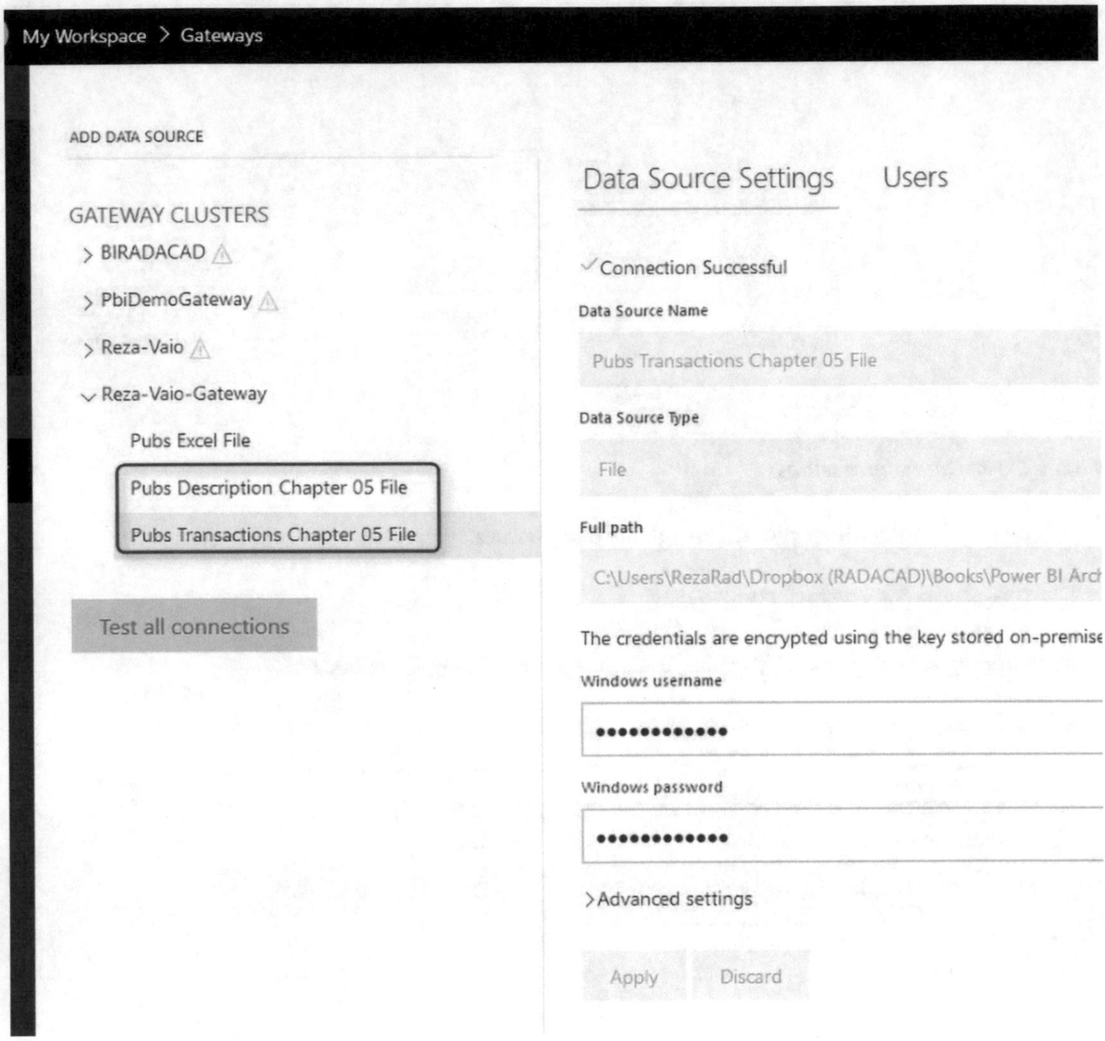

Figure 3-16. *Adding all the data sources under the gateway*

Scheduled Refresh

After adding all the sources, you can connect this gateway to the dataset within the Scheduled Refresh configuration of the dataset, as shown in Figure 3-17.

Figure 3-17. *Scheduled Refresh of the Power BI dataset in the Power BI Service*

After connecting the gateway, you can set a scheduled refresh. As shown in Figure 3-18, a refresh can be scheduled weekly or daily, with a maximum number of refreshes of eight times a day (with Power BI Premium, you can refresh it up to 48 times a day).

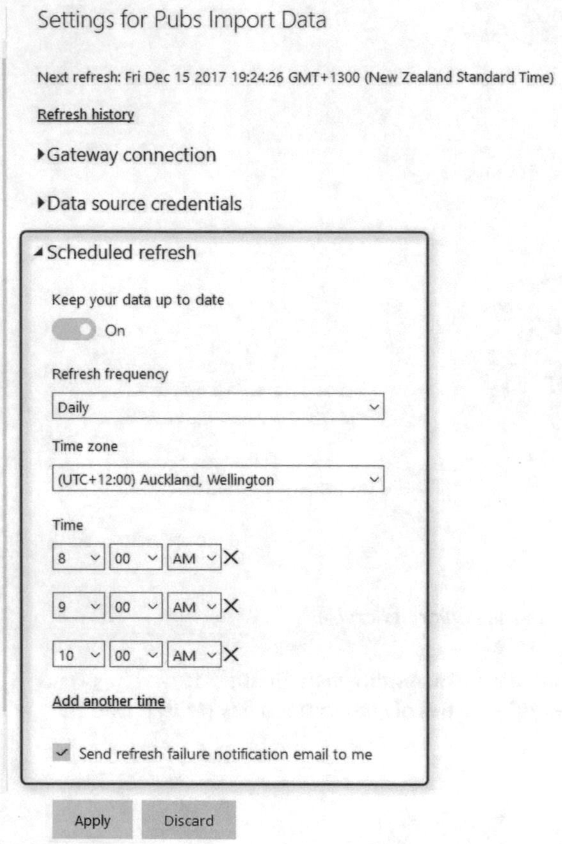

Settings for Pubs Import Data

Next refresh: Fri Dec 15 2017 19:24:26 GMT+1300 (New Zealand Standard Time)

Refresh history

▶ Gateway connection

▶ Data source credentials

▲ Scheduled refresh

Keep your data up to date

On

Refresh frequency

Daily

Time zone

(UTC+12:00) Auckland, Wellington

Time

8   00   AM   ✕

9   00   AM   ✕

10   00   AM   ✕

Add another time

☑ Send refresh failure notification email to me

Apply   Discard

Figure 3-18. *Scheduling a refresh configuration*

After setting up the Scheduled Refresh, you can see the next refresh and the last refresh time in the dataset properties, as shown in Figure 3-19.

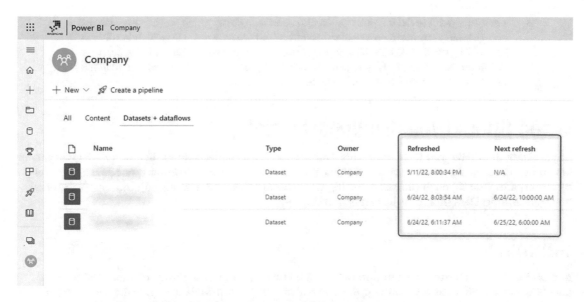

Figure 3-19. *Checking times for the next and the last refresh of Power BI datasets*

Advantages and Disadvantages of Import Data

Let's wrap things up and look at the pros and cons of Import Data are, as well as the scenarios in which this connection type is useful. This section is a wrap-up of what is explained above, just a quick review of those;

Advantages of Import Data

- **Speed: In-Memory Engine:** An advantage of the Import Data connection type is its super-fast response time. Remember that this is an in-memory technology, so querying data from memory is much faster than querying from disk. This method of connection is the fastest method of connection in Power BI.

- **Flexibility: DAX and Power Query:** With this method, Power Query and DAX are fully functional. Power Query and DAX are two dominant components of Power BI. In fact, without these two elements, Power BI is just a visualization tool. The existence of Power Query and DAX make it an extraordinary tool that can cover all analytics requirements. When you use Power BI with other types of connections, these two components aren't fully functional. Import Data gives you the flexibility to do data manipulation with Power Query and perform analytical calculations with DAX.

Disadvantages of Import Data

- **The requirement to schedule a data refresh:** In many BI scenarios, data will be refreshed overnight or on a scheduled basis. However, sometimes you need the data to be updated without delay. Import Data is not capable of doing that. With Import Data, the dataset must be refreshed and it can be scheduled to refresh up to eight times a day (or 48 times a day with Power BI Premium).

- **Very-large-scale data:** If your dataset is massive, let's say petabytes of data, and the compression engine of Power BI cannot fit it into the allowed size (which is 1GB per model for pro, and 400GB per model for premium), you must change the type of connection. Alternatively, you can choose to be part of a Power BI Premium capacity and leverage a larger dataset allowance with that option.

When Should You Use Import Data?

Import Data should be your first choice when you're choosing a connection type in Power BI. It gives you flexibility, power, and performance and avoiding it comes at big costs. Try to import your data into Power BI; if you cannot do it (maybe the size is too big, or a real-time dashboard is needed), you can try the other methods. Import Data should be the first option you try.

Summary

In this chapter, you learned about Import Data or Scheduled Refresh. With this type of connection, your data is imported into memory. However, the data will be compressed, and the copy of the data in memory is usually smaller than the actual data source size. Because this method copies the data into memory, you do need to set a scheduled refresh for this model.

Import Data or Scheduled Refresh is the fastest method, the most agile way of working with Power BI, and the most thoroughly functional connection type in Power BI. It allows you to combine multiple data sources with Power Query, write analytical calculations with DAX, and visualize the data. This method is super-fast because reading data from memory is always faster than reading it from disk.

However, the Import Data mode has a couple of limitations—the need to refresh data is one of them, and the other one is the size limitation of the Power BI files. Size limitation can be lifted when using the Power BI premium capacity, or by changing to other types of connections, which I explain in the next few chapters.

CHAPTER 4

DirectQuery

In the previous chapter, you learned about the Import Data or Scheduled Refresh connection type. In this chapter, you learn about the second type of connection, DirectQuery. This type of connection is supported by a limited number of data sources, and it mainly targets systems with huge amounts of data. DirectQuery is different from Live Connection, which is covered in the next chapter.

What Is DirectQuery?

DirectQuery is a type of connection in Power BI that does not load data into the Power BI model. If you remember from the previous chapter, Power BI loads data into memory (when Import Data or Scheduled Refresh is used as the connection type). DirectQuery doesn't consume memory because a second copy of the data is not stored. With DirectQuery, Power BI is directly connected to the data source. Anytime you see a visualization in a report with DirectQuery, the data has come straight from a query sent to the data source.

Which Data Sources Support DirectQuery?

Unlike Import Data, which is supported in all types of data sources, DirectQuery is only supported by a limited number of data sources. You cannot create a connection as a DirectQuery to an Excel File. Usually, data sources that are relational database models, or have a modeling engine, support DirectQuery mode. Here are some of the data sources supported through DirectQuery:

- Amazon Redshift
- Azure HDInsight Spark
- Azure SQL Database
- Azure SQL Data Warehouse
- Google BigQuery
- IBM Netezza
- Impala
- Oracle Database
- SAP Business Warehouse
- SAP HANA
- Snowflake

© Reza Rad 2023
R. Rad, *Pro Power BI Architecture*, https://doi.org/10.1007/978-1-4842-9538-0_4

- Spark

- SQL Server

- Teradata Database

- Vertica

This list may change. With every new update of Power BI, some new data sources may be added to the DirectQuery-supported lists of Power BI.[1]

How to Use DirectQuery

To run this example, you need a SQL Server instance installed. You can download the SQL Server Developer Edition at `www.microsoft.com/en-us/sql-server/sql-server-downloads`. Then set up the `AdventureWorksDW` database on it. You can get this database from `github.com/microsoft/sql-server-samples/tree/master/samples/databases/adventure-works/data-warehouse-install-script`.

This book is not about installing and configuring SQL Server or setting up the database on it. So, I'm not going to explain how to do that. This section covers the Power BI part of the example.

Open the Power BI Desktop and, under Get Data, select SQL Server, as shown in Figure 4-1.

Figure 4-1. *Getting data from SQL Server*

---

[1] View the up-to-date list at `docs.microsoft.com/en-us/power-bi/connect-data/power-bi-data-sources`.

The very first query you get when connecting to SQL Server data source includes an option for choosing the Data Connectivity mode. Select DirectQuery, as in Figure 4-2. You also need to add your server name. If your SQL Server instance is the default instance on your machine, you can use (.) for the server.

Figure 4-2. *Selecting DirectQuery in Power BI*

Note that data sources that support DirectQuery also support Import Data. (All data sources support Import Data.)

In the Navigator window, you can select some tables from the AdventureWorksDW database, such as DimDate and FactInternetSales, as I selected in Figure 4-3.

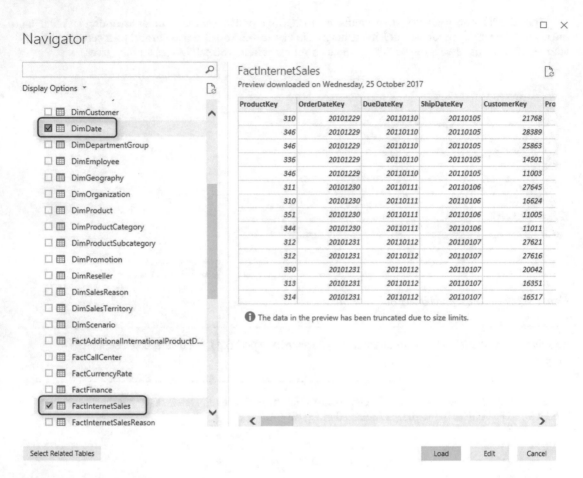

Figure 4-3. *Selecting tables in DirectQuery mode*

After selecting tables, click Load. The Data Load dialog in this connection mode is much faster because there is no need to load data into memory. This time, only metadata will be loaded into Power BI. The data remains on SQL Server.

No Data Tab in DirectQuery Mode

One of the first things you will notice in the DirectQuery mode, shown in Figure 4-4, is that there is no Data tab (the middle tab on the left side navigation of Power BI).

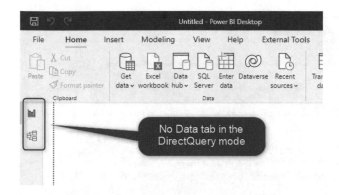

Figure 4-4. *No Data tab in the DirectQuery mode*

The Data tab shows you the data in the Power BI model. However, with DirectQuery, there is no data stored in the model. At the bottom-right side of the Power BI Desktop, shown in Figure 4-5, note that there is a note about the DirectQuery connection.

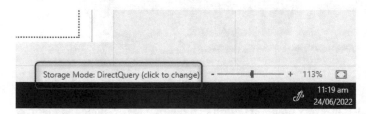

Figure 4-5. *DirectQuery is enabled*

How DirectQuery Works

With DirectQuery enabled, every time you see a visualization, Power BI sends a query to the data source, and the result of that comes back. You can check this process in SQL Profiler. SQL Profiler is a tool that you can use to capture queries sent to your SQL Server database. Figure 4-6 shows an example Power BI report on a DirectQuery model.

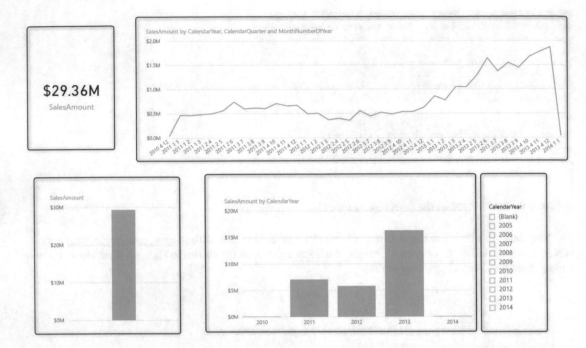

Figure 4-6. *Sample Power BI report*

Running a SQL Profiler will show you that, every time you refresh that report page or change something, there is one query for every visualization (see Figure 4-7)!

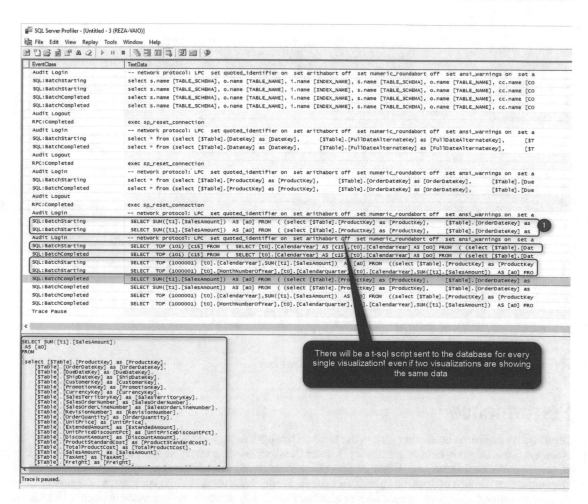

Figure 4-7. *Capturing queries sent to the database with SQL Profiler. There is a SQL Query for each visualization sent to the data source*

You can see in Figure 4-7 that in the SQL Profiler, five queries have been sent to the database. As Figure 4-7 also makes clear, even if two visualizations are showing the same thing, they send two separate queries to the database. As seen in Figure 4-8 for each visualization, one query will be produced.

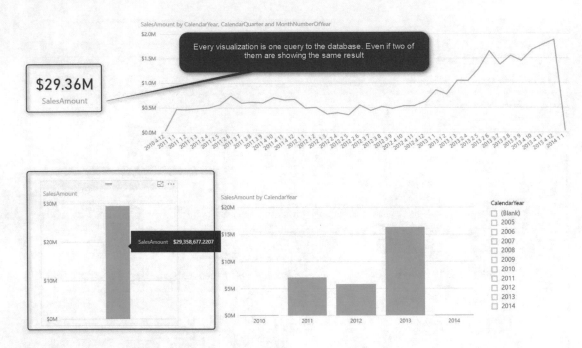

Figure 4-8. *Every visualization sends a query to the database*

Performance

DirectQuery performs much slower than the Import Data option. Import Data loads data into memory. It is always faster to query data from memory (Import Data), rather than querying it from disk (DirectQuery). However, to determine how much faster Import Data is, you need to know more about the implementation. Depending on the size of data, the specification of the server that the database is running on, the network connection speed, and other factors such as whether there is any database optimization applied to the data source, the answer might be entirely different.

Performance Tuning on the Data Source

The critical point to understand is that this type of connection is the slowest, and if you decide to use it, you must immediately think about performance tuning your database.

Using DirectQuery without performance tuning the source database is a big mistake.

To understand the need for performance tuning, let's go through an example. Assume that you have a large table in a SQL Server database, a table with 48 million rows in it. You want to query the Sum of Sales column from that table.

Figure 4-9 demonstrates the performance you get if you have a normal index on the table with 48 million records.

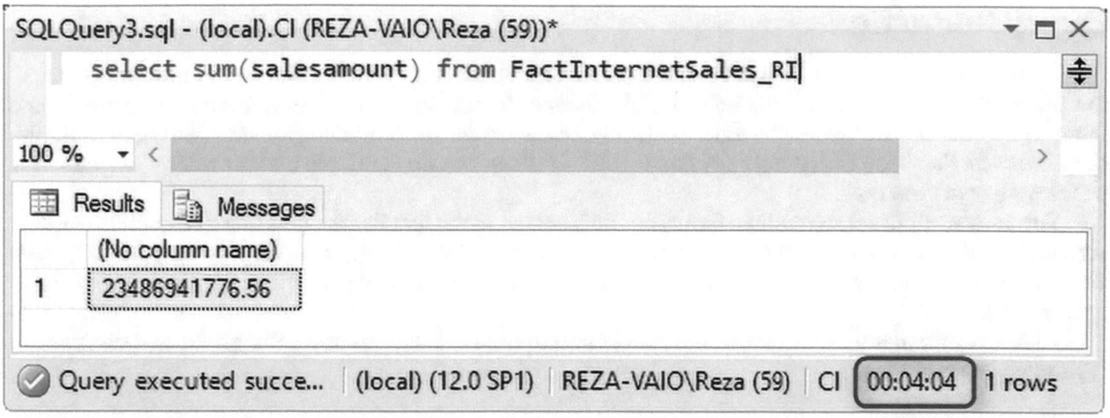

Figure 4-9. *Table with a regular index*

A regular select sum from this table with 48 million records takes four minutes and four seconds to run. The same query responds in less than a second when you have a Clustered Column Store index. It shows significantly improved performance when you have a Clustered Column Store index on the same table with the same amount of data rows, as shown in Figure 4-10.

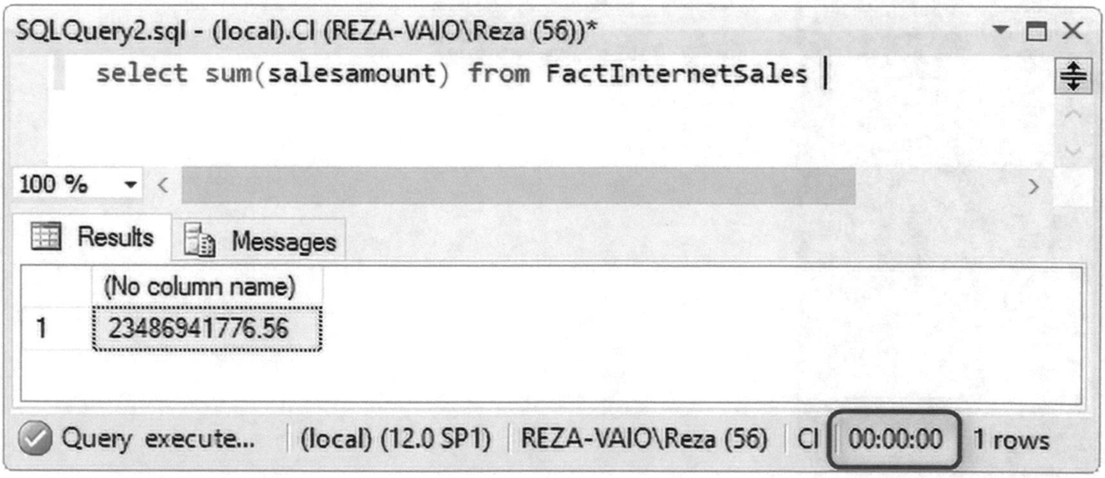

Figure 4-10. *Table with a clustered column store index*

I'm not going to teach you all performance tuning in this chapter, and I can't do it because you have to read books, blog posts, and watch videos to learn all that. That is a whole different topic on its own. The most important thing is that performance tuning is different for each data source. Performance tuning for Oracle, SQL Server, and SSAS are entirely different. Your friend for this part is Google, and the vast amount of free content available on the Internet for you to study.

Query Reduction

One of the newest features added to Power BI helps reduce the number of queries sent to the database in the DirectQuery mode. The default behavior of a slicer or filter in Power BI is to select an item in the slicer or filter, so that other visuals are filtered immediately. In the DirectQuery mode, it means it will send multiple queries to the database with every selection in filter or slicer. Sending multiple queries will reduce the performance of your report.

You may want to select multiple items, but only selecting the first item means that five queries will be sent to the database. Then, after selecting the second item, another five queries will be sent to the database. The speed, as a result, will be twice as slow. To fix this issue, you can set a property in the Options of your Power BI file.

Click the File menu in the Power BI Desktop, and then select Options and Settings. From there, choose Options (see Figure 4-11).

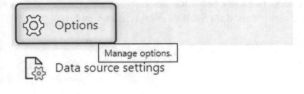

Figure 4-11. *Power BI file options*

Then click Query Reduction on the left side (the last item, as shown in Figure 4-12).

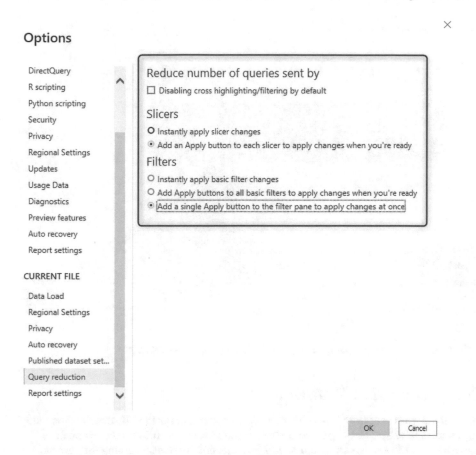

Figure 4-12. *Query reduction for DirectQuery mode*

I do not recommend using the first item in most cases. The first item will disable cross highlighting/filtering by default. When selecting the first option, the main functionality of Power BI, which is cross highlighting/filtering, will not work. Cross-highlighting/filtering means that, when you click a visual, other visuals will be either filtered or highlighted. This feature makes the Power BI an interactive visualization tool. If you have some visuals that don't need to interact with each other, enabling this option could reduce the number of queries sent to the database.

The second and third options, however, are beneficial, especially when you have multi-select slicers and filters. When you choose this option, your filters or slicers will have an Apply button on them. Changes will not apply until you click the Apply button, and then all the queries will be sent to the database. This option is highly recommended when you have a multi-selection slicer or filter. You can even choose to have one single Apply button for the entire Filter pane, which can be very helpful in query reduction. This is depicted in Figure 4-13.

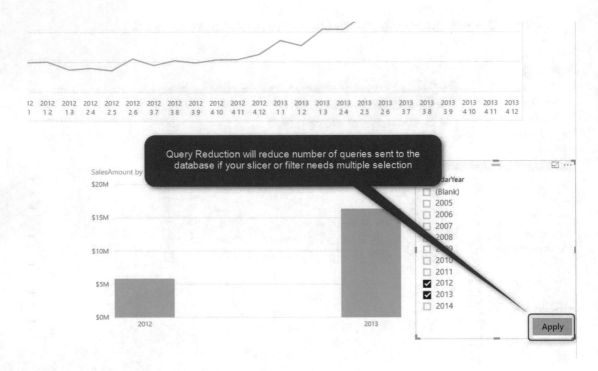

Figure 4-13. *Query reduction sends queries only once the Apply button has been clicked*

Maximum Connections Per Data Source

The number of concurrent queries sent from Power BI to the data source is important. If you allow too many concurrent queries, you are applying a very high load on the data source. On the other hand, if you have created a report page with over 15 visuals, you would need 15 concurrent queries (assuming they are not slicers, and query reduction won't reduce the number of queries).

You can set the number of concurrent queries per data source in the Power BI file options, as highlighted in Figure 4-14.

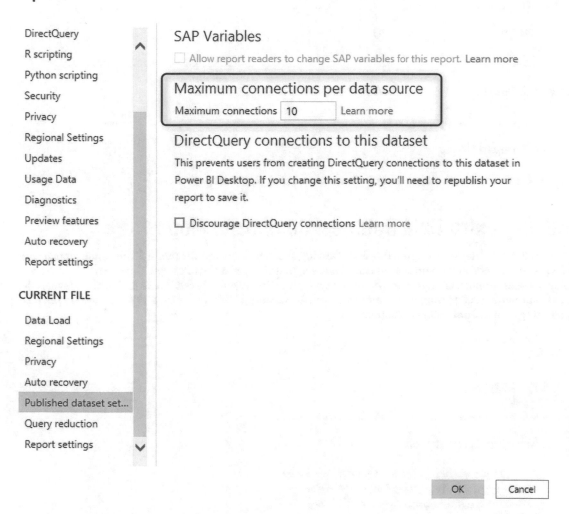

Figure 4-14. *Maximum connections per data source in the DirectQuery mode*

This setting is for the published Power BI file. A published Power BI report can be opened by multiple users. This also means increasing the concurrent connections. When you set this number, you have to take into account not only the number of visuals on the page and the performance of the data source, but also the number of concurrent report users.

Depending on your Power BI license and the environment, there are some limits to this number, as shown in Figure 4-15.

ENVIRONMENT	UPPER LIMIT (ACTIVE CONNECTIONS PER DATA SOURCE)
Power BI Pro	10
Power BI Premium	30
Power BI Report Server	10

Figure 4-15. *Maximum connections per data source setting for DirectQuery*

Adding Extra Data Sources: Composite Mode

Back in the older days of using the Power BI Desktop, if DirectQuery was the mode of the connection, it was not possible to add any other data sources. However, that changed a few years ago. You can now add extra data sources (Import, or any other connection types) to a DirectQuery-based Power BI file. This changes the file to something called *composite mode*. However, the warning shown in Figure 4-16 will be visible when you bring data in from other data sources.

Figure 4-16. *Adding more data sources into the DirectQuery-based file*

Composite mode is a very powerful way to build Power BI files. It uses part of the data using a DirectQuery connection and other parts of the data using an Import Data connection. Often—even in large-scale data source scenarios—there are small tables for dimensions. Dimensions in such cases can be imported while the big fact tables are used as a DirectQuery. You can learn more about composite mode in the next chapters. In Figure 4-17, `DimCustomer` is an Import Mode table, and `DimDate` and `FactInternetSales` use DirectQuery.

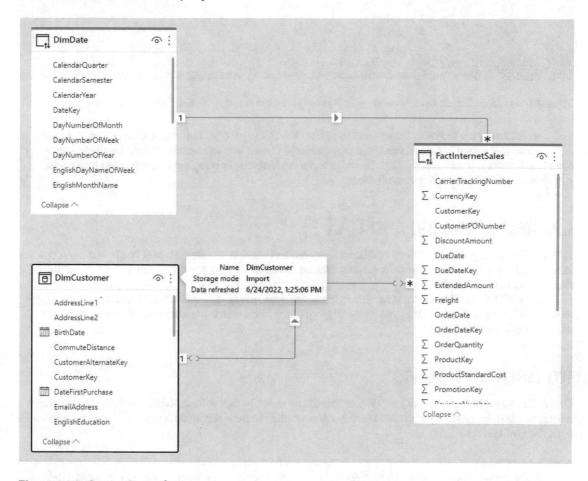

Figure 4-17. *Composite mode*

Limited Power Query

With DirectQuery, you can apply data transformations in the Query Editor window. However, not all transformations are supported. To find out which transformations are supported and which are not, you have to check the data source first. Some of the data sources don't support any transformations, such as SAP Business Warehouse. Other transformations, such as the SQL Server database, support more transformations.

If you use a transformation that is not supported, you'll get an error message that says, "This step results in a query that is not supported in DirectQuery mode." See Figure 4-18.

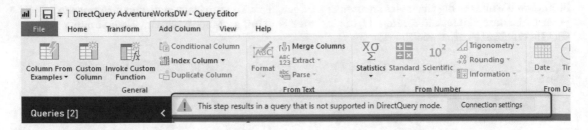

Figure 4-18. *Not all data transformations in Power Query are supported with DirectQuery data sources*

Transformations in Power Query are limited in DirectQuery mode. This depends on the data source.

As mentioned earlier, when you use a DirectQuery connection, you usually should think of another data transformation tool, such as SQL Server Integration Services, to bring data transformed into a data warehouse before connecting Power BI to it.

Limited Modeling and DAX

DAX and Modeling are also limited in DirectQuery mode. Creating calculated tables is allowed in composite mode, and the default Date hierarchy is not available. Some of the DAX functions, such as parent-child functions, are not available.

Some of the complex DAX measures might cause performance issues in DirectQuery mode. It is better to start with simple measures such as simple aggregations first, test the performance, then gradually add more complex scenarios.

No Refresh Needed

One of the advantages of DirectQuery is that there is no need for data refresh to be scheduled. Every time a user looks at the report, a query is sent to the database and the most recent data is shown. There is no need for a data refresh schedule.

When the automatic refresh happens with dashboards, the DirectQuery connection will be refreshed every 15 minutes or more. For reports, data will be updated any time a new query is sent to the database.

Large Scale Dataset

DirectQuery is best used with a massive amount of data. Because the data is not loaded into the memory, there is no limitation on the size of the data source. Any limitation comes from the data source itself. You can have petabytes of data with a DirectQuery connection. However, you need to consider performance tuning in the data source, as mentioned.

The lack of size limitation is the main reason to use DirectQuery. DirectQuery is slower and less flexible, with fewer features than Power Query and DAX. Overall, DirectQuery is good option only when the other two types of connections cannot be used.

These days, especially after composite mode became available in Power BI, it is very rare to see a pure DirectQuery-only method used in a Power BI dataset. The better approach is to use DirectQuery for large tables and use Import Data for smaller tables and then create a composite mode.

Summary

Power BI supports three types of connections. In this chapter, you learned about DirectQuery, which is one of the connection types. DirectQuery does not store a second copy of the data in memory. It keeps the data in the data source. With DirectQuery, anything you see in the report is sent to the database through T-SQL scripts. If you have ten visualizations in your report, it posts ten queries to the database and returns the result.

DirectQuery supports a huge amount of data. Because the data is not stored in the memory, the only limitation on the data size is the limitation of the data source itself. You can easily have petabytes of data in a database and connect to it from Power BI. Another advantage of DirectQuery is that there is no need for a scheduled refresh. Data is updated any time the report is refreshed with queries sent to the database, so there is no need for scheduling a refresh.

DirectQuery has many limitations and downsides. With DirectQuery, the speed of Power BI reports is much slower. DirectQuery is limited in using modeling features of Power BI such as DAX, calculated tables, built-in date tables, and Power Query functionalities. DirectQuery is less flexible and has fewer features. Using DirectQuery means you get slower reports, with less functionality on the Power BI side.

DirectQuery is only recommended if the other two connections (Import Data or Live Connection) cannot be applied. In the next chapter, I explain Live Connection. If you decide to use DirectQuery, it is better to use another integration tool and do all the data transformation before loading data into the source database. Also, it is better to take care of all the calculations in the data source itself.

DirectQuery is only recommended if the other two types of connections (Import Data or Live Connection) cannot be applied. DirectQuery is better used in combination with Import Data through a composite mode.

To close this summary, here is the list of pros and cons of DirectQuery:

Advantages

- Large scale dataset; size limitation only for the data source

- No need for data refreshes

Disadvantages

- Power Query transformations are limited

- Modeling is limited

- DAX is limited

- Slower speed of the report

CHAPTER 5

Live Connection

Live Connection is another type of connection in Power BI. This connection is similar to DirectQuery because it doesn't store data in memory. However, it is different from DirectQuery, because it includes the analytical engine of SQL Server Analysis Services Tabular. With this method, you get benefits from both worlds—large-scale model size and the analytical power of Analysis Services. In this chapter, you learn about the details of Live Connection, including things that you need to consider and how to set it up when working with a gateway.

What Is Live Connection?

Live Connection is used with three types of data sources. It does not store a second copy of the data in memory. Data is kept in the data source, and visualizations query the data source from Power BI. The types of data sources supported by this type of connection are as follows:

- Azure Analysis Services

- SQL Server Analysis Services Tabular

- SQL Server Analysis Services Multi-Dimensional

- Power BI Service Dataset

These four types are the SQL Server Analysis Services (SSAS) technology. You cannot use Live Connection with the SQL Server database engine. However, the SSAS technology can be cloud-based (Azure Analysis Services) or on-premises (SSAS on-premises).

Create a Report with Live Connection

To create a Live Connection example, you need to install the SQL Server Analysis Services Tabular model. You can download the SQL Server trial for 180 days using this link: `www.microsoft.com/en-us/sql-server/sql-server-downloads`.

After installing a SSAS Tabular instance, you can restore the `AdventureWorks` Tabular model on it. The database can be accessed and downloaded from `github.com/Microsoft/sql-server-samples/releases/download/adventureworks-analysis-services/adventure-works-tabular-model-1200-full-database-backup.zip`.

This book does not go into details of how to set up or install SQL Server or the SSAS Tabular model.

© Reza Rad 2023
R. Rad, *Pro Power BI Architecture*, https://doi.org/10.1007/978-1-4842-9538-0_5

Open a Power BI Desktop and choose Get Data, Analysis Services, as shown in Figure 5-1.

Figure 5-1. *Getting data from Analysis Services*

When connecting to a SQL Server Analysis Services database, choose Connect Live, as shown in Figure 5-2.

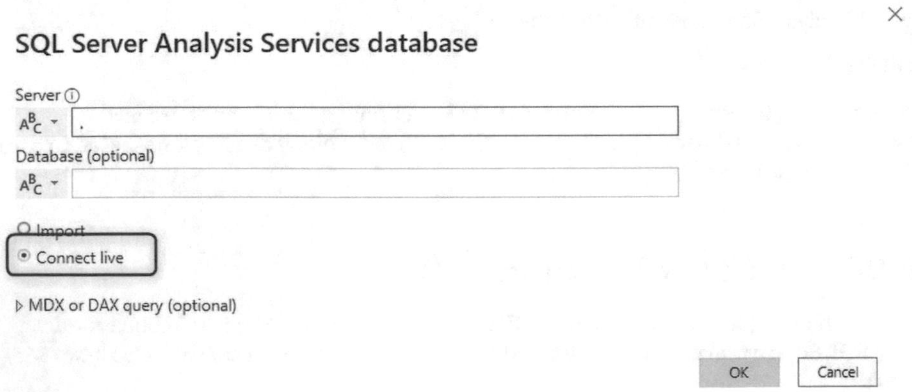

SQL Server Analysis Services database

×

Server ①

A^B_C ▾   .

Database (optional)

A^B_C ▾

○ Import

⦿ Connect live

▷ MDX or DAX query (optional)

OK   Cancel

Figure 5-2. *Connecting live to Analysis Services*

The SSAS installed on my machine is in the tabular instance name, which is why I use the server name `.\tabular`. For your machine, the setup might be different. In the Navigator window, select the Adventure Works Internet Sales model (see Figure 5-3).

Navigator

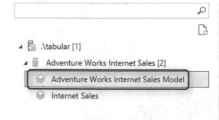

.\tabular [1]
  Adventure Works Internet Sales [2]
    Adventure Works Internet Sales Model
    Internet Sales

Adventure Works Internet Sales Model
Last Modified: 11/10/2016 22:03:51

This perspective contains the following dimensions and measures
Customer, Date, Geography, Internet Sales, Product, Product Category, Product Subcategory, Days Current Quarter to Date, Days in Current Quarter, Internet Distinct Count Sales Order, Internet Order Lines Count, Internet Total Units, Internet Total Discount Amount, Internet Total Product Cost, Internet Total Sales, Internet Total Margin, Internet Total Tax Amt, Internet Total Freight, Internet Previous Quarter Margin, Internet Current Quarter Margin, Internet Previous Quarter Margin Proportion to QTD, Internet Previous Quarter Sales, Internet Current Quarter Sales, Internet Previous Quarter Sales Proportion to QTD, Internet Current Quarter Sales Performance, Internet Current Quarter Margin Performance

OK   Cancel

Figure 5-3. *Selecting the model from Analysis Services*

Note that you just choose a model, not tables. The model includes multiple tables, with their relationships, hierarchies, and calculations, and they will all be connected to Power BI. You can verify on the bottom-right side of the Power BI Desktop that it is a live connection. Figure 5-4 shows you what to look for.

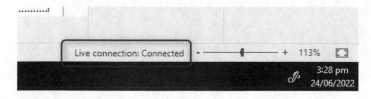

Figure 5-4. *Live Connection is enabled*

Live Connection Behind the Scenes

Consider the Power BI report shown in Figure 5-5.

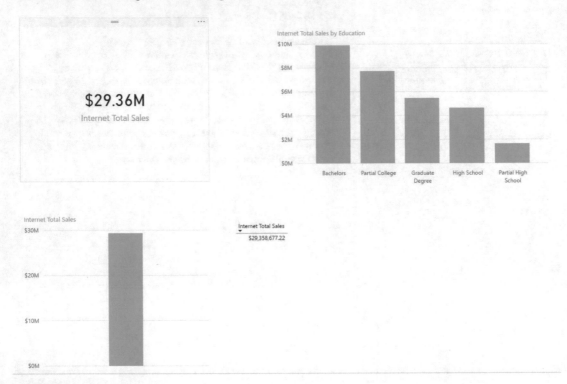

Figure 5-5. *Sample Power BI report*

You can run SQL Profiler on Analysis Services to capture all the DAX queries sent to the database. Figure 5-6 features queries posted to the database for the report in Figure 5-4.

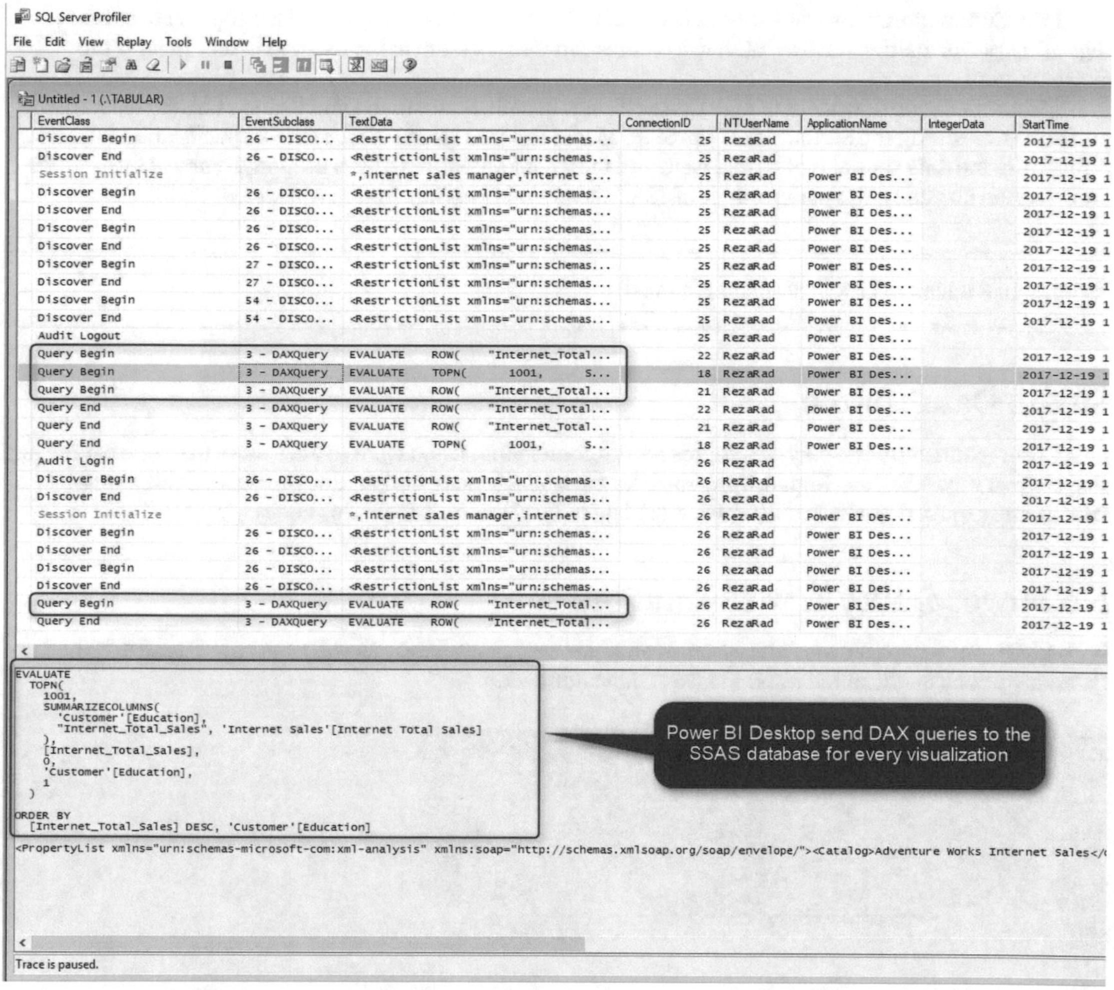

Figure 5-6. DAX codes sent to the Analysis Services database

As with DirectQuery, the Power BI Desktop will send a query for every visualization to the database. However, because these queries run on an analytical engine, you can typically expect faster results (this might be different depending on many factors).

Performance

Live Connection can work faster than DirectQuery in many scenarios. However, in every implementation, many factors affect the performance, and there are always exceptions. In general, because Live Connection connects to an analytical engine, calculations and analytical results are faster than a query from the database.

Using Live Connection to SSAS Tabular is usually faster because the data is stored in the memory of the machine that runs SSAS Tabular. However, this depends on network bandwidth and how calculations and model are implemented, so it might change.

Live Connection, however, is not as fast as Import Data. Import Data is the fastest possible option regarding performance in Power BI. A live connection is the second in the list, and DirectQuery is the slowest option.

Although the performance of Live Connection is usually better than DirectQuery, I highly recommend performance tuning the SSAS Model. The SSAS Model can perform fast if the server specification is at the right scale, the data model is designed well, and the calculations are written properly. If any of these items aren't tuned correctly, the performance of SSAS server and Live Connection will suffer.

Performance tuning in Live Connection is a must.

Single Data Source

Live Connection supports only one source for the connection. If you want to have more than one connection source, you can either use Import Data from the Analysis Services, or create a composite mode using DirectQuery to Analysis Services (which is explained in a later chapter in this book).

No Power Query Transformations

With Live Connection, Power Query transformations are not available. As you can see in Figure 5-7, the Edit Queries options are disabled when in Live Connection mode.

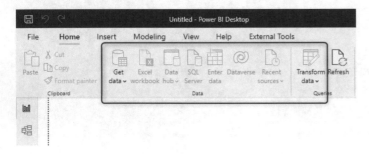

Figure 5-7. *No Power Query in Live Connection mode*

All the data transformations needs must be handled before loading data into an SSAS model. Because SSAS is not a data transformation tool, you can use SSIS to do the data transformations before loading data into the data warehouse, and then process data from the data warehouse into an SSAS data model. Figure 5-8 contains a sample scenario.

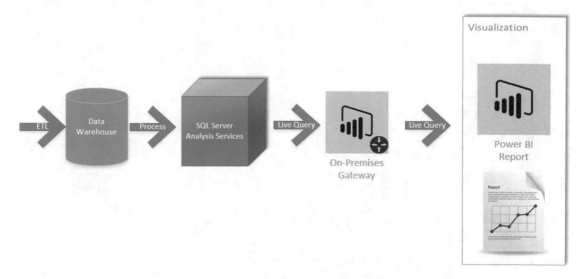

Figure 5-8. *Enterprise use of Live Connection with a data warehouse and ETL*

With Live Connection, you don't need to select each table separately. All the tables in the model will be available, as you can see in the model diagram in Figure 5-9.

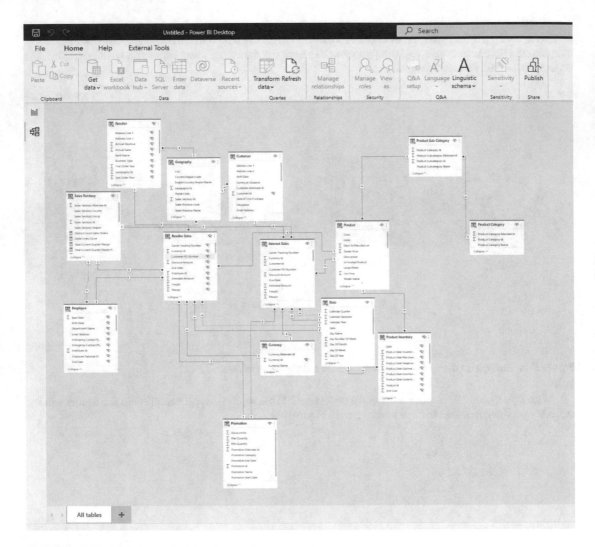

Figure 5-9. *Model diagram for Live Connection*

Modeling and Report-Level Measure

With Live Connection, modeling in Power BI is very limited. You can only create measures. The type of measure that you create a Live Connection is called a report-level measure. Report-level measures are only for this Power BI report. If you create another Power BI report connected live to the same data source, you cannot use the report-level measures that were built in the previous Power BI report.

To create a report-level measure, click Add New Measure from the Modeling tab, as shown in Figure 5-10.

Figure 5-10. *Report-level measures*

As you can see in the example in Figure 5-10, I created a report-level measure to calculate sales year to date. The code is as follows:

```
Sales YTD = TOTALYTD(
    [Internet Total Sales],
    'Date'[Date])
```

The same code, when sent to SSAS, can be fetched with SQL Profiler, as follows:

```
DEFINE MEASURE 'Customer'[Sales YTD] =
  (/* USER DAX BEGIN */
TOTALYTD(
    [Internet Total Sales],
    'Date'[Date])
/* USER DAX END */)
EVALUATE
  TOPN(
    502,
    SUMMARIZECOLUMNS(
      ROLLUPADDISSUBTOTAL('Date'[Date], "IsGrandTotalRowTotal"),
      "Internet_Total_Sales", 'Internet Sales'[Internet Total Sales],
      "Sales YTD", 'Customer'[Sales YTD]
    ),
    [IsGrandTotalRowTotal],
    0,
    'Date'[Date],
    1
  )
ORDER BY
  [IsGrandTotalRowTotal] DESC, 'Date'[Date]
```

Report-level measures are not bound to the SSAS model. They are only for the current Power BI file; in other files they must be created again.

Report-level measures are flexible and give the users a self-service functionality. However, they reduce the governance and centralized modeling feature of Live Connection. One good use case for a report-level measure is to create conditional formatting in the visualization.

Publishing the Report and Gateway Configuration

Let's now look at how to publish and configure this report in the Power BI Service. Publishing the report here is like publishing any other report. Later in this chapter, you learn how to set up the gateway. Let's go straight to the point of adding data sources.

Create the Data Sources

Now you'll create the data sources. You might think that one gateway is enough for connecting to all the data sources in a domain. That is right. However, you still need to add a data source to that gateway for each source. The source can be a SQL Server database, and Analysis Services database, and so on. In this example, we build a data source for SQL Server Analysis Tabular on-premises. Before going through this step, I installed AW Internet Sales Tabular Model 2014 on my SSAS Tabular and want to connect to it.

To create a data source, click Add Data Source from the Manage Gateways window (you have to select the proper gateway first), as shown in Figure 5-11.

Figure 5-11. *Creating a data source under the gateway*

Then enter the data source's details, as shown in Figure 5-12. I named this data source AW Internet Sales Tabular Model 2014, then entered my server name and database name. Then I used Windows authentication with my domain user <domain>\username and the password. You should see a successful message after clicking Apply. The domain name that I used is BIRADACAD (my SSAS Tabular domain), and the user was PBIgateway, which is a user of the BIRADACAD domain (username: BIRADACAD\PBIgateway). This is an administrator for the SSAS Tabular (explained in next few paragraphs).

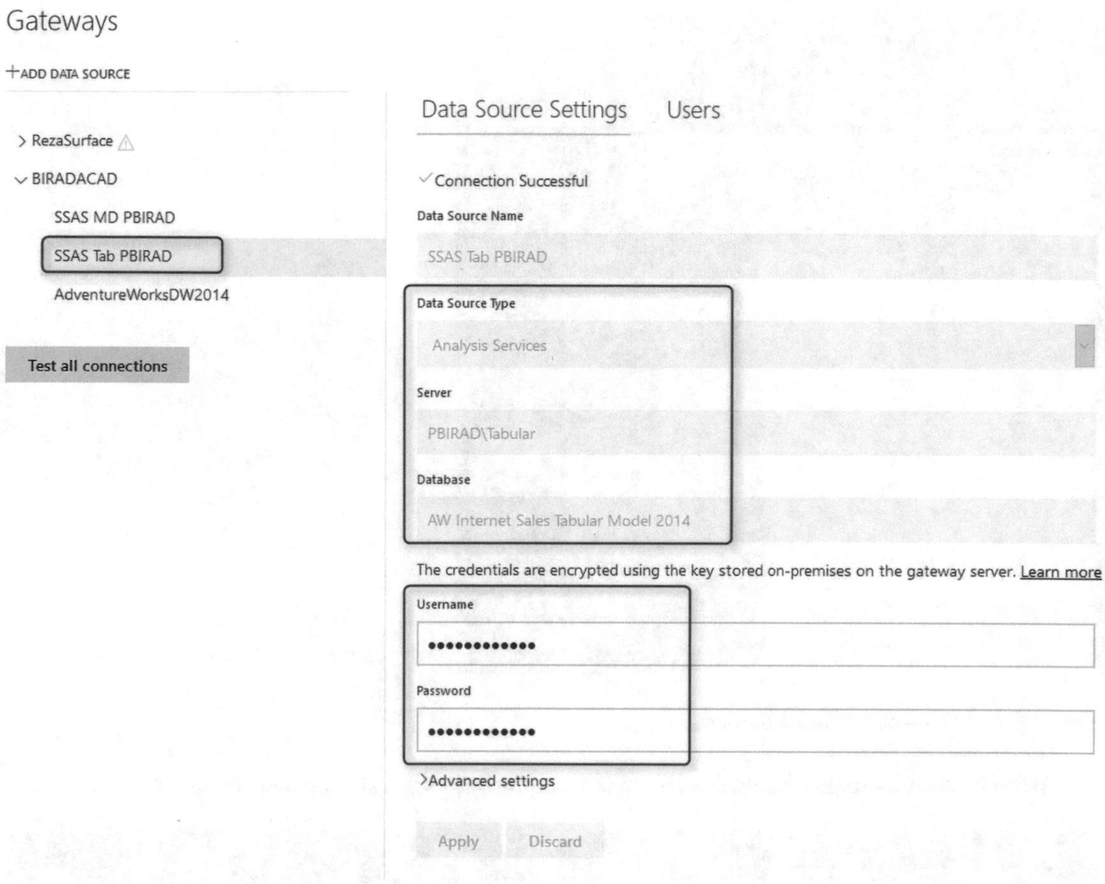

Gateways

+ADD DATA SOURCE

> RezaSurface ⚠

∨ BIRADACAD

    SSAS MD PBIRAD

    SSAS Tab PBIRAD

    AdventureWorksDW2014

Test all connections

Data Source Settings   Users

✓ Connection Successful

Data Source Name

SSAS Tab PBIRAD

Data Source Type

Analysis Services

Server

PBIRAD\Tabular

Database

AW Internet Sales Tabular Model 2014

The credentials are encrypted using the key stored on-premises on the gateway server. Learn more

Username

•••••••••••••

Password

•••••••••••••

>Advanced settings

Apply   Discard

Figure 5-12. *Data source configuration*

Note that the user account that you are using should meet these conditions:

- It should be a domain user.

- The domain user should be an administrator in SSAS Tabular.

You can set the administrator for SSAS Tabular by right-clicking the SSAS Tabular instance in SSMS and then choosing the Properties option (see Figure 5-13).

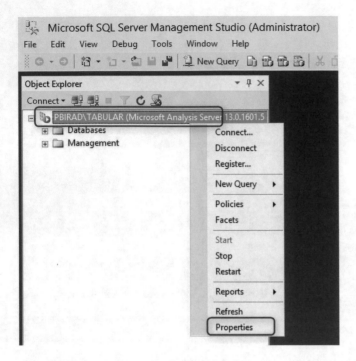

Figure 5-13. *Properties of SSAS Server*

In the Security settings tab, add the user to the administrators list, as shown in Figure 5-14.

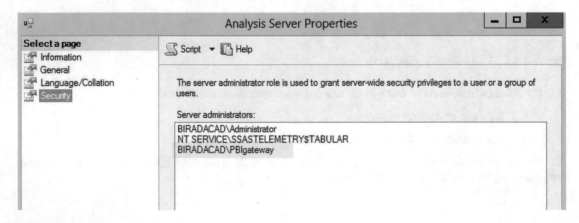

Figure 5-14. *Security settings in SSAS Server*

Using EffectiveUserName

The gateway account is used to access the Power BI cloud service from the on-premises SSAS Tabular. However, this account by itself isn't enough for data retrieval. The gateway passes the EffectiveUserName from Power BI to the on-premises SSAS Tabular, and the result of the query is returned based on the access of the EffectiveUserName account to the SSAS Tabular database and model. Figure 5-15 illustrates how this works.

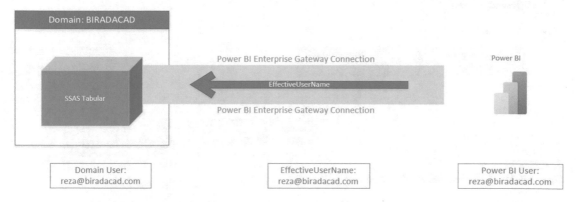

Figure 5-15. *Using EffectiveUserName*

By default, EffectiveUserName is the username of the user who is logged in to Power BI, or in other words, EffectiveUserName is the Power BI account. The Power BI account should have proper access to the SSAS Tabular database to fetch the required data. If the Power BI account is from the same domain as the SSAS Tabular, there is no problem, and security configuration can be set in the SSAS Tabular. However, if the domains are different, you have to perform UPN mapping.

UPN Mapping

Your SSAS Tabular is part of a domain (because that's how Live Connection works), and that domain might be the same domain that your Power BI user account uses. If you are using the same domain user for the Power BI account, you can skip this step. However, if the domains are different, as shown in Figure 5-16, you have to perform UPN mapping.

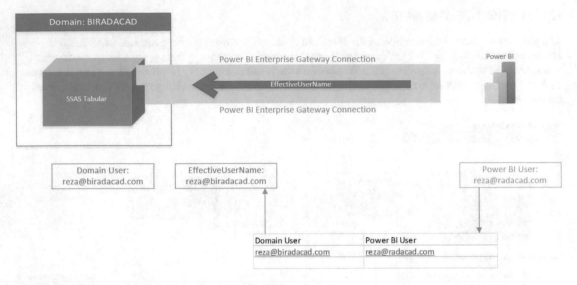

Figure 5-16. *UPN mapping table required*

UPN mapping maps the Power BI accounts to your local on-premises SSAS Tabular domain accounts. This example doesn't use the same domain account as the Power BI account, so UPN mapping must be set up, as shown in Figure 5-17.

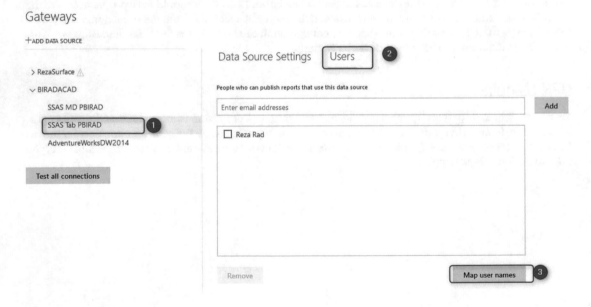

Figure 5-17. *Mapping usernames in the data source*

Then in the Mapping pane, I create a new mapping that maps my Power BI user account to reza@biradacad.com, which is my local domain for the SSAS Tabular server (see Figure 5-18).

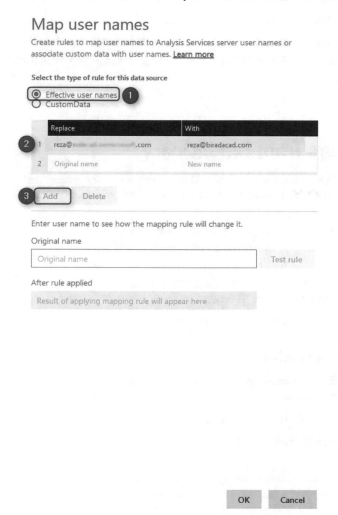

Figure 5-18. *UPN mapping setting in the Power BI Service*

With this username mapping, reza@biradacad.com will be passed as EffectiveUserName to the SSAS Tabular.

Live Connection to Power BI Service

Another type of live connection is to connect to a dataset published in the Power BI service. This dataset is then treated as an SSAS instance. The dataset in the Power BI service is hosted in a shared Azure Analysis Services (AAS) cloud environment. When you connect to it from the Power BI Desktop, it is like connecting to an instance of SSAS with a live connection.

For this option, you need to be logged in to the Power BI Desktop. You will see a list of datasets that you built, and you can choose one.

After connecting to the dataset, you will see the Live Connection message on the bottom-right side of the Power BI Desktop. This method works similarly to the connection to SSAS with Live Connection.

Connecting to another dataset in the Power BI Service with Live Connection is the recommended approach for a multi-developer environment. One user can build the model, and other users can work on various Power BI files. I explain more about this in upcoming chapters.

How Live Connection Differs from DirectQuery

One of the mistakes that many Power BI developers make is to consider DirectQuery and Live Connection the same. These two types of connections are different in many ways. Here is a list of differences between these two:

- DirectQuery is a connection mainly to non-Microsoft databases or analytical engines, or to relational databases (such as SQL Server, Teradata, Oracle, SAP Business Warehouse, and so on).

- Live Connection is a connection to four sources: SSAS Tabular, SSAS Multi-Dimensional, Azure Analysis Services, and Power BI dataset.

- DirectQuery still has limited Power Query functionality with some data sources (such as SQL Server databases).

- Live Connection has no Power Query features in it.

- You can create some simple calculated columns in DirectQuery; these will be converted to T-SQL scripts behind the scenes.

- You cannot create calculated columns in Live Connection.

- You can use report-level measures and leverage all DAX functions in a Live Connection instance.

- In DirectQuery mode, you can have limited measure abilities. For more complex measures, you must check the performance (and some of the functions such as parent-child functions are not available). Some complex measures might slow performance down significantly.

- DirectQuery mode is usually slower than Live Connection.

- A Live Connection instance is usually less flexible than DirectQuery mode.

As you see, the list explains how these two types of connections differ.

Summary

In this chapter, you learned about Live Connection. This type of connection is only available for four data sources—Azure Analysis Services, SSAS Tabular, SSAS Multi-Dimensional, and Power BI datasets. This type of connection is much more limited than DirectQuery, because you have no access to the Power Query Editor.

However, Live Connection provides a better solution than DirectQuery, because the ability to write DAX code is fully possible if the SSAS Tabular is used as a data source. With Live Connection, you get the benefits of both worlds—because data is not stored in the Power BI, the size limitation of Import Data does not apply. Also, because the SSAS Tabular can leverage DAX, and the analytical power of Power BI is based on DAX, the analytical engine of this solution is very efficient.

A Live Connection instance is faster than DirectQuery in most cases. However, it can be still slower than Import Data in the performance (depending on the SSAS server specification and the connection between the report and the server). The recommendation is to start with Import Data, and if it's not possible, use Live Connection. If neither of those can be used (for example if you are working with a huge amount of data, and the SSAS is not available because the Microsoft toolset is not used for analytics in your company), choose the last option, which is DirectQuery. However, always remember to use DirectQuery through a composite mode.

CHAPTER 6

Composite Model

In the early days of developing Power BI solutions, you could choose the DirectQuery or Import Data connection types, but not both. In 2018, Power BI added a breakthrough feature called *composite model*. Using this feature, you can have part of your Power BI dataset connected directly to a data source, and another part imported. Along with this change, you can also choose the storage mode for each entity. In this chapter, you learn about composite model—what it is and how it works.

What Is Composite Model?

A composite model in Power BI means that part of your model can be a DirectQuery connection to a data source (for example, SQL Server database), and another part can use Import Data (for example, an Excel file). Previously, when you used DirectQuery, you couldn't even add another data source into the model. See Figure 6-1.

With composite model, your very large tables can use a DirectQuery connection, without needing to import them, and you can import smaller tables so they are quickly accessible.

Composite Model in Power BI

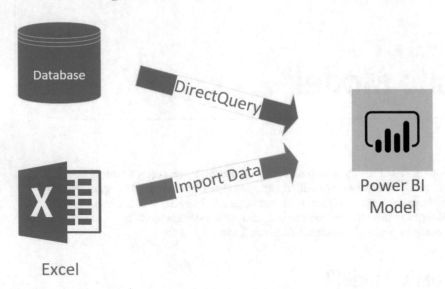

Figure 6-1. *Composite model combines DirectQuery and Import Data*

Why Use Composite Model?

To answer this question, you first need to consider the benefits of the Import Data and DirectQuery modes. Import Data is good for super-fast data analysis and is flexible, while DirectQuery is good for big data tables and data freshness. See Figure 6-2.

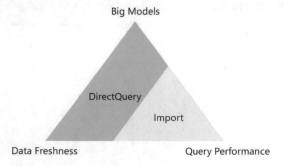

Figure 6-2. *DirectQuery and Import Data have different advantages*

Composite model combines the good things of Import and DirectQuery into one model. Using composite model, you can work with big data tables in DirectQuery, and still import smaller tables using Import Data. See Figure 6-3.

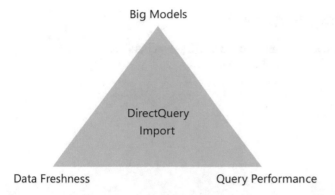

Figure 6-3. *Composite model improves performance and works with big data tables at the same time*

Using composite model, you can have tables with different connection types, some using Import Data and some using DirectQuery. See Figure 6-4.

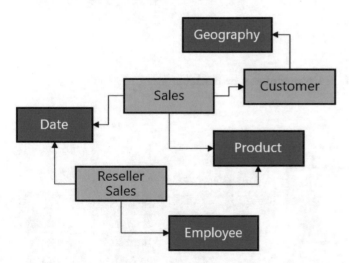

Figure 6-4. *In composite model, some of the tables can be in Import Data mode, and others can use DirectQuery (the red tables use Import Data, and the gray tables use DirectQuery)*

Having big data tables with DirectQuery and smaller tables with Import Data is much better than doing everything purely with DirectQuery, because in pure DirectQuery mode, performance is slow. In composite model, the smaller tables can be used as Import Data to improve the performance. This also comes with a new storage mode, called *Dual*, which you learn about it a bit later in this chapter.

How Does Composite Model Work?

Figure 6-5 depicts a Power BI file using a DirectQuery connection to a SQL Server database (AdventureWorksDW in this example).

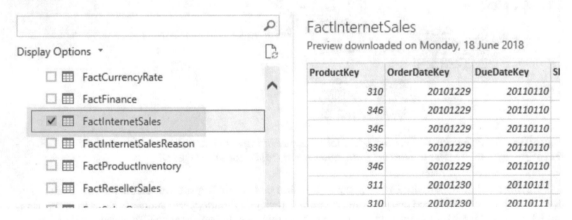

Figure 6-5. *DirectQuery source*

In Figure 6-6, I selected the FactInternetSales table from this database.

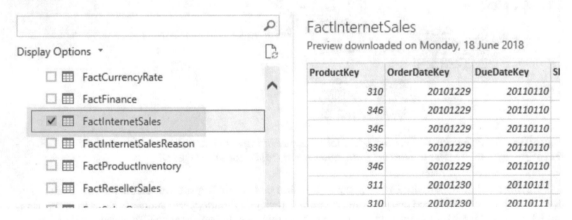

Figure 6-6. *Selecting DirectQuery tables*

In the Power BI Desktop, after loading the table, you can see (on the right-bottom corner) that it uses using the DirectQuery storage mode (see Figure 6-7).

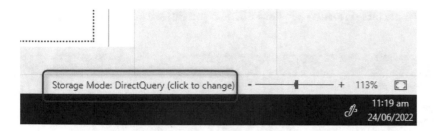

Figure 6-7. *Using DirectQuery storage mode*

The second table gets data from Excel, as shown in Figure 6-8.

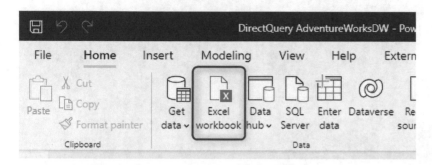

Figure 6-8. *Getting data from an Excel workbook*

Next, select `DimCustomer` from the Excel file (this Excel file is the Excel version of the `AdventureWorksDW` database). As soon as you bring a table in from another data source, you will be notified that there is a potential privacy risk, whereby the data from one data source may be used to pass parameters into another data source, as shown in Figure 6-9.

Figure 6-9. *Potential security risk warning when combining data from different sources*

After you click OK, the new data table is loaded into Power BI, and you can see in Figure 6-10 that the mode changes to Mixed.

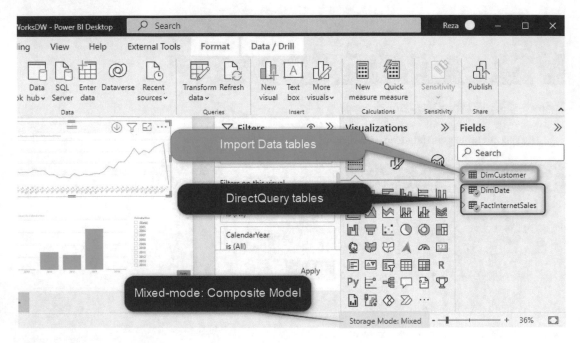

Figure 6-10. *Mixed mode*

The mixed mode of composite model indicates that the fact table is *not* loaded into Power BI. It will be queried each time from the SQL Server database table. The dimension, however, is already imported into the Power BI model and needs to be refreshed each time. If you refresh your model, you will see that the only table(s) that are refreshed are the Import Data tables, as shown in Figure 6-11.

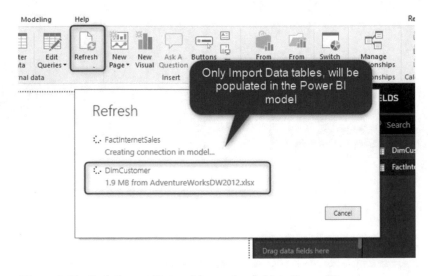

Figure 6-11. *Only Import Data tables are loaded into Power BI*

Using this option, you can see the Data tab (which you can't use in mere DirectQuery mode), and you can see only the Import Data tables there (see Figure 6-12).

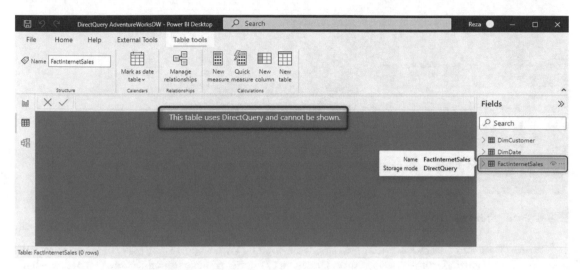

Figure 6-12. *The Data tab shows import tables only*

You can have the big data tables of the model come from a DirectQuery source, and it doesn't matter if they are billions of rows, because they are not loaded into Power BI. Small tables can be imported into Power BI for better performance.

Dual Storage Mode

With composite model, you may wonder where the data is stored in every table and how it works behind the scenes. Each table in Power BI has a storage mode. You can select a table and determine the storage mode for that table. The storage mode is Import, DirectQuery, or Dual.

If you go to the Model tab in the Power BI Desktop and click a table, you can see the Storage mode in the Properties pane, under the Advanced section. As Figure 6-13 demonstrates, there are three options: Import, DirectQuery, and Dual.

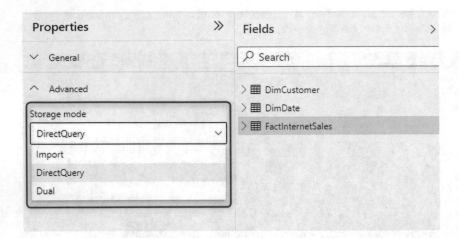

Figure 6-13. *Storage modes*

Import Data and DirectQuery are understandable enough. With Import Data, every time you refresh the data, it will be imported from the data source. DirectQuery queries directly from the source no matter what visual you use. So what is Dual mode?

If you try to change the mode of an import table to Dual, as shown in Figure 6-14, you'll see that this change is not possible.

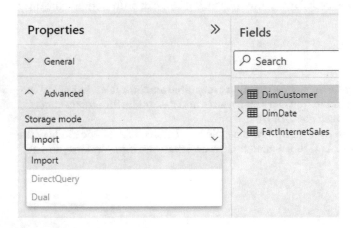

Figure 6-14. *Storage mode cannot be changed for import tables*

Dual mode is only an option for DirectQuery data sourced tables.

When you change the storage mode of a DirectQuery table to Dual (as demonstrated in Figure 6-15), it will create a copy of that table in the Power BI model. But unlike with Import Data, there is a copy in memory, and there is still the main table in the DirectQuery source.

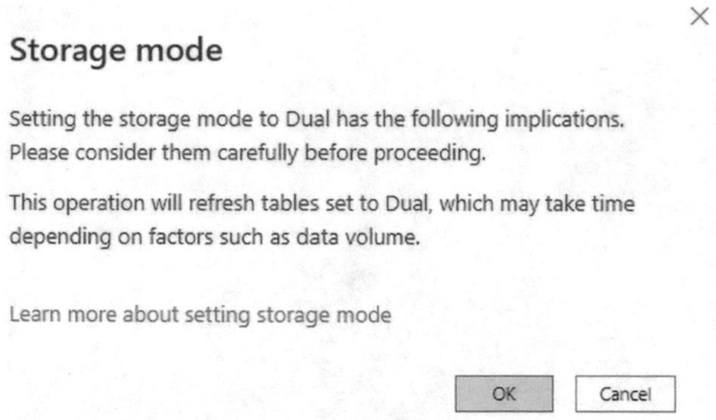

×

Storage mode

Setting the storage mode to Dual has the following implications.
Please consider them carefully before proceeding.

This operation will refresh tables set to Dual, which may take time
depending on factors such as data volume.

Learn more about setting storage mode

OK	Cancel

Figure 6-15. *Changing to Dual storage mode*

Dual storage mode works like DirectQuery or Import Data, depending on what other tables related to it are used in the visualization. If you have a visual that has columns from Import tables and a Dual table, the Dual table will act like an Import. If you have a visual that has columns from DirectQuery tables and a Dual table, the Dual table will act like a DirectQuery table. This ensures that you get the best performance when working with smaller tables (such as dimension tables) in Dual storage mode.

Modeling with the Power BI Composite Model

The following sections outline some points to consider when performing data modeling with a Power BI composite model.

Relationships in the Power BI Composite Model

You can create relationships between tables from different data sources and using different storage modes. Figure 6-16 shows how DimCustomer (Import Data) is connected to FactInternetSales (DirectQuery) and DimDate (Dual).

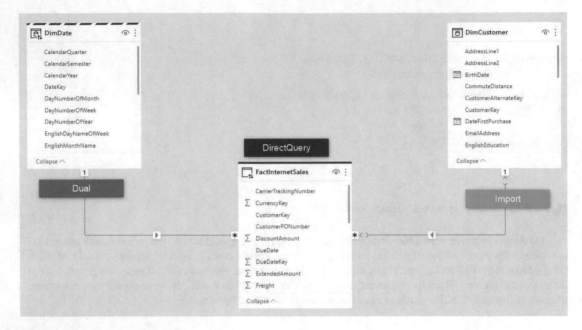

Figure 6-16. *Relationships in a Power BI composite model*

The cardinality of the relationship can be anything you want—one-to-many, many-to-one, one-to-one, and many-to-many.

Calculations and DAX

Calculated tables are available in composite model. These tables will be in Import mode, and their expression can be anything that DAX allows. You can also create calculated tables using the Power Query Editor.

Calculated tables are refreshed at the scheduled refresh time of the Power BI dataset.

Depending on where you create the calculated columns, they have some limitations. If you create a calculated column in an Import table or a calculated table, there will be no limitations. However, if you create a calculated column in a DirectQuery table, only columns from the same table can be used.

DirectQuery to Power BI Datasets

In composite model, you can create a DirectQuery connection to a Power BI dataset. This is different from a live connection to the Power BI dataset. A DirectQuery to a Power BI dataset enables you to import the Power BI dataset into the composite model, which enables you to do further data modeling on the chained dataset (see Figure 6-17). This concept is explained in a later chapter of this book.

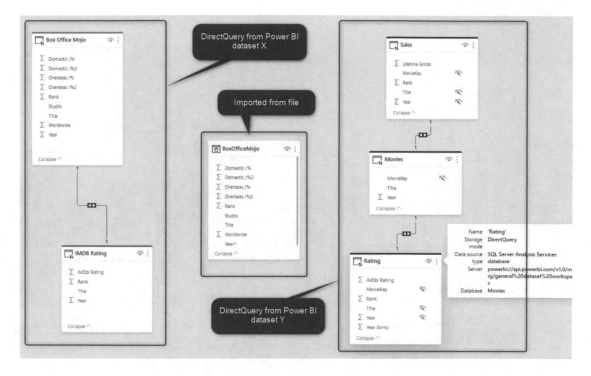

Figure 6-17. *DirectQuery to a Power BI dataset in composite model*

Summary

In summary, combining DirectQuery tables and Import Data tables in one Power BI model is called composite model or mixed mode. With this feature, you can leverage the option for using Dual storage mode to keep a copy of a DirectQuery table in memory. This is good for answering quick slicing and dicing questions.

DirectQuery was not a common method when it came to working with data in Power BI, especially because this mode couldn't originally combine multiple data sources. But now with composite model, DirectQuery is faster. If you have big data tables, I definitely recommend exploring composite model. Composite model can even go one step further in performance when aggregations are used.

Composite model is better than a pure DirectQuery approach. This option gives you performance and big data, all in one data model.

You learn more about this approach in the following chapters.

CHAPTER 7

■ ■ ■

DirectQuery for Power BI Datasets and Analysis Services

One of the recent features added to Power BI is the DirectQuery for Power BI datasets and Analysis Service. In other words, it's a composite model for Power BI datasets. This chapter explains what this means, how it's useful, and how it works in detail.

Power BI with Import Data

Most Power BI users import data from their sources into Power BI. This option provides the ultimate flexibility in modeling. If you use this approach, you can customize the tables using Power Query transformations, create relationships the way you want, write DAX calculations, and finally do visualizations. The Import Data mode of Power BI gives you untainted power and flexibility. In an earlier chapter of this book, I explained the Import Data mode in detail.

One Important Problem with Import Data

Importing data is fantastic, but nothing comes without side effects. With Import Data, one of the big problems is that every self-service user will start to import data into their own data model, and soon you end up with many data models, a lot of duplications, and silos of Power BI models everywhere. Many of those models might do the same thing over and over. See Figure 7-1.

© Reza Rad 2023
R. Rad, *Pro Power BI Architecture*, https://doi.org/10.1007/978-1-4842-9538-0_7

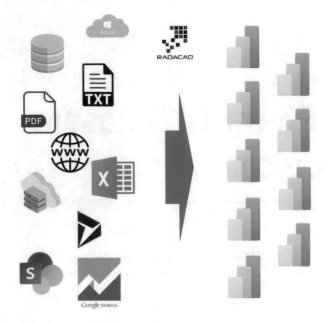

Silos of Power BI files

- All imported data
- From different sources, some sources the same
- Many repeated calculations
- No consistency
- Lots of redundancy
- Not a single source of truth
- Lots of extra time, effort and budget spent
- Not all results are the same
- Low trust in Power BI results

Figure 7-1. *The problem with silos of Power BI files*

Power BI Using Live Connection

An approach that comes in very handy to solve these problems is to have a Power BI report with a live connection to another dataset. This dataset can be a Power BI dataset hosted on the Power BI Service, an Azure Analysis Services dataset, or a SSAS dataset hosted on-premises. The Power BI report in this case would visualize the data from the main model.

Using Power BI as a live connection means that users cannot change the model and build their own. So there won't be a problem with inconsistency and there won't be silos of data models. There is one or a few central models only. In an earlier chapter of this book, I explained what a live connection means for Power BI.

Big Limitation of Live Connection

Live Connection is great for governing the Power BI implementation and avoiding silos. However, it is not a useful option for self-service users, because they cannot import other data sources and build variations on top of it. The most they can do is create report-level measures. A chapter later in this book explains how to import data from a Power BI dataset so that these types of users can still leverage some of the calculations done in the central model.

DirectQuery for Power BI Datasets or Analysis Services Datasets

Now that you have the background information, let's talk about the main topic. This feature, which was first announced in December 2020, allows you to create a new dataset that uses the central dataset. You can also bring your variations into it. See Figure 7-2.

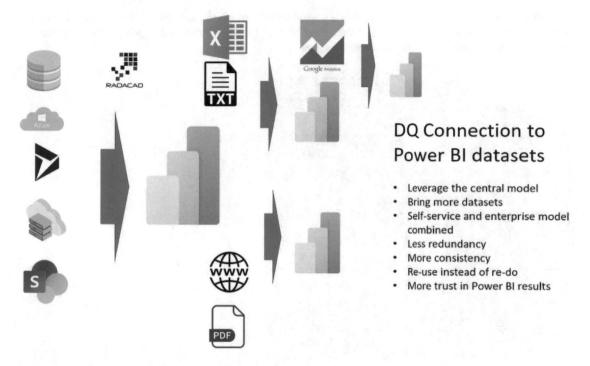

Figure 7-2. *DirectQuery for Power BI Datasets and Analysis Services*

This feature allows self-service users to reuse the existing model and add more options to it in a new model. Instead of reinventing the wheel, they add more components to the existing model. This is where the two worlds of self-service and Enterprise BI come together.

As an example, say a developer on the BI team builds a data model that has some entities about Sales from the SQL Server database, Dynamics 365, Azure blob storage, SharePoint, and a few other sources. This model can be used directly to create a report, or it can be used by a self-service user who wants to use other data from Excel and CSV files and have a more complete visualization for a specific use.

The model built by that self-service user can also be customized by another self-service user. As you see in Figure 7-2, this feature provides layers of implementation and development, rather than having to redo everything.

Why Is This Feature a Big Deal?

This feature allows you to:

- Leverage the central model

- Bring in more datasets

- Combine the self-service and enterprise models
- Have less redundancy
- Have more consistency
- Reuse instead of redo
- Have more trust in the Power BI results

This feature is more than a feature—this is where the two worlds of Enterprise BI and self-service BI come together, as illustrated in Figure 7-3. Instead of blocking each other's way and going their own ways, now these two help each other reach a common goal.

Figure 7-3. *Self-service BI and Enterprise BI come together with DirectQuery for Power BI Datasets and Analysis Services*

How It Works Under the Hood

Using this feature, you'll have a new copy of the data model that gets part of the data as a DirectQuery source from the Power BI dataset connection, and another part of the data from the data sources you import. There are limitations to this function at the time of writing this chapter. However, these limitations will be lifted one by one, gradually.

Not from My Workspace

The first thing you need to consider is that this feature doesn't work for datasets located in My Workspace, as shown in Figure 7-4. Right now, if you host a dataset in My Workspace, a connection to that dataset will be a normal live connection and you can't combine other data sources with it.

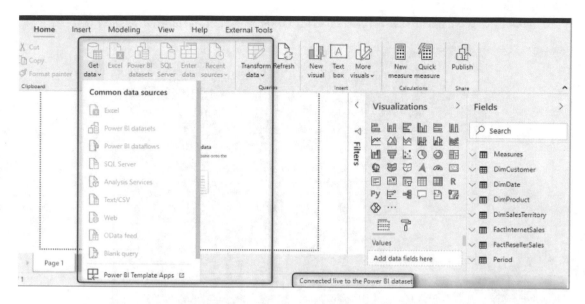

Figure 7-4. *DirectQuery to Power BI Dataset is not supported for datasets hosted in My Workspace*

This limitation will likely be lifted in the future, based on mentions in Microsoft's documentation. However, even if this is not a limitation when you read this book, I strongly advise you not to use it.

Imagine someone built a dataset and published it to My Workspace. Then others used that dataset to build something on top of it. If that person leaves the organization, it will be hard to get a hold of the original dataset. Having a dataset that is used as a source of other datasets in My Workspace is not recommended.

Creating a DirectQuery to Power BI Dataset

Creating a DirectQuery connection to a Power BI dataset is simple. From Get Data, choose Power BI Datasets, as shown in Figure 7-5.

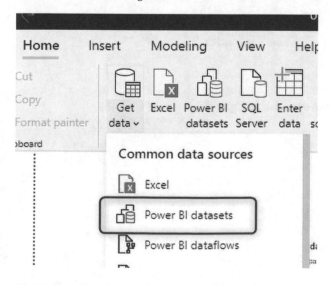

Figure 7-5. *Getting data from a Power BI dataset*

This will give you a normal live connection to the Power BI dataset, as shown in Figure 7-6.

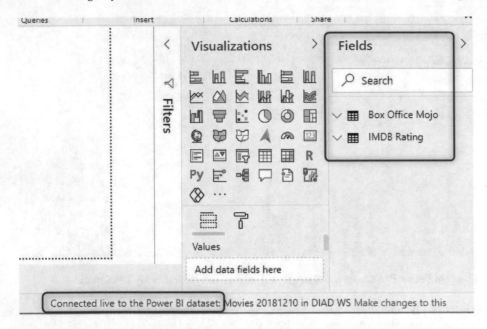

Figure 7-6. *Live connection to the Power BI dataset*

You can now get data from another dataset, as shown in Figure 7-7.

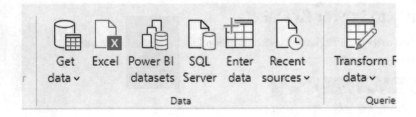

Figure 7-7. *Getting data from another dataset*

Or you can click Make Changes to this Model, as shown in Figure 7-8.

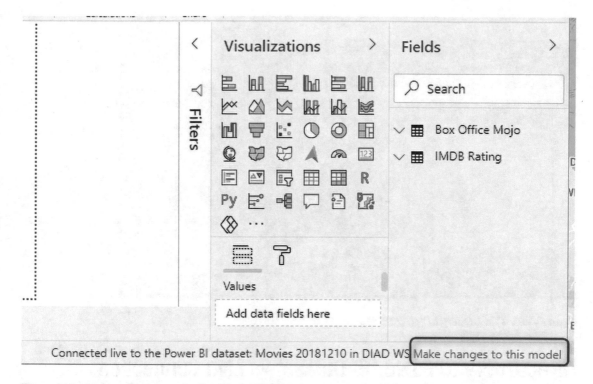

Figure 7-8. Making changes to the live Power BI dataset connection model

Using either of these options will show you the message that this operation will create a local dataset copy with the ability to change, as Figure 7-9 indicates.

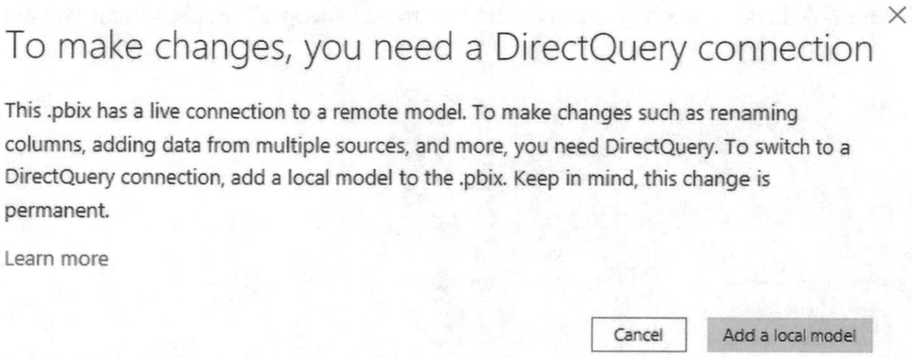

To make changes, you need a DirectQuery connection

This .pbix has a live connection to a remote model. To make changes such as renaming columns, adding data from multiple sources, and more, you need DirectQuery. To switch to a DirectQuery connection, add a local model to the .pbix. Keep in mind, this change is permanent.

Learn more

Cancel   Add a local model

Figure 7-9. Adding a local model (DirectQuery to Power BI dataset)

This action will change the storage mode of your Power BI dataset tables to DirectQuery, as shown in Figure 7-10.

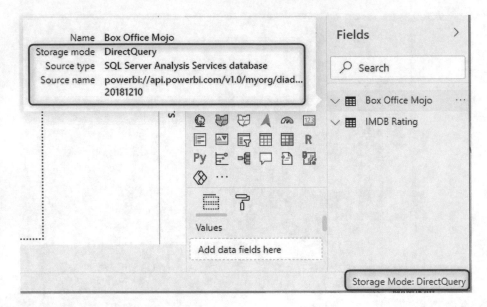

Figure 7-10. *DirectQuery to Power BI dataset*

DirectQuery to Power BI Dataset vs Live Connection to Power BI Dataset

With Live Connection to Power BI dataset, the only thing you can do is create report-level measures. Anything else has to be done in the original model.

With DirectQuery to Power BI dataset, you can add other data sources, columns, measures, tables, and so on, as shown in Figure 7-11. In other words, you can build a new model on top of the existing one with the changes you want.

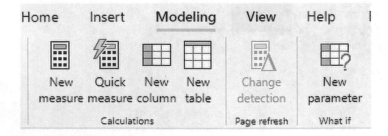

Figure 7-11. *Changes in the model using DirectQuery to Power BI dataset*

Multiple DirectQuery Connections Are Supported

You can have part of the model coming from one Power BI dataset, and another part coming from another dataset, as shown in Figure 7-12. You can also import some other tables. The new model view of Power BI shows these very nicely, with different color headings for each category.

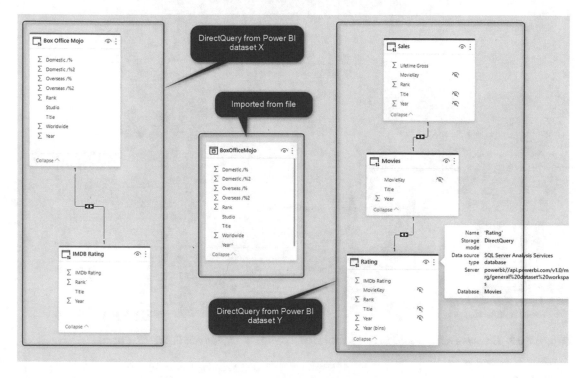

Figure 7-12. *Composite model using DirectQuery to Power BI dataset*

Creating a Relationship Between Different Data Sources

As you can see in Figure 7-13, you can easily create relationships between tables from different sources.

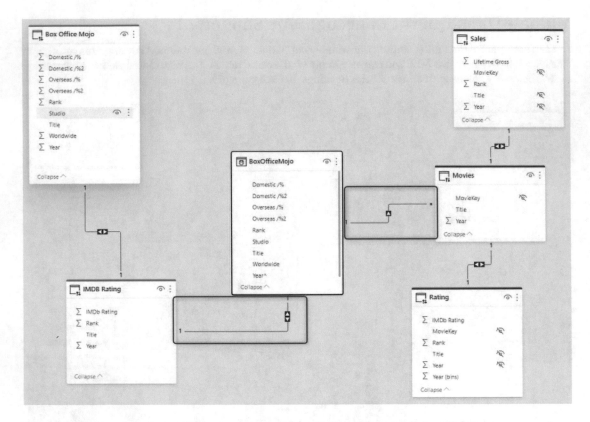

Figure 7-13. *Creating relationship in composite model using DirectQuery to Power BI dataset*

Publish to Service

The new data model, when published to service, requires some steps compared to other types of Power BI datasets. The following sections explain these steps.

Error: There Is No Gateway

For the visuals that have anything from the DirectQuery Power BI dataset, you may see an error saying, "There is no gateway," as highlighted in Figure 7-14.

Figure 7-14. *The "there is no gateway" error for DirectQuery to Power BI datasets*

To solve this error, go to the dataset's setting, as shown in Figure 7-15.

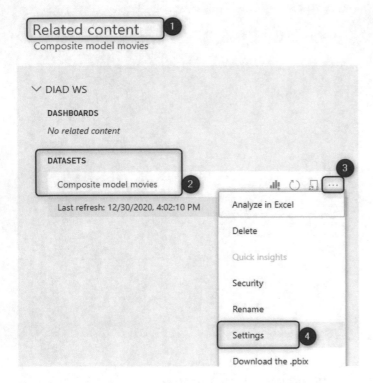

Figure 7-15. *Dataset's settings*

Remember that you need a gateway for any data source located on-premises and imported, as indicated in Figure 7-16. Select that in the gateway. Do not select a gateway option for your Power BI datasets.

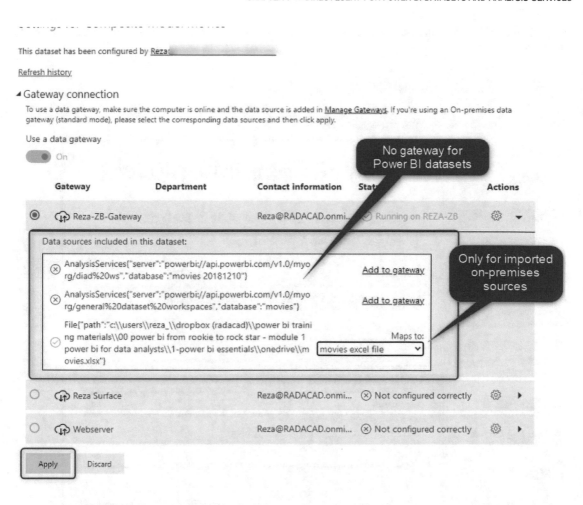

Figure 7-16. *Fixing the gateway error for DirectQuery to Power BI dataset*

If you are new to the gateway, there is a chapter about Power BI Gateway later in this book.

Data Source Credentials

After setting up the gateway, you need to set the credentials for the Power BI datasets, as shown in Figure 7-17.

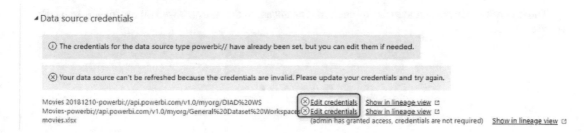

Figure 7-17. *Setting up data source credentials for Power BI datasets*

Select OAuth2 and enter the Power BI account credentials that have access to the datasets, as shown in Figure 7-18.

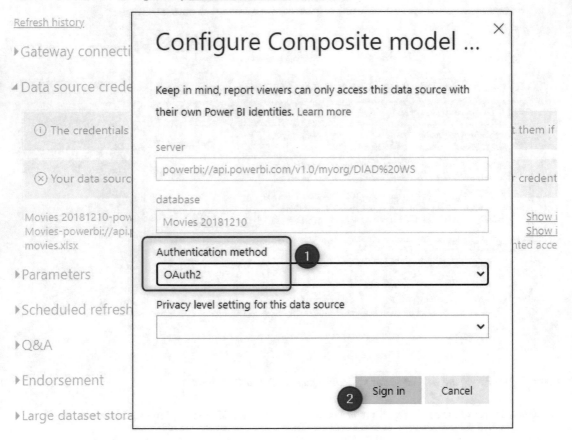

Figure 7-18. Entering credentials for DirectQuery to Power BI dataset

The credentials simply create the connection. The access to the data is based on the logged-in user's access to the data.

Lineage View

You can also see lineage view, which shows you all the data sources in your composite Power BI model. See Figure 7-19.

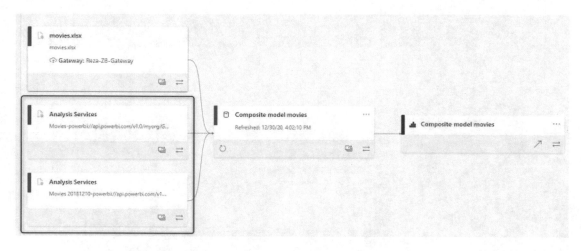

Figure 7-19. *Lineage view for a Power BI dataset*

After following these steps, the report will appear. See Figure 7-20 as an example.

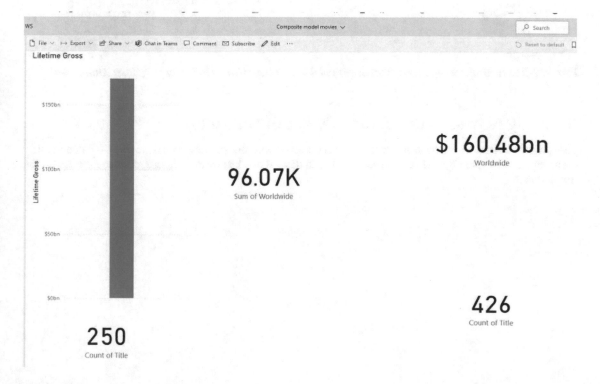

Figure 7-20. *Composite model report appears without errors*

Sharing the Report

This type of report can be shared like any other. However, sometimes, depends on the sharing configurations, the user gets the output shown in Figure 7-21.

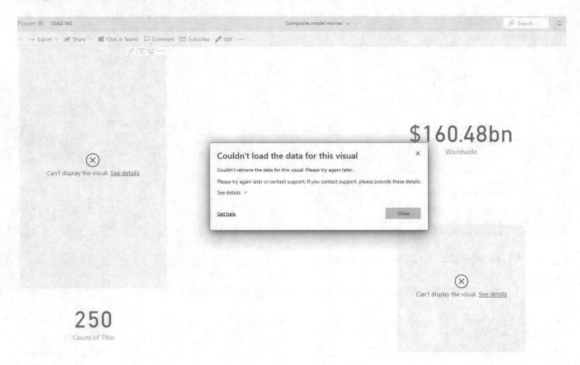

Figure 7-21. *Error when sharing a composite model with a DirectQuery to Power BI dataset connection*

Building Access to the Source Power BI Datasets

This happens often when the user who the report is shared with doesn't have access to one of the Power BI datasets. As shown in Figure 7-22, you can go to each dataset one by one and choose Manage Permission for that dataset.

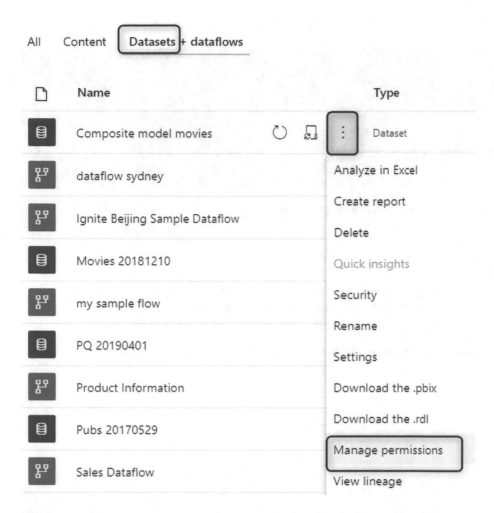

Figure 7-22. *Managing permissions of the sources of the Power BI datasets*

If the user doesn't have build access, enable it for them, as demonstrated in Figure 7-23. They should then be able to access the dataset just fine.

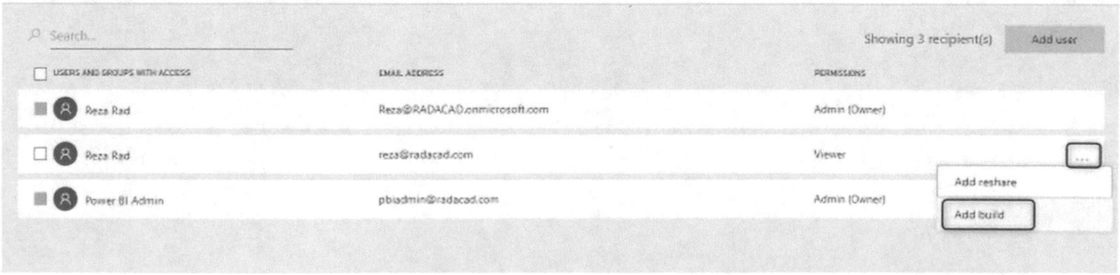

Figure 7-23. *Adding build access to the Power BI dataset*

With build access, the user can see the report properly, as shown in Figure 7-24.

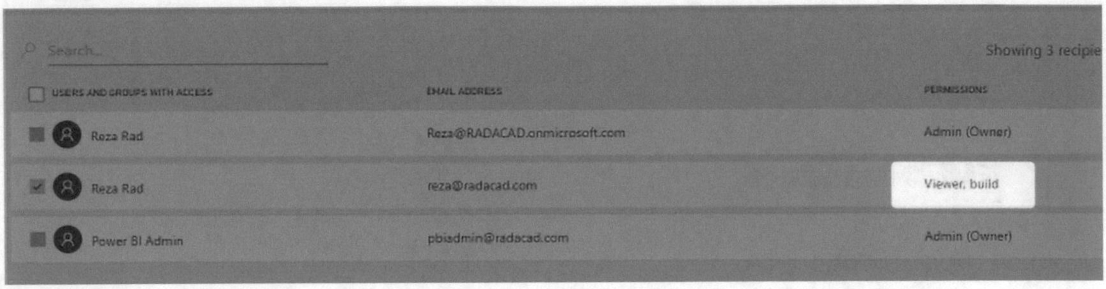

Figure 7-24. *User has build access to the Power BI dataset*

Summary

This feature is a major milestone in developing Power BI solutions in any organization. This feature can help you build less redundant code, have better consistency across your analysis, reuse whatever has been done so far, and customize on top of it. This feature significantly changes the way Power BI is used in a development environment.

In the next chapter, you learn about the differences between all the connection types in Power BI.

CHAPTER 8

■ ■ ■

Choosing the Right Connection Type: DirectQuery, Live, Import, or Composite Model

Power BI supports different methods for connecting data. That is why the decision to choose the right method is always a tough one. You have learned about of DirectQuery, Live Connection, Import Data, and composite model. Which situations would you choose one over the other? What are the pros and cons of each? What are the best practices for choosing each? Which one is faster? Which one is more flexible? I always get a lot of questions like these in my courses, conference talks, and blog posts. In this chapter, you get answers to all of these questions and more. This chapter will help you choose the right data connection methodology and architecture for your Power BI solution.

Why Is This a Tough Decision?

If Power BI had only one way to connect to data sources, you choice would be easy. You would never need to choose between methods and find the right one. However, Power BI supports multiple methods for connecting to data: DirectQuery, Live Connection, Import Data (or some call it Scheduled Refresh), and composite model. Many of you might still think that DirectQuery and Live Connection are the same, however, they are different. You learn about their differences in this chapter. Each method has benefits and drawbacks. Depending on the scenario that you are implementing, you might choose one over the others. Changing from one method to another can be a time-consuming task once you're in the implementation process. So the best approach is to choose the best method from the beginning.

Choosing the right method is an important step for your Power BI Solution Architecture. You need to make this decision in the early phases, before starting the implementation process. In this chapter, I explain in detail every method and answer the following questions:

- What is Import Data/Schedule Refresh?

- What is DirectQuery?

- What is Live Connection?

- What is the difference between Live Connection and DirectQuery?

- Pros and cons of each method

- Which method performs the fastest?

© Reza Rad 2023
R. Rad, *Pro Power BI Architecture*, https://doi.org/10.1007/978-1-4842-9538-0_8

- Which method is the most flexible?

- Which method is the most scalable?

- What are the architecture scenarios to use for each method?

- What is the role of the gateway?

What Is Import Data (Scheduled Refresh)?

This method has two names—some call it Import Data and some call it Scheduled Refresh. With this method, data from the source is loaded into Power BI. Loading data in Power BI consumes memory and disk space. If you are developing Power BI on your machine with the Power BI Desktop, it is the memory and disk space of your machine. If you are publishing the report on a website, it is the memory and disk space of the Power BI cloud machines.

If you have 1 million rows in a source table, and you load that data into Power BI with no filtering, you end up having the same amount of data in Power BI. If you have a database with 1,000 tables, however, you only load ten of those tables in Power BI, you get memory consumption for only those ten tables. The bottom line is that you spend memory and disc space equal to how much data you load into Power BI.

Compression Engine of xVelocity

The first assumption that you might come to after reading this explanation about Import Data is that, if you have a database with 100GB and import it into Power BI, you will have a 100GB file in Power BI. This is not true. Power BI leverages the compression engine of xVelocity and works on a column-store in-memory technology. The column-store in-memory technology compresses data and stores it in a compressed format. You could have a 1GB Excel file and when you import it into Power BI, your Power BI file ends up being 10MB. This is mainly because of the compression engine of Power BI. However, the compression rate varies. It depends on many things—the number of unique values in the column, the data types, and many other situations. A later chapter explains the compression engine in detail.

The short read for this part is this: Power BI stores compressed data. The size of the data in Power BI will normally be much smaller than the size in the data source.

Important Pros and Cons of This Method

Power BI Is Fully Functional

With this method, you get full functionality of Power BI. You can use Power Query to combine data from multiple sources, or DAX to write advanced time intelligence expressions and visualizations. There is no limitation on the functionality of Power BI with this method. You can use all its components.

Size Limitation

With this method, you have a limitation on the size of the model. Your Power BI model (or let's say the file) cannot be more than 1GB (if you are not using Power BI Premium capacity or Premium Per User licenses). You usually have up to 10GB in your account; however, the files can be up to 1GB. Power BI Premium allows you to have up to 400GB loaded on the Power BI website (Premium Per User allows up to 100GB). If you are using Power BI Report Server, the size limitation is 2GB. However, remember that 1GB in the Power BI file is not equal to 1GB of data in the source. (As mentioned in the compression engine section.)

This Is the fastest Method

This connection method is the fastest option possible. Data is loaded into the memory of the server and report queries are evaluated from the data loaded into memory. There are no lags or slowness with this method (as long as you designed your Power BI model with no performance issues).

What Is DirectQuery?

DirectQuery is a direct connection to the data source. Data is not stored in the Power BI model. Power BI will be a visualization layer, which queries the data from the data source every time. Power BI only stores the metadata of tables (table names, column names, relationships...), not the data. The Power BI file size is much smaller, and you will likely never hit the size limitation because there is no data stored in the model.

DirectQuery is possible using only a few data sources. Some of the data sources that support DirectQuery from Power BI include:

- Amazon Redshift
- Azure HDInsight Spark
- Azure SQL Database
- Azure SQL Data Warehouse
- IBM Netezza
- Impala
- Oracle Database
- SAP Business Warehouse
- SAP HANA
- Snowflake
- Spark
- SQL Server
- Teradata Database

Important Pros and Cons of This Method

Scalability: The Main Advantage

This method does not have a size limitation. Mainly because no data is stored in the Power BI file, so you never get an issue with the size of data. You can have data sources with petabytes of data in SQL Server, Oracle, or any other supported data sources and connect to them from Power BI.

Limited Functionality: Few Power Query Operations, Mainly Visualization

This method does not have the full functionality of Power BI. With this method, you have only two tabs in Power BI Desktop—Report and Relationship. You can change the relationship in this mode.

In Power Query, you are limited to the number of operations. The majority of the operations that cannot be folded cannot be used. To learn more about query folding, visit radacad.com/not-folding-the-black-hole-of-power-query-performance. With this mode, however, you have full visualization support.

Slow Connection

A big disadvantage of this method is that the connection is slower than with other types of connections. Note that every visual sends a query to the data source and the data comes back. You usually have more than one visual in your report, and when slicing and dicing, you are sending queries to the data source. Performance tuning the data source is a must when using this model.

To show a small example of performance tuning, Figure 8-1 shows the performance I get when I have a normal index on my table with 48 million records.

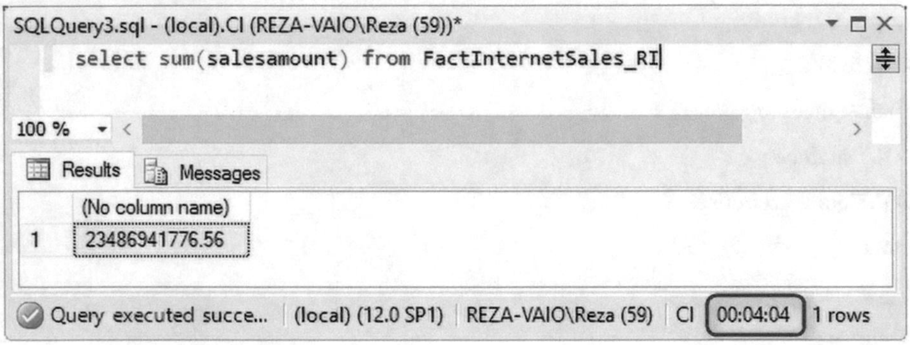

Figure 8-1. *A regular index*

A regular select sum from my table with 48 million records takes four minutes and four seconds to run. The same query responds in less than a second when I have a Clustered Column Store index, as you can see in Figure 8-2. You'll see significantly improved performance when you have a Clustered Column Store index on the same table with the same amount of data rows.

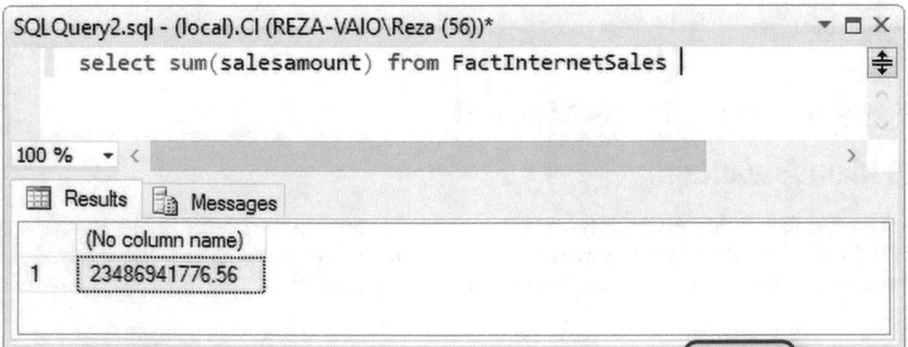

Figure 8-2. *Performance boost with a Clustered Column Store index*

This chapter doesn't teach you about performance tuning; you'll have to read books, blog posts, and watch videos to learn about it. That is a whole different topic on its own. The most important thing to remember is that performance tuning is different for each data source. Performance tuning for Oracle, SQL Server, and SSAS is totally different. Your friend for this part is Google, and the vast amount of free content available on the Internet for you to study.

What Is Live Connection?

Live Connection is similar to DirectQuery in the way that it works with the data source. It does not store data in Power BI, and it queries the data source every time. However, it is different from DirectQuery. Live Connection is only supported for these data sources:

- Azure Analysis Services

- SQL Server Analysis Services (SSAS) Tabular

- SQL Server Analysis Services (SSAS) Multi-Dimensional

- Power BI Dataset in the Service

Because these data sources are modeling engines themselves, Power BI connects to these and fetches all model metadata (measure names, attribute names, relationships...). With this method, you need to handle all your modeling requirements in the data source; Power BI just surfaces that data through visualization.

Important Pros and Cons of This Method

Big Model Size with OLAP or Tabular Engine

The main benefit of this model is that you can have a big-sized data model, and you can leverage the modeling layer of SSAS. SSAS Tabular will give you DAX, and Multi-Dimensional will give you MDX. With either of these two languages, you can cover all your calculations and modeling needs. This method has better modeling features than DirectQuery. In DirectQuery, there is no DAX or MDX. All the calculations need to be done on the database side. Doing calculations on the database side is often much more complex than doing them in the analytical expression language.

No Power Query, Just Visualization

The big disadvantage of this method is that you do not have access to Power Query.

Report-Level Measures

You get report-level measures with this type of connection, which give you the ability to write DAX measures. However, you might want to keep them in the data source to keep your model consistent.

Report-level measures are a great feature because users can create measures without having to call the BI developer. However, these measures are not added to the dataset. These are just for the report. So for consistency of your model, you might want to keep measure creation as part of your SSAS data source model.

Composite Model: The Best of Both Worlds

Power BI enables you to combine DirectQuery sources and Import Data sources into one dataset, as Figure 8-3 illustrates. Compositing gives you the performance and flexibility of Import Data, and the scalability and large data size of DirectQuery.

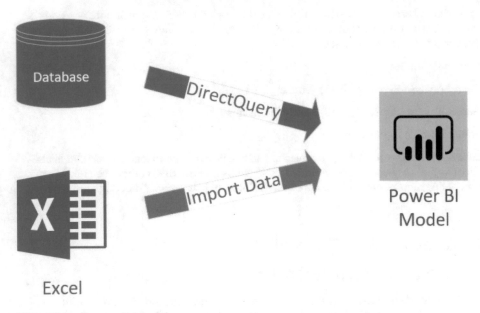

Figure 8-3. *Composite model*

Composite model not only supports DirectQuery to data sources such as SQL Server and other DirectQuery sources, it also enables you to use DirectQuery to the Power BI Dataset. This enables you to create a chained dataset from the main Power BI dataset. See Figure 8-4.

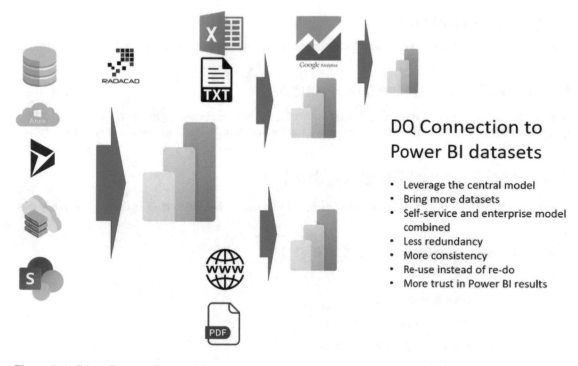

DQ Connection to Power BI datasets

- Leverage the central model
- Bring more datasets
- Self-service and enterprise model combined
- Less redundancy
- More consistency
- Re-use instead of re-do
- More trust in Power BI results

Figure 8-4. *DirectQuery to Power BI Dataset*

Composite model has many useful features, and it is highly recommended that you build a composite model for any of your DirectQuery data sources. This can be as simple as keeping the smaller tables in Import Data mode (such as dimension tables). This also enables you to create aggregated (and imported) versions of your DirectQuery tables for better performance.

Differences Between Live Connection and DirectQuery

Now that you know about all different types of connections, let's look at the differences between Live Connection and DirectQuery:

- DirectQuery is a direct connection to data sources such as SQL Server, Oracle, IBM, and so on.

- Live Connection is a direct connection to the Analysis Services model (Azure AS, SSAS Tabular, Multi-Dimensional, or a Power BI Report published service).

Relationship Configuration

With DirectQuery, you can still configure relationships in some cases. With Live Connection, you have no relationship ability. This should be handled in the data source. Because the Analysis Services is a modeling engine, you can build more than just a relationship there. Things such as hierarchies, measures, and columns can be created in the data source for the Live Connection and then be used in Power BI.

Report-Level Measures

With some types of SSAS live connections (to tabular model or Power BI Service), you get report-level measures.

No Power Query in Live Connection

In DirectQuery, you still can do simple Power Query transformations. However, in Live Connection, Power Query is not available. All you can do is change the source data model to another model or another server.

Pros and Cons of Each Method

I have already explained the main pros and cons in each section. This section reviews them all in handy lists.

Import Data or Scheduled Refresh

Advantages

- Fastest possible connection
- Power BI is fully functional
- Combines data from different sources
- Full DAX expressions
- Full Power Query transformations

Disadvantages

- Power BI file size limitation (this is different for Premium and Pro)

DirectQuery

Advantages

- Large-scale data sources are supported. No size limitation
- Pre-built models in some data sources can be used instantly

Disadvantages

- Very limited Power Query functionality
- Slower connection type: Performance tuning in the data source is must

Live Connection

Advantages

- Large-scale data sources supported. No size limitation as far as SSAS supports
- Many organizations already have SSAS models, so they can use them as a Live Connection without the need to replicate into Power BI

- Report-level measures
- MDX or DAX analytical engines in the data source of SSAS can be a great asset for modeling compared to DirectQuery

Disadvantages

- No Power Query
- Cannot combine data from multiple sources
- Slower connection type: Performance tuning in the data source is must

Which Method Is the Best and Fastest?

Import Data is the fastest possible option. Data is loaded into the memory of the server and all queries are resolved immediately. Live Connection is the next option in this list, especially if the SSAS Tabular or Power BI Service is used, because these two are in-memory technologies and perform faster than the Multi-Dimensional option.

DirectQuery is the slowest type of connection. You have to consider the performance tuning of your data source. However, DirectQuery can be combined with Import Data to boost the performance of your reports. I recommend you use aggregated import tables to even make things faster when querying big data tables.

The winner in this case is Import Data. The Import Data parts of the composite model go into the same category.

Which Method Is More Flexible?

With Import Data, you get the full functionality of Power BI, including full power query transformations, DAX measures, and visualizations.

Direct Query and Live Connection are the next on this list because they both give you something. DirectQuery provides a few Power Query options. Live Connection provides report-level measures.

The winner here is again Import Data. However, a composite model can have part of the data imported. So the flexibility on that part of the data is exactly the same as Import Data.

Which Method Is More Scalable?

The Import Data method has a size limitation. If you aren't using Power BI Premium, this method is not scalable. With DirectQuery and Live Connection, you get better scalability. Data sources support a large amount of data. The winners here are Live Connection and DirectQuery.

Which Architecture Scenarios Are Best for Each Method?

Import Data for Agility and Performance

Import Data has a fully functional Power BI and great performance. If your dataset is not huge, you can easily use this method and produce reports very quickly.

Live Connection for an Enterprise Solution

Many enterprises already have pre-built models in the SSAS Tabular or Multi-Dimensional options. These models can easily be used in a Power BI Live Connection.

Even if your company hasn't started the AAS (Azure Analysis Services) or SSAS solution, and you are dealing with a huge dataset, this option is better than Direct Query. In SSAS, you have the analytical expression languages of MDX or DAX to cope with lots of calculations and modeling challenges. Figure 8-5 shows a sample architecture that can be used with this method.

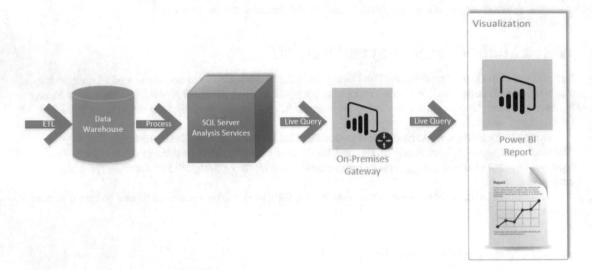

Figure 8-5. *Enterprise use of a Power BI live connection to Analysis Services*

Live Connection for Team Development

Even if you are not working in an enterprise environment with a dedicated BI team, you may find there are many benefits to using Live Connection. If you are working on an analytics project with multiple report authors and team members, you will enjoy a lot of benefits by sharing a dataset with a live connection. The dataset can then be consumed by report authors using the Get Data command from a Power BI Dataset and a live connection.

Direct Query for Non-Microsoft Sources

The DirectQuery connection is not used very much in Microsoft solution architecture settings. The main reason is that if you have a Microsoft-based solution architecture, you will probably use SSAS to leverage its analytical engine. DirectQuery mode is used mainly in non-Microsoft architectures, such as Oracle, IBM, or SAP HANA systems.

Even when you decide to use DirectQuery, I strongly recommend not using pure DirectQuery. Always combine DirectQuery tables with smaller import tables (dimensions or aggregated tables). This normally results in better performance when querying data in the reports.

What Is the Role of the Gateway?

Regardless of the type of connection you use (Import Data, DirectQuery, or Live Connection), if the data source is located on-premises, you need a gateway for it. Otherwise, you do not. To learn more about setting up a gateway, see the related chapter later in this book.

Summary

You've learned about the different types of connections—Live Connection, Import Data, DirectQuery, and Composite Model. You've learned their differences, pros and cons, and scenarios in which each should be used. There are still a lot of details for each method. In this chapter, I tried to explain everything in general to give you a holistic view. For more detailed information about each connection, read the previous chapters about each connection type. Now that you know about the connection types, the following chapters cover the important elements of the Power BI architecture—datasets, dataflows, and datamarts.

CHAPTER 9

■ ■ ■

Dataflows

Dataflows are an important component of the Power BI architecture. Using them can enhance the development and maintenance of your Power BI solution significantly. However, there are many Power BI implementations that don't use this functionality, even though more than three years have passed since it was released. In this chapter, you learn what a dataflow is and why you should use it.

What Is a Dataflow?

A dataflow is the data transformation service that runs on the cloud *independent* of the Power BI dataset or solution. This data transformation service leverages the Power Query engine and uses the Power Query online and UI to do the data transformation, illustrated in Figure 9-1.

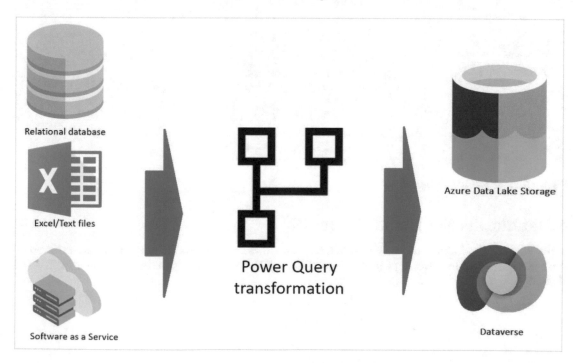

Figure 9-1. A dataflow is a data transformation in the cloud that's independent of the Power BI dataset

© Reza Rad 2023
R. Rad, *Pro Power BI Architecture*, https://doi.org/10.1007/978-1-4842-9538-0_9

One might say that the Power BI dataset, when published to the service, also runs the data transformation online. Would it then be a dataflow? The answer is no. Because Power Query, which is part of the Power BI dataset, is loading data into the dataset directly. With a dataflow, the destination is not a dataset. It can be Azure Data Lake Storage or a dataverse (or some other storage types explained later). This makes the dataflow the independent data transformation component of Power BI.

A Dataflow Is Service-Only (Cloud-Only) Object

You cannot author or create a dataflow using the desktop tools such as the Power BI Desktop. The only way to create a dataflow is to do it in the cloud. In the Power BI Service, you can do it in a workspace. A dataflow created in the service (shown in Figure 9-2) can be used in the desktop tools (to connect and get data).

Figure 9-2. Creating a dataflow

A Dataflow Is Not Just for Power BI

In the Power BI world, we call them Power BI dataflows. However, dataflows are not just for Power BI. You can create dataflows in Power Apps (called Power Platform Dataflows). This process is illustrated in Figure 9-3.

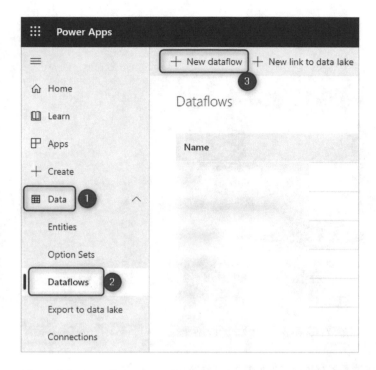

Figure 9-3. Dataflows created in Power Apps

Calling the dataflows by the platform in which you create them is not a common method. Instead, dataflows have two categories—Standard and Analytical.

Where Do Dataflows Store Data?

Dataflows do not store the data in the Power BI dataset. As you read earlier, the dataflow acts independently of the Power BI dataset. There must be another storage for the dataflow objects. The storage for a dataflow can be Azure Data Lake Storage or dataverses (There are other storage options available in Dataflow Gen2 as part of the release wave plan for Microsoft Fabric).[1]

You don't need an extra license to get the data storage option for a dataflow. If you use the Power BI Pro license, there will be an internal Azure Data Lake storage available for your dataflow tables. If you use Power Apps licenses, you will have storage available in the dataverse to use for your dataflows.

Other Microsoft services, such as Power Platform, can then connect to the dataflow, as shown in Figure 9-4.

---

[1] docs.microsoft.com/en-us/power-platform-release-plan/2022wave2/data-integration/ load-azure-sql-database-dataflows

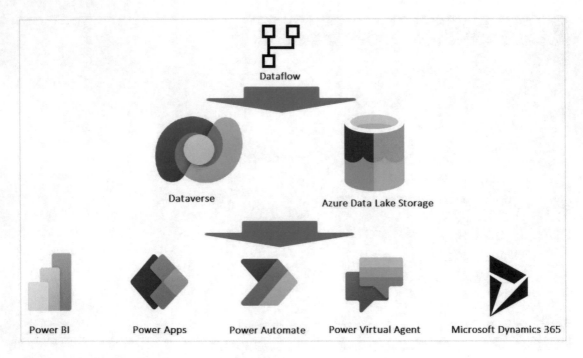

Figure 9-4. *A dataflow stores data in Azure Data Lake storage or dataverses*

Standard vs. Analytical Dataflows

Dataflows are characterized by Standard or Analytical. This categorization is not only based on the storage option of the dataflow but also on some of the functionalities available in each option. Analytical dataflows give you more analytical power, such as Computed entity[2] and AI functions in the dataflow[3]. The Standard dataflow store the data in dataverses only. There are a few other differences, too, but they are beyond the scope of this book.

Table 9-1 is a summary of these dataflows.

---

[2] To learn more about a computed entity, visit radacad.com/linked-entities-and-computed-entities-dataflows-in-power-bi-part-4

[3] To learn more about dataflow AI functions, visit radacad.com/ai-in-dataflow-power-bi-webservice-auto-azure-ml-part2

Table 9-1. *Standard vs. Analytical Dataflows*

Operation	Standard	Analytical
How to create	Power Platform dataflows	Power BI dataflowsPower Platform dataflows by selecting the Analytical Entity checkbox when creating the dataflow
Storage options	Dataverse	Power BI provided Azure Data Lake Storage for Power BI dataflows, Dataverse provided Azure Data Lake Storage for Power Platform dataflows, or customer provided Azure Data Lake storage
Power Query transformations	Yes	Yes
AI functions	No	Yes
Computed entity	No	Yes
Can be used in other applications	Yes, through the dataverse	Power BI dataflows: Only in Power BIPower Platform dataflows or Power BI external dataflows: Yes, through Azure Data Lake Storage
Mapping to standard Entity	Yes	Yes
Incremental load	Default incremental-loadPossible to change using the Delete rows that no longer exist in the query output checkbox at the load settings	Default full-loadPossible to set up incremental refresh by setting up the incremental refresh in the dataflow settings
Scheduled Refresh	Yes	Yes, the possibility of notifying the dataflow owners upon failure

Dataflows Are Powered by Power Query Online

Dataflows are powered by Power Query Online. Every transformation is completed by the dataflow engine, and the UI provided for doing the transformation is the Power Query Editor Online. There are more than 80 data sources available using dataflows, some of which are shown in Figure 9-5.

Figure 9-5. *Data sources for dataflows*

The online Power Query Editor enables you to do most of the transformations through the GUI. However, you can also use the Advanced Editor and work with the M script directly. See Figure 9-6.

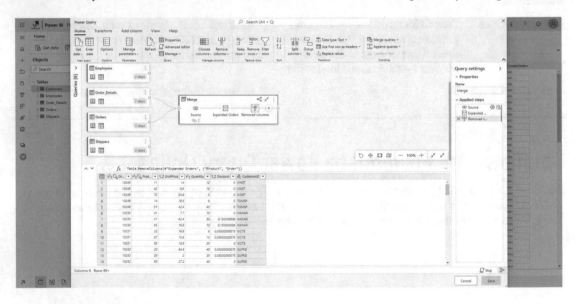

Figure 9-6. *Power Query Editor online*

Dataflows Can Be Used in Power BI, Excel, and Other Services

Depending on the type of dataflow, you can get data from it in a Power BI Desktop (or a Power BI Dataset), as in Figure 9-7, in Excel, and in some other services. This makes the dataflow a fully-independent component on its own.

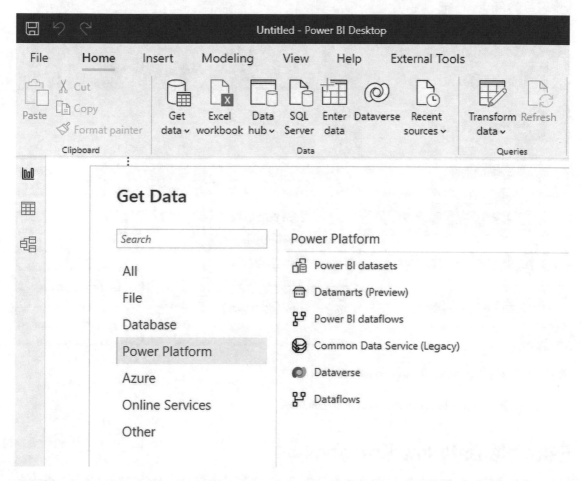

Figure 9-7. *Getting data from a dataflow in the Power BI Desktop*

In Excel, the same thing is available, as shown in Figure 9-8.

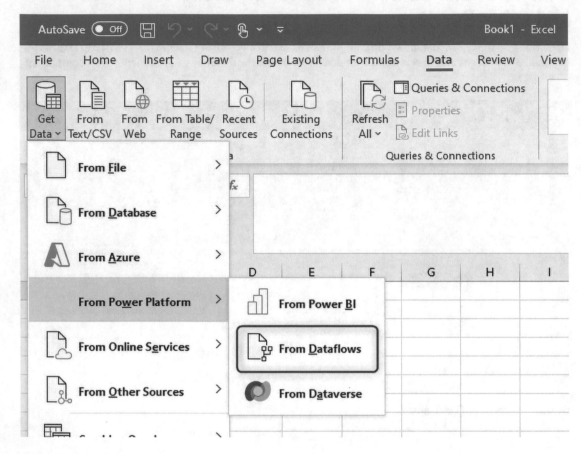

Figure 9-8. *Getting data from a dataflow in Excel*

The next sections discuss the use cases of dataflows.

Example Dataflow Scenarios

Now comes the big question of why you should use a dataflow. What is the point of it? I find it best to explain using examples.

Using One Power Query Table in Multiple Power BI Reports

Have you ever had the need to use one Power Query table in multiple Power BI reports? Of course you did. If you worked with Power BI for some time, you know that tables generated through Power Query are only part of one Power BI file. If you want to use the same table in another file, with a combination of some other tables that is not in the first file, you need to replicate the Power Query transformations (or copy and paste the M script) into the new *.pbix file. You may think, no I don't, but Figure 9-9 shows an example—Date Dimension!

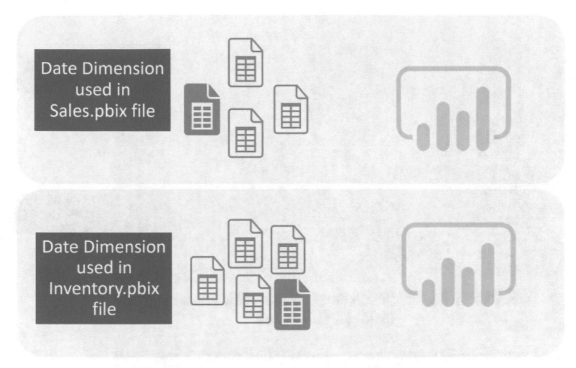

Date Dimension transformation executed multiple times, when only once is needed

Figure 9-9. A table that is needed in multiple Power BI files

Date dimension is a table that you use in a *.pbix, let's say for Sales Analysis, and in another *.pbix for inventory reporting, and another *.pbix for HR data analysis. What do you do in these situations? Copy the script of Date Dimension in all of these files? What if after a year, you decide to add a transformation or a column to the date dimension? Then you need to replicate this change in all *.pbix files that you have, otherwise, your code will become inconsistent. It would have been much better if you did the transformation once, stored the output somewhere, and then reused it. As Figure 9-10 demonstrates, this is exactly what dataflows can do for you!

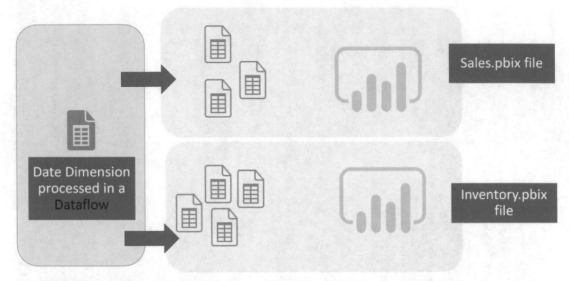

Date Dimension transformation executed only once, and then used multiple times

Figure 9-10. *Processing the common table in the dataflow and reusing it in multiple PBIX files*

Reusable tables or queries across multiple Power BI files are one of the best candidates for dataflows.

Different Data Sources with Different Refresh Schedules

What do you do if you have a dataset that includes two tables with different schedule options? For example, the Sales transactions table comes from the SQL Server database changes every day, and you need to refresh this data every day. However, the mapping table used for some of the products and maintained by the product team changes every quarter. If you have both of these queries in one *.pbix file, you have no other choice but to refresh at the maximum frequency needed, which is once a day.

However, what if there were a mechanism that could refresh the mapping table every quarter, apply all needed transformations, and store it in a table. Then every day you just need to read it. Dataflows can do that for you; with one query running the data transformation script and loading it into a destination table. This can be scheduled for whatever plan you need. Figure 9-11 illustrates this scheduling feature.

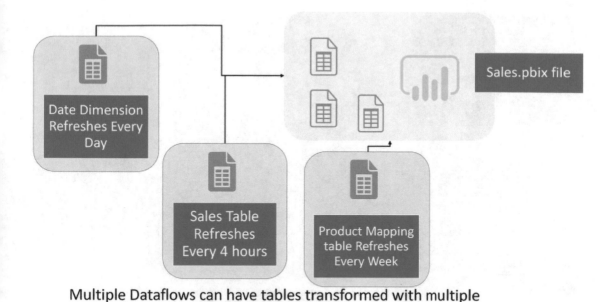

Multiple Dataflows can have tables transformed with multiple schedule options

Figure 9-11. *You can have multiple dataflows for different scheduled refresh settings*

Dataflows can run the extract, transformation, and load (ETL) process on a different schedule for every query (or table).

Centralized Data Warehouse

With the evolution of Power BI and other self-service technologies, many companies started to implement a BI system without having a data warehouse. However, if the number of BI systems increases, the need for a centralized data warehouse appears quickly. A data warehouse is a specifically designed database that stores data in the format needed for reporting. In traditional BI systems, one of the phases of building a BI system, and one of the most important phases, is to create a centralized data warehouse. The ETL process will extract data from the data sources and load it into the centralized data warehouse. All reporting solutions then use the data warehouse as the single source of truth.

Dataflows can be an important part of building a centralized data warehouse for your Power BI solution. You can build the structure you want through Power Query scripts in a dataflow. Dataflows then run those scripts and store the data in output tables. Output tables of the dataflow can act as a centralized data warehouse for your *.pbix files. Alternatively, you can have your own Azure Data Lake storage and configure it the way that you want, with the structure of tables that you want, and get a dataflow to load data into those tables. See Figure 9-12.

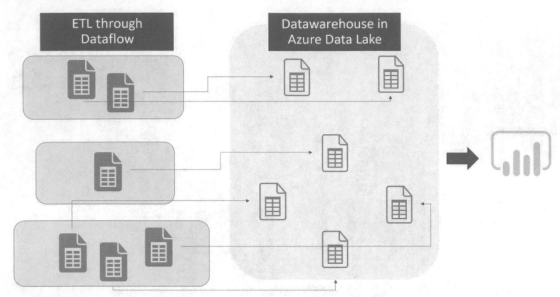

Dataflow Fuels the Azure Data Lake as the ETL fuels the Data Warehouse

Figure 9-12. *Dataflows can feed data into your data warehouse*

Dataflows can be the ETL engine that fuels the centralized data warehouse in Azure Data Lake storage.

Power BI datamarts are a new component of Power BI, and they can be a much better replacement for dataflows when used for Data Warehouse purposes. I suggest strongly reading about datamarts in future chapters of this book.

Getting Started with Dataflows in Power BI

This section provides hands-on experience with dataflows and explains how dataflows work. First, you'll see how to create a dataflow. The first thing you need to know is that the dataflow creation and maintenance process is happening in the Power BI Service, not in the desktop, because dataflows are not part of any report or *.pbix file.

Developing and editing dataflows is possible through the Power BI service (not the desktop).

The second important thing you need to know is that dataflows can be created only in an app workspace. You cannot create a dataflow in My Workspace. So either create one or navigate to an app workspace. As you can see in Figure 9-13, I am in an app workspace called dataflow. The name of the app workspace can be anything you want.

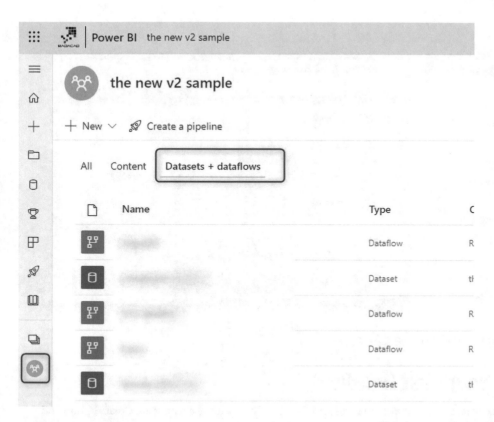

Figure 9-13. Dataflows should be created in an organizational workspace

---

Dataflows are only available in an app workspace (not in My Workspace).

In the Datasets + Dataflows tab, you can see any dataflows you created. If you don't see the Dataflow tab, even in an app workspace, then there is something else you need to consider—the administrator's control of the dataflow.

Administrator's Control

Power BI administrators can turn off and on the creating and use of the dataflow for users in the tenant. So if you don't see the Dataflows option, it is probably because the Power BI administrator has turned that feature off. Contact your administrator to get that enabled. At the time of writing this book, this option can be only turned on or off for the entire organization (like many other options in the tenant setting at the very first few months of their appearance), but I believe this feature is available for a select group of people (like many other options in the tenant settings in the future).

In the Admin Portal of Power BI service, under Tenant Settings, there is a configuration option for dataflows, as shown in Figure 9-14.

Admin portal

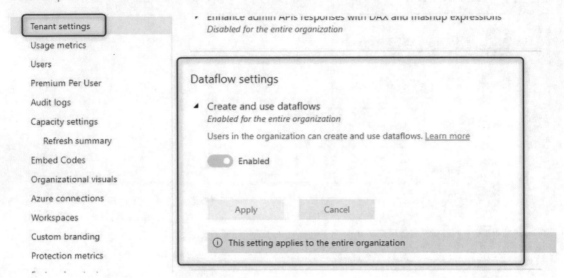

Tenant settings

Usage metrics

Users

Premium Per User

Audit logs

Capacity settings

   Refresh summary

Embed Codes

Organizational visuals

Azure connections

Workspaces

Custom branding

Protection metrics

Figure 9-14. *Tenant settings for dataflows*

Creating Your First Dataflow

Now that you are ready, you can start building your first dataflow. Start by clicking the Create option and choosing Dataflow, as shown in Figure 9-15.

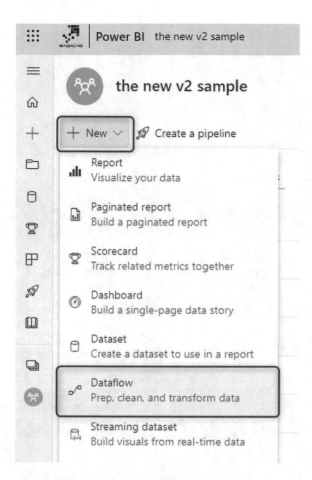

Figure 9-15. *Creating a dataflow in the workspace*

Each dataflow acts like a job schedule process. It has one or more transformations in it and can be scheduled. These transformations can write data into entities and tables. In Figure 9-16, you can see that there is an option to Define New Tables. Let's start with that.

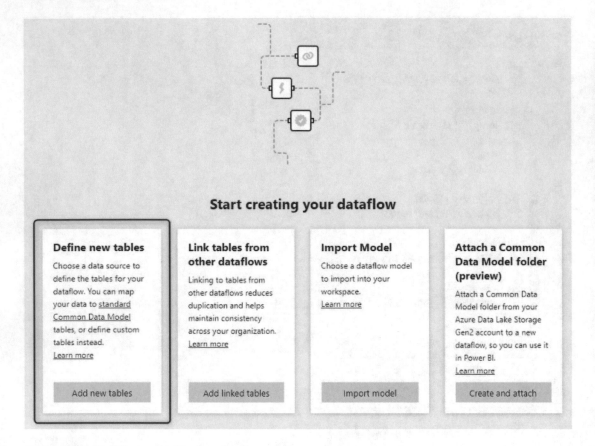

Figure 9-16. *Defining new tables in a dataflow*

Click Add New Tables. You can see a list of all supported data sources. (Recently in an update, many more data sources were added to the list). As you can see in Figure 9-17, the interface is very similar to the Get Data interface of the Power BI Desktop.

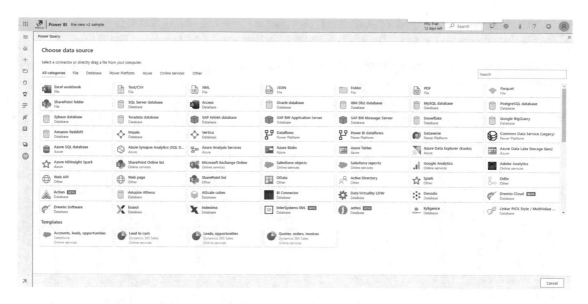

Figure 9-17. *Data sources available for dataflows*

Sample Datasets

For this example, you will be using an OData source, because it doesn't need a gateway set up or need additional setup requirements. Select OData[4] as the data source type, and in the URL part, enter the following address—`services.odata.org/V3/Northwind/Northwind.svc/`—as shown in Figure 9-18.

Connect to data source

OData Other	**Connection settings** URL `services.odata.org/V3/Northwind/Northwind.svc/` Connection credentials On-premises data gateway (none) ↻ Authentication kind Anonymous

Figure 9-18. *Getting data from OData*

---

[4] OData is a dataset that is available through API, and its output can include one or more tables. Many data transformation tools can read data from OData. Power Query (or in this case, a dataflow) also has an OData data source connection.

After this step, you should see a screen that is very similar to the Navigator window in the Power Query Editor. On this screen, you will see a list of all tables and can start exploring them—see Figure 9-19.

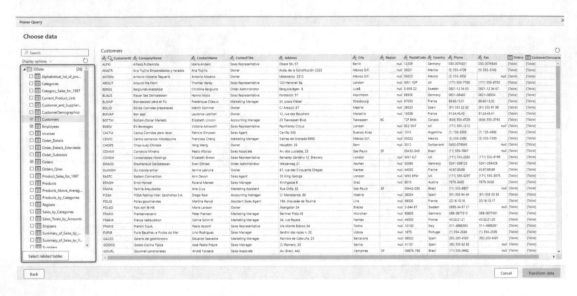

Figure 9-19. *Selecting tables for transformation*

In this example, select the Customers, Employees, and Orders tables and then click Transform Data.

Power Query Editor Online

As you can see in Figure 9-20, after selecting tables, you will see a screen that is very similar to the Power Query Editor, but an online version of it. You can see the Queries pane, the Steps (Query Settings) pane, the Data Preview pane, and the Data Transformation pane. There have been recent updates to the graphical interface of the Power Query Editor online.

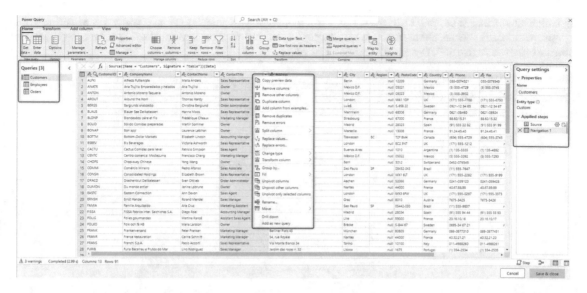

Figure 9-20. *Power Query Editor online*

In this example, I selected the three tables with no transformation and clicked Done. You can see all the tables in this dataflow. In dataflows, these are called entities. For every entity, you can specify Incremental Refresh if you want. You can then save your dataflow, as shown in Figure 9-21.

Figure 9-21. *Saving your dataflow*

Setting Up a Gateway

If your data is sourced from an on-premises (local domain) source, you need to have a gateway set up, as shown in Figure 9-22. You can read information about the gateway in a later chapter in this book. The difference here with Power Query in the Power BI Desktop is that, because you are developing the file locally, you can connect to an on-premises data source in the Power BI Desktop and start developing your solution, and then after publishing it to the service, you can set up the gateway. However, in a dataflow, because everything is happening in the service, you need to have a gateway set up if you are connecting to an on-premises data source. Otherwise, you cannot pass the first step. If you are connecting to an online data source (such as Azure SQL Database), you don't need a gateway.

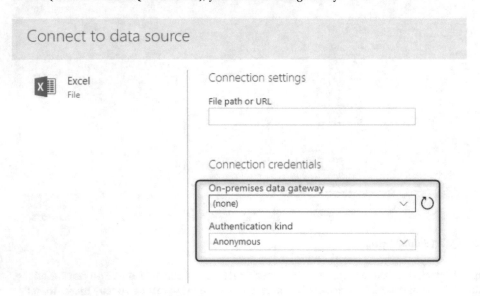

Figure 9-22. *Gateway setup for the dataflow tables*

Blank Query as the Data Source

One way to transfer your Power Query scripts to dataflow is to select () Blank Query as the data source, as shown in Figure 9-23, and copy and paste the M script from your Power Query tables to the dataflow. However, be mindful that not all Power Query transformations are supported yet. You may need to make some changes.

Figure 9-23. *Startting the dataflow table with a Blank Query*

This script (see radacad.com/download/13519/) is creating a basic date dimension. (You can learn more about it at radacad.com/all-in-one-script-to-create-date-dimension-in-power-bi-using-power-query.) You can copy and paste it into the blank query in the dataflow. See Figure 9-24.

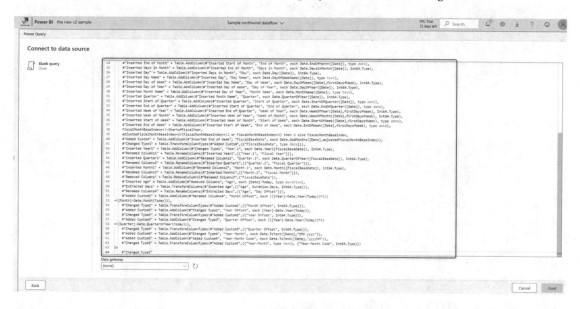

Figure 9-24. *Copying and pasting the M script into the blank query*

Dataflow should be able to show you a list of steps based on the script, although this depends on the functions used in the script and whether they are already supported in dataflow. See Figure 9-25.

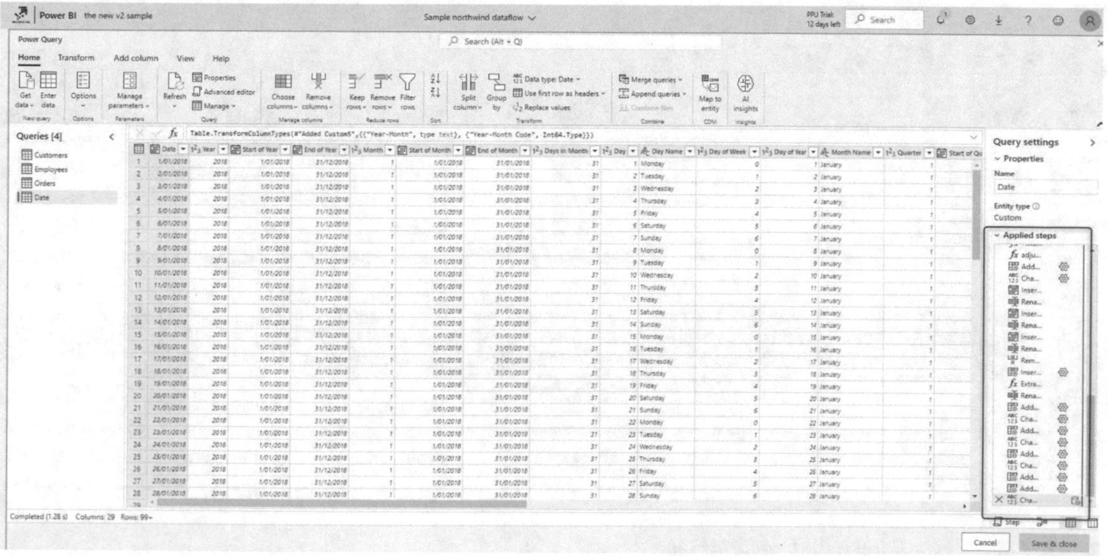

Figure 9-25. *Applied steps in the online Power Query Editor*

You can also see that there is a very useful diagram view in the Power Query Editor online that demonstrates all the steps and the data at each step. See Figure 9-26.

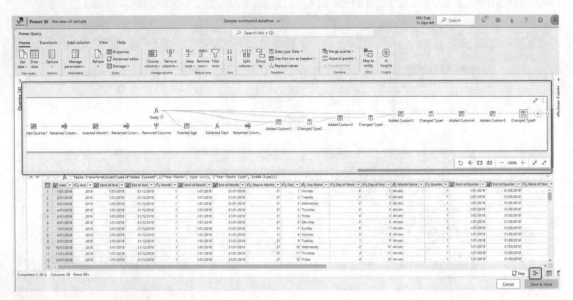

Figure 9-26. *Diagram view in the online Power Query Editor*

Scheduled Refreshes

You can configure dataflow refreshes at each dataflow level (not at the entity level), as shown in Figure 9-27.

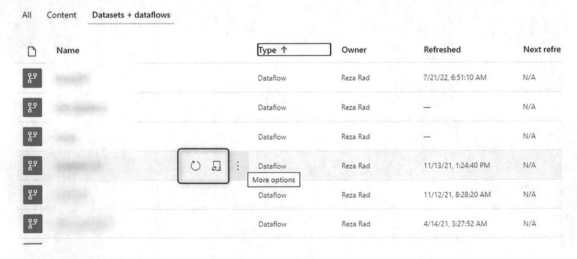

Figure 9-27. *Scheduled refresh of dataflows*

Get Data from Dataflow in the Power BI Desktop

In the Power BI Desktop, you can get data from the dataflows under the common data sources, as shown in Figure 9-28.

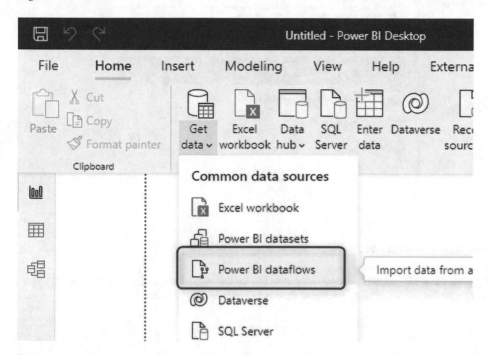

Figure 9-28. *Getting data from Power BI dataflows under the common data sources*

Under the Power Platform, you can choose Power BI dataflows. Note that there is also an option for dataflows in general, which includes Power Platform dataflows, as shown in Figure 9-29.

Get Data

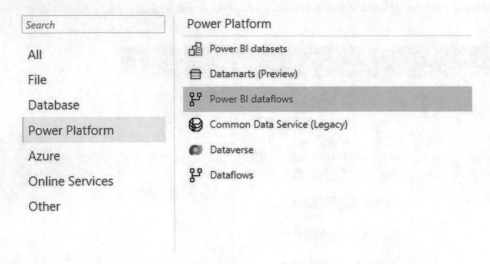

Figure 9-29. *Getting data from dataflows using the Power Platform menu option*

After entering your Power BI credentials, you can then see all the workspaces with dataflows under it, and you can select the tables you want from each dataflow, as shown in Figure 9-30.

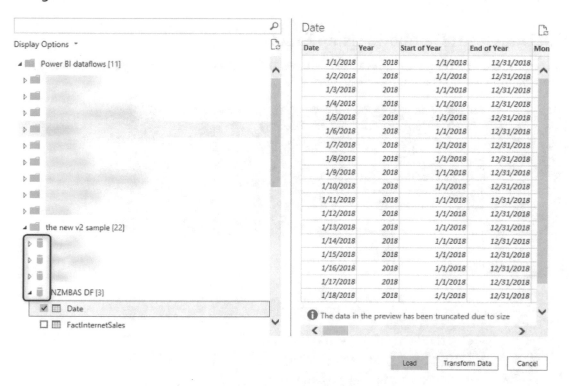

Figure 9-30. *Selecting the dataflow to get the data from the Navigator window*

Each dataflow is like a database, and you can have multiple tables in it. Once you get the data from the dataflow, the Power Query in the Power BI Desktop will simply import the data (but not the transformations) from the dataflow table, as Figure 9-31 shows.

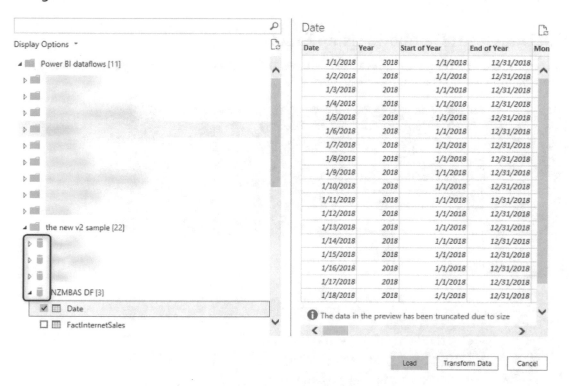

Figure 9-31. *Importing data from the dataflows*

It is possible to have a DirectQuery connection to the Dataflow tables as well, but that requires a Premium license.

Get Data from Dataflows Using Excel

You can also use Excel to get data from a dataflow table. This option gives you access to both Power BI and Power Platform dataflows in one place. See Figure 9-32.

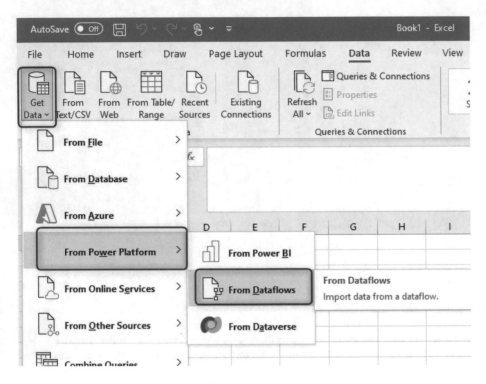

Figure 9-32. *Getting data from dataflows in Excel*

After entering the credentials, you can choose the dataflow from Environments (for Power Platform Dataflows) or Workspaces (for Power BI Dataflows). See Figure 9-33.

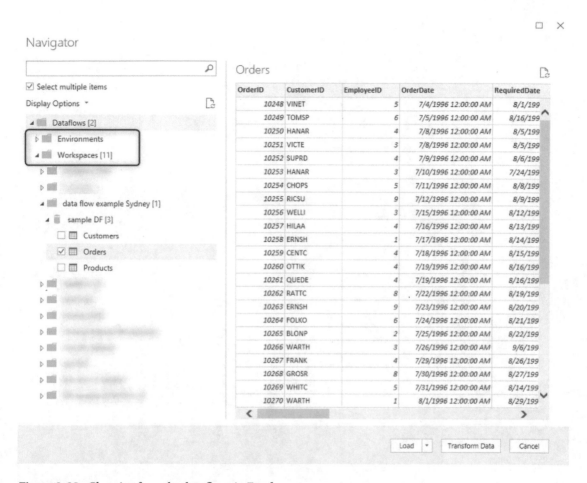

Figure 9-33. *Choosing from the dataflows in Excel*

Summary

Dataflows provide the data transformation engine of Power BI, which is independent of other Power BI objects. Dataflows are powered by the Power Query engine and the Power Query Editor online. Using dataflows, you can separate the ETL layer of the Power BI implementation from the rest of the work. Using dataflows is highly recommended because you can reuse your existing tables in multiple files. Dataflows are not just for Power BI, then can be used in Excel too, and they can be created in the Power Platform. Dataflows come in two categories—Standard and Analytical. In this chapter, you learned how to create a dataflow.

CHAPTER 10

■ ■ ■

Shared Datasets

Have you ever wanted to reuse part of a model in another report? Imagine two report visualizers on your team who want to create Power BI report visualizations from your data model. You have already done some modeling and calculations. How can this be done the best way without high maintenance costs? The answer is a shared dataset in Power BI. In this chapter, you learn about the following:

- What a shared dataset is in Power BI

- How a shared dataset can help with Power BI development

- Where the shared dataset is in the Power BI architecture

- How the shared dataset works behind the scenes in the Power BI service

- What certified and promoted datasets are

What Is the Dataset in Power BI?

When you create a Power BI report (a *.PBIX file) and the data connection mode is Import Data, the report has two components—a report and a dataset. When you are in the Power BI Desktop environment, you can't see the separation that easily unless you go to the task manager and see the dataset running behind the scenes under the Power BI Desktop task threads, as shown in Figure 10-1.

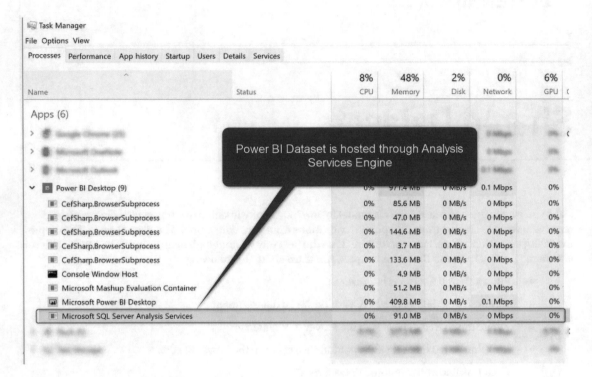

Figure 10-1. *The Task Manager showing the Microsoft SQL Server Analysis Service running behind the scenes of the Power BI Desktop*

However, when you publish the PBIX file into the service (the Power BI website), you can easily see that there are two objects—a report and a dataset.

- The *report* is the visualization layer of your Power BI implementation

- The *dataset* includes the data, tables, relationships, calculations, and connections to the data source (see Figure 10-2).

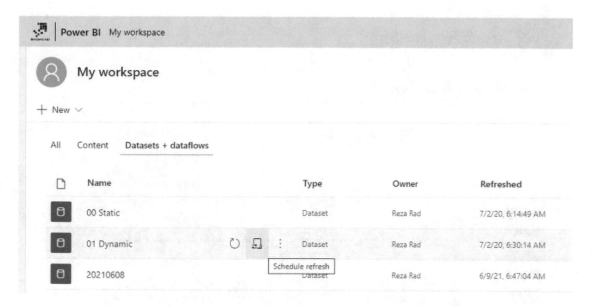

Figure 10-2. Datasets in the Power BI Service

You can schedule the refresh for the dataset and connect to on-premises sources (through a gateway) or cloud-based sources.

What Is Included in the Dataset?

So far, you know that a dataset is a separate object from the report. However, precisely which parts of the development are in the dataset? Here are some of the components that are part of the dataset:

- The connection to the data source

- Tables and their data

- Calculated columns, tables, and measures

- Hierarchies

- Formatting and settings of the fields (visibility, formatting, display folders, sort by column, data category, and so on)

- Relationships

Anything that somehow is related to the data is part of the dataset.

What Is a Shared Dataset?

Now that you know about the dataset, let's talk about the shared dataset. A shared dataset is a dataset that's shared between multiple reports. You can create a new report from an existing dataset through the Power BI website, as demonstrated in Figure 10-3. This will create a report without a dataset. In fact, the dataset of that report is the dataset that you are creating the report from. This type of report is also called a *thin* report.

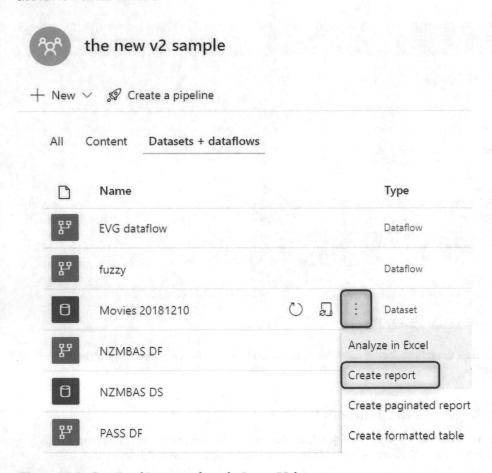

Figure 10-3. Creating thin reports from the Power BI dataset

A thin report is a report without a dataset. This type of report is usually connected live to an existing dataset.

You can also create thin reports from the Power BI Desktop. To do this, you can choose Power BI Dataset under the Data Hub, as shown in Figure 10-4.

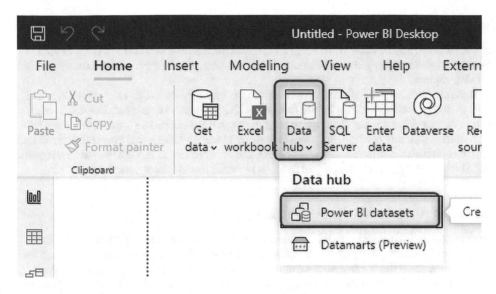

Figure 10-4. *Creating thin reports from the Power BI Desktop*

Thin reports have the same attributes as the Power BI reports connected using Live Connection. They give you the ability to create report-level measures, but beyond that, the modeling is limited, unless you create a composite model using DirectQuery to a Power BI dataset.

When a shared dataset is refreshed, all of the associated reports will have new data. A shared dataset is one step closer to the multi-developer tenant in the Power BI environment. Figure 10-5 shows an example of a shared dataset.

Figure 10-5. *Power BI Shared dataset*

How Do You Create a Shared Dataset?

Any Power BI dataset can be a shared dataset. To use it as a shared dataset, first you need to publish your PBIX file to the Power BI Service. After publication, you will have a dataset and a report. The dataset can then be used to create other reports.

If you want to create a dataset without a report, at the time of writing this book, it is not possible to do that using Power BI Desktop. You can create a Power BI file (which includes the dataset and report in one), and then publish it to the service. After publishing it to the service, you can delete the report associated with that dataset. The challenge with this method, however, is that any future updates to the Power BI dataset and republishing will also republish the report again, and you need to then remove it. It might be easier to ignore the report associated with the dataset. Or simply just use that report to troubleshoot your dataset.

Sharing Datasets Across Multiple Workspaces

For a long time, sharing datasets was only possible inside a workspace. You could not use a dataset from one workspace as the source for a report in another workspace. However, the feature became available a few years ago, and you can now share the dataset across multiple workspaces. When you get data from a Power BI dataset through the Power BI Desktop, as shown in Figure 10-6, you can select which dataset you want to get the data from.

Figure 10-6. *Getting data from a Power BI Dataset*

External Dataset: How Does Shared Dataset Work Behind the Scenes?

When you get data from a Power BI dataset in workspace 1, and then save your report in workspace 2, you will see something called an *external* dataset (it was previously called a linked dataset). The fact is that what you see is just a link. Power BI will bring the link to that dataset into the new workspace. This link helps you understand when the dataset gets refreshed.

Figure 10-7 demonstrates what an external dataset looks like in Lineage View.

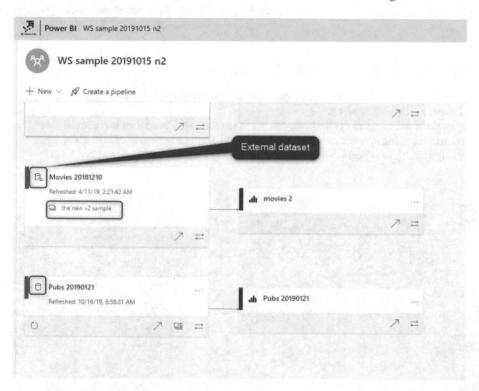

Figure 10-7. *An external dataset in Power BI*

An external dataset is not a copy; it is a link to the original dataset.

Why Use Shared Datasets?

Now the million-dollar question is why should you use a shared dataset? What is good about it? What are its main benefits? Let's answer these questions through an example.

Let's assume you are the Power BI developer of the Sales.PBIX file on your team. Your team recently hired a data analyst with good visualization skills named Maggie. Maggie wants to build some visualization on your Sales.PBIX file, However, you want to do some modeling (writing calculations, bringing more tables, adding relationships, and so on) at the same time. How can you do this?

Suppose you give Maggie a copy of your Sales.PBIX file and call it Maggie's Sales.PBIX. She can build new visualizations, but now her version will be different from your Sales.PBIX file. What if you wanted to merge your changes (new calculations and tables) into her file? This brings lots of headaches because you're managing two versions of the same file.

Instead of copying files, you can create a shared dataset, and Maggie can create a Power BI thin report connected to the same dataset. This way, maintaining the solution will be much easier in the future. Whenever you update your dataset, Maggie needs to refresh the file to get the new changes. A shared dataset separates the modeling layer of your Power BI solution from the rest of it. It's like a dataflow, which separates the ETL layer.

Shared Datasets in the Power BI Architecture

In a later chapter, I explain how dataflow and shared datasets can play an important role in the multi-developer tenant of Power BI implementation.

In a nutshell, using the dataflow ensures that you can bring the data well prepared in a central area, which you can call a centralized data warehouse in the Azure Data Lake. Using the shared datasets, you can build data models that multiple reports can use. Figure 10-8 shows how the architecture works in diagram view.

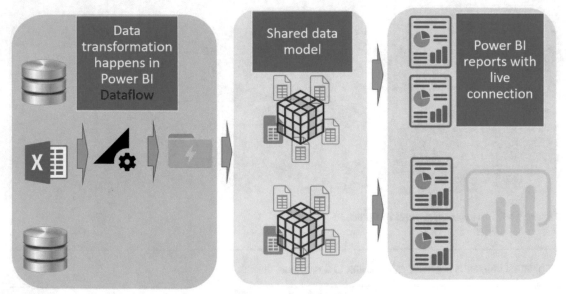

Power BI Solution Architecture

Figure 10-8. *Power BI Solution Architecture diagram*

Instead of having silos of Power BI reports and files everywhere, you can build an architecture that works best with multiple developers, has less data, code, and logic redundancy, and is easier to maintain. I highly recommend reading this chapter to learn more about this architecture and learn how the shared dataset located in this architecture is a key element.

Endorsement: Certified and Promoted Datasets

When Power BI developers get data from a Power BI dataset, they see all the datasets from all workspaces that they have access to. This might be a bit confusing. There might be many datasets shared in the environment. The developer might wonder which of those they can use.

A labeling system is added to the Power BI datasets, which helps in this scenario. You can mark some of the datasets as certified or promoted. To certify a dataset, an approval process can ensure the dataset has passed some of the tests. You can clarify through this labeling system which datasets are good to be used as the source and which are not. You can build the concept of Gold, Silver, and Bronze datasets. Gold datasets are fully tested, and reconciled, whereas a Bronze dataset hasn't been through any testing yet.

To use this labeling system, the creator of the dataset can go to the dataset's settings area, as Figure 10-9 demonstrates.

Figure 10-9. *Dataset settings*

In the settings, you can set the Endorsement level, as shown in Figure 10-10.

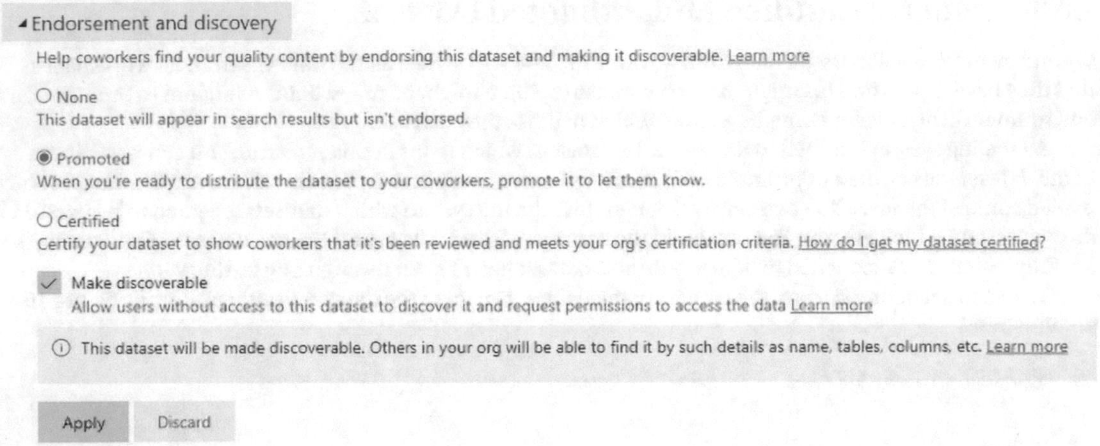

◢ Endorsement and discovery

Help coworkers find your quality content by endorsing this dataset and making it discoverable. Learn more

○ None
This dataset will appear in search results but isn't endorsed.

◉ Promoted
When you're ready to distribute the dataset to your coworkers, promote it to let them know.

○ Certified
Certify your dataset to show coworkers that it's been reviewed and meets your org's certification criteria. How do I get my dataset certified?

☑ Make discoverable
   Allow users without access to this dataset to discover it and request permissions to access the data Learn more

ⓘ This dataset will be made discoverable. Others in your org will be able to find it by such details as name, tables, columns, etc. Learn more

Apply   Discard

Figure 10-10. *Power BI dataset endorsement*

As you can see, the Certified option might not be available. The Power BI tenant administrator has the authority to enable labeling and give out access in the Tenant Settings. Take a look at how to enable access in Figure 10-11.

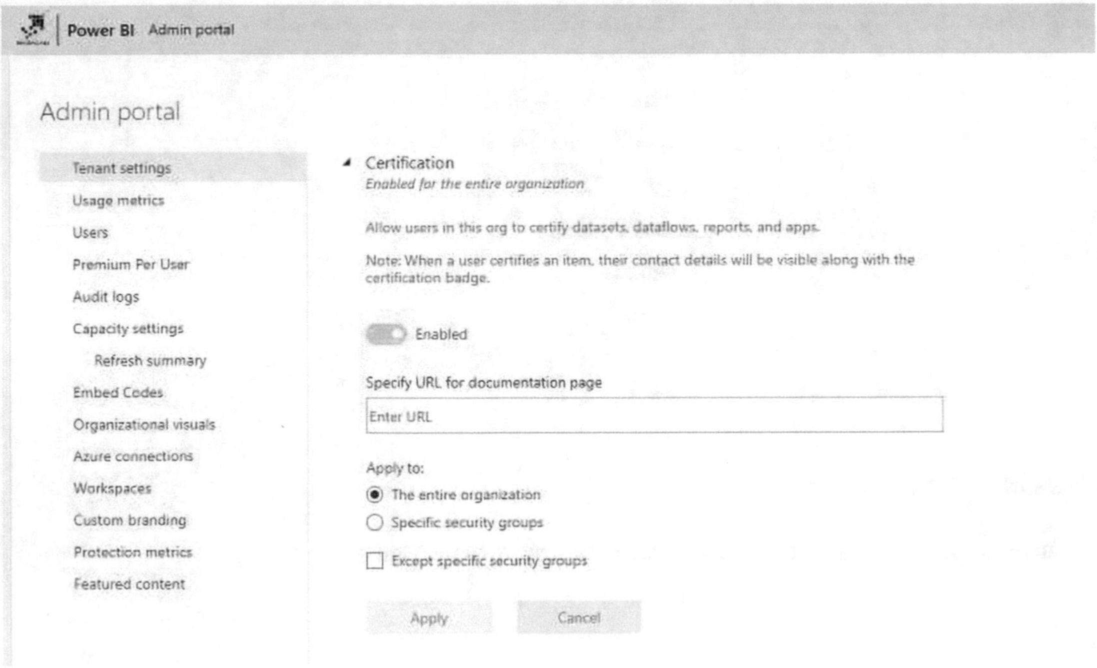

Power BI Admin portal

Admin portal

Tenant settings	◢ Certification
Usage metrics	*Enabled for the entire organization*
Users	
Premium Per User	Allow users in this org to certify datasets, dataflows, reports, and apps.
Audit logs	Note: When a user certifies an item, their contact details will be visible along with the certification badge.
Capacity settings	
Refresh summary	⬤ Enabled
Embed Codes	
Organizational visuals	Specify URL for documentation page
Azure connections	Enter URL
Workspaces	
Custom branding	Apply to:
Protection metrics	◉ The entire organization
Featured content	○ Specific security groups
	☐ Except specific security groups
	Apply Cancel

Figure 10-11. *Admin setting determining who can certify datasets in the Power BI Service*

You can also determine if promoted or certified content is discoverable throughout the tenant under the same Tenant Settings of the Admin Portal, as shown in Figure 10-12.

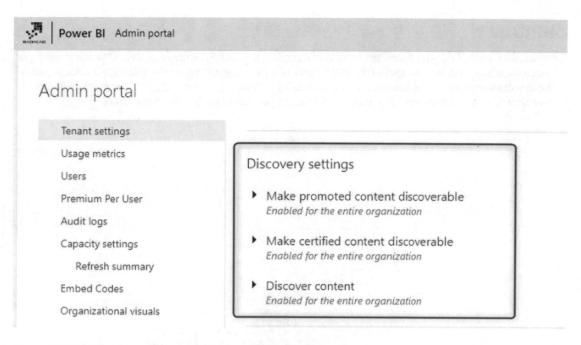

Figure 10-12. *Discovery settings in the Power BI admin portal*

The endorsement labeling system, shown in Figure 10-13, helps Power BI developers determine what is the level of certification that a dataset must be used as a shared dataset, and then can select based on that; see Figure 10-13.

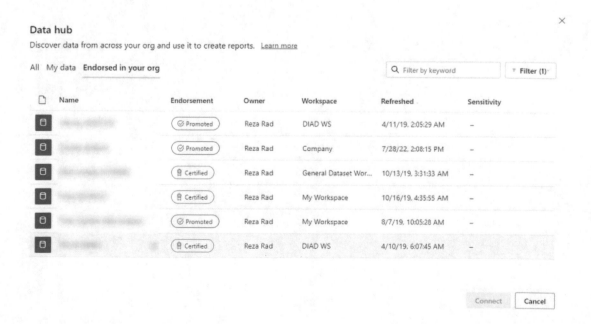

Figure 10-13. *Filtering the datasets by the endorsement in the Power BI Desktop*

Summary

You can use a shared dataset to create centralized data models serving multiple reports. You can reduce the maintenance time, the redundancy of the code, and the data using this approach. Having a labeling system of the certified or promoted dataset is also a great way to put some process and governance in place and ensure that the shared datasets have been through some process of testing and reconciling.

CHAPTER 11

Datamarts

One of the newest additions to Power BI is the datamart. Power BI datamarts are more than just another feature; they are a major milestone where the development of Power BI solutions are revolutionized. They help both citizen data analysts and developers. This chapter explains what datamarts are and how they help you with your Power BI implementations.

Power BI for the Citizen Data Analyst

Power BI came to the market in 2015 with the promise of being a tool for citizen data analysts. A citizen data analyst is someone who does not have a developer background but understands the business and the data related to that business. Power BI (and many other self-service tools) target this type of audience.

You don't need to be a developer to use the Power BI Desktop. It's so easy and straightforward that even by just opening the tool and clicking here and there you can easily learn how to use it. If you read a few guides, you can build your first report and dashboard using Power BI. That is exactly the promise that Microsoft offered with Power BI.

Governance and Reusability

As time goes by in your Power BI development cycle and you build more Power BI files, you may realize that you need something else. Building everything in a Power BI file is simple, but maintenance is problematic. What if you want to reuse a table in another Power BI file? What if you want to reuse a measure or expression in another report?

That is why Power BI offers separate components that build the full architecture of Power BI development, components, features, and technologies, such as thin reports (reports that don't have a dataset and connect live to another dataset), shared datasets (datasets that can be used to feed data into multiple reports), dataflows (the data transformation engine in the cloud), composite model (combining a shared dataset with additional data sources), and so on. All of these technologies create a better development lifecycle for Power BI developers. Figure 11-1 shows this Power BI multi-layered architecture.

© Reza Rad 2023
R. Rad, *Pro Power BI Architecture*, https://doi.org/10.1007/978-1-4842-9538-0_11

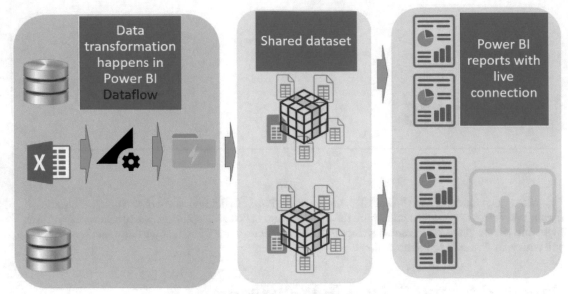

Power BI Solution Architecture

Figure 11-1. *Power BI Solution architecture with separate layers*

Although all these components are fantastic features in the Power BI ecosystem, there is still a need for a database or a data warehouse as a central repository of the data. The need for this repository comes from many different aspects—keeping the integrated data structured in a relational database, having a central database with all the data from other source systems in it, creating views to cover particular needs for reports, and more.

What are Datamarts in Power BI?

Datamarts are used to close the database gap in the Power BI ecosystem, but they are much more than that. If you want just a database, you can design it in an Azure SQL database or other platforms. The problem is that you need to build the database in a tool such as SSMS (SQL Server Management Studio), then have an ETL process (such as dataflows, ADF, or SSIS) to feed data into that database, and then the Power BI dataset using the Power BI Desktop. As you can see in Figure 11-2, datamarts give you a single unified platform to build all of these without needing another tool, license, or service. Datamarts make Power BI enough for you to do all your BI requirements, but with less control over how the database is implemented.

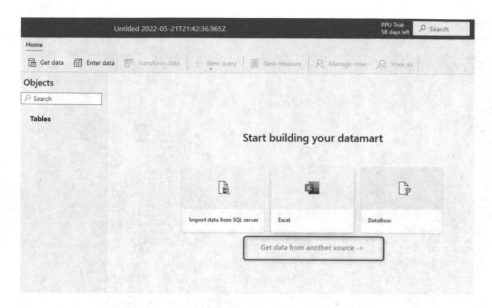

Figure 11-2. *Building a datamart*

A Power BI datamart is a combined set of dataflows, an Azure SQL database, a Power BI dataset, and a Web UI that manages and builds all these functionalities, as depicted in Figure 11-3.

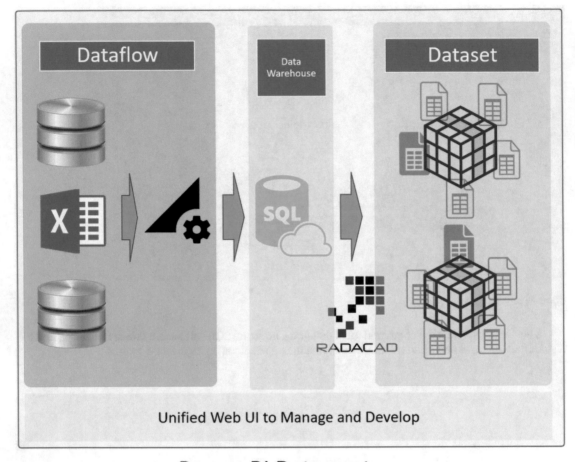

Power BI Datamart

Figure 11-3. *Datamart components*

The data warehouse term I use here sometimes causes confusion. Some will use the term data warehouse for huge databases that need to scale with technologies such as Azure Synapse. However, the term data warehouse here means the database or repository where you store the star-schema-designed tables of dimension and fact tables for the BI model. These tables can be big or small.

Who Are Datamarts for?

If you are wondering who datamarts are for, or who can use them, the following sections explain a few scenarios.

Power BI Datamart for the Citizen Data Analyst

Daniel is a data analyst at a small to mid-size company. His background is not in development. He knows the business though. He understands how the business operates and he understands the data related to the business. He wants to build dashboards and reports in Power BI. If he does all that in the Power BI Desktop, soon he will realize that there isn't good governance around such a structure. His company doesn't have a data warehouse as such, and no BI team to build such a thing. He can use a Power BI datamart to have a fully governed architecture with dataflows (transformation and ETL layer), an Azure SQL Database (data warehouse or dimensional model), a Power BI dataset (the analytical data model), and reports. All of these can be developed using the UI of the Power BI Service. Daniel does not need to open any other tool or service; he does not need to learn SQL Server database technology or any other technologies except the Power BI itself. This is an example of a datamart empowering a citizen data analyst to build a Power BI solution that is scalable, governed, and self-service at the same time.

Power BI Datamart for Enterprises

Arwen is a data analyst at a large enterprise with a data warehouse and BI team. However, every time Arwen asks for a change in the centralized data model from the BI team, it takes months if not years to get the results (because of the bottleneck of requests). Now using datamart, Arwen can build her data warehouse with the data transformation layer and everything in a way that can be consumable for future projects or by colleagues using Power BI. The solution will be governed by the Power BI service, the BI team can implement a process for certifying datamarts and, as a result, Arwen can not only implement quicker but also can help the BI team reduce their backlog. Power BI datamarts empower both Arwen and the BI team to implement faster Power BI solutions in a fully-governed structure.

Power BI Datamart for Developers

Peter is a BI developer. He knows how to work with databases and write T-SQL queries. He can use the Web UI of the datamart to write T-SQL queries to the Azure SQL database. Or he can use the database connection and connect to the database using a tool such as SSMS. He can also connect to the dataset built by the datamarts using the XMLA endpoint using SSMS, Tabular Editor, or any other tools to enhance the data model and take it to the next level. Power BI datamarts empower Peter in his development work throughout his Power BI implementation.

What Are the Features of Datamarts that Empower Power BI Development?

Throughout this chapter thus far, you have learned about some of the features of datamarts that empower the Power BI developers. The following sections explain these features separately.

Datamarts Complete the BI Ecosystem

Datamarts use the dataflows for data transformation, an Azure SQL database for the data warehouse (or dimensional model), and the Power BI dataset for the analytical data model. Finally, the Power BI report can connect to the dataset. This builds a complete four-layer implementation in Power BI, as shown in Figure 11-4.

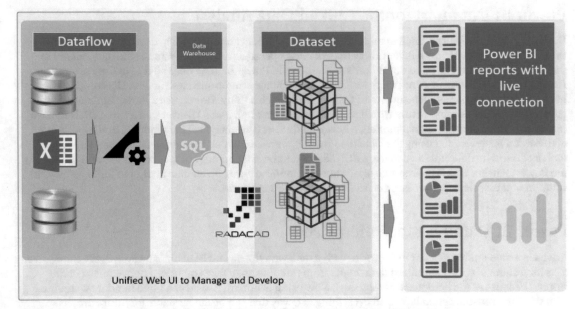

Power BI Solution Architecture using Datamart

Figure 11-4. *Datamart in the Power BI architecture*

One Place to Manage and Build, No Other Tools Needed

The user interface to build datamarts is web-based. You don't even need to install the Power BI Desktop. You can use any operating system (Mac, Windows, or even a tablet). You build the entire Power BI solution, from getting data from data sources all the way to building the reports, using the same UI in the Power BI Service. You don't need SSMS, Visual Studio, Power BI Desktop, and so on. See Figure 11-5.

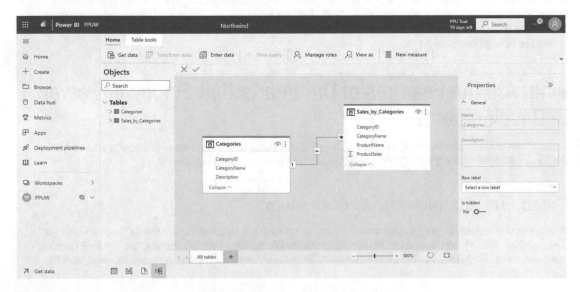

Figure 11-5. *Single unified UI to manage everything: datamarts*

Although at the early stages of building datamarts, there are some functionalities that are not yet %
possible using the Web UI, this will improve in the near future.

One License Is Enough

Datamarts build an Azure SQL database for you, but you don't need to purchase a separate license from
Azure Portal. You don't even need to have an Azure subscription. Power BI datamarts give you all of that
using the Power BI Premium capacity, or Premium Per User license. The database, the Dataflow, and the
dataset are all part of your Power BI license.

The Vast Horizon and the Future of Datamarts

Datamart is just the beginning of many wonderful features to come. Imagine features such as Slowly
Changing Dimension (SCD) and inferred dimension members handling implementations. You can think
about monitoring the dataflow processes in a way that the incremental refresh data that is processed every
night is stored in log tables and you can troubleshoot any potential problems easily.

Think about what features can be enabled now that there is a single Web UI enabled for the developers,
version control, and the ability for team members to work on the same Power BI project simultaneously.
This is all on the horizon. These features do not exist yet in datamarts. However, datamarts can be the base
on which all these amazing features can be built.

Governance

Like many other objects in the Power BI workspace, datamarts can have governance aspects such as
endorsements and sensitivity labels. If the datamart is marked with specific organizational sensitivity labels,
and the link is somehow sent by mistake to someone who isn't part of the organization and should not see
the data, that is all covered by the sensitivity labels and configurations of Microsoft Azure behind the scenes.

Getting Started with Power BI Datamarts

So far, you learned what a datamart is and the use cases in a Power BI implementation. In this section, you
experiment with datamarts and learn through an example how they work. The interesting thing in all the
steps that follow is that you only need a web browser to build a datamart.

Premium Workspace

Power BI datamarts are only accessible through a Premium workspace. You either need to have a Premium
capacity workspace or create a workspace using a Premium Per User (PPU) account, as you can see in
Figure 11-6. If you don't have a PPU account, you can easily apply for a 60 day trial through the Power BI
Service.

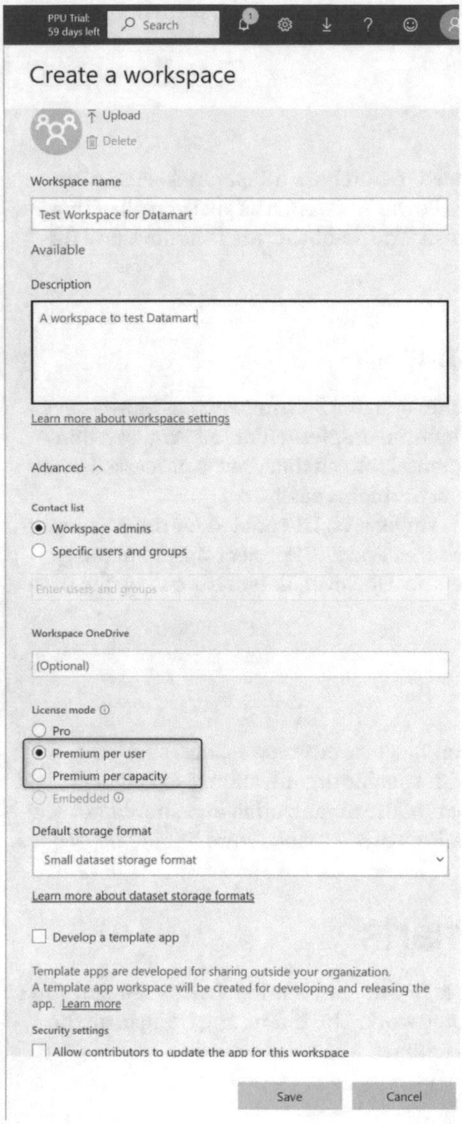

Figure 11-6. *Creating a workspace to test a Power BI datamart*

A workspace with Premium settings usually has an icon representing this fact, as shown Figure 11-7.

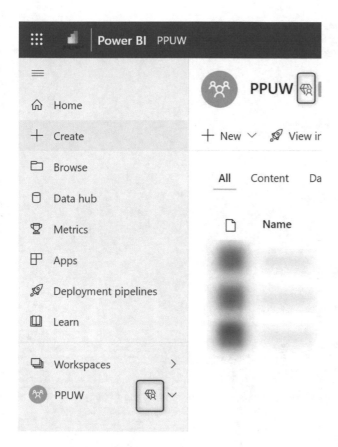

Figure 11-7. *The Power BI premium workspace icon*

Creating a Datamart

Click New, and from the list, select Datamart, as shown in Figure 11-8.

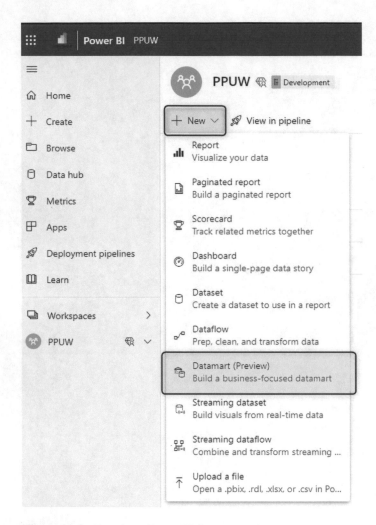

Figure 11-8. *Creating a Power BI datamart*

Note that the ability to create datamarts can be enabled or disabled through the Tenant Settings of the Power BI admin portal, as shown in Figure 11-9.

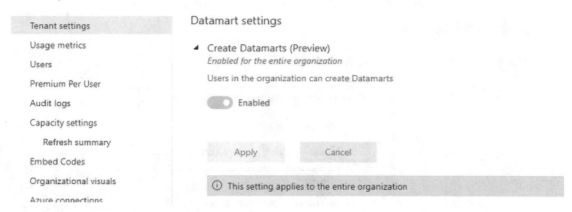

Figure 11-9. *Enabling datamart creation in the Power BI Tenant*

Get Data: Power Query Online

When you create a datamart, the first thing you do is to choose where to get the data. You can start by getting data from a dataflow, Excel, SQL Server, or pretty much any other data source that Power BI offers a connector to (more than 150 sources). To do this, select the Get Data from Another Source.

This will open dataflow's familiar Get Data window, where you select the source, as depicted in Figure 11-10.

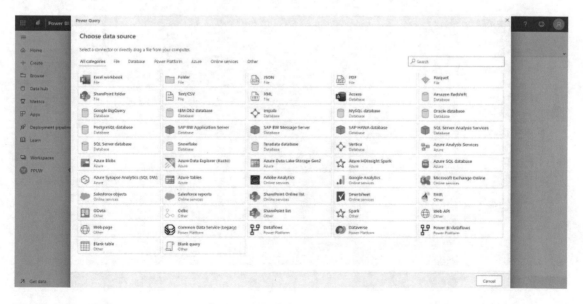

Figure 11-10. *Data source connectors for Power BI datamarts*

For this example, I use OData as a source and this URL: `services.odata.org/Northwind/Northwind.svc`. Enter it, as shown in Figure 11-11.

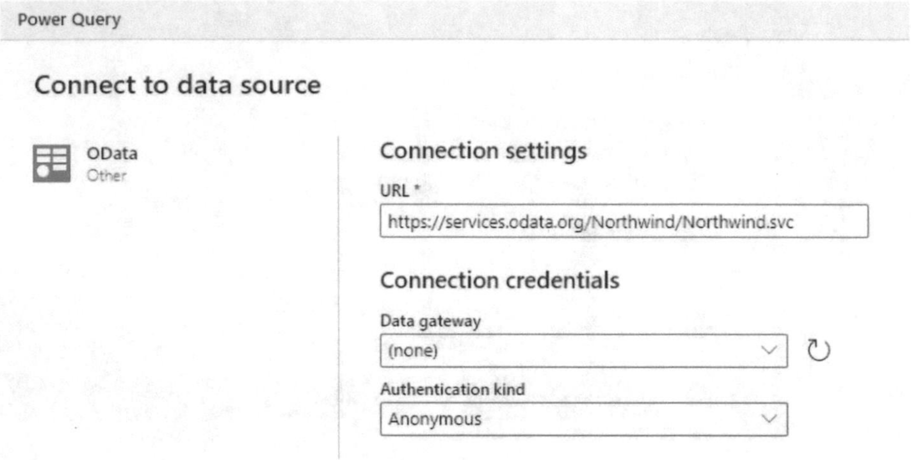

Power Query
Connect to data source
OData
Other
Connection settings
URL *
https://services.odata.org/Northwind/Northwind.svc
Connection credentials
Data gateway
(none)
Authentication kind
Anonymous

***Figure 11-11.** OData source for a Power BI datamart*

Choose the data tables you need. I am using the Orders tables and some related tables; see Figure 11-12.

Choose data
Orders
Select related tables
Back
Cancel
Transform data

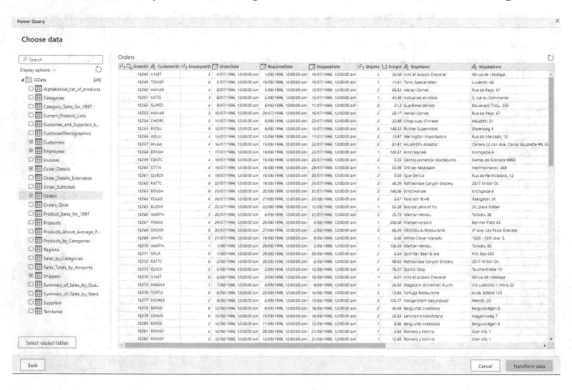

***Figure 11-12.** Power Query Navigator window*

As you can see in Figure 11-13, the next step will reveal the Power Query Editor online version, which enables to do all the transformations you need.

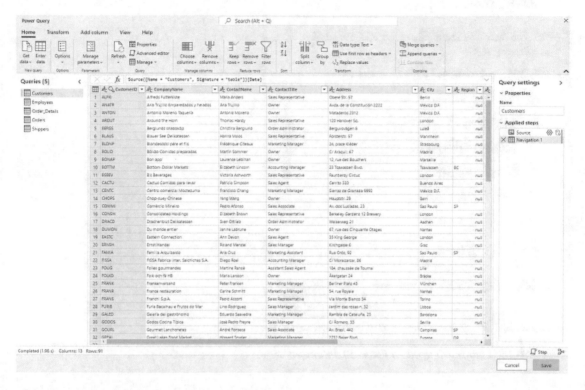

Figure 11-13. *Power Query Editor online version*

The data will then be loaded into the datamart, as shown in Figure 11-14.

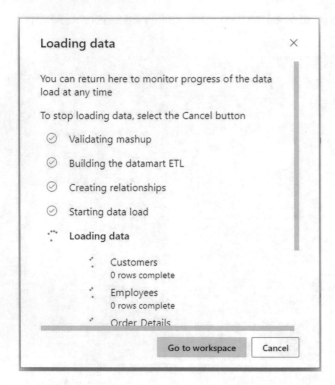

Figure 11-14. *Loading data into a Power BI datamart*

The Datamart Editor

Once the data is loaded into the datamart, you can see the Power BI Datamart Editor (see Figure 11-15). This editor will improve a lot in the future I believe. However, even right now, the editor has some mind-blowing features and capabilities. I explain these features as the chapter unfolds.

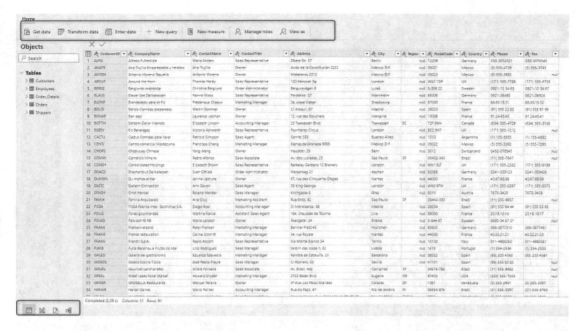

Figure 11-15. *The Power BI Datamart Editor*

The Data View Tab

The first tab is the Data View, which is like the Data tab in the Power BI Desktop. This is the place where you can see the data rows in each table. That is the view you see in Figure 11-15.

You can add data to this datamart using the Get Data option, or use Transform Data to get back to the Power Query Editor. You can also enter data directly as a table if you want.[1] These options are shown in Figure 11-16.

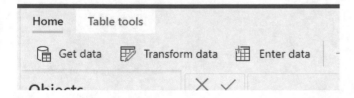

Figure 11-16. *The Get Data and Transform Data options for Power BI datamarts*

Creating a New Query

An interesting capability of datamarts is creating new queries. A new query is like a new table generated through the Power Query process. It might be a combined version of a table or a transformed version of one table (see Figure 11-17). You can of course do that already in Power BI Desktop using the Power Query Editor. However, the reason it is called New Query here is that, behind the scenes, it is created as a view in the Azure SQL database.

---

[1] Learn more at radacad.com/create-a-table-in-power-bi-using-enter-data-and-how-to-edit-it

183

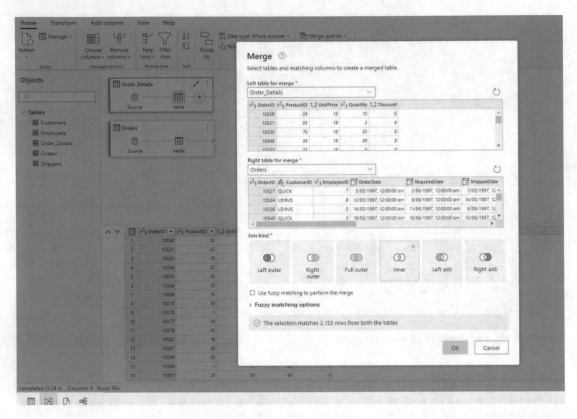

Figure 11-17. *Data transformation using Power Query Editor online to create a new query in a Power BI datamart*

Figure 11-18 shows what you see in the second tab.

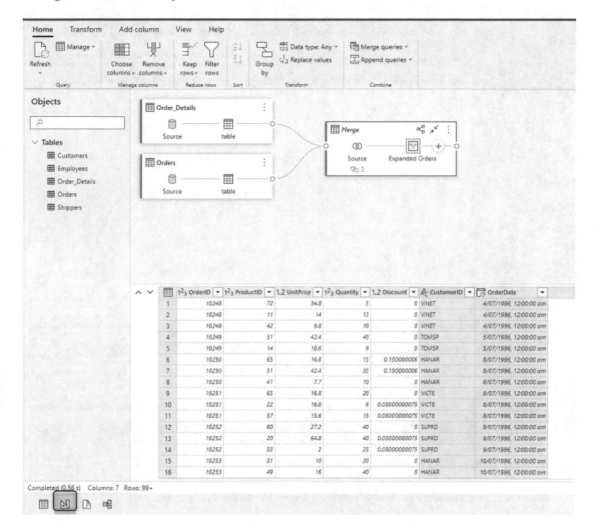

Figure 11-18. *Creating a new query in a Power BI datamart*

Writing T-SQL Queries

Power BI datamarts create an Azure SQL database behind the scenes. You can write queries in T-SQL statements in the third tab, shown in Figure 11-19.

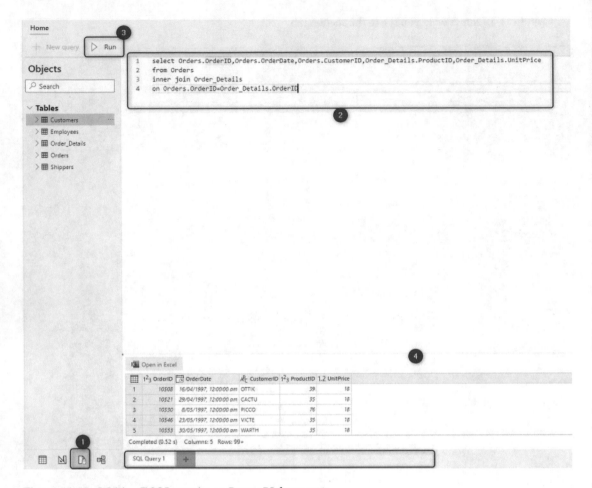

Figure 11-19. Writing T-SQL queries on Power BI datamarts

Power BI enables citizen data analysts and developers to use this component.

Model Diagram and Relationship Editor

The unified UI for datamarts enables you to write T-SQL queries, see the data, and transform data. It also enables you to define the relationship and build the diagram of the model, adding configurations for fields and tables all in one Web UI. Figure 11-20 shows the scope of what datamarts offer.

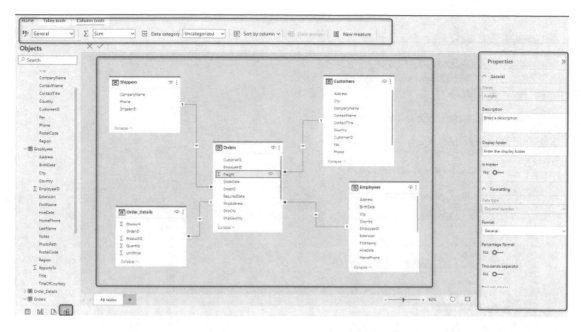

Figure 11-20. The Model tab in the Power BI Datamart Editor

The interesting fact here is that you create relationships only once, but the datamart behind the scenes will create it in both the Azure SQL database and in the subsequent Power BI dataset.

Creating Measures and Writing DAX Expressions

You can create measures using the Datamart Editor, as shown in Figure 11-21, and the Expression Editor will help you with the DAX function library and the IntelliSense to write whatever you want.

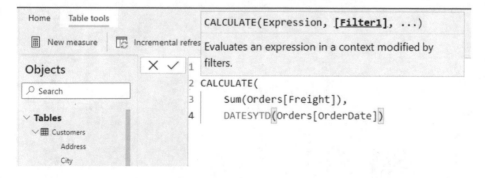

Figure 11-21. Writing DAX measures in Power BI datamarts

Incremental Refresh: One Setup for All

Incremental refresh enables you to set up a delta load rather than loading the entire data. When you use dataflows and datasets separately, you need to set incremental refreshes in them one by one. However, using the Datamart Editor, you can set the Incremental Refresh once, and it sets it everywhere for you. You can see what this process setup looks like in action in Figure 11-22.

187

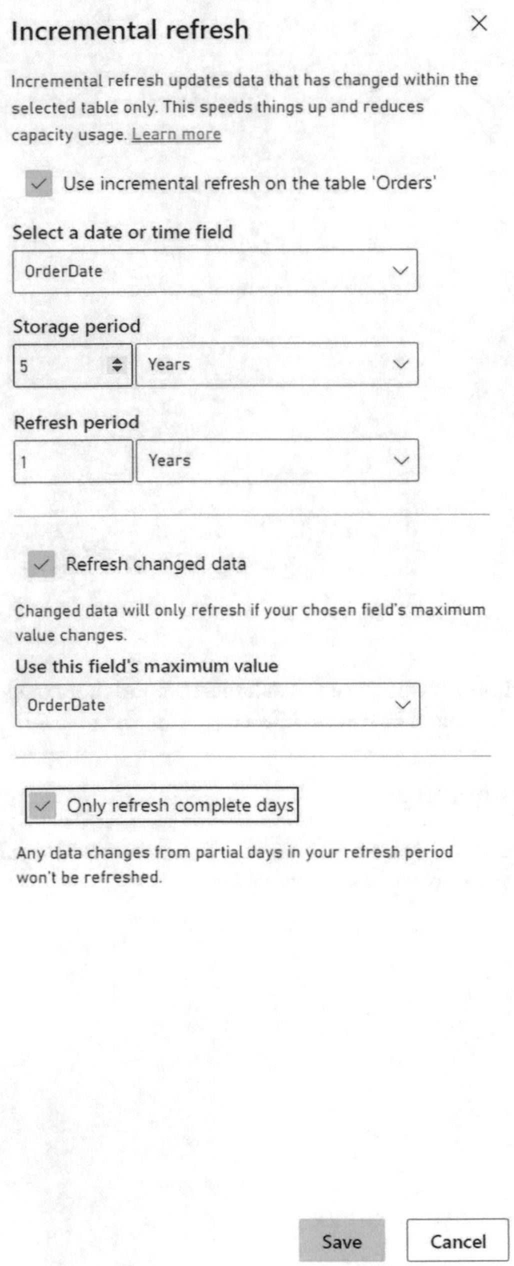

Incremental refresh   ✕

Incremental refresh updates data that has changed within the
selected table only. This speeds things up and reduces
capacity usage. Learn more

☑ Use incremental refresh on the table 'Orders'

Select a date or time field

OrderDate	∨

Storage period

5 ⇕	Years	∨

Refresh period

1	Years	∨

☑ Refresh changed data

Changed data will only refresh if your chosen field's maximum
value changes.

Use this field's maximum value

OrderDate	∨

☑ Only refresh complete days

Any data changes from partial days in your refresh period
won't be refreshed.

Save	Cancel

Figure 11-22. Incremental refresh setup for Power BI datamarts

Row-Level Security: In Databases and Datasets

Another interesting feature of datamarts is that you don't need to set up Row-level security in two different places (in the database and the dataset). As shown in Figure 11-23, you set it once in the datamart, and it will implement it in both places for you.

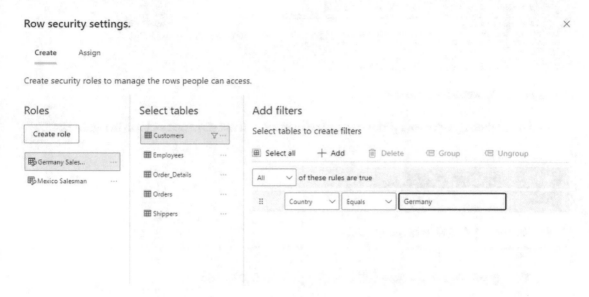

Figure 11-23. *Row-level security setup process in datamarts*

The process of assigning roles to users all happens in one place. Unlike using the Power BI Desktop for role creation and then the Power BI service for assignment. However, the difference is that you don't use DAX expressions for RLS. This is because these RLS settings are originally for the Azure SQL database and the associated dataset follows that.

You can test and view a specific role if you want, as shown in Figure 11-24.

Figure 11-24. *Creating roles and testing them using the Power BI Datamart Editor*

You can rename the datamart by clicking the current title and changing it, as shown in Figure 11-25.

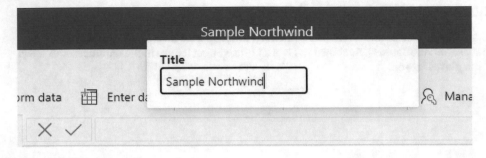

Figure 11-25. *Renaming a datamart*

Congratulations, you've built your first Power BI datamart. It will show up as shown in Figure 11-26.

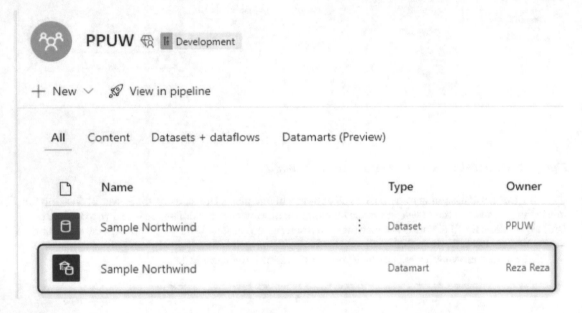

Figure 11-26. *The Power BI datamart in the service*

Power BI Datamart Components

What is a Power BI datamart underneath? Can you connect to the database generated by the datamart? How can the dataset that's associated with the datamart be used? Is there a linage view? This section of this chapter answers these questions and you will learn about datamart's components.

Power BI Datamarts Under the Hood

When you create a datamart, three objects are created behind the scenes: a dataflow, an Azure SQL database, and a dataset (see Figure 11-27). Some of these components are exposed as individual components, and some are hidden.

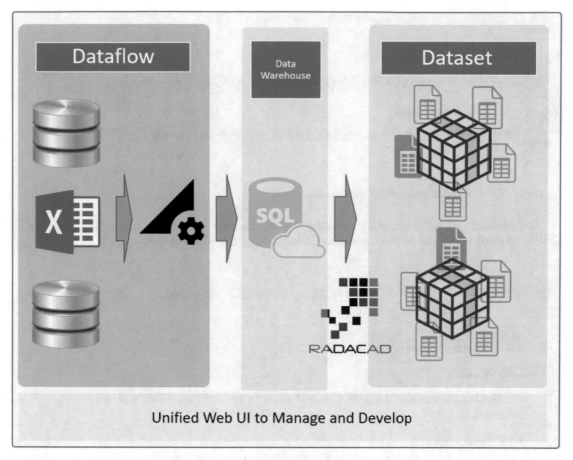

Power BI Datamart

Figure 11-27. *Power BI datamart's components*

The Power BI Dataset

When you create a datamart, the most obvious component of it can be seen separately, and that is the Power BI dataset, as shown in Figure 11-28.

All
Content
Datasets + dataflows
Datamarts (Preview)
Name
Type
Owner
Sample Northwind
Dataset
PPUW
Sample Northwind
Datamart
Reza Reza

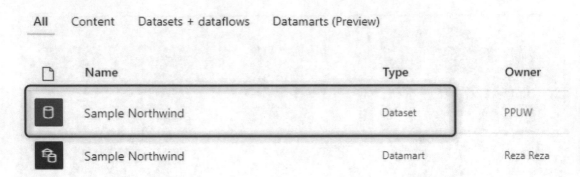

Figure 11-28. *The dataset associated with the datamart*

You can also connect to the dataset using the Power BI Desktop (like a normal dataset), or using the XMLA endpoint, which can be found under the Datasets setting, as shown in Figure 11-29.

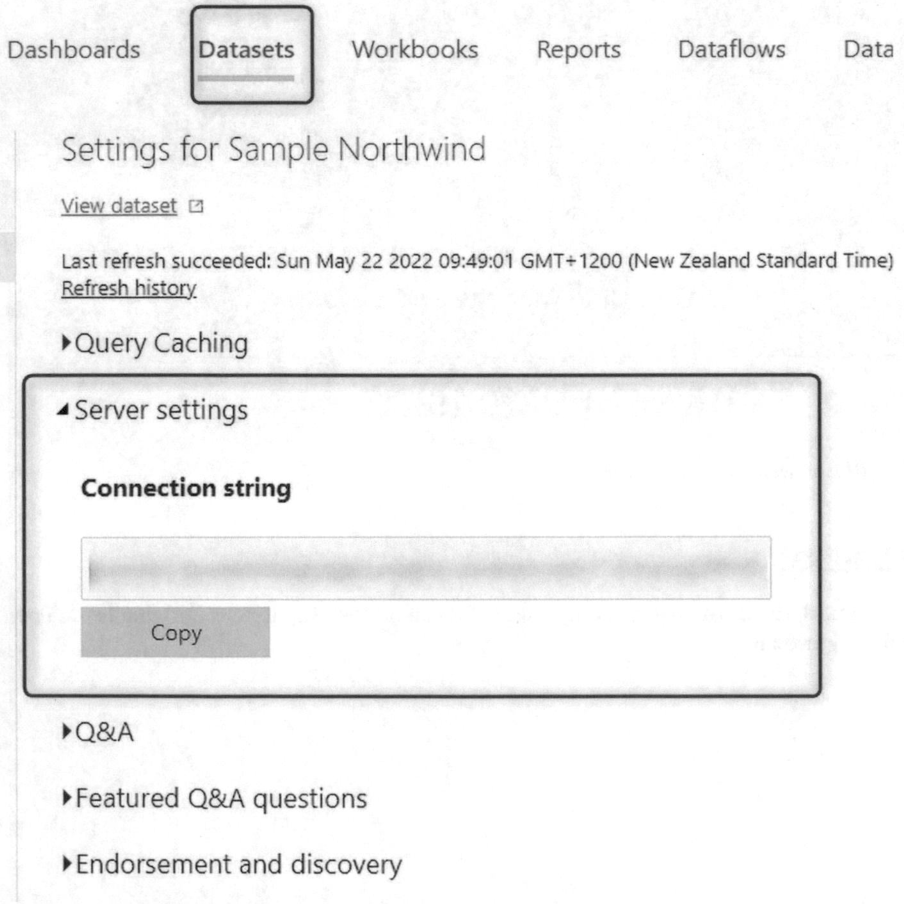

Dashboards
Datasets
Workbooks
Reports
Dataflows
Data
Settings for Sample Northwind
View dataset
Last refresh succeeded: Sun May 22 2022 09:49:01 GMT+1200 (New Zealand Standard Time)
Refresh history
Query Caching
Server settings
Connection string
Copy
Q&A
Featured Q&A questions
Endorsement and discovery

Figure 11-29. *Power BI dataset settings*

This connection string then can be used with SSMS, Visual Studio, Tabular Editor, Power BI Helper, and many other tools to connect to the Power BI dataset.

The dataflow and the Azure SQL database are not that easy to find inside the Power BI service (apart from the Datamart Editor). But there are ways to connect to them.

Connecting to the Azure SQL Database

To find the connection to the Azure SQL database, click the more options button on the Datamart and select Settings, as shown in Figure 11-30.

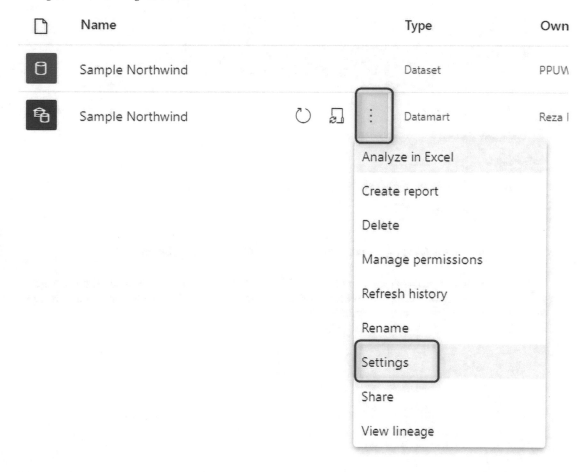

Figure 11-30. *Power BI datamart settings*

Then under Server Settings, you'll find the Connection string, as shown in Figure 11-31.

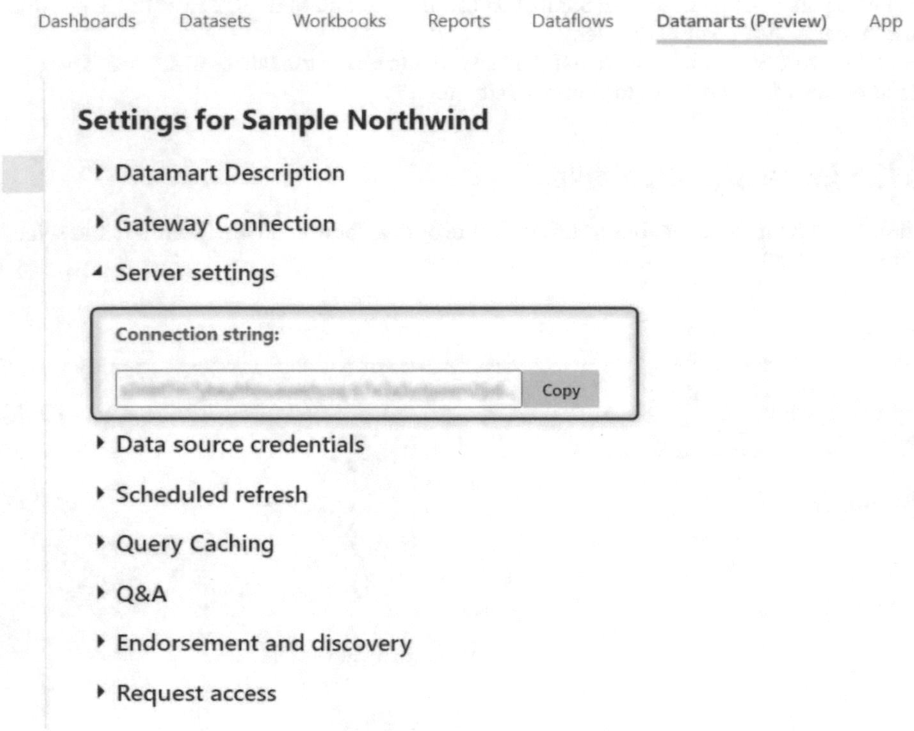

Dashboards   Datasets   Workbooks   Reports   Dataflows   **Datamarts (Preview)**   App

Settings for Sample Northwind

▸ Datamart Description

▸ Gateway Connection

◢ Server settings

Connection string:

[_____] Copy

▸ Data source credentials

▸ Scheduled refresh

▸ Query Caching

▸ Q&A

▸ Endorsement and discovery

▸ Request access

Figure 11-31. Finding the Azure SQL database connection from the Power BI datamart

This connection can be used with other tools, such as SSMS (SQL Server Management Studio). Note that you should be using Azure Active Directory–Universal with MFA for authentication and your Power BI account as the username, as shown in Figure 11-32.

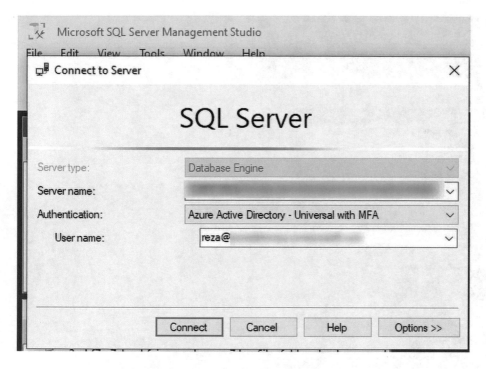

Figure 11-32. Connecting to the Azure SQL database of a Power BI datamart

You can then see the database with the objects in it. The tables are hidden at first as an extra safety measure. However, there is a view per table that you can see, plus other metadata tables such as relationships. See Figure 11-33.

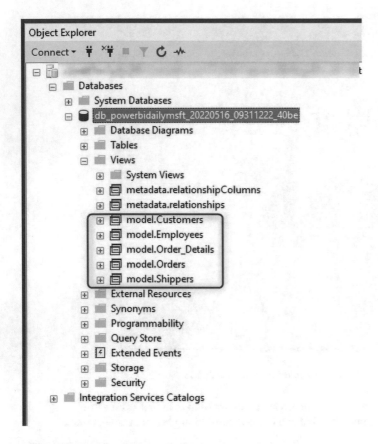

Figure 11-33. *The datamart's database structure*

Similar to any Azure SQL database, you can view the script of the views, such as the model.Customers. You can see in Figure 11-34 that even in the script, the row-level security implementation can be visible.

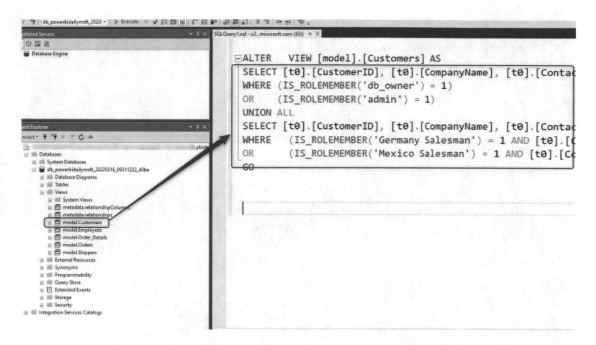

Figure 11-34. *Views in an Azure SQL database of the datamart*

There are limitations that ensure that you don't change anything in this structure that would cause the datamart to fail.

Building Reports from Datamarts

There are multiple ways to create reports from a datamart. You can go to the Data Hub and click the datamart, as shown in Figure 11-35.

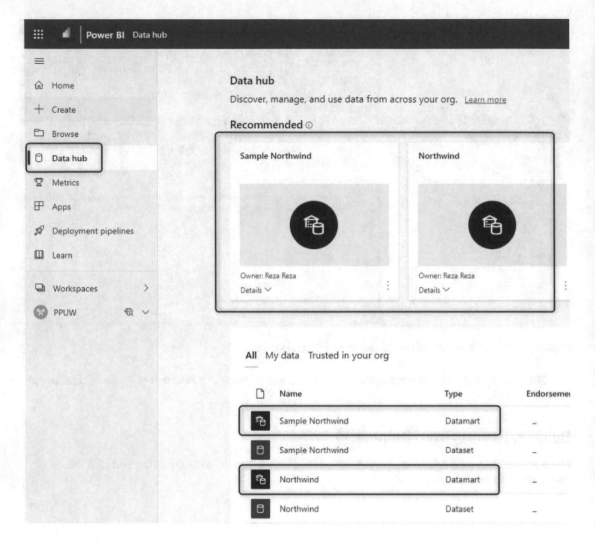

Figure 11-35. *Datamarts in the Power BI Data Hub*

In the datamart's details, you can see the SQL connection string and create a report from scratch, which will be connected to this datamart, as shown in Figure 11-36.

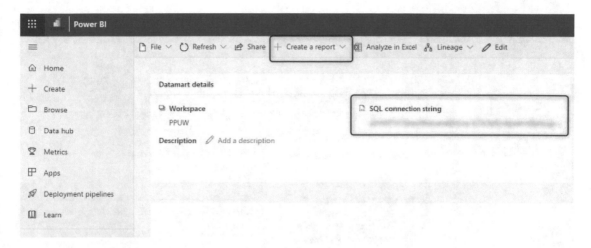

Figure 11-36. *Creating a report from a Power BI datamart*

The report will automatically connect to the tables in the dataset, as shown in Figure 11-37.

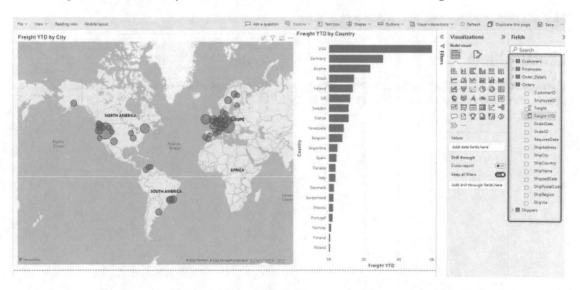

Figure 11-37. *Creating a Power BI report in the Power BI Service from a datamart*

The report can be also created from the dataset associated with the datamart, or from the Power BI Desktop by choosing Get Data from Power BI dataset, as you see in Figure 11-38.

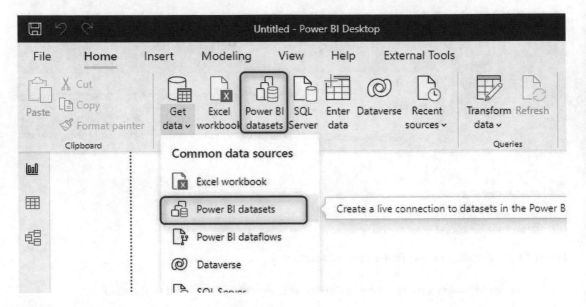

Figure 11-38. *Getting data from a Power BI dataset*

Lineage View

If you are on the datamart, on the dataset associated with it, or on any of the reports connected to that dataset, you can see the Lineage view, as shown in Figure 11-39.

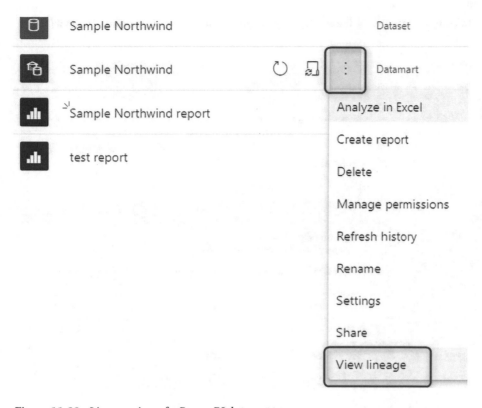

Figure 11-39. *Lineage view of a Power BI datamart*

In Figure 11-40, you can see that the datamart is populating data from an OData source and feeding it into a dataset. There are three reports generated from that dataset. The dataflow part of the datamart and the Azure SQL database is hidden from this diagram (they are parts of the datamart).

Figure 11-40. *Power BI Lineage view*

Also in the Data Hub, when you click the datamart, you can see all the reports generated from it (see Figure 11-41).

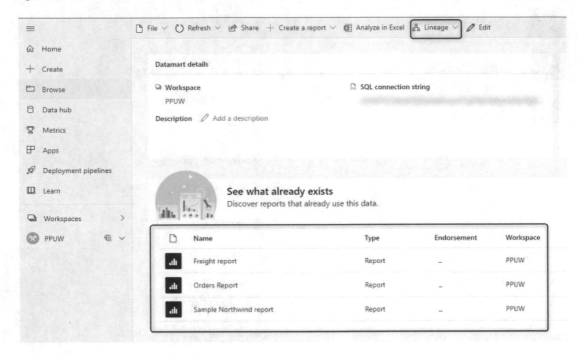

Figure 11-41. *The Datamart details in the Power BI Data Hub*

Summary

This chapter was about Power BI datamarts. It explained what a datamart is, what features it includes, and who should use it. I strongly believe that datamarts revolutionize the way we develop Power BI solutions. Datamarts are the future of building Power BI solutions in a better way.

In the second part of the chapter, you learned how to create a Power BI datamart and about the features inside the Datamart Editor. As you saw from an example, datamarts provide a single unified editor experience, from getting data and transforming it, to writing queries, creating relationships, and event managing things such as row-level security.

Finally, you've learned what is under the hood of Power BI datamarts: a dataflow, an Azure SQL database, and a dataset. You can connect to some of these components using other tools. In this chapter, you learned some methods for doing that. You can also build a report that connects to the dataset created by the datamart, and see the entire Lineage view.

CHAPTER 12

The Multi-Layer Architecture

Using Power BI is simple. However, using it properly requires a good architecture. In a multi-developer environment, the architecture of a Power BI implementation should allow multiple developers to work on the same solution at the same time. On the other hand, the Power BI architecture should be designed so that different layers can be decoupled for better integration. This chapter explains how dataflows, datamarts, and shared datasets can help build such an architecture in Power BI.

Challenges of Using a Single PBIX File for Everything

Before I start explaining the architecture, it is important to understand the challenge and think about how to solve it. The default usage of Power BI involves importing data into the Power BI data model and then visualizing it. Although there are other modes and other connection types, Import Data is the most popular option. However, there are challenges when using a PBIX file with everything in one file, as illustrated in Figure 12-1. Here are some:

- Multiple developers cannot work on the same PBIX file at the same time. (Multi-developer issue.)

- Integrating the single PBIX file with another application or dataset would be very hard. (Ongoing maintenance issue.)

- All data transformations happen inside the model, and the refresh time is slower. (Performance issue.)

- The only way to expand visualization is by adding pages to the model, and you would end up with hundreds of pages. (Complexity issue.)

- Every change, even a small change in the visualization, means deploying the entire model. (Deployment issue.)

- Creating a separate Power BI file with some parts referencing the model would not be possible; as a result, you would create a lot of duplication. (Ongoing maintenance issues.)

- If you wanted to reuse some of the tables and calculations in other files in the future, it won't be easy to maintain when everything is in one file. (Lack of flexibility issue.)

- And many others.

© Reza Rad 2023
R. Rad, *Pro Power BI Architecture*, https://doi.org/10.1007/978-1-4842-9538-0_12

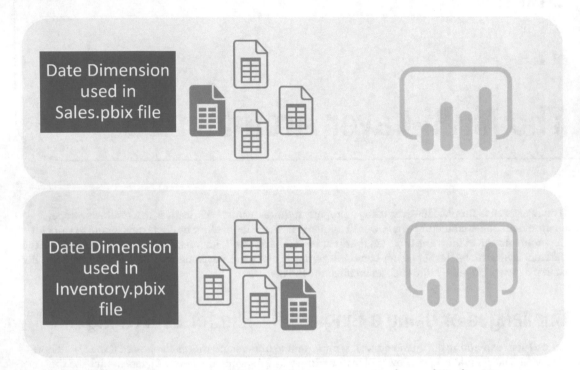

Date Dimension transformation executed multiple times, when only once is needed

Figure 12-1. *An example of one table needed in multiple Power BI files*

Suppose you are the only Power BI developer in your organization and are working on a small model that won't grow into multiple Power BI files in the future. In that case, you can keep everything in one file. However, I do not recommend keeping everything in one file if the scenario is different.

Using Dataflows to Decouple the Data Preparation Layer

Power Query is used for data preparation in the world of Power BI. Based on my experience and what I have seen from other implementations, you will spend 70 percent of your time on data preparation for a proper data model. That means if you are doing a Power BI implementation for ten months, then seven months will be spent on data preparation with Power Query! You don't want that time to be wasted and duplicated for another work. You want to maintain the efforts you have made for your data preparation.

Instead of doing your data preparation as part of a Power BI file, which will link that work only to that file, you can do it through a Power BI dataflow, as shown in Figure 12-2. Power BI dataflows run Power Query independently from Power BI files. The independence of dataflows from a Power BI file means that you can do data preparation for one entity only once and use it multiple times! In other words, you can use the dataflow to decouple the Power BI system's data preparation (or ETL) layer from the Power BI file. After doing the data preparation using the dataflow, the Power BI files can get data from it using the Get Data option from the dataflow.

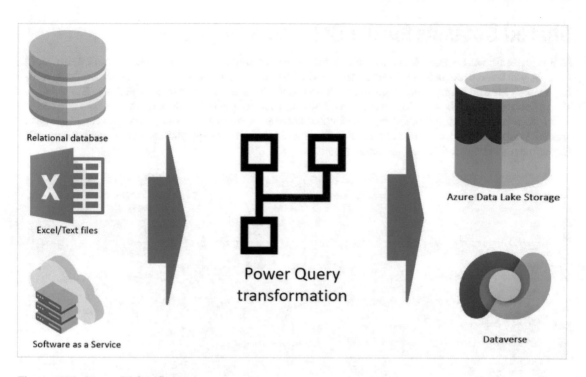

Figure 12-2. *Power BI dataflows*

Figure 12-3 features a diagram of using dataflows with multiple Power BI files.

Date Dimension transformation executed only once, and then used multiple times

Figure 12-3. *Shared tables can be processed in a dataflow and then reused in multiple Power BI files*

Shared Datasets for the Data Modeling Layer

Although dataflows create shared data sources for Power BI models, if you want to create multiple Power BI models, you need to set field-level formatting inside the Power BI file. You need to create DAX calculations inside each file and create hierarchies and any other modeling requirements inside the Power BI model. These settings cannot be done in the dataflow. These are parts of the Power BI dataset.

Instead of doing all the modeling and calculations in each Power BI file separately, you can leverage the shared dataset concept, shown in Figure 12-4. The shared dataset concept enables you to create a Power BI file with a model only and no visualization pages.

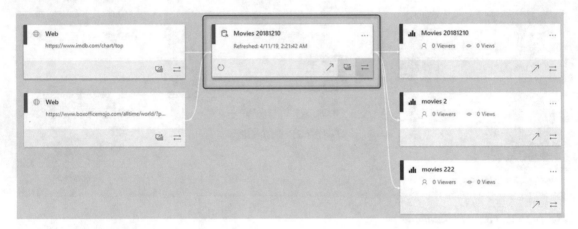

Figure 12-4. *A Power BI shared dataset*

A shared dataset then can be used in multiple Power BI reports as a centralized model. You don't need to duplicate your DAX calculations, hierarchies, and field-level formatting using the shared dataset. The shared dataset will act like a modeling layer of your Power BI solution.

Thin Power BI Reports, Paginated Reports, and the Analyze in Excel Option

Now that you have the Power BI data model in a shared dataset, you can create Power BI reports that get data from that shared dataset. This process is shown in Figure 12-5. These reports will create a live connection to that dataset. These are called thin reports.

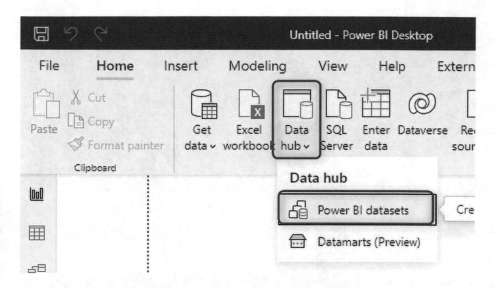

Figure 12-5. *Creating thin reports with a live connection to Power BI shared datasets*

You can create multiple thin reports by getting data from the shared dataset. This enables multiple report visualizers to build visualizations at the same time.

Not only can you create Power BI reports on top of the shared dataset, but you can also create paginated reports. As you can see in Figure 12-6, you connect to the same Power BI dataset in Excel.

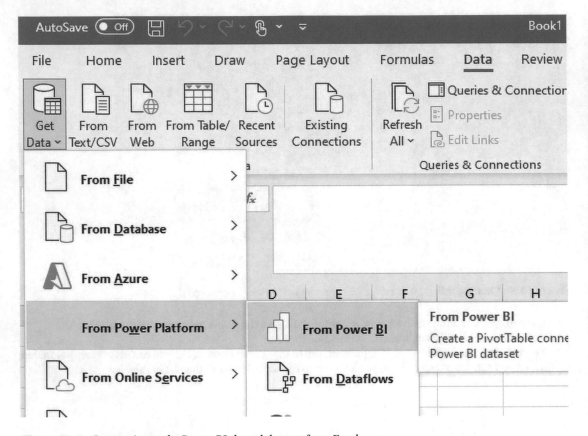

Figure 12-6. *Connecting to the Power BI shared dataset from Excel*

Power BI Architecture with Dataflows, Shared Datasets, and Thin Reports

As a result, I recommend the multi-layered Power BI architecture shown in Figure 12-7. This architecture doesn't include datamarts (which are explained later in this chapter) because the licensing for datamarts might require a different setup.

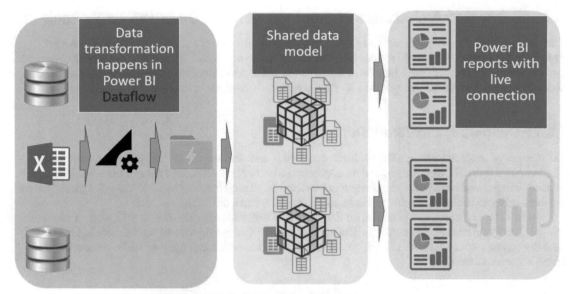

Power BI Solution Architecture

Figure 12-7. *The Power BI Solution Architecture with dataflows and a shared dataset*

This architecture uses layers as follows:

- Dataflow for the ETL or data preparation layer

- Shared dataset for the data modeling layer

- Get Data from Power BI dataset for the visualization layer (thin reports), paginated reports, or the Analyze option in Excel

Benefits of a Multi-Layered Architecture

Every architecture plan has its pros and cons. The following sections covers some of the benefits of this architecture.

Decoupling the Data Preparation Layer Using Dataflows

The development time you put using Power Query will be preserved and can be used in other Power BI models. The dataflow stores the data in an Azure Data Lake. Decoupling the data preparation from the modeling means that you can apply changes to the data transformation with minimum effect on the other layers (modeling).[1]

---

[1] Moving shared data tables to a Power Query dataflow is a recommended approach I have previously written about. Learn more at radacad.com/move-your-shared-tables-to-dataflow-build-a-consistent-table-in-power-bi.

A Multi-Layered Architecture Without the Need for Other Developer Tools

You can use SSIS, Azure Data Factory, or other ETL tools to take care of the data preparation process. However, the power of Power BI resides in its simplicity. Everyone with fair knowledge of Power Query can use dataflow. You don't need to be a C# or SQL Server developer to work with this tool. When you build a shared dataset, you are still using Power BI. All the skills you need are in the Power BI skillset.

Multi-Developer Environments

The proposed architecture supports multiple developers simultaneously on one Power BI solution. You can have multiple ETL developers (or data engineers) working on dataflows, data modelers working on the shared dataset, and multiple report designers (or data visualizers) building reports. They don't need to wait for each other to finish their work and then continue. They can work independently.

In this environment, everyone can do the job they are skilled to do. The dataflow developer requires Power Query and M skills but not DAX. The data modelers need to understand the relationships and DAX, and the report visualizer needs to understand the art of visualization and tips and tricks on how to build informative dashboards.

Reusing Calculations and Modeling with Shared Datasets

Having a centralized model will reduce the need for writing DAX calculations repeatedly. You do the modeling once and reuse it in multiple reports. On the other hand, you are sure that all reports are getting their data from a reconciled and fully tested model, or in other words, it is a gold data model.

Minimum Redundancy, Maximum Consistency, and Low Maintenance

A solution implementation that reduces the need for code duplication (using dataflows and a shared dataset) and reusing the existing code (using Get Data from the dataflows and datasets) will be highly consistent. Maintenance of such an implementation is possible with minimal effort.

Enhancing the Architecture Using Power BI Datamarts

Datamarts take the architecture of Power BI implementation to the next level by bringing one unified UI to build the dataflow, the data warehouse using an Azure SQL database, and the shared dataset. Because datamarts require premium (PPU or Premium capacity) licensing, I do not explain them in the original version of the architecture.

If you have the required licensing, I recommend using datamarts, which will introduce the data warehouse as the fourth layer of the Power BI architecture, as shown in Figure 12-8.

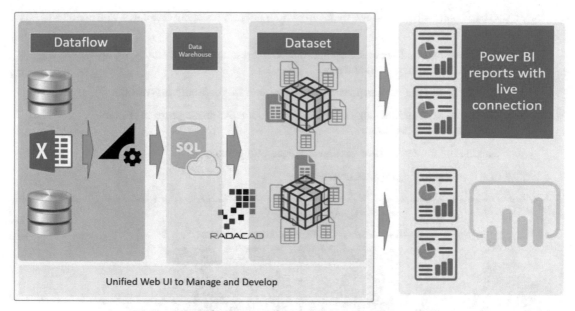

Power BI Solution Architecture using Datamart

Figure 12-8. Power BI solution architecture using datamarts

Datamarts are explained in the previous chapter, which I recommend you study.

Layered Architecture for Dataflow

This architecture includes three layers (or four if you use datamarts). However, this can be expanded into many more layers in a real-world situation. The Data Preparation layer, which is done by dataflow, can split into multiple layers.[2]

Staging Dataflows

One of the key points in any data integration system is to reduce the number of reads from the source operational system. In a traditional data integration architecture, this reduction is made by creating a new database, called a *staging database*. The purpose of the staging database is to load data as is from the data source into the staging database on a regular schedule. The rest of the data integration will then use the staging database as the source for further transformation and convert it to the dimensional model structure.

I recommended that you follow the same approach using dataflows. Create a set of dataflows that are responsible for loading data as is from the source system (and only for the tables you need). The result is then stored in the storage structure of the dataflow (either Azure Data Lake Storage or a dataverse). This change ensures that the read operations from the source system are minimal.

---

[2] I explain this concept in my article at docs.microsoft.com/en-us/power-query/dataflows/
best-practices-for-dimensional-model-using-dataflows*

Next, you can create other dataflows that source their data from staging dataflows. The benefits of this approach include:

- Reducing the number of read operations from the source system and reducing the load on the source system as a result.

- Reducing the load on data gateways if an on-premises data source is used.

- Having an intermediate copy of the data for reconciliation purposes in case the source system data changes.

- Making the transformation dataflows source-independent.

Figure 12-9 shows how staging dataflows works.

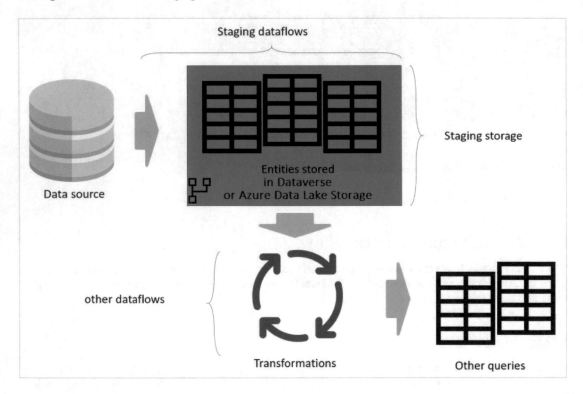

Figure 12-9. *Staging dataflows*

Figure 12-9 emphasizes staging dataflows and staging storage, and it shows the data being accessed from the data source by the staging dataflow. Entities are being stored in either Cadavers or Azure Data Lake Storage. These entities are then transformed along with other dataflows, which are sent out as queries.

Transforming Dataflows

When you've separated your transformation dataflows from the staging dataflows, the transformation will be independent of the source. This separation helps if you're migrating the source system to a new system. All you need to do in that case is change the staging dataflows. The transformation dataflows are likely to work without any problems because they're sourced only from the staging dataflows.

This separation also helps when the source system connection is slow. The transformation dataflow, shown in Figure 12-10, won't need to wait to get records coming through a slow connection from the source system. The staging dataflow has already done that part, and the data will be ready for the transformation layer.

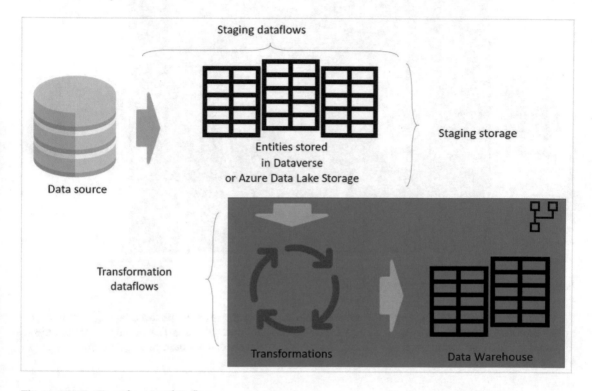

Figure 12-10. *Transforming dataflows*

Layered Dataflow Architecture

A layered architecture is an architecture in which you perform actions in separate layers. The staging and transformation dataflows can be two layers of a multi-layered dataflow architecture. Trying to do actions in layers ensures minimum maintenance is required. When you want to change something, you just need to change it in the layer in which it's located. The other layers should all continue to work fine.

Figure 12-11 shows a multi-layered architecture for dataflows in which their entities are then used in Power BI datasets.

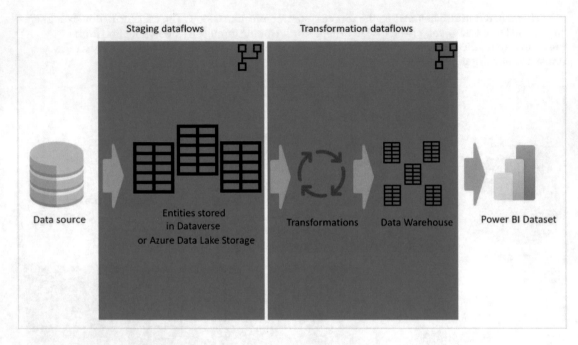

Figure 12-11. *Layered architecture of a dataflow*

The dataflow layered architecture is not only helpful when you are using the three-layered architecture, but also when you use the four-layered architecture with a datamart. A datamart can get data from dataflows that are ingesting data from some other transformation dataflow, which are then getting data from the data source using staging dataflows.[3]

Chained Datasets

Power BI datasets can also be implemented in multiple layers, by way of chained datasets. Chained datasets are datasets that use the DirectQuery to Power BI Dataset scenario. These chained datasets can be further modeled or can include data from other sources. This is particularly helpful in scenarios in which data analysts use a centralized model built by the BI team and extend it to a smaller chained model for their use cases. See Figure 12-12.

---

[3] Information about layered dataflow architecture borrows from my previous work, found at docs.microsoft.com/en-us/power-query/dataflows/best-practices-for-dimensional-model-using-dataflows*

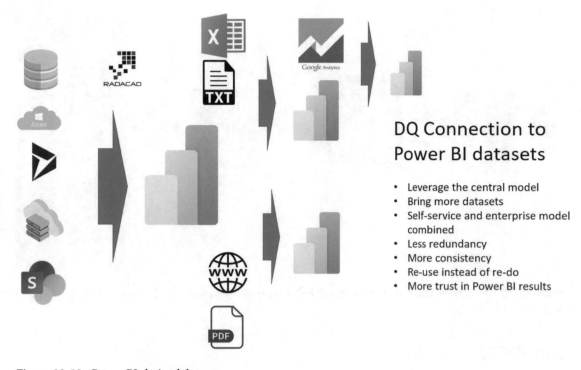

Figure 12-12. *Power BI chained datasets*

As you see in Figure 12-12, the dataflow and the dataset can become multiple layers. The number of layers in the architecture is not important. Designing layers in a way that leads to less maintenance and more reusable objects and components is the critical thing to consider when you design the architecture of a Power BI solution.

What About Enterprise Architecture?

You might already use Power BI in an enterprise solution using Azure Data Factory or SSIS as the ETL tool, SSAS as the modeling tool, and Power BI Live Connection as the visualization tool (see Figure 12-13). Such an architecture is similar to what Figure 12-13 shows. If you already have that architecture in place, I recommend you proceed.

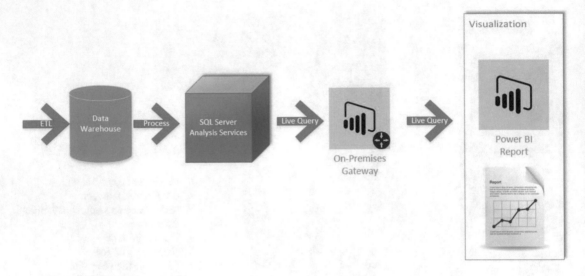

Figure 12-13. *Enterprise architecture for a Power BI implementation using other tools and services for ETL and data modeling*

Summary

Implementing a Power BI solution is simple. However, maintaining it is not! You must have a proper architecture if you want low maintenance, highly scalable, consistent, and robust Power BI implementation. This chapter explained the benefits of a proposed architecture that leverages dataflows for the data preparation layer and shared datasets for the data modeling layer. The architecture can also be enhanced using Power BI datamarts. The proposed architecture will require minimum maintenance efforts—it is highly scalable. I strongly recommend you consider using this architecture in your implementations.

■ ■ ■

CHAPTER 13

Datamarts vs. Dataflows vs. Datasets

Datamarts, dataflows, and datasets are all Power BI components that deal with data. I have presented about these a lot, and one of the questions I get is what is the difference between them? In this chapter, you learn the differences between these three components, when and where you use each, and how they work together with the other components of Power BI.

What Is a Dataflow?

A Power BI dataflow is the data transformation component in Power BI. It is a Power Query process that runs in the cloud, independent of the Power BI report and dataset, and it stores the data into Azure Data Lake storage (or a dataverse). Dataflows are not limited to Power BI; they can be created and used in other services such as Power Platform (Power Apps). Dataflows give you the transformation engine of Power Query plus the storage option. Dataflows give you a reusable ETL (Extract-Transform-Load) component. Figure 13-1 shows an overview of dataflows.

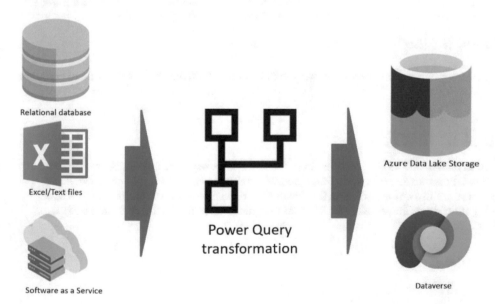

Figure 13-1. *A Power BI dataflow*

To learn more about dataflows, I recommend the earlier chapter in this book.

© Reza Rad 2023
R. Rad, *Pro Power BI Architecture*, https://doi.org/10.1007/978-1-4842-9538-0_13

What Is a Dataset?

A Power BI dataset is the object that contains the connection to the data source, data tables, the data itself, the relationship between tables, and DAX calculations. Usually, a Power BI dataset is hidden from the Power BI Desktop view but can easily be seen in the Power BI Service. A Power BI dataset is used commonly when sharing a model between multiple visualization objects (such as multiple Power BI reports, paginated reports, and Excel reports). The ability to use a shared dataset will give you a reusable modeling layer in Power BI. Figure 13-2 shows how datasets appear in your workspace.

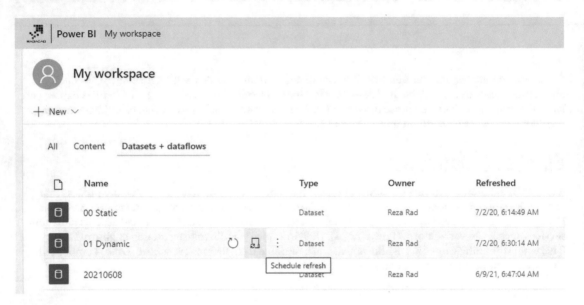

Figure 13-2. *A Power BI dataset*

To learn more about datasets and how they are used in Power BI, read the chapter about them earlier in this book.

What Is a Datamart?

A Power BI datamart is a recently added component to the Power BI ecosystem. Power BI datamarts are a combination of dataflows, an Azure SQL database (acting like a data warehouse), and a dataset. Power BI datamarts also come with a unified editor in the Power BI Service. Power BI datamarts are more like containers around other components of Power BI (dataflows, datasets, and an Azure SQL database), as illustrated in Figure 13-3.

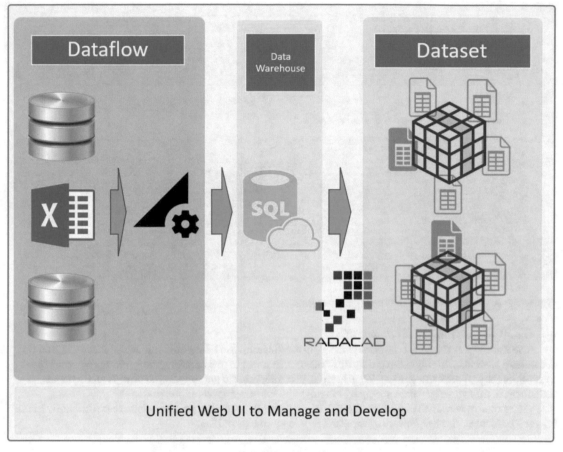

Power BI Datamart

Figure 13-3. *A Power BI datamart*

To learn more about datamarts, read the earlier chapter in this book.

Differences Between Dataflows and Datasets

Datamarts, dataflows, and datasets are Power BI components that store and work with data. Now that you know what they are, let's look at the differences between these three components.

A dataflow is the Power Query component.

Dataflows decouple the Power Query logic and code from the Power BI file so that it can be used in multiple files. You can get data from many different data sources, do the transformations using Power Query online, get the data in the shape you want, set a scheduled refresh for it, and load it into storage options (such as Azure Data Lake storage or a dataverse). See Figure 13-4.

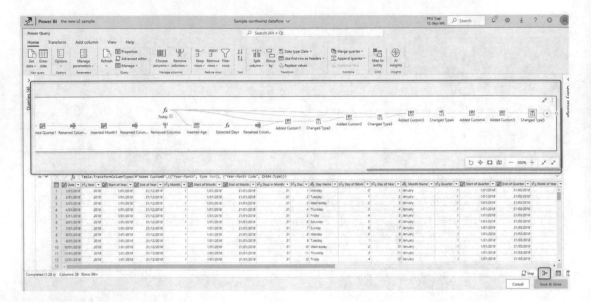

Figure 13-4. Dataflows are the Power Query component

Dataflows are not just for Power BI.

The dataflow is the only component of the three that can also be created outside of Power BI. You do not need a business intelligence or data analysis requirement to use dataflows. Sometimes you may need a dataflow for just data integration. For example, you may want to get data from some source systems, transform it, and store it in data storage. This might be for other applications to use.

Dataflows in Power BI can be used for data analysis purposes, but you can also create dataflows in the Power Platform under the Power Apps portal, as shown in Figure 13-5.

Figure 13-5. *Dataflows in the Power Apps portal*

Datasets replace DAX calculations and relationships.

Using a shared dataset, you can reuse the DAX calculations and relationships you created for one model in other Power BI files. If you want to reuse the DAX measures, the calculated columns and tables, the hierarchies, the field-level formatting, and the relationships defined in your model for multiple files, shared datasets do that for you. You can connect multiple reports to a shared dataset and reuse the data model, as shown in Figure 13-6.

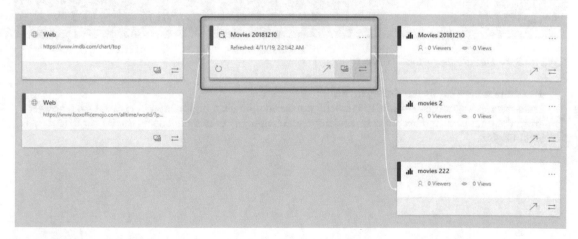

Figure 13-6. *Shared datasets replace your DAX and any calculations*

Why not use DirectQuery from the source instead of a dataset?

The question that normally comes to mind is, what if you already have a data warehouse? Or even if there is no data warehouse, what if you consider the storage of your dataflow a data warehouse? Can you connect DirectQuery to that? Isn't a Power BI dataset an unnecessary layer on top of that? Why would you need Power BI datasets in those cases?

Power BI datasets use in-memory engine storage for the data. The in-memory storage for the data ensures the best performance in the report and visualization, as the interaction in the report would be the fastest. It also includes a powerful calculation language called DAX that helps with some analytical requirements and calculations. So even if you already have a data warehouse, I still highly recommend using a dataset on top of that.

Dataflows represent the ETL layer.

Dataflows represent the Data Transformation layer in your Power BI implementation, highlighted in Figure 13-7. The terminology for this layer is ETL (Extract, Transform, Load). It will extract data from the data sources, transform the data, and load it into the CDM.

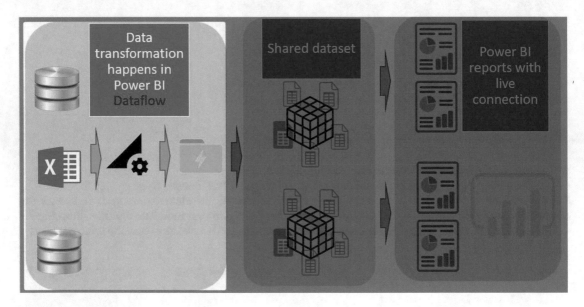

Figure 13-7. *Dataflows are the ETL layer*

Datasets represent the modeling layer.

Datasets represent the layer of all the calculations and modeling, highlighted in Figure 13-8. They get data from the dataflow (or other sources) and build an in-memory data model using the Power BI (Analysis Services) Engine.

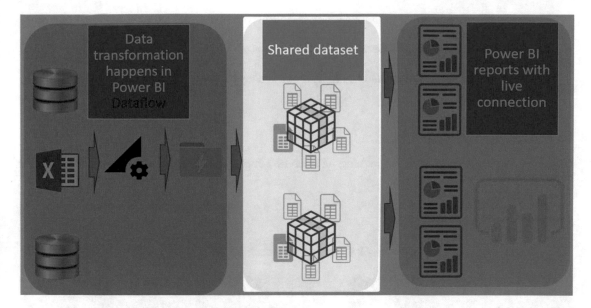

Figure 13-8. *Datasets make up the modeling layer*

Dataflows feed data into the dataset.
The result of the dataflow will be fed into a dataset for further modeling; a dataflow by itself is not a visualization-ready component.

Datasets feed data into visualizations.
Because the dataset is an in-memory model built and is ready for visualization, its result is used to build a visualization.

Dataflows access the data source directly.
Unless you use a linked or computed entity, a dataflow usually gets data directly from the data source.

Datasets can access data from the dataflow.
Although a dataset can directly get data from a data source, it is a best practice that a shared dataset gets the data from dataflows. This supports a multi-developer implementation of Power BI.

A dataflow developer needs Power Query skills.
One of the reasons to use dataflows and shared datasets is to decouple the layers, so you have multiple developers building the Power BI solution at the same time. In such an environment, the skillset needed for a dataflow developer include Power Query and how to build Star-Schemas, and so on. No DAX or visualization skills are required for dataflow developers.

A dataset developer needs DAX and modeling skills.
On the other hand, the dataset developer needs to know everything about the relationships in Power BI and the calculations in Power BI using DAX. Although the dataset developer can know Power Query and visualization, it does not need to be their primary skill.

Dataflow users are called data modelers.
The dataflow's result can be used for data modelers. It is not a great approach to give the output of dataflow to report visualizers. The dataflow has to be loaded into a model with proper relationships and calculations added to it.

Dataset users are called report visualizers.
The result of a dataset is ready for report visualizers. They can have a live connection to the shared dataset and build their visualizations from it.

Dataflows solve the problem of having multiple versions of the same table in different PBIX files.

Using a dataflow, you reduce the need to copy and paste your Power Query scripts into other files. You can reuse a table in multiple files.

Datasets solve the problem of having multiple versions of the same DAX code in different PBIX files.

Using a shared dataset, you can have multiple reports using the same calculations and data model without duplicating the code.

Dataflows vs. Datasets

Dataflow and datasets are not the same thing. As Table 13-1 demonstrates, there are considerable differences between them.

Table 13-1. Dataflows vs. Datasets

Dataflow Vs. Dataset

Dataflow	Dataset
Replacement of your Power Query layer	Replacement of your modeling, relationship, DAX expressions
ETL Layer	Modeling Layer
Feeds Data to the Dataset	Feeds the Visualization Layer
Access the data source directly (usually)	Access the data from dataflow (best practice)
Dataflow developer needs to have Power Query skills	Dataset developer needs DAX and modelling skills
Users of dataflow are data modelers	Users of dataset are report visualizers
Dataflow solves the problem of having multiple version of the same table in different PBIX files	Dataset solves the problem of having multiple version of the same DAX code in different PBIX files

They are two separate, essential components of Power BI and both have their places in the Power BI architecture for a multi-developer scenario. Figure 13-9 shows a representation of their essential-but-separate roles. Dataflows and datasets are not replacements for each other; they are the complements of the other.

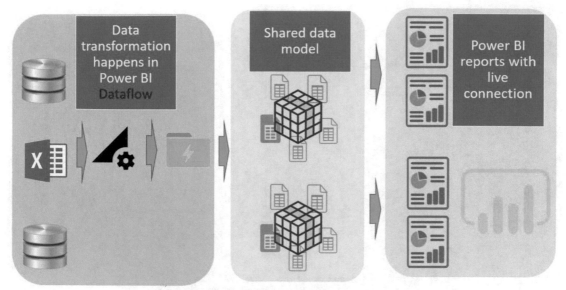

Power BI Solution Architecture

Figure 13-9. *The Power BI Solution architecture with dataflows and datasets*

What About Datamarts?

You learned a lot about the differences between dataflows and datasets. But what about datamarts? Shouldn't they be in the comparison list?

Power BI datamarts are more like containers of components rather than single objects (see Figure 13-3). When you create a Power BI datamart, you are creating a dataflow, an Azure SQL database, and a dataset. This means that the datamart benefits from the features mentioned for dataflows and datasets. Datamarts also have an extra component: they store data in the Azure SQL database. After processing by the dataflow, the data is loaded into the Azure SQL database. Some call this a data warehouse, and some may even call this a datamart. But Power BI datamarts include all these components: dataflows, an Azure SQL database, and a dataset.

Power BI Datamart Components

Power BI datamarts also provide a unified Web UI to build and manage all these components. With the addition of the datamart, the multi-developer architecture of Power BI looks more like Figure 13-10.

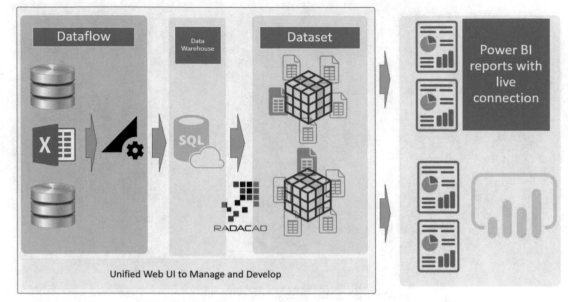

Power BI Solution Architecture using Datamart

Figure 13-10. *Power BI solution architecture using datamarts*

You might wonder whether datamarts will replace datasets and dataflows. The next section considers this question.

Will Dataflows Be Replaced by Datamarts?

No. Certainly not. A dataflow is a component by itself. As mentioned, you can build and use a dataflow without needing a BI solution. Datamarts are normally useful when you are building a BI solution. You may just want to integrate some tables into storage and reuse them in other applications; in that case, you can use a dataflow by itself.

Another use case of a dataflow by itself is that even if you have a datamart, you may still want to implement multiple layers of dataflows for staging and transformation. Having multiple layers of dataflows (see Figure 13-11) provides an effective technique in data source isolation and reuse of dataflow components.

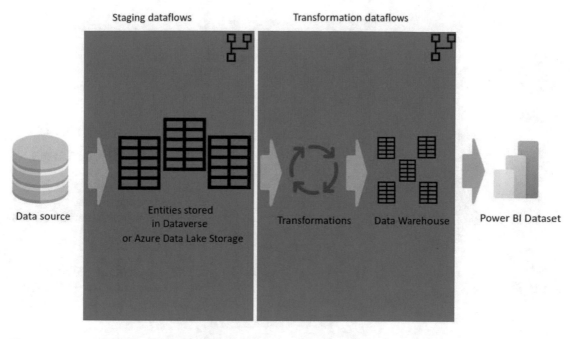

Figure 13-11. *Multi-layered dataflow architecture*

Are Datasets Being Replaced by Datamarts?

The answer to this question is also no. Although it is now easier to create a dataset from the unified UI of the datamart, that doesn't reduce the need for the dataset to be a separate component of its own. There are plenty of use cases for a dataset as a component on its own. Imagine you are implementing an architecture in which the data transformation is done using another service (such as Azure Data Factory), and the data warehouse is in Azure Synapse. You can still use Power BI datasets to build the data model and calculations on top of that without building a full datamart.

Another use case is that even if you use a Power BI datamart, you may still create chained datasets on top of your existing dataset. These chained datasets are DirectQuery to Power BI datasets (which in this case is part of a datamart), but they can include other data sources. Chained datasets (see Figure 13-12) are a very useful way to work with self-service data analysts in an enterprise organization.

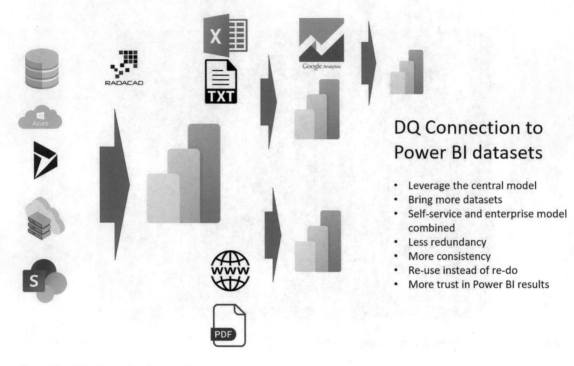

Figure 13-12. Power BI chained datasets

Summary

Now is time for the million-dollar question; which one of these components should you use? Each of these comes with some benefits, as you've learned. Let's answer this question using a scenario.

James is a BI developer who is building a new BI solution. His implementation includes stages such as getting data from the source, doing transformations, loading data into a data warehouse, writing calculations in the model, and visualization. Power BI datamarts enable him to build most of that in one unified structure but still use a multi-layered approach that can be easily maintained in the future.

After some time, James realizes that the data transformation side of his implementation is heavy. He wants the data transformation to be isolated from the data source so that if the source changes, his solution will still work with minimal changes. So, he uses staging and transformation dataflows in his architecture.

James has some colleagues who are business analysts in other departments. They want to use the dataset that James provided as the main source, but add data sources and calculations to it. They create chained datasets on top of that.

This scenario uses all three components in an architecture. Choosing which components you need is mainly based on what reusable components you have and where you want to use them.

CHAPTER 14

Paginated Reports

If you want to print a Power BI report and have a tabular visual in your report (such as a table or matrix), your options are limited. Fortunately, the Power BI Paginated Report feature can help with that. This chapter explains the paginated report and the differences between it and a normal Power BI report, plus situations that you need to use each.

What Is a Paginated Report in Power BI?

If you look at Figure 14-1, you can see two objects in the Power BI service. They both are report type, but they have different icons.

Figure 14-1. Two types of reports in the Power BI Service

The Movies to Print report is a paginated report. Paginated reports, although they look like normal reports, are a different type of report in Power BI.

Paginated reports are created using another tool (not using the Power BI Desktop) and for a different use case. Paginated reports are designed for pixel-perfect printing. They are ideal for exporting to PDF or printing, especially when the data presented in the report is multiple pages (such as a table with thousands of rows). That is why they are called paginated. You can design the report over multiple pages. You can set page headers and footers and categorize them so that certain information goes into certain report pages.

Figure 14-2 shows an example paginated report.

Contoso Suites

123 Coffee Street
Buffalo,NY 98052
USA
Telephone 012345678
http://www.contososuites.com

Owl Wholesales
123 Violet Road , Phoenix, CO 85003 USA

Invoice CIV-000676 000007-1
30 November 2019

Payment terms: Net 45 days
Payment due 1/14/2020

$321,113.52

ITEM	DESCRIPTION	QUANTITY		SALES PRICE	DISCOUNT	AMOUNT
D011	Lens	2	Each	2	0	4.00
L0001	Mid-Range Speaker	35	Each	500	0	17,500.00
P0001	Acoustic Foam Panel	117	Each	37	0	4,329.00
D0003	Standard Speaker	23	Each	220	0	5,060.00
T0001	Speaker cable 10	65	Each	500	0	32,500.00
D0004	High End Speaker	12	Each	2000	0	24,000.00
T0004	Television M120 37" Silver	53	Each	350	0	18,550.00
T00002	Projector Television	23	Each	3750	0	86,250.00
T0005	Television HDTV X590 52" White	33	Each	2890	0	95,370.00
T0003	Surround Sound Receiver	56	Each	450	0	25,200.00

SALES SUBTOTAL AMOUNT		4.00
SALES TAX		12,350.52
USD TOTAL		**321,113.52**

Sales invoice notes

METHODS OF PAYMENT

Electronic payment	Check
Payment reference **US-009**	Make check payable to **Contoso**
Sort code	**Suites**.
Account No. 34567	Write reference **US-009** on the check.

OTHER INFORMATION

Tax registration no.	**1234123400**
Our reference	**Karl Bystrom**

Figure 14-2. *Power BI paginated report sample*

Paginated reports are created using the Power BI Report Builder. This is a different editor than the Power BI Desktop and has to be downloaded and installed separately.

Why Paginated Reports?

As you already know, you can use the Power BI Desktop to create any report you want. So you might wonder why you would need to create paginated reports. To answer this, you must understand how printing works with a normal Power BI report.

Say you have a normal Power BI report (a report that is created using the Power BI Desktop), and your report looks like Figure 14-3.

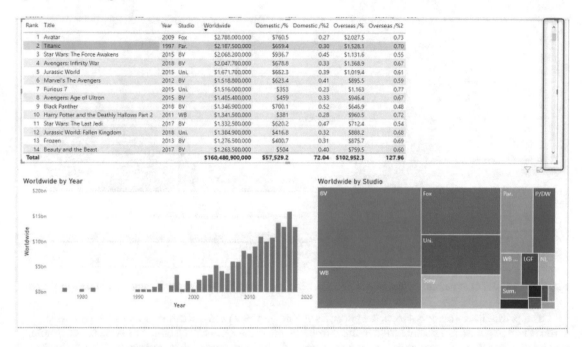

Figure 14-3. *Power BI report with table visuals*

Figure 14-3 shows a table visual in the Power BI report. Only a few rows in that table can be presented on the screen, so it includes a scroll bar on the right. In the context of an interactive report, you can easily scroll down to get to the records you want, or you can filter the report using slicers or other visuals.

However, the printed version of the report would look like Figure 14-4.

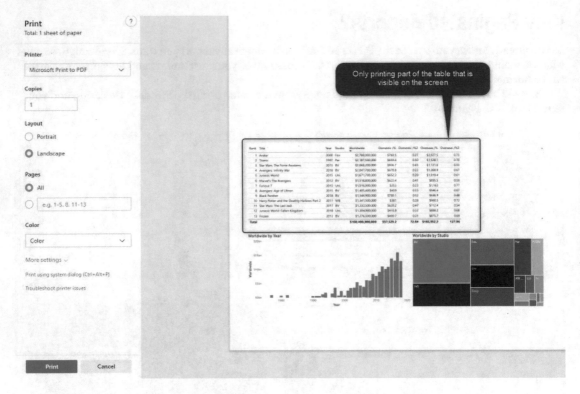

Figure 14-4. *Printed version of the Power BI report includes only the part of table rows visible on the screen*

The printed version only shows the few rows visible on the screen. All other rows, which you must scroll down to get to, are not included in the output. Printing the content of a table or matrix is not simple; you need pagination. You may need page headers and footers and some other settings. This is why there are paginated reports in Power BI. A paginated report can be designed exactly as you want to print it in the output. See Figure 14-5.

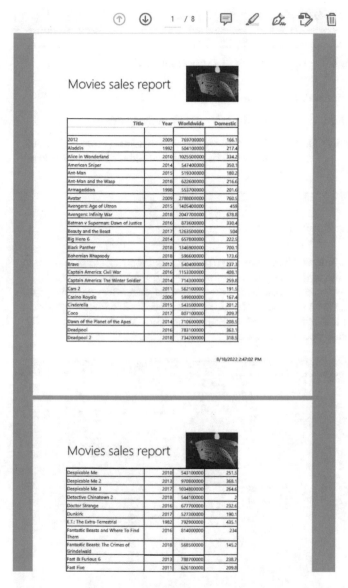

Figure 14-5. *A printed output of a Power BI paginated report*

Differences Between Power BI Reports and Paginated Reports

Although these two are reports hosted in the Power BI service, they are generated for different purposes and have different capabilities. Table 14-1 summarizes a few key differences.

Table 14-1. *Power BI Reports vs. Paginated Reports*

	Power BI Report	**Paginated Report**
It can be created Using	Power BI DesktopPower BI Service	Power BI Report BuilderVisual Studio
License needed	Power BI Free, Pro, Premium, PPU	Premium, PPU
Ideal for	Interactive analytical reports	Pixel-perfect print-ready reports
Design Process	Powerful and user-friendly GUI of the Power BI Desktop	Powerful but not user-friendly (more developer-focused) UI of Report Builder or Visual Studio
File extension	.PBIX	.RDL

Do You Need a Paginated Report?

If you need to print your reports on occasion, you will likely need to use paginated reports. One of the main reasons that users print reports is to carry them to the meetings, discuss them, and show them to others. When using Power BI mobile applications, especially if you design mobile-friendly reports, you can certainly have normal Power BI reports that can be carried to meetings (by phone), be discussed (with annotation on them), and shown to others. See the example in Figure 14-6. My experience shows that mobile-friendly Power BI reports can replace many (but not all) paginated reports.

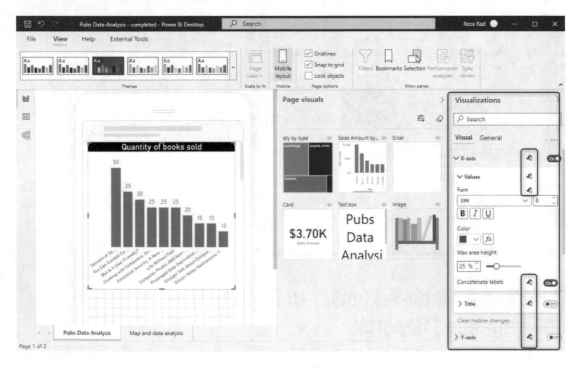

Figure 14-6. *Designing mobile-friendly reports in the Power BI Desktop*

If, after designing and adopting mobile-friendly Power BI reports, you still feel you need printed reports, it's time to create paginated reports.[1]

Architecture Best Practice: One Dataset to Rule Them All

If you create paginated reports, I urge you to consider the best architecture practices. The best architecture for development is the one that requires less maintenance and reuses components as much as possible. I explained how a dataset could be shared in multiple Power BI objects in the multi-layered architecture chapter and the shared dataset chapter.

Paginated reports can get data from a Power BI dataset. I strongly advise you to do that because your normal Power BI and paginated reports are sourced from the same dataset. Any changes to that dataset will then be available to both reports, as Figure 14-7 makes clear.

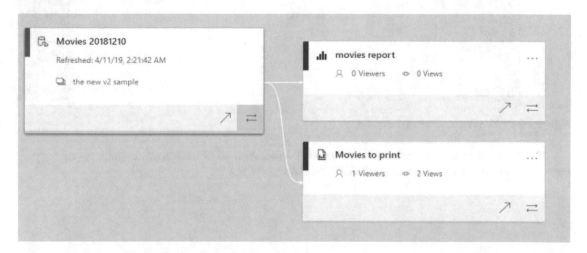

Figure 14-7. *Paginated reports and Power BI reports are sourced from a single shared dataset*

If you use this design, you can build a powerful reporting system. The Power BI report can be the interactive landing page report for the users. If they want more paginated details, you can build a master-detail scenario, passing details using parameters to the paginated report and navigating between these two. This is a great way to combine the power of both types of reports into one analytical system.

The Power BI Report Builder

Your tool to create a paginated report is called the Power BI Report Builder. This tool (before the age of Power BI) was called the Reporting Services Report Builder, or SSRS Report Builder. It is a lightweight tool for creating print-ready reports. However, compared to the Power BI Desktop, the Report Builder is not a user-friendly tool. You can download and install the Power BI Report Builder from aka.ms/pbireportbuilder.

As Figure 14-8 shows, this tool has a wizard that you use to start building a report. Usually, this is a good starting point if you are a beginner.

---

[1] To learn more about designing and adopting mobile-friendly Power BI reports, visit radacad.com/power-bi-design-tip-design-for-mobile-device.

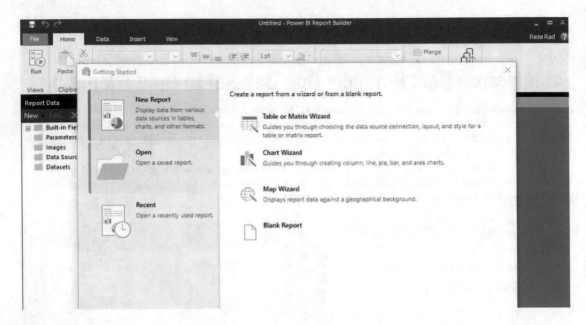

Figure 14-8. *The Power BI Report Builder*

The Report Builder has settings and configurations that are used to create a print-ready report. Figure 14-9 offers a sample view of the designer and its capabilities.

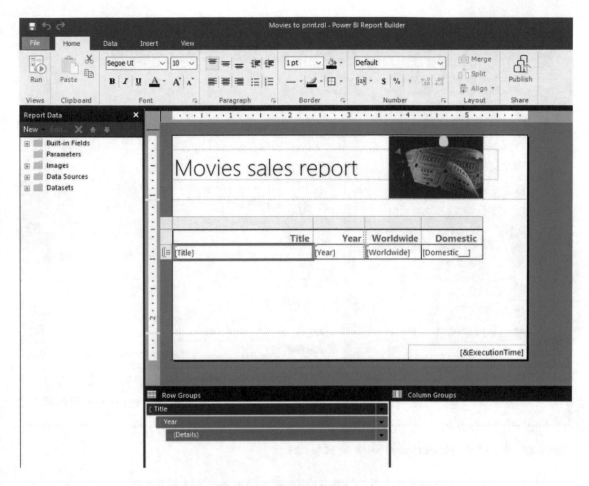

Figure 14-9. *An example of the designer for the Report Builder*

This differs from the Power BI environment, where things are more drag-and-drop, interaction-friendly. Remember that the Report Builder was created during the age of SQL Server Reporting Services, and the UI is older.

In Report Builder, you can get data from a Power BI dataset, which is what I recommend you do; see Figure 14-10.

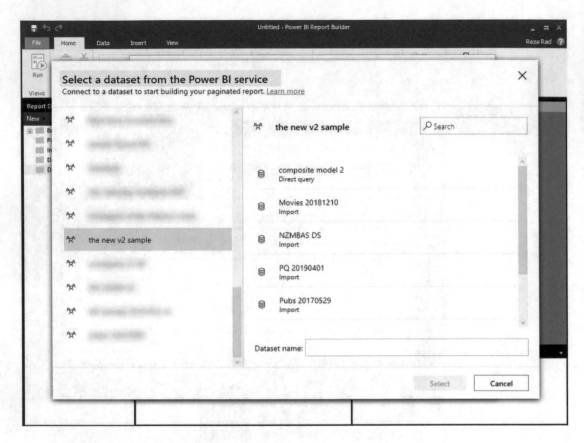

Figure 14-10. *Select a dataset from the Power BI service*

After building your report, you can publish it to the service, as Figure 14-11 shows.

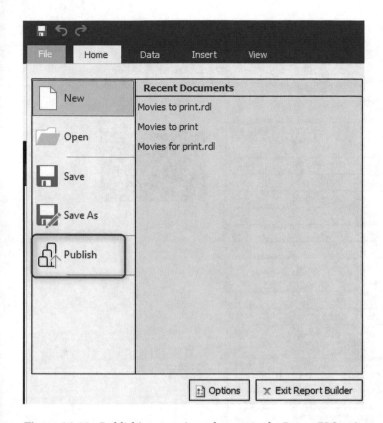

Figure 14-11. *Publishing a paginated report to the Power BI Service*

Publishing is only possible in Premium or PPU workspaces. Figure 14-12 shows a view of a paginated report.

Figure 14-12. Power BI paginated report in the Power BI Service

The learning curve for paginated reports is longer and steeper than for the Power BI Desktop. Some of the changes you can do only in Visual Studio. Many of the configurations are not as user-friendly as the Power BI Desktop. However, paginated reports are SSRS reports by nature, and SSRS is a very powerful visualization engine. There are books of over a thousand pages covering that technology.

Summary

Paginated reports are pixel-perfect, print-friendly reports. These reports are designed using Power BI Report Builder (and they can also be extended using Visual Studio). They are not usually as interactive as the normal Power BI reports, but they are perfect for printing. Before creating these reports, always think twice whether you actually need print-ready reports. Maybe accessible reports (such as mobile-friendly reports) would serve you better. If you are creating paginated reports, use shared datasets to access a good, layered architecture for your Power BI solution.

CHAPTER 15

■ ■ ■

Excel and Power BI Integration

Power BI and Excel are longtime friends of each other, not only because Power BI components come from add-ins introduced in Excel, but also because of how these two tools interact from the Power BI Service. This chapter is not about using Power Query or Power Pivot components in Excel. This chapter discusses the interaction between Excel and Power BI through the service.

Power BI and Excel integration through the service allows users to use Excel as their slicing and dicing tool while connected to a live Power BI dataset. On the other hand, you can pin a range of cells from an Excel document into the Power BI dashboard. Excel files also can be uploaded to the Workbook tab of the Power BI service. In this chapter, you learn the following ways that Excel and Power BI interact with each other through the Power BI Service:

- Analyze in Excel feature
- Publish to Power BI from Excel
- Import Excel into the Power BI Desktop

The Analyze in Excel Feature

Every company has users with good Excel experience. Excel users can use Excel to connect to the Power BI dataset and then use the Excel features such as PivotTable and PivotChart to slice and dice the data. The connection to the Power BI dataset is a live one, which means whenever users refresh the Excel file, they get the most up-to-date data from the Power BI service. Let's look at how the Analyze in Excel feature works in action.

The Analyze in Excel Feature from the Power BI Service

You can initiate the Analyze in Excel feature from a Power BI Service report or a dataset. Log in to the Power BI Service and click the More options of a dataset (or a report). Choose the Analyze in Excel option, as shown in Figure 15-1.

© Reza Rad 2023
R. Rad, *Pro Power BI Architecture*, https://doi.org/10.1007/978-1-4842-9538-0_15

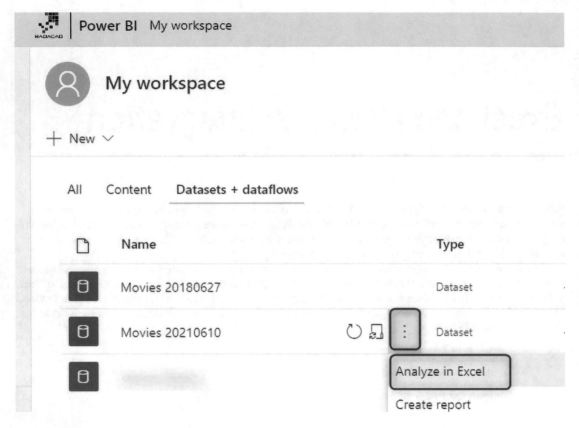

Figure 15-1. *Analyze in Excel from Power BI report or dataset*

Power BI will generate an Excel file in OneDrive and create a connection from that Excel file to the Power BI dataset. As shown Figure 15-2, you get a notification when the Excel file is ready. (If you don't have OneDrive for Business in your tenant, then clicking Analyze in Excel will download the workbook to your local computer.)

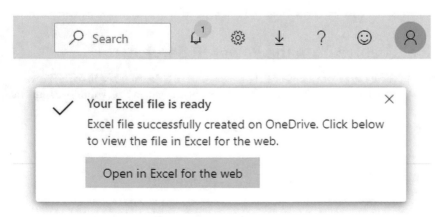

Figure 15-2. *Opening Analyze in Excel*

This file, by default, is opened in Excel online (the web version). However, you can download the file and store it locally. When you open the file, you get a warning about the data coming from outside of this workbook (Power BI Dataset), as shown in Figure 15-3.

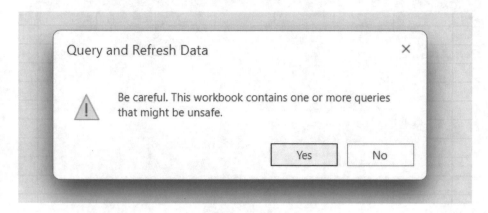

Figure 15-3. *Data is coming from outside of the Excel workbook*

Once you click Yes, you will see an Excel workbook with a PivotTable, which is the data sourced from the Power BI dataset in the service (see Figure 15-4). Analyze in Excel will use the same Power BI account username and password that you used to access the report (because the Power BI account is an Office 365 account).

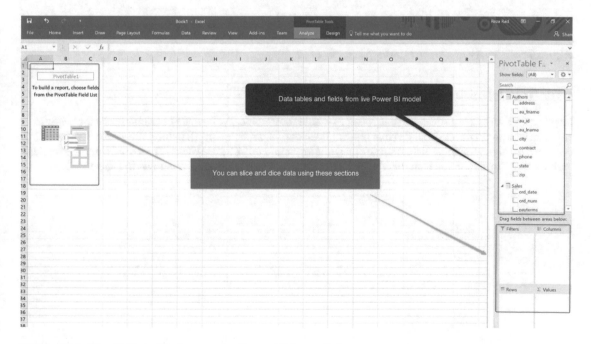

Figure 15-4. *PivotTable in Excel presenting Power BI dataset's data*

Drag the data fields into the slicing and dicing area (under the fields pane), and you will see a result in PivotTable. This result is fetched live from the Power BI dataset in the Power BI service. See Figure 15-5.

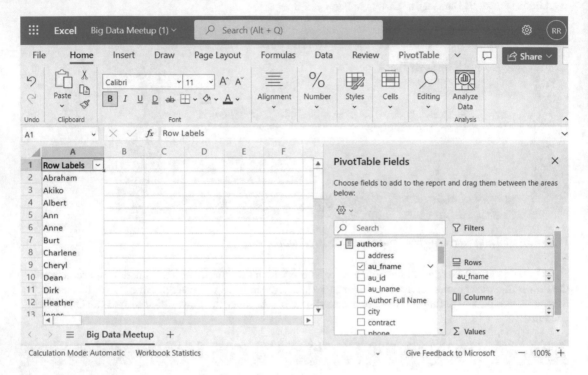

Figure 15-5. *Power BI data in tabular format in Excel*

Implicit Measures Don't Work in Excel

Implicit measures are a measure that Power BI creates automatically. Power BI automatically applies auto summarization on numeric fields (that haven't been part of a relationship). Behind the scenes, Power BI creates a measure for those fields; these measures are called implicit measures. These measures are marked with a small Sum or Sigma icon beside their name in the Power BI Desktop, as shown in Figure 15-6.

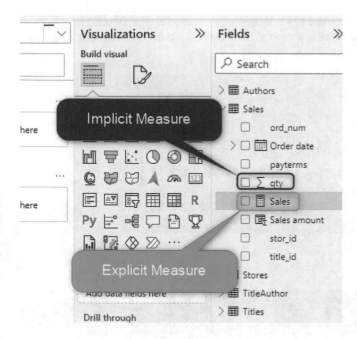

Figure 15-6. *Implicit vs. explicit measures in Power BI*

The implicit measure cannot be used in the Analyze in Excel feature; if you try dragging them to a PivotTable, you will see individual values instead of the aggregation. This limitation is illustrated in Figure 15-7.

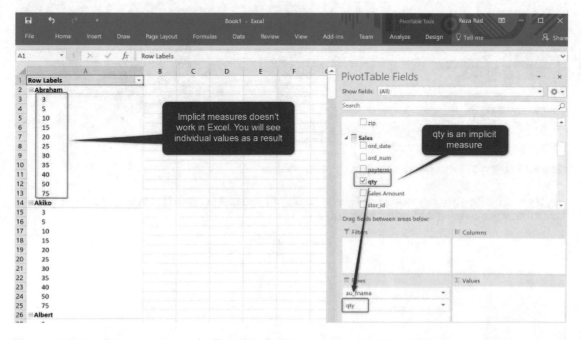

Figure 15-7. *Implicit measures aren't allowed in the Value section of the PivotTable*

However, if you create explicit measures (which are DAX measures created by you), similar to Figure 15-8, you can then use them in PivotTables as a normal measure and see the correct result, such as in Figure 15-9.

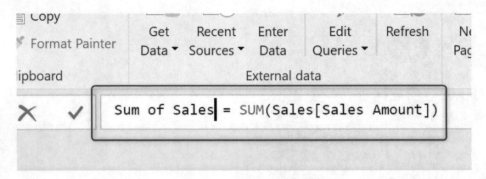

Figure 15-8. *An explicit measure*

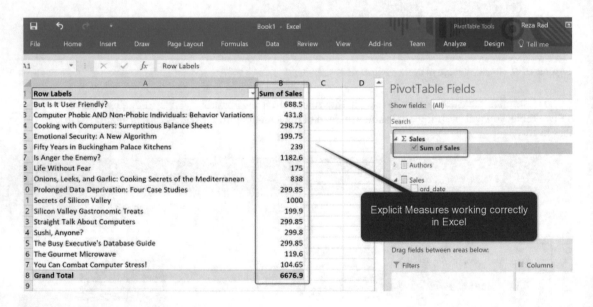

Figure 15-9. *Explicit measures work correctly in PivotTables*

If you consider that some users use Excel as their front-end tool to connect to Power BI models, you have to consider creating the Explicit measure.

Excel Is Connected Live to the Power BI Model in the Service

The wonderful thing about the Excel connection to the Power BI Service is that the connection is live. Using a live connection means Excel fetches the data directly from the dataset in the Power BI service. Any time you refresh the Excel file, you get the most up-to-date data from the service. This feature is completely different from the Export to Excel option. The Export to Excel option you see on visuals in the Power BI service only downloads data offline. However, Analyze in Excel is an online and live connection to the dataset.

You can check the connection properties in the Data tab, under the Connections, Properties section, as shown in Figure 15-10.

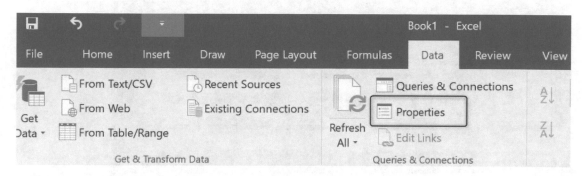

Figure 15-10. *Getting properties of the connection from Excel*

The Connection properties will have an Azure address with the ID of the dataset in the Power BI service. You can even use this connection in any other Excel file to connect to the same dataset. See Figure 15-11.

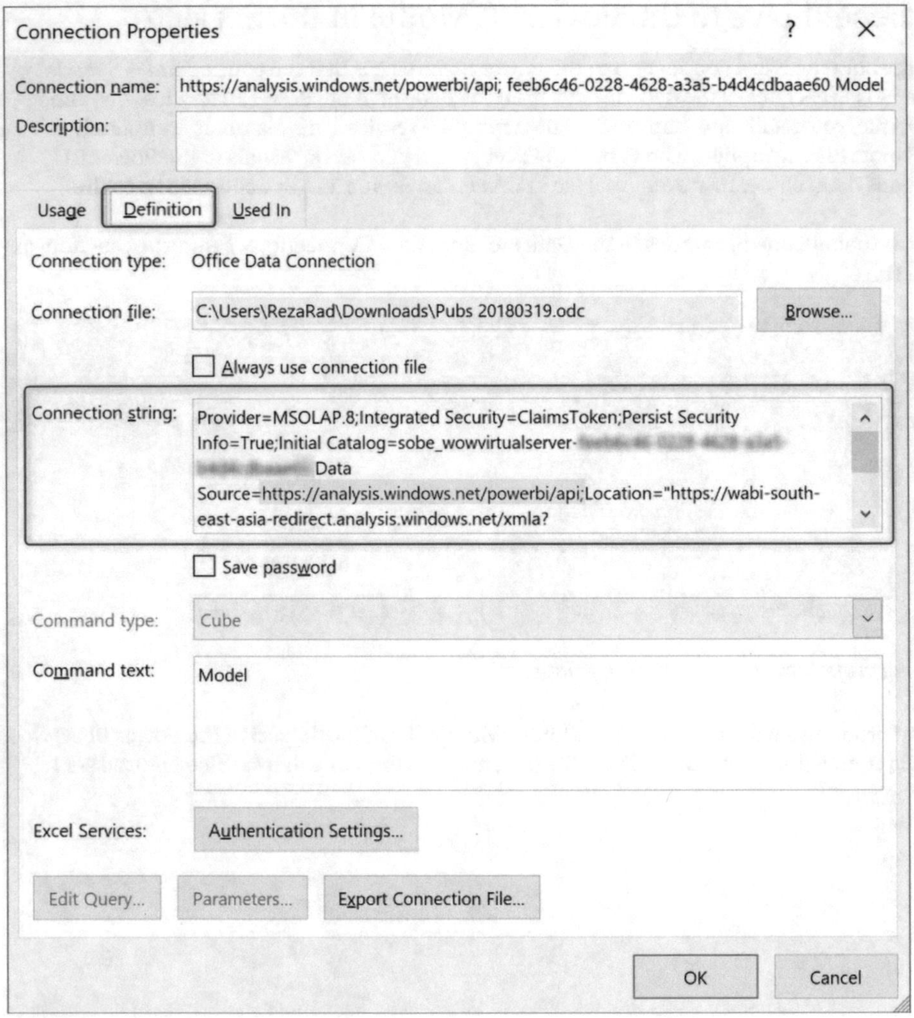

Figure 15-11. *Excel is connected to Azure Analysis Services (where the Power BI dataset is hosted)*

Getting Data from Power BI Dataset

Another very similar approach to Analyze in Excel is getting data from the Power BI dataset in Excel. If you have an Excel file and you want to do some data analysis on the data of a Power BI dataset, you can go to the Data tab and choose Get Data. Then choose From Power Platform, Dataset, as shown in Figure 15-12.

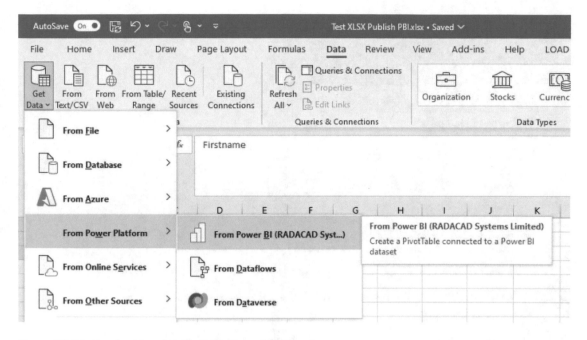

Figure 15-12. *Excel getting data from the Power BI dataset*

This will show you the list of Power BI datasets that you have access to, as shown in Figure 15-13) and you can select any of those.

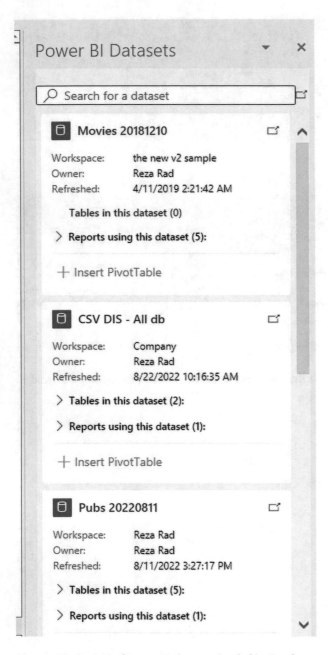

Figure 15-13. *List of Power BI datasets loaded in Excel*

Doing this will create a live connection to the Power BI dataset (similar to a thin report).

Getting Data from a Power BI Dataflow

Using Excel, you can also connect to a Power Platform dataflow and get data from it, as Figure 15-14 demonstrates.

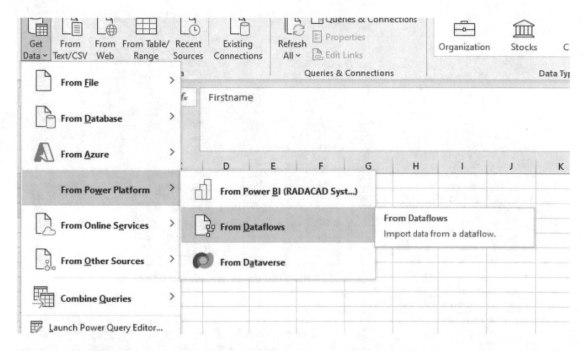

Figure 15-14. *Excel can get data from the Power Platform and Power BI dataflows*

The Navigator window will show you the Power Platform dataflows (under Environments) and Power BI dataflow (under workspaces), as shown in Figure 15-15.

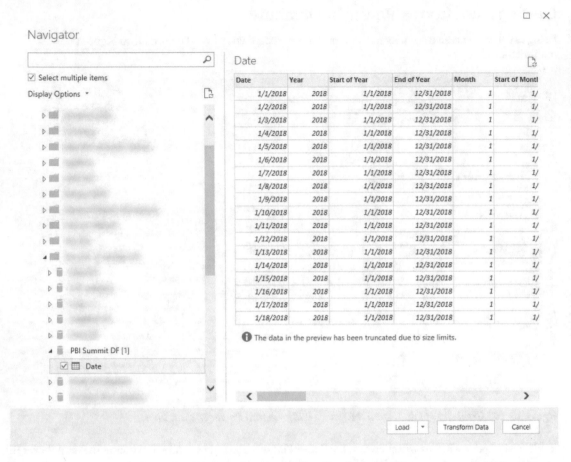

Figure 15-15. Power Platform dataflows listed in the Excel connector for dataflows

Why is Analyze in Excel Better than Using Export Data?

There are many reasons that Analyze in Excel is a better option than exporting data. The following sections explore some of those reasons.

Analyze in Excel is Live

As soon as you export data from a Power BI report or dataset, you create a snapshot of the data. If the report refreshes the next day, your exported data is no longer up-to-date. It is offline and outdated.

However, when you use Analyze in Excel, the data is fetched live from the Power BI dataset in the service. You can see that in the connection properties of Excel. You can check the connection properties in the Data tab, under the Connections, Properties section. The Connection properties will have an Azure address with the ID of the dataset in the Power BI service. You can even use this connection in any other Excel file to connect to the same dataset.

Export Data Is Limited to 150,000 Rows

Export data has a limitation on the number of rows. Analyze in Excel doesn't. You are connected to the model live. It looks like a live connection to the SSAS Tabular; you can do whatever you want with the data.

The export is limited to 150K rows if you export to Excel and 30K rows for CSV files.

Export Data Is Limited to Specific Visuals and Fields

When you use Export Data, you only do it from a specific visual. The fields in that visual (or related fields) are exported. When you use Analyze in Excel, you have access to all the tables, columns, and calculated fields and measures in Excel.

Analyze in Excel is the entire model: all the tables and calculations.

Export Data Is Not Secure

You might export data using an account that has access to everything and then share the exported data file with someone who should not have access to the data. Because the security and the data are decoupled when you use the export data, there is no security around it. You have to be careful to secure the exported data yourself. That said, Power BI has the system to apply sensitivity labels using other Azure services, which can help. Analyze in Excel uses Power BI account credentials.

However, when you use Analyze in Excel, you have to log in with your Power BI account. You can see the data only if you have access to it.

Analyze in Excel Supports Row-Level Security

Because users log in from Excel, when they use the Analyze in Excel feature, they will only see the part of the data they are allowed to see. That means if row-level security is enabled on the data, users will only see their part of the data, and nothing more (as long as they don't have Edit access on the dataset).

Analyze in Excel Uses Shared Datasets

When you use the Analyze in Excel feature, you use the shared Power BI dataset from the Excel frontend. Whenever the dataset refreshes, you get the new data. You get the updates if the dataset gets a new table or field.

As Figure 15-16 shows, Analyze in Excel works well with multi-layered architecture for Power BI development. The visualization layer can be Power BI reports, paginated reports, or even Excel.

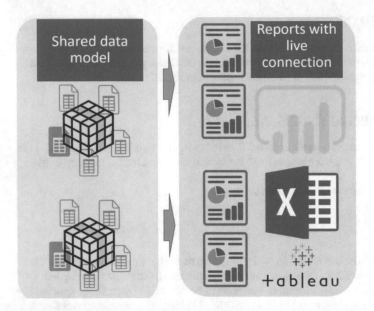

Figure 15-16. *Analyze in Excel works well with the Multi-Layered architecture for Power BI*

Publish to Power BI from Excel

Not only can Excel read data from the Power BI Service, but also it can publish data into Power BI. This is possible in the Excel 2016 editions or Office 365 editions of Excel. Once you click the Publish button from the File menu, you will see an option to publish into Power BI, as shown in Figure 15-17.

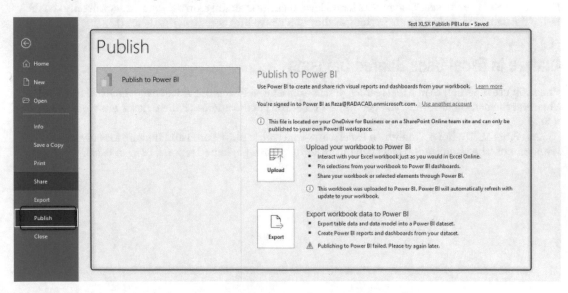

Figure 15-17. *The Publish to Power BI option from Excel*

Upload Your Workbook to Power BI

If you have an Excel workbook file, which you want to keep beside your Power BI objects (reports, dashboards, and datasets), this option is for you. You can upload the workbook into the Power BI workspace using this option. (See Figure 15-17 as an example.) Once the process is complete, the Excel workbook will be accessible from the Power BI workspace and can be opened and edited in Excel online. See Figure 15-18.

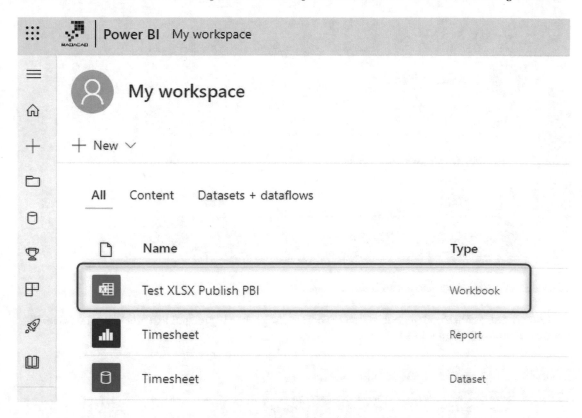

Figure 15-18. *Uploading an Excel workbook into the Power BI workspace*

The Excel workbook, as mentioned, can be opened and edited or viewed online, as shown in Figure 15-19.

Figure 15-19. *Opening an Excel workbook from the Power BI workspace*

Export Workbook Data to Power BI

Here comes the exciting feature; not only can you upload the Excel file as a workbook, but you can also export it as a Power BI dataset. To do this, you must have data in the Excel file as tables. The table data will then be exported into a Power BI dataset from Excel (and it can be updated by updating the Excel file). See Figure 15-20.

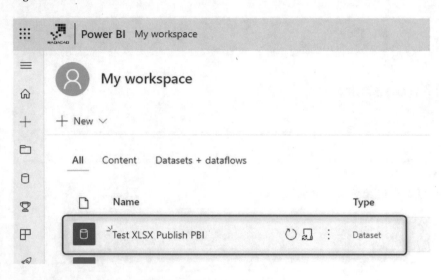

Figure 15-20. *Exporting workbook data into Power BI*

After these publish options, you will see a short message showing the publish process to the Power BI Service, as shown in Figure 15-21.

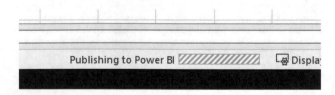

Figure 15-21. *The progress of publishing to Power BI from Excel*

These two options might not be very commonly used, but they certainly bring an interesting aspect to the integration between Excel and Power BI.

Import Excel into the Power BI Desktop

I cannot discuss the Excel and Power BI integration options without mentioning the most important developer option. You can import an Excel model, which includes a PowerPivot model, into Power BI. The Import into Power BI doesn't just import the data from Excel, it imports the entire model, including all the tables, relationships, and calculations, into a Power BI report. This scenario is a very handy option when you have an existing PowerPivot model in Excel, as shown in Figure 15-22.

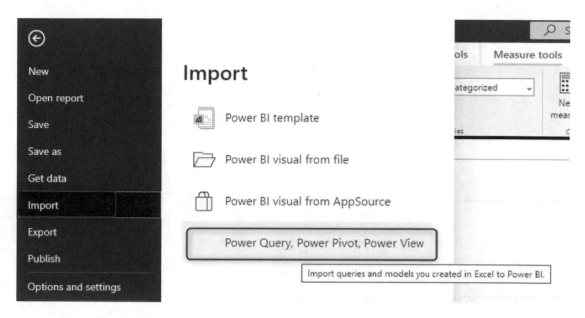

Figure 15-22. *Import Power Query, Power Pivot, and Power View into the Power BI Desktop*

Importing an Excel workbook is a very easy and straightforward process. The only important note in this process is that your Excel file should not be password-protected.

Summary

In this chapter, you learned that Excel and Power BI can work together. Each of the modes of integration will give you some features. Analyze in Excel allows you to slice and dice the data model of the Power BI Service easily from Excel through PivotTables and PivotCharts. Excel can publish the entire workbook or the data part as a dataset into Power BI. Both of the features will be well received by any business users who are good with Excel as a frontend tool. Last but not least, you can import an entire Excel PowerPivot model with all tables, relationships, and calculations into a Power BI report instead of having to recreate it.

CHAPTER 16

■ ■ ■

Real-Time Streaming Datasets in Power BI

Power BI datasets can use the Import Data, DirectQuery, or Live Connection connection types. However, there is also one specific type of dataset that is different, called a *streaming dataset*. A streaming dataset is used with a real-time dashboard and comes with various setups and configurations. This chapter talks about this type of dataset.

Real-time vs. Live or DirectQuery

The first question I get most often when I explain the real-time dataset is, "What is the difference between real-time, Live, and DirectQuery?" The common belief is that a Live Connection is real-time. This is not true. One of the best ways of understanding the differences is as follows:

- In a Live Connection or DirectQuery connection report or dashboard, when you refresh the visual (which can be done either by refreshing the report itself or by clicking a visual or slicer that triggers a query from the data source), you get the most up-to-date data. The report or dashboard can also be scheduled to refresh automatically so that you have the most up-to-date data on scheduled interval.

- A real-time dashboard will update automatically as soon as the new data row appears in the dataset. This new data row can come from various methods, such as pushing through a REST API of Power BI, stream analytics, or other streaming services such as PubNub. A real-time dashboard does not need a scheduled refresh.

One big difference you can spot in these types of connections is that a real-time dataset doesn't wait for a refresh, it pushes the data directly to the dashboard, and the dashboard shows that change immediately. In a Live or DirectQuery connection, you get the most up-to-date data whenever you ask for it, and that is by refreshing the report. (Although, even if you don't refresh the report, perhaps you are looking at the data that was refreshed less than an hour ago.)

A real-time dataset is mainly used in scenarios where the change has to be visible as soon as it happens. Let's say you have a temperature sensor in a room. You want to have a Power BI dashboard that shows the temperature changes in a line chart as soon as they change. A real-time streaming dataset is necessary here.

Live or DirectQuery connections are used when you want up-to-date data. If you do not have an IoT device that sends the data as soon as it appears, and your purpose is to see the most up-to-date data in your report and dashboard whenever you look at it, a Live or DirectQuery connection is best. (Of course, there are differences between the Live Connection and DirectQuery, which I explained in previous chapters.)

© Reza Rad 2023
R. Rad, *Pro Power BI Architecture*, https://doi.org/10.1007/978-1-4842-9538-0_16

Many businesses will ask for a real-time dashboard, but they really need a Live or DirectQuery connection. Use the definitions and the differences described here as your reference when making this decision. As a Power BI architect, you should understand the requirements, read between the lines, and come up with the best solution for the business needs.

In the rest of this chapter, you learn how to set up and use a real-time streaming dataset in Power BI.

Sample Scenario

For the real-time streaming scenario of this chapter, I explain this procedure and how to implement it:

- A Microsoft form is shared with users to get feedback on their Power BI roles and salaries.

- Power Automate is used to pass the feedback posted in the form (as soon as it arrives) to the Power BI streaming dataset.

- The Power BI streaming dataset receives the feedback and presents it in real-time on a dashboard.

This scenario might not be the most common, but it is one of the simplest to understand because it doesn't require much coding, and the components can be easily accessed without needing a special license for those tools and services.

Capturing Inputs with a Microsoft Form

I used a Microsoft form to capture the user's input (see Figure 16-1).

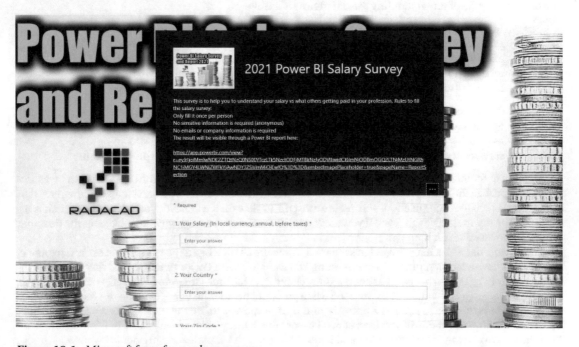

Figure 16-1. *Microsoft form for a salary survey*

The form shown in Figure 16-1 is used for this fictitious Power BI 2021 Salary Survey[1]. You can create a form like this in Microsoft Forms by going to `forms.office.com/`.[2]

The Power BI Streaming Dataset

To capture the form's data and send it to Power BI, you need to create a streaming dataset with the same set of fields. A streaming dataset cannot be created in the Power BI Desktop. You have to log in to the Power BI Service and create the streaming dataset from there, as shown in Figure 16-2.

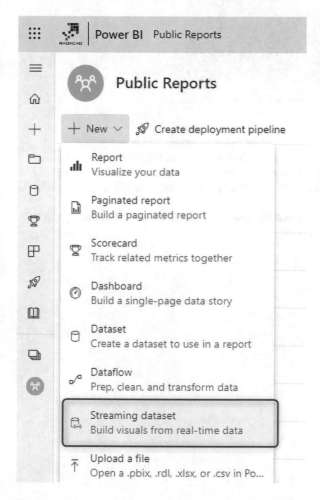

Figure 16-2. *Creating a streaming dataset in Power BI*

---

[1] `radacad.com/power-bi-salary-survey-and-report-2021`
[2] `forms.office.com/`

There are three ways to create a streaming dataset in Power BI, as illustrated in Figure 16-3.

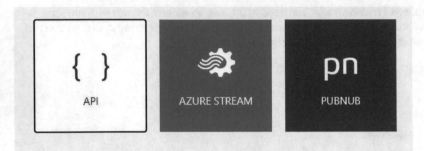

Figure 16-3. Power BI streaming dataset options

It is important to understand how the Power BI streaming dataset works behind the scenes, which I explain later in this chapter. For now, consider these three methods as three different data streaming service providers—Azure Stream Analytics, PubNub, and Power BI Rest API. This example uses the Power BI Rest API.

In the next step, you need to name this streaming dataset and set up the fields and their data types; see Figure 16-4.

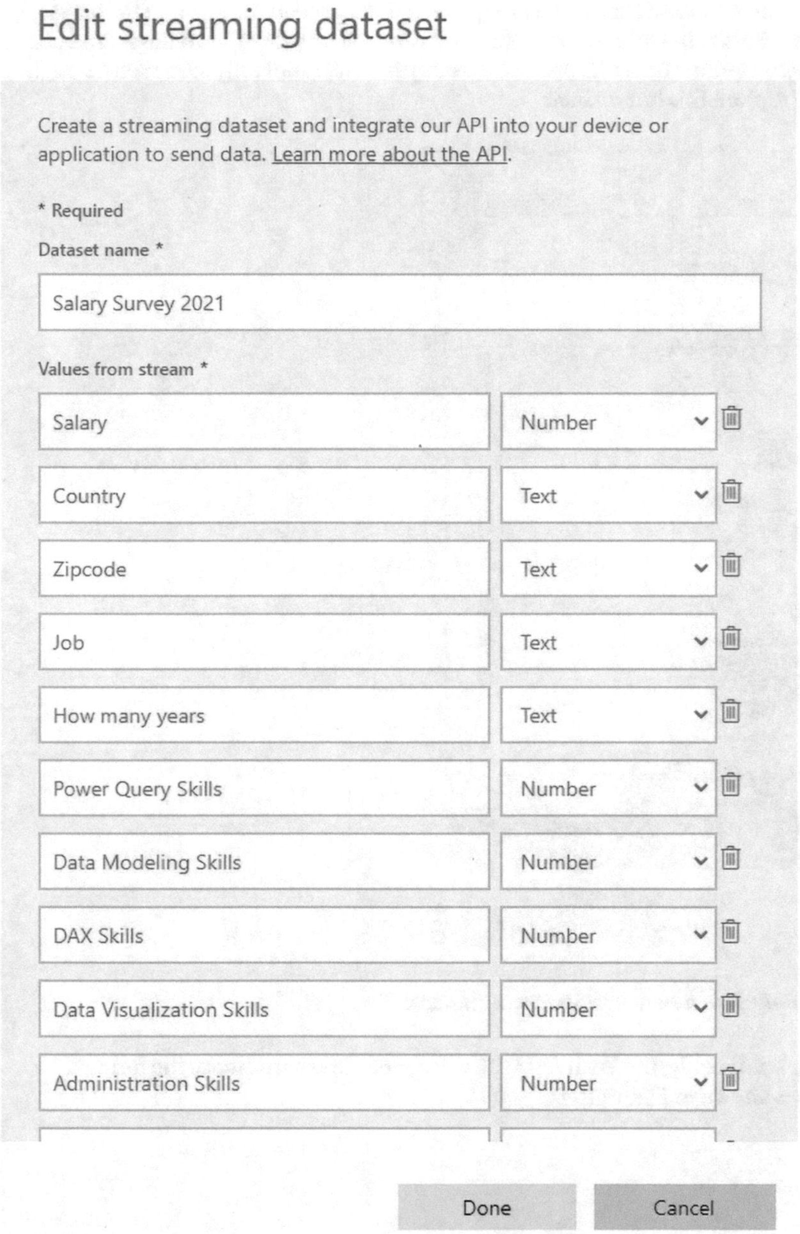

Edit streaming dataset

Create a streaming dataset and integrate our API into your device or application to send data. Learn more about the API.

* Required

Dataset name *

Salary Survey 2021

Values from stream *

Salary	Number ⌄ 🗑
Country	Text ⌄ 🗑
Zipcode	Text ⌄ 🗑
Job	Text ⌄ 🗑
How many years	Text ⌄ 🗑
Power Query Skills	Number ⌄ 🗑
Data Modeling Skills	Number ⌄ 🗑
DAX Skills	Number ⌄ 🗑
Data Visualization Skills	Number ⌄ 🗑
Administration Skills	Number ⌄ 🗑

Done	Cancel

Figure 16-4. *Setting up the streaming dataset in Power BI*

The data type for fields is a limited set of Text, Number, or Datetime. The streaming dataset is different from a normal Power BI dataset.

Once you create the fields, you can see a sample record generated underneath them in JSON format (see Figure 16-5 for an example). This is the format that the record data will be sent to the dataset. You can also see a Historical Data Analysis option. Turn this on. This means that data is not only streamed through this dataset but is also stored. I explain this option later.

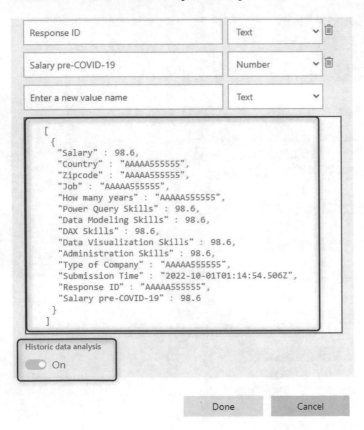

Figure 16-5. Historical data analysis in a Power BI streaming dataset

When the dataset is created and ready, the Push API URL will appear. You can choose the format for sending data to it as a sample, as shown in Figure 16-6.

API info on Salary Survey 2021

Use the API endpoint URL and one of the examples shown below to send data to your streaming dataset. For more information, read our API documentation and integration guide.

Push URL

https://api.powerbi.com/beta/ ▬▬▬▬▬▬▬▬▬ /data

Raw	cURL	PowerShell

```
[
  {
    "Salary" :  98.6,
    "Country" :  "AAAAA555555",
    "Zipcode" :  "AAAAA555555",
    "Job" :  "AAAAA555555",
    "How many years" :  "AAAAA555555",
    "Power Query Skills" :  98.6,
    "Data Modeling Skills" :  98.6,
    "DAX Skills" :  98.6,
    "Data Visualization Skills" :  98.6,
    "Administration Skills" :  98.6,
    "Type of Company" :  "AAAAA555555",
    "Submission Time" :  "2022-10-01T01:19:58.513Z",
    "Response ID" :  "AAAAA555555",
    "Salary pre-COVID-19" :  98.6
  }
]
```

Figure 16-6. *Pushing URL details for Power BI Dataset*

The Push URL is the API URL that other applications should use to pass data rows (or push them) into this dataset. This example uses Power Automate to push data to this dataset.

Power Automate Pushes Data to the Power BI Dataset

You can use many applications to push data into the streaming dataset, such as a C# application, PowerShell scripts, and so on. However, for simplicity, this example uses Power Automate, which you can access from make.powerautomate.com/. Power Automate is a service in the Power Platform toolset for If-Then-Else flow definitions. Here, you use it to set up a flow. If there is an entry in the form, then Power Automate will push that record to the streaming dataset in Power BI.

You can use the template in Power Automate (see Figure 16-7), which has the process you want. You just need to enter your credentials and environment details in it.

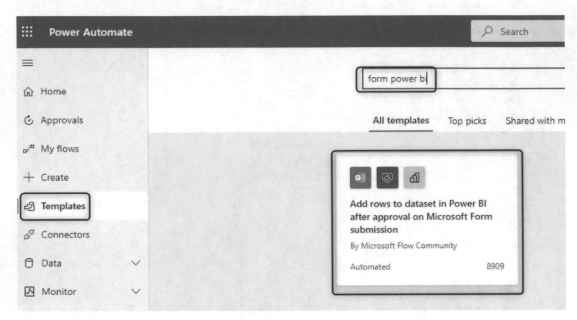

Figure 16-7. *Using a template in Power Automate*

The flow definition is simple. As shown in Figure 16-8, it has three steps: connect to the Microsoft form when a new response is submitted, read the response, and push it to the Power BI dataset.

Figure 16-8. *Pushing data to the Power BI streaming dataset using Power Automate*

As you can see, the Add Rows to Power BI Dataset component generates the data row and pushes it to the streaming dataset in Power BI. This flow will run automatically as soon as a Microsoft form entry is entered (this is set by the When a New Response Is Submitted trigger).

The Power BI Real-Time Dashboard

The last step is creating a Power BI Dashboard to show the real-time changes. This dashboard is similar to the other dashboards in Power BI. The only difference is that it is sourced from the streaming dataset. The dashboard can be created from a report, or it can be created as a blank, and then you can add a tile connecting to a streaming data source, as shown in Figure 16-9. Then you can select the streaming dataset for it.

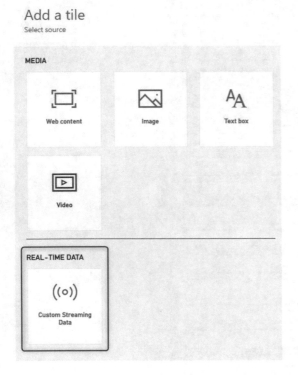

Figure 16-9. *Dashboard connected to streaming dataset*

There are just a few charts and visuals you can use for a streaming dataset tile, which are listed in Figure 16-10.

Add a custom streaming data tile

Choose a streaming dataset > Visualization design

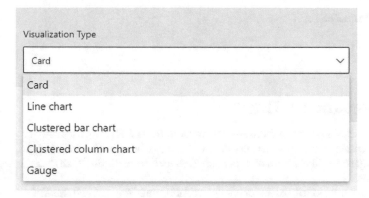

Figure 16-10. *Visuals that can connect to streaming datasets*

You can now test the solution. Go to your form, enter a result, and see if the result immediately appears in the Power BI dashboard (depending on what part of the result you chose to show in the dashboard).

Streaming Dataset Types

One of the most important aspects of a streaming dataset is understanding the types of datasets. The streaming dataset can have three types—Push, Streaming, and Hybrid.

Push Datasets

When this dataset is created, the Power BI service automatically creates a database to store the data. For this type of real-time dataset, you can create reports.

Streaming Datasets

With this dataset, the data is only stored in a temporary cache, which would expire. This dataset has no underlying database. You cannot create reports from this dataset; you can only create a dashboard.

Hybrid Datasets

This dataset is a combined version of Push and Streaming. With this dataset, there is a temporary cache for the data that is coming and going, and there is also a database to store the data. You can create this by enabling the Historic Data Analysis option when creating the streaming dataset. This is the type of dataset used in the scenario in this chapter.

Understanding these three types of datasets is important because, if you want to also store the streaming data for further report creation and data analysis, then a Hybrid dataset is what you need instead of a Streaming dataset.

Streaming Services

You can use three services for a real-time dataset for Power BI:

- Power BI streaming dataset and REST API
- Azure Stream Analytics
- PubNub

Power BI Streaming Dataset and REST API

The example in this chapter uses the Power BI streaming dataset with Power BI REST API. This uses only Power BI objects and services. You don't need any additional services or licenses. However, there are some limitations. For example, you can have up to 1 million rows of data pushed every hour with the Push dataset; the request size also has some limitations.

Using the Power BI REST API does not necessarily mean using Power Automate. You can call the API using any other application. [3]

Azure Stream Analytics

Azure Stream Analytics is the data streaming service of Microsoft Azure. It can be used for Power BI and many other tools and services in the Microsoft toolset. You can use this service to capture data input from IoT devices, for example, and pass part of that data to Power BI and another part to Azure Machine Learning for data mining. I wrote an article about a sample solution with Azure Stream Analytics and Power BI at `radacad.com/stream-analytics-and-power-bi-join-forces-to-real-time-dashboard`.

PubNub

PubNub is a streaming service that is not only for Microsoft. It integrates with many tools and services. You can check out the website for the details of how this service works.

Creating Calculations on Real-Time Datasets

A streaming dataset is not like a normal Power BI dataset. In a normal Power BI dataset, you can use the Power BI Desktop to write DAX calculations and use Power Query to transform the data. A streaming dataset, however, is different. When you work with a streaming dataset, you are limited. There are some workarounds in writing calculations, which I explain in this section.

Writing Calculations Using Q&A

The first workaround is to use Q&A to write simple calculations. The big development problem with the streaming dataset is that you don't have a PBIX file (see Figure 16-11). You cannot open this solution in the Power BI Desktop. And as a result, you cannot bring in other datasets, modify or edit the data using Power Query, or write calculations using DAX.

---

[3] Learn more about how to use a C# application to push data to a streaming dataset in Power BI: `radacad.com/monitor-real-time-data-with-power-bi-dashboards`; `radacad.com/integrate-power-bi-into-your-application-part-6-real-time-streaming-and-push-data`

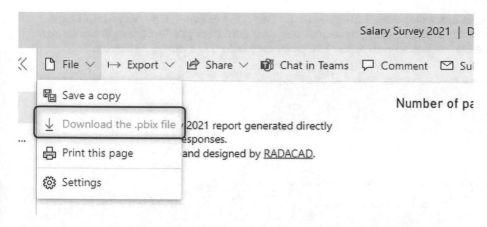

Figure 16-11. *You cannot download a PBIX file of a streaming Power BI dataset*

The download option is not even available from the dataset (see Figure 16-12).

	Name		Type

All   Content   **Datasets + dataflows**

	Name		Type
🗄			Dataset
🗄			Dataset
🗄			Dataset
🗄			Dataset
🗄			Dataset
🗄	Salary Survey 2021	⋮	Dataset
🗄			

Create report

Delete

Manage permissions

Quick insights

Edit

API Info

Figure 16-12. *You cannot download a Power BI streaming dataset or report*

Although you cannot write calculations, you can use Q&A. Q&A in Power BI is a very useful way to analyze data and build visualizations by just asking questions.[4] Q&A gives you the existing field's list and understands some calculations, so you can use it to create calculations in a streaming dataset.

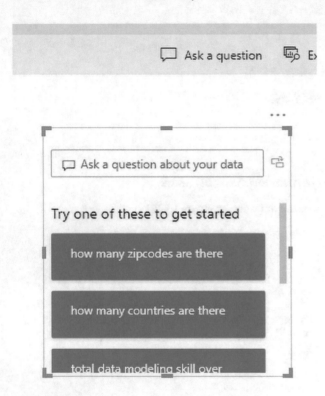

Figure 16-13. *Using Q&A in the Power BI Service*

As you can see in Figure 16-4, I can subtract the two fields—Salary and Salary pre-COVID-19—and add more criteria to my visual. This creates the calculation and uses it in that visual.

---

[4] Learn more about Q&A at radacad.com/qa-visual-in-power-bi-desktop

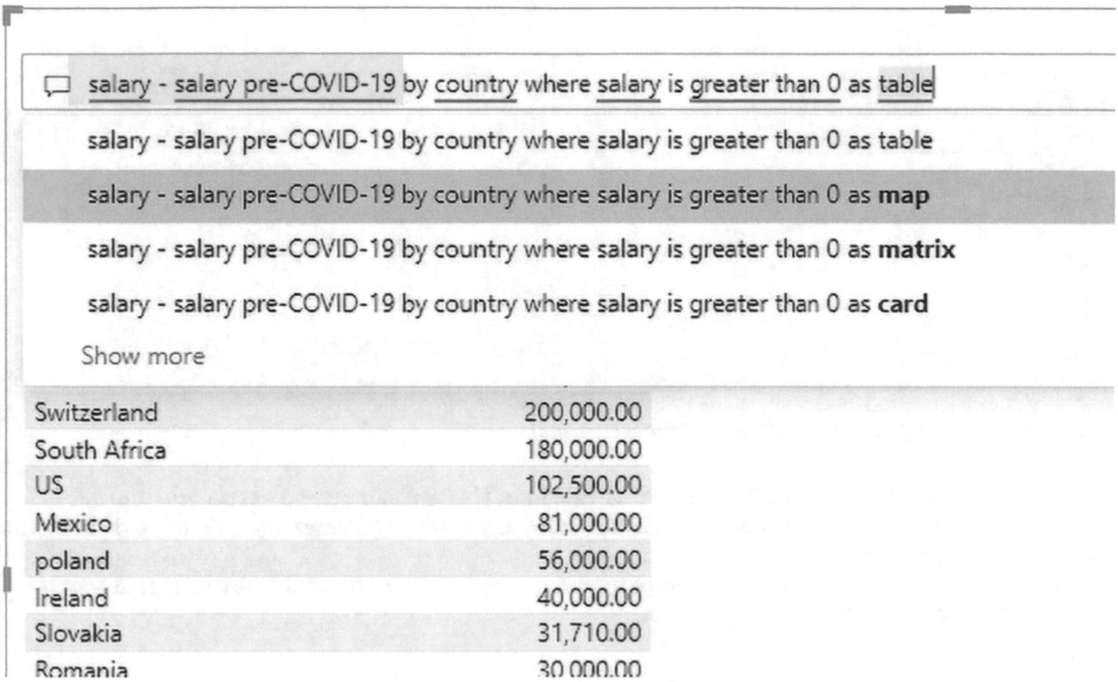

💬 salary - salary pre-COVID-19 by country where salary is greater than 0 as table|

salary - salary pre-COVID-19 by country where salary is greater than 0 as table

salary - salary pre-COVID-19 by country where salary is greater than 0 as **map**

salary - salary pre-COVID-19 by country where salary is greater than 0 as **matrix**

salary - salary pre-COVID-19 by country where salary is greater than 0 as **card**

Show more

Switzerland	200,000.00
South Africa	180,000.00
US	102,500.00
Mexico	81,000.00
poland	56,000.00
Ireland	40,000.00
Slovakia	31,710.00
Romania	30,000.00

Figure 16-14. *Running calculations in Q&A*

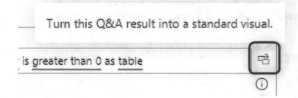

Turn this Q&A result into a standard visual.

is greater than 0 as table

Figure 16-15. *Turning the Q&A result into a standard Power BI visual*

When I convert that visual into a normal visual using the button highlighted in Figure 16-15, the standard visual will include the calculation, as shown in Figure 16-16.

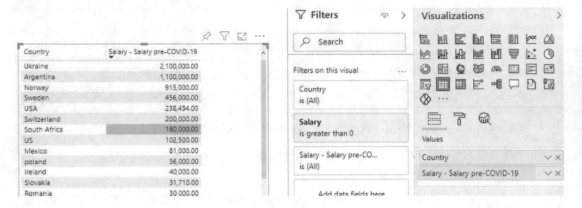

Figure 16-16. Calculation in a standard Power BI visual

This will not of course support all types of calculations. I believe many complex scenarios are not supported. However, the ability to do simple calculations in a streaming dataset (that otherwise there was no other way to do) is great.

If the calculation that you are after is too complex for the Q&A, you should do the calculation before sending the data row to the streaming dataset.

Live Connection to a Streaming Dataset

The second method is to create a report with a live connection to the Power BI dataset. This type of connection won't be real-time anymore, and it works when you have a Push or Hybrid dataset.

If the calculation you are after is a complex dynamic calculation, you can write DAX expressions for it. This can be done using a live connection to the streaming dataset and the Power BI Desktop, as shown in Figure 16-17.

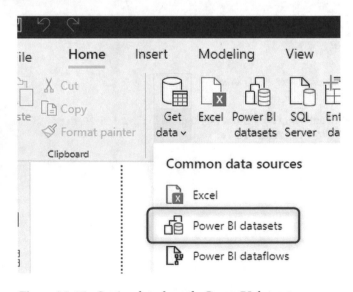

Figure 16-17. Getting data from the Power BI dataset

The streaming dataset can then be used as the source of the live connection, as shown in Figure 16-18.

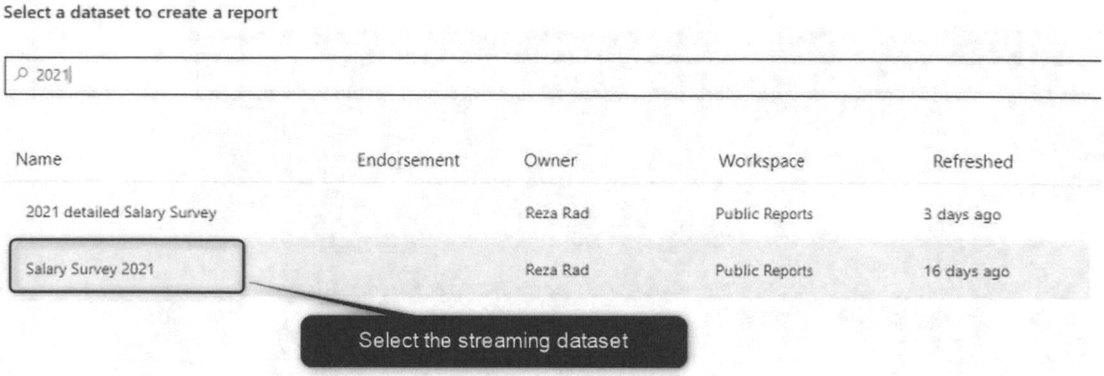

Select a dataset to create a report

| 🔍 2021| |

Name	Endorsement	Owner	Workspace	Refreshed
2021 detailed Salary Survey		Reza Rad	Public Reports	3 days ago
Salary Survey 2021		Reza Rad	Public Reports	16 days ago

Select the streaming dataset

Figure 16-18. Choosing a streaming dataset as the source of the live connection

This will create a live connection to the streaming dataset, as shown in Figure 16-19.

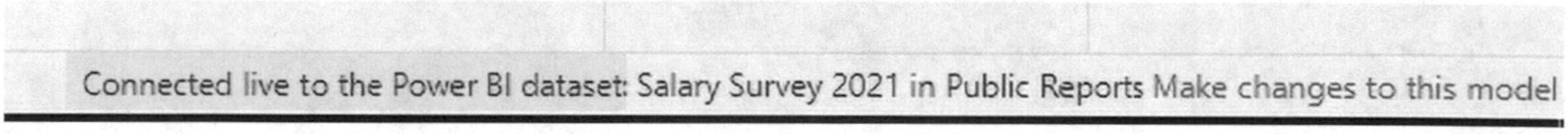

Connected live to the Power BI dataset: Salary Survey 2021 in Public Reports Make changes to this model

Figure 16-19. Live connection created to the streaming dataset

When the live connection is created, you can write DAX measures using normal measures or quick measures, as highlighted in Figure 16-20.

```
1  List of Salary values =
2  VAR __DISTINCT_VALUES_COUNT = DISTINCTCOUNT('RealTimeData'[Salary])
3  VAR __MAX_VALUES_TO_SHOW = 3
4  RETURN
5      IF(
6          __DISTINCT_VALUES_COUNT > __MAX_VALUES_TO_SHOW,
7          CONCATENATE(
8              CONCATENATEX(
9                  TOPN(
10                     __MAX_VALUES_TO_SHOW,
11                     VALUES('RealTimeData'[Salary]),
12                     'RealTimeData'[Salary],
13                     ASC
14                 ),
15                 'RealTimeData'[Salary],
16                 ", ",
17                 'RealTimeData'[Salary],
18                 DESC
19             ),
20             ", etc."
21         ),
22         CONCATENATEX(
23             VALUES('RealTimeData'[Salary]),
24             'RealTimeData'[Salary],
25             ", ",
26             'RealTimeData'[Salary],
27             DESC
28         )
29
```

Figure 16-20. Writing DAX measures on a live connection to a Power BI streaming dataset

Would it Be Real-Time?

One important consideration here is that the report generated this way won't be a real-time report or dashboard. This would be a live connection to the real-time dataset. That means any dashboard created on top of it would be refreshed with the frequency that's set at the dashboard level. Every time you browse the report, you will have the report from the data at that moment.

DirectQuery to the Streaming Dataset: Even More Flexibility

The ability to write measures is great. However, sometimes, you want to create columns too, and maybe include another data table to combine with this data. Using DirectQuery to Power BI dataset, you can do this, as Figure 16-21 indicates.

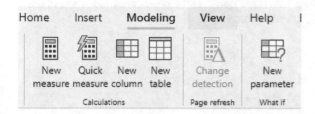

Figure 16-21. *Changes in the model using DirectQuery to the Power BI dataset*

You can have a table as the DirectQuery connection to the streaming Power BI dataset, which enables you to import other data tables and have a more complete solution; see Figure 16-22.

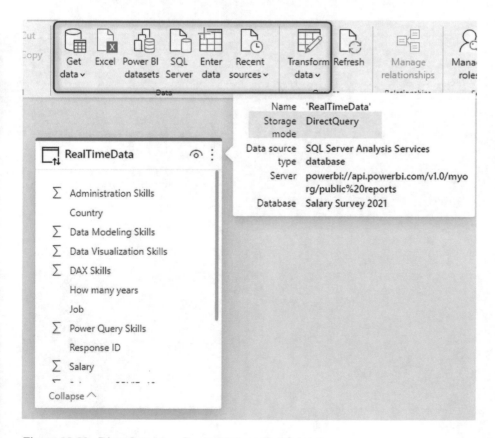

Figure 16-22. *DirectQuery to a Power BI streaming dataset*

Summary

A real-time streaming dataset is different from a Live or DirectQuery connection. Using this dataset, you can see changes immediately after the data changes. The push data API or other streaming services can help you achieve this. The streaming dataset can also store the data in a database for further analysis. A streaming dataset is not like a normal Power BI dataset; it comes with limitations. It is important to know when to use a real-time streaming dataset versus Live and DirectQuery datasets.

■■■

CHAPTER 17

Performance Tuning with Aggregations

Power BI is not only a solution for small datasets—it also caters to big datasets. If the volume of data is huge, you can switch to DirectQuery mode. Because DirectQuery does not store a copy of the data in the memory of the machine that runs the Power BI model, Power BI will send queries back to the data source for every page rendered in the report.

However, as Figure 17-1 depicts, DirectQuery mode is slow. Consider a page with three, four, or five visuals. That page will send five queries to the data source with every change in the filtering context, such as changing the slicer, clicking a column chart to highlight part of it, or refreshing the page. Sending queries to the data source for every interaction makes DirectQuery mode very slow. Because of that, DirectQuery is not the best way to connect in Power BI. My suggestion is to use DirectQuery only when the other methods cannot be used.

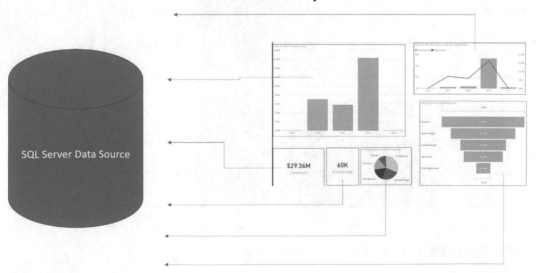

Figure 17-1. *DirectQuery has a downside*

R. Rad, *Pro Power BI Architecture*, https://doi.org/10.1007/978-1-4842-9538-0_17

Earlier in this book, you read about another type of connection in Power BI, called composite mode. Composite mode allows part of the model to use DirectQuery (for large tables) and part of the model to use Import Data (for smaller tables). This way, you get better performance when you work with smaller tables because they query the in-memory structure of the data.

However, the table(s) that are part of the DirectQuery connection are still slow. Composite mode comes with a fantastic feature called *aggregations*. Aggregations speed up the DirectQuery sourced tables in a composite model. With aggregations, you can create layers of pre-aggregated values, which can be stored in memory and performed faster.

How Does Aggregation Work?

Imagine a fact table with 250 million rows. Such a fact table is big enough to be considered a good candidate for a DirectQuery connection. You don't want to load such a big table into memory, and the Power BI file size probably exceeds the 1GB limitation. Now, think about your reporting solution for a second. Do you always query this fact table at the finest or minimum granular level? Do you always look at single transaction in this table when you run a report on it?

The answer is likely no. Most of the time, you query the data by other fields or columns. For example, you might query the Sales value in the fact table by Year, as shown in Figure 17-2. Or you might query the fact table's values by the customer's education category. Or you might query the values in the fact table by each product. When you consider real-world scenarios, you are usually querying the fact table by aggregations of dimension tables.

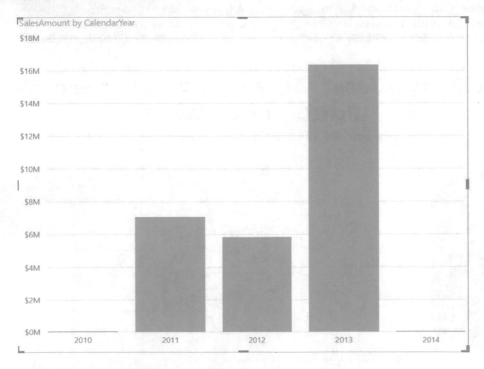

Figure 17-2. *Querying SalesAmount from the fact table by CalendarYear*

Figure 17-3 is querying SalesAmount from the fact table by the CalendarYear from DimDate.

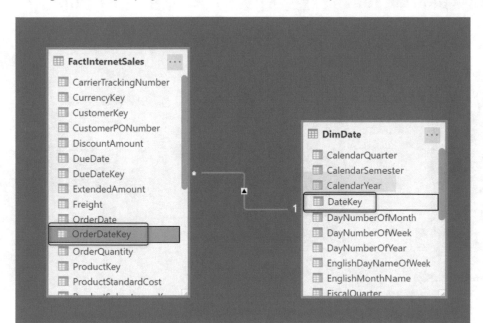

Figure 17-3. *Creating relationships*

Aggregated Table

So, if you are querying only by CalendarYear, you can create an aggregated table. The aggregated table can pre-calculate the Sum of SalesAmount for every CalendarYear. In this example, you would have a table with five rows. One row for each year, from 2010 to 2014. The aggregated table is so small (five rows) that it can be easily imported into memory, and whenever you query that table, you'll get a super-fast result.

You might also query this by quarter. You may want to drill down into the month, week, or even every day. That is fine. Considering there are 365 days in each year, you have a table with 5×365 rows. This would be a table including 1827 rows maximum (you may have one or two leap years in the period as well). The aggregated table size is still very tiny (fewer than 2000 rows) compared to a fact table with 250 million rows (see Figure 17-4). You can still import your aggregated table into memory. Such a table will cover all the data analysis you want every day.

Sales by Year will hit the aggregated table in the memory

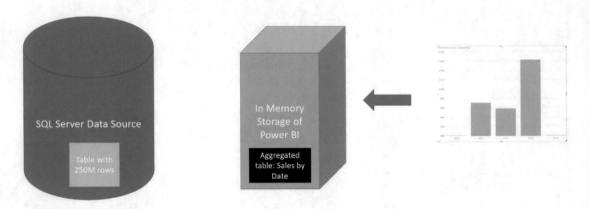

Figure 17-4. *Aggregated table*

Layers of Aggregation

You may need to create other aggregations by other dimensions too. B because dimensions are much smaller than the fact table, your aggregated tables will always be smaller than the fact table. These aggregated tables are your layers of aggregation in the model.

The golden rule for a composite model in Power BI is, do not use a lower-level table if there is an aggregation on top of it that can be used for the query.

If you are querying a DirectQuery table with 250 million rows, but you are only querying it by date, then Power BI acts differently. Power BI will not send a query to the data source of the fact table. Instead, it will query the aggregated table in memory, as shown in Figure 17-5, and you'll get a fast response. Power BI only switches to the table underneath if aggregated tables cannot answer the question.

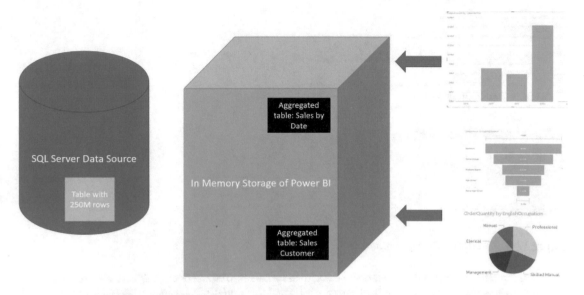

Figure 17-5. *Querying aggregated tables*

The overall process for using an aggregation is as follows:

- Creating an aggregation table
- Creating relationships necessary for the aggregation table and the DirectQuery table
- Setting the Storage mode of the aggregated and dimension tables
- Configuring the aggregation

The process is explained in detail in the following sections.

Step 1: Create the Aggregated Table

If you want to follow the example scenario here, you need a SQL Server database named AdventureWorksDW. I made some changes to my dataset so it's bigger, so I can show you the functionality of aggregations. You can download the database link from here:

radacad.com/files/adventureworksdw2012.bak

Sample Model

This sample model analyzes the data in FactInternetSales (which is the big fact table). First create a Power BI report with a DirectQuery connection to SQL Server, as shown in Figure 17-6.

SQL Server database

Server ⓘ

.

Database (optional)

AdventureWorksDw2012

Data Connectivity mode ⓘ

○ Import

● DirectQuery

> Advanced options

Figure 17-6. *Creating a Power BI report with DirectQuery*

With the DirectQuery option, select the FactInternetSales, DimCustomer, DimDate, DimProduct, DimProductCategory, DimProductSubCategory, DimPromotion, and DimGeography tables (the selections will be viewed, as shown in Figure 17-7).

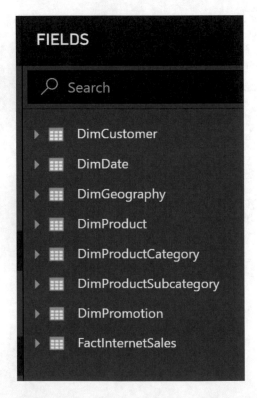

FIELDS

🔍 Search

▸ ▦ DimCustomer

▸ ▦ DimDate

▸ ▦ DimGeography

▸ ▦ DimProduct

▸ ▦ DimProductCategory

▸ ▦ DimProductSubcategory

▸ ▦ DimPromotion

▸ ▦ FactInternetSales

Figure 17-7. *Selecting tables through DirectQuery*

Tables loaded into Power BI will have relationships. I limited the relationship between `DimDate` and the `FactInternetSales` table to one active relationship based on `DateKey` (in `DimDate`) and `OrderDateKey` (in `FactInternetSales`). The diagram of these relationships is shown in Figure 17-8.

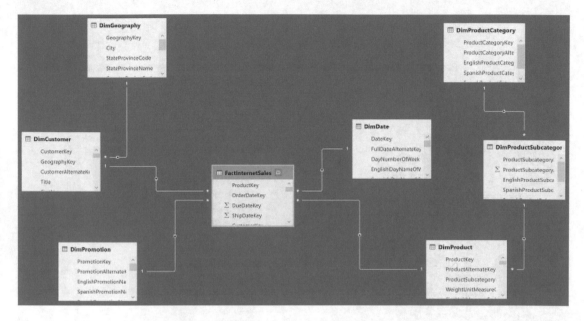

Figure 17-8. *Diagram of the table relationships*

What Is an Aggregated Table?

An aggregated table is a table in Power BI aggregated by one or more fields from the DirectQuery source table. In this case, the aggregated table is grouped by specific fields from the `FactInternetSales` table. You can use various methods to create an aggregated table. You can create an aggregated table with T-SQL statements from SQL Server, or you can create one in Power Query. Or you can even create one in DAX using `Summarize` or `GroupBy` or other aggregation functions. You can create an aggregated table in all other data transformation tools and query languages. Since this example does everything with Power BI, I create the aggregated table using Power Query.

An aggregated table can be created in the data source with T-SQL queries, or in Power Query, or anywhere else that you can create a grouped table.

Creating an Aggregated Table

Go to the Power Query Editor and select the `FactInternetSales` table. The aggregated table created in this example is going to include three fields—`OrderDateKey`, `CustomerKey`, and `ProductSubCategoryKey`. The first two fields exist in `FactInternetSales`. Using relationship columns, you can retrieve that last table.

Scroll to the right in the `FactInternetSales` table columns to find Product, then click Expand. In the Expand options, simply select `ProductSubCategoryKey`. These steps are shown in Figure 17-9.

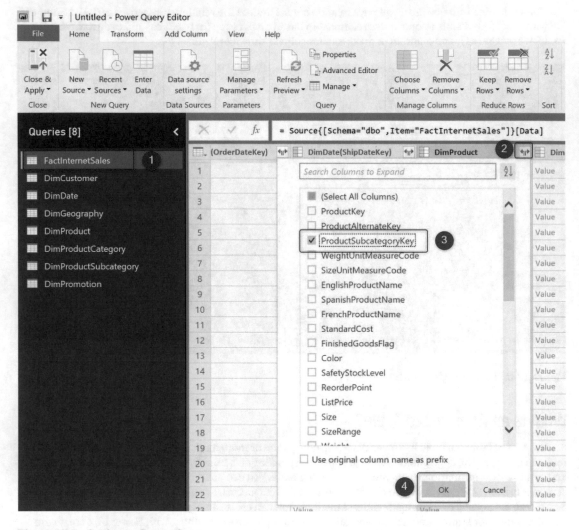

Figure 17-9. *Setting up Power Query*

Now that you have ProductSubCategoryKey in the table, you can apply the Group By. But if you use Group By in the existing query, you will change it to the aggregated table. You do, however, need to keep the existing table intact. So you'll create a REFERENCE from the existing FactInternetSales table.[1] Name it Sales Agg and then you'll run the Group By on Sales Agg. In the Transformation tab, click Group By, as shown in Figure 17-10.

---

[1] To learn more about reference and how it differs from duplicate, visit radacad.com/
reference-vs-duplicate-in-power-bi-power-query-back-to-basics

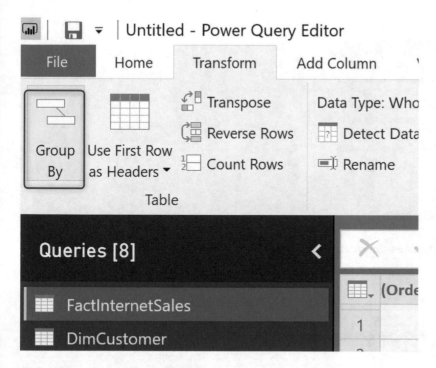

Figure 17-10. Initiating Group By

When the Group By dialog box pops up, choose Advanced, as shown in Figure 17-11.

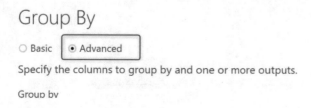

Figure 17-11. Selecting an advanced Group By

Choose OrderDateKey, CustomerKey, and ProductSubcategoryKey in the Group By fields, as Figure 17-12 shows.

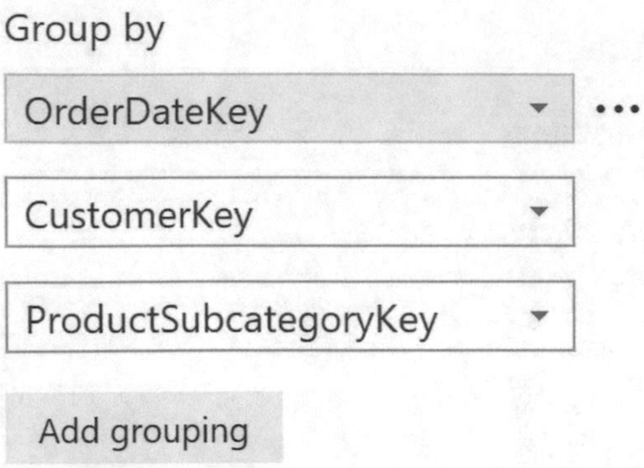

Group by

| OrderDateKey ▼ | ••• |

| CustomerKey ▼ |

| ProductSubcategoryKey ▼ |

Add grouping

Figure 17-12. *Group By field selection*

Then add four aggregations, as shown in Figure 17-13.

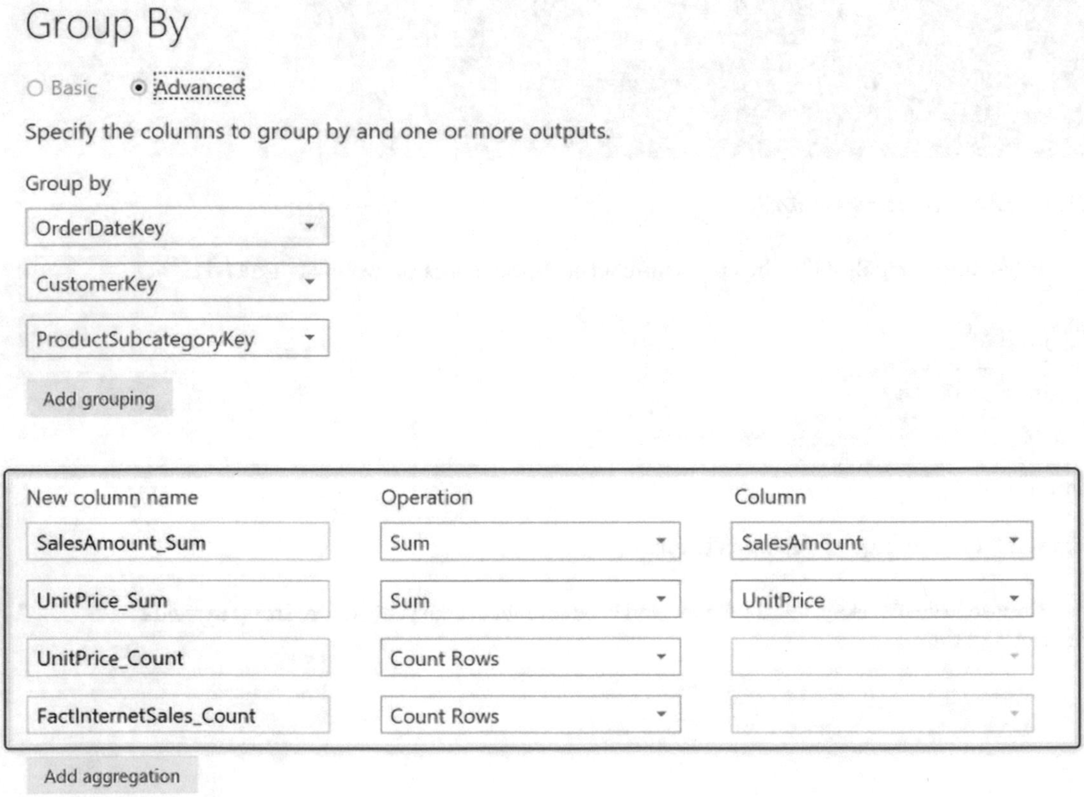

Group By

○ Basic   ● Advanced

Specify the columns to group by and one or more outputs.

Group by

| OrderDateKey ▼ |

| CustomerKey ▼ |

| ProductSubcategoryKey ▼ |

Add grouping

New column name	Operation	Column
SalesAmount_Sum	Sum ▼	SalesAmount ▼
UnitPrice_Sum	Sum ▼	UnitPrice ▼
UnitPrice_Count	Count Rows ▼	▼
FactInternetSales_Count	Count Rows ▼	▼

Add aggregation

Figure 17-13. *Adding aggregations*

Let's call this table the Sales Agg table. Figure 17-14 shows the Sales Agg table.

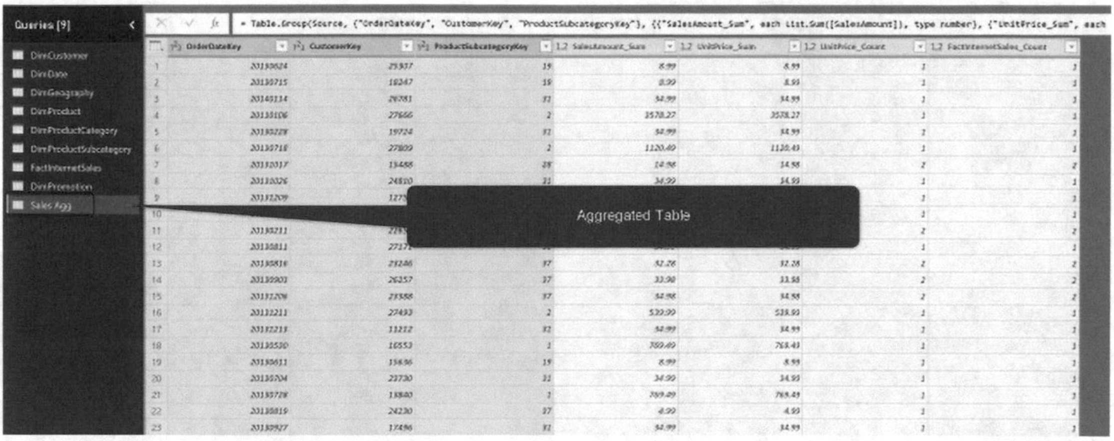

Figure 17-14. *Sample aggregated table*

Key Consideration for Upcoming Steps

Aggregation columns in the aggregated table should follow specific rules.

Rule #1: Exact Match for Data Types of Aggregations by Sum, Min, Max, or Average

Columns that you apply an operation on, such as Sum, Average, Min, or Max, should have exactly the same data type as the original source column after the aggregation. If they don't, change the data types to have the same. For example, the SalesAmount field in FactInternetSales must have a Decimal data type, as shown in Figure 17-15.

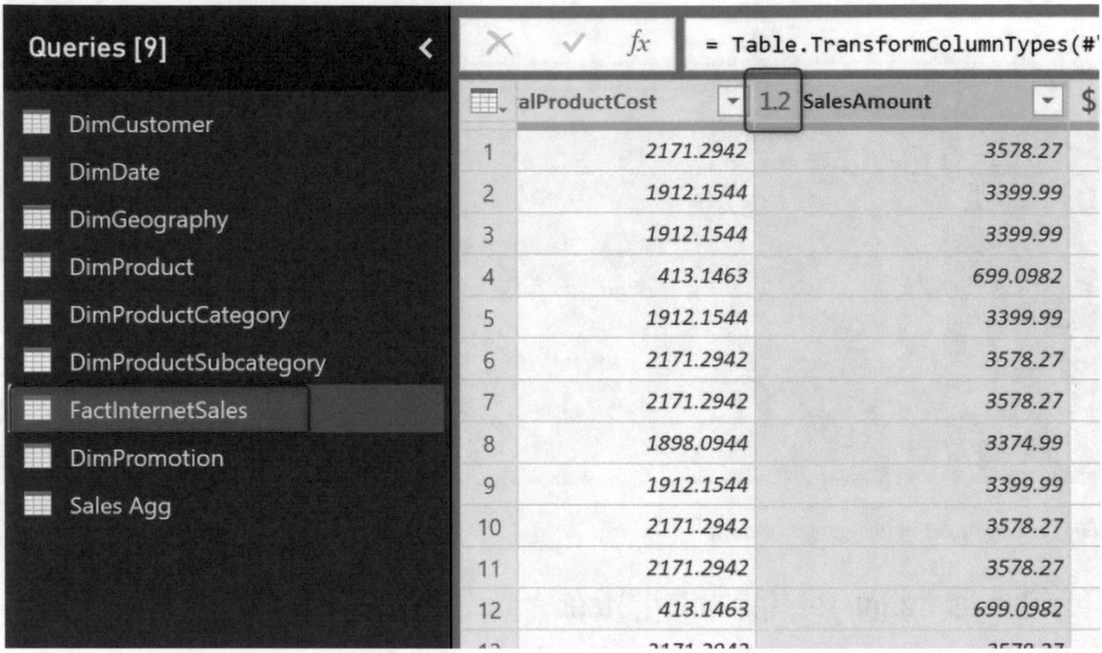

Figure 17-15. *Confirming that the columns use the decimal data type*

The SalesAmount_Sum column in the Sales Agg table should also have the same data type. In this case, it's Decimal, as shown in Figure 17-16.

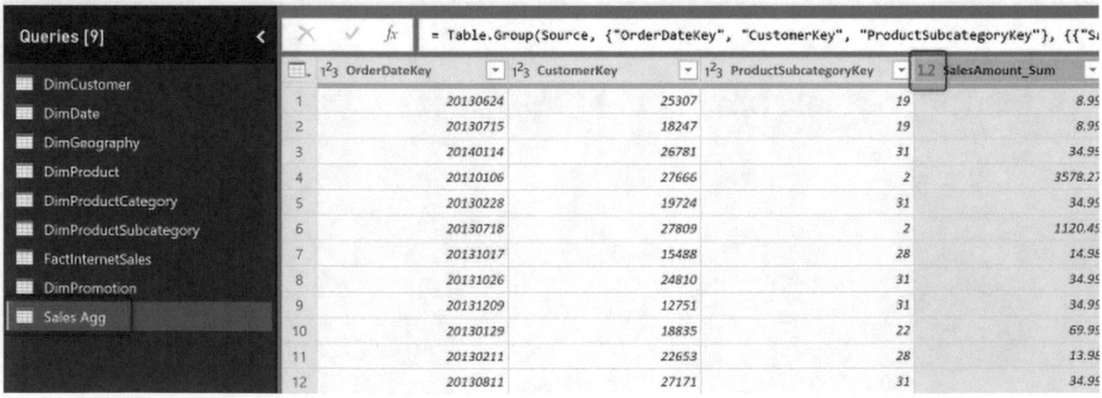

Figure 17-16. *The data type of SalesAmount_Sum is decimal*

Note that having the Decimal data type is not important to this rule. It is important that both data types match exactly. This process, in this example, should be completed for the SalesAmount_Sum and UnitPrice_Sum columns.

Rule #2: The Whole Number Data Type Is Mandatory for Aggregations by Count

Any aggregations that use Count as their aggregation function should have the data type of the whole number or, let's say, Integer. The sample table has two columns with the Count function, as shown in Figure 17-17.

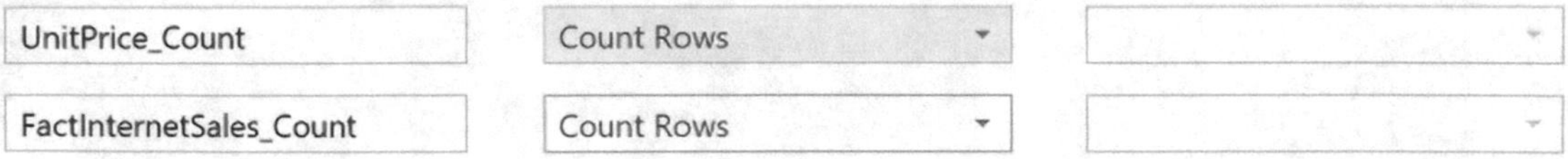

| UnitPrice_Count | Count Rows ▾ | ▾ |
| FactInternetSales_Count | Count Rows ▾ | ▾ |

Figure 17-17. *Sample columns with the Count function*

Make sure that these two columns have a Whole Number data type after the Group By transformation, as shown in Figure 17-18.

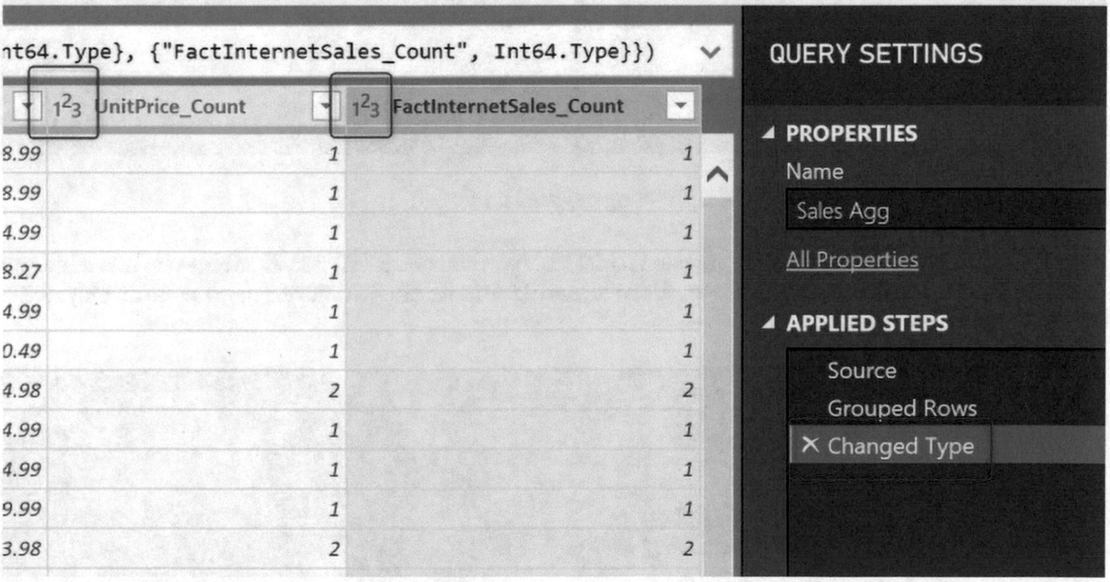

Figure 17-18. *Column using whole number data types*

These two rules are important in the next steps of configuring an aggregation in Power BI.

An Aggregated Table Is an Import Table

The aggregated table you created is called Sales Agg. Because this table is much smaller than the FactInternetSales table, it can be stored in memory. This way, you get the best query response time when you query something at the aggregated level.

Your data model in Power BI should now show the aggregated table, as shown in Figure 17-19.

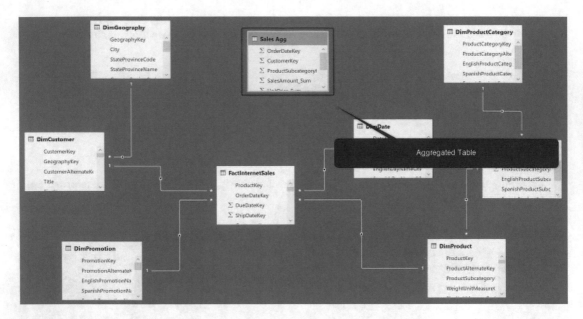

Figure 17-19. *Completed data model with the aggregated table*

Congratulations, you built an aggregated table! Now you can create relationships between this table and the three dimension tables: `DimCustomer`, `DimDate`, and `DimProductSubcategory`. Figure 17-20 displays the full relationship diagram.

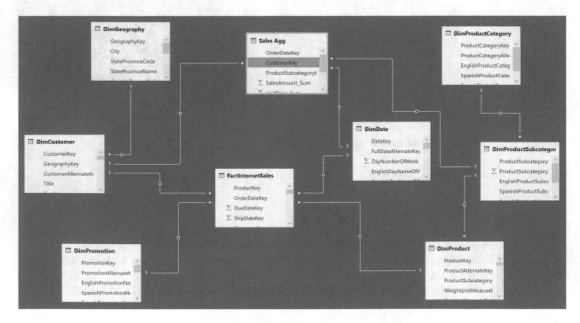

Figure 17-20. *Diagram of relationships between the aggregate table and the dimension tables*

Dual Storage Mode; The Most Important Configuration for Aggregations!

Step 2: Power BI Aggregations

An aggregated table can be a layer on the DirectQuery source table. This table needs to have a proper relationship set up with other tables and also the proper storage mode configuration. Configuring the storage mode of the composite model is a critical part of setting up the aggregation. The storage mode configuration of Import Data and DirectQuery is self-explanatory, but what about Dual Storage mode? The next sections explain in detail what Dual mode is. Let's dig in.

What Is Storage Mode?

Storage mode in Power BI tables determines where the data of that table is stored and how queries are sent to the data source. You can determine the storage mode of a table by hovering the mouse on it in the Power BI Desktop in the fields section, as shown in Figure 17-21.

Figure 17-21. *One way to confirm the table storage mode*

You can also determine the storage mode by right-clicking the table and selecting properties, as shown in Figure 17-22.

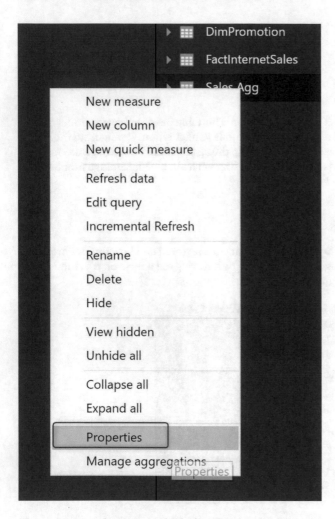

Figure 17-22. *Alternate method of confirming the storage mode, step one*

In the Properties pane, you can see the Storage Mode drop-down list (see Figure 17-23).

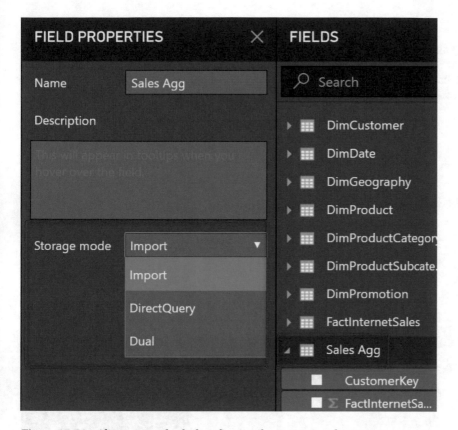

Figure 17-23. *Alternate method of confirming the storage mode, step two*

There are three storage modes:

- Import
- DirectQuery
- Dual

Import Data

Import and DirectQuery are the obvious options in this list. For example, If a table's storage mode is Import Data, then it means the data of that table will be stored in the in-memory storage of the Power BI server (the machine that runs the Power BI engine). Every query to the data will query the in-memory structure, not the data source.

Suppose you have a table sourced from SQL Server that uses the Import Data storage mode. Then a copy of that data will be stored in the memory engine of Power BI. Whenever you refresh a visualization in the Power BI report, it will query the in-memory structure rather than sending the query to the SQL Server data source.

DirectQuery

Tables with the DirectQuery storage mode keep the data in the data source. FactInternetSales stores the data in the SQL Server data source in the example dataset. If you have a visualization from a table with this storage mode, Power BI will send a T-SQL query to the data source and get the results. For example, Figure 17-24's visualization in the Power BI report is just a card visual of the SalesAmount field in FactInternetSales.

Figure 17-24. *The SalesAmount field comes from the FactInternetSales table*

Because this table uses the DirectQuery storage mode, if you run SQL Profiler simultaneously (to capture queries sent to the data source), you'll get a query captured to the SQL Server database, as shown in Figure 17-25.

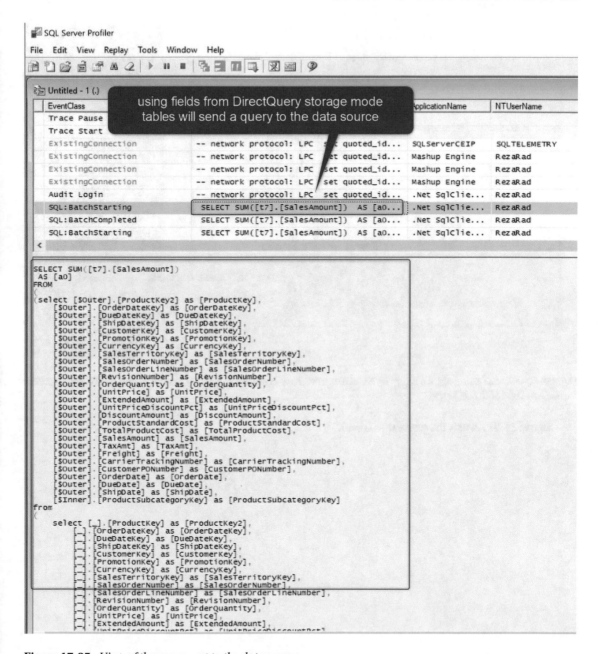

Figure 17-25. *View of the query sent to the data source*

Query from Multiple DirectQuery Tables

If you have multiple tables with DirectQuery storage mode, the result will be a query sent to the data source for that combination. Figure 17-26 includes a column chart by SalesAmount from FactInternetSales (DirectQuery) and CalendarYear from DimDate (DirectQuery).

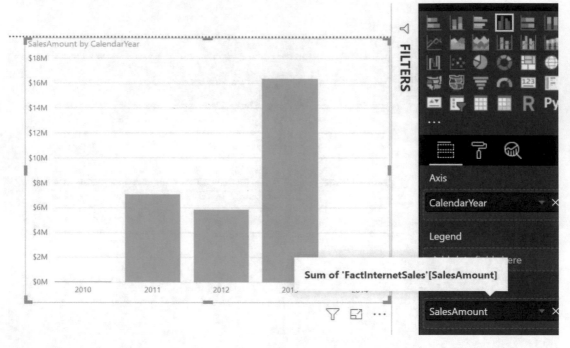

Figure 17-26. *Sample column chart by SalesAmount from FactInternetSales (DirectQuery) and CalendarYear from DimDate (DirectQuery)*

Figure 17-27 reveals the query that is sent.

Figure 17-27. *Query sent to the data source*

Caution: Combining DirectQuery and Import

So far, with these examples, everything happens as expected. Nothing strange happens. However, combining fields from DirectQuery sourced tables with Import storage mode tables would be strange. As an example, the Sales Agg table is an Import Data table. The purpose of creating this table is to query faster from the in-memory structure. If you create a visual that contains something from the Sales Agg table, as shown in Figure 17-28, no query will be sent to the data source. It all happens in memory, as expected.

Figure 17-28. *The Sales Agg table visual will not trigger a query*

As Figure 17-29 shows, SQL Profiler doesn't catch any queries sent to the data source.

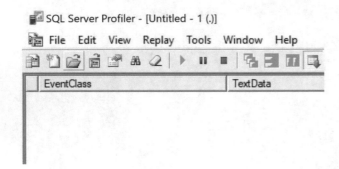

Figure 17-29. *No queries are tracked*

However, the behavior is different if, as shown in Figure 17-30, you have a visual that gets data from the Sales Agg table and a DirectQuery table such as DimDate.

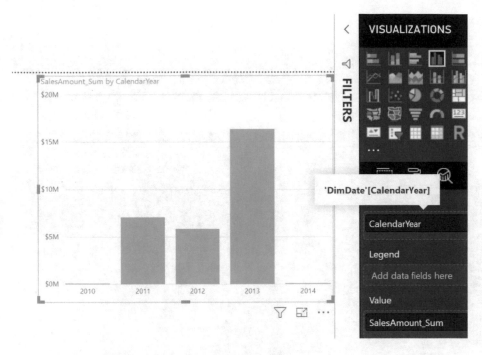

Figure 17-30. *Visual of the Sales Agg table and a DirectQuery table*

This time, you see a T-SQL query tracked in SQL Profiler, querying the DimDate in the SQL Server database (see Figure 17-31).

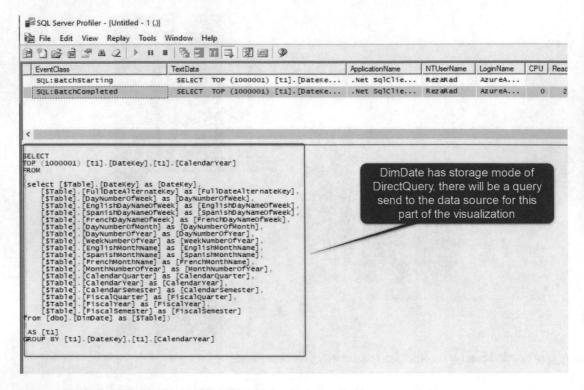

Figure 17-31. *T-SQL query tracked in SQL Profiler*

This is not what you would expect to see. The purpose of the Sales Agg table is to speed up the process from DirectQuery mode, but you are still querying the `DimDate` from the database. So, what is the solution? Do you change the storage mode of `DimDate` to Import Data? If you do that, what happens to the connection between `DimDate` and `FactInternetSales`? You want that connection to work as DirectQuery, of course.

Now that you learned about the challenge, it is a good time to talk about the third storage mode, Dual.

Dual Storage Mode

The Dual storage mode is built to cover a scenario like the one just discusses. With Dual storage mode, one table can act either as DirectQuery or Import Data, respective to the relationship to other tables. Dual storage mode is the secret sauce of composite mode and aggregation in Power BI. Let's see how this mode works.

If you change the storage mode of `DimDate` to Import Data, you get the issue of sending the query to the data source when you are querying `FactInternetSales`. If you change the storage mode of `DimDate` to DirectQuery, then even for Sales Agg, you are sending the query to the data source. The solution is to change the storage mode of the common dimension tables to Dual.

When you set the storage mode of a table such as `DimDate` to Dual, you get a warning that this process may take some time (see Figure 17-32). By changing the storage mode to Dual, you get a copy of that table in memory.

✕

Storage mode

Setting the storage mode to Dual has the following implications. Please consider them carefully before proceeding.

This operation will refresh tables set to Dual, which may take time depending on factors such as data volume.

Learn more about setting storage mode

| OK | Cancel |

Figure 17-32. *Setting storage to Dual triggers a warning*

The copy of that table in memory acts like an Import table. There will be another version of that table that works through DirectQuery, though. It looks like you have two identical tables, one for Import Data and another for DirectQuery.

What would be the impact of having two tables on reporting? The same visual you had before in the previous example is now working through the in-memory engine, as shown in Figure 17-33.

Figure 17-33. *Dual storage mode for the DimDate table*

As you can see in Figure 17-34, no queries are sent to the data source for this table.

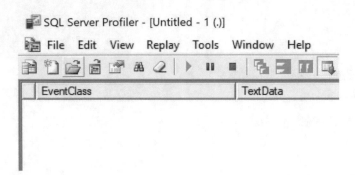

Figure 17-34. *No queries are tracked*

Because this table is connected to an Import table (Sales Agg), the Dual storage mode acts like an Import table storage (see Figure 17-35). Everything is queried from memory.

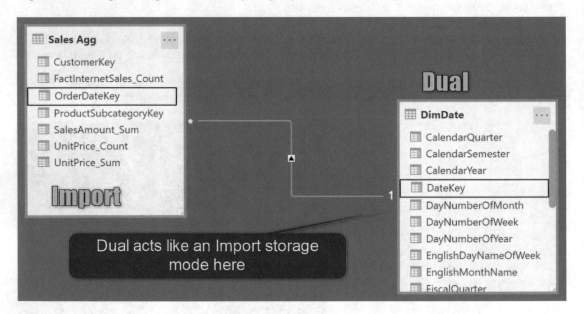

Figure 17-35. *Dual storage behaves like an import table storage*

Say you have the Dual storage mode table, used in a visualizing alongside a DirectQuery table, similar to Figure 17-36.

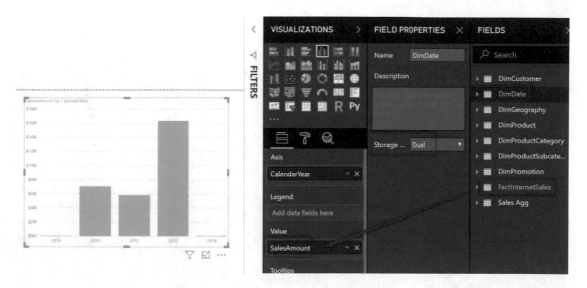

Figure 17-36. *Visualization of data from a table using Dual storage mode*

This visualization will send a query to the data source, as you can see in the SQL Profiler track featured in Figure 17-37.

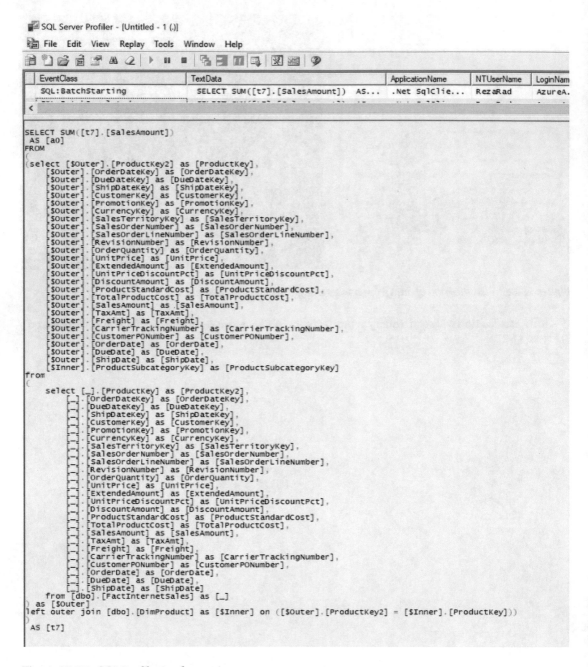

Figure 17-37. *SQL Profiler tracks queries*

In this scenario, the Dual storage mode acts like a DirectQuery because it comes with a connection to a DirectQuery sourced table, as Figure 17-38 demonstrates.

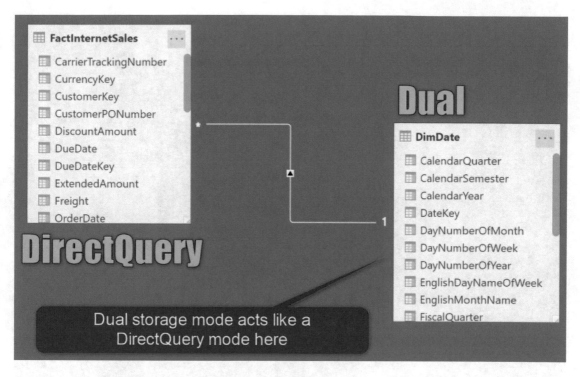

Figure 17-38. *Dual mode behaves like DirectQuery mode*

Now you can see why this mode is called Dual. Sometimes it acts like Import and sometimes like DirectQuery, depending on the table that is combined through the visualization. See Figure 17-39.

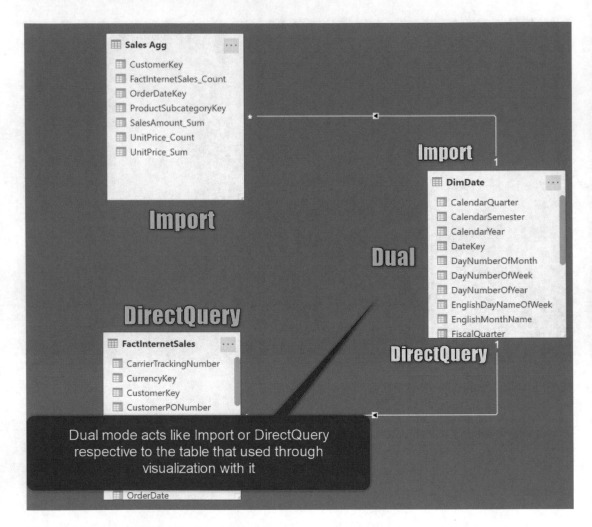

Figure 17-39. *Dual mode can behave in two ways*

If you don't care about the details, and you just want to know how to get the aggregations working, the answer is easy. All tables connected to both Sales Agg (the aggregation table, which is Import), and FactInternetSales (the big fact table, which is DirectQuery) should be set to the Dual storage mode. This way, they can act both ways, depending on the situation.

All tables connected to Import table (aggregation) and DirectQuery table (big fact table) should be set to Dual storage mode.

In this example, Dual storage mode is used with DimDate, DimProductSubcategory, and DimCustomer. However, when you apply Dual storage mode to DimCustomer, a message pops up saying that DimGeography will also be set as Storage mode (see Figure 17-40). That is correct; other tables that are related to this through a many-to-one relationship need to be set to Dual too.

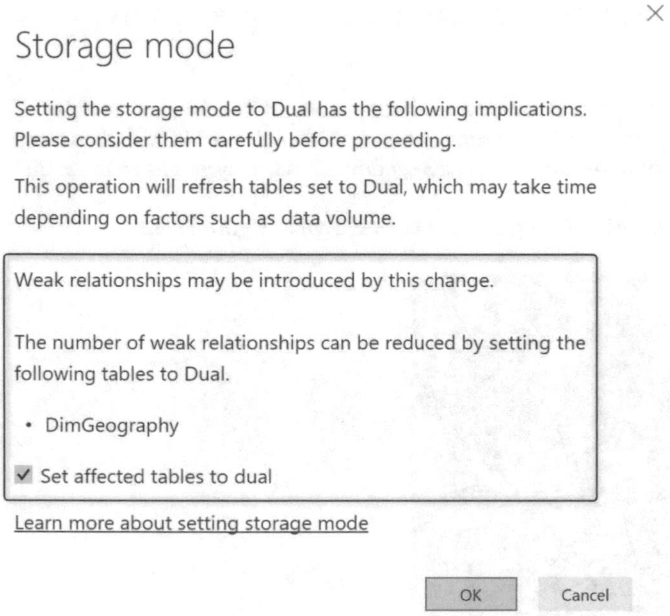

Storage mode

✕

Setting the storage mode to Dual has the following implications. Please consider them carefully before proceeding.

This operation will refresh tables set to Dual, which may take time depending on factors such as data volume.

> Weak relationships may be introduced by this change.
>
> The number of weak relationships can be reduced by setting the following tables to Dual.
>
> - DimGeography
>
> ☑ Set affected tables to dual

Learn more about setting storage mode

OK   Cancel

Figure 17-40. *Storage mode alert*

The same process happens with `DimProductSubcategory` and `DimProductCategory`. In the sample diagram and model, all tables selected in Figure 17-41 are set to Dual storage mode.

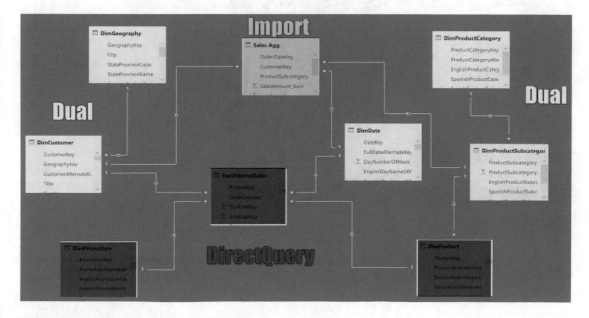

Figure 17-41. *Tables set to Dual storage mode*

Step 3: Configure Aggregation Functions and Test Aggregations in Action

The aggregated table is created and has proper relationships and storage modes. However, Power BI is unaware of this aggregation (remember you can create the aggregation outside of Power BI with the Group By clause in T-SQL). You have to let Power BI know about this aggregation. That is why you need to set up and configure it.

Right-click the Sales Agg table and select Manage Aggregations, as shown in Figure 17-42.

Figure 17-42. *Managing aggregations*

In the Manage Aggregations window, you can choose aggregation functions and fields that the function will be applied to (see Figure 17-43).

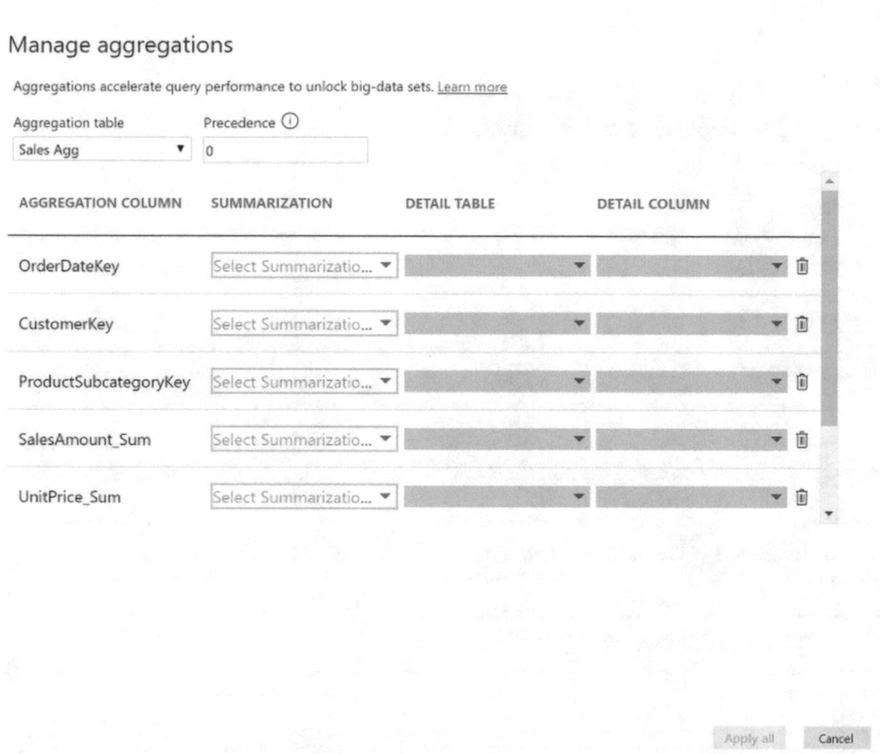

×

Manage aggregations

Aggregations accelerate query performance to unlock big-data sets. Learn more

Aggregation table	Precedence ⓘ
Sales Agg ▼	0

AGGREGATION COLUMN	SUMMARIZATION	DETAIL TABLE	DETAIL COLUMN	
OrderDateKey	Select Summarizatio... ▼	▼	▼	🗑
CustomerKey	Select Summarizatio... ▼	▼	▼	🗑
ProductSubcategoryKey	Select Summarizatio... ▼	▼	▼	🗑
SalesAmount_Sum	Select Summarizatio... ▼	▼	▼	🗑
UnitPrice_Sum	Select Summarizatio... ▼	▼	▼	🗑

Apply all   Cancel

Figure 17-43. *Selecting aggregations*

This aggregation configuration should match the aggregation configuration on the aggregated table. What does that mean? When creating the aggregated table, you created a Group By with the setup shown in Figure 17-44.

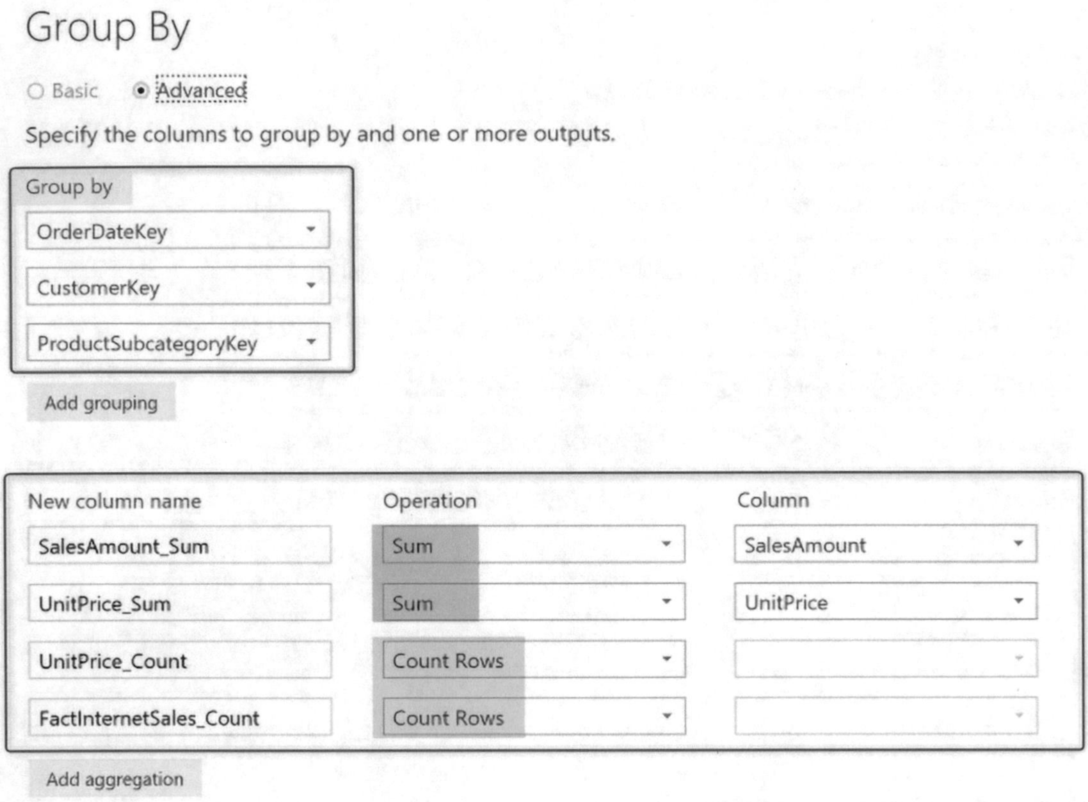

Group By

○ Basic   ◉ Advanced

Specify the columns to group by and one or more outputs.

Group by
OrderDateKey ▾
CustomerKey ▾
ProductSubcategoryKey ▾

Add grouping

New column name	Operation	Column
SalesAmount_Sum	Sum ▾	SalesAmount ▾
UnitPrice_Sum	Sum ▾	UnitPrice ▾
UnitPrice_Count	Count Rows ▾	▾
FactInternetSales_Count	Count Rows ▾	▾

Add aggregation

Figure 17-44. *Aggregation setup*

As you can see in Figure 17-44, you have three fields that are the Group By fields—OrderDateKey, CustomerKey, and ProductSubcategoryKey. These fields should be marked as Group By on their respective related field in the FactInternetSales table (the original fact table). See the highlighted portion of Figure 17-45.

Manage aggregations

Aggregations accelerate query performance to unlock big-data sets. Learn more

Aggregation table   Precedence ⓘ

| Sales Agg ▾ | | 0 |

AGGREGATION COLUMN	SUMMARIZATION	DETAIL TABLE	DETAIL COLUMN
OrderDateKey	GroupBy ▾	FactInternetSales ▾	OrderDateKey ▾ 🗑
CustomerKey	GroupBy ▾	FactInternetSales ▾	CustomerKey ▾ 🗑
ProductSubcategoryKey	GroupBy ▾	FactInternetSales ▾	ProductSubcategory... ▾ 🗑

Figure 17-45. *Setting Group By fields*

Then you should set up aggregation functions according to the original grouping configuration. For `SalesAmount_Sum` and `UnitPrice_Sum`, the aggregation should be set as Sum to their respective fields in the `FactInternetSales` table, as shown in Figure 17-46.

Manage aggregations

Aggregations accelerate query performance to unlock big-data sets. Learn more

Aggregation table   Precedence ⓘ

| Sales Agg ▾ | | 0 |

CustomerKey	GroupBy ▾	FactInternetSales ▾	CustomerKey ▾ 🗑
ProductSubcategoryKey	GroupBy ▾	FactInternetSales ▾	ProductSubcategory... ▾ 🗑
SalesAmount_Sum	Sum ▾	FactInternetSales ▾	SalesAmount ▾ 🗑
UnitPrice_Sum	Sum ▾	FactInternetSales ▾	UnitPrice ▾ 🗑

Figure 17-46. *Setting aggregation as Sum*

Rule #1: The Detail column must be the same data type of the grouped column to use the Sum function

At the time of creating the aggregated table, I mentioned that if you are using SUM as aggregation, the data type of the column after aggregation (`SalesAmount_Sum`) should be the same data type as the original column (`SalesAmount`).

If you don't follow this rule, the column will be grayed out in the list of columns, and you cannot select it. Change the data type first, then come back to set it.

For the other two columns—UnitPrice_Count and FactInternetSales_Count—the aggregation is Count and the table is FactInternetSales, as Figure 17-47 demonstrates:

Figure 17-47. *Aggregation is set to Count*

Rule #2: The data type of the column must be Whole Number (Integer) if you used the Count function
If you created any aggregated result using Count, that column's data type should be a whole number. Otherwise, the Count function in the manage aggregations will be grayed out. After configuring everything, your Manage Aggregations window should look like Figure 17-48.

Manage aggregations

Aggregations accelerate query performance to unlock big-data sets. Learn more

Aggregation table
Sales Agg ▼

Precedence ⓘ
0

AGGREGATION COLUMN	SUMMARIZATION	DETAIL TABLE	DETAIL COLUMN	
OrderDateKey	GroupBy ▼	FactInternetSales ▼	OrderDateKey ▼	🗑
CustomerKey	GroupBy ▼	FactInternetSales ▼	CustomerKey ▼	🗑
ProductSubcategoryKey	GroupBy ▼	FactInternetSales ▼	ProductSubcategory... ▼	🗑
SalesAmount_Sum	Sum ▼	FactInternetSales ▼	SalesAmount ▼	🗑
UnitPrice_Sum	Sum ▼	FactInternetSales ▼	UnitPrice ▼	🗑

Figure 17-48. *The Manage Aggregations window, set up correctly*

Hiding the Aggregated Table

The final step is to hide the aggregated table! You created the aggregated table for Power BI to automatically switch from the DirectQuery big fact table to the small Import Data aggregated table. However, this is just behind the scenes. The user should know nothing about this process. As shown in Figure 17-49, hide the Sales Agg table to make this experience seamless from the user's point of view. Power BI will automatically do this in the recent version of the Power BI Desktop.

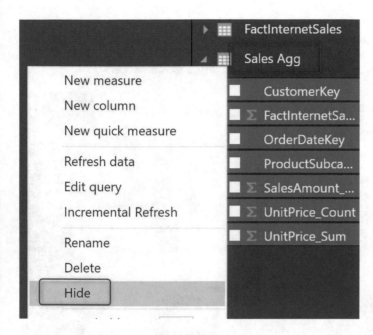

Figure 17-49. *Hiding the aggregated table from the users*

The user will see nothing about this table. The list of tables in the fields section contains only one fact table, called FactInternetSales. See Figure 17-50.

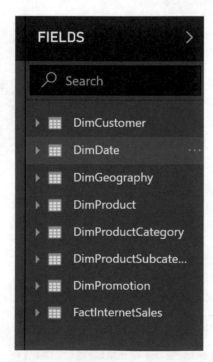

Figure 17-50. *Aggregated table successfully hidden from view*

Testing the Result

Now is the time to test how the aggregation works in action. The report in Figure 17-51 has all kinds of visualizations from FactInternetSales and SalesAmount sliced and diced by education and occupation (from DimCustomer), CalendarYear (from DimDate), ProductSubcategory, and ProductCategory.

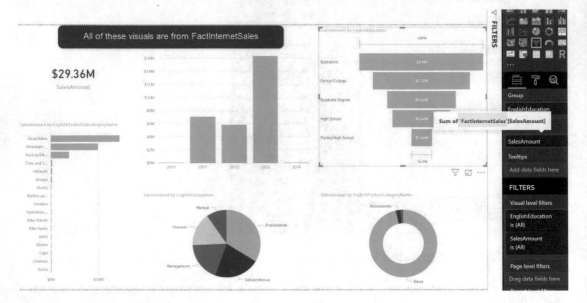
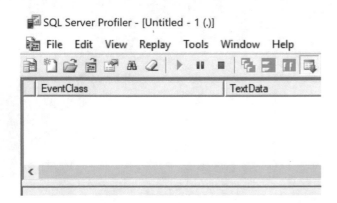

Figure 17-51. *Report with visualizations fetched from an aggregated table*

I have SQL Profiler running all the time, and Figure 17-52 shows the result.

Figure 17-52. *No query is sent to the DirectQuery source*

This is how the aggregated table works behind the scenes. Since all of these visuals are slicing and dicing the data by fields in the aggregated table (CustomerKey, OrderDateKey, and ProductSubcategoryKey), the result will always be automatically fetched from the aggregated table. Even though the Sales Agg table is not used in these visualizations.

If, however, I have a visualization that uses a different field that's not in the aggregated table, it is time to query from the data source. Figure 17-53 looks at every promotion.

SalesAmount	EnglishPromotionName
$27,307,607.0825	No Discount
$30,992.91	Touring-1000 Promotion
$14,847	Touring-3000 Promotion
$2,005,230.2282	Volume Discount 11 to 14
$29,358,677.2207	

Figure 17-53. *Visualization of a field that is not in aggregation*

SQL Profiler tracks the query, as shown in Figure 17-54.

Figure 17-54. *Query tracked in SQL Profiler*

So here you go; you have an aggregation that speeds up the performance of the DirectQuery sourced table. Nothing stops you from creating multiple levels of aggregation. It is recommended to do so, especially in scenarios where a different combination of fields will be used by different users or visuals.

Multiple Layers of Aggregations

Aggregations speed up the model. However, the aggregated table is not just one table; it can be multiple layers of aggregations—aggregation by date, aggregation by date and product, aggregation by date, product, and customer. Multiple layers ensure that you always have the best performance result possible, and you only query the DirectQuery data source for the most atomic requests. Let's see how this process is possible and helpful.

Second Aggregation Layer

The second aggregation layer added to this includes promotion options. Figure 17-55 shows the Group By settings for this second aggregation table in Power Query.

Figure 17-55. Sample group settings for another aggregation table

You have to load the table into Power BI and create relationships to `DimDate`, `DimCustomer`, `DimProductSubcategory`, and `DimPromotion`. See Figure 17-56.

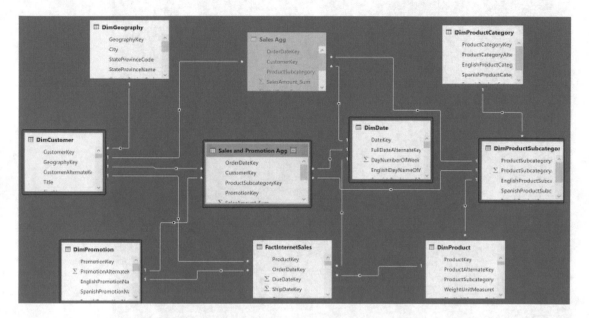

Figure 17-56. *Sample relationship diagram*

Set the storage mode of `DimPromotion` to Dual, as shown in Figure 17-57. It is important to use Dual storage mode. With this setup, Power BI for aggregation-based analysis uses the in-memory copy of `DimPromotion`, and for the atomic transaction levels, it uses the DirectQuery version of it.

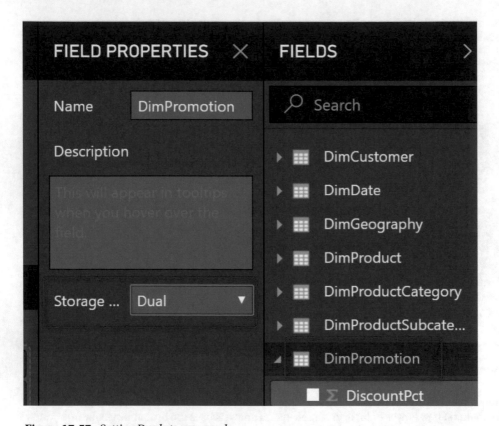

Figure 17-57. *Setting Dual storage mode*

After setting up relationships and storage modes, you need to manage the aggregations on the Sales and Promotion Agg tables (this is the second aggregation table). See Figure 17-58.

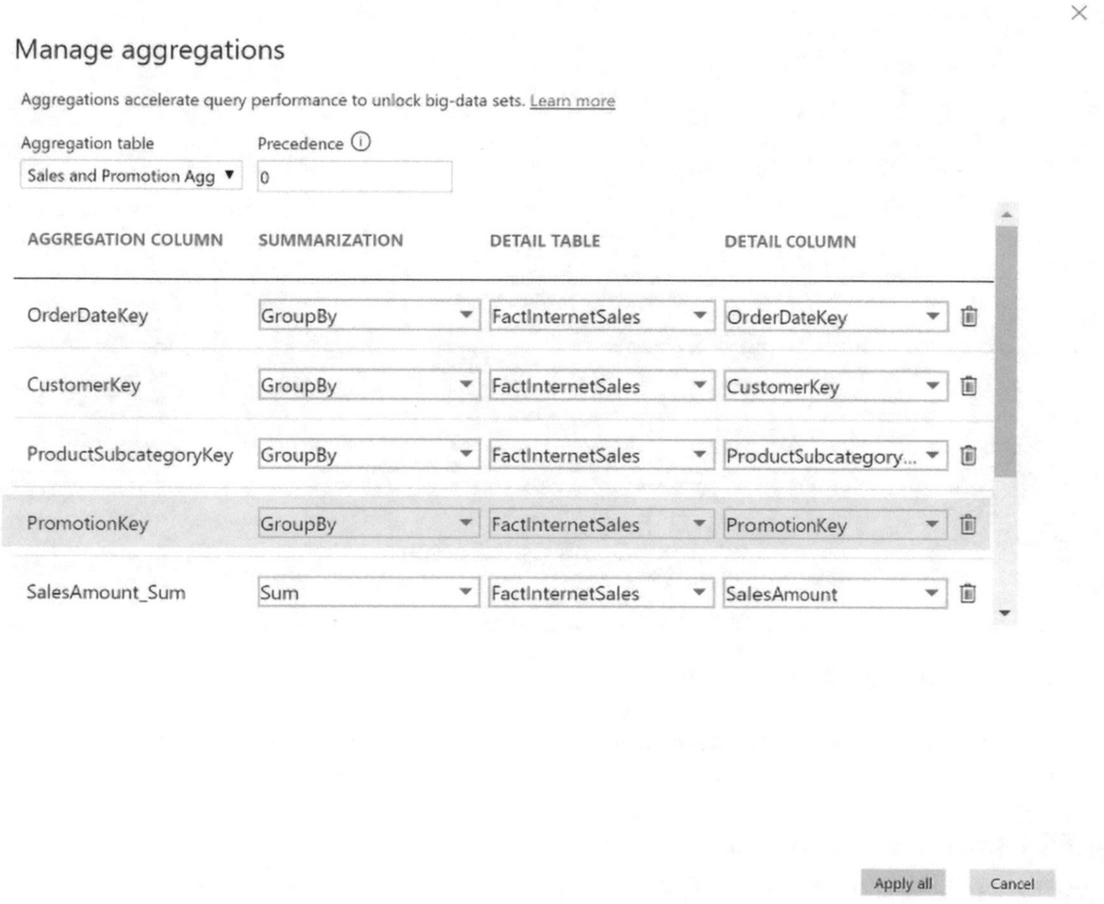

Manage aggregations

Aggregations accelerate query performance to unlock big-data sets. Learn more

Aggregation table   Precedence ⓘ

| Sales and Promotion Agg ▼ | | 0 |

AGGREGATION COLUMN	SUMMARIZATION	DETAIL TABLE	DETAIL COLUMN	
OrderDateKey	GroupBy ▼	FactInternetSales ▼	OrderDateKey ▼	🗑
CustomerKey	GroupBy ▼	FactInternetSales ▼	CustomerKey ▼	🗑
ProductSubcategoryKey	GroupBy ▼	FactInternetSales ▼	ProductSubcategory... ▼	🗑
PromotionKey	GroupBy ▼	FactInternetSales ▼	PromotionKey ▼	🗑
SalesAmount_Sum	Sum ▼	FactInternetSales ▼	SalesAmount ▼	🗑

Apply all   Cancel

Figure 17-58. Managing the aggregations

Everything in Figure 17-58 is similar to the aggregation setup you saw for the Sales Agg table. For this example, the only addition is the Group By action on PromotionKey.

Precedence Setup

When you have multiple layers of aggregation, you must set their precedence. The aggregated table you want to take the highest priority should have the highest precedence. In this case, Sales Agg can be 1, and Sales and Promotion Agg can be 0.

Testing the result

With this setup, you can have visualizations that use promotions, Customer, Date, and ProductSubcategory and are still sourced from the aggregation. Figure 17-59 offers one example.

FirstName	LastName	EnglishPromotionName	SalesAmount	FullDateAlternateKey	EnglishProductSubcategoryName	EnglishProduct
Aaron	Adams	No Discount	$34.99	Sunday, 28 April 2013	Helmets	Accessories
Aaron	Adams	No Discount	$53.99	Sunday, 28 April 2013	Jerseys	Clothing
Aaron	Adams	No Discount	$28.98	Sunday, 28 April 2013	Tires and Tubes	Accessories
Aaron	Alexander	No Discount	$69.99	Friday, 13 December 2013	Shorts	Clothing
Aaron	Allen	No Discount	$3,399.99	Friday, 2 December 2011	Mountain Bikes	Bikes
Aaron	Baker	No Discount	$49.99	Monday, 9 September 2013	Jerseys	Clothing
Aaron	Baker	No Discount	$1,700.99	Monday, 9 September 2013	Road Bikes	Bikes
Aaron	Bryant	No Discount	$8.99	Wednesday, 24 April 2013	Caps	Clothing
Aaron	Bryant	No Discount	$49.99	Wednesday, 24 April 2013	Jerseys	Clothing
Aaron	Bryant	No Discount	$34.99	Friday, 26 July 2013	Helmets	Accessories
Aaron	Bryant	No Discount	$39.99	Friday, 26 July 2013	Tires and Tubes	Accessories
Aaron	Butler	No Discount	$14.98	Thursday, 26 December 2013	Bottles and Cages	Accessories
Aaron	Campbell	No Discount	$34.99	Tuesday, 10 September 2013	Helmets	Accessories
Aaron	Campbell	No Discount	$1,120.49	Tuesday, 10 September 2013	Road Bikes	Bikes
Aaron	Carter	No Discount	$34.99	Sunday, 22 December 2013	Helmets	Accessories
Aaron	Carter	No Discount	$4.99	Sunday, 22 December 2013	Tires and Tubes	Accessories
Aaron	Chen	No Discount	$34.99	Saturday, 13 July 2013	Helmets	Accessories
Aaron	Chen	No Discount	$4.99	Saturday, 13 July 2013	Tires and Tubes	Accessories
Aaron	Coleman	No Discount	$21.98	Thursday, 5 December 2013	Fenders	Accessories
Aaron	Coleman	No Discount	$34.99	Thursday, 5 December 2013	Helmets	Accessories
Aaron	Coleman	No Discount	$4.99	Thursday, 5 December 2013	Tires and Tubes	Accessories
Aaron	Collins	No Discount	$3,578.27	Tuesday, 25 January 2011	Road Bikes	Bikes
Aaron	Collins	No Discount	$34.99	Saturday, 16 November 2013	Helmets	Accessories
Aaron	Collins	No Discount	$49.99	Saturday, 16 November 2013	Jerseys	Clothing
Aaron	Collins	No Discount	$2,384.07	Saturday, 16 November 2013	Touring Bikes	Bikes
Total			**$29,358,677.2207**			

Figure 17-59. Sourced from the aggregation

This kind of visualization will not send a query to the DirectQuery source, as you can see in Figure 17-60.

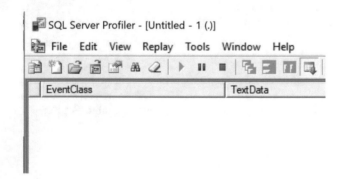

Figure 17-60. Query not sent to the source

How about the Precedence of Execution?

When you have multiple aggregation layers, determining which one runs first is important. As an example, let's assume some numbers. These are not real numbers; these just help you understand the scenario. The big fact table (FactInternetSales) uses DirectQuery mode and has 250 million rows. And the Sales Agg table has only 10,000 rows. But the Sales and Promotion Agg table has 1,000,000 rows. In such a scenario, when you are querying something that can be answered with the table with 10K rows (Sales Agg), you have to use that, because it would be much faster than the table with 1M rows (Sales and Promotion Agg). Therefore, you need to set up the precedence of execution. Smaller aggregation tables should be the source of analysis first.

Query Hits the First Aggregated Table in Memory

Figure 17-61 shows the Power BI page using Gender (from DimCustomer) and SalesAmount (from FactInternetSales).

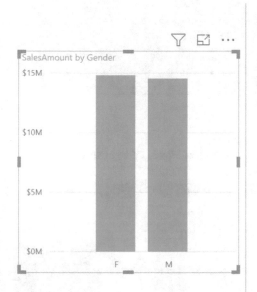

Figure 17-61. *Sample visual*

The visual in Figure 17-61 will query the aggregated table behind the scenes, not the FactInternetSales table. In this case, it will query the Sales Agg table. Figure 17-62 shows the behind-the-scenes query sent to the VertiPaq engine (result generated from SQL Profiler).

query Begin	3 - DAXQuery	2018-12-11 09:16:25...	2018-12-1:
VertiPaq SE Query Begin	0 - VertiP...	2018-12-11 09:16:25...	2018-12-1:
VertiPaq SE Query Begin	10 - Inter...	2018-12-11 09:16:25...	2018-12-1:
VertiPaq SE Query End	10 - Inter...	2018-12-11 09:16:25...	2018-12-1:
VertiPaq SE Query End	0 - VertiP...	2018-12-11 09:16:25...	2018-12-1:
Query End			

```
SET DC_KIND="DENSE";
SELECT
SUM([Sales Agg (2460)].[SalesAmount Sum (2563)]) AS [$Measure0], COUNT()
FROM [Sales Agg (2460)];
```

Figure 17-62. *Querying the aggregated table*

In this example, the query hits the first aggregated table in memory, as Figure 17-63 clearly illustrates.

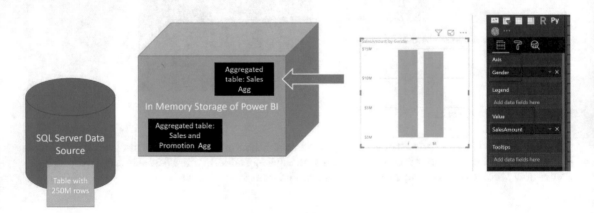

Figure 17-63. *Query path*

Query Hits the Second Aggregated Table in Memory

Figure 17-64 offers another visual that uses EnglishPromotionType (from DimPromotion) and SalesAmount (from FactInternetSales).

Figure 17-64. *Another sample visualization*

The result this time cannot be fetched from the Sales Agg table (because `DimPromotion` is not there as the Group By function), so it will be queried from the second aggregated table—Sales and Promotion Agg—as highlighted in Figure 17-65.

Figure 17-65. *Querying the second aggregated table*

In this instance, the query hits the second aggregated table in memory, as illustrated in Figure 17-66.

Query hits the second aggregated table in the memory

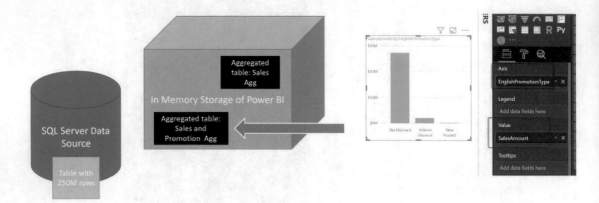

Figure 17-66. *Query path to the second aggregated table*

Query Hits the DirectQuery Table in the Source

Figure 17-67 uses EnglishProductName (from DimProduct) and SalesAmount (from FactInternetSales).

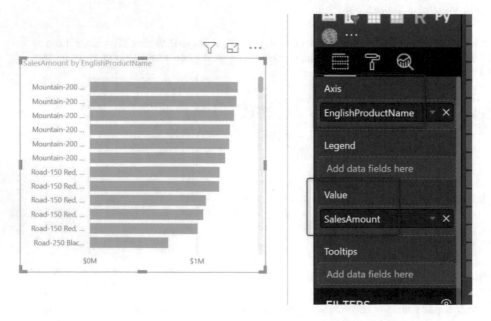

Figure 17-67. *A final sample visualization*

The result this time cannot be fetched from any of the aggregated tables, so it comes directly from the DirectQuery source table—FactInternetSales—as shown in Figure 17-68.

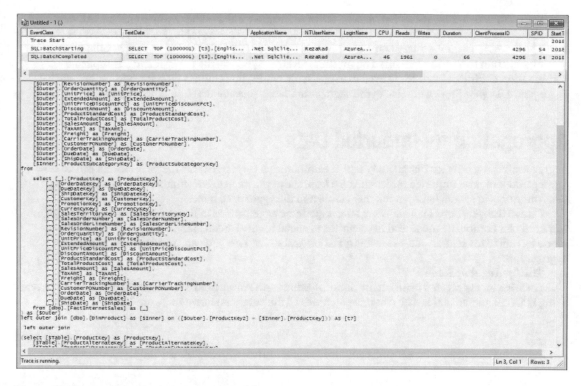

Figure 17-68. *From the DirectQuery source table*

In the last example, the query hits the DirectQuery table in the data source; see Figure 17-69.

Query hits the DirectQuery table in the data source

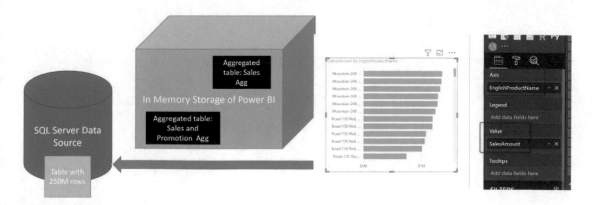

Figure 17-69. *Query path toward data source*

Power BI is switching nicely between layers of aggregated tables without you noticing it. All these operations are happening behind the scenes. The user will feel that one table (FactInternetSales) is serving all queries, and the query response time will be super-fast (with the help of aggregations).

Aggregation can be implemented on multiple levels to speed up the performance. If a specific combination of dimension fields is used in user visualizations, that combination is a good candidate for aggregation. Depending on the size of the aggregation table, precedence should be followed.

Aggregation for Imported Data

Aggregation is not only for DirectQuery tables. Sometimes a very large table that is imported can be slow. Aggregated tables on imported tables can also improve performance. For situations like that, you need to use DAX measures to switch between the main table and the aggregated table.

One of the questions I normally get after explaining aggregations in Power BI is, does the aggregation work only for composite mode and in scenarios to speed up the DirectQuery? Or does it work in Import mode as well? This section addresses this question and shows how you can speed up your model with aggregation.

The Aggregated Table

Creating an aggregated table can be done anywhere—in Power Query, in the backend data source, and using DAX calculated tables. The fact table includes all the columns shown in Figure 17-70.

Figure 17-70. *Sample fact table*

In this case, the aggregated table is the GROUPED-BY version of that table with fewer columns (which are grouped by key columns and aggregations), as shown in Figure 17-71.

Figure 17-71. *The resulting aggregated table*

No Manage Aggregations in Imported Mode

When you create aggregation on an imported table versus DirectQuery table, one of the differences is the Manage Aggregation option, previewed in Figure 17-72. This feature, which is also called aggregation awareness, works only if the main table is DirectQuery.

Figure 17-72. *The Manage Aggregations window*

This doesn't mean that you cannot use aggregations in the Import Data model. It just means that this feature (which is Power BI's ability to find the aggregated table when the main table is queried) doesn't work, and you have to do it in another way.

DAX Measures Instead of Manage Aggregation

You don't have the aggregation awareness of Power BI in all imported models. However, you can use DAX measures to do almost anything. You can use a simple IF statement with another function that checks what tables are filtered, to switch between the aggregated and the main table.

To understand how it works, first look at the model in Figure 17-73.

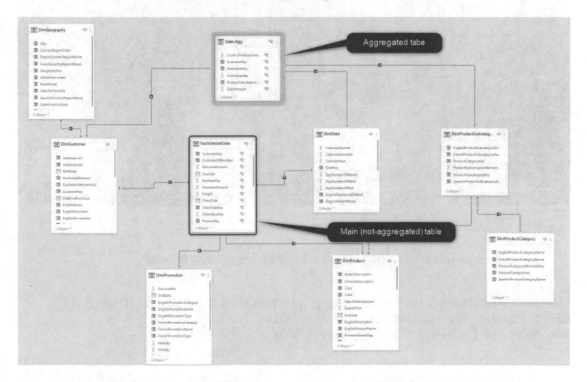

Figure 17-73. *Sample model of tables*

In this model, the Sales Agg is an aggregated table, which includes the grouped by data dimDate, dimCustomer, and dimProductSubCategory. This means that if you use anything from these tables, as well as DimGeography and DimProductCategory, you can get what you want from the Sales Agg table.

However, if you slice and dice the data by DimPromotion or DimProduct, then you would need FactInternetSales; see Figure 17-74.

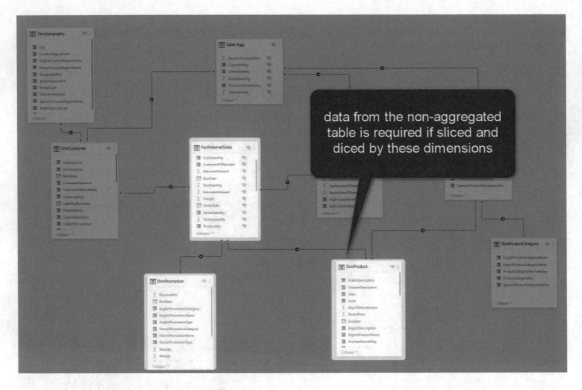

data from the non-aggregated table is required if sliced and diced by these dimensions

Figure 17-74. Sample model with sliced data

This can be done using an IF statement and a filter-checking function in DAX;

```
Sales = IF(
ISCROSSFILTERED(DimPromotion[PromotionKey]) || ISCROSSFILTERED(DimProduct[ProductKey]),
SUM(FactInternetSales[SalesAmount]), // main table
SUM('Sales Agg'[SalesAmount]) // aggregated table
)
```

This expression uses the main (non-aggregated) table if any of the fields from DimPromotion or DimProduct are used in a visualization. (ISCROSSFILTERED will check if any combination of fields from that table filters the output.) The expression will use the aggregated table otherwise.

After these steps, the two main and aggregated tables can be hidden from the report view (see Figure 17-75).

Figure 17-75. *Table selection*

Testing the Aggregation

To check if you are fetching data from an aggregated table or non-aggregated table, you can create another measure as follows:

```
Sales from which table = IF(
ISCROSSFILTERED(DimPromotion[PromotionKey]) || ISCROSSFILTERED(DimProduct[ProductKey]),
"FactInternetSales",
"Sales Agg"
)
```

This measure can now be used in a tooltip, and Figure 17-76 shows how it works.

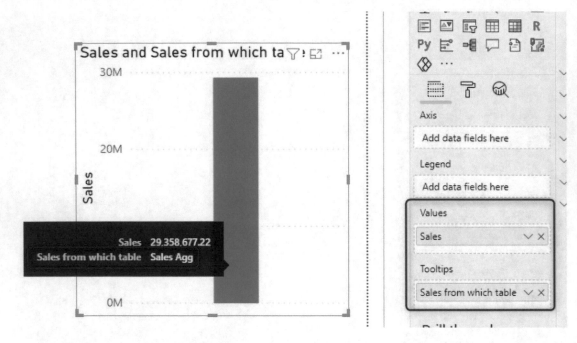

Figure 17-76. *Testing using tooltips*

If you slice and dice data by anything other than `DimProduct` and `DimPromotion`, the calculation result will come from Sales Agg, as shown in Figure 17-77.

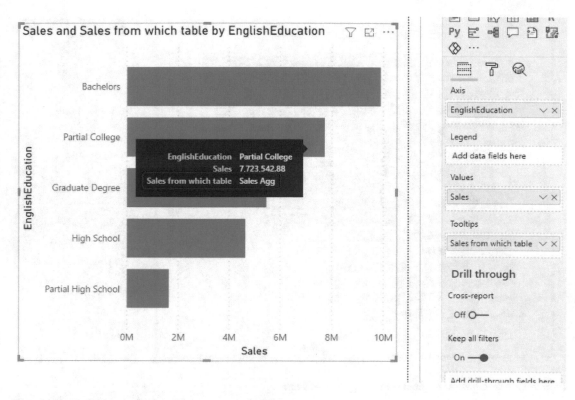

Figure 17-77. *Data results from the aggregated table*

If you filter data by any of the `DimProduct` or `DimPromotion` fields, you will get the data from a non-aggregated table, as shown in Figure 17-78.

Figure 17-78. *Data results from a non-aggregated table*

Multiple Layers of Aggregations Are Also Possible

Using the DAX measure approach, multiple layers of aggregation are also possible. All you need to do is add more conditions to your IF expression. You can also use SWITCH and get the result from the relevant aggregated table.

In addition to good data modeling, proper DAX calculations, and having calculations in their rightful places, aggregation is another way to speed up the performance of your model. If you are dealing with large tables, aggregations help reduce the number of rows to process for the calculation.

Automatic Aggregation

Creating aggregations in Power BI highly depends on using columns and tables in the report. Performance tuning advice is to start creating aggregations on those columns mostly used in visuals. The good news is that Power BI can automate this process for you. It is called *automatic aggregation.*

Automatic aggregation is the process in which Power BI checks the usage logs of the columns and tables in the Power BI dataset and creates automatic aggregation tables based on that. This requires minimum effort from you as a developer. It will all be handled very simply by Power BI. You can enable this from the dataset settings feature, as demonstrated in Figure 17-79.

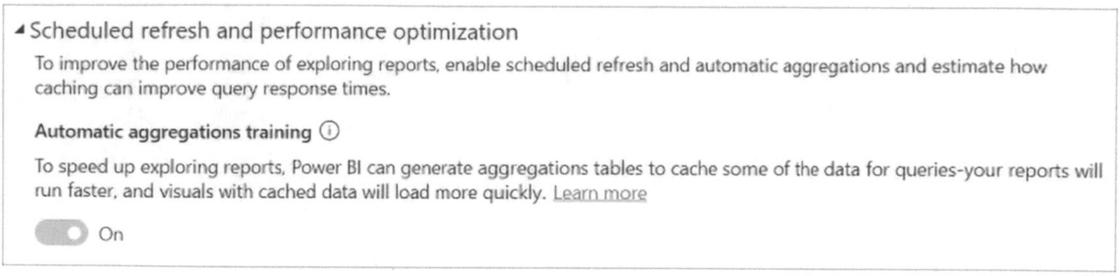

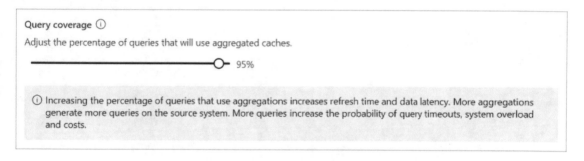

Figure 17-79. *Enabling automatic aggregation*

There is a setting for how much query coverage you want to get with the automatic aggregation, as Figure 17-80 shows.

Figure 17-80. *Setting up query coverage for automatic aggregation*

Summary

Aggregation is a game-changer in the performance and speed of Power BI solutions when the data source table is huge. With the help of aggregations, you can have layers of pre-calculations stored in memory and ready to respond to queries from users. The DirectQuery data source will be used for the atomic transaction queries. Aggregation is not just for DirectQuery models; it can also improve the performance of Import Data models.

CHAPTER 18

■ ■ ■

Big Data with Incremental Refresh and Hybrid Tables

The default configuration for the Power BI dataset is to wipe out the entire data and reload it again on each refresh. This can be a long process if you have a big dataset. Hybrid tables in Power BI keep part of the data in DirectQuery, and the rest of the data is imported for data freshness and performance. This chapter explains how to set up Incremental Refresh in Power BI. You also learn about hybrid tables. Incremental Refresh is not just used in Power BI datasets but also in dataflows and datamarts. In this chapter, you learn how to load only part of the changed data instead of loading the entire data each time.

What Is Incremental Refresh?

When you load data from the source into the destination (Power BI), there are two methods: Full Load and Incremental Refresh. Full Load fetches the entire dataset each time and wipes out the previous data. When I say the entire dataset, I mean after all the Power Query transformations because there might be some filtering in Power Query. When I talk about the entire data, I am referring to whatever data loads into the Power BI dataset.

If the dataset is small, or the refresh process is quick, then using Full Load is not a problem. The problem happens when your dataset is big, or the refresh process takes too long. Imagine you have a large dataset that includes 20 years of data. Data from 20 years ago likely won't change, or even the data from 5 years ago, and sometimes even a year ago. Why reprocess data that never changes? Why reload data that isn't being updated? Incremental Refresh is the process of loading only the part of the data that could change and adding it to the previous dataset, which is no longer changing.

Incremental Load splits the table into partitions. The number of partitions is based on the settings applied at the time of Incremental Refresh. For example, if you want to refresh only last year's data, a yearly partition will likely be created for every year, and the one for the current year will be refreshed on a scheduled basis.

Hybrid Tables

If you need data freshness (near real-time) on a big table, there is an option for you. You can design your table to keep both your DirectQuery and Import Data in a single table. The DirectQuery part ensures near real-time data, and the imported part ensures the best performance in Power BI.

Hybrid tables are partitioned, so their most recent partition is a DirectQuery from the data source, and their historical data is imported into other partitions. This is different from dual storage mode. This is a table whereby part of it is imported, and part of it is DirectQuery. Hybrid tables can only be applied on a table that is configured for Incremental Refresh.

© Reza Rad 2023
R. Rad, *Pro Power BI Architecture*, https://doi.org/10.1007/978-1-4842-9538-0_18

Configuring Incremental Refresh

Table with Date Field(s)

To set up Incremental Refresh, you must have one or more tables with a date field. The date field is used to implement a partial refresh of the data. For example, let's say you have a FactSales table. You want to load all sales made earlier than a year ago just once, but everything from a year ago to now, you want to load regularly. You need to have a date field in your table. Often, this field will be called something like CreatedDate, ModifiedDate, OrderDate, PublishDate, and so on.

A data source that supports query folding

Query folding is when the Power Query transformations are translated to the data source language (such as T-SQL when querying from SQL Server). Although you can implement Incremental Refresh on any data source, even if it is does not support query folding, it would be pointless to do so. The main point of Incremental Refresh is that Power BI reads the data that has changed rather than reading the entire data from the source. With a data source that supports query folding, that is possible because Power BI can query only the recent part of the data. However, if your data source doesn't support query folding (for example, it is a CSV file), then Power BI will read the entire set of data anyway.

Licensing Requirement

You don't need a Premium or PPU license to use Incremental Refresh. You can even set it up using a Power BI Pro license. However, hybrid tables require a Power BI Premium or PPU capacity.

Limitations: Things to Know Beforehand

One important limitation to consider is that after setting up Incremental Refresh, you can no longer download the PBIX file from the service. That's because the data is now partitioned (see Figure 18-1). This also makes sense because the data size is likely too large for downloading.

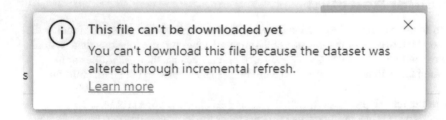

Figure 18-1. *PBIX download limitation*

Setting Up Incremental Refresh

To set up Incremental Refresh, you go through some steps in the Power BI Desktop and then in the Power BI Service. Let's look at these steps one by one.

Parameters in Power Query

You need to use Power Query parameters to set up an Incremental Refresh in Power BI. You need to create two parameters with the reserved names of RangeStart and RangeEnd. (Note that Power Query is a case-sensitive language.) Go to Transform Data in your Power BI Desktop solution, as shown in Figure 18-2.

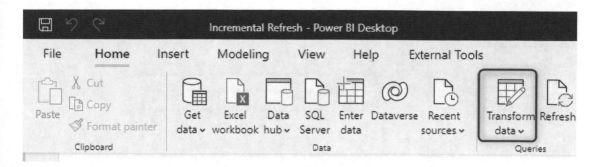

Figure 18-2. *Setting up parameters (choose Transform Data)*

Click New Parameter, as shown in Figure 18-3.

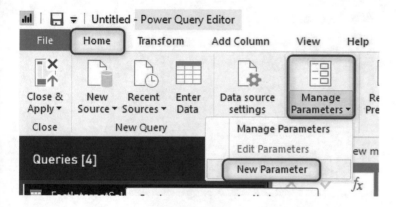

Figure 18-3. *Setting up parameters (choose New Parameter)*

Then, as shown in Figure 18-4, create two parameters with the DateTime data type, called RangeStart and RangeEnd, and set a default value for each. The default values can be anything.

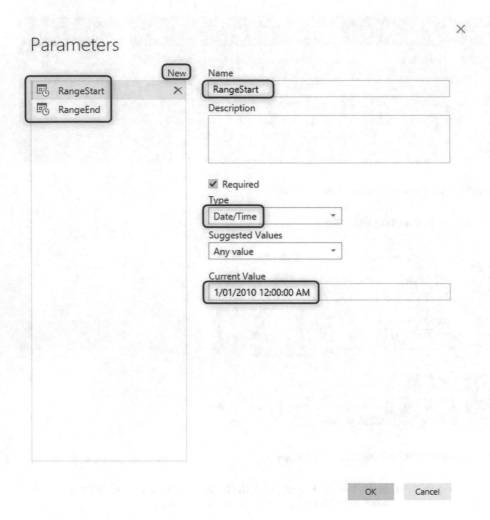

Figure 18-4. *Setting up parameters (choose RangeStart and RangeEnd)*

Filter Data Based on the Parameters

After creating the two parameters, you need to filter the data of the date field based on these two parameters. For example, in the FactInternetSales table, I can filter OrderDate using column filtering, as Figure 18-5 demonstrates.

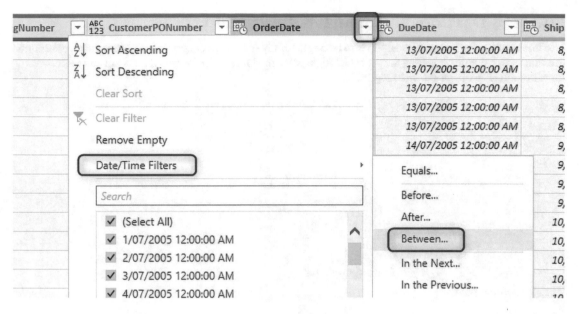

Figure 18-5. *Filtering data*

You can use a Between filter and the RangeStart and RangeEnd parameters, as shown in Figure 18-6.

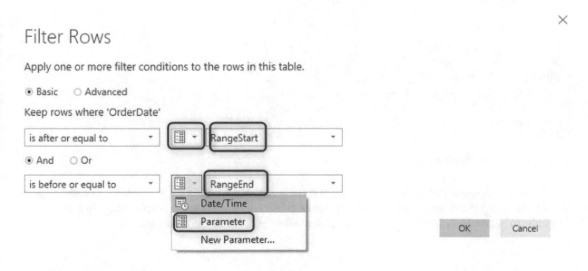

Figure 18-6. *Filtering options*

After this action, your data in the table will be filtered based on the default values you set for the RangeStart and RangeEnd parameters. However, don't worry about that for now. These two parameters will be overwritten with the configuration you make in the Incremental Refresh setting of the Power BI Desktop.

Power BI Desktop Incremental Refresh Setup

The final step in the Power BI Desktop is to close and apply the Power Query Editor window and determine the Incremental Refresh setting for the table. Right-click the table in the Power BI Desktop and select Incremental Refresh, as shown in Figure 18-7.

Figure 18-7. *Selecting Incremental Refresh*

In the Incremental Refresh and Real-Time Data window, start by selecting the table. If the table doesn't include the RangeStart and RangeEnd parameters used in the filter criteria, you can't configure it. For example, in Figure 18-8, DimCustomer doesn't give me the option to do the configuration.

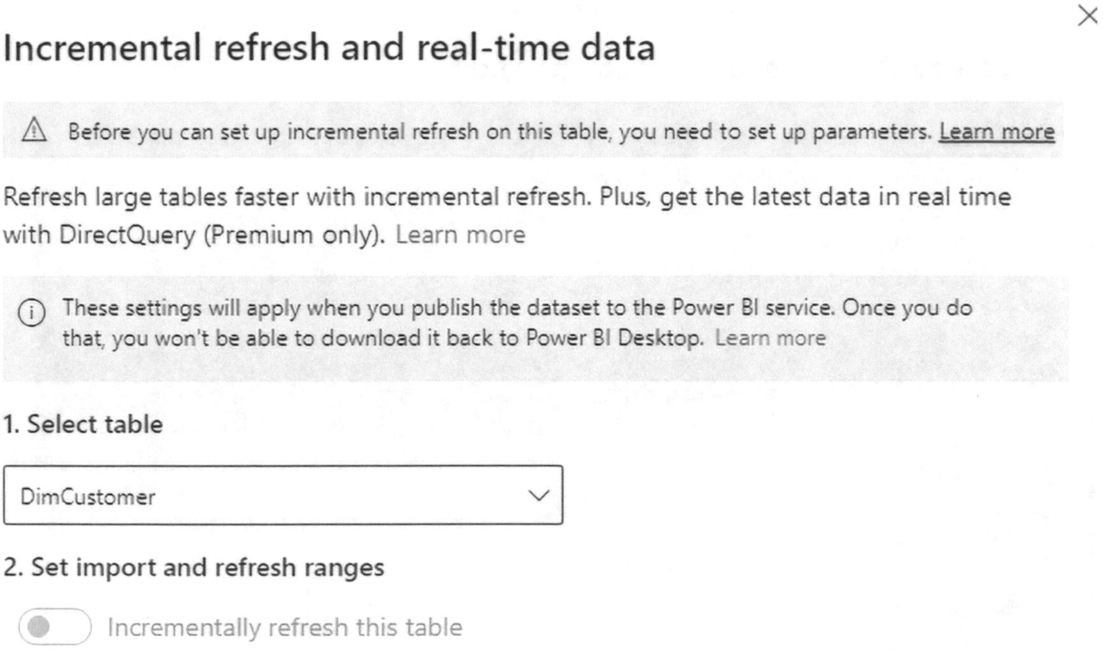

×

Incremental refresh and real-time data

⚠ Before you can set up incremental refresh on this table, you need to set up parameters. Learn more

Refresh large tables faster with incremental refresh. Plus, get the latest data in real time with DirectQuery (Premium only). Learn more

ⓘ These settings will apply when you publish the dataset to the Power BI service. Once you do that, you won't be able to download it back to Power BI Desktop. Learn more

1. Select table

DimCustomer ⌄

2. Set import and refresh ranges

◖ Incrementally refresh this table

Figure 18-8. Parameters needed to set up in Incremental Refresh

However, I can configure FactInternetSales because I did filter the OrderDate field of this table based on the parameters. There are two things to notice at this step: If your data source supports query folding, then Incremental Refresh works best. If not, it is not recommended to use it. Large volumes of data can come from a relational data store system, and query folding lets you load only the subset of the data that you need.

Another thing to note is the Get the Latest Data in Real-Time with DirectQuery option, which requires Premium or PPU licensing. And finally, remember that you cannot download a PBIX file from the service when Incremental Refresh is set up.

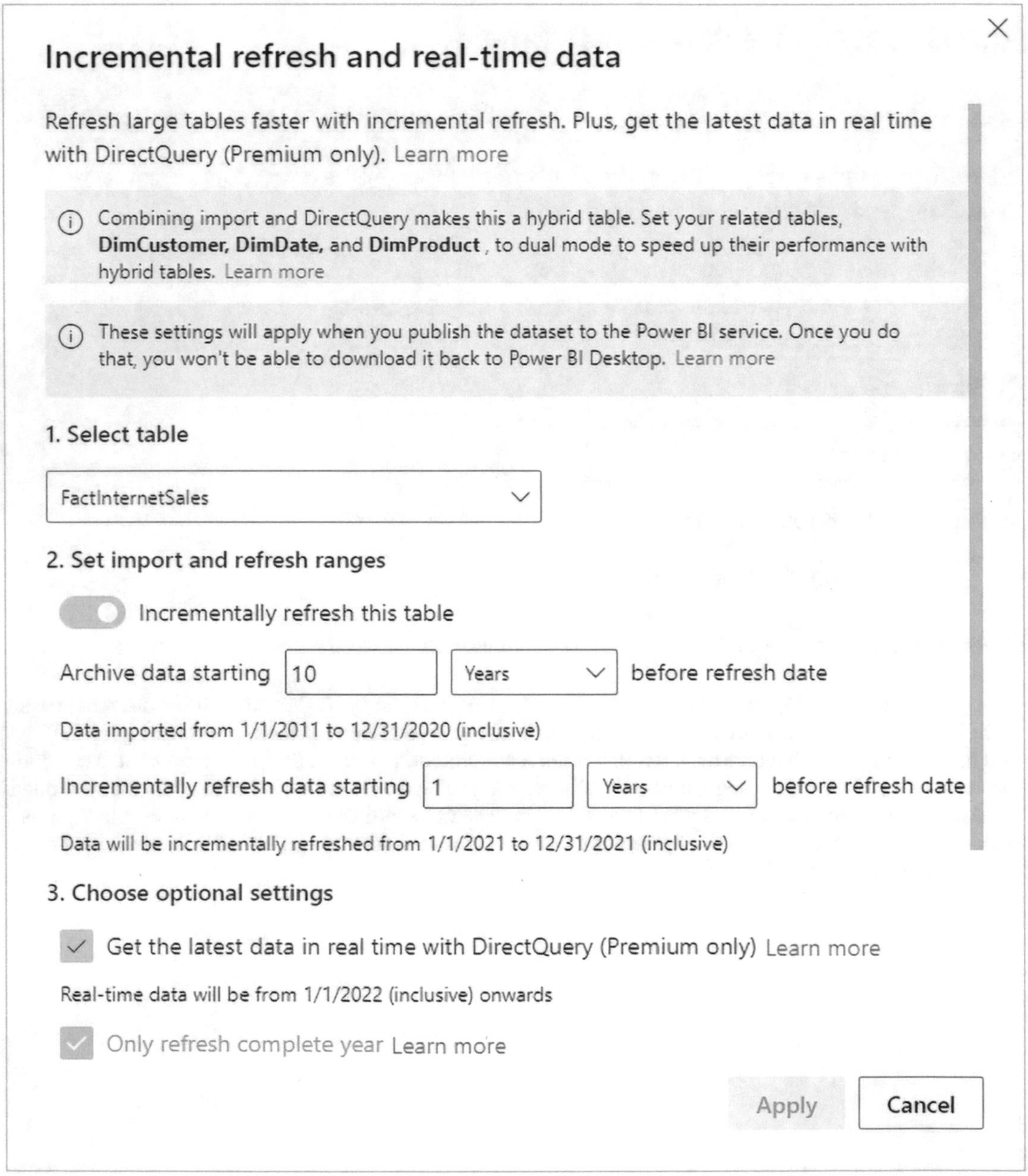

Figure 18-9. *Incremental Refresh settings*

Configuring Incremental Refresh is easy. You set up which rows to store (load only once and store them) and which rows to refresh (reload every time); see Figure 18-10.

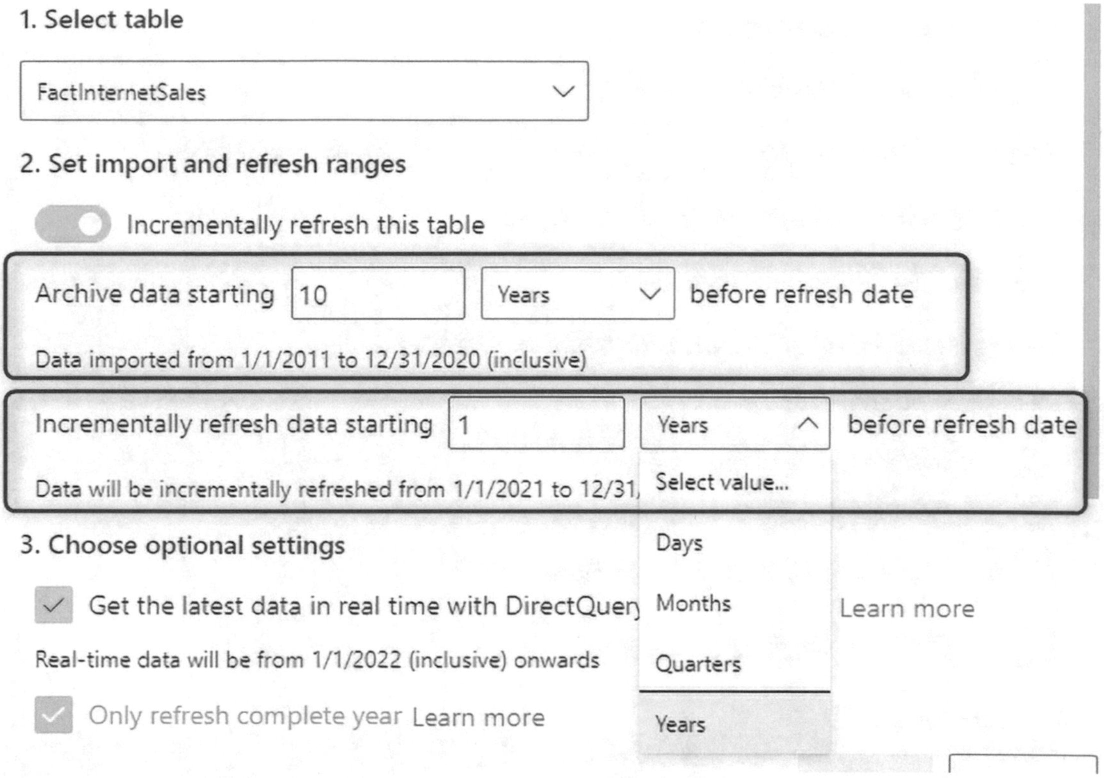

1. Select table

FactInternetSales ⌄

2. Set import and refresh ranges

⬤ Incrementally refresh this table

Archive data starting | 10 | Years ⌄ | before refresh date

Data imported from 1/1/2011 to 12/31/2020 (inclusive)

Incrementally refresh data starting | 1 | Years ⌃ | before refresh date

Data will be incrementally refreshed from 1/1/2021 to 12/31,

Select value...

3. Choose optional settings

✓ Get the latest data in real time with DirectQuery

Days

Months   Learn more

Real-time data will be from 1/1/2022 (inclusive) onwards

Quarters

✓ Only refresh complete year Learn more

Years

Figure 18-10. Selecting refresh specifics

Hybrid Table Setup

You have one more configuration if you want to set up your table as a hybrid table. This requires a Premium or PPU license. Select the Get the Latest Data in Real-Time with DirectQuery option, as shown in Figure 18-11. Your dataset must have been published into a Premium or PPU workspace. Once you set this configuration, you can see the period of real-time data and a diagram of the timeline of your setup.

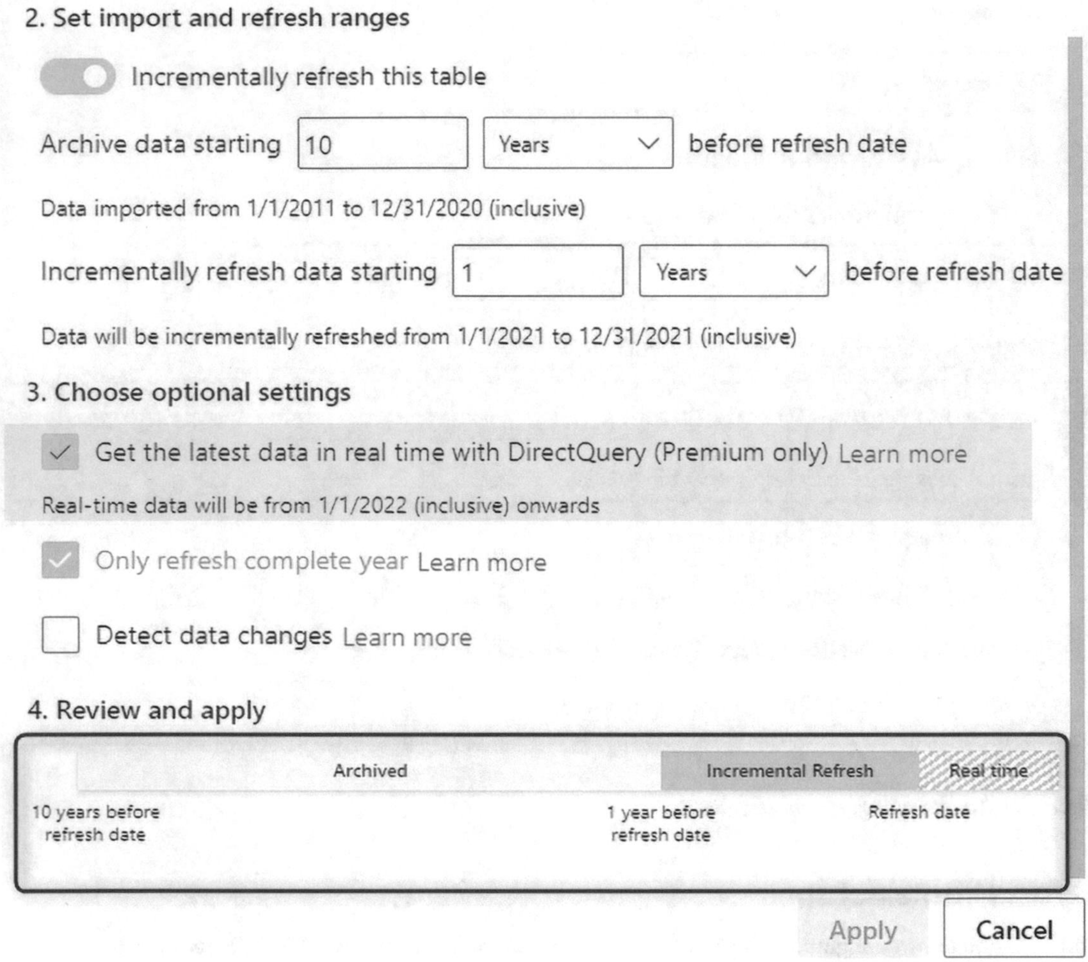

2. Set import and refresh ranges

Incrementally refresh this table

Archive data starting `10` | Years ⌄ | before refresh date

Data imported from 1/1/2011 to 12/31/2020 (inclusive)

Incrementally refresh data starting `1` | Years ⌄ | before refresh date

Data will be incrementally refreshed from 1/1/2021 to 12/31/2021 (inclusive)

3. Choose optional settings

☑ Get the latest data in real time with DirectQuery (Premium only) Learn more

Real-time data will be from 1/1/2022 (inclusive) onwards

☑ Only refresh complete year Learn more

☐ Detect data changes Learn more

4. Review and apply

Archived	Incremental Refresh	Real time
10 years before refresh date	1 year before refresh date	Refresh date

Apply   Cancel

Figure 18-11. Hybrid table settings

After enabling this on your dataset, it can only be published to a Premium or PPU workspace.

Incremental Refresh for Multiple Tables

You can set up the Incremental Refresh for multiple tables. You don't need more parameters; the two existing RangeStart and RangeEnd parameters are enough. You just need to set the filter in any other tables you want to refresh incrementally. See Figure 18-12.

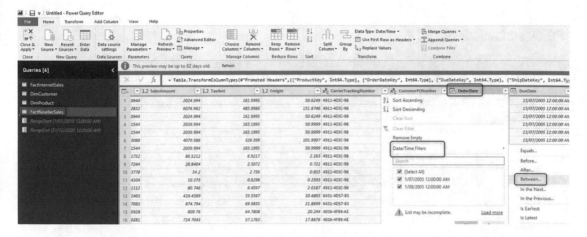

Figure 18-12. *Filter tables using the same DateTime parameters*

You then set up the configuration in the Power BI Desktop for each table, as demonstrated in Figure 18-13.

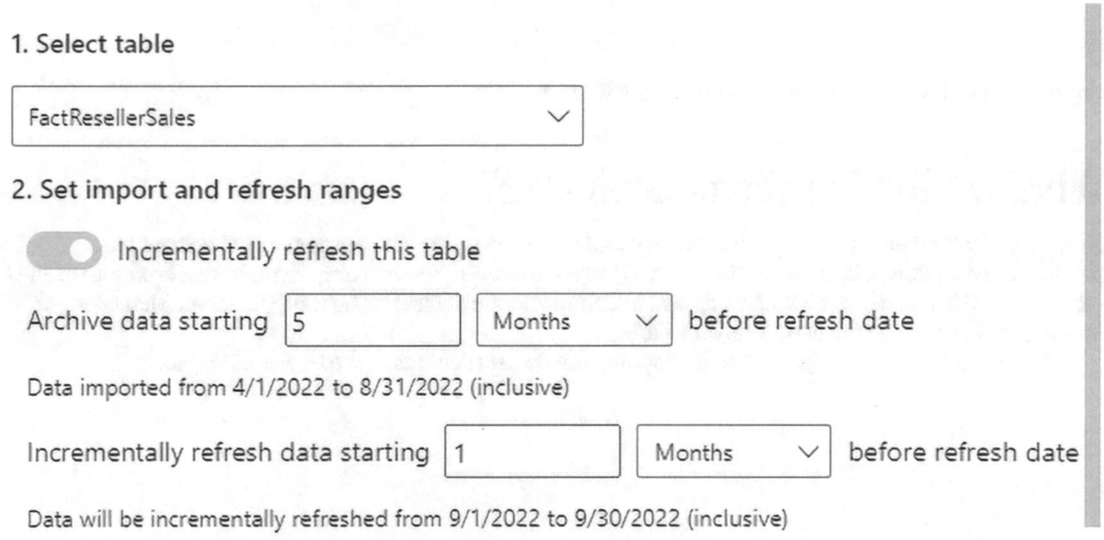

1. Select table

FactResellerSales

2. Set import and refresh ranges

⬤   Incrementally refresh this table

Archive data starting   5   Months   before refresh date

Data imported from 4/1/2022 to 8/31/2022 (inclusive)

Incrementally refresh data starting   1   Months   before refresh date

Data will be incrementally refreshed from 9/1/2022 to 9/30/2022 (inclusive)

Figure 18-13. *Configuring Incremental Refresh for each table*

Note that although you are using the same `RangeStart` and `RangeEnd` parameters, the Store and Refresh configurations for the Incremental Refresh can be different for each table.

Publish to Service

After configuring everything, you can publish the Power BI file to the service. Note that if you use hybrid tables, you can only publish to Premium workspaces, as indicated in Figure 18-14.

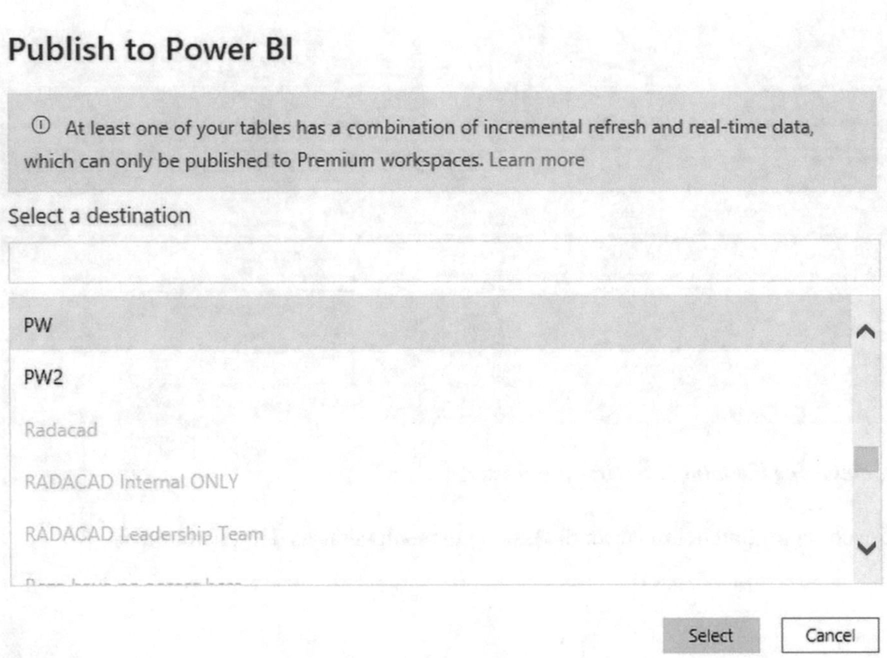

×

Publish to Power BI

ⓘ At least one of your tables has a combination of incremental refresh and real-time data, which can only be published to Premium workspaces. Learn more

Select a destination

PW	∧
PW2	
Radacad	
RADACAD Internal ONLY	
RADACAD Leadership Team	∨

Select   Cancel

Figure 18-14. Hybrid tables require a Premium license

What Do the Partitions Look Like?

Now that you have set up Incremental Refresh and the hybrid table settings, you can check out the partitions in the Power BI dataset. The method I used to show this works only if you have a Premium or PPU workspace. You can use the XMLA endpoint to connect to the dataset using the SQL Server Management Studio (SSMS) and see the partitions on a table.

As Figure 18-15 shows, you begin by opening the dataset settings in the Power BI Service.

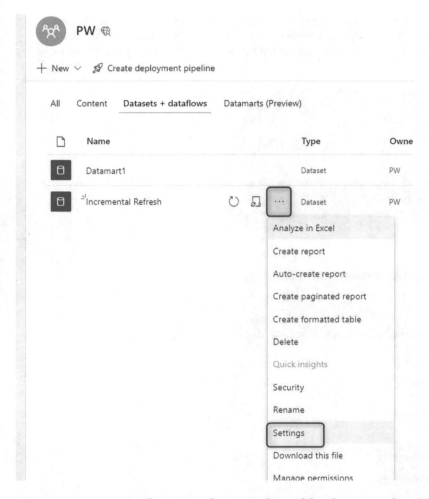

Figure 18-15. Beginning the process of accessing the model and partitions from SSMS

In the Dataset settings, expand Server Settings and copy the connection string (if you don't see this section, your workspace may not be a Premium or PPU workspace). See Figure 18-16.

◢ Server settings

Connection string

powerbi://api.powerbi.com/v1.0,

Copy

Figure 18-16. Copying the connection string

Open SSMS, create a connection to Analysis Services, and paste the connection string as the server name. Then set authentication to Azure Active Directory–Universal with MFA. Finally, use your Power BI email as the username. After authentication, you can see your dataset in the SSMS. Expand the tables, as shown in Figure 18-17.

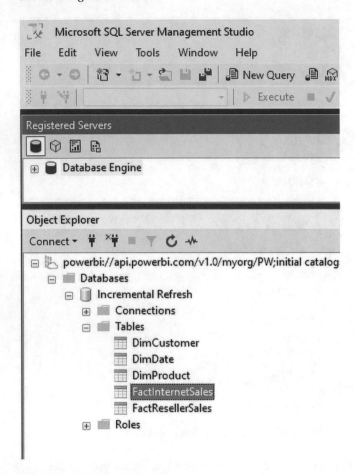

Figure 18-17. *The model is visible in SQL Server Management Studio*

Right-click a table (such as FactInternetSales) and select Partitions (see Figure 18-18).

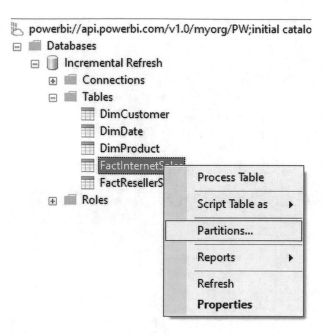

Figure 18-18. *Opening partitions*

You will then be able to see the partitions, which may appear as shown in Figure 18-19.

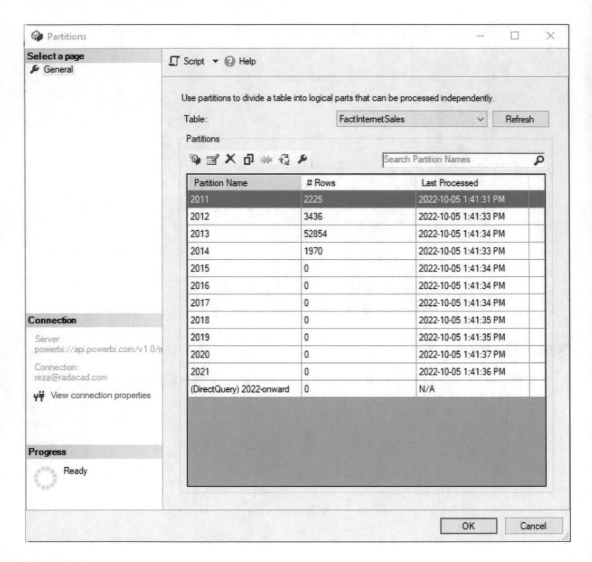

Figure 18-19. *View of the partitions*

If your table has a single partition, perhaps it doesn't have Incremental Refresh set up on it. If your table has hybrid table settings, the last partition will be a DirectQuery partition (which is what you see in Figure 18-19).

Detecting Data Changes

Incremental Refresh makes processing much faster, because it reduces the number of rows being loaded into the dataset. However, there is still one better way to do that. Suppose you have a ModifiedDate (or UpdatedDate) column in your table. In that case, the Incremental Refresh process can monitor that field and only get rows whose date/time is after the last date/time in that field in the previous refresh. To enable this process, you enable Detect Data Changes and then choose the ModifiedDate or UpdatedDate column from the table, as shown in Figure 18-20. Notice that this is different from OrderDate and TransactionDate. Not all tables have a suitable field like this.

Detect data changes Learn more
Only refresh data in the last 1 year if the maximum value of this datetime column changes:
DueDate
OrderDate
ShipDate
h complete year Learn more
Apply all

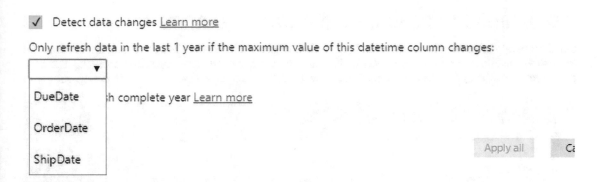

Figure 18-20. *Enabling the Detect Data Changes option*

Only Refresh When Period Is Complete

Depending on the period you selected when you set up the Incremental Refresh, you can choose to just refresh when the period is complete. For example, in the `FactInternetSales` field shown in Figure 18-21, I set the refresh period to Year. Then I can set the option to Only Refresh the Complete Period. Even if it was in February 2019, it would only refresh the data up to December 2018 (because that is the last date that I have a complete year of data for).

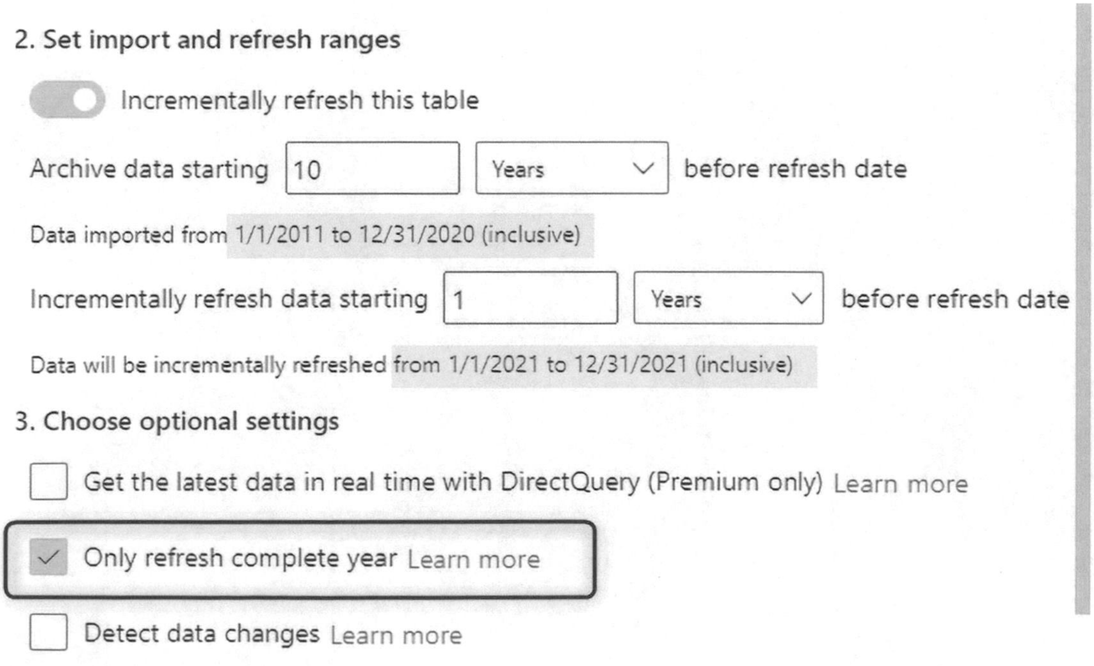

2. Set import and refresh ranges
Incrementally refresh this table
Archive data starting
10
Years
before refresh date
Data imported from 1/1/2011 to 12/31/2020 (inclusive)
Incrementally refresh data starting
1
Years
before refresh date
Data will be incrementally refreshed from 1/1/2021 to 12/31/2021 (inclusive)
3. Choose optional settings
Get the latest data in real time with DirectQuery (Premium only) Learn more
Only refresh complete year Learn more
Detect data changes Learn more

Figure 18-21. *Setting the refresh period*

Incremental Refresh for Dataflows or Datamarts

Recall that dataflows are ETL processes in the cloud for the Power BI Service. You can set up the Incremental Refresh for dataflows, and it is even easier to do. You don't need to create the RangeStart and RangeEnd parameters. You just go to the Incremental dataflow Refresh setting directly, as shown in Figure 18-22.

Figure 18-22. *Setting up Incremental Refresh for dataflows is relatively simple*

You can see in Figure 18-23 that the same Incremental Refresh settings are available for dataflows.

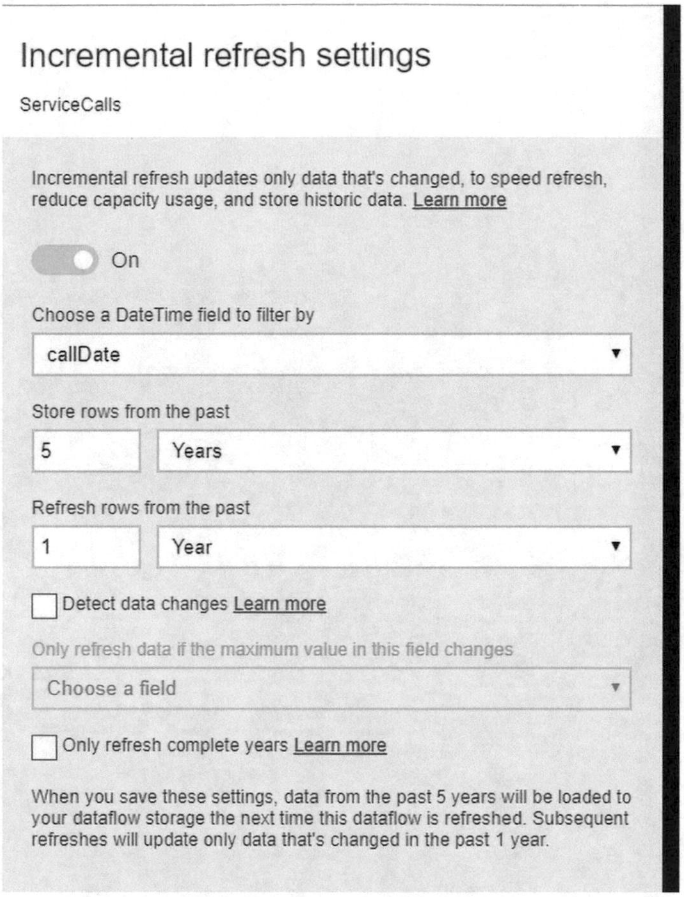

Figure 18-23. *Incremental Refresh settings available for dataflows*

A similar Incremental Refresh setting can be configured for datamarts.

Summary

Setting up Incremental Refresh in Power BI allows you to load only part of the data regularly and store the unchanged data. This process makes your refresh time much faster. However, there are some requirements for it. You must have a date field in your table. It is recommended only when the data source supports query folding. You can do this configuration on a Power BI dataset or in Power BI dataflows and datamarts. If you do this on a dataset, after publishing the dataset, you cannot download the PBIX file.

Hybrid tables can be an addition to your Incremental Refresh setup. They are helpful in accessing the most up-to-date data using the DirectQuery partition while the historical data is stored as Import Data in other partitions. From the Power BI point of view, these are all part of a single table.

CHAPTER 19

■ ■ ■

Development Best Practices

Regardless of your job function (developer, consultant, or architect), following certain practices with Power BI ensures a good quality solution. This chapter explains some of those best practices, including why they are helpful and links for how to use them. These tips are related to developing a Power BI solution, not deploying, publishing, or sharing the solution.

Reuse Tables Generated in Power Query

If you are using Power Query to connect to the data source and transform the data, then it is likely that you will create a table that you may need in another file in the future. If you use Power Query inside the Power BI Desktop for transformation, then reusing the table in other PBIX files will be a challenge. Your only choice would be to copy and paste the codes into the new file. This would create another issue—redundancy of the Power Query code.

The proper way to connect to the data source and reuse data in other Power BI files is to use dataflows. Dataflows run on the cloud, and the data is stored in a destination such as Azure Data Lake Storage or a dataverse. If a table is generated in the Power Query of the dataflow, it can be used easily in multiple Power BI files.

The wrong way to reuse tables: copying and pasting Power Query tables between PBIX files.

The right way to reuse tables: creating Power Query tables in dataflow and getting data from them in PBIX files.

Reuse DAX Calculations

DAX is the language for writing calculations in Power BI. You can use DAX to write calculations such as year-over-year changes and percentages, percentage of the total, or rank of customers by their yearly revenue. Writing calculations in DAX takes time, and you may likely need to reuse a calculation in multiple reports.

Creating copies of the PBIX file every time you need to reuse a calculation is not ideal. The better approach is to create a shared dataset with the DAX calculations and then create thin reports with live connections to that shared Power BI dataset. Using a shared dataset ensures that all the reports use the same DAX calculations. If you need to make a change, it is only necessary in the shared dataset. Maintaining a solution like this is much easier.

The wrong way to reuse DAX calculations: copying and pasting them between PBIX files.

The right way to reuse DAX calculations: creating a shared Power BI dataset and connecting to it live as a Power BI thin report.

Use Power Query Functions for Reusable Data Transformation

There are likely a specific set of data transformation steps for multiple data sources. For example, the Sales data has the same structure for all the branches of a company. Each Sales field is in a different database (or in a different Excel or CSV file). You can develop a set of data transformations and reuse them inside Power Query using custom functions.

Power Query custom functions are reusable pieces of Power Query transformation steps. A function can have input parameters (or it might not have any parameters if it is a generator function) and can generate output. The output of the custom function can then be used in other queries.

Custom functions reduce the need for rewriting a piece of code or transformation. As a result, maintaining that code is easier. If you need to make a change, you only have to do that inside the Power Query custom function. You can reuse the custom function in multiple places inside the Power BI file.

If you use a custom connector, you can include the custom function in it so that you can use that custom function even in multiple PBIX files.

The wrong way: copying and pasting the Power Query transformation between tables.

The right way: creating a Power Query custom function and reusing it in multiple places.

Parametrize the Data Transformation Process Using Power Query Parameters

Your data source might change from one server to another, or the folder that Power BI gets the Excel files from moves to a shared folder on a server, or the email address that Power BI gets data from Exchange might change. In any of these cases, changing the data source from the previous value to the new value is a hassle. You would have to open the Power BI file in the Power BI Desktop, change the data source settings, or even go into Power Query Editor to make such changes.

If you use Power Query parameters where you think the value might change, you can change the parameter value, even outside of Power Query. If your file is already published to the service, then under the Dataset Settings, there is a place where you can change the values of parameters before the next refresh of the Power BI dataset.

Using Power Query parameters enables you to parameterize the values in the data transformation. These can be the data source names, paths, server names, table and column names, and many other values that are likely to change.

The wrong way: using values (such as server names, folder paths, and other values that are likely to change) directly in Power Query.

The right way: creating Power Query parameters for values likely to change and using parameters in Power Query.

Categorize Power Query Using Power Query Groups (or Folders)

Categorize Power Query objects (tables, parameters, functions, lists, records, and so on) in folders. In Power Query, these folders are called *groups*. You can create as many groups as you want. The method by which you create the group is dependent on you. Some prefer creating groups per data source (such as all the tables from SQL Server data source under one folder), and others prefer creating groups per table functions (such as all product tables from all data sources under one folder). Some generic groups, such as final tables (the group that includes all enable-load queries) or temp tables (the group that includes all disable-load queries) are also common.

Be sure to determine your standard for defining groups and use them to categorize your Power Query object structure.

Disable the Load of Temp Tables in Power Query

Power BI loads everything into the memory. If you have a table in Power Query that you are not using directly, but are using it to load data into another table, consider disabling its load. For example, suppose you are building a product table by merging a product category, subcategory, and product details. In that case, you can disable those three tables' loads, especially if the data that you need will be available in the product table at the end.

Disabling the load of a table won't load it into the memory of the Power BI dataset. The table will still be part of the refresh process in Power Query. Disabling the load of temp tables leads to a significant performance improvement in the Power BI model. Adding unnecessary tables to Power BI not only affects performance, but it also makes the model complicated and confusing (you may select the Product ID from a table that is not the primary product table).

Only Load What You Need for Reporting: Filter the Data

If you are loading 20 years of sales transactions just in the hopes that someday, someone will use them in visualization, rethink your approach. It might be better to filter this data for the last few years that you need (such as the last three years) and then create a Power Query parameter to change it if required.

Reducing the amount of data loaded into Power BI leads to a significant performance improvement. Just load the data that you need.

The same rule also applies to tables with hundreds of columns. If you need five columns from a table, don't import the entire table. This is a common mistake when getting data from CRM or ERP systems, where the tables are wide. You can use Power Query to load more columns or tables in the future if needed.

Use Reference and Duplicate in Their Rightful Places

There are two ways to copy a table in Power Query—Duplicate and Reference. Duplicate creates an identical copy of the table without a link to the original table. You can change this new table without any concerns about the main query. Reference keeps the transformation in the primary table, and the new table is a link to the original table. This is used when you want to apply a set of transformations on a currently existing query and still follow the transformations of the primary query. Choosing between Reference and Duplicate is a crucial choice.

Multi-Layer Architecture Everywhere

A best practice when reusing components is to design them in layers. When you have a component in a layer, you can replace it easily, change it easily without needing heavy maintenance, and reuse it easily. Dataflows used for shared Power Query tables or shared datasets for Power BI thin reports are examples of multi-layer architecture.

However, the multi-layer architecture is not just about using dataflows and datasets. Anywhere in your architecture, think of methods that make reusability easier. For example, if the data source is likely to change from SQL Server or Oracle, it might make the change easier if you create a data staging layer using dataflows. The staging layer can then be easily changed without much change needed in the transformations or other layers.

Datasets can be in layers themselves. If you get data from a dataset and apply some changes to it, you've created a chained dataset. This way, you are creating layers of Power BI datasets.

Sync Slicers

If you are using the same slicer across multiple pages, it makes sense to sync slicers. Syncing slicers means that if you change the values of the slicer on one page, you don't have to redo that change on another page. The slicers will be synced.

Syncing slicers can also help when creating a slicer page. This is particularly helpful if the number of fields you want to define a slicer on is too many to be part of a report page. In this case, you can create a single page with all the slicers, then sync it with the other pages and use buttons and bookmarks to go back and forth to the slicer page.

Use a Theme File

Many organizations use company color codes . You may also want to set some predefined styles for font sizes, colors, borders, and other visual effects in your report. It is not good to set these for each page and visual one by one. Maintaining a solution like that wouldn't be easy, and if someone else wants to follow your standards, they would have a hard time doing so.

You can instead create a Power BI theme for your visual standards. A Power BI theme can include colors, fonts, and other generic visual properties you want to synchronize across the pages. The theme can then be stored as a JSON file and be reused for other PBIX files. All you need to do to reuse it is to browse for the theme and apply it.

If you create a theme for a team of developers, it is a good idea to keep the file in a shared folder so that everyone can access and reuse it.

Use a Background Image for Report Pages

In addition to the theme file, it is common to use background images for report pages. You can design a background image with the border, color, header, and footer you want and design sections for visual settings. Then this background image can easily be used in report pages to give them a professional yet consistent look. The report user won't be distracted when moving from one page to another with a different look. Your entire report will look like an application, with a constant look and feel.

Incorporate Conditional Formatting Using DAX, Parameters, and Tables

Visualization is more than just beautiful charts and graphs; it is the art of conveying the right message to the users. The right message can sometimes be passed by color-coding values of a visual like a table or matrix visual. In Power BI, you can use conditional formatting to make some values more visible than others by color coding them.

Conditional formatting can be done by hard-coding values directly into the visual configuration (which is not recommended), or it can be done using DAX measures, parameter tables, and what-if parameters. The latter is a better approach for conditional formatting, because if you do the conditional formatting based on a DAX measure, you can use the same DAX measure in other pages and visuals and have a consistent look across your reports. The color codes can be stored in tables for more straightforward configuration and maintenance too.

Create a Measure Table

Measures can get lost inside a Power BI data model that has many tables. It can sometimes be hard to determine which table you created measures in. If you cannot remember the measure name, you will have to expand each table and scan the measure names gradually. This can be avoided by using a measure table.

A measure table is a blank table (which can be created anywhere—Power Query, data source, DAX, and so on) with no data. The valuable objects in this table are measures. Once you create this table, you can move all the measures in it. This way, you can find the measures all in one place.

You can also use the display folders in addition to the Measure table. Display folders give you folders and subfolders for better categorization.

Create and Use Hierarchies

Suppose you have a product category, subcategory, and product name. You may want to combine these three fields in multiple visuals. Perhaps in some of them, you want to have the ability to drill down in these three levels. Instead of going to each product and dragging and dropping these three fields one by one, you can create a hierarchy of these three fields and reuse that hierarchy in other visuals.

Although you can achieve the same outcome by dragging and dropping the three fields separately, creating the hierarchy will give you consistency across your report and will make it easier to use the fields in other visuals. If you want to use two levels of hierarchy in one visual, you can easily adjust them at the visual level. Hierarchies are part of the data model and they unify field use.

Set Auto Summarization at the Field Level

Numeric fields are automatically aggregated in Power BI unless they are used in a relationship or some other conditions are applied to them. This is very helpful for fact fields, such as Sales and Budget fields. However, If you use a Date table with the Year column numeric, or if you have a parameter table with the Age column on it, you won't want the Year or the Age columns to be automatically summarized when using it in Power BI reports.

It is best to set the auto summarization (or auto aggregation) on each field, based on that field at the model level. That way, when you use the field in visuals, they follow the right summarization. This is a simple configuration to apply, but it helps in future reporting and visualization.

Consider Using a Custom Date Table

Although Power BI comes with a default Date table, for many advanced use cases, you will need extensions of a Date table. If you want to slice and dice data by weekdays and weekends, run holiday data analysis, or investigate many other scenarios, they require a custom Date table.

You can create the custom Date table using Power Query, DAX, or even the data source. If you use Power Query to create a custom Date table, it would be better to do it in a dataflow so that you can reuse it in other files. Once you create the custom Date table, make sure to mark it as a Date table so that the Time Intelligence calculations work correctly. Also disable the Auto-Date/Time option in Power BI.

Design Mobile Reports

Power BI reports are designed for interactivity. The new era of reporting and dashboarding does not rely on offline reporting methods, such as printed papers. Nowadays, using technologies such as Power BI, report users can access live, interactive reports and dashboards from their mobile devices everywhere. This not only reduces the need for printing, but it also helps users contribute to the reports and send feedback to the developers.

Although Power BI reports are mobile-friendly by default, in order to view them in their best mode on a mobile device, the report developer has to design the mobile view of the report and dashboard. This is a simple yet effective process. Report pages can have different configurations and settings for desktop and mobile views (such as different font sizes and layouts).

Creating mobile-friendly views for your reports and dashboards is a big step toward the adoption of Power BI in your organization.

Use Aggregations for Big Tables

If you are working with large tables and the reports are slow because of the enormous amount of rows in tables, you need to consider using aggregations. Aggregations can be done on top of large tables (DirectQuery or Import Data tables). Aggregation is a grouped version of the original table based on just a few columns. This grouped table (aggregated table) is a layer between the visualization and the main table. Because the aggregated table is smaller, querying data from it is faster. If the visualization values can be fetched from the aggregated table, then the aggregated table will be used. Otherwise, the main table will be used. This way, calculations and visualizations are faster. You can have multiple layers of aggregations to support different visualizations.

Defining aggregations on big tables in Power BI is a crucial performance-tuning step in Power BI modeling. Aggregations can also be automatically generated based on field use. The auto-aggregation feature can be enabled as a Power BI Premium functionality.

Use Incremental Refresh and Hybrid Tables When Possible

Loading all the data of a table might take a long time, especially if the table has many rows. Instead of reloading the entire data every time, you can reload only the data that has changed, and the historical data can be loaded once. This process is called Incremental Refresh. Using Incremental Refresh, you can load historical data (let's say for the past ten years) only once and then reload the last period (let's say the last year) every time the dataset refreshes. This process makes the dataset refresh time much faster. This is mainly helpful with the data sources that support query folding because, in that case, instead of reading the many years of data, you only read and transfer one year of data each time.

Hybrid tables can also accompany Incremental Refresh. Hybrid tables store part of their data in real-time using DirectQuery to the source table (usually the most recent period of data) and the remaining data is imported. Hybrid tables are suitable for scenarios where data freshness is also needed in a table with many rows and where Incremental Refresh is already set up.

Design Star-Schema Models

Designing the structure of tables and their relationships is one of the primary tasks of every BI system. A common best practice in designing the table structure is called Star-Schema. In this type of design, tables are categorized into two types—Dimension and Fact tables. Fact tables include the numeric and additive measures and the dimensions, including the descriptive fields that slice and dice the data of the fact table. The relationship between Dimension and Fact tables is one-to-many from the Dimension table to Fact table. There can be multiple dimensions per Fact table, and there can be multiple Fact tables inside the model. The design of Dimension and Fact tables is dependent on the reporting requirements.

Avoid Both-Directional Relationships

A vital performance consideration in a Power BI dataset is avoiding both-directional relationships. The direction of a relationship in Power BI is how the filter propagates between the tables. Sometimes, to get the values of a field from another field in another table, you may feel the need to change the direction of the relationship. However, changing a relationship to both-directional comes at the cost of performance, as well as ambiguity and confusion in the data model.

    A star-schema-designed model usually doesn't need both-directional relationships. However, on rare occasions, if required, it can be evaluated separately, and the solution can be designed without a both-directional relationship. Using DAX functions such as `CrossFilter` inside a measure can also be a remedy for scenarios where the both-directional relationship seems your only recourse. Using the measure instead of changing the direction of the relationship can result in better performance, because that measure might not be used in all the report pages, so the performance reduction may not occur all the time.

Clean Up Your Models

It is a good idea to review your models over time. In the review, you may find fields that are not used anymore and measures and calculations that are created for test purposes and can be removed. Cleaning up your model is a task that can be done over time. Fortunately, many community tools can help you with this process. I use Power BI Helper, which is a free tool for this purpose; it has many other helpful Power BI development features.

PART III

Deployment and Collaboration

CHAPTER 20

■ ■ ■

The Power BI Service

The Power BI toolset comes in many shapes and forms. There is a Power BI Desktop application, a Power BI mobile app, the Power BI Report Server, and the Power BI Service (along with some other applications and components). This chapter explains the Power BI Desktop, Power BI reports, the Power BI Service, and more.

The Power BI Desktop: A Report Authoring Tool

The report authoring experience in Power BI is usually performed in a desktop application called the Power BI Desktop. Note that Microsoft is working hard to create a similar experience of it as a web version. You can install the Power BI Desktop on your machine for free. You don't pay a cent to use it. You don't even need an account. All you need to do is download and install it. Figure 20-1 offers a look at the application in action.

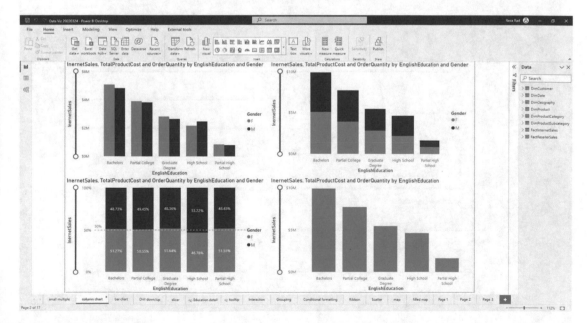

Figure 20-1. *The Power BI Desktop is for authoring and developing reports*

© Reza Rad 2023
R. Rad, *Pro Power BI Architecture*, https://doi.org/10.1007/978-1-4842-9538-0_20

The Power BI Desktop has everything you need to create reports. However, the next step after creating the report is sharing it with others, even if that means just simply showing the results to others. You might also want to make your reports available on other devices, such as your mobile device.

Power BI files created in the Power BI Desktop application can be saved as *.PBIX files and then reopened using the Power BI Desktop application. However, you should not use that method to share the Power BI report with users. That would require them to install the Power BI Desktop on their machines, and there are some problems with that:

- The Power BI Desktop is a report authoring tool. Even if the users can install it, they would have too much power. They could edit and change the report. Then they would come to you to fix their problem.

- Users are meant to use the report everywhere—on their mobile devices, tablets, and so on. The Power BI Desktop cannot be installed on all of these tools.

Hosting Options for Power BI Reports

To share a Power BI report correctly, you must host it somewhere. Then the hosted report can be viewed by users using a web browser or the Power BI mobile application. This is the right way to share reports and would not lead to any of the problems mentioned in the last section.

There are two hosting options for Power BI reports—cloud-based hosting (called the Power BI Service or website) and on-premises hosting (called Power BI Report Server). See Figure 20-2.

Figure 20-2. *The Power BI Service is a cloud-based app that is accessible from all devices*

What Is the Power BI Service?

The Power BI Service (or, as some call it, the Power BI website) is the cloud-based hosting environment for Power BI reports, datasets, dashboards, and more. This cloud-hosting environment is provided by Microsoft and is part of the Microsoft cloud service offering (in Azure and Microsoft 365). You can see the portal in Figure 20-3.

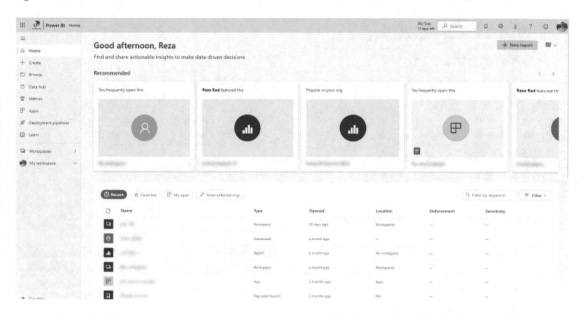

Figure 20-3. *The Power BI Service portal*

In the Power BI Service, organizations are separated using tenants. Tenants can be managed by using the Azure Active Directory portal or the Microsoft 365 portal. Under tenants, there are users. These users are Azure Active Directory users.

You can access the Power BI service at `app.powerbi.com/`.

In addition to users and authentications, there is the concept of workspaces in the Power BI Service. A *workspace* is like a shared folder between a team of users. This can be a place to share some of the Power BI content. There are many ways to share Power BI content that is published to the Power BI service. Figure 20-4 shows just one of those sharing options.

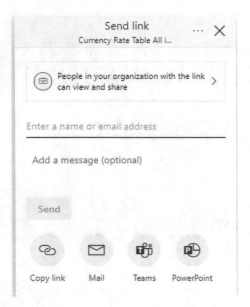

Figure 20-4. *Sharing content in the Power BI Service*

The Power BI Service allows security to be applied at the workspace or object level. There are tenant configurations and settings that can be applied to govern the entire organization's use of Power BI objects.

Publish Reports to the Service

Reports created in the Power BI Desktop can easily be published to the Power BI Service, as shown in Figure 20-5. You can even create objects directly in the Power BI Service, such as dashboards as landing pages for multiple reports.

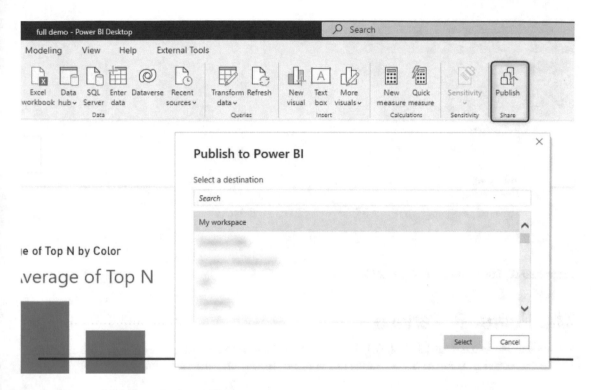

Figure 20-5. *Publishing to the Power BI Service*

Capacity-Based or User-Based

To use the Power BI Service, you must have a Power BI license (see Figure 20-6). There are two types of licenses for Power BI—capacity-based and user-based licensing. Capacity-based licensing is usually better for organizations with hundreds of users or more, and user-based licensing is good for small- to medium-sized businesses. Although, for some of the operations, in addition to the capacity-based licensing, you would also need to get user-based licensing.

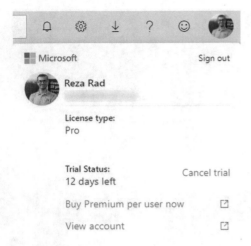

Figure 20-6. *User profile and Power BI licensing*

The Power BI Service

The Power BI Service is not just a place to host reports. It does much more than that. Many of the enterprise features of Power BI were developed for the Power BI Service. Among these are components such as:

- Dataflows

- Shared datasets

- Datamarts

- Metrics

- Data lineage

- Content certification

- Sensitivity labels

- Deployment pipelines

- Workspaces

- Apps

These components and features are Power BI Service-only features. They enable you to better govern Power BI adoption and provide a better architecture for the Power BI implementation. However, to use some of these, you may need premium licensing. In the following sections, some of the most important items are explained.

Template Apps

One of the more useful features available in the Power BI Service are template apps. Template apps are prebuilt Power BI reports and data models. Third parties have created these prebuilt reports. You may need to purchase some of them, but many are free. These templates, some of which are shown in Figure 20-7, enable you to connect to your data source without needing to create the report and get the analysis ready.

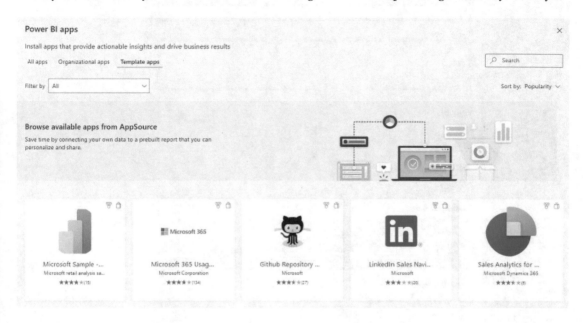

Figure 20-7. *Power BI template apps*

Apps

Delivering the Power BI content to the user can be organized in packages called apps. Each app can contain multiple Power BI reports and other content. As shown in Figure 20-8, the app can be designed with a background color and theme, and you can set the landing page and audience when creating the app.

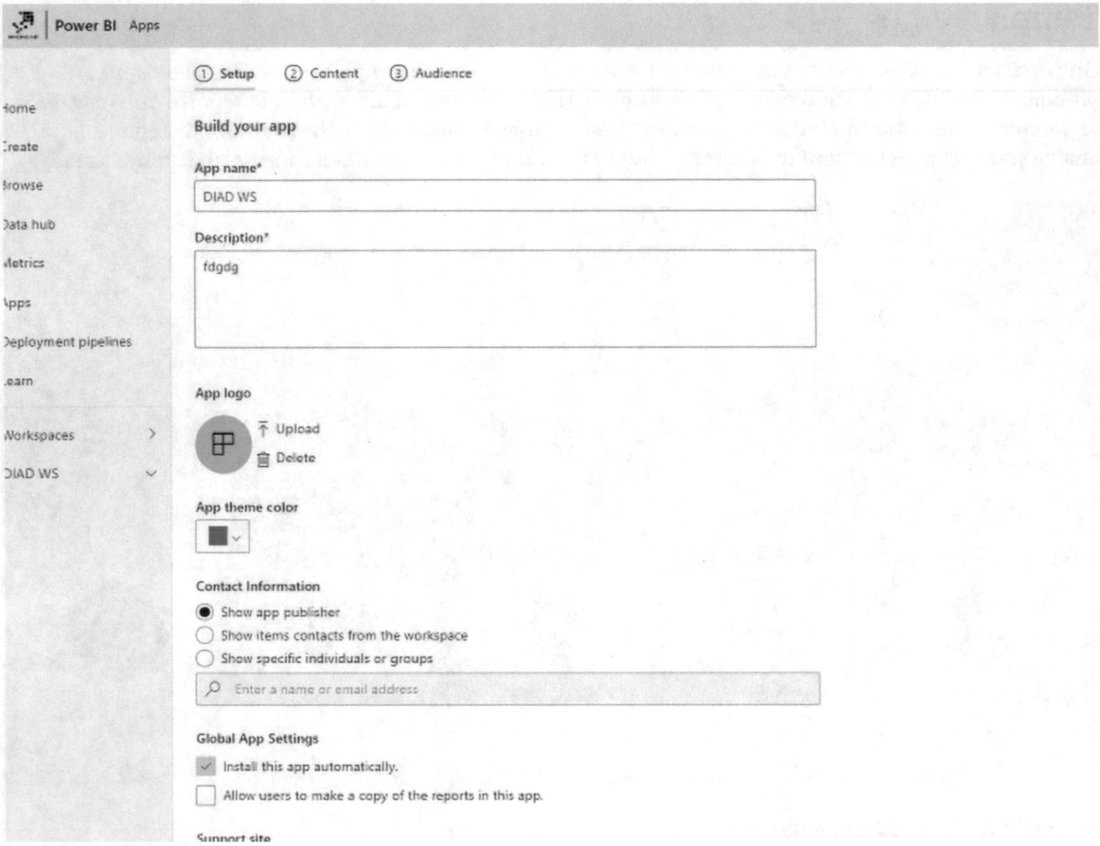

Figure 20-8. A Power BI app

Workspaces

Power BI workspaces are collaborative environments for teams using the Power BI Service. This is where teams can share Power BI content, review and edit each other's work, and deploy the changes to other environments. Each member of a team can have different levels of access in these shared environments, depending on their roles. See Figure 20-9.

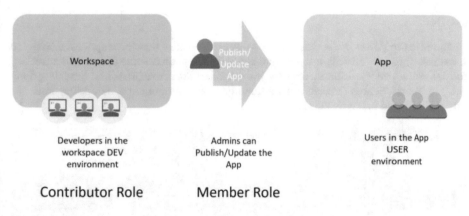

Figure 20-9. *Power BI workspace*

Dataflows

Dataflows are the cloud-based ETL operations that use the Power Query engine. Instead of copying the data transformation between multiple Power BI files, you can use dataflows for shared tables as a central place for data transformation and to store the data. Power BI files can get data from the dataflow. Dataflows play an important role in a multi-layered Power BI architecture, as illustrated in Figure 20-10.

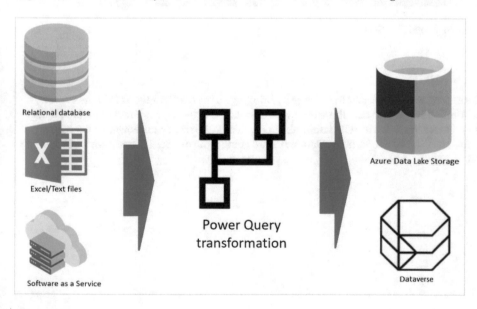

Figure 20-10. *Power BI dataflow*

377

Shared Datasets

Once a dataset is published to the Power BI Service, it can be reused to create a new thin report. A thin report is a report without a dataset, or in other words, a report that connects live to an existing Power BI dataset or other tabular data model. When you use a shared dataset, you can reuse the calculations and modeling done in that dataset in multiple reports. Shared datasets are another important component of a multi-layered Power BI architecture, as illustrated in Figure 20-11.

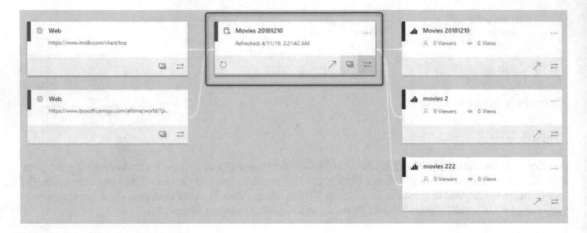

Figure 20-11. *Power BI shared datasets*

Datamarts

Datamarts make modeling Power BI easier to manage by bringing all the configurations into the Power BI Service with one unified editor to create the dataflows and datasets together, as shown in Figure 20-12. Internally, the data is stored in an Azure SQL database, which comes as part of your Power BI licensing. You do not need to license the database separately. Datamarts are going to be the next-generation way to build Power BI data models.

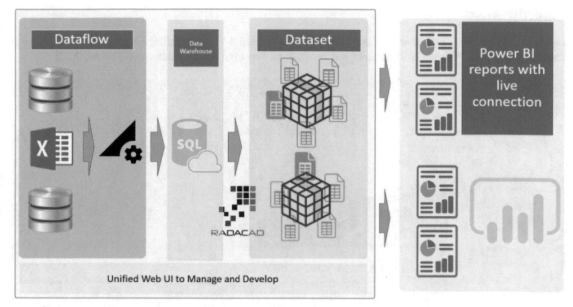

Power BI Solution Architecture using Datamart

Figure 20-12. *A Power BI datamart in the Power BI multi-layered architecture*

Deployment Pipelines

To ensure that users aren't impacted by the changes done by developers immediately, it is essential to separate the development environment from the user environment. In some organizations, there are often three environments with names like Dev, Test, and Production. When you have multiple items in your Dev environment, pushing the changes into the next environment (Test or Production) can be managed easily using deployment pipelines. Deployment pipelines consider your Dev, Test, and Production workspaces and compare the changes between these environments. This process makes deployment easier to control. See Figure 20-13.

Figure 20-13. *Deployment pipelines*

Dashboards

The Power BI Service offers another layer of visualization called the dashboard. Dashboards can be the landing pages for multiple reports or they can be used for real-time visualizations (see Figure 20-14).

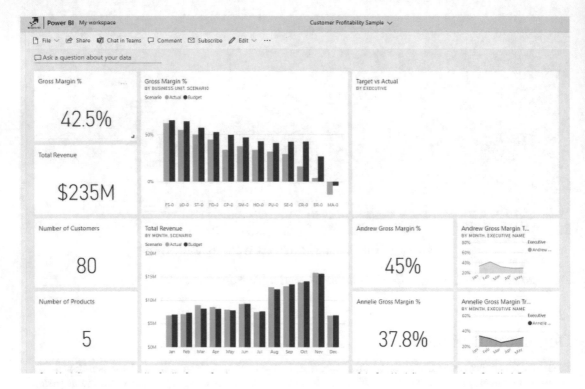

Figure 20-14. *A Power BI dashboard*

Using dashboards is optional; however, they come with additional options such as data alerts and auto-refresh of tiles.

Metrics

Power BI has a comprehensive component for showing KPIs (Key Performance Indicators) and scorecards. This component was previously called Power BI Goals; now it's called Power BI Metrics. A sample metrics landing page is shown in Figure 20-15. Using Power BI Metrics, you can view all aspects of a KPI, such as its values, targets, trends, statuses, and rules that define whether the value is on track or behind. The metric can use a Power BI shared dataset as its source.

Figure 20-15. *Power BI Metrics*

Content Certification

The Power BI Service also offers some data governance settings and configurations. One of these is called *content certification*. Power BI objects such as datasets, dataflows, reports, and apps can be promoted for others to use, and even certified by a certain group in the organization. As shown in Figure 20-16, the Power BI tenant administrator can determine which members can certify the content. This helps in the adoption and usage of content and helps other users find reliable content.

◢ Certification
Enabled for the entire organization

Allow users in this org to certify datasets, dataflows, reports, and apps.

Note: When a user certifies an item, their contact details will be visible along with the certification badge.

◯● Enabled

Specify URL for documentation page

Enter URL

Apply to:
◉ The entire organization
◯ Specific security groups

☐ Except specific security groups

Apply   Cancel

Figure 20-16. *Power BI content certification*

Data Lineage

Because there are many data-related components available in the Power BI Service, it's easy to be confused about where the data is coming from—which dataset and dataflow fetches that data and from which data source. The Power BI Service offers a Data Lineage view, shown in Figure 20-17, that can be used to see these details. The Data Lineage view is still a work in progress and I believe it will be enhanced in the future, as some cases aren't yet supported.

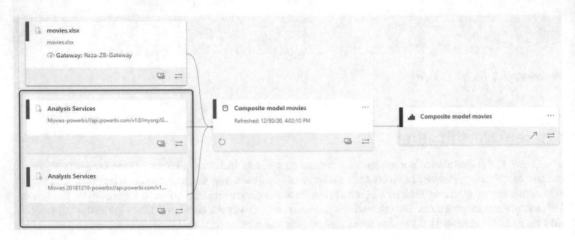

Figure 20-17. *Power BI Data Lineage view*

Summary

The Power BI Service is one of two hosting options for Power BI content. The Power BI Service hosts the Power BI content in the cloud and is used in the majority of cases, instead of the Power BI Report Server (which is the on-premises hosting solution for Power BI content). The Power BI Service comes with all the features and configurations needed for a hosting platform (user access, tenant-level configurations, workspaces, categorizing the content, sharing, and more). It also comes with extra useful features and components. These extra components play an important role in Power BI adoption and implementation. Some of these components are dataflows, shared datasets, datamarts, metrics, dashboards, deployment pipelines, content certification, workspaces, and apps. These extra components and the regular updates to the Power BI Service make it an important part of Power BI adoption in many organizations.

CHAPTER 21

■ ■ ■

The Power BI Report Server

Power BI is not only a cloud-based reporting technology. Due to the demand to have data and reporting solutions on-premises, Power BI also has the option to be deployed on-premises. Power BI on-premises hosting is handled via the Power BI Report Server. This chapter covers using Power BI in a fully on-premises solution with the Power BI Report Server.

This chapter will teach you everything you need to know about the on-premises world of Power BI. You learn how to install the Power BI Report Server, learn all the requirements and configurations for the Power BI Report Server to work correctly, and learn about all the pros and cons of this solution. At the end of this chapter, you will be able to decide if Power BI on-premises is the right choice for you, and if it is, you will be able to set a Power BI on-premises solution up and run it.

What Is the Power BI Report Server?

Power BI reports can be hosted in two environments—cloud-based and on-premises. The cloud-based Power BI hosting is called the Power BI Service. The on-premises option is called the Power BI Report Server.

The Power BI Report Server is a specific edition of SQL Server Reporting Services that can host Power BI reports. To run Power BI Report Server, you don't need an SQL Server installation disk; the Report Server comes with its own setup files. You can download the setup files, which is explained in the next section. The Power BI Report Server can host Power BI Reports and Reporting Services (SSRS) Reports, also called *paginated reports*.

With the Power BI Report Server, there will be an instance of the Power BI Desktop installation. The Power BI Desktop edition that comes with the Report Server is used to create Power BI reports. Otherwise, reports cannot be hosted on the report server. The good news is that the Power BI Desktop Report Server edition is regularly updated, and its experience will be very similar to the Power BI Desktop.

© Reza Rad 2023
R. Rad, *Pro Power BI Architecture*, https://doi.org/10.1007/978-1-4842-9538-0_21

Requirements for Setting It Up

You need to download the latest edition of the Power BI Report Server from this link, as shown in Figure 21-1:

    https://powerbi.microsoft.com/en-us/report-server/

You will have two installation items—the Power BI Report Server and the Power BI Desktop Report Server edition (which comes in 32-bit and 64-bit versions).

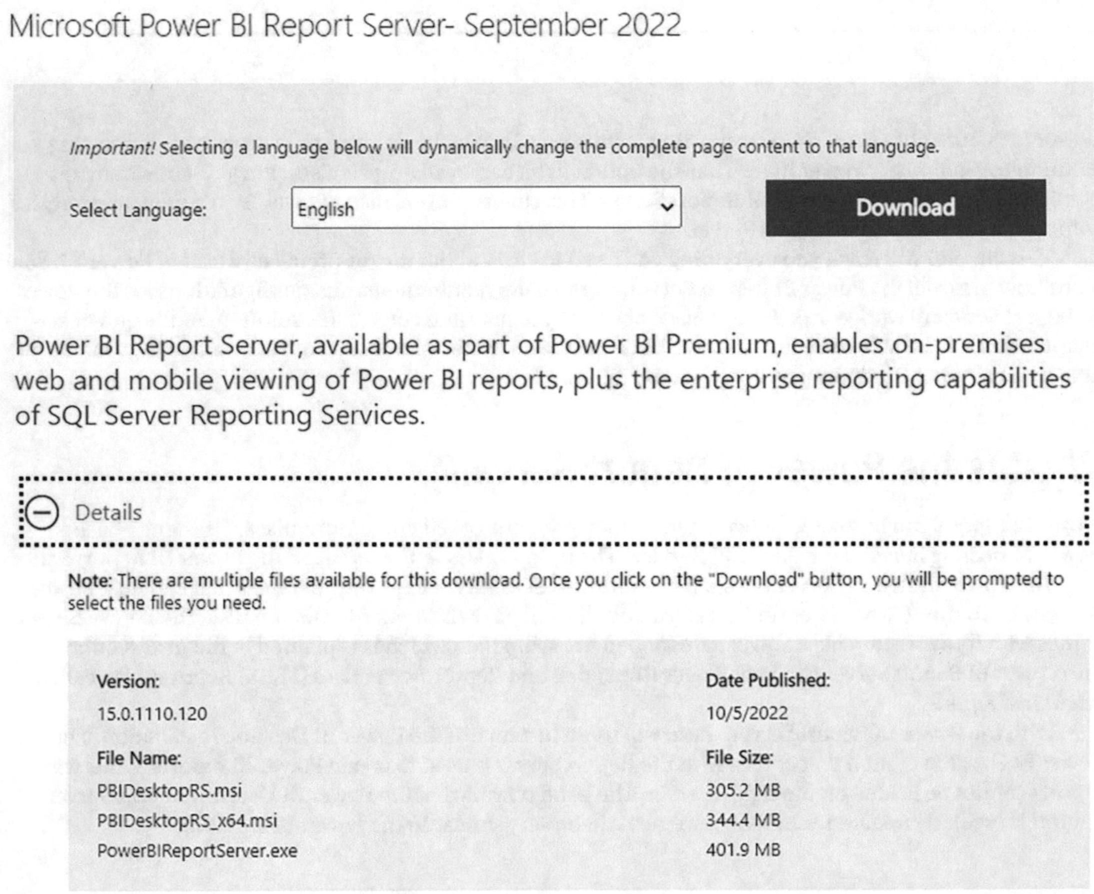

Microsoft Power BI Report Server- September 2022

Important! Selecting a language below will dynamically change the complete page content to that language.

Select Language: English   Download

Power BI Report Server, available as part of Power BI Premium, enables on-premises web and mobile viewing of Power BI reports, plus the enterprise reporting capabilities of SQL Server Reporting Services.

⊖ Details

Note: There are multiple files available for this download. Once you click on the "Download" button, you will be prompted to select the files you need.

Version:	Date Published:
15.0.1110.120	10/5/2022

File Name:	File Size:
PBIDesktopRS.msi	305.2 MB
PBIDesktopRS_x64.msi	344.4 MB
PowerBIReportServer.exe	401.9 MB

Figure 21-1. *Downloading the Power BI Report Server*

Installing the Power BI Report Server

Setting up the Power BI Report Server is simple. You just run the setup file and continue the instructions, as shown in Figure 21-2.

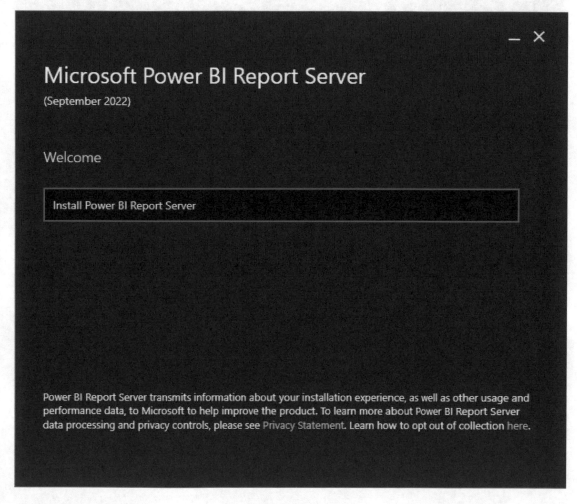

Figure 21-2. *The Power BI Report Server installation process*

As shown in Figure 21-3, you can choose the evaluation edition (valid for six months) or get the licensed version (licensing of the Power BI Report Server is explained later in this chapter).

Figure 21-3. Selecting the edition of the Power BI Report Server to install

Earlier in this chapter, I mentioned that you don't need to install SQL Server to get the Power BI Report Server. However, the SQL Server database engine is needed for the report server to run, as shown in Figure 21-4. If you don't have SQL Server, don't worry; this setup process will install the database engine automatically.

Figure 21-4. *The Power BI Report Server requires an instance of the SQL Server database engine*

The remaining installation steps are straight-forward (see Figure 21-5).

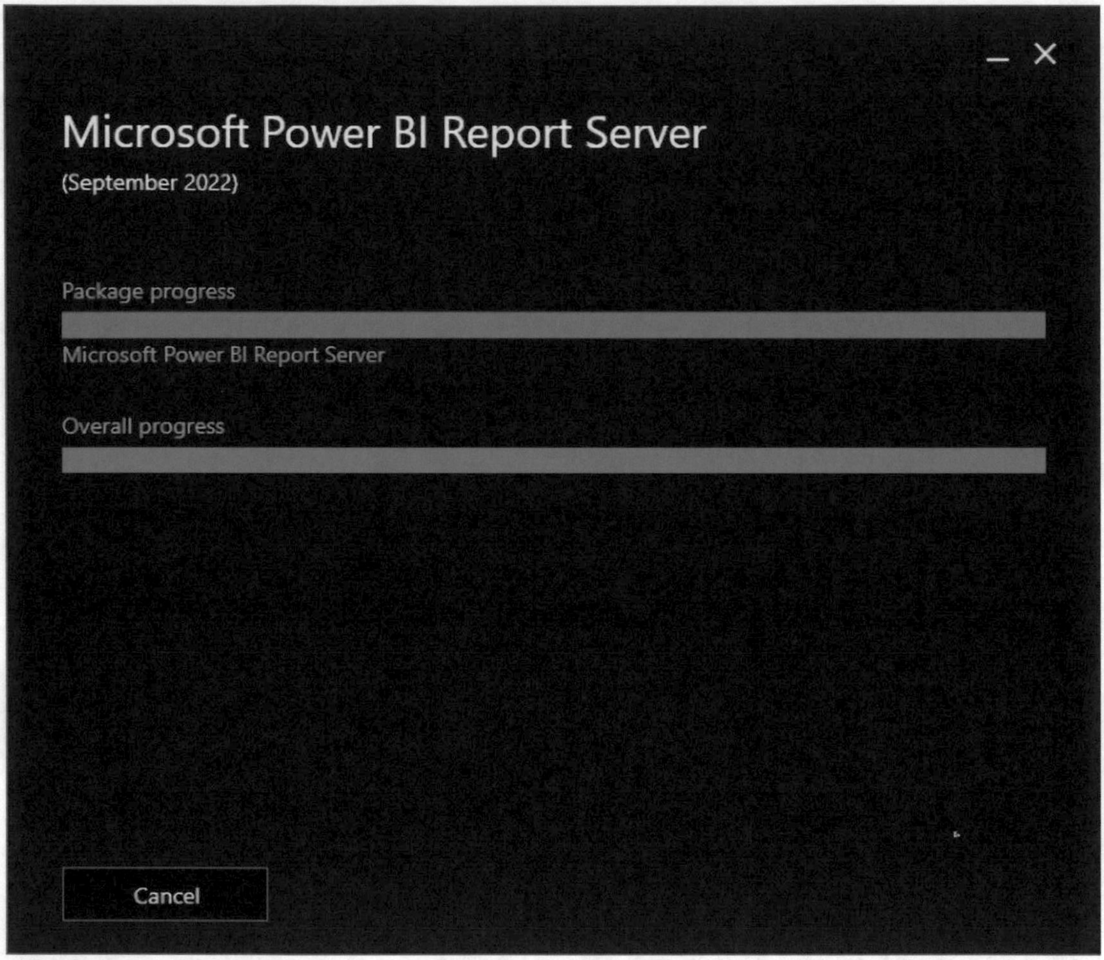

Microsoft Power BI Report Server

(September 2022)

Package progress

Microsoft Power BI Report Server

Overall progress

Cancel

Figure 21-5. The installation process of the Power BI Report Server

After completing the setup, you can open the configuration section by clicking Configure Report Server, as highlighted in Figure 21-6. The instruction asks you to restart and then go to the Report Server. Both options are fine. If you decide to restart your server, then after the restart, choose Start ➤ Programs ➤ Report Server Configuration Manager.

Figure 21-6. *Configuring Report Server*

Configuring the Power BI Report Server

To configure the Report Server, you need to connect to the server you just installed. As Figure 21-7 shows, the instance name of this server is PBIRS.

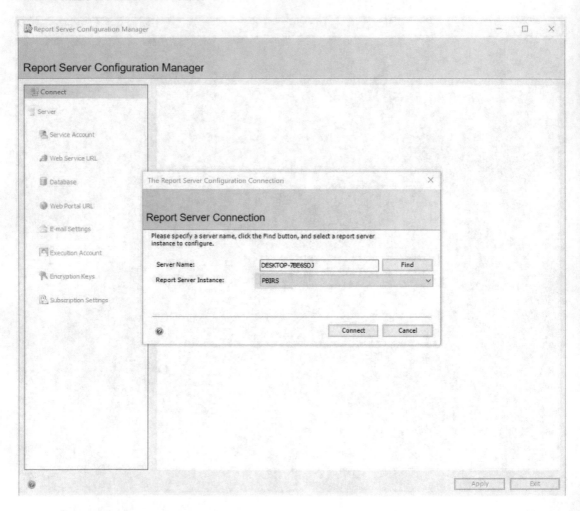

Figure 21-7. *Connecting to the Report Server*

After connecting to the server, it is time to configure it. The first step is to configure databases. To configure the database, click Database on the left side and then choose Change Database, as indicated in Figure 21-8.

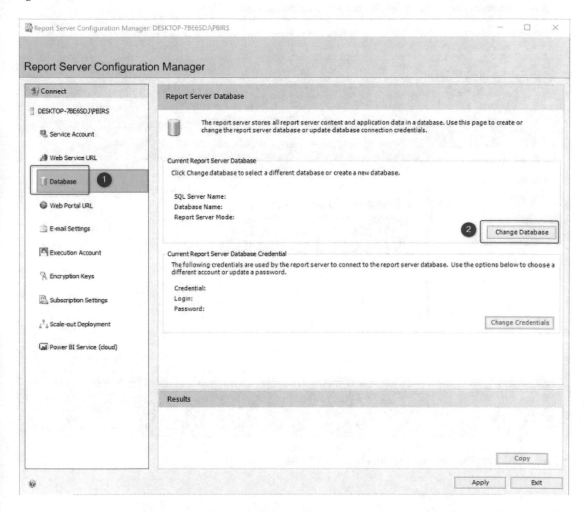

Figure 21-8. *Setting up the database for the Report Server*

Database Set Up

You can create databases for the Report Server using the Change Database wizard. As shown in Figure 21-9, select the option to Create a New Report Server Database and then click Next.

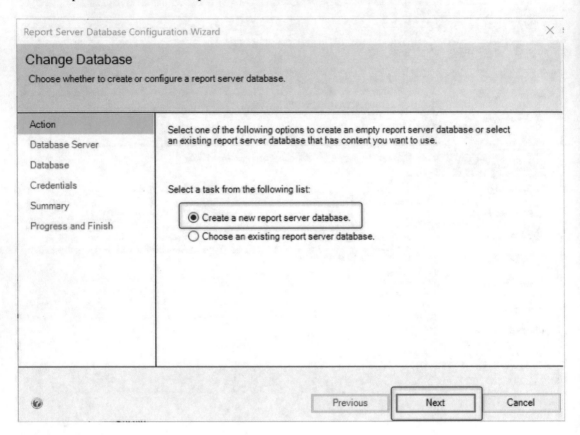

Figure 21-9. Creating the database for the Report Server

In the next step, you need to connect to the SQL Server database instance where the Report Server databases will be created. If you have only one local instance of the SQL Server database, you can connect to it with a single dot (a single dot indicates the local database server). If you have multiple instances, you should enter the database server and the username and password. You can also test the connection afterwards to make sure everything is correct. Figure 21-10 shows this alternate process.

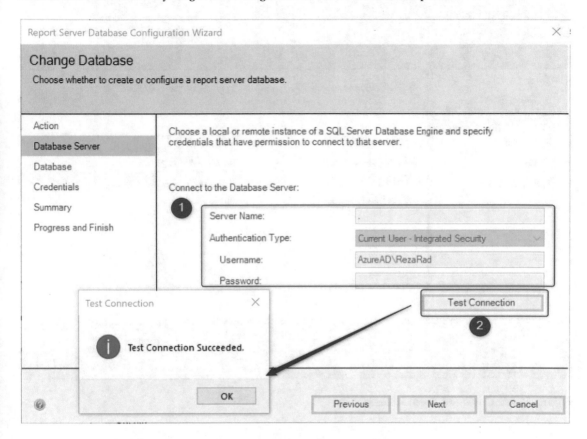

Figure 21-10. The database is successfully created and tested

In the next step, choose the database name (the default is ReportServer) and continue, as shown in Figure 21-11.

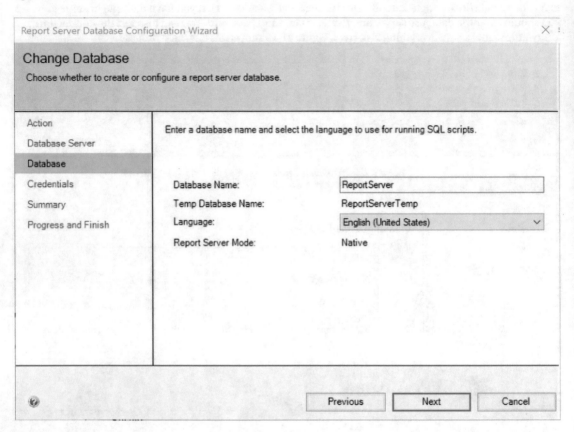

Figure 21-11. *Creating a temp database*

There will always be a second database called the Temp database; you don't need to configure anything about it. Continue with the wizard. In the next step, set the credentials and continue, as indicated in Figure 21-12.

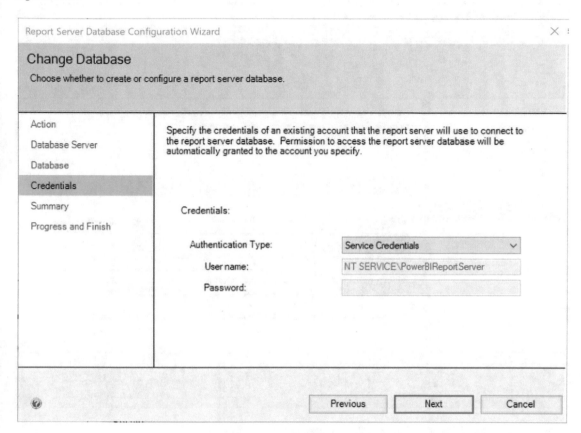

Figure 21-12. *Credentials to connect to the database server*

After confirming things in the Summary step, the setup will continue and finish. Figure 21-13 shows that the database has been successfully set up.

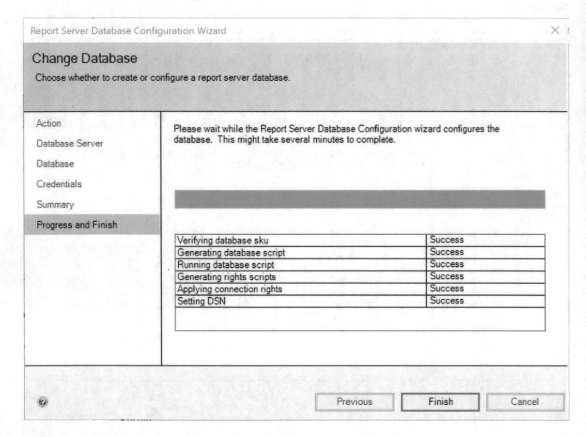

Figure 21-13. *Database setup has completed successfully*

Click Finish. The database setup is done now; the next step is to set up the URLs.

Web URL Set Up

The Report Server needs web portals, and you need to set up the URLs for it, for the web service, and for the web portal.

Web Service Set Up

To create the web service, click the Web Service URL on the left side, as shown in Figure 21-14.

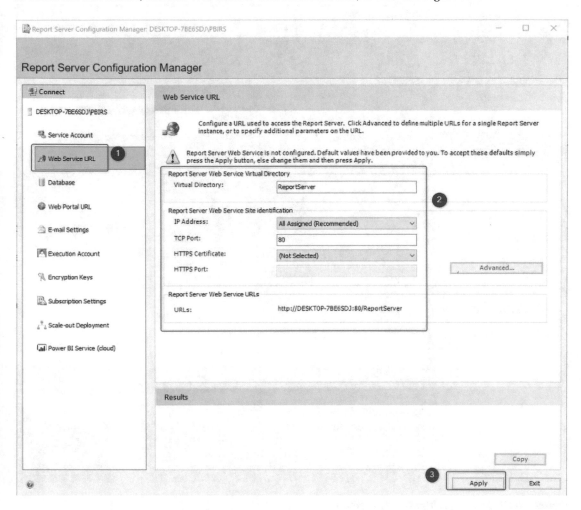

Figure 21-14. *Getting started with Report Server configuration*

You can set up configurations such as the address of the server, the port that this web service will run, and other configurations. If you choose a basic setup, you don't need to change anything here; simply click Apply.

Changing the configuration is only required when you want to set it up on a different port or server with a specific configuration. If you want to do that, it is best to consult with your web admin.

After successfully completing this step, you should see messages and an URL that you can click to open the Report Server's web service, as shown in Figure 21-15.

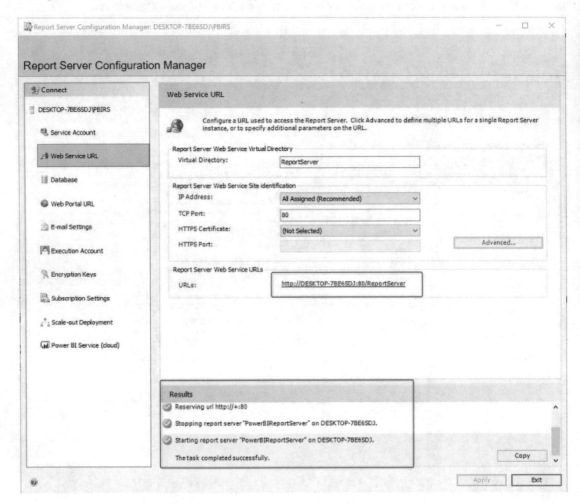

Figure 21-15. *Successful Report Service setup*

If you click the URL, you should see that the web service's page up and running without any issues or errors. It will look similar to Figure 21-16.

Figure 21-16. *The Power BI web service page preview*

On the Report Server's page, you won't see anything except the version of the Report Server and its name. Later, when you upload Power BI files, you'll be able to see the content.

Web Portal Set Up

To set up the web portal, click the Web Portal URL on the left side. You can do some configuration if you want for the service, and then click Apply, as outlined in Figure 21-17.

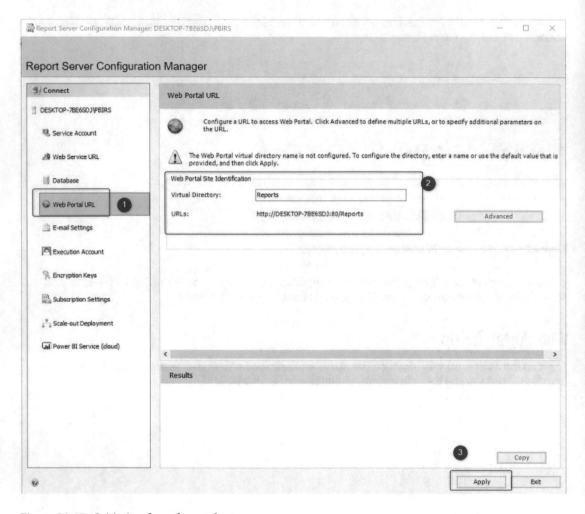

Figure 21-17. *Initiating the web portal setup process*

Similar to the web server setup process, if you want to do the advanced setup, consult with your web admin.

If the setup finishes successfully, you see the success message, and you can click the web portal URL, highlighted in Figure 21-18, to open it in a browser window.

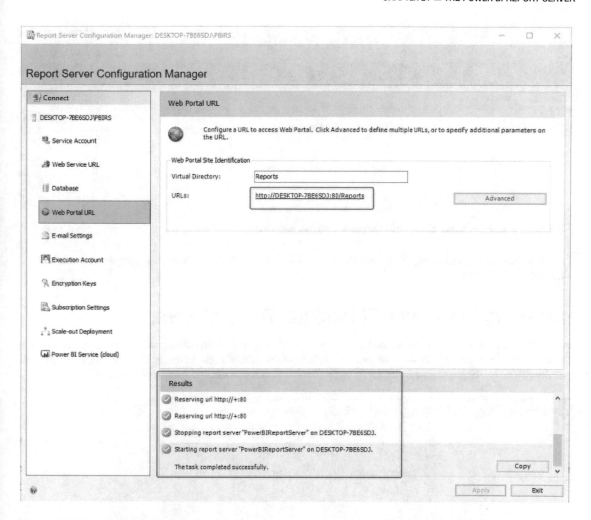

Figure 21-18. *Successful web portal setup*

The web portal should show you the environment of the Power BI Report Server's admin view. As you can tell from Figure 21-19, there is no content on the server yet; later in this chapter, you'll learn how to add content.

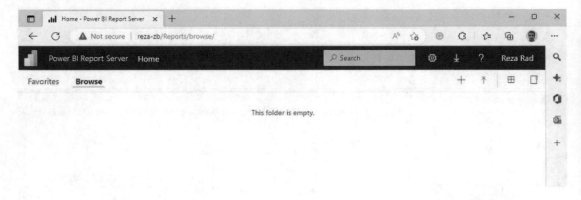

Figure 21-19. *The Power BI Report Server web portal preview*

Installing and configuring the Power BI Report Server is now finished. You can close the Report Server Configuration Manager.

Installing the Power BI Desktop Report Server

Power BI reports that you can host in the Report Server need to be developed with a specific edition of the Power BI Desktop called the Power BI Desktop Report Server. You get this edition of the Power BI Desktop from the same link you download the Report Server from. You'll begin the installation process as shown in Figure 21-20.

Figure 21-20. *Installation of the Power BI Desktop Report Server*

After a successful installation, you can open the Power BI Desktop Report Server. The Power BI Desktop Report Server is similar to the normal Power BI Desktop, with a slight difference, as shown in Figure 21-21.

Figure 21-21. *The Power BI Desktop Report Server*

Developing Reports with the Power BI Report Server

You can start creating a report in the Power BI Desktop Report Server, similar to how you do it in the normal Power BI Desktop. The report development experience in these two editions is very similar. You can even open a report developed with a normal Power BI Desktop in the Power BI Desktop Report Server. A sample report is shown in Figure 21-22.

Figure 21-22. *The Power BI Desktop Report Server*

The Power BI Desktop Report Server is slightly behind the Power BI Desktop. When features are added to the Power BI Desktop, it takes a few months before they are implemented in the Power BI Desktop Report Server (Power BI Desktop updates every month, but the Power BI Desktop Report Server updates every four months). One of the features you will lose in this edition is the Power BI Desktop preview feature. Because the Report Server cannot run the preview features, these items are unavailable here.

You can run the normal Power BI Desktop and the Power BI Desktop Report Server simultaneously on your system. Figure 21-23 illustrates how they differ.

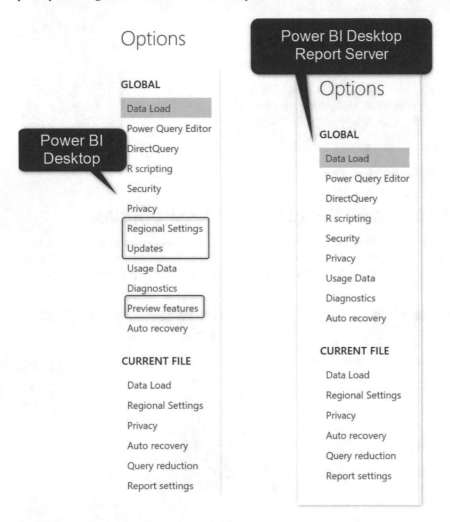

Figure 21-23. *The Power BI Desktop versus the Power BI Desktop Report Server*

Publish Report to the Report Server

There are two ways to publish the Power BI report to the report server. One way is from the Power BI Desktop Report server edition. First, you need to set up the URL to your report server. Go to the File menu and select Power BI Report Server from Open Report, as shown in the Figure 21-24.

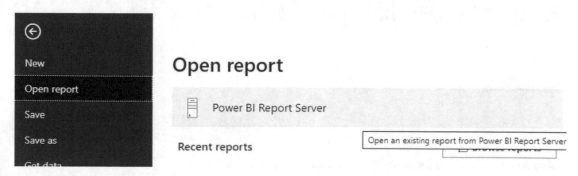

Figure 21-24. *Opening a report from the Power BI Report Server*

In this window, you can connect to a report server. Enter the web portal URL from the step of configuring the report server (see Figure 21-25).

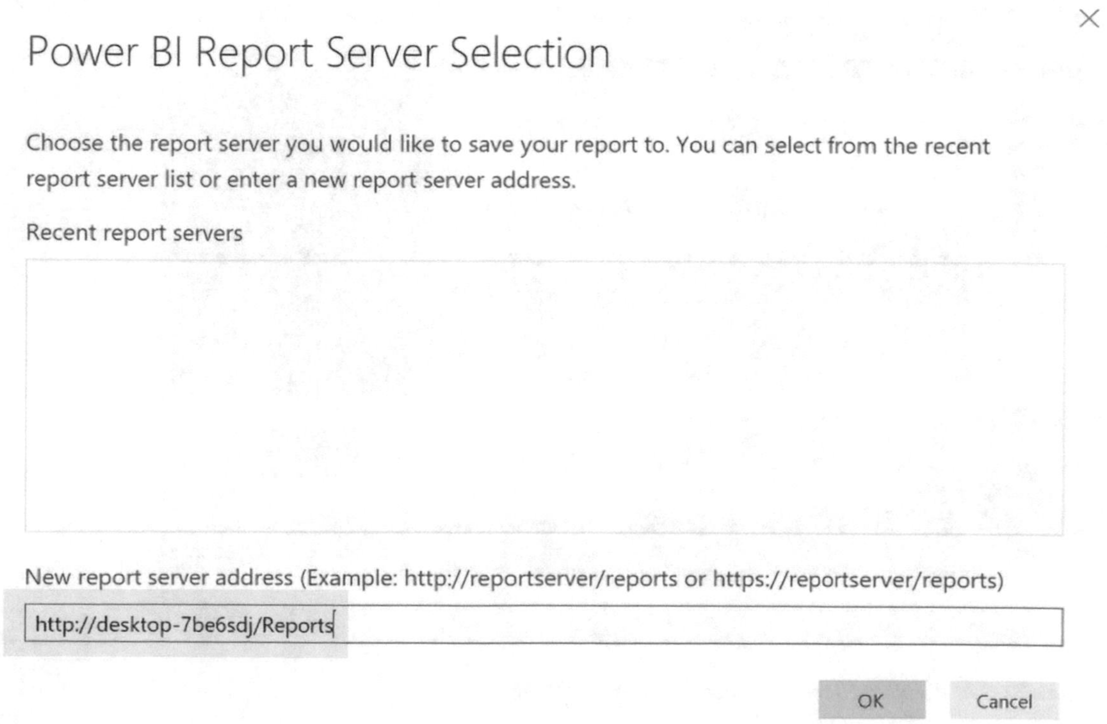

Power BI Report Server Selection   ×

Choose the report server you would like to save your report to. You can select from the recent report server list or enter a new report server address.

Recent report servers

New report server address (Example: http://reportserver/reports or https://reportserver/reports)

http://desktop-7be6sdj/Reports

OK   Cancel

Figure 21-25. *Publishing reports to a report server*

Like the method mentioned in Figure 21-25, you can go to Save As, select Power BI Report Server as your destination, and save your report there.

After successful deployment, you will see a message with a link to the report, previewed in Figure 21-26.

Figure 21-26. *The report was successfully published to the Report Server*

The report hosted on the Power BI Report Server is a fully interactive report like a Power BI report hosted in the service. Figure 21-27 shows a sample report.

Figure 21-27. *A Power BI report hosted in the Power BI Report Server*

The second way to publish a Power BI report to the Report Server is to use the Upload item in the Power BI Report Server; you can use the Upload option from the web portal, as shown in Figure 21-28.

Figure 21-28. *Upload a report using the Report Server's web portal*

Managing Datasets on the Report Server

A Power BI report published to the Report Server can be configured to refresh. To do this, open the Report Server web portal, and as shown in Figure 21-29, click More Info for the Power BI report.

Figure 21-29. *Configuring the Power BI report on the Power BI Report Server*

In the Manage tab of a report, you can configure the data source configuration, the connection to the data source, and schedule a refresh if required (see Figure 21-30).

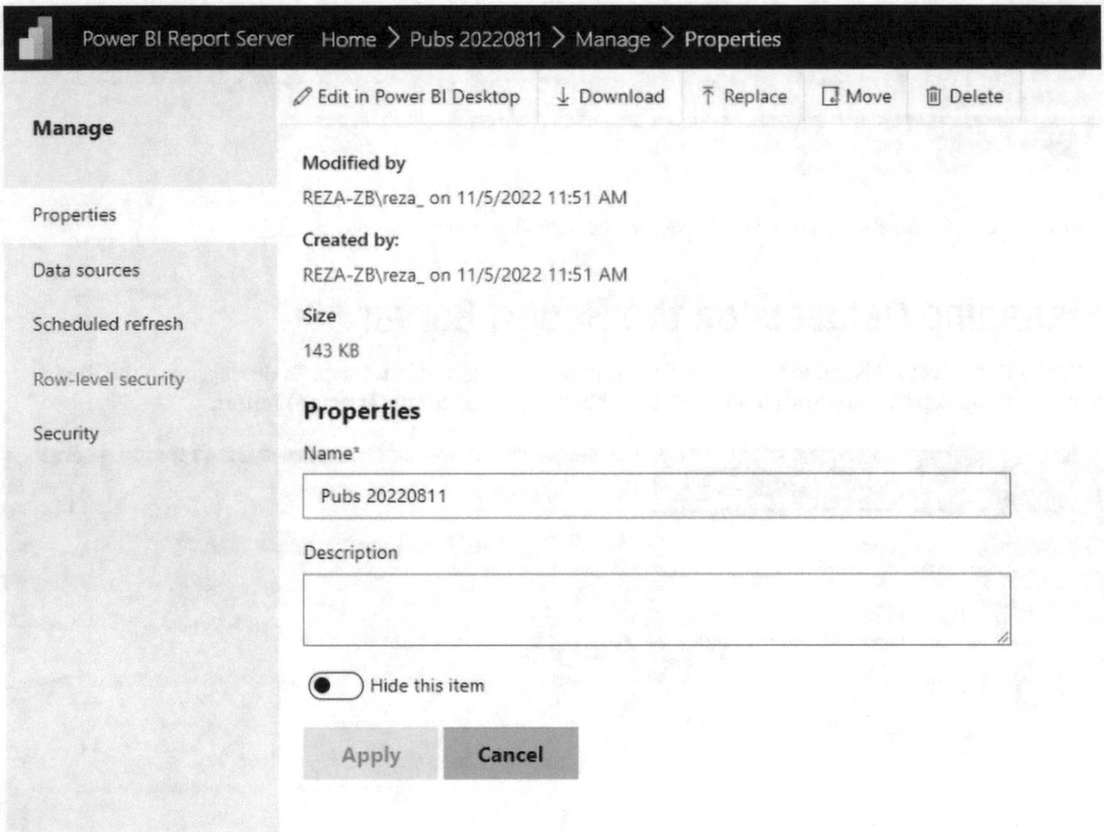

Figure 21-30. *Managing data source configuration*

Schedule Refresh Requirement

If your report is sourced from a file, as shown in the example in Figure 21-31, you may have some requirements to fulfill before you can schedule it for a refresh. You would need to source the file from a network path.

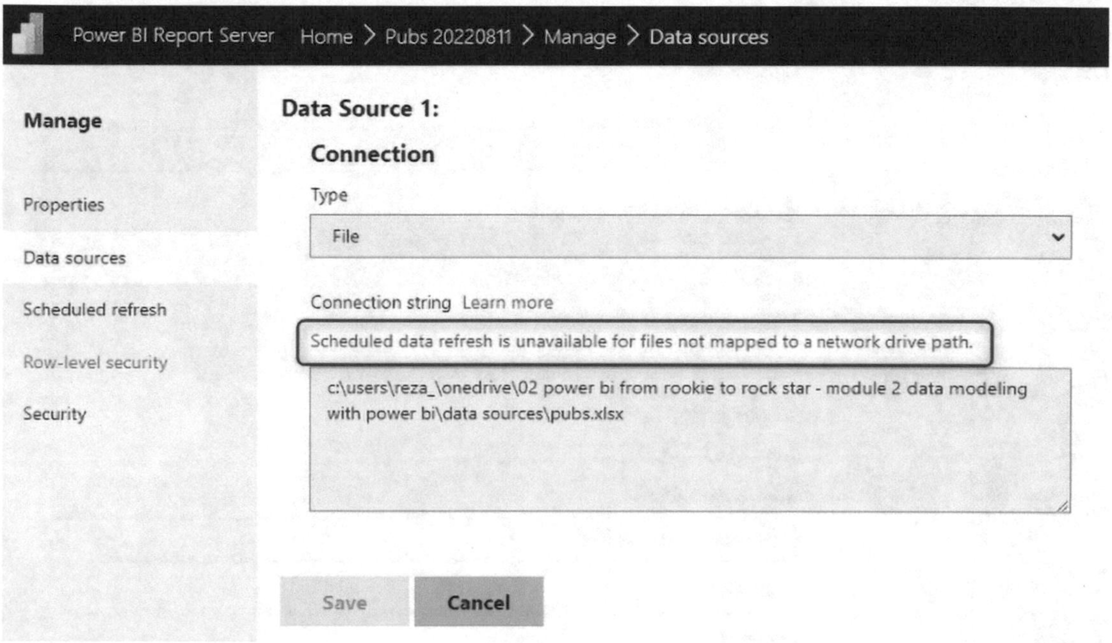

Figure 21-31. Use a network drive path for the file addresses

If you use a network-shared path to access the source file, you can set up the connection to the file, as shown in Figure 21-32.

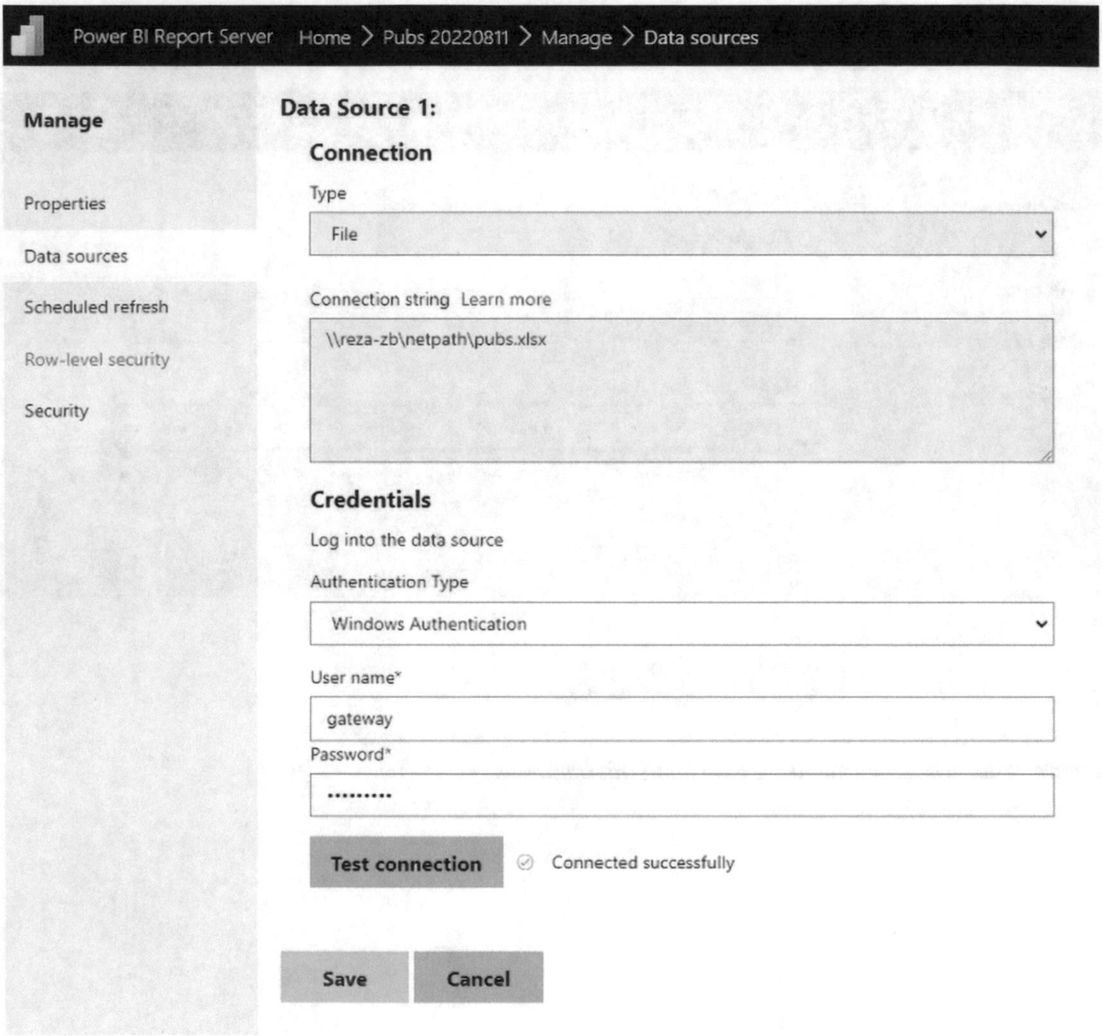

Figure 21-32. *Setting up the data source credentials in the Power BI Report Server*

Make sure to click Save after this step. Otherwise, you won't be able to schedule the refresh process. Then you can click the Scheduled Refresh and create a scheduled refresh plan. See Figure 21-33.

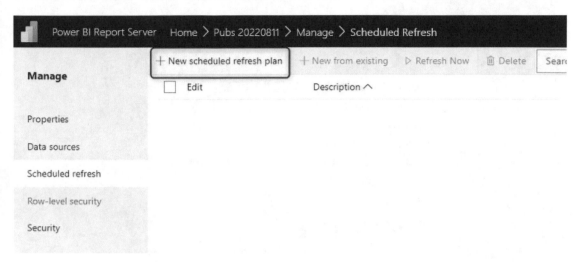

Figure 21-33. *Create a scheduled refresh plan for the Power BI Report*

The Scheduled Refresh feature of the Report Server has many more options than the Power BI Service; you can schedule hourly, daily, weekly, monthly, or any custom period. You can choose the start and end date and many other configurations. Figure 21-34 shows the available options.

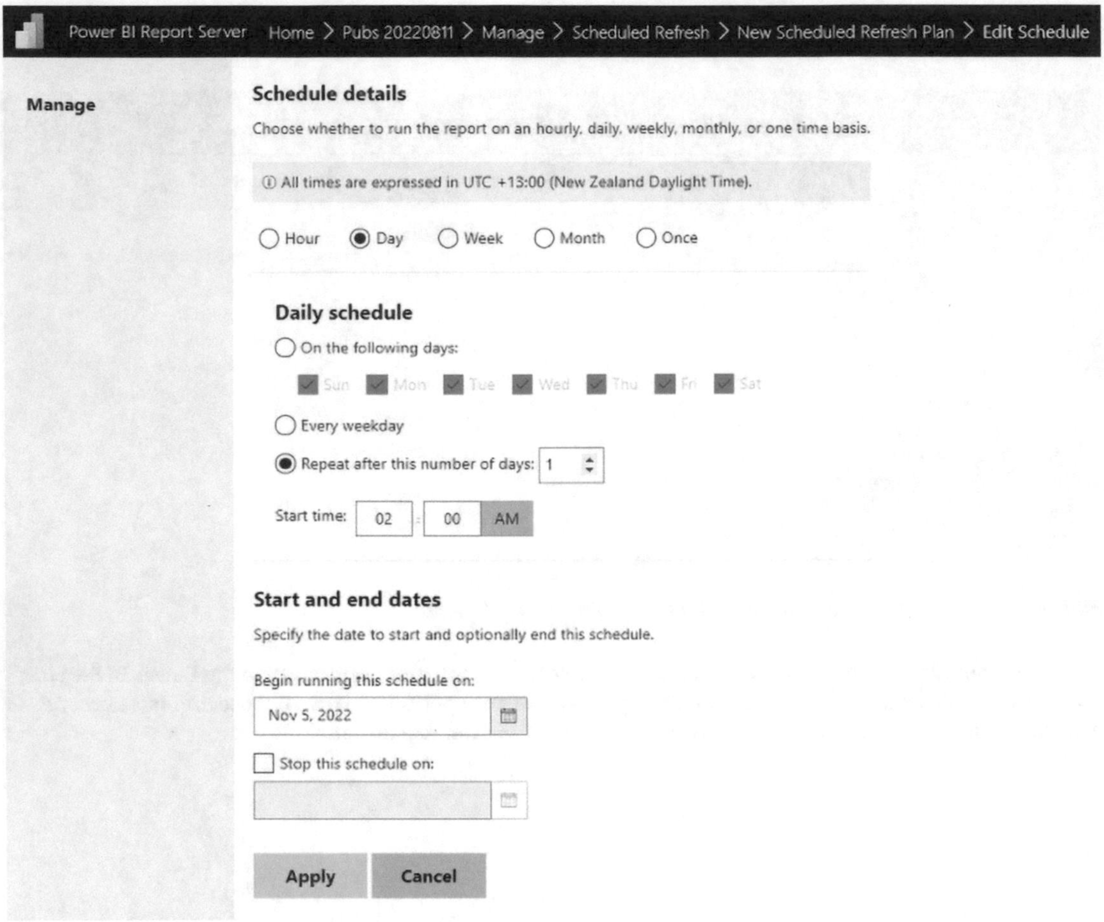

Figure 21-34. *Setting the schedule details for the refresh plan*

For a scheduled refresh plan to be successful, the SQL Server Agent service must be up and running. In the Scheduled Refresh section, you will also see a list of configurations and their status.

Pros and Cons of the Report Server

As you saw, the Report Server environment is similar in some ways (data source settings, scheduled refresh, security, and sharing) to the Power BI Service. The Power BI Report Server comes with advantages and disadvantages.

No Gateway Is Needed

You read that right; you do not need a gateway with the Power BI Report Server. A gateway is only for all connections from the Power BI Service. Gateways are responsible for connecting the dataset from the Power BI Service to the data source on-premises. With the Power BI Report Server, everything is hosted on-premises. You do not need to install or configure a gateway.

412

All Types of Connections Are Supported

With the very early releases of the Power BI Report Server, you could only create a live connection to SQL Server Analysis Services from Power BI reports. Now, you can use any connection (except the composite model). The example you saw earlier in this chapter used Import Data and scheduled the report to refresh. You can also use the DirectQuery connection or Live Connection to the Power BI Report Server.

The Power BI Report Server Is a Fully On-Premises Solution

I wrote the first draft of this chapter while flying on a 17-hour flight, my first leg from New Zealand to the UK, with no Internet connection. All of the examples and screenshots were taken without an Internet connection. The Power BI Report Server is a fully on-premises solution. You will not publish your reports to the Power BI website, and you will not need a cloud-based technology.

The Power BI Report Server is an on-premises technology choice for companies not yet ready to move to cloud-based technologies.

The Power BI Service Features Are Not Available

The Power BI Report Server has many great features. However, it also has some drawbacks. One of the main drawbacks of the Power BI Report Server is its isolation from the Power BI Service. You won't get great features of the Power BI website on the Report Server. The website has features such as usage metrics of the report, Power BI apps, Q&A and quick insights, and many others that are not available in the Report Server.

Here is a list of some of the main features that are not included in the Power BI Report Server:

- Analyze in Excel
- Composite model
- Dashboards
- Workspaces
- Apps
- Template apps
- Shared datasets
- Q&A
- Cross-report drill through
- Preview features
- Metrics
- Dataflows
- Datamarts

Licensing the Report Server

The Power BI Report Server comes in two types of licensing—Power BI Premium and SQL Server Enterprise License with Software Assurance.

Summary

The Power BI Report Server is an on-premises reporting technology. With the Power BI Report Server, you can use interactive Power BI reports on on-premises servers. This type of technology is based on SQL Server Reporting Services technology. You will need to set up the Power BI Report Server alongside a specific edition of Power BI Desktop.

There are some pros and cons of the Report Server. With the Power BI Report Server, you can host reports fully on-premises without needing a Power BI website. You do not need a gateway, and all types of connections (Scheduled Refresh, DirectQuery, and Live Connection) are supported (except the composite model). However, the Power BI Report Server doesn't have all the features and functionalities available in the Power BI Service.

The Power BI Report Server needs specific licensing from Power BI Premium or SQL Server Enterprise license with software assurance.

CHAPTER 22

■ ■ ■

Power BI Gateways

Power BI is a data analysis tool that connects to many data sources. Suppose the data source for Power BI is located on-premises. In that case, the connection from the cloud-based Power BI Service to the on-premises data source should be created with an application called a *Gateway*. This chapter explains what a Gateway is, the types of the Gateways, their differences, installing a Gateway, and scheduling a dataset with that Gateway.

What Is a Gateway?

Power BI Gateways connect Power BI cloud-based data analysis technology and the data source on-premises. A Gateway is an application that can be installed on any server in the local domain. The Gateway is responsible for creating the connection and passing data through.

Do You Always Need a Gateway?

You don't need a Gateway in all scenarios, only when the data source is on-premises. For online or cloud-based data sources, no Gateway is required. For example, if you are getting data from CRM online, you don't need a Gateway. However, if you are getting data from a SQL Server database located on your local domain server, you need a Gateway. For Azure SQL DB, you don't need a Gateway. However, a SQL Server database on an Azure Virtual Machine is considered on-premises and needs a Gateway.

Types of Gateways

Power BI Gateways come in two modes—personal mode and standard mode. The difference between these two is not the paid or licensing plan. Both Gateways are free to use. The difference is the way that you want to use the Gateway. Personal mode is mainly used for one-person use, not for a team. On-premises standard Gateway, on the other hand, is a good choice when you want to work in a collaborative environment. Let's look at their differences in detail. In Table 22-1, the on-premises mode is the standard mode of a Power BI on-premises Gateway.

© Reza Rad 2023
R. Rad, *Pro Power BI Architecture*, https://doi.org/10.1007/978-1-4842-9538-0_22

Table 22-1. Personal versus Standard On-Premises Modes

	Personal Mode	On-premises Mode
Target Persona	Business Analyst who wants to set up and use gateway to run his/her reports	BI Admins to set up the gateway for their companies Multiple BI developers to use the gateway for their reports
Usage	Analyst	BI Admin Developer
Connection Type	Import Data or Scheduled Refresh	Import Data or Schedule Refresh Live Connection DirectQuery
Management	Per user data source management	Central data source management
Monitoring/Control	No monitoring/Control	Central Monitoring and Control
Services Supported	Power BI only	Power BI PowerApps Microsoft Flow Azure Logic Apps

Personal Mode

When you install a Gateway in personal mode, you can use it yourself only. You can connect it to local data sources such as SQL Server, Excel, and other data sources. However, the Gateway installed in personal mode only supports one type of connection—Import Data or Scheduled Refresh. This Gateway is only used for Power BI; you cannot use it for other applications.

Because this Gateway is personal, you cannot use it in a team development scenario. Multiple developers cannot leverage this Gateway. You can create reports and connect them to this Gateway and share it with multiple users. However, only one developer can use the Gateway. That is why it is called personal mode.

Installing the personal mode and configuring it is easier than the on-premises Gateway. When you install the Gateway in personal mode, you don't have the configuration option to set data sources. There is no place to configure it after installation. This Gateway uses the same credentials as the person who installed it. This Gateway mode is meant to be used for business analysts with the least hassle to get their reports published and refreshed.

This type of Gateway is usually for one business analyst who wants to publish Power BI reports and schedule them to refresh and share them with users. There are not many configuration options, it's easy to set up, and its single developer features make it a good option for such scenarios.

On-Premises Standard Mode

Power BI's on-premises Gateway recommends the standard mode. This mode of installation supports a multi-developer environment. Multiple developers can use the Gateway. This Gateway type is built for team development; you can have a Gateway administrator. There is a central configuration section for Gateways to add data sources and control them.

On-premises Gateways support not only Power BI but also PowerApps, Azure Logic Apps, and Microsoft Flow, which are other Microsoft cloud-based technologies.

On-premises Gateways also support all types of connections from Power BI. The Import Data or Scheduled Refresh is supported, as well as DirectQuery and Live Connection.

This type of Gateway is for enterprise usage of Power BI or where Power BI needs to be used alongside other applications such as PowerApps. Multiple developers can work with the same Gateway if the administrator authorizes them to do so. More centralized control and monitoring exist for this type of Gateway.

Gateway Execution Flow

Figure 22-1 shows the architecture of this Gateway.

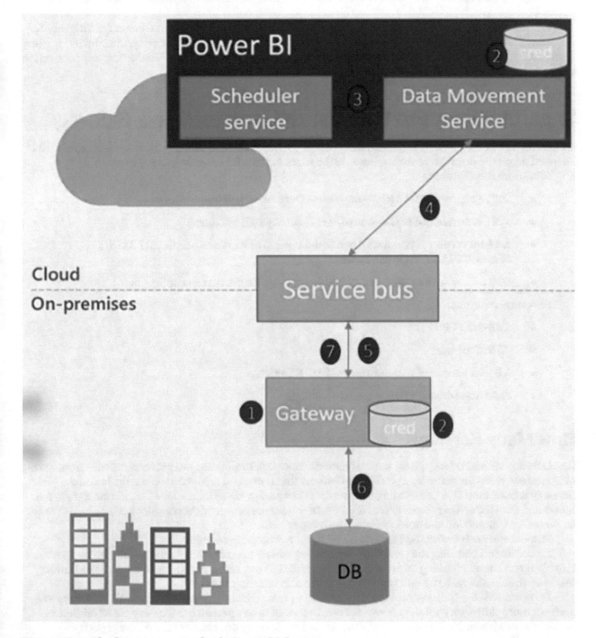

Figure 22-1. *The flow of execution for the Power BI Gateway*

Gateways are installed on a machine in the on-premises domain. During this installation, credentials are stored in local and Power BI Services.

Credentials entered for the data source in Power BI are encrypted and then stored in the cloud. Only the Gateway can decrypt the credentials.

The Power BI Service kicks off a dataset refresh; this happens through a scheduler service in Power BI.

Data movement service analyzes the query and pushes it to the appropriate service bus instance. There is a queue of requests on the service bus. The Gateway pulls the bus for pending requests. The Gateway gets the query and executes it on the data source. After getting the result, the Gateway pushes that back to Power BI.

When the Gateway pulls the bus to check if there are any pending requests, the bus cannot trigger the Gateway. The reason for this architecture is security. If the bus can trigger the Gateway, the inbound security ports need to be open, which is not a good practice for security. So, you can say that the Gateway connection is very secure because it only uses outbound ports.

Important Points to Consider Before Installing a Gateway

A Gateway can be installed on any machine in the on-premises domain. However, it is not recommended to be installed on the domain controller. Here are the requirements for a Gateway installation.

Minimum requirements:

- .NET Framework 4.7.2 (Gateway release December 2020 and earlier)

- .NET Framework 4.8 (Gateway release February 2021 and later)

- A 64-bit version of Windows 8 or a 64-bit version of Windows Server 2012 R2 with current TLS 1.2 and cipher suites

- 4GB disk space for performance monitoring logs (in the default configuration)

Recommendations:

- An 8-core CPU

- 8GB of memory

- A 64-bit version of Windows Server 2012 R2 or later

- Solid-state drive (SSD) storage for spooling

How Many Gateways Are Required?

One Gateway should be enough for many situations. However, sometimes you get more benefits from having more Gateways. As an example, if you have a Gateway that is used for scheduled data refresh, and the same Gateway is used for a Live Connection, then you get slow performance for the Live Connection if there is a scheduled data refresh in process at that time. So, in this scenario, you might consider having one Gateway for your Live Connection and another for a scheduled refresh.

The Gateway can be installed only on 64-bit Windows operating systems.

I recommend choosing the version of the Gateway you need on that machine carefully. If it is a server, I highly recommend installing an on-premises standard Gateway rather than a personal one. The Gateway machine should always be up and running to handle data refresh queries.

Do not install the Gateway on a machine that is connected through a wireless network. Gateways will perform more slowly on a wireless network. Ports that need to be open for the Gateway are all outbound ports: TCP 443 (default), 5671, 5672, and 9350-9354. The Gateway does not require inbound ports.

Installing Gateways

You can download the Power BI Gateway from this link:

powerbi.microsoft.com/en-us/gateway/

Or you can find the link when you log in to the Power BI Service. Under Download, choose Data Gateway, as shown in Figure 22-2.

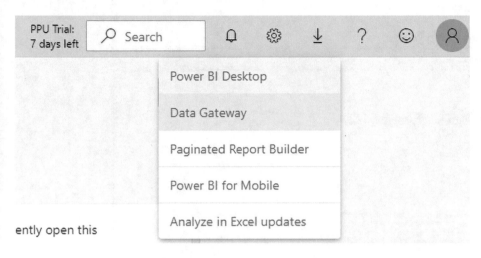

Figure 22-2. *Downloading the Power BI Gateway*

After downloading and running the installation file, you will see the options you can configure.

For this example, you are going to install the on-premises recommended Gateway option because it supports Live Connection and DirectQuery.

After choosing the Gateway type, the installer downloads the files required for installation, and then you can continue the installation. You need to choose a folder to install the Gateway. In this example, you'll use the default. The installation process is simple. After installation, you need to register your Gateway.

To register your Gateway, you need to sign in using your Power BI email account, as shown in Figure 22-3.

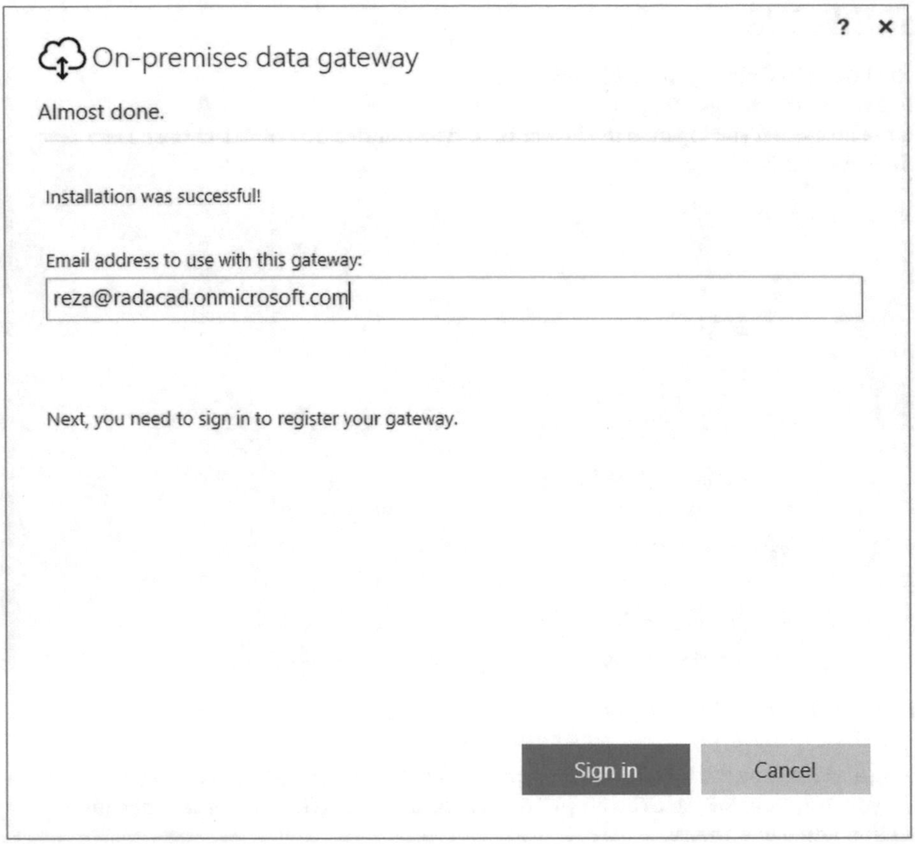

Figure 22-3. Signing in with a Power BI account

You can then register a new Gateway or migrate or restore an existing Gateway. Select Register a New Gateway and continue. You need to enter two important pieces of information:

- **Gateway name:** A name that can remind you where this Gateway is installed. For example, `Reza-Vaio-Gateway`.

- **Recovery key:** This is a very important key required for recovering the Gateway later. If you want to uninstall it and install it again, or if you want to move the Gateway from one machine to another without the hassle of changing all the connections, then keep the Gateway name and recovery key in a safe place.

You can also add the Gateway to an existing Gateway cluster. This option is for having high availability through Gateways. For this example, leave that unchecked, as shown in Figure 22-4.

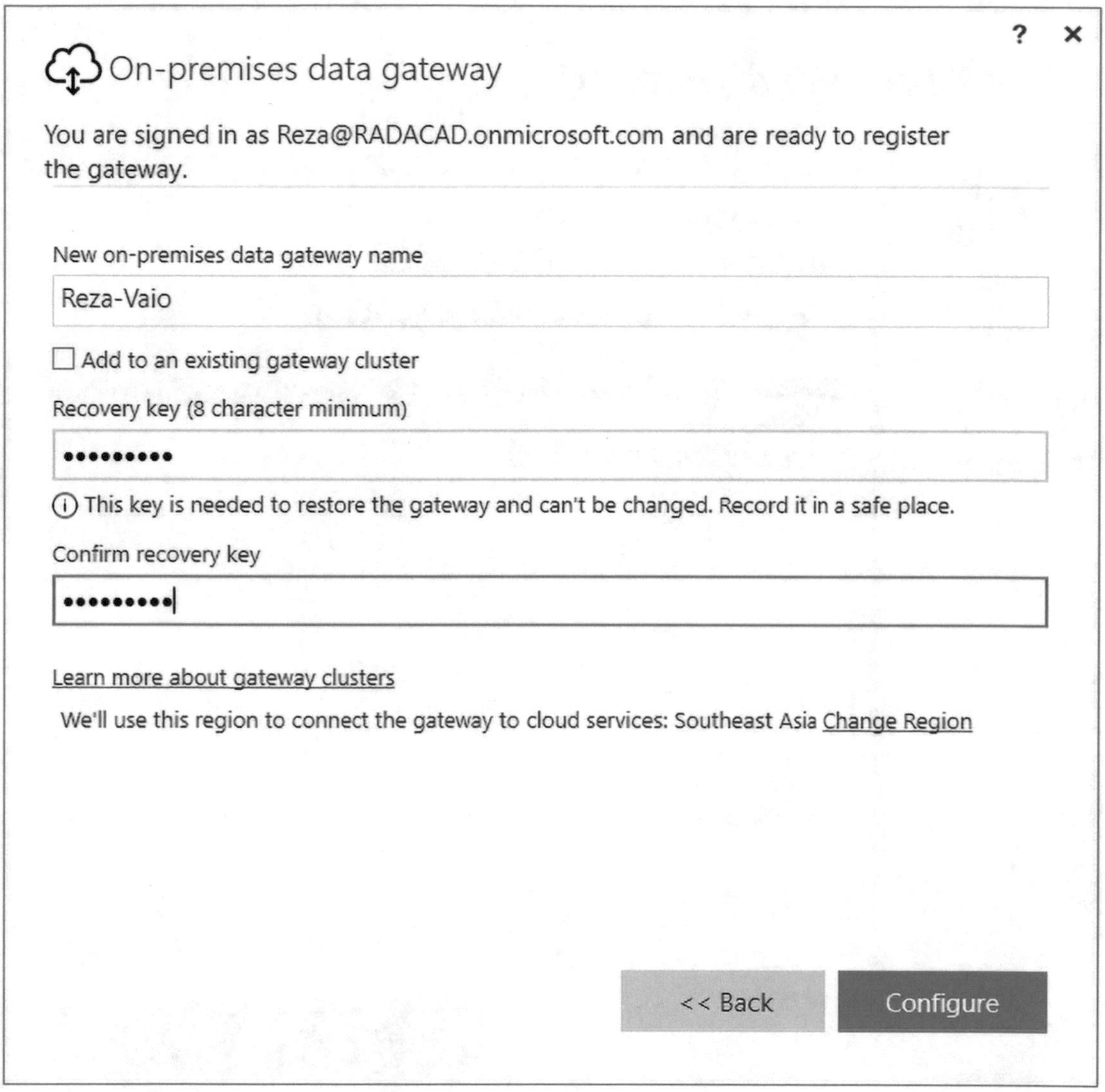

Figure 22-4. *Registering a new Gateway*

After successfully registering your Gateway, you should see a message that says that the Gateway is online and ready to go, as shown in Figure 22-5.

Figure 22-5. *Power BI on-premises Gateway status*

Now you can see the Gateway in the Power BI service under your account as well. In the Power BI Service, click the Setting icon, and then choose Manage Gateways, as shown in Figure 22-6.

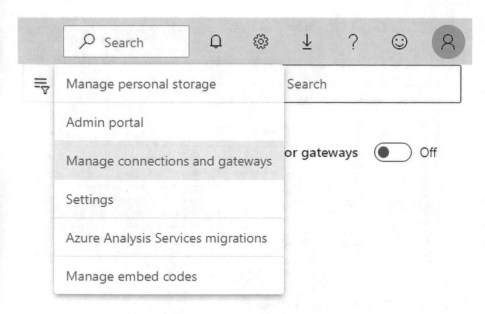

Figure 22-6. *Managing Gateways from the Power BI Service*

You should see all the Gateways set up under your account. In Figure 22-7, you can see that I have a few Gateways in my account.

Figure 22-7. *Managing Gateways in the Power BI Service*

If you are the tenant administrator, you can turn the Tenant Administration for Gateways option on and see and manage all the Gateways under your organization's tenant, even if you are not the direct administrator of that Gateway. This is demonstrated in Figure 22-8.

Figure 22-8. *Seeing all the Power BI Gateways under the tenant*

Adding Data Sources

The Gateway itself is just for creating the connection from the cloud to the local domain. In order for your datasets to refresh through this Gateway, you need to add the data sources. Data sources are connections to every on-premises database, file, folder, and so on, that is used in Power BI as a connection.

To add data sources to the Gateway, you first need to check the Power BI file and see what data sources have been used. One easy way of finding that out is to open the `*.pbix` file in the Power BI Desktop.

After opening the file, choose Edit Queries ➤ Data Source Settings (see Figure 22-9).

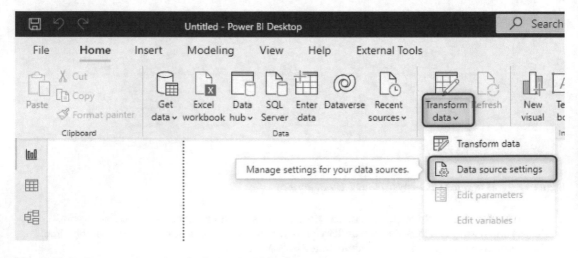

Figure 22-9. *Data source settings in the Power BI Desktop*

In the Data Source Settings area, you will see all the data sources used in the current file. Click every data source, click Change Source, and then copy the path for the file, as demonstrated in Figure 22-10.

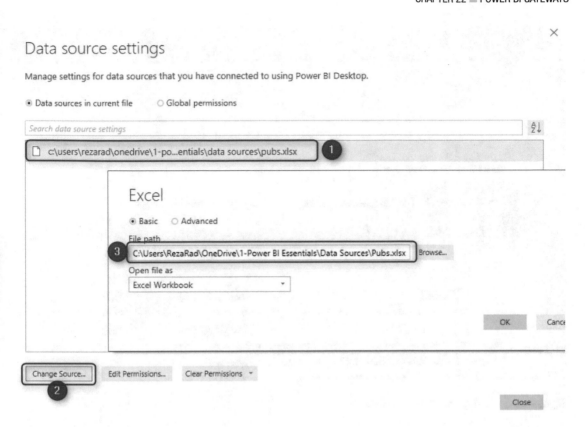

Figure 22-10. *Exploring data source settings*

As demonstrated in Figure 22-11, you can go to the Power BI Service, Manage Gateway section, select the Gateway you installed previously, and then click Add Data Source.

Figure 22-11. *Adding a data source*

In Add Data Source tab, you need to set some options. The name of the data source is only important for remembering it later. The first important option is Data Source Type. In this example, I choose File because my source is an Excel file. However, this can be a SQL Server database or any other data source.

After choosing the data source type, you need to enter other configurations for that source. I used the file, so I need to specify the full path of the file. This path should be the path of the file from the machine where the Gateway is installed. If the file is in a shared folder path, then that path should be accessible from the machine where the Gateway is installed. This should also be the same path used in the data source configuration of the Power BI Desktop.

You need to enter a username and password to access the data source as well. In this case, because I used a file, the username and password should be the local username and password that have access to that data source from the machine where the Gateway is installed. The username should always have a domain name leading it (domain\username), as shown in Figure 22-12.

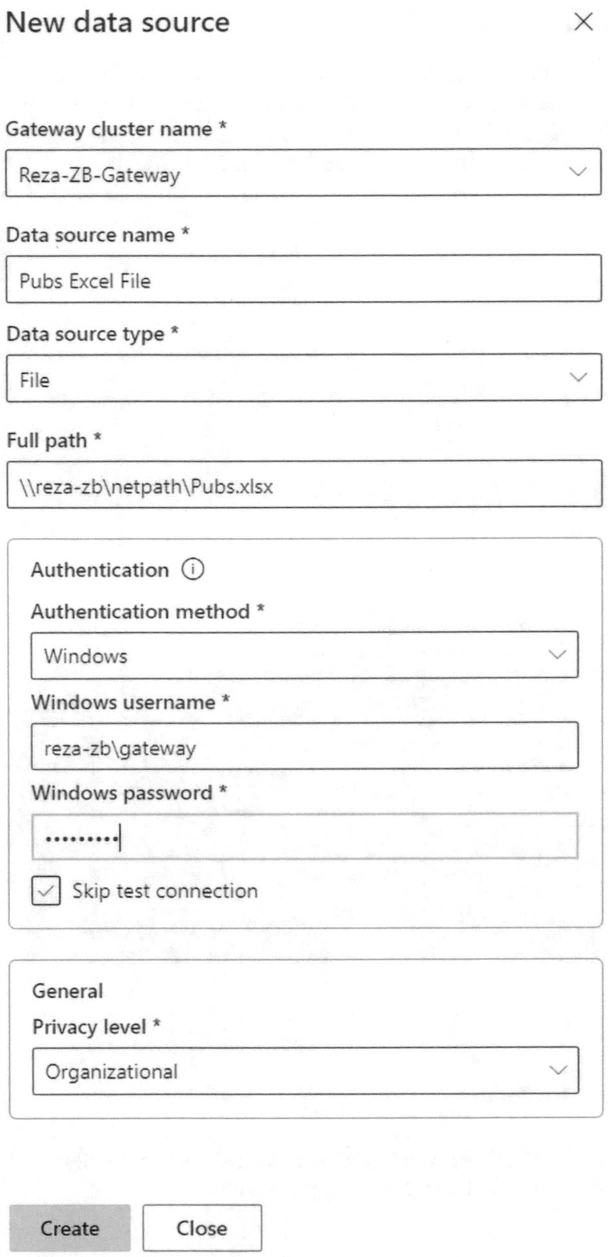

New data source ✕

Gateway cluster name *

Reza-ZB-Gateway ⌄

Data source name *

Pubs Excel File

Data source type *

File ⌄

Full path *

\\reza-zb\netpath\Pubs.xlsx

Authentication ⓘ

Authentication method *

Windows ⌄

Windows username *

reza-zb\gateway

Windows password *

•••••••••|

☑ Skip test connection

General

Privacy level *

Organizational ⌄

Create   Close

Figure 22-12. *Setting up data sources properly*

If everything is set up correctly, you should see a message that says that the connection was successful. *Important note: If you have multiple sources, you must go through this process for every source.*

Set Up a Gateway Connection to the Dataset

After adding the required data sources, you can create the connection through the Gateway. You should select the data source to configure the Power BI Service. You can then set the dataset in the Power BI Service.

Click Gateway Connection. If your Gateway has all the data sources needed for this dataset, you will see it under Use a Data Gateway, and you can select it, then click Apply, as highlighted in Figure 22-13.

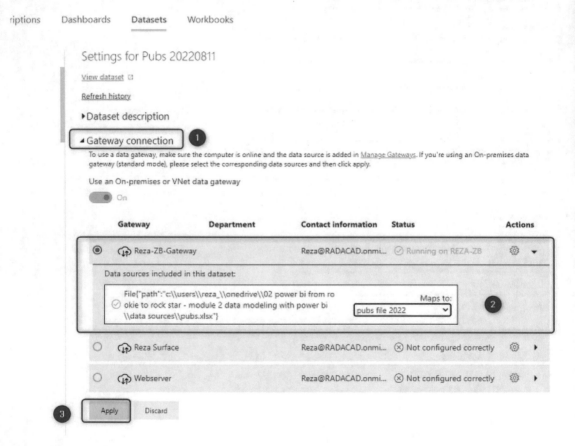

Figure 22-13. *Mapping the Gateway's data source to the dataset*

You have now configured your dataset to refresh through this Gateway. You can test it by manually refreshing your dataset. To manually refresh your dataset, find it in your workspace (see Figure 22-14).

Figure 22-14. *Testing the refresh of the Power BI dataset*

After finding your dataset, click Refresh. The last refresh time should update with no error if everything is set up correctly. Congratulations! You have set up the Gateway for your dataset.

Users and Access Controls for Gateways

There are multiple levels of controls to user access when it comes to Power BI Gateways.

Gateway Installers

By default, anyone in your organization can install a Gateway (they need a Power BI account). However, as the tenant administrator, you can control this by clicking Manage Gateway Installers, as shown in Figure 22-15.

Figure 22-15. *Managing the Gateway installers in the organization*

In Figure 22-16, you can see that when you turn this option on, you can choose the group or people who can install Gateways.

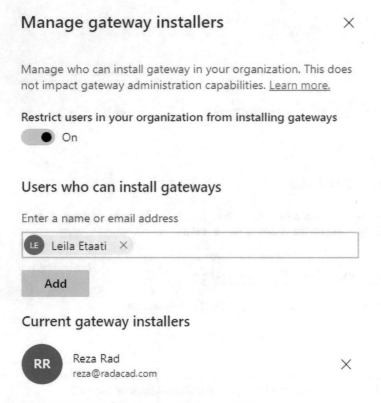

Figure 22-16. *Controlling installing capabilities*

This is good for organizations with many Power BI users, and the control of the installation of the Gateway is better to be governed.

Gateway Users

Each Gateway can have three access types for the users, as shown in Figure 22-17.

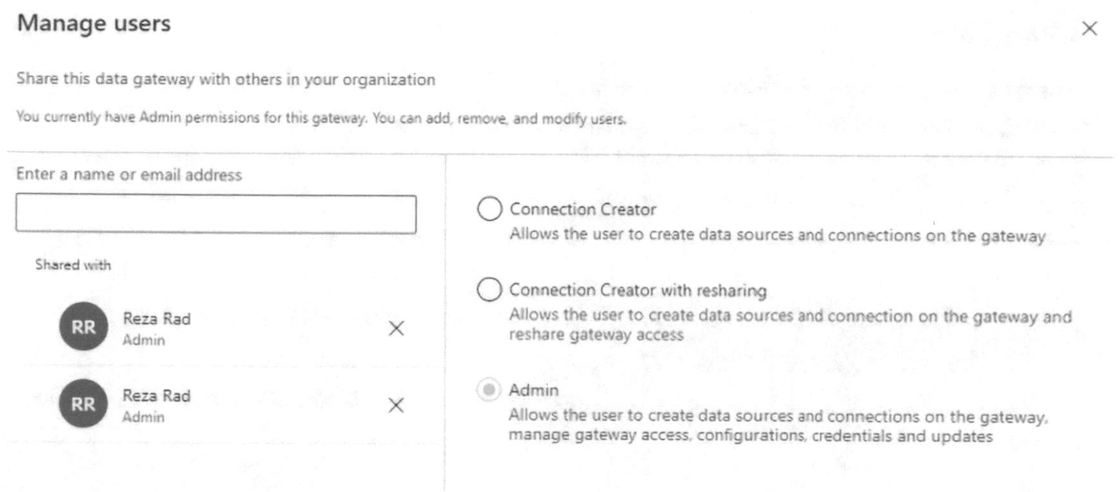

Manage users ✕

Share this data gateway with others in your organization

You currently have Admin permissions for this gateway. You can add, remove, and modify users.

Enter a name or email address

Shared with

RR Reza Rad
Admin ✕

RR Reza Rad
Admin ✕

○ Connection Creator
Allows the user to create data sources and connections on the gateway

○ Connection Creator with resharing
Allows the user to create data sources and connection on the gateway and reshare gateway access

◉ Admin
Allows the user to create data sources and connections on the gateway, manage gateway access, configurations, credentials and updates

Figure 22-17. *User access to the Power BI Gateway*

Gateway Connection Creator

This type of user can create data sources under the Gateway and use them for a connection to the datasets and dataflows.

Gateway Connection Creator with Resharing

In addition to creating data sources and using them in connections, this user can also reshare access to the Gateway.

Gateway Admin

This user has full control of the Gateway. In addition to adding and removing data sources, this user can manage access to the Gateway, control the settings, and remove the Gateway.

Data Source Users

In addition to giving access at the Gateway level, you can give users access at the data source level. This is more granular access and is helpful when a user only needs permission or access to a few data sources and not the entire Gateway. The data source users can also have three types of access, as shown in Figure 22-18.

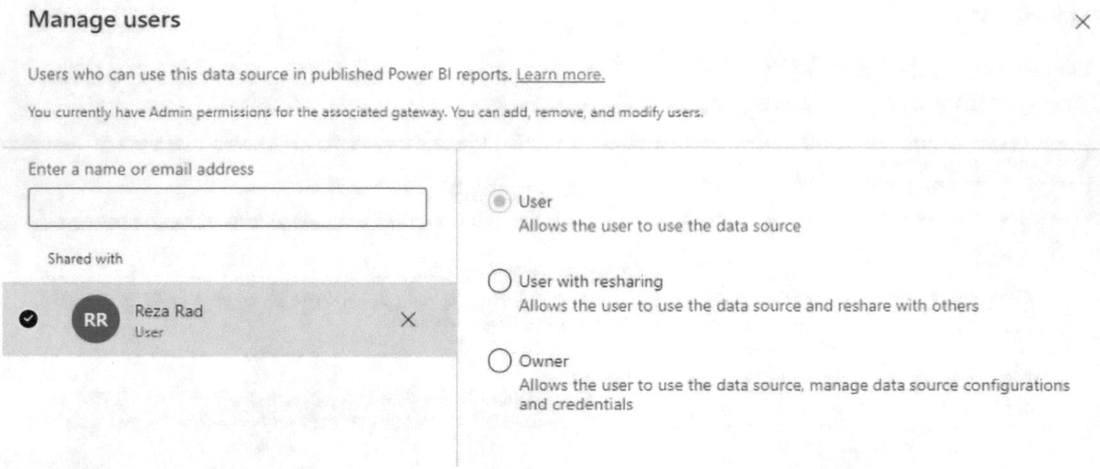

Manage users   ✕

Users who can use this data source in published Power BI reports. Learn more.

You currently have Admin permissions for the associated gateway. You can add, remove, and modify users.

Enter a name or email address

[   ]

Shared with

| ✔ | RR | Reza Rad
User | ✕ |

○ User
Allows the user to use the data source

○ User with resharing
Allows the user to use the data source and reshare with others

○ Owner
Allows the user to use the data source, manage data source configurations and credentials

Figure 22-18. *Data source users in a Power BI Gateway*

- **User:** This is just a pure user of the data source. This user cannot change the data source defined under the Gateway but can use it to connect to a Power BI dataset or dataflow.

- **User with resharing:** In addition to being the user, this user can also reshare this data source with other users.

- **Owner:** This user has full control of the data source itself but not of other data sources or the Gateway.

You must understand the differences between data source users and Gateway users and correctly assign access to users based on their use cases. Too much access can sometimes be challenging for a user not trained to use it with caution.

Additional Settings for Gateway

There are a few other important additional settings for the Gateway, shown in Figure 22-19. An explanation for each setting follows.

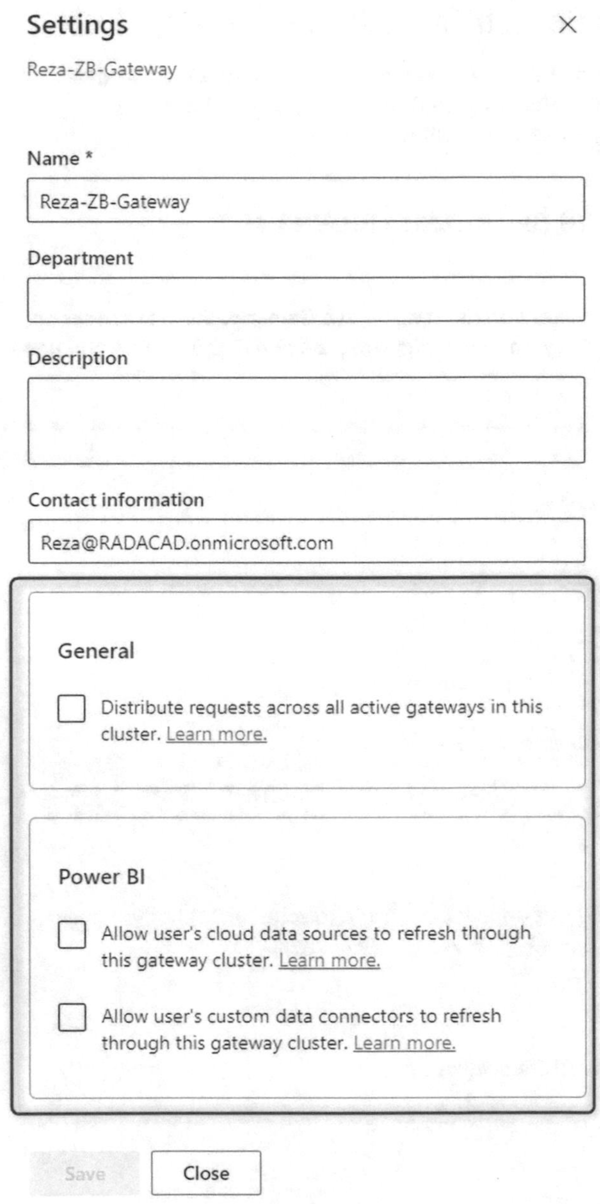

Settings ✕

Reza-ZB-Gateway

Name *

Reza-ZB-Gateway

Department

Description

Contact information

Reza@RADACAD.onmicrosoft.com

General

☐ Distribute requests across all active gateways in this cluster. Learn more.

Power BI

☐ Allow user's cloud data sources to refresh through this gateway cluster. Learn more.

☐ Allow user's custom data connectors to refresh through this gateway cluster. Learn more.

Save   Close

Figure 22-19. *Additional settings for Power BI Gateways*

Distribute Requests Across All Active Gateways in This Cluster

This sets load balancing on the Gateways. This is very helpful if the Gateway is under many parallel requests. When you set up a Gateway cluster (a group of Gateway installations bundled together to serve as one Gateway), you can enable this functionality. To learn more about load balancing, visit learn.microsoft. com/en-nz/data-integration/gateway/service-gateway-high-availability-clusters#load-balance-across-gateways-in-a-cluster.

Allow User's Cloud Data Sources to Refresh Through This Gateway Cluster

When you need to combine multiple data sources in a single Power Query table (when one of the data sources is on-premises and another is cloud-based), enabling this option will give you that ability. Otherwise, you may need to create two separate queries and combine them.[1]

Allow User's Custom Data Connectors to Refresh Through This Gateway Cluster

You can build your own Power Query custom connector and use it through a Gateway. You need to set up the custom connector settings in the installed Gateway, shown in Figure 22-20, and in the service, you need to enable this option.

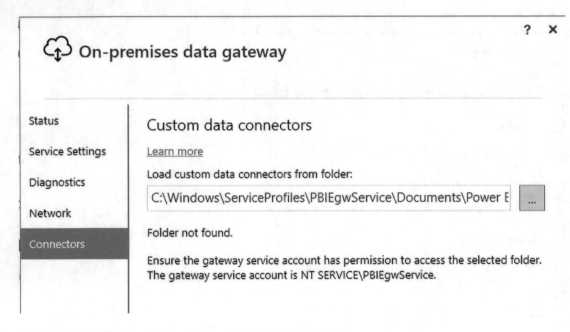

Figure 22-20. Using a custom connector in a Power BI Gateway

---

[1] Learn more about it at learn.microsoft.com/en-nz/power-bi/connect-data/service-gateway-mashup-on-premises-cloud

Troubleshooting

There are a few scenarios in which you may face an issue when setting up the Gateway. This section explains them:

- You cannot see the Gateway when you go to your dataset setting, most probably because you did not add all the data sources needed for that dataset. Go to the Power BI Desktop and check whether you have added all the data sources.[2]

- Gateway has a logging system that can be helpful when an issue comes up. You can enable additional logging and access the Gateway logs from the on-premises data Gateway installed in the application. This process is shown in Figure 22-21.[3]

---

[2] Analysis Services Live Connection with Gateway requires more configuration, which I explain in this article: radacad.com/step-by-step-walk-through-on-premises-live-sql-server-connection-with-power-bi-enterprise-gateway

[3] There are a few known issues with the on-premises Gateway, which you can read more about here: docs.microsoft.com/en-us/power-bi/service-gateway-onprem-tshoot
as well as a few known issues with the personal Gateway, which you can read more about at docs.microsoft.com/en-us/power-bi/personal-gateway

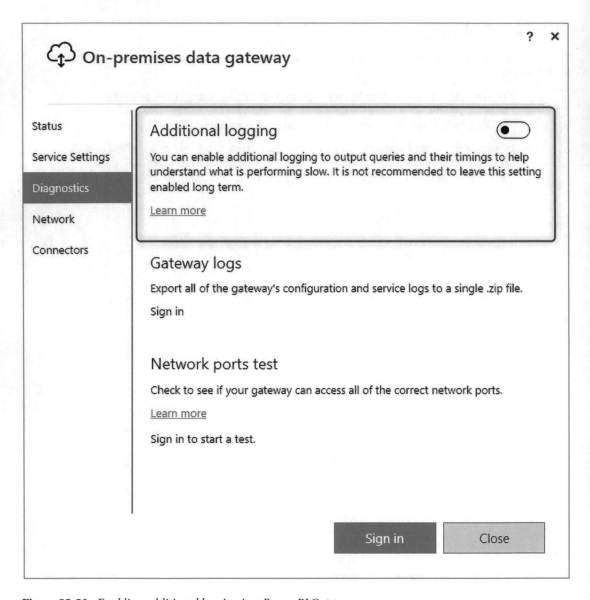

Figure 22-21. *Enabling additional logging in a Power BI Gateway*

Summary

In this chapter, you've learned about Gateways. Gateways connect the Power BI cloud-based dataset and the data source on-premises. You learned that Gateways are only required for on-premises connections. There are two modes to install a Gateway—personal and recommended (on-premises). You learned that the on-premises recommended Gateway can serve more than one developer at a time and can be used for Power BI, PowerApps, and a few other applications. It also supports multiple connection types.

The chapter also explained the installation and configuration of the Gateway and connected one Power BI dataset to it. The key to using a Gateway is to add all the required data sources under it and then map them to the dataset.

CHAPTER 23

■ ■ ■

Power BI Licensing

There are many ways to license Power BI. Users often do not understand which features are included in which licensing plans. In this chapter, you learn about all the different licensing plans for Power BI, the scenarios in which to use the licensing, and scenarios in which you may need to change your chosen licensing plan. This chapter is intended to help you to find the most cost-effective licensing plan for your requirements. You learn about the following licensing options:

- Power BI Free
- Power BI Pro
- Power BI Premium Per User
- Power BI Embedded
- Power BI Premium
- Power BI Report Server Only licensing

Two Types of Licensing

Power BI licensing can be separated into two main categories:

- User-based licensing
- Capacity-based licensing

To understand this, let's look at the Power BI Service setup. Power BI Service is a cloud-based hosting solution for Power BI objects. This cloud-based hosting solution offers two options for Power BI users—they can either use a shared capacity of resources (CPU, memory, and all the shared resources of the cloud computing for the Power BI service in the cloud), or they can use capacity that is dedicated just for themselves and not shared with anyone else. When you choose user-based licensing, you are using a shared capacity. Capacity-based licensing allows you to use a capacity dedicated to yourself. These two types of licensing also have some interactions. For example, reports hosted in a dedicated capacity can be published by a user-based license and consumed by a user-based license. You learn more about this later in this chapter.

It is essential to say that these two types of licensing are mainly designed for the Power BI Service. If you intend to use Power BI as a full on-premises option (using Power BI Report Server), there is a separate licensing option, which you learn about later in this chapter.

All the prices mentioned in this chapter are based on USD.

© Reza Rad 2023
R. Rad, *Pro Power BI Architecture*, https://doi.org/10.1007/978-1-4842-9538-0_23

The Power BI Desktop

Note that the Power BI Desktop, which is the tool for authoring and creating the data model, the report, and the PBIX files, is free. You do not even need an account to use it. It is free to use for anyone worldwide; no signup is needed; you can download and install it.

There is a log-in/sign-in option when you open the Power BI Desktop, but you can skip that, and you can still use the Power BI Desktop. A few of the features, such as browsing the gallery of custom visuals, might not be available if you are not signed in, but you can still use the main capabilities of the Power BI Desktop, which involve creating Power BI models and reports.

Why Do I Need a License if the Power BI Desktop Is Free?

The Power BI Desktop creates reports, it does not consume them. The Power BI Desktop is a developer tool. Although you can install it on the end user's machine and give them the PBIX file to view it, the Power BI Desktop is not designed to be an end user tool. Here are some reasons why:

- The Power BI Desktop cannot be installed on all devices (phones or some tablets, for example). This is important because many end users want to use mobile devices to consume reports.

- The Power BI Desktop empowers users to edit and change datasets and reports. The end user might unknowingly remove something from the report or change something that causes it to stop working correctly. Ideally, an end user tool should not allow users to change reports.

- If you use the Power BI Desktop to build the model, your model isn't following the best practices of the multi-layered architecture, and you are creating silos of reports in your organization. This is likely to cause a big failure in the Power BI adoption across your organization.

- There isn't a way to add security around the PBIX file shared outside of your organization.

- There isn't a way to track and monitor the usage of the Power BI reports.

- You will end up with many versions of the PBIX files floating around, and users will likely be confused about which version is correct.

- And many other issues.

Unfortunately, in some organizations, the Power BI Desktop is still used for sharing and consuming reports. This must be stopped; this list explains just a few of the issues involved with this procedure. So, how should you share reports with other users?

To share the reports with other users, you must deliver them from a hosting solution to which you can add governance, security, and architecture. You need a hosting solution that can give you the options to share a read-only version of a report if needed and also give you the option to push changes and updates through a developer channel. Power BI offers two hosting options—the Power BI Service and the Power BI Report Server. To use either of these two, you need a Power BI license.

Now that you understand why licensing is needed in the world of Power BI, let's talk about the details.

User-Based Licensing

User-based licensing comes in three flavors:

- Power BI Free

- Power BI Pro

- Power BI Premium Per User

These three options provide a different range of features. Power BI's user-based licensing options are under Office 365 user management. That means that the Office 365 administrator of an organization can assign licenses to the users.

Power BI Free

Certain features in Power BI are free to use (apart from the Power BI Desktop); however, you need a free Power BI license. The Power BI administrator or the Office 365 administrator can assign free licenses. You can also sign up for a free Power BI account if your organization allows you to do so.

A free Power BI account will give you access to the Power BI Service. You can publish and host your reports in the service. You can see the reports using a web browser or the Power BI mobile app. However, you cannot share the report with others.

If you have a free Power BI account and want to see a report that's been shared with you, depending on how the report is shared and where it is hosted, you might be able to see it using your Power BI Free account. I explain that ambiguity more later in this chapter.

Note that there is a free way to share Power BI content without needing Power BI user accounts, called Publish to Web. This method is not secure and is not recommended for confidential data. This chapter covers the licensing required to share confidential reports and data throughout an organization.

Power BI Pro

Power BI Pro is the per-user subscription for Power BI. At the time of writing this chapter, it costs $9.99 USD per user per month. With Power BI Pro, you can get everything that a free account has, plus many other Power BI Service features, as well as other methods of sharing reports. A Pro license is designed for developers.

Sharing

With Power BI Pro, you can use all sharing methods except Power BI Embedded (which comes with a different licensing option). You can use Simple Sharing, Workspaces, Power BI Apps, and Embed in SharePoint Online. If you have a Power BI Pro license, you can share the reports internally or externally (if you're allowed to by the Power BI Administrator). However, if you share a report with someone else, they must also have a paid Power BI license to view the reports. If you have a Pro license and share a report with a free user, they cannot see it unless they upgrade to the Pro user or Premium per user. (There is an exception to this, which is when the report is hosted in a dedicated premium capacity, in which the free users can consume the Power BI content through apps, and I explore this option later in this chapter.)

Developer Functions in the Service

With Power BI Pro, you get some integration features of Power BI, such as Analyze in Excel, highlighted in Figure 23-1. If a member of your developer team wants to connect to the Power BI dataset using Excel and analyze it, they can do so.

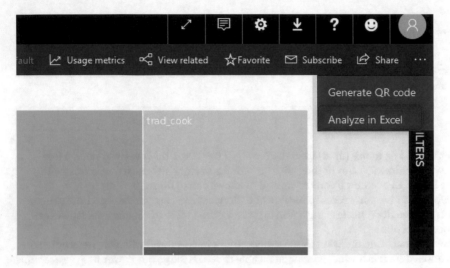

Figure 23-1. *Power BI Pro gives you all the authoring features (such as Analyze in Excel) and sharing options*

With a Pro license, you can create workspaces, as shown in Figure 23-2, or be part of a workspace. A Power BI workspace is like a development environment. You can collaborate with other developers in workspaces.

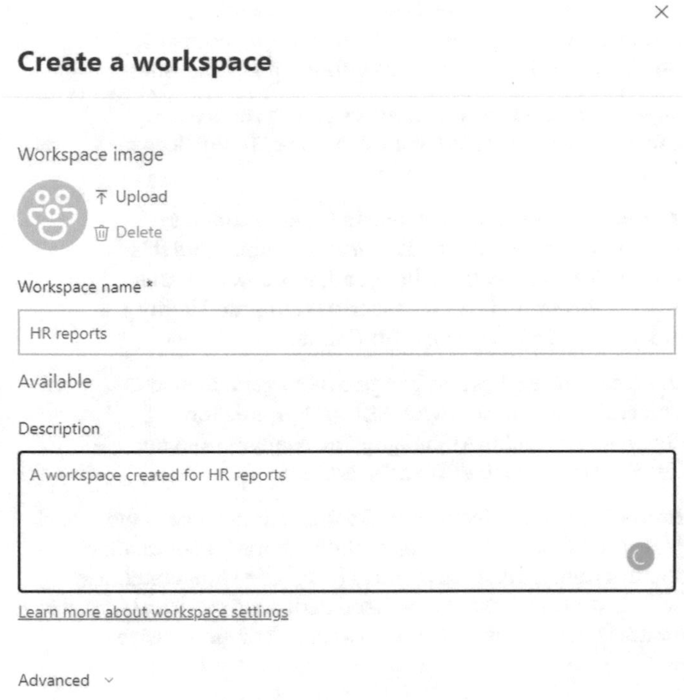

×

Create a workspace

Workspace image

⌁ Upload

🗑 Delete

Workspace name *

HR reports

Available

Description

A workspace created for HR reports

◔

Learn more about workspace settings

Advanced ⌄

Figure 23-2. *The Power BI Pro license enables you to use workspaces*

A Pro license also includes actions so you can maintain your Power BI objects, such as the model size of 1GB in a capacity of 10GB, the use of dataflows, paginated reports, shared datasets, monitoring, and some governance around the objects.

Power BI Pro Licenses Are Designed for Developers

A Pro license enables you to use most of the features that a Power BI developer needs. You may, however, need a higher-level license to use some of the advanced features of Power BI. The Premium Per User license (in short, PPU) is designed for advanced features of Power BI at a user-based licensing option. At the time of writing this chapter, the cost for a PPU license is $20 USD per user per month.

Power BI PPU: Premium Per User

Although the Power BI Pro license gives you most of the features you need for Power BI development in an organization, some features are still not included.

- **Bigger model size:** If you use the Power BI Pro, your model size cannot exceed 1GB. This is a compressed size of the PBIX file; however, if you are dealing with a lot of data, that size might not fit your purpose. With a PPU license, you can have a model size of 100GB.

- **More refreshes:** Sometimes, the eight refreshes of the Power BI dataset offered by the Power BI Pro license is not enough; you may need to refresh it more frequently. The PPU license gives you up to 48 refresh times a day, plus unlimited API refreshes.

- **AI functions:** Some AI functionalities in Power BI work with cognitive services in Azure. To use some of those features, you need a PPU license. A Power BI Pro license doesn't cover those features.

- **Datamarts and advanced dataflow features:** The most recent announcements about Power BI datamarts reveal a new way of building Power BI solutions, and this is limited only to PPU and Premium licenses. On the other hand, if you want to use some of the advanced features of the Power BI dataflows; such as Computed Entity and Enhanced Compute Engine, you need a PPU license (or Premium).

- **Deployment pipelines:** You can create an application lifecycle management system in Power BI by assigning workspaces to the development, test, and production environments. You can have deployment pipelines managing the changes from one environment to another. This feature is limited to PPU and Premium.

PPU offers many more features than Pro. Some of these features make the maintenance of the model in the Power BI service more accessible (deployment pipelines), some of them offer a better architecture (advanced dataflow and datamarts), and some of them offer extra features (such as AI functionalities). Microsoft introduced PPU for companies with fewer users who do not need dedicated capacity but still want to use premium functionalities. I think the extra features that PPU provides are so comprehensive that I recommend it to organizations.[1]

Capacity-Based Licensing

The next category of licensing in Power BI is the capacity-based licensing option. It is offered in two ways:

- Power BI Embedded

- Power BI Premium

Each of these options has different SKUs, pricing levels, and tiers. The main thing is that the capacity-based licensing options cannot be used alone; you need to combine them with a user-based license. For example, you need a Power BI Pro license for the developer hosting the Power BI reports in a workspace with a Power BI Premium capacity.

Power BI Embedded

If you ever want to embed Power BI content into a custom application and use a custom application's user management, Power BI Embedded is the licensing plan for you (see Figure 23-3). This licensing plan is based on page renders.

---

[1] Explaining PPU and its use cases would take an entire chapter unto itself. I encourage you to read my article about Power BI PPU at radacad.com/what-is-premium-per-user-license-for-power-bi-and-what-is-it-good-for

Embedded Dashboard

The following dashboard is the first dashboard found in the given group. Please feel free to change the code to match your needs.

Figure 23-3. *Power BI Embedded licensing is calculated based on page renders*

Every refresh on the page that has Power BI content in it is a page render; if you select a slicer, that causes another page render. If you click a column in a column chart and that causes interactivity of other charts, then that is another page render.

With Power BI Embedded, you can reserve buckets of page renders per peak hour. Table 23-1 lists the costs at the time of writing this chapter.

Table 23-1. *Power BI Embedded Tiers and Pricing In USD[2]*

Node Type	Virtual Cores	Memory	Frontend/Backend Cores	Peak Renders per Hour	Price
A1	1	3GB RAM	0.5 / 0.5 [1]	1 – 300	$1.0081/hour
A2	2	5GB RAM	1 / 1 [1]	301 – 600	$2.0081/hour
A3	4	10GB RAM	2 / 2	601 – 1,200	$4.0242/hour
A4	8	25GB RAM	4 / 4	1,201 – 2,400	$8.0565/hour
A5	16	50GB RAM	8 / 8	2,401 – 4,800	$16.13/hour
A6	32	100GB RAM	16 / 16	4,801 – 9,600	$32.26/hour

The pricing in Table 23-1 may scare you, and you may immediately think of not going through the embedded path. However, there are some scenarios in which Power BI Embedded can be a more cost-effective option than Pro. Here is an example:

---

[2] azure.microsoft.com/en-us/pricing/details/power-bi-embedded/

Assume that you have 100 users for your Power BI solution. Your users are not connecting simultaneously to use Power BI reports. You may have maximum page renders of 300 per hour if you use Embedded. In such a case, Embedded for that scenario would cost you about $700 USD per month, whereas the Power BI Pro for 100 users would be $1000 USD per month. This means saving $3,600 USD per year. Power BI Embedded can be more cost-effective than Pro.

An important note to consider when you think about Embedded is the hidden cost of a web developer. Power BI Embedded brings Power BI content embedded into your custom application, and who is going to do that? A web developer. If later on through the path, you want to change the way that users are working with the application, who is going to make that change? A web developer.

Power BI Embedded gives you the ability to embed Power BI content into a custom application and share it based on a custom user management through that application.

Power BI Premium

Power BI Pro is expensive when you have a large user base, and Embedded needs constant maintenance by a web developer. If you have a large user base (say 10,000 users), Power BI Premium is the best licensing option for you. Power BI Premium is designed for large user base scenarios where the data size is huge.

Power BI Premium is not priced per user, it is per node. In Power BI Premium, you pay for nodes, which have dedicated capacity and resources. Table 23-2 shows the existing nodes and their details at the time of writing this chapter.

Table 23-2. Power BI Premium Licensing Tiers

Capacity		Dataset				Dataflow	Export API
Capacity SKUs	V-cores	Max memory (GB)[1, 2, 3]	DirectQuery/Live connection (per second)[1, 2]	Max memory per query (GB)[1, 2]	Model refresh parallelism[2]	Dataflow parallel tasks[5]	Max concurrent pages[6]
EM1/A1	1	3	3.75	1	5	4	20
EM2/A2	2	5	7.5	2	10	8	25
EM3/A3	4	10	15	2	20	16	35
P1/A4	8	25	30	6	40	32	55
P2/A5	16	50	60	6	80	64	95
P3/A6	32	100	120	10	160	64	175
P4/A7[4]	64	200	240	10	320	64	200
P5/A8[4]	128	400	480	10	640	64	200

Pricing starts at P1 nodes, which cost $5K USD per month, P2 is twice that price, and P3 is twice P2. As you see, the licenses are in two categories of EM (lightweight for embedding purposes), and P SKUs (what premium nodes are normally called). If you use Premium licenses, you can also use Embedded features.

Power BI Premium includes all the features that PPU offers, plus some other exciting options. The most important of them is the ability to share content with free users.

Sharing Content with Free Users

This is perhaps the most significant advantage of the Premium license over PPU. Suppose you have Power BI content hosted in a workspace. If your workspace is a Premium workspace (connected to a Premium capacity), you can create an app on the workspace and share the workspace's content through that app with the end users, even if they don't have a paid Power BI license. They can have a Power BI Free account. In other words, a Power BI report hosted in a Premium-capacity workspace can be shared with thousands of free Power BI account holders.[3]

Premium Calculation Scenario

It can be difficult to determine how many nodes you need, or how big the nodes need to be, when creating your Power BI solution. Figure 23-4 offers an example calculation for 10,000 users.

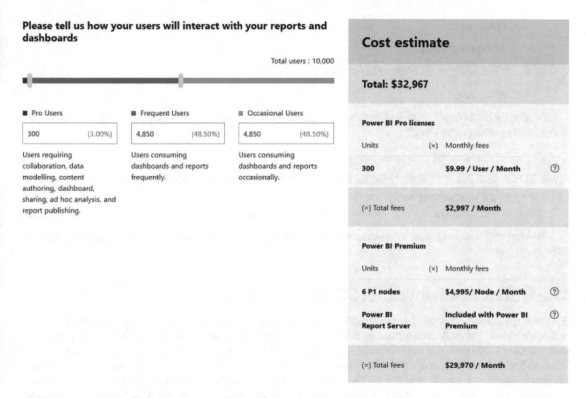

Figure 23-4. *Sample Pro BI costs*

If you compare the total costs of $33K per month with $100K per month ($100K per month if all 10,000 users purchase Power BI Pro), you can see how Power BI Premium can be more cost-effective with a larger user base scenario. The idea behind creating the Power BI Premium licensing is that users who are only reading a report should not pay Pro pricing.

---

[3] I explain this in more detail in my article at radacad.com/the-read-only-license-for-power-bi

Extra Features in Premium

Power BI Premium also provides some extra features. Some of these features have been released, and some are still in progress and in the roadmap:

- Dedicated Power BI resources

- Massive dataset storage and no user quotas: 100TB storage

- More frequent dataset refreshes: 48 times a day rather than 8 times a day

- Power BI Report Server licensing to use Power BI Report Server on-premises

- Support for larger datasets (up to 400GB)

- Datamarts

- AI functionalities

- The ability to share organizational apps with free users

- Autoscale

Autoscale enables you to add vCores to your capacity as the need arises (this feature requires the Power BI Premium per capacity Gen2).

Power BI Premium licensing is designed for large user base scenarios. This licensing tier gives you many extra features as well as incremental load.

To read more about Power BI Premium, read my blog post at radacad.com/power-bi-premium-is-it-for-you-or-not.

The Difference Between A SKUs and P/EM SKUs

You perhaps noticed that there are similarities in A, EM, and P SKUs over the pricing tables for Premium and Embedded and wondered about the differences between them. You can embed Power BI reports into web pages in more than one way. One method requires users to log in using their organizational accounts (such as Secure Embed), another method doesn't need the users to have Power BI accounts at all, and the application can manage the users itself. To use organizational accounts, you need to use EM or P licenses. However, for the application to have its own user management, EM, P, or A licenses can be used. A licenses are part of the Azure offering, whereas the EM or P licenses are part of Office's offering. An A license is billed hourly, whereas the EM and P licenses are on monthly billing periods.

Table 23-3 features several scenarios in which to use different SKUs.

Table 23-3. *Scenarios to Use Each SKU for Power BI Licensing[4]*

Scenario	Azure	Office
	(A SKU)	(P and EM SKUs)
Embed for your customers (app owns data)	✓	✓
Embed for your organization (user owns data)	✗	✓
Microsoft 365 apps (formerly known as Office 365 apps) • Embed in Teams • Embed in SharePoint	✗	✓
Secure URL embedding (embed from Power BI service)	✗	✓

Table 23-4 lists some capacity considerations for each SKU.

Table 23-4. *Capacity Considerations for Each SKU[5]*

Payment and usage	Power BI Embedded	Power BI Premium	Power BI Premium
Offer	Azure	Office	Office
SKU	A	EM	P
Billing	Hourly	Monthly	Monthly
Commitment	None	Yearly	Monthly or yearly
Usage	Azure resources can be: • Scaled up or down • Paused and resumed	Embed in apps, and in Microsoft applications	Embed in apps, and in Power BI service

SQL Server Enterprise Edition Plus Software Assurance

The combination of SQL Server Enterprise Edition and software assurance provides you with licensing for Power BI Report Server (see Figure 23-5). The Power BI Report Server is the on-premises hosting solution for Power BI. Contact your Microsoft contact for these products.

---

[4] learn.microsoft.com/en-us/power-bi/developer/embedded/embedded-capacity
[5] learn.microsoft.com/en-us/power-bi/developer/embedded/embedded-capacity

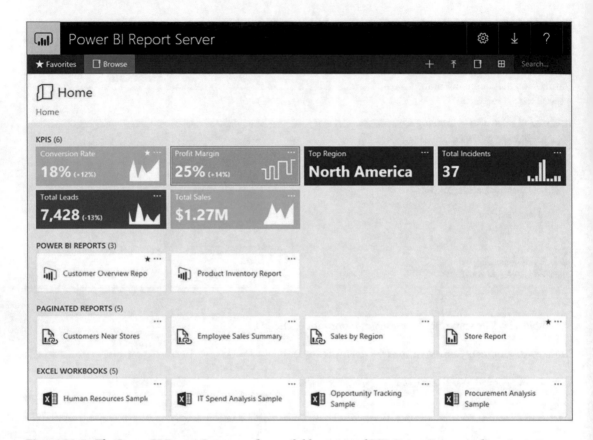

Figure 23-5. *The Power BI Report Server can be available as part of SQL Server Enterprise licensing*

If you already have SQL Server Enterprise Edition licensing in your organization, and you intend to use Power BI only on-premises using the Power BI Report Server, buying Software Assurance is the more cost-effective option.

Summary

You learned about six different licensing plans for Power BI in this chapter. You learned what features are included in each plan and in which situations they are most cost-effective. Table 23-5 summarizes the features in each licensing plan.

Table 23-5. *Power BI Licensing Comparison Table*

	Power BI Free	Power BI Pro	Power BI Premium Per user	Power BI Embedded (A SKU)	Power BI Premium Per capacity (EM and P SKU)	SQL Server Enterprise with Software Assurance
Power BI Desktop	Yes	Yes	Yes	Yes	Yes	
Power BI Mobile app	Yes	Yes	Yes		Yes	
Dataflow		Yes	Yes	Yes	Yes	
Incremental Refresh		Yes	Yes	Yes	Yes	
Deployment Pipelines			Yes	Yes	Yes	
XMLA endpoint read/write			Yes	Yes	Yes	
Datamart			Yes	Yes	Yes	
Advanced AI (text analytics, image detection...)			Yes	Yes	Yes	
Secure Embed					Yes	
Autoscale					Yes	
Consume content without paid user license				Yes	Yes	
Embed in custom application				Yes	Yes	
Paginated Reports		Yes	Yes	Yes	Yes	Yes
Report Server					Yes	Yes
maximum model size	1 GB	1 GB	100 GB	400 GB	400 GB	As per server spec
Refresh rate		8/day	48/day	48/day	48/day	unlimited
Maximum storage	10 GB / user	10 GB / user	100 TB	100 TB	100 TB	As per server spec

Last but not least, if you want to set up a free environment in which you can try Power BI Service features, you can use the Power BI Sandbox.[6]

---

[6] This sits beyond the scope of this book. Learn more about it at `https://radacad.com/power-bi-sandbox-an-environment-to-learn-power-bi-service-for-free`

CHAPTER 24

■ ■ ■

Power BI Admin Portal and Tenant Settings

In the world of Power BI, there are some configurations in the Desktop tool and in the service. One of the more critical configurations is the Tenant Settings of the Power BI administrator panel. Tenant Settings include a list of highly important configurations across your Power BI tenant. If you don't configure the settings properly, it might result in leaking data, authorizing people who should not be authorized to see reports, and many other catastrophic scenarios. In this chapter, you learn about the configurations available in Tenant Settings and the recommended options for each.

Power BI Administrator

By default, the Office 365 administrator is the Power BI administrator. However, you can add a specific Power BI administrator by selecting the Power BI administrator role from the Office 365 Portal. Here are the details of assigning a Power BI administrator role to a user.

Log in to portal.office.com with an Office 365 administrator account. Go to the Admin panel. Find the user in the list of active users and select them from the list, as shown in Figure 24-1.

Figure 24-1. *Assigning the Power BI administrator role*

Next, click Manage Roles. Under Admin Center Access, expand the Show All by category. Then, from the list, select Power BI Administrator.

You can also use PowerShell scripts to assign the Power BI administrator role to a user.

Tenant Settings

The Power BI administrator can access Tenant Settings from the Power BI Service. To do that, you need to click the Setting icon and choose Admin Portal, as shown in Figure 24-2.

Figure 24-2. *Navigating to Power BI Admin Portal*

From the Admin Portal, you can click Tenant Settings, as depicted in Figure 24-3 (note that you can access this page only if you are a Power BI administrator). If you are not a Power BI administrator, under Admin Portal, you will perhaps just see the capacity settings.

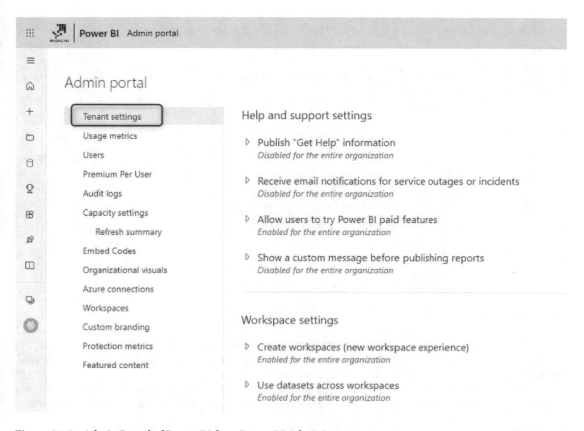

Figure 24-3. *Admin Portal of Power BI for a Power BI Administrator*

Tenant Settings are categorized into groups. Since the first public release of Power BI until now, many features have been added to the Power BI, and with new additions come new configurations. Over time, the Tenant Settings configuration list has gradually expanded to a long list of options. The following sections explain some of the most important aspects of these configurations.

Help and Support Settings

You can set links to be used for help and support throughout your organization. When a user in your tenant logs in to the Power BI Service and click the Help icon, they can be redirected to a specific URL or page you want them to see for documentation or FAQs. To set these up, use the Get Help information setup, as shown in Figure 24-4.

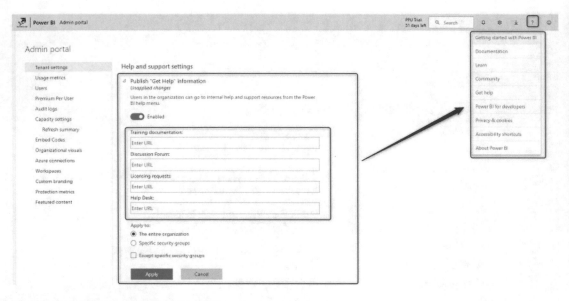

Figure 24-4. *Setting up the Get Help links in the Power BI Service*

The settings you apply here are then be used in the Get Help links that are available in the Power BI Service. You can set the settings for the entire organization or for only a specific group of people (this type of categorization exists in most of the configurations of the Tenant Settings).

As shown in Figure 24-5, there are other options that mostly affect your support or development team by allowing them to try some of the new paid features or get a message when they want to publish a report.

Help and support settings

▷ Publish "Get Help" information
Disabled for the entire organization

▷ Receive email notifications for service outages or incidents
Disabled for the entire organization

▷ Allow users to try Power BI paid features
Enabled for the entire organization

▷ Show a custom message before publishing reports
Disabled for the entire organization

Figure 24-5. *Additional help and support settings on the Power BI Tenant Settings page*

Workspace Settings

Workspaces are the heart of collaboration in the Power BI Service environment. It is better to control who can create the workspace (see Figure 24-6). This is one of the options that I recommend only be enabled for the Power BI development group in your organization. However, using datasets across workspaces is a very good option for the entire organization. This will enable users to use a shared dataset and avoid creating silos of Power BI objects.

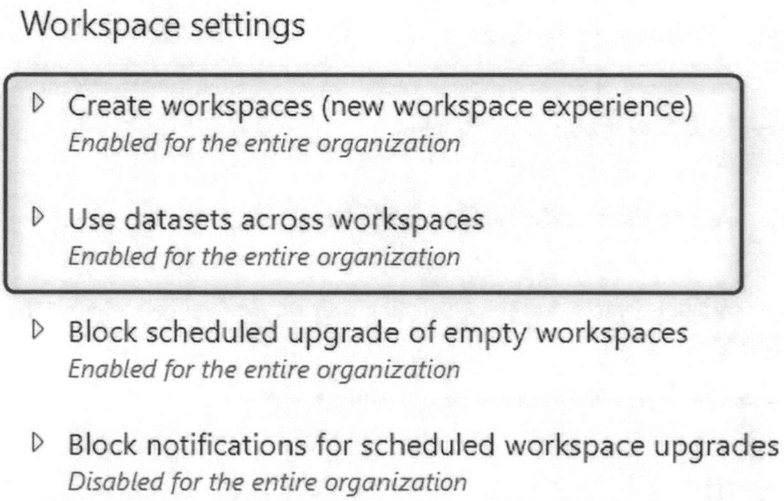

Workspace settings

▷ Create workspaces (new workspace experience)
Enabled for the entire organization

▷ Use datasets across workspaces
Enabled for the entire organization

▷ Block scheduled upgrade of empty workspaces
Enabled for the entire organization

▷ Block notifications for scheduled workspace upgrades
Disabled for the entire organization

Figure 24-6. *Workspace settings on the Power BI Tenant Settings page*

Information Protection

You can enable sensitivity labels in Power BI. This feature uses Microsoft Purview Information Protection, which has a separate licensing structure. Figure 24-7 offers a preview of the Information Protection options. It requires some prerequisite setup,[1] and then you can use the option provided in this section.

---

[1] learn.microsoft.com/en-us/power-bi/enterprise/service-security-enable-data-sensitivity-labels

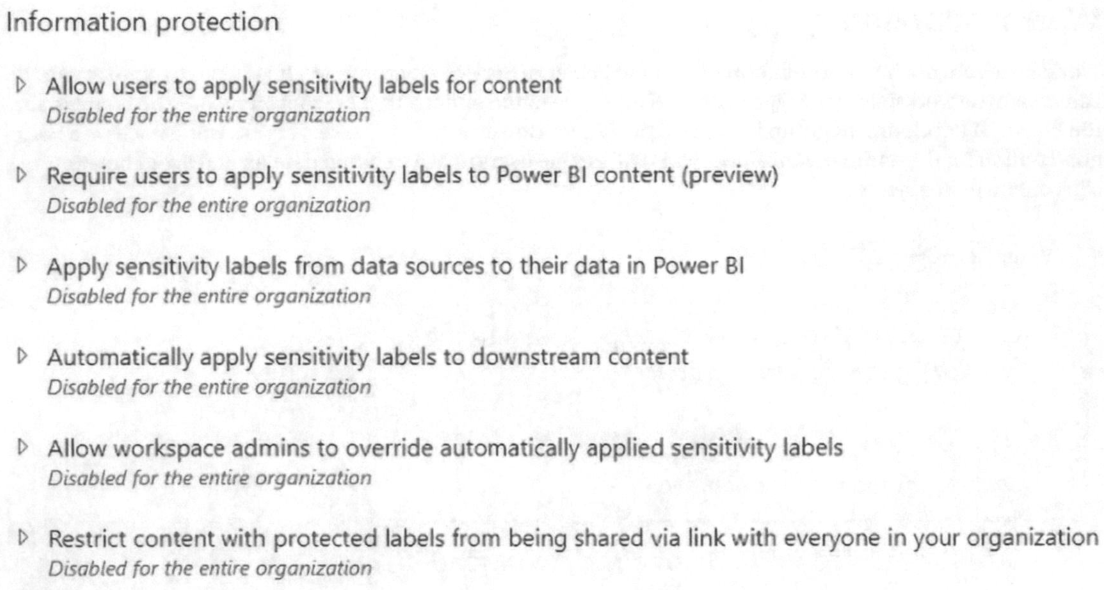

Information protection

▷ Allow users to apply sensitivity labels for content
Disabled for the entire organization

▷ Require users to apply sensitivity labels to Power BI content (preview)
Disabled for the entire organization

▷ Apply sensitivity labels from data sources to their data in Power BI
Disabled for the entire organization

▷ Automatically apply sensitivity labels to downstream content
Disabled for the entire organization

▷ Allow workspace admins to override automatically applied sensitivity labels
Disabled for the entire organization

▷ Restrict content with protected labels from being shared via link with everyone in your organization
Disabled for the entire organization

Figure 24-7. *Information protection settings on the Power BI Tenant Settings page*

Export and Sharing Settings

This is a large section of settings; it includes configurations regarding sharing across your tenant (except sharing with apps or other methods), the ability to export or copy and paste, and more.

External Users

There are a few options to allow external users to access Power BI, and even to enable them to manage and edit your Power BI content. Figure 24-8 offers a look at these options. Set these as you need.

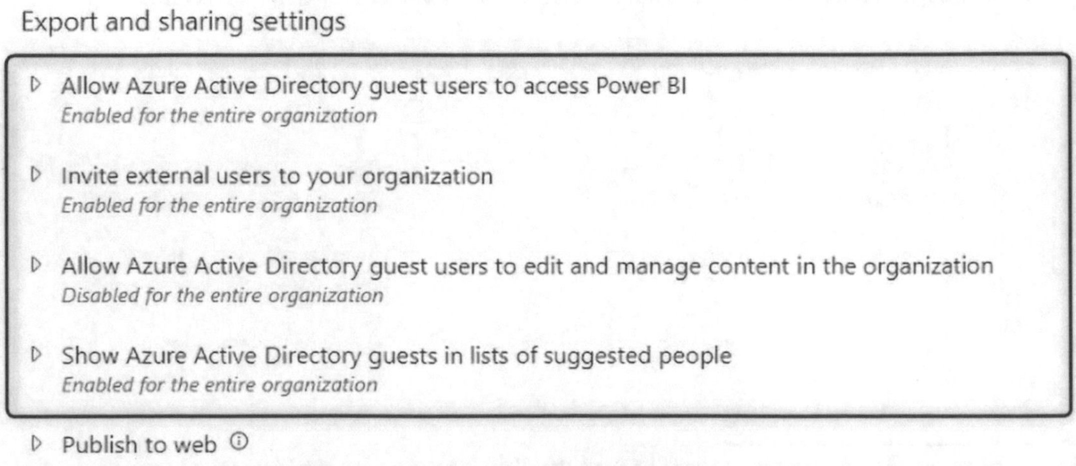

Export and sharing settings

▷ Allow Azure Active Directory guest users to access Power BI
Enabled for the entire organization

▷ Invite external users to your organization
Enabled for the entire organization

▷ Allow Azure Active Directory guest users to edit and manage content in the organization
Disabled for the entire organization

▷ Show Azure Active Directory guests in lists of suggested people
Enabled for the entire organization

▷ Publish to web ⓘ

Figure 24-8. *External user configurations on the Power BI Tenant Settings page*

Publish to Web

This configuration, shown in Figure 24-9, is often a good enough reason to access the Tenant Settings page. By default, everyone in your organization can publish their reports on the web! If you don't know about Publish to Web, it's covered in later chapter in this book. Publish to Web makes the Power BI content publicly available. This is a very dangerous option to always have on. You must make sure that you either disable this option or allow a very restricted group of people to use it.

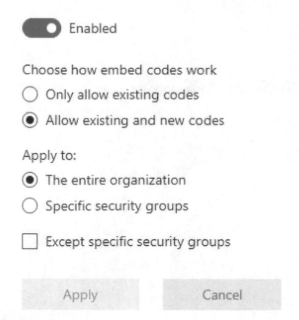

◿ Publish to web ⓘ
   Enabled for the entire organization

   People in your org can publish public reports on the web. Publicly published reports don't require authentication to view them.

   Go to Embed Codes in the admin portal to review and manage public embed codes. If any of the codes contain private or confidential content remove them.

   Review embed codes regularly to make sure no confidential information is live on the web. Learn more about Publish to web

   ⬤◯ Enabled

   Choose how embed codes work
   ◯ Only allow existing codes
   ◉ Allow existing and new codes

   Apply to:
   ◉ The entire organization
   ◯ Specific security groups

   ☐ Except specific security groups

   [Apply]   [Cancel]

Figure 24-9. Publish to Web settings for the Power BI tenant

Export, Copy, Print, and Integrate Data

There are options for enabling and disabling exporting functionalities such as Export to Excel or to CSV, as well as the ability to download reports, create a live connection to a dataset, export reports as different formats and print.

Some of these configuration options are shown in Figure 24-10, but there are more in the list, such as allowing DirectQuery to connect to Power BI dataset to create a chained dataset, to enable the integration with Microsoft Teams and PowerPoint.

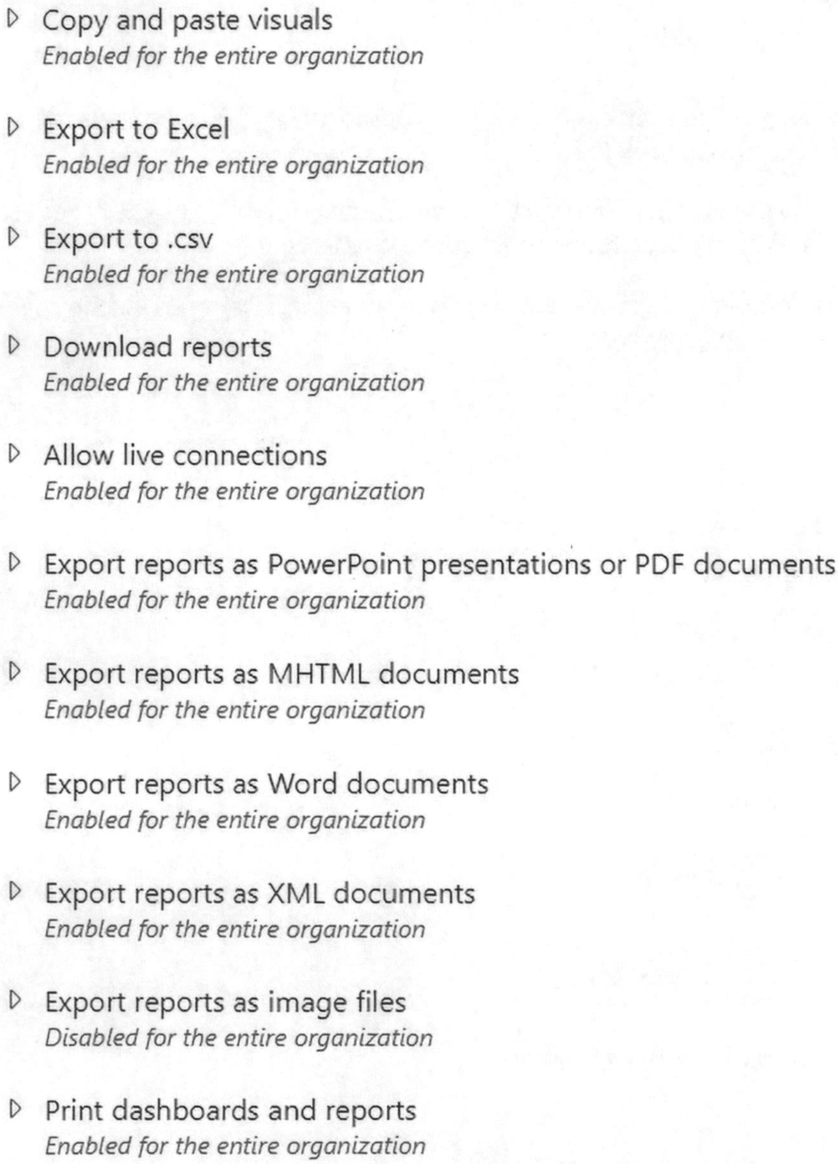

▷ Copy and paste visuals
Enabled for the entire organization

▷ Export to Excel
Enabled for the entire organization

▷ Export to .csv
Enabled for the entire organization

▷ Download reports
Enabled for the entire organization

▷ Allow live connections
Enabled for the entire organization

▷ Export reports as PowerPoint presentations or PDF documents
Enabled for the entire organization

▷ Export reports as MHTML documents
Enabled for the entire organization

▷ Export reports as Word documents
Enabled for the entire organization

▷ Export reports as XML documents
Enabled for the entire organization

▷ Export reports as image files
Disabled for the entire organization

▷ Print dashboards and reports
Enabled for the entire organization

Figure 24-10. *Export data settings on the Power BI Tenant Settings page*

Certifications

Your Power BI contents can be marked as certified, which shows that they have been through a process of testing and quality checks. It is important that only a certain group within the organization be able to certify Power BI objects. I explain this later in the chapter that covers certification and endorsements.

In addition to this setting, there are some important discovery options, shown in Figure 24-11, including Make Promoted Content and Certified Content Discoverable.

Discovery settings

▷ Make promoted content discoverable
   Enabled for the entire organization

▷ Make certified content discoverable
   Enabled for the entire organization

▷ Discover content
   Enabled for the entire organization

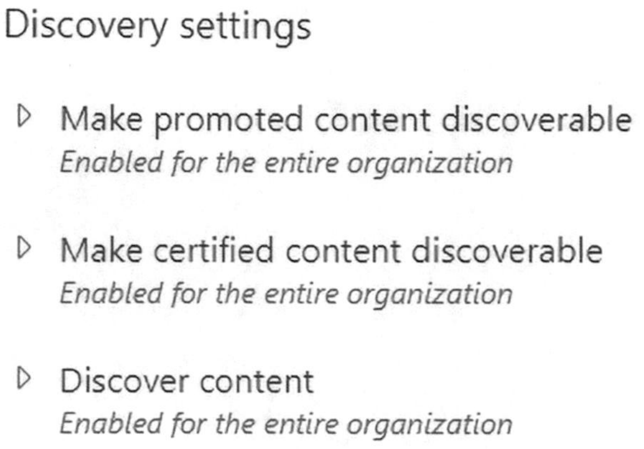

Figure 24-11. *Certification Discovery settings in Power BI*

Content Pack and App Settings

Content Pack and Power BI Apps are ways to share Power BI reports.[2] The Content Pack method is almost obsolete, and the Power BI App method is a prevalent way of sharing. In this section, you can configure this method of sharing, as shown in Figure 24-12.

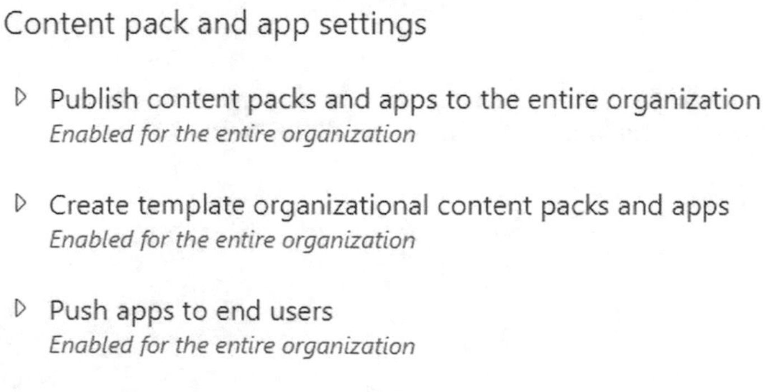

Content pack and app settings

▷ Publish content packs and apps to the entire organization
   Enabled for the entire organization

▷ Create template organizational content packs and apps
   Enabled for the entire organization

▷ Push apps to end users
   Enabled for the entire organization

Figure 24-12. *App settings in the Power BI Tenant Settings page*

---

[2] To learn more about Content Pack, visit radacad.com/content-pack-sharing-self-service-and-governance-together

Push Apps to End Users

Shown in Figure 24-13, this setting is one of the very new options added to the Tenant Settings. Without this option selected, Power BI apps won't automatically be pushed to the end user's apps section. When you turn this option on, any apps created will be automatically pushed to your users. You don't need to get the app from each user's profile individually. This is a very good option to be turned on. However, you might want to limit it to a specific group in the organization.

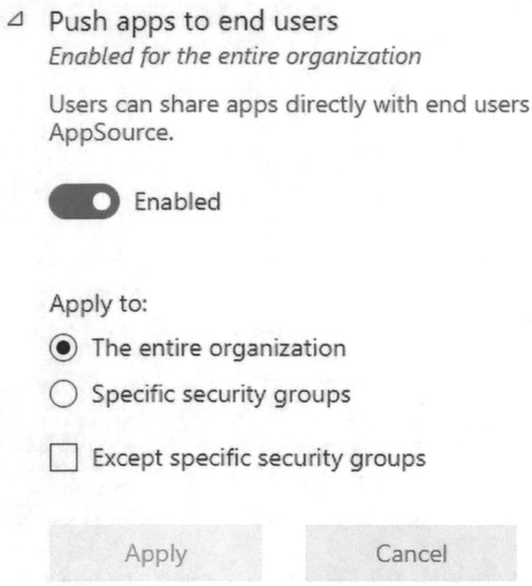

◿ Push apps to end users
Enabled for the entire organization

Users can share apps directly with end users without requiring installation from AppSource.

◖● Enabled

Apply to:

◉ The entire organization

○ Specific security groups

☐ Except specific security groups

| Apply | Cancel |

Figure 24-13. *Push apps to end users*

Integration Settings

Configurations in the Integration Settings area, featured in Figure 24-14, are related to integrating Power BI with other technologies, such as ArcGIS, XMLA endpoint, Azure Maps, Snowflake, Redshift, Google BigQuery, and so on.

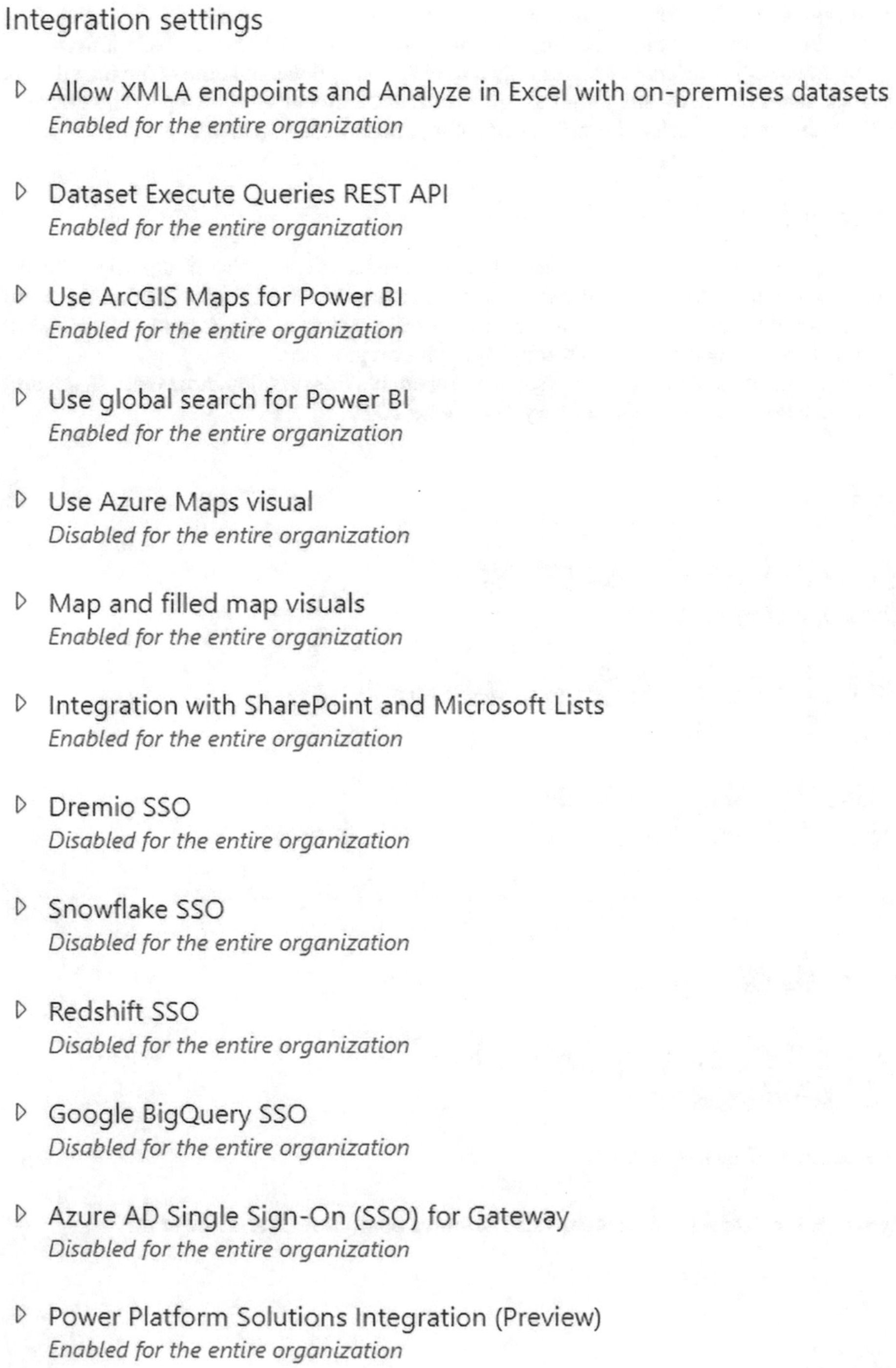

Integration settings

▷ Allow XMLA endpoints and Analyze in Excel with on-premises datasets
Enabled for the entire organization

▷ Dataset Execute Queries REST API
Enabled for the entire organization

▷ Use ArcGIS Maps for Power BI
Enabled for the entire organization

▷ Use global search for Power BI
Enabled for the entire organization

▷ Use Azure Maps visual
Disabled for the entire organization

▷ Map and filled map visuals
Enabled for the entire organization

▷ Integration with SharePoint and Microsoft Lists
Enabled for the entire organization

▷ Dremio SSO
Disabled for the entire organization

▷ Snowflake SSO
Disabled for the entire organization

▷ Redshift SSO
Disabled for the entire organization

▷ Google BigQuery SSO
Disabled for the entire organization

▷ Azure AD Single Sign-On (SSO) for Gateway
Disabled for the entire organization

▷ Power Platform Solutions Integration (Preview)
Enabled for the entire organization

Figure 24-14. *Integration settings on the Power BI Tenant Settings page*

Some of these options are very helpful and essential to use, such as the XMLA endpoint. This gives you the ability to connect to the Power BI dataset using third-party tools and build a better data model in Power BI. Some of them are specific to visuals, such as Map and Filled Map. Because some of the map data is processed in the servers, it requires the tenant admin to agree with that term before allowing it. The same is true for sign-on abilities with services such as Snowflake, Redshirt, and Google BigQuery.

Custom Visual Settings

Custom visuals, as shown in Figure 24-15, are great add-ins. Custom visuals are built by third parties. Not all custom visuals are supported well. Also, some of the custom visuals are paid. As the Power BI administrator, you may want to restrict your tenant's usage of custom visuals by changing this option. Or you may only want to allow certified custom visuals (which have been through a validation process).

You can also control the usage of R and Python visuals. If you enable this function, note that using R and Python visual also requires a Power BI personal gateway. See Figure 24-15.

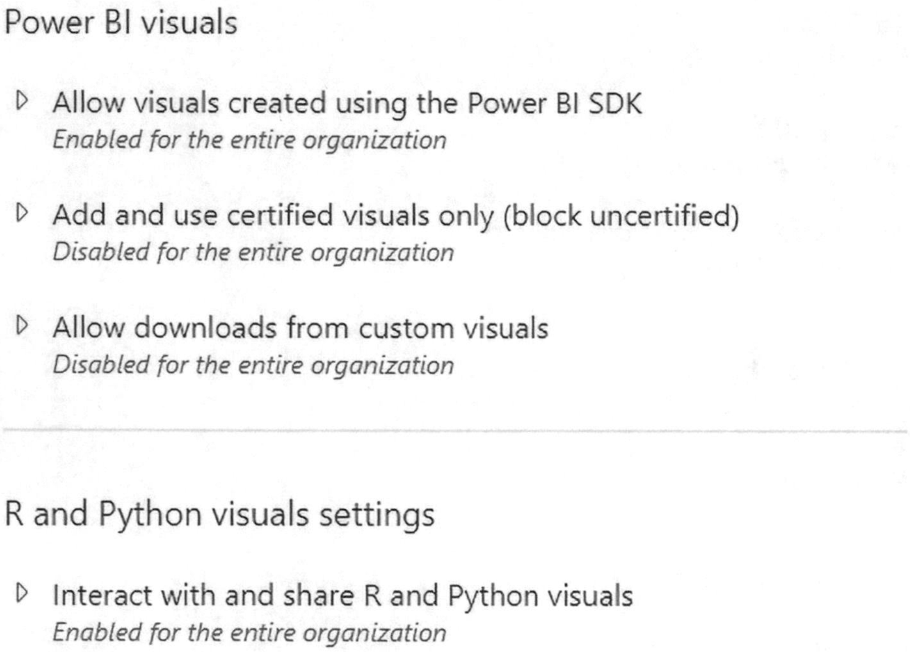

Power BI visuals

▷ Allow visuals created using the Power BI SDK
Enabled for the entire organization

▷ Add and use certified visuals only (block uncertified)
Disabled for the entire organization

▷ Allow downloads from custom visuals
Disabled for the entire organization

R and Python visuals settings

▷ Interact with and share R and Python visuals
Enabled for the entire organization

Figure 24-15. *Custom visual settings in Power BI*

There are many visuals for R, and Leila Etaati has also written a book about R and Power BI.[3]

---

[3] radacad.com/online-book-analytics-with-power-bi-and-r

Audit and Usage Settings

The Power BI usage metrics work with audit logs and give you a detailed analysis of the usage and consumption of your Power BI content. Options in this section are related to the audit log and usage metrics. You can enable the usage for content creators (which is recommended to be on), and enable per-user data in the usage metrics (which helps to identify user activities).

Create Audit Logs for Internal Activity Auditing and Compliance

The audit logs are created by this option, and users can use it for monitoring and data analysis.

Usage Metrics for Content Creators

Content creators are people who create Power BI reports, dashboards, and datasets. By default, content creators have access to the usage metrics report monitoring the usage of their content. You can change the option if you want to turn off this feature.

Per-User Data in Usage Metrics for Content Creators

Usage metrics data can also include the per-user individual metrics. Per-user data is useful, especially if you want to monitor usage by users to see if they are using the content shared with them. Figure 24-16 shows an example of a usage metrics report with per-user data.

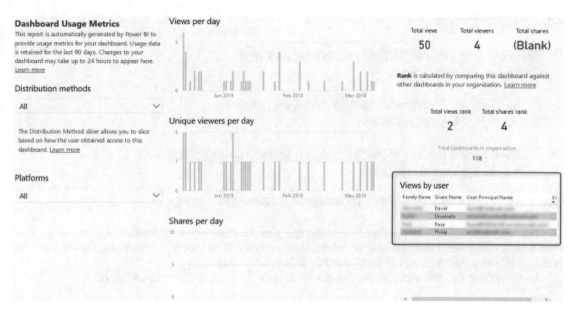

Figure 24-16. *Usage metrics with user data*

Developer Settings

As a developer, you can leverage Power BI Embedded API and embed reports or dashboards into an application. This is a powerful feature, and it can be turned on or off from here. To learn more about Power BI Embedded, read the chapter related to that in this book. See Figure 24-17 for a look at the developer and admin API settings.

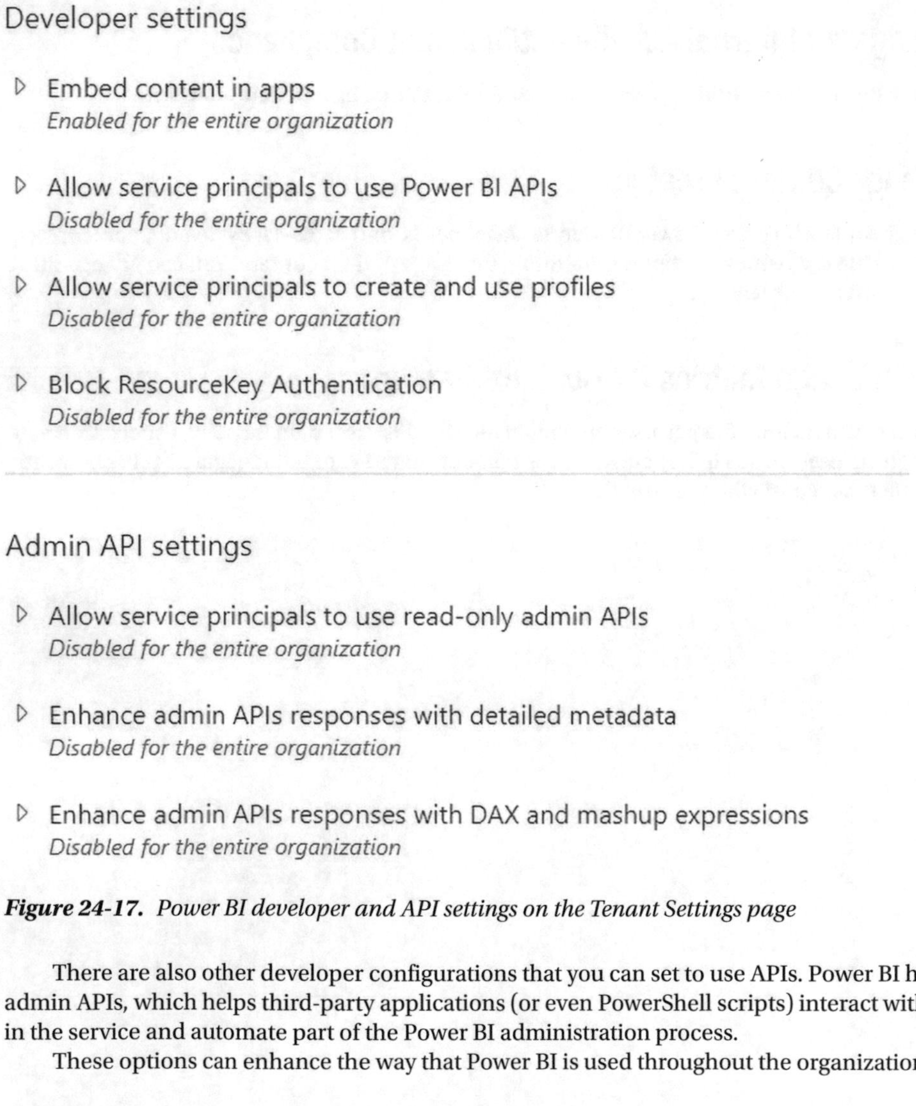

Developer settings

▷ Embed content in apps
Enabled for the entire organization

▷ Allow service principals to use Power BI APIs
Disabled for the entire organization

▷ Allow service principals to create and use profiles
Disabled for the entire organization

▷ Block ResourceKey Authentication
Disabled for the entire organization

Admin API settings

▷ Allow service principals to use read-only admin APIs
Disabled for the entire organization

▷ Enhance admin APIs responses with detailed metadata
Disabled for the entire organization

▷ Enhance admin APIs responses with DAX and mashup expressions
Disabled for the entire organization

Figure 24-17. *Power BI developer and API settings on the Tenant Settings page*

There are also other developer configurations that you can set to use APIs. Power BI has a good list of admin APIs, which helps third-party applications (or even PowerShell scripts) interact with Power BI objects in the service and automate part of the Power BI administration process.

These options can enhance the way that Power BI is used throughout the organization.

Dataflow, Template Apps, and Datamarts

There are many configurations that enable or disable the use and creation of objects such as dataflows, datamarts, metrics, template apps, and many of the new and preview features in Power BI.

Usage Metrics

The Admin Portal also has other sections that are helpful for a Power BI administrator. One monitoring part of the Admin Portal is the usage metrics of all Power BI content across the tenant. This can be accessed from the Admin Portal by clicking Usage Metrics, as shown in Figure 24-18.

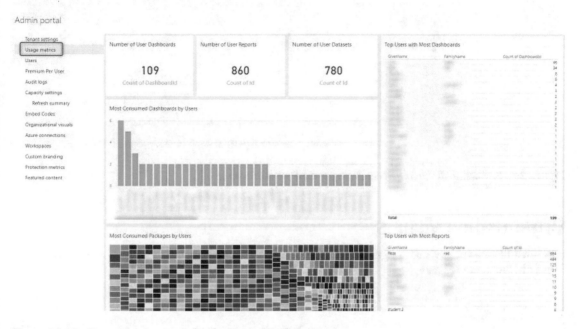

Figure 24-18. *Usage metrics report for the Power BI administrator*

The usage metrics here are different from the usage metrics for each dashboard and report. The usage metrics for the Power BI administrator provide an overall monitoring view of which users use most of the content, and which dashboards or reports have been used most often. How many dashboards, reports, or data sets exist in the tenant? This will reveal information about workspaces and more. The usage metrics reporting however, is not flexible and you cannot customize it.

Embed Codes

If you enabled the Publish to Web feature of Power BI in the tenant settings, you need to monitor the content that users publish using this option. The Embed Codes section of the Admin Portal, featured in Figure 24-19, tells you which reports are published to the web by which user. You can see the report or delete the embed code (deleting the embed code will not delete the report, it will only unpublish it from the web link).

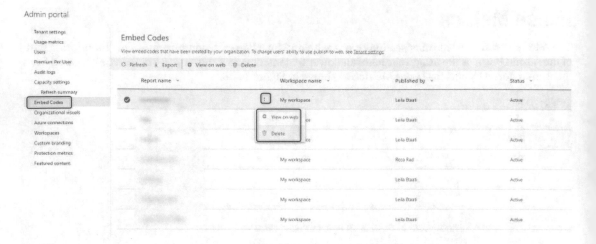

Figure 24-19. *Seeing all the embed codes across the Power BI tenant*

Organization Visuals

You can add a Power BI visual designed by your organization, as shown in Figure 24-20. You need the
`*.pbiviz` file to upload here.

Figure 24-20. *Adding a custom Power BI visual*

Then you can enter the details of the visual, as shown in Figure 24-21.

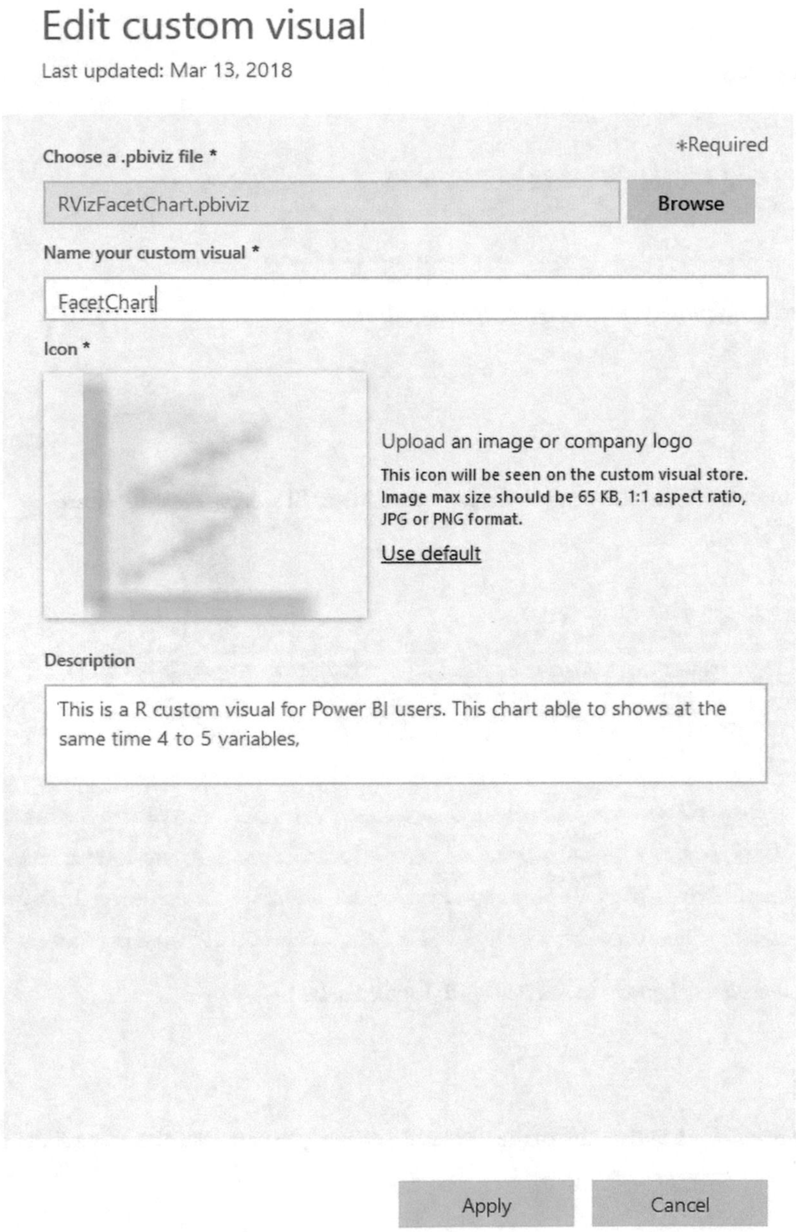

Edit custom visual

Last updated: Mar 13, 2018

*Required

Choose a .pbiviz file *

| RVizFacetChart.pbiviz | **Browse** |

Name your custom visual *

FacetChart

Icon *

Upload an image or company logo

This icon will be seen on the custom visual store.
Image max size should be 65 KB, 1:1 aspect ratio,
JPG or PNG format.

Use default

Description

This is a R custom visual for Power BI users. This chart able to shows at the
same time 4 to 5 variables,

Apply   Cancel

Figure 24-21. *Finalizing the custom visuals*

These visuals will then be available in the Power BI Desktop from the My Organization tab, as shown in Figure 24-22.

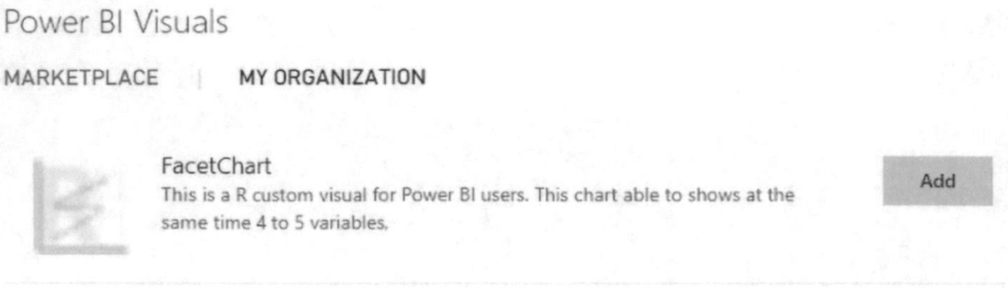

Power BI Visuals

MARKETPLACE | MY ORGANIZATION

FacetChart
This is a R custom visual for Power BI users. This chart able to shows at the same time 4 to 5 variables.

[Add]

Figure 24-22. *Custom visuals can be found on the My Organization tab*

Workspaces

Figure 24-23 shows that, as the tenant admin, you can see the full list of Power BI workspaces if they are defined under a Premium capacity.

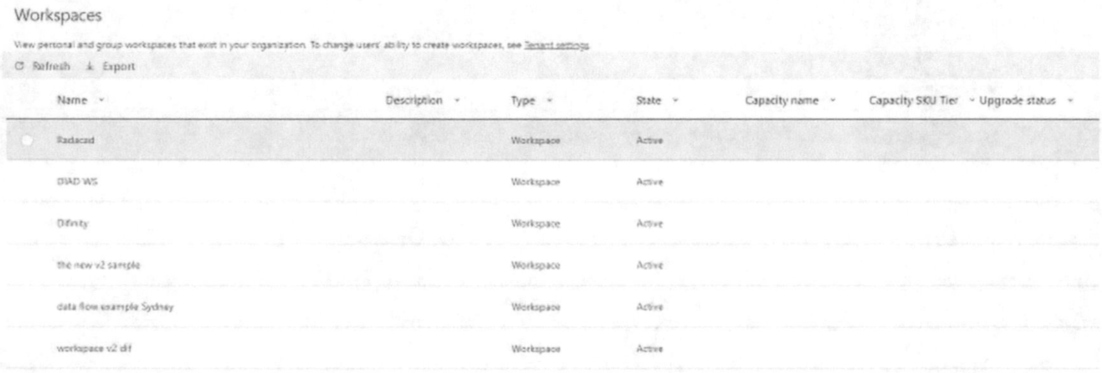

Workspaces

View personal and group workspaces that exist in your organization. To change users' ability to create workspaces, see Tenant settings.

↻ Refresh   ↓ Export

Name ∨	Description ∨	Type ∨	State ∨	Capacity name ∨	Capacity SKU Tier ∨	Upgrade status ∨
Radacad		Workspace	Active			
DIAD WS		Workspace	Active			
Difinity		Workspace	Active			
the new v2 sample		Workspace	Active			
data flow example Sydney		Workspace	Active			
workspace v2 dif		Workspace	Active			

Figure 24-23. *The full list of Power BI workspaces in the Power BI Admin Portal*

Custom Branding

If you want to add your organization's logo and colors to the Power BI Service, you can easily do so, as shown in Figure 24-24.

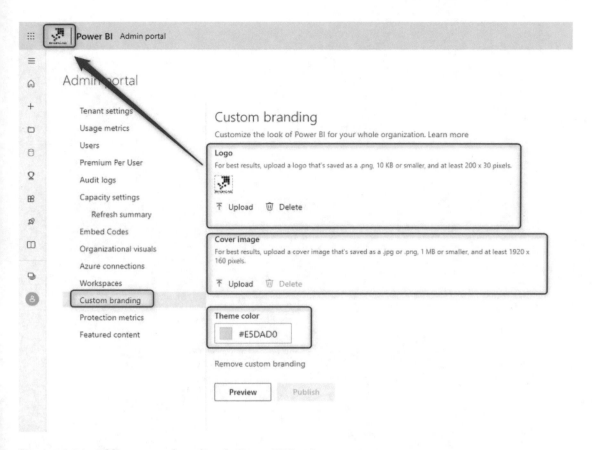

Figure 24-24. *Adding custom branding the Power BI Service*

Summary

Power BI administrators have access to specific parts of the Admin Portal, such as Tenant Settings, Manage Embed Codes, Organization Visuals, Usage Metrics, and more. The Tenant Settings area has many configurations and you need to be careful when using these options. For example, Publish to Web and the integration settings are important options to consider. The Admin Portal and Tenant Settings are updated in each version of the Power BI Service. There were some options that I did not explain in this chapter, as their use is either obvious or is related to a different topic (for example, Azure connections are related to creating external dataflow in Power BI that stores the data in your own Azure Data Lake storage subscription).

CHAPTER 25

■ ■ ■

PowerShell Cmdlets for Power BI

Power BI has a set of PowerShell Cmdlets that help automate part of the operations with Power BI. However, PowerShell is not a familiar technology. In the world of Power BI, we are used to working with graphical options and settings provided in the tools and the service. However, using commands provided for Power BI in a command/scripting tool such as PowerShell can be an excellent asset to a Power BI administrator, architect, and developer. In this chapter, you learn about the PowerShell Cmdlets for Power BI.

PowerShell

> *PowerShell is a task automation and configuration management program from Microsoft, consisting of a command-line shell and the associated scripting language.* [1]

PowerShell has become a common tool for administrators over the past few years. As an administrator, there are many libraries that you can access using PowerShell modules. PowerShell's scripting and command line experience are not as complicated as learning a programming language (such as C#.NET). This results in an easy-to-use tool that provides great power in configuration and task automation. Learning PowerShell is a topic that is outside of this chapter.[2]

PowerShell Cmdlets for Power BI

PowerShell includes modules that provide access to certain functionalities. Consider these modules like libraries. Each module gives you access to certain objects and configurations in the Power BI Service.

For example, one module gives you access to the list of workspaces in the Power BI Service, and another helps you with the reports inside the workspace. You can use a module to capture activities through the Power BI tenant in your organization. You can use a combination of these modules to extract a report from one workspace and then export it to another.

Table 25-1 shows the list of the modules.[3]

---

[1] en.wikipedia.org/wiki/PowerShell

[2] The PowerShell documentation is a good place to start: learn.microsoft.com/en-us/powershell/

[3] learn.microsoft.com/en-us/powershell/power-bi/overview?view=powerbi-ps

Table 25-1. *PowerShell Modules for Power BI*

Description	Module Name
Rollup module for Power BI Cmdlets	MicrosoftPowerBIMgmt
Admin module for Power BI Cmdlets	MicrosoftPowerBIMgmt.Admin
Capacities module for Power BI Cmdlets	MicrosoftPowerBIMgmt.Capacities
Data module for Power BI Cmdlets	MicrosoftPowerBIMgmt.Data
Profile module for Power BI Cmdlets	MicrosoftPowerBIMgmt.Profile
Reports module for Power BI	MicrosoftPowerBIMgmt.Reports
Workspaces module for Power BI	MicrosoftPowerBIMgmt.Workspaces

If you install the first module, it includes all the other modules. You can also choose to install modules as you need. To use the modules in Table 25-1, you must meet the following requirements:

- Windows PowerShell v3.0 and up with .NET 4.7.1 or above

- PowerShell Core (v6) and up on any OS platform supported by PowerShell Core

Getting Started

Let's go through a sample use of these modules. To start, open Windows PowerShell ISE (this is a more user-friendly version of Windows PowerShell). If you don't have this application, use the normal Windows PowerShell. It is better if you start this application as an administrator, as shown in Figure 25-1.

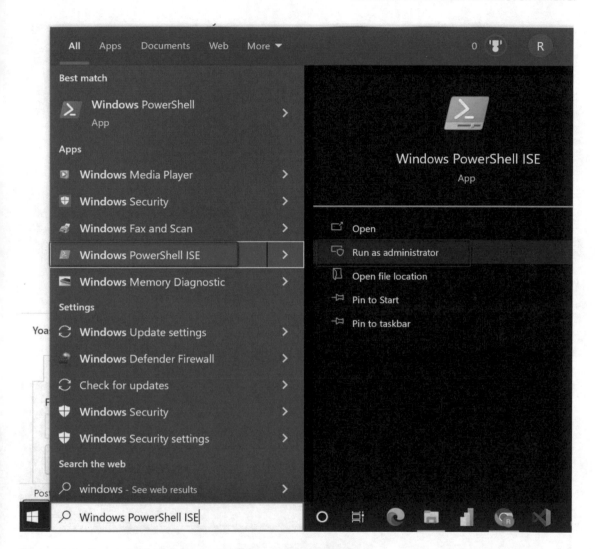

Figure 25-1. *Opening Windows PowerShell ISE as administrator*

This will open the application (see Figure 25-2), in which you can either type the commands (also called Cmdlets) or use the list on the right side and select from the Cmdlets. (Note that this list is only available in ISE, the basic Windows PowerShell doesn't come with it.)

Figure 25-2. Windows PowerShell ISE

To get the modules, you can use the Install-Module Cmdlet as follows:

```
Install-Module -Name MicrosoftPowerBIMgmt
```

You can then confirm the installation of the module, as shown in Figure 25-3.

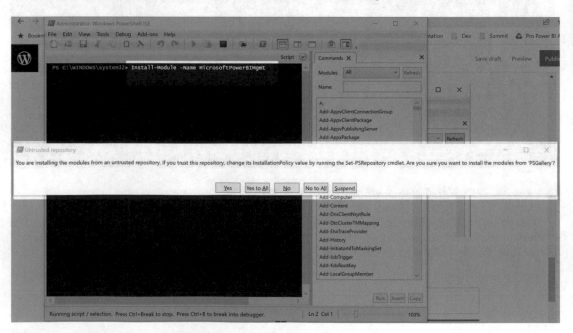

Figure 25-3. Installing Power BI modules for PowerShell

This step will install the module. If you already have the module installed and want to update it to the most recent version, use the Update-Module Cmdlets with the same parameters.

To use the Power BI Cmdlets, you first need to log in to Power BI using the Connect-PowerBIServiceAccount Cmdlet as follows:

```
Connect-PowerBIServiceAccount
```

Or, if you prefer to use the list of modules in the PowerShell ISE, refresh the modules list, select the Power BI Profile module, and then select the Cmdlet. You can either run the command from here or insert it, which will insert in the command line. Figure 25-4 outlines these steps.

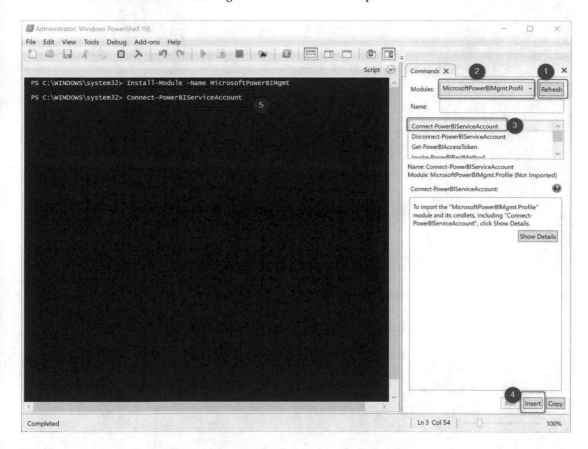

Figure 25-4. *Using the list of Cmdlets in PowerShell ISE*

If you choose a Cmdlet that requires parameters, the UI will also have places to enter those details.

Use the sign-in box to use your account for the Power BI (see Figure 25-5). If your account is a Power BI administrator, it might give you tenant results in your command execution. Otherwise, you can still use your non-admin Power BI account to use some of the commands.

Figure 25-5. *Log in using the Power BI account*

If the login is successful, you will see your tenant ID and username, as shown in Figure 25-6.

Figure 25-6. *The output of the Connect-PowerBIServiceAccount Cmdlet*

Now you can test some of the Cmdlets and see the results. For example, the following Cmdlet gives you a list of all the workspaces (these are the workspaces that you have access to, not all the workspaces in the organization):

```
Get-PowerBIWorkspace -All
```

The output is a list of workspaces, their names with IDs, and other information, as shown in Figure 25-7.

```
Id                    : 63678ecc-f862-4fb4-a463-a1e72badb8fa
Name                  : Community
Type                  : Workspace
IsReadOnly            : False
IsOrphaned            : False
IsOnDedicatedCapacity : False
CapacityId            :

Id                    : d8aeefb1-1052-476b-9d0e-dcddde69b623
Name                  : PW
Type                  : Workspace
IsReadOnly            : False
IsOrphaned            : False
IsOnDedicatedCapacity : True
CapacityId            : 6C533637-8A43-4B09-88CF-67D689A04CBB

Id                    : d3847ea9-b624-48c1-b025-37b1bff5ede1
Name                  : PW2
Type                  : Workspace
IsReadOnly            : False
IsOrphaned            : False
IsOnDedicatedCapacity : True
CapacityId            : 6C533637-8A43-4B09-88CF-67D689A04CBB

Id                    : 48e4d0ce-84e1-472c-a306-a23abe4cf5ad
Name                  : PPU WS
Type                  : Workspace
IsReadOnly            : False
IsOrphaned            : False
IsOnDedicatedCapacity : True
CapacityId            : 6C533637-8A43-4B09-88CF-67D689A04CBB

Id                    : 36f1f927-13c8-4c1c-a4aa-d0b2bdd7ecca
Name                  : WS DIS
Type                  : Workspace
IsReadOnly            : False
IsOrphaned            : False
IsOnDedicatedCapacity : True
CapacityId            : 6C533637-8A43-4B09-88CF-67D689A04CBB

PS C:\WINDOWS\system32>
```

Figure 25-7. *Getting a list of all workspaces for a Power BI user*

Example: Export a List of All Workspaces in the Organization as a CSV File

If your account is a Power BI Administrator account, you can use a parameter for scope and set that to Organization. This will give you all the workspaces in your tenant (even if you don't have access to those workspaces and other users in your organization created them):

```
Get-PowerBIWorkspace -Scope Organization -All
```

As mentioned, you can also select this Cmdlet in the list on the right side and see all the other parameters (see Figure 25-8).

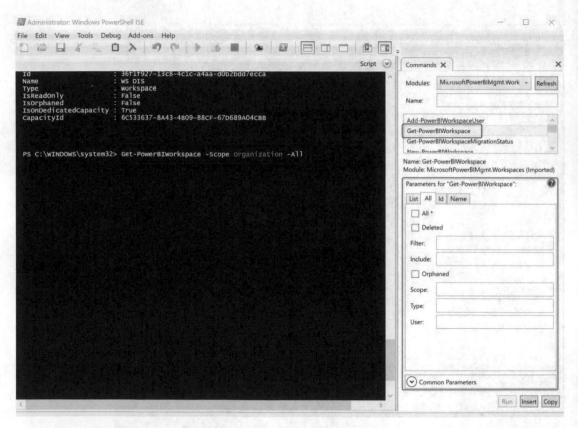

Figure 25-8. *Getting all the Power BI workspaces in the organization*

This command might take some time to run if you have many workspaces in your organization.

Now comes the power of PowerShell itself. This output is great, but what if you could export the output as a file, which you could use for other applications and purposes? Many modules and Cmdlets in PowerShell can help you with general tasks like that. The following example uses the ConvertTo-Csv Cmdlet with the Out-File parameter, which specifies the path of the CSV file.

```
Get-PowerBIWorkspace -Scope Organization -All | ConvertTo-Csv | Out-File
c:\PowerBIWorkspaces.csv
```

This command gives you a CSV file export of all workspace details, as demonstrated in Figure 25-9.

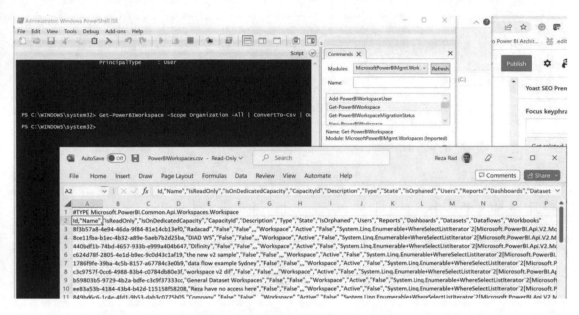

Figure 25-9. *Exporting all the Power BI workspaces to a CSV file*

Isn't this helpful? Now imagine if you could schedule these simple few lines of script to run every night from a server and store a list of workspaces. Now you have an application that stores the history of workspace changes throughout time in your organization. It is needless to say that you can generate the filename using the date and timestamp. So, if you have a history of all workspaces throughout the entire organization at any point in time, you can schedule the script. The next example shows how to schedule a PowerShell script using Task Scheduler.

Example: Deploy a Power BI Report from One Workspace to Another

PowerShell Cmdlets for Power BI can also create deployment pipeline solutions. This, then, can be a good replacement for the Deployment Pipeline feature, which is a Premium function in Power BI (of course, building something as comprehensive as that might take a while using the PowerShell Cmdlets).

I am going to show you part of this as an example. Let's say you want to export a single report from one workspace to another. You can use a combination of Cmdlets for this purpose, including Get-PowerBIReport and Export-PowerBIReport.

You need to know the workspace ID to get a Power BI report from a workspace. The workspace ID is a unique identifier. As Figure 25-10 shows, this ID can be recognized in the page URL when you are inside the workspace.

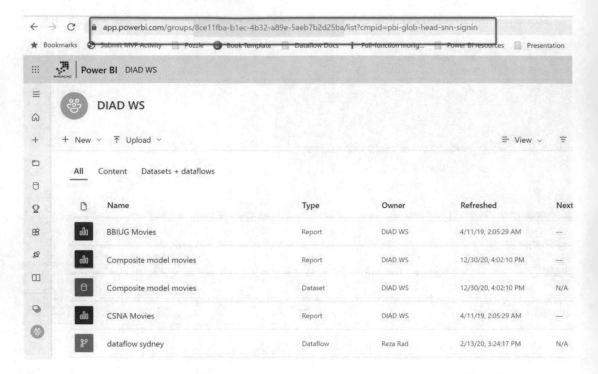

Figure 25-10. *Getting the workspace ID*

The same workspace ID is also returned as the result of PowerShell Cmdlets such as Get-PowerBIWorkspace, as shown in Figure 25-11.

```
Id                    : 6a6aa149-1ed8-446c-a235-41a3d1f5ca83
Name                  : DPS WS
Type                  : Workspace
IsReadOnly            : False
IsOrphaned            : False
IsOnDedicatedCapacity : False
CapacityId            :
```

Figure 25-11. *Getting the workspace ID from PowerShell Cmdlets*

This workspace ID can now be used as a parameter for the Get-PowerBIReport Cmdlet to give you the list of all the reports in the workspace.

```
Get-PowerBIReport -WorkspaceId <id of your workspace>
```

Figure 25-12 shows the output.

```
                  aw5kb5uzLm5rucrsimveymvkkmvnumvyzxmrons rbw9kzxJurwirrzwqrumkyuwusrnvzrwarrw
                  vOcmljc1ZoZxhOIjpOcnVlfxO%3d
DatasetId :       74a44663-0659-4032-8907-0a5f66bad515

Id        :       9d6555ee-2419-418c-9af2-faa88b7637ab
Name      :       CSNA Movies
webUrl    :       https://app.powerbi.com/groups/8ce11fba-b1ec-4b32-a89e-5aeb7b2d25ba/report
                  s/9d6555ee-2419-418c-9af2-faa88b7637ab
EmbedUrl  :

DatasetId :       39ef290c-6c77-4547-80f3-a53a92eb3156

Id        :       d782b9e0-870d-4bbe-9441-ee48f313ae93
Name      :       Composite model movies
webUrl    :       https://app.powerbi.com/groups/8ce11fba-b1ec-4b32-a89e-5aeb7b2d25ba/report
                  s/d782b9e0-870d-4bbe-9441-ee48f313ae93
EmbedUrl  :

DatasetId :       d13dbba9-4f60-4efb-bb42-d20424be977a


PS C:\WINDOWS\system32>
```

Figure 25-12. *Getting a list of Power BI reports in a workspace*

To export the PBIX file of one of these reports, you can use the report ID and the output filename as follows:

```
Export-PowerBIReport -Id <report Id> -OutFile "c:\CSNA Movies.pbix"
```

This downloads the PBIX file for that report into the local path (see Figure 25-13).

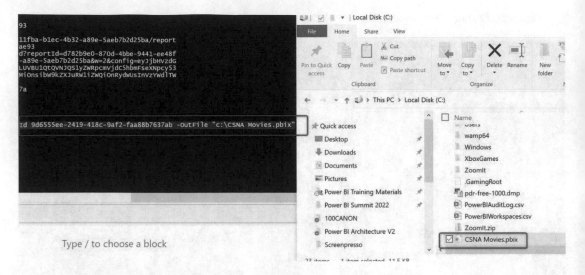

Figure 25-13. *The PBIX file was exported using the PowerShell Cmdlet*

Now you can publish this PBIX file to another workspace. You need the workspace ID of the destination workspace, and you can use the following Cmdlet:

```
New-PowerBIReport -Path "C:\CSNA Movies.pbix" -WorkspaceId <workspace id>
```

The report is now copied into this destination workspace, as shown in Figure 25-14.

Figure 25-14. *Publishing the Power BI report into a workspace*

This action is different from the Copy-PowerBIReport Cmdlet. The difference between these two is that the Copy Cmdlet creates a live connection to the dataset in the source workspace, whereas the method just explained creates a copy of the dataset.

This method can be expanded into looping through all the reports in the source workspace and exporting them into the destination workspace, like a full deployment pipeline from the Development environment into the Test or Production environment. However, explaining such a process is outside of this chapter's scope.

Are PowerShell Cmdlets the Same as REST APIs in Power BI?

The answer to this question is yes and no. These Cmdlets are designed on the basis of the REST API functions. However, far more capabilities are available in the REST APIs than in the PowerShell Cmdlets. PowerShell Cmdlets are kind of a layer on top of REST APIs. There is not a Cmdlet for every REST API; there are functions that you can only do through REST API.

One big benefit of PowerShell Cmdlets compared to REST API, however, is that to use the PowerShell Cmdlets, you don't need to be a C# or VB.NET developer. PowerShell scripts are much simpler to use and learn. An administrator can use them with a little practice.

However, if you need more extensive usage of APIs, REST APIs through a custom application is the way to go. If you have seen the capabilities in the Power BI Helper,[4] which helps with documentation in the service[5] and exports reports from one workspace to another,[6] those are implemented using the .NET REST API

Summary

In a nutshell, Power BI has a set of modules and Cmdlets for PowerShell. These are simple to use and, combined with the generic Cmdlets in Power BI, gives you capabilities such as the scenarios mentioned in this chapter (creating deployment scripts or generating documentation on a time-based schedule). Learning PowerShell is not as complex as learning a programming language. This, combined with the ability to connect to Power BI Service objects from PowerShell, enables Power BI administrators and developers to leverage these functionalities and automate some scenarios. The Cmdlets and modules are still a work in progress; however, they are always behind the REST API functionality. If you need more extensive capabilities through programming, REST API is a better option.

---

[4] Learn more: `https://radacad.com/power-bi-helper`
[5] Learn more: `https://radacad.com/document-the-power-bi-tenant-objects-workspace-reports-datasets-dataflows-with-no-code`
[6] Learn more: `https://radacad.com/copy-workspace-publish-to-multiple-workspaces-download-all-pbix-files-and-much-more-in-power-bi-helper-april-edition`

■ ■ ■

CHAPTER 26

Power BI REST API

You can interact with Power BI objects in the Power BI Service through a set of APIs called the Power BI REST API. The Power BI REST API can help automate tasks, build tools that work with Power BI, configure Power BI outside of the platform, and embed Power BI into third-party applications. This chapter describes the REST API and explains why it is useful with a few examples.

The Power BI REST API

A REST API is a type of web service that can be used with or without parameters and provide responses about a specific area. In the case of Power BI, the Power BI REST API is a set of web services that can work with the Power BI objects in the Power BI Service. There are many Power BI use cases for the REST API. Some examples follow:

- Refreshing the dataset automatically when it fails

- Refreshing the dataset immediately after successfully finishing the refresh of all related dataflows

- Creating a deployment pipeline

- Embedding a Power BI report or dashboard into a web application

- Automating documentation of Power BI Service objects

- Sending data rows to a streaming dataset in the Power BI Service

- Extracting the use of Power BI objects by the users

- And many other scenarios

Power BI REST APIs can be used in programming (.NET or other languages), PowerShell, and other tools. Most of the use cases for the APIs are through a programming language. This chapter doesn't go into detail about the program in which you invoke the REST API. Instead, this chapter focuses on where to get the information.

Getting Started

To start working with REST API for Power BI, you can go to learn.microsoft.com/en-us/rest/api/power-bi/. This is the link to the documentation for the REST API. The REST API operation is categorized into groups to find the function you are looking for easily, as shown in Figure 26-1.

Operation group	Description
Admin	Operations for working with administrative tasks.
Apps	Operations for working with Apps.
Available Features	Operations that return available features.
Capacities	Operations for working with capacities.
Dashboards	Operations for working with dashboards.
Dataflow Storage Accounts	Operations for working with dataflow storage accounts.
Dataflows	Operations for working with dataflows.
Datasets	Operations for working with datasets.
Embed Token	Operations for working with embed tokens.
Gateways	Operations for working with gateways.
Groups	Operations for working with groups.
Imports	Operations for working with imports.
Pipelines	Operations for working with deployment pipelines.
Push Datasets	Operations for working with push datasets.
Reports	Operations for working with reports.
Template Apps	Operations for working with Template Apps.
Users	Operations for working with users.

Figure 26-1. *Power BI REST API operation groups*

This list is updated regularly, and you can expect more functions and operations to be available through the REST API in the future. Once you click an operation group, you will see all the functions under that group, as shown in Figure 26-2.

Clone Report	Clones the specified report from My workspace.
Clone Report In Group	Clones the specified report from the specified workspace.
Delete Report	Deletes the specified report from My workspace.
Delete Report In Group	Deletes the specified report from the specified workspace.
Export Report	Exports the specified report from My workspace to a Power BI .pbix or .rdl file.
Export Report In Group	Exports the specified report from the specified workspace to a Power BI .pbix or .rdl file.
Export To File	Exports the specified report from My workspace to the requested file format.
Export To File In Group	Exports the specified report from the specified workspace to the requested file format.
Get Datasources	Returns a list of data sources for the specified paginated report (RDL) from My workspace.
Get Datasources In Group	Returns a list of data sources for the specified paginated report (RDL) from the specified workspace.
Get Export To File Status	Returns the current status of the Export to File job for the specified report from My workspace.
Get Export To File Status In Group	Returns the current status of the Export to File In Group job for the specified report from the specified workspace.
Get File Of Export To File	Returns the file from the Export to File job for the specified report from My workspace.
Get File Of Export To File In Group	Returns the file from the Export to File In Group job for the specified report from the specified workspace.
Get Page	Returns the specified page within the specified report from My workspace.
Get Page In Group	Returns the specified page within the specified report from the specified workspace.
Get Pages	Returns a list of pages within the specified report from My workspace.
Get Pages In Group	Returns a list of pages within the specified report from the specified workspace.
Get Report	Returns the specified report from My workspace.
Get Report In Group	Returns the specified report from the specified workspace.
Get Reports	Returns a list of reports from My workspace.
Get Reports In Group	Returns a list of reports from the specified workspace.
Rebind Report	Rebinds the specified report from My workspace to the specified dataset.
Rebind Report In Group	Rebinds the specified report from the specified workspace to the specified dataset.
Take Over In Group	Transfers ownership of the data sources for the specified paginated report (RDL) to the current authorized user.
Update Datasources	Updates the data sources of the specified paginated report (RDL) from My workspace.
Update Datasources In Group	Updates the data sources of the specified paginated report (RDL) from the specified workspace.
Update Report Content	Updates the content of the specified report from My workspace with the content of a specified source report.
Update Report Content In Group	Updates the content of the specified report from the specified workspace with the content of a specified source report.

Figure 26-2. *The REST API functions for Power BI reports*

The list in Figure 26-2 is for the REST API functions for Power BI reports. If you compare this list to the Power BI Cmdlets for PowerShell reports, you can see how extensive the REST API list is. This shows you immediately that the REST API is more powerful than the PowerShell Cmdlets for Power BI (although the PowerShell Cmdlets are easier for non-programmers to use).

A helpful feature in the Microsoft documentation for these REST APIs is that you can try a REST API function from the web page see (Figure 26-3). This way, you can call the function in your environment using your Power BI account and see if it is what you are looking for.

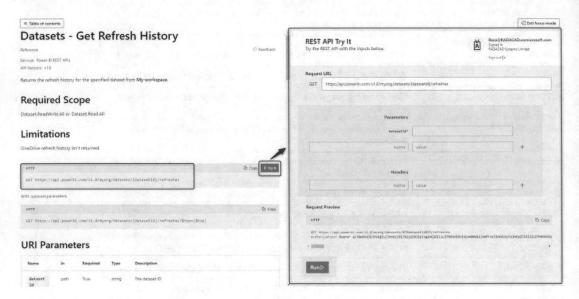

Figure 26-3. *Trying a REST API function through a browser*

For example, if you run the Get Refresh History API for a sample dataset, you can get the response through the Try window in the browser (see Figure 26-4).

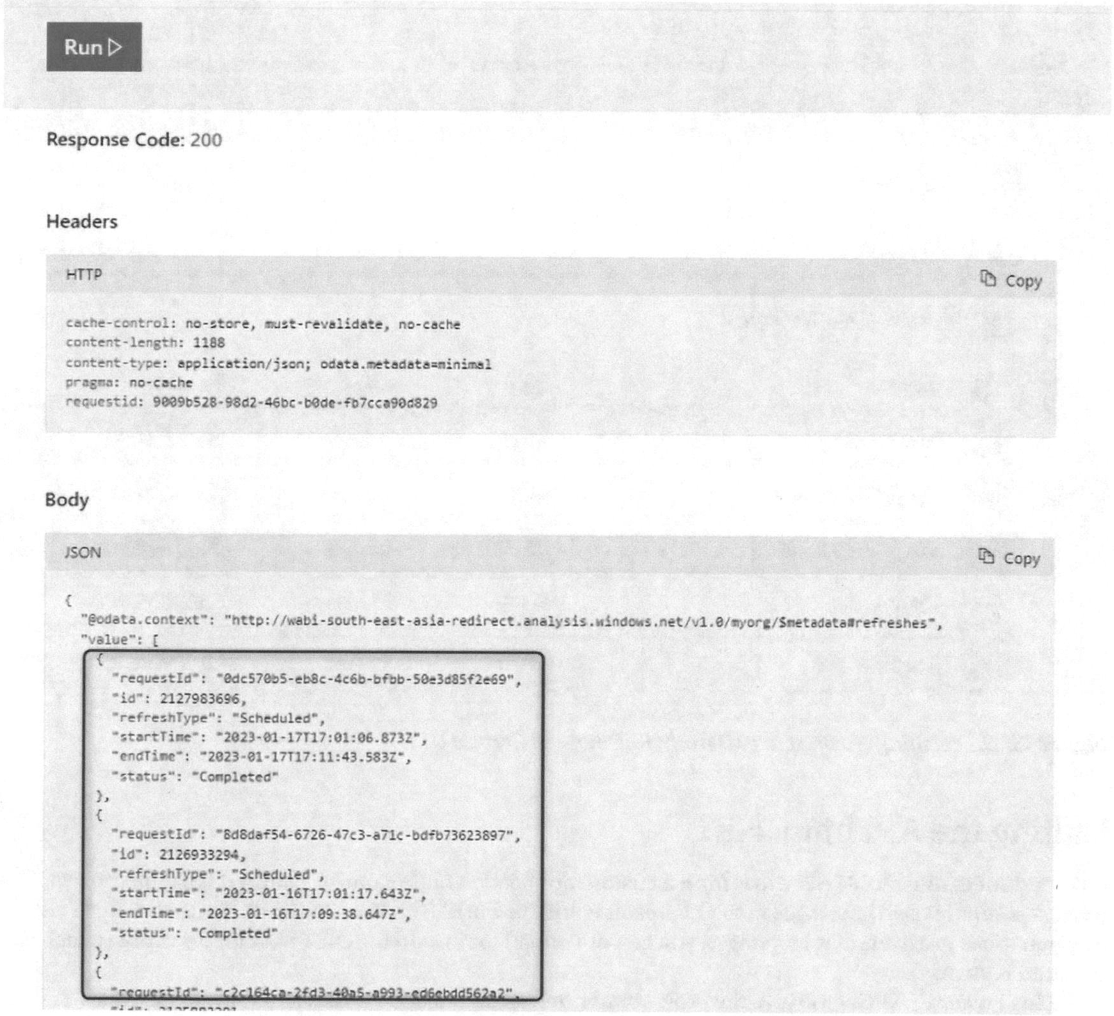

Run ▷

Response Code: 200

Headers

HTTP   📋 Copy

```
cache-control: no-store, must-revalidate, no-cache
content-length: 1188
content-type: application/json; odata.metadata=minimal
pragma: no-cache
requestid: 9009b528-98d2-46bc-b0de-fb7cca90d829
```

Body

JSON   📋 Copy

```
{
  "@odata.context": "http://wabi-south-east-asia-redirect.analysis.windows.net/v1.0/myorg/$metadata#refreshes",
  "value": [
    {
      "requestId": "0dc570b5-eb8c-4c6b-bfbb-50e3d85f2e69",
      "id": 2127983696,
      "refreshType": "Scheduled",
      "startTime": "2023-01-17T17:01:06.873Z",
      "endTime": "2023-01-17T17:11:43.583Z",
      "status": "Completed"
    },
    {
      "requestId": "8d8daf54-6726-47c3-a71c-bdfb73623897",
      "id": 2126933294,
      "refreshType": "Scheduled",
      "startTime": "2023-01-16T17:01:17.643Z",
      "endTime": "2023-01-16T17:09:38.647Z",
      "status": "Completed"
    },
    {
      "requestId": "c2c164ca-2fd3-40a5-a993-ed6ebdd562a2",
```

Figure 26-4. *The REST API sample results in the web browser*

Some APIs require the ID of the objects in the Power BI service. These IDs are the unique identifier codes that can be fetched through the URL of the object in the Power BI Service (see Figure 26-5) or through the response of some other API functions.

Figure 26-5. *Fetching a workspace ID from the Power BI Service URL*

Calling the API from .NET

As mentioned, most REST API use is from a custom application or program. C# and VB.NET are the two most commonly used languages in the Microsoft world for the REST API of Power BI. To use the REST API through these programming languages, you can download (or install) the .NET SDK for Power BI (which is updated regularly).

This Power BI NuGet will give the programmer the list of functions to use, as shown in Figure 26-6.

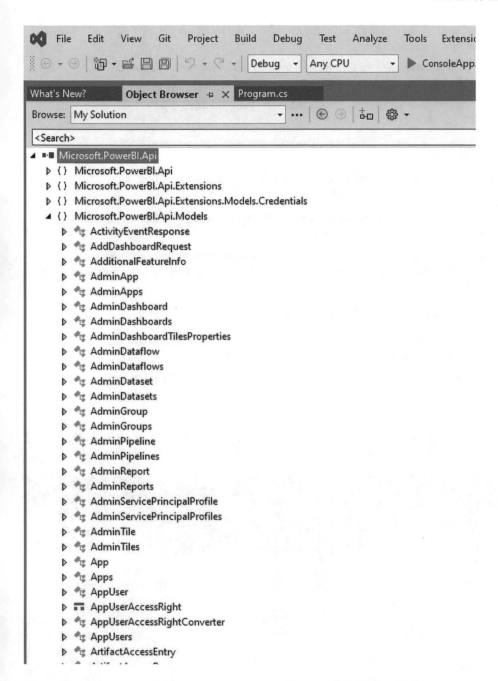

Figure 26-6. *The Power BI functions and classes in the Power BI SDK for .NET*

An example of such an application is the Power BI Helper, which uses the functions in the .NET SDK of Power BI to get the Power BI service documentation.

To get started with the .NET SDK of Power BI, you must register an application for Power BI in your organization's tenant active directory. Then you must complete the authentication process. If you are interested in learning more about it and seeing some samples of working with the .NET SDK of Power BI, read this article series:

- Part 1: Register the Application (radacad.com/integrate-power-bi-into-your-application-part-1-register-your-app)

- Part 2: Authentication (radacad.com/integrate-power-bi-into-your-application-part-2-authenticate)

- Part 3: Embed Content (radacad.com/integrate-power-bi-into-your-application-part-3-embed-content)

- Part 4: Refresh the Dataset (radacad.com/integrate-power-bi-into-your-application-part-4-refresh-data-set)

- Part 5: Manage the Data Source (radacad.com/integrate-power-bi-into-your-application-part-5-data-source-management)

- Part 6: Send Data Rows to Real-Time Streaming Datasets (radacad.com/integrate-power-bi-into-your-application-part-6-real-time-streaming-and-push-data)

Embedding into a Custom Application

A common use case for the REST API of Power BI is embedding the report or dashboard into a custom web application. The Power BI documentation has two good resources for that:

- Power BI Embedded analytics documentation-See learn.microsoft.com/en-us/power-bi/developer/embedded/

- Power BI Playground—See playground.powerbi.com/en-us/

The first link contains all the documentation you need for Power BI Embedded. The Power BI Playground (see Figure 26-7) is an interesting place to run embedded code as a test in the browser.

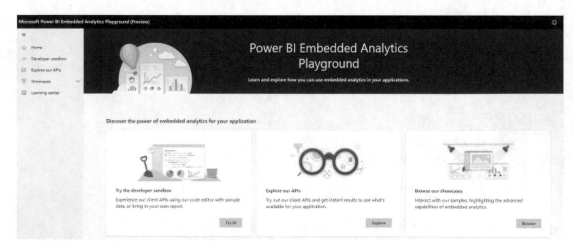

Figure 26-7. *The Power BI Embedded Analytics Playground*

The playground environment gives you a sandbox to see how code results perform in the application, get sample codes, and even run the code for your tenant, as shown in Figure 26-8.

Figure 26-8. *Testing codes in the Power BI Embedded Playground*

Power Automate

Some of the most common REST API functions for Power BI are streamlined through Power Automate. Power Automate is a service for designing flow and automation. You can, for example, use the Power BI functions in Power Automate to do tasks like the following:

- Export Power BI paginated reports using Power Automate (learn.microsoft.com/en-us/power-bi/collaborate-share/service-automate-paginated-integration)

- Export and email reports using Power Automate (learn.microsoft.com/en-us/power-bi/collaborate-share/service-automate-power-bi-report-export)

Power Automate includes a user-friendly UI; you don't need to be a programmer to work with the Power BI functions. An example of using Power Automate functions for Power BI is using Power Automate to trigger when a Microsoft Form is submitted and send the result to a real-time streaming Power BI dataset.

PowerShell to Call REST API

Another way to call the REST API is through a PowerShell command called Invoke_RestMethod. Check out the documentation of this function to learn how to use it at learn.microsoft.com/en-us/powershell/module/microsoft.powershell.utility/invoke-restmethod?view=powershell-7.3.

Summary

Power BI REST APIs are web services that can work with the Power BI Service objects (such as workspaces, datasets, dataflows, reports, and more). Using the REST API, a programmer can use a custom application to automate configurations for a Power BI Service solution and extend the solution to another level. Things that are not possible through the normal GUI of the Power BI service might be possible through the REST API.

■ ■ ■

CHAPTER 27

Power BI Audit Log for the Tenant

The Power BI dashboard and reports come with a usage metric, so you can see how users used this content. There is another report for usage metrics across the entire tenant, which you can see if you have access to the Power BI Administrator account under Admin Panel in the Power BI Service. However, what if you want to create your own detailed usage metrics report across the entire tenant? If you want to see across all workspaces in the tenant, you need a different approach. This information is not easily accessible in the Power BI Service. This chapter explains how to extract the Audit Log from Office 365, export it into text files, and create a Power BI report from it. Or in other words, how to create a custom usage metrics report across the tenant.

The Problem

Let's first consider the issue. Each report and dashboard has a usage metrics report, which shows where and when and by whom the content was used. You can usually find it at the top of the dashboard or report in the Power BI Service, as shown in Figure 27-1.

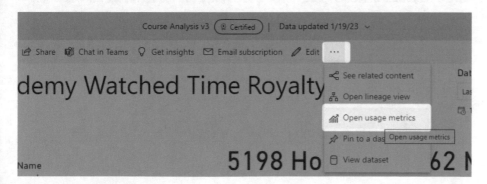

Figure 27-1. Viewing usage metrics

Figure 27-2 shows an example of a usage metrics report.

Figure 27-2. Usage metrics for a report in the Power BI Service

I previously wrote an article and explained how you can customize this report and create your version of this report using Save As, and then edit the report. Figure 27-3 shows a customized usage metrics report that I created.

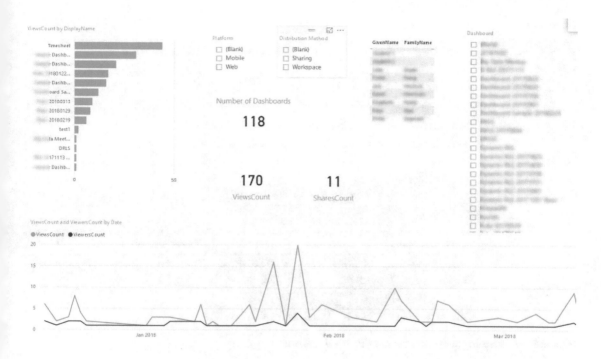

Figure 27-3. *A customized usage metrics report*

However, there is still a big challenge. This report will show me the usage metrics only in the current workspace, not in other workspaces. I would have to produce this report in each workspace separately!

Usage metrics of reports and the dashboard, even after customizing, show only the current workspace's data, not all workspace data.

On the other hand, if you have access to the Power BI Administrator account, under Admin Portal, you can find the usage metrics of all reports and dashboards across the tenant (see Figure 27-4).

Admin portal

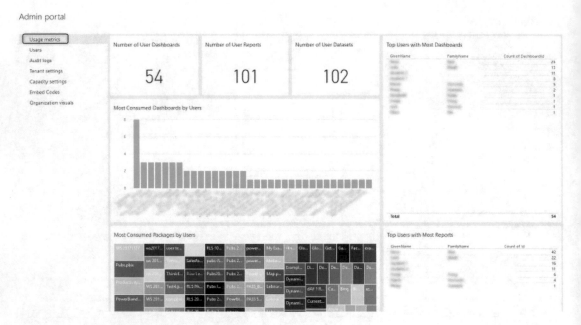

Figure 27-4. *Viewing usage metrics via the Admin Portal*

The challenge with this report is that you cannot customize it.

The usage metrics in the Admin Portal give you the metrics related to all content in the Power BI tenant, but that report is customizable and lots of details are missing.

Considering these two points, you are looking for a way to get a usage metrics report that gives you information about all the activities in the Power BI tenant. Let's consider how this is possible.

The Audit Log

The Power BI Service leverages the Office 365 logging system. The Power BI activities are already logged into Office 365; you just need to find them. If you have an account with sufficient privilege to the Audit Log, you can go to Admin Portal, and under Audit Log, access the Audit Log through the Microsoft 365 Admin Center. See Figure 27-5.

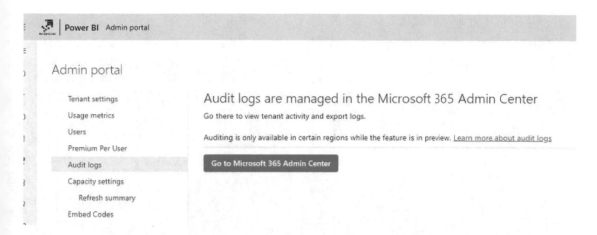

Figure 27-5. *Link to Audit Log from the Power BI Admin Portal*

This will open the Audit Log search in the Office Portal (see Figure 27-6).

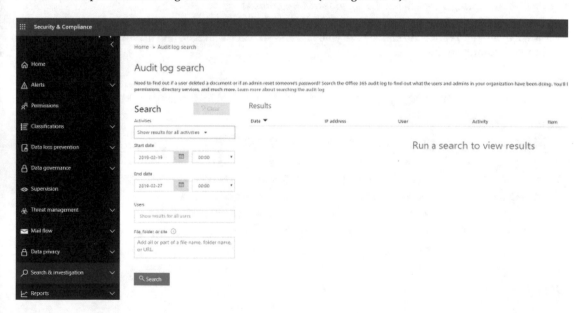

Figure 27-6. *The Audit Log search dialog*

Now you can search for the activities by selecting them in the Activities drop-down list, as shown in Figure 27-7.

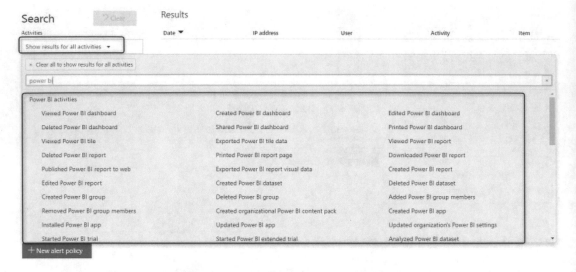

Figure 27-7. *Selecting activities via the Activities drop-down list*

You can also add other criteria, such as your search's start and end date and users to search. Figure 27-8 shows some example output.

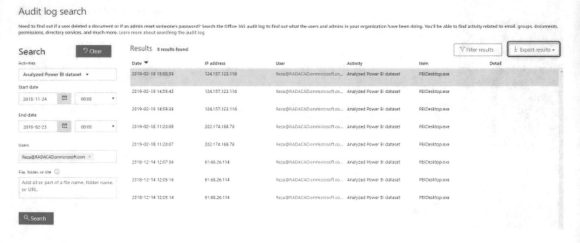

Figure 27-8. *Output based on example search criteria*

This output can then be exported as a source of a Power BI report. However, you cannot export all Power BI activities of all users. You will get an error like the one shown in Figure 27-9.

Audit log search

Need to find out if a user deleted a document or if permissions, directory services, and much more. Le

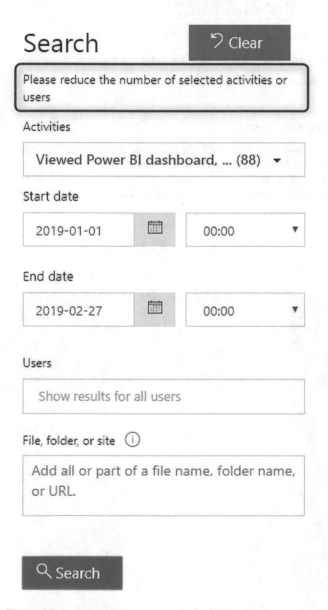

Figure 27-9. *Error message generated when trying to export all activity by all Power BI users*

Exporting the log data manually, and partially each time, is not practical, so you need another way to extract the Audit Log information.

Using PowerShell to Extract the Audit Log

There is more than one way to extract the Audit Log. Here are some methods:

- Using Office 365 Audit Log PowerShell Cmdlets (used in this chapter)

- Using Power BI Cmdlets for PowerShell

- Using the REST API for Power BI

- Using a third-party tool, such as Power BI Helper

These methods can all be used to export the Audit Log. The method I explain here uses the Office 365 Audit Log Cmdlets for PowerShell. This method can also extract logs about all other parts of Office 365.

PowerShell is an expression-based tool that automates some of the work for admins. PowerShell can be used to access the Office 365 Audit Log. First of all, you need to open PowerShell as an administrator (see Figure 27-10).

Figure 27-10. Running PowerShell as the administrator

Then start the following script (needed only once for a machine):

```
Install-Package ExchangeOnlineManagement
Import-Module ExchangeOnlineManagement
```

After installing and importing the module, you can then log in to your Power BI account using the following command (see Figure 27-11):

```
Connect-ExchangeOnline -UserPrincipalName <Power BI email account>
```

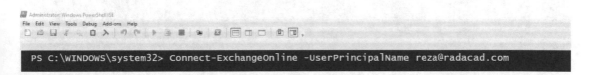

Figure 27-11. *Log in to the Office 365 account using the PowerShell Cmdlet*

To access the entire Audit Log across the tenant, you need access to the admin account. This is the same account you use in the previous script.

After successfully logging in, you can start accessing the Audit Log. To do that, you need another package, called ExchangePowerShell. Install and Import (see Figure 27-12) uses the following script (needed only once per machine):

```
Install-Package ExchangePowerShell
Import-Module ExchangePowerShell
```

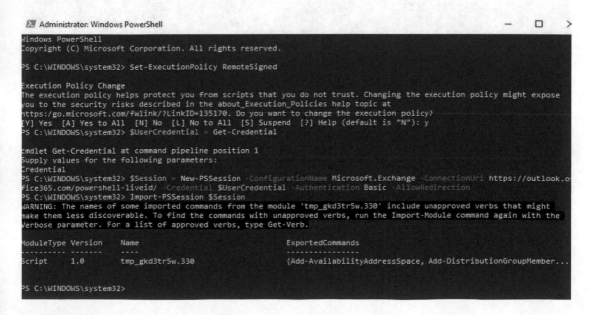

Figure 27-12. *The Install and Import package*

As the final step, you can read the Audit Log using the Search-UnifiedAuditLog function:

```
Search-UnifiedAuditLog -StartDate (Get-Date).AddDays(-90) -EndDate (Get-Date) -RecordType
PowerBIAudit -ResultSize 10
```

This will give you only ten rows of the Audit Log (I have limited the result size to ten), as shown in Figure 27-13.

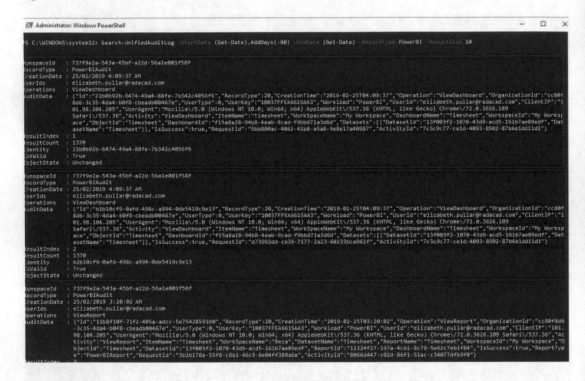

Figure 27-13. *Reading an Audit Log using the Search-UnifiedAuditLog function*

As you can see in Figure 27-13, you will have a list of log activities with a field named AuditData, which includes anything about the activity, including the object name and ID, the operation, the time and date of the operation, users who performed the operation, and the result of the operation.

The next step is to format this data and export it to a CSV file:

```
Search-UnifiedAuditLog -StartDate (Get-Date).AddDays(-90) -EndDate (Get-Date) -RecordType
PowerBIAudit -ResultSize 5000 | ConvertTo-Csv | Out-File c:\PowerBIAuditLog.csv
```

This will export the output of 5,000 log entries in the period of the last three months to CSV format, as illustrated in Figure 27-14.

```
#TYPE Deserialized.Microsoft.Exchange.Data.ApplicationLogic.UnifiedAuditLogEvent
"PSComputerName","RunspaceId","PSShowComputerName","RecordType","CreationDate","UserIds","Operations","AuditData",
"outlook.office365.com","737f9e2a-543a-45bf-a22d-56a1e001f58f","False","PowerBIAudit","26/02/2019 12:08:30 AM","Re
"outlook.office365.com","737f9e2a-543a-45bf-a22d-56a1e001f58f","False","PowerBIAudit","25/02/2019 4:09:37 AM","eli
"outlook.office365.com","737f9e2a-543a-45bf-a22d-56a1e001f58f","False","PowerBIAudit","25/02/2019 4:09:37 AM","eli
"outlook.office365.com","737f9e2a-543a-45bf-a22d-56a1e001f58f","False","PowerBIAudit","25/02/2019 3:20:02 AM","eli
"outlook.office365.com","737f9e2a-543a-45bf-a22d-56a1e001f58f","False","PowerBIAudit","25/02/2019 3:09:24 AM","eli
"outlook.office365.com","737f9e2a-543a-45bf-a22d-56a1e001f58f","False","PowerBIAudit","25/02/2019 1:08:07 AM","eli
"outlook.office365.com","737f9e2a-543a-45bf-a22d-56a1e001f58f","False","PowerBIAudit","25/02/2019 12:02:45 AM","el
"outlook.office365.com","737f9e2a-543a-45bf-a22d-56a1e001f58f","False","PowerBIAudit","22/02/2019 4:08:22 AM","eli
"outlook.office365.com","737f9e2a-543a-45bf-a22d-56a1e001f58f","False","PowerBIAudit","22/02/2019 3:41:36 AM","Re:
"outlook.office365.com","737f9e2a-543a-45bf-a22d-56a1e001f58f","False","PowerBIAudit","22/02/2019 3:07:06 AM","eli
"outlook.office365.com","737f9e2a-543a-45bf-a22d-56a1e001f58f","False","PowerBIAudit","22/02/2019 1:05:52 AM","eli
"outlook.office365.com","737f9e2a-543a-45bf-a22d-56a1e001f58f","False","PowerBIAudit","22/02/2019 12:07:32 AM","e
"outlook.office365.com","737f9e2a-543a-45bf-a22d-56a1e001f58f","False","PowerBIAudit","21/02/2019 11:03:53 PM","e
"outlook.office365.com","737f9e2a-543a-45bf-a22d-56a1e001f58f","False","PowerBIAudit","21/02/2019 10:08:38 PM","e
"outlook.office365.com","737f9e2a-543a-45bf-a22d-56a1e001f58f","False","PowerBIAudit","21/02/2019 9:04:35 PM","eli
"outlook.office365.com","737f9e2a-543a-45bf-a22d-56a1e001f58f","False","PowerBIAudit","21/02/2019 8:05:22 PM","eli
"outlook.office365.com","737f9e2a-543a-45bf-a22d-56a1e001f58f","False","PowerBIAudit","21/02/2019 4:44:53 AM","eli
"outlook.office365.com","737f9e2a-543a-45bf-a22d-56a1e001f58f","False","PowerBIAudit","21/02/2019 4:05:13 AM","eli
"outlook.office365.com","737f9e2a-543a-45bf-a22d-56a1e001f58f","False","PowerBIAudit","21/02/2019 3:03:41 AM","eli
```

Figure 27-14. *Formatting data and exporting it to a CSV file*

Here are a few tips about the export process in Figure 27-14:

- The default time period that Office 365 keeps the Audit Log is 90 days. You can change it if you want.

- The export only supports up to 5,000 Audit Log transactions. You need to split it into multiple exports if you have more than that.

The Power BI Report for the Audit Log

Now that you have a CSV file of all the Audit Logs, you can use that as a data source in Power BI. Open a new Power BI file and get the data from the CSV file (see Figure 27-15).

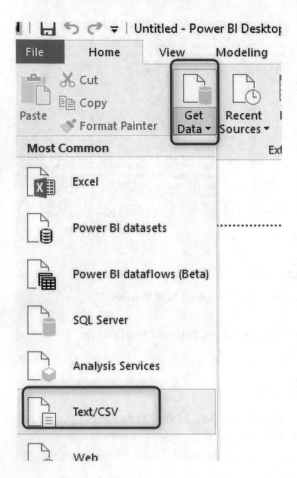

Figure 27-15. *Getting data from an existing .csv file*

After selecting the source file, click Transform Data to go to the Power Query Editor window (see Figure 27-16).

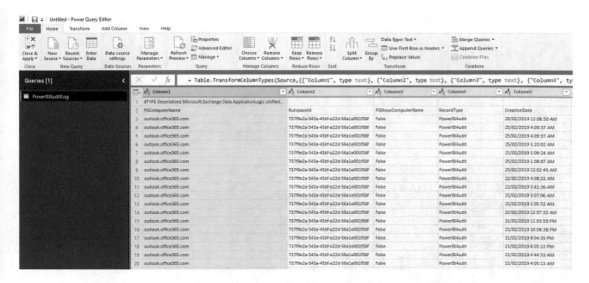

Figure 27-16. *The Power Query Editor window*

Remove the top row, as it doesn't contain any useful information (see Figure 27-17).

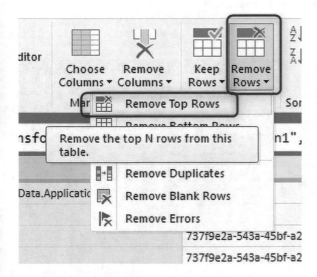

Figure 27-17. *Removing the top row of the .csv file*

In the next step, go to the Transform tab and choose Use First Row as Headers (see Figure 27-18).

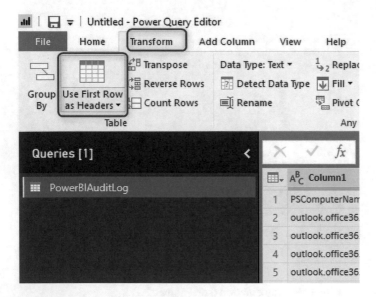

Figure 27-18. *Selecting Use First Row as Headers from the Transform tab*

You will see the log output shown in Figure 27-19.

PSComputerName	Runspaceld	PSShowComputerNa...	RecordType	CreationDate	UserIds	Operations	AuditData
1 outlook.office365.com	7379e2a-543a-45bf-a22d-56a1e001f58f	FALSE	PowerBIAudit	26/02/2023 12:08:30 AM	Reza@RADACAD.onmicrosoft.co...	ViewUsageMetrics	["id": "bb57afd8-9215-
2 outlook.office365.com	7379e2a-543a-45bf-a22d-56a1e001f58f	FALSE	PowerBIAudit	25/02/2023 4:09:37 AM	elizabeth.pullar@radacad.com	ViewDashboard	["id": "21b0b92b-6474-
3 outlook.office365.com	7379e2a-543a-45bf-a22d-56a1e001f58f	FALSE	PowerBIAudit	25/02/2023 4:09:37 AM	elizabeth.pullar@radacad.com	ViewDashboard	["id": "b3fc03cf9-0a1b-
4 outlook.office365.com	7379e2a-543a-45bf-a22d-56a1e001f58f	FALSE	PowerBIAudit	25/02/2023 3:20:02 AM	elizabeth.pullar@radacad.com	ViewReport	["id": "11bff10f-71f2-
5 outlook.office365.com	7379e2a-543a-45bf-a22d-56a1e001f58f	FALSE	PowerBIAudit	25/02/2023 3:09:24 AM	elizabeth.pullar@radacad.com	ViewDashboard	["id": "3d523cbf-ea2b
6 outlook.office365.com	7379e2a-543a-45bf-a22d-56a1e001f58f	FALSE	PowerBIAudit	25/02/2023 2:08:07 AM	elizabeth.pullar@radacad.com	ViewDashboard	["id": "bb5bb85c-1605
7 outlook.office365.com	7379e2a-543a-45bf-a22d-56a1e001f58f	FALSE	PowerBIAudit	25/02/2023 12:02:45 AM	elizabeth.pullar@radacad.com	ViewDashboard	["id": "bf9b2dd9-cfe5-
8 outlook.office365.com	7379e2a-543a-45bf-a22d-56a1e001f58f	FALSE	PowerBIAudit	22/02/2023 4:08:22 AM	elizabeth.pullar@radacad.com	ViewDashboard	["id": "1b13cb90-7ba9
9 outlook.office365.com	7379e2a-543a-45bf-a22d-56a1e001f58f	FALSE	PowerBIAudit	22/02/2023 3:41:36 AM	Reza@RADACAD.onmicrosoft.co...	ViewUsageMetrics	["id": "a30aeb72-eb3c
10 outlook.office365.com	7379e2a-543a-45bf-a22d-56a1e001f58f	FALSE	PowerBIAudit	22/02/2023 3:07:06 AM	elizabeth.pullar@radacad.com	ViewDashboard	["id": "c9f690ed-3fa4-
11 outlook.office365.com	7379e2a-543a-45bf-a22d-56a1e001f58f	FALSE	PowerBIAudit	22/02/2023 2:05:52 AM	elizabeth.pullar@radacad.com	ViewDashboard	["id": "d452f318-54b4
12 outlook.office365.com	7379e2a-543a-45bf-a22d-56a1e001f58f	FALSE	PowerBIAudit	22/02/2023 12:07:32 AM	elizabeth.pullar@radacad.com	ViewDashboard	["id": "7a5cac40-e8c8
13 outlook.office365.com	7379e2a-543a-45bf-a22d-56a1e001f58f	FALSE	PowerBIAudit	21/02/2019 11:03:53 PM	elizabeth.pullar@radacad.com	ViewDashboard	["id": "4926874e-7f4a
14 outlook.office365.com	7379e2a-543a-45bf-a22d-56a1e001f58f	FALSE	PowerBIAudit	21/02/2019 10:08:38 PM	elizabeth.pullar@radacad.com	ViewDashboard	["id": "f6d052e6-a493
15 outlook.office365.com	7379e2a-543a-45bf-a22d-56a1e001f58f	FALSE	PowerBIAudit	21/02/2019 9:04:35 PM	elizabeth.pullar@radacad.com	ViewDashboard	["id": "631aa78d-286d
16 outlook.office365.com	7379e2a-543a-45bf-a22d-56a1e001f58f	FALSE	PowerBIAudit	21/02/2019 8:05:22 PM	elizabeth.pullar@radacad.com	ViewDashboard	["id": "e73d7f92-2447-
17 outlook.office365.com	7379e2a-543a-45bf-a22d-56a1e001f58f	FALSE	PowerBIAudit	21/02/2019 4:44:53 AM	elizabeth.pullar@radacad.com	ViewReport	["id": "83a61d91-09ac
18 outlook.office365.com	7379e2a-543a-45bf-a22d-56a1e001f58f	FALSE	PowerBIAudit	21/02/2019 4:05:13 AM	elizabeth.pullar@radacad.com	ViewDashboard	["id": "94e8fbdc-24fa-
19 outlook.office365.com	7379e2a-543a-45bf-a22d-56a1e001f58f	FALSE	PowerBIAudit	21/02/2019 3:03:41 AM	elizabeth.pullar@radacad.com	ViewDashboard	["id": "27f2e847-ca1c-
20 outlook.office365.com	7379e2a-543a-45bf-a22d-56a1e001f58f	FALSE	PowerBIAudit	21/02/2019 1:06:34 AM	elizabeth.pullar@radacad.com	ViewDashboard	["id": "90fc5a75-3cd5-
21 outlook.office365.com	7379e2a-543a-45bf-a22d-56a1e001f58f	FALSE	PowerBIAudit	21/02/2019 12:06:38 AM	elizabeth.pullar@radacad.com	ViewDashboard	["id": "61fc3aff-5680-
22 outlook.office365.com	7379e2a-543a-45bf-a22d-56a1e001f58f	FALSE	PowerBIAudit	20/02/2019 11:09:17 PM	elizabeth.pullar@radacad.com	ViewDashboard	["id": "3f1354ae-8dcb-
23 outlook.office365.com	7379e2a-543a-45bf-a22d-56a1e001f58f	FALSE	PowerBIAudit	20/02/2019 9:37:12 PM	elizabeth.pullar@radacad.com	ViewReport	["id": "cfec6e1f-6598-
24 outlook.office365.com	7379e2a-543a-45bf-a22d-56a1e001f58f	FALSE	PowerBIAudit	19/02/2019 2:04:56 AM	reza@radacad.com	AnalyzedByExternalApplication	["id": "7c115920-f205-
25 outlook.office365.com	7379e2a-543a-45bf-a22d-56a1e001f58f	FALSE	PowerBIAudit	19/02/2019 2:00:39 AM	Reza@RADACAD.onmicrosoft.co...	AnalyzedByExternalApplication	

Figure 27-19. *The Power BI log output*

As you can see, there is some generic information, and the main details are all in the AuditData field. The AuditData field is formatted as JSON. Let's remove all the other fields and only keep the AuditData (see Figure 27-20).

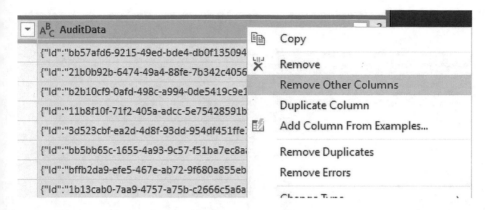

Figure 27-20. *Removing all fields except for AuditData*

Because the field is in JSON format, you can choose the Parse JSON option, as illustrated in Figure 27-21.

Figure 27-21. *Using the Parse JSON option*

JSON data will be as a record in every cell, and you can expand it to underlying columns, as depicted in Figure 27-22.

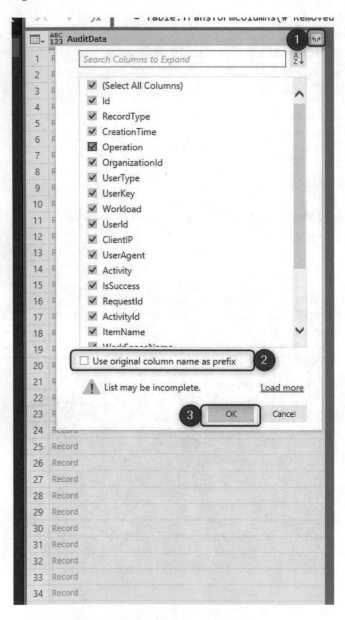

Figure 27-22. Expanding JSON data to underlying cells

Figure 27-23 shows all the Audit Log data.

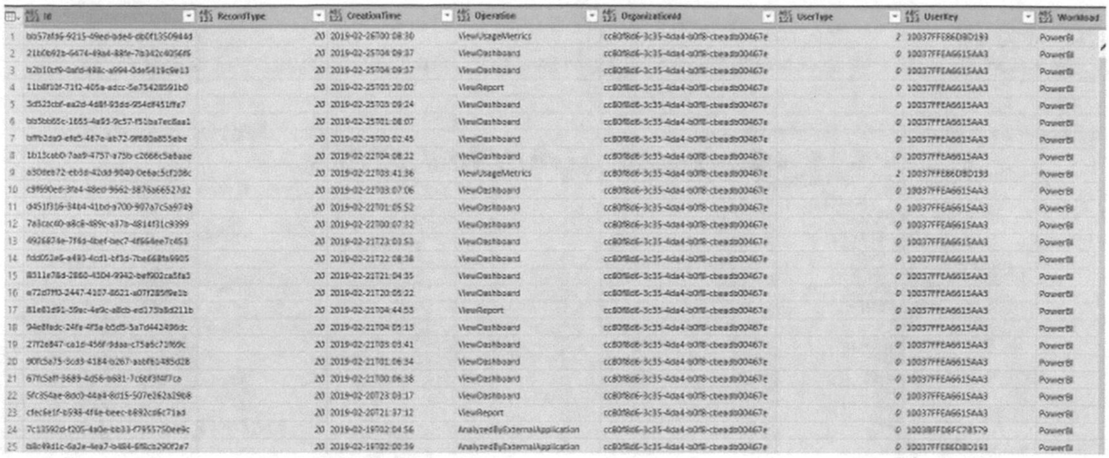

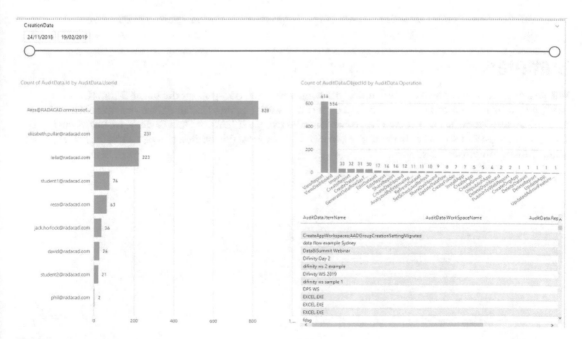

Figure 27-23. *Displaying all the Audit Log data*

The remaining steps involve visualizing this data. Figure 27-24 shows some sample visualizations I created. This report shows all users and their operations on certain items (report, dataset, dashboard, and workspaces).

Figure 27-24. *Sample data visualization showing all users and their activities*

Figure 27-25 shows all the objects and the operations on them with the list of users.

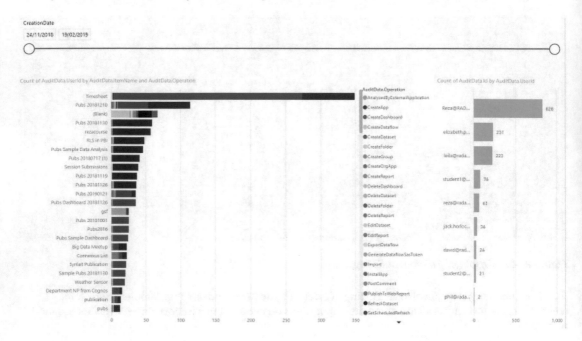

Figure 27-25. *Sample data visualization showing all objects and operations performed on them*

Summary

Yes, you can create your own custom audit and usage metrics reports across the entire tenant from all workspaces. You can leverage PowerShell to export the Audit Log into CSV and then use that as the source for the Power BI report. This process can be automated using SSIS, Azure Data Factory, or Task Scheduler. This information is also available through Power BI Helper. Also, PowerShell can be useful for getting much other information from the service.

CHAPTER 28

■ ■ ■

XMLA Endpoint

The XMLA Endpoint is still too technical for many Power BI report developers. Many people come to me asking what exactly an XMLA endpoint is and what it's used for. This chapter explains the XMLA Endpoint in detail. Let's dig in.

Behind the Scenes of a Power BI Dataset

To understand what an XMLA Endpoint is and what it does for you, you need to understand the backstage of a Power BI dataset. By backstage, I mean what is behind the Power BI report that you see.

A Power BI report is a visualization element connected to an in-memory dataset behind the scenes. (I am talking about the most common method of using Power BI, which is Import Data.) The in-memory dataset behind the scenes has all the data loaded into the memory, with all calculations, relationships, and connections to the data source. When you open a *.PBIX file, behind the scenes, there are two elements—a report (the visualization part) and a dataset (the data model). This separation is visible in the Power BI Desktop app resource details, accessed from the Task Manager (see Figure 28-1).

Task Manager

File Options View

Processes Performance App history Startup Users Details Services

Name	Status	15% CPU	49% Memory	2% Disk
> 🌐 Google Chrome (32)		0.6%	1,426.5 MB	0.1 MB/s
∨ 📊 Power BI Desktop (9)		1.1%	1,105.4 MB	0 MB/s
📈 Microsoft Power BI Desktop		0.1%	448.3 MB	0 MB/s
▣ CefSharp.BrowserSubprocess		0.1%	165.8 MB	0 MB/s
▣ CefSharp.BrowserSubprocess		0%	138.0 MB	0 MB/s
▣ Microsoft SQL Server Analysis Services		0%	118.1 MB	0 MB/s
▣ CefSharp.BrowserSubprocess		0%	105.2 MB	0 MB/s
▣ Microsoft Mashup Evaluation Container		0%	70.9 MB	0 MB/s
▣ CefSharp.BrowserSubprocess		0.9%	50.4 MB	0 MB/s
🖥 Console Window Host		0%	4.9 MB	0 MB/s
▣ CefSharp.BrowserSubprocess		0%	3.8 MB	0 MB/s

Figure 28-1. *Viewing resource details in the Task Manager*

© Reza Rad 2023
R. Rad, *Pro Power BI Architecture*, https://doi.org/10.1007/978-1-4842-9538-0_28

As you can see in Figure 28-1, a Microsoft SQL Server Analysis Services task is running under the Power BI Desktop list. A Power BI report stores its data in memory, which is managed by the Microsoft SQL Server Analysis Services Engine. (Let's call it by its shorter, more familiar, name—SSAS.) Even if you run the Power BI Desktop on a machine that doesn't have SSAS installed, you will see this service because the Power BI Desktop automatically installs a version of SSAS.

A Power BI dataset is hosted through a SQL Server Analysis Services Engine.

When you publish your `*.pbix` file to the Power BI Service, you will also see this separation of the data model (the dataset) and the visualization (the report), as shown in Figure 28-2.

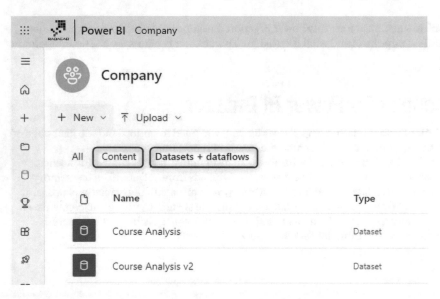

Figure 28-2. *The separation of the dataset and the report (content) in the Power BI Service*

When you host your report (or publish it) in the Power BI Service, the dataset will be managed by a version of SSAS installed on a cloud machine that you don't see (or, better to say, a version of Azure Analysis Services).

SSAS Is More Than What You See

Now that you know a Power BI dataset is an SSAS model behind the scenes, the next question is, what is the point? Or what is the benefit of it? To understand that, let's look at SSAS more closely.

SSAS is a modeling engine in Microsoft SQL Server. It's more than 20 years old and is a mature technology. SSAS is a server-side modeling technology. The model is hosted on a server, and the client tools can work with it. Through many years, the two most common client tools to work with SSAS are SQL Server Data Tools (SSDT) and SQL Server Management Studio (SSMS), the latter of which is shown in Figure 28-3.

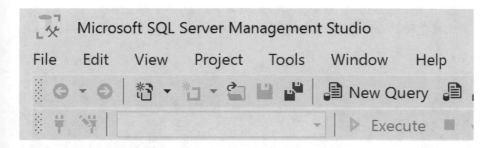

Figure 28-3. *The SQL Server Management Studio UI*

These tools not only build the model in SSAS but also manage it. When it comes to management, that includes monitoring, controlling, backing up, and restoring the model, and many other features. Figure 28-4 shows a view of an SSAS database (model) from SSMS.

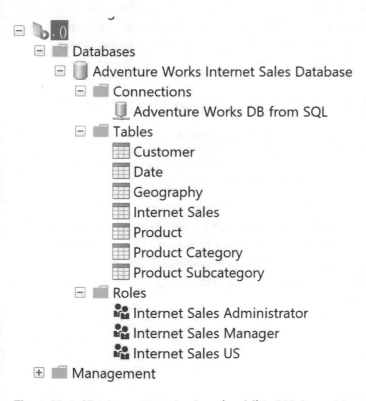

Figure 28-4. *Viewing an SSAS database (model) in SQL Server Management Studio*

SSAS models can be monitored using queries and commands called Dynamic Management Views (DMV). For example, the command in Figure 28-5 shows all the users querying or working with this SSAS model.

```
Select * from $System.discover_sessions
```

100 % ▾ ◁

☐ Messages ☷ Results

SESSIO...	SESSIO...	SESSIO...	SESSION_USER_NAME	SESSIO...	SESSIO...	SESSIO...	SESSIO...	SESSIO...	SESSIO...	SESSIO...	SES
E9AC0...	798	8	AzureAD\RezaRad	Advent...	22		6/04/20...	187863	6/04/20...	6/04/20...	0
EB9134...	827	11	AzureAD\RezaRad	Advent...	3		6/04/20...	48806	6/04/20...	6/04/20...	15
29C2DF...	831	12	AzureAD\RezaRad	Advent...	3		6/04/20...	48389	6/04/20...	6/04/20...	0

Figure 28-5. *Executing a command that shows all users querying or working with the SSAS model*

SQL Server Analysis Services is a server-side technology that gives you a lot of details about the model. It can be monitored through client tools using scripts and commands such as Dynamic Management Views.

Can I Access the SSAS Model of My Power BI Dataset?

You learned so far that your Power BI dataset is an SSAS model behind the scenes. You also learned that you can control and monitor SSAS models using client tools. However, when the Power BI dataset is hosted in the Power BI Service, how can you connect to that SSAS model? How can you control, manage, or monitor it? Or, even more importantly, why is it important to do it? See Figure 28-6.

If you can connect to the SSAS model of your Power BI dataset, you can connect to the data model directly. You can see how many users are using it. You can see what processes take longer and which ones are slow. You can leverage all those monitoring features to build a better model moving forward. There are two common ways to connect to the Power BI dataset hosted in the service—the Power BI Desktop (using Get Data from the Power BI dataset) and Excel (using Analyze in Excel).

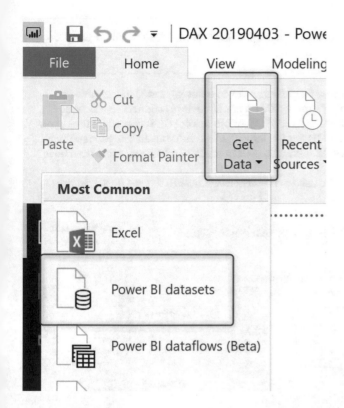

Figure 28-6. *Connecting to a Power BI dataset hosted in a service*

Both of these tools are reporting tools. You can (somehow) run monitoring queries from these tools, but these are not built for that purpose. You will have better control if you can access this through other client tools. The good news is that now you can! That's where XMLA Endpoint comes in to play.

XMLA Endpoint

XMLA stands for Extensible Markup Language for Analysis. Now is a good time to explain what an XMLA Endpoint is. An XMLA Endpoint creates a connectivity channel for other tools and services (which can be third-party tools) to the SSAS model. An XMLA Endpoint is available for SSAS models hosted through SQL Server and has been used for a long time. You can use a tool such as SSMS and connect to the local SSAS engine. Without an XMLA Endpoint, access to the SSAS model will be very limited and probably unsupported.

An XMLA Endpoint creates a connectivity channel for other tools and services (which can be third-party tools) to the SSAS model.

The good news is that XMLA Endpoints are available for Power BI datasets hosted in the Power BI Service. It means you can use any client tools that support XMLA connectivity to connect to Power BI datasets. When I say any, I mean it. In addition to SSMS or SSDT, or Microsoft SQL Server client tools, you can use third-party tools, such as DAX Studio and Power BI Helper, as well as Tableau! Yes, you read that right. You can use Tableau to connect to a Power BI dataset hosted in the Power BI Service and then have your visualization in Tableau.

Figure 28-7 says it all. All of these tools can be used to connect to a Power BI dataset hosted in the service.

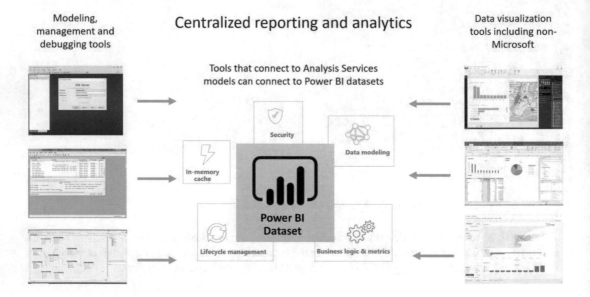

Figure 28-7. The various tools that can be used to connect to a Power BI dataset hosted in the service

In other words. the Power BI dataset is not just for Power BI tools; it can be the source for any other tools that have XMLA connectivity support—Tableau, SSMS, Power BI Helper, and more.

How Does an XMLA Connection Work?

There are two types of connections for an XMLA Endpoint—Read and Read/Write. The XMLA functionality is limited to Premium licensing. The Read connection enables you to read data from the dataset, which can be useful for monitoring and querying. The Read/Write connection enables you to change the dataset, such as adding calculation groups or object-level security to the Power BI dataset.

The XMLA Endpoint URL

If you go to a Premium capacity allocated workspace, under the Premium Capacity, you will see the XMLA Endpoint connection URL (see Figure 28-8).

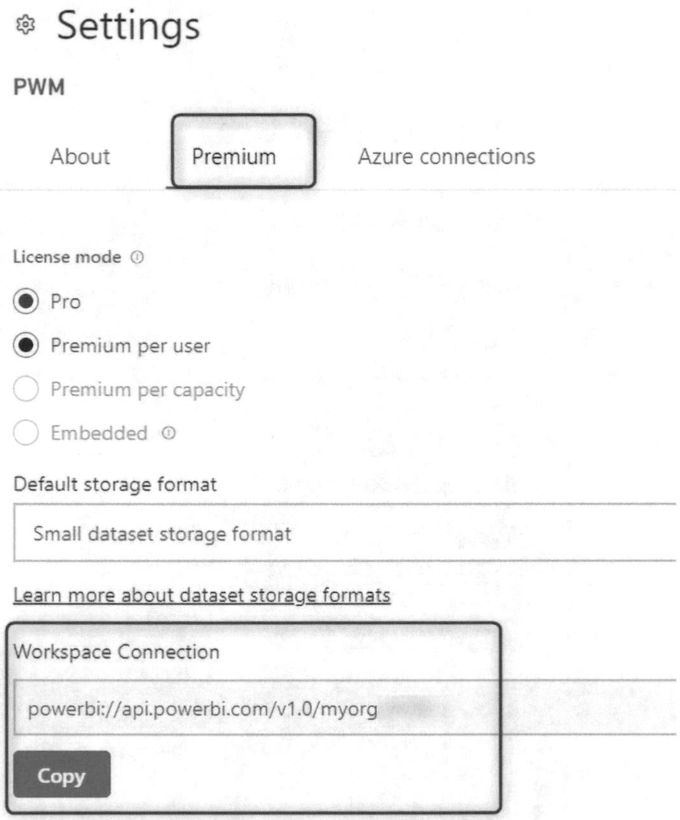

⚙ **Settings**

PWM

| About | **Premium** | Azure connections |

License mode ⓘ

⦿ Pro

⦿ Premium per user

◯ Premium per capacity

◯ Embedded ⓘ

Default storage format

Small dataset storage format

Learn more about dataset storage formats

Workspace Connection

powerbi://api.powerbi.com/v1.0/myorg

Copy

Figure 28-8. *The XMLA Endpoint connection URL*

The format is as follows:

```
powerbi://api.powerbi.com/v1.0/myorg/<workspace name>
```

The workspace name can have spaces and is case sensitive. For example:

```
powerbi://api.powerbi.com/v1.0/myorg/Reza SAMPLE workspace
```

Admin Control under Capacity Configuration

Your capacity admin should enable you to use an XMLA Endpoint. This is possible from the Admin Portal by choosing Capacity Setting, selecting the capacity, and then choosing Workloads. If you are using Premium Per User licensing, there is a place to set this under the Admin Portal from Premium Per User (see Figure 28-9).

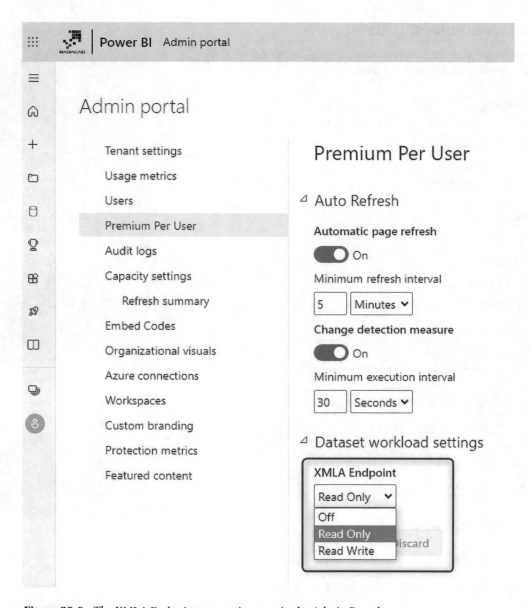

Figure 28-9. *The XMLA Endpoint connection type in the Admin Portal*

Client Tools

You should have a client tool for this type of connection. You can use a tool such as SSMS. However, you need SSMS 18.0 RC1 or above, which can be downloaded from docs.microsoft.com/en-us/sql/ssms/download-sql-server-management-studio-ssms?view=sql-server-2017#ssms-180-rc1. The client tools must have installed the libraries listed at docs.microsoft.com/en-us/azure/analysis-services/analysis-services-data-providers to be able to connect.

Sample Connection

Figure 28-10 shows a sample of the connection created using an XMLA Endpoint through SSMS.

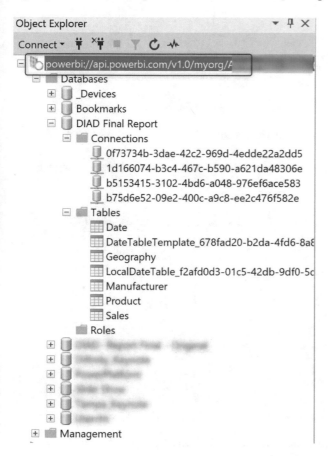

Figure 28-10. *Example connection created using an XMLA Endpoint through SSMS*

As an example, Figure 28-11 shows a query that lists how many users are using this dataset with DMVs.

SESSIO...	SESSIO...	SESSIO...	SESSION_USER_NAME	SESSIO...	SESSIO...	SESSIO...	SESSIO...	SESSIO...	SESSIO...	SESSIO...	SES
E9AC0...	798	8	AzureAD\RezaRad	Advent...	22		6/04/20...	187863	6/04/20...	6/04/20...	0
EB9134...	827	11	AzureAD\RezaRad	Advent...	3		6/04/20...	48806	6/04/20...	6/04/20...	15
29C2DF...	831	12	AzureAD\RezaRad	Advent...	3		6/04/20...	48389	6/04/20...	6/04/20...	0

Figure 28-11. *Example query showing how many individuals are using this dataset via DMVs*

The Power BI Helper

The Power BI Helper can also connect to an XMLA Endpoint, as shown in Figure 28-12.

Figure 28-12. *The Power BI Helper connecting using an XMLA Endpoint*

It can also give you documentation and information about the datasets in this workspace, as shown in Figure 28-13.

Figure 28-13. *Using the Power BI Helper to view documentation and information about datasets in the workspace*

Summary

Using XMLA Endpoints, you can use client tools to control, manage, and monitor Power BI datasets in the service. Also, a Power BI dataset can be used as the data model for other visualization tools, such as Tableau. XMLA Endpoints can be read-only for querying and logging purposes or read-write for making changes to the model.

CHAPTER 29

■ ■ ■

Dashboard and Report Sharing

Power BI provides multiple ways to share content with users. Each sharing method has its pros and cons and can be used for specific scenarios. Some sharing methods can be used together to build a framework for sharing. This chapter discusses the most basic way to share Power BI content. This method is called dashboard (or report) sharing. Dashboard sharing is the easiest way to share; however, it may not always be the best way. In this chapter, you'll learn how this method works, its pros and cons, and the scenarios for using it.

Power BI Content Owner

Before going through dashboard sharing, you need to understand how content security works in Power BI. When you publish a `*.pbix` report to the Power BI Service, especially when you publish it under My Workspace, no one else can see or access your report. You can decide with whom you want to share this report.

All Power BI content (reports, dashboards, and datasets) has an owner; the content owner is the person who created and published that content to Power BI. The owner has full access to the content. The owner can share that content with others as needed.

How Does Dashboard Sharing Work?

Dashboard or report sharing, as the name implies, is based on a dashboard. You can only share a dashboard or report using this method, not a dataflow or a datamart. Consider that you have a dashboard like the one shown in Figure 29-1, and you want to share it. Note the share link in the top-right corner of the dashboard.

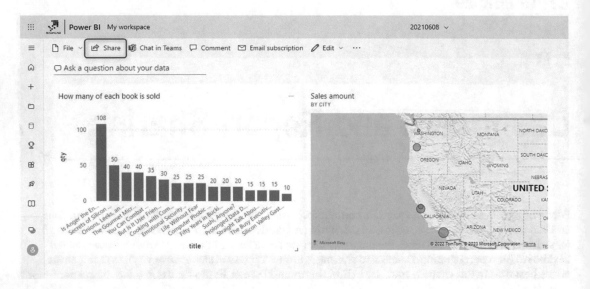

Figure 29-1. *Sharing from a dashboard page in Power BI*

Dashboard sharing has a few options you can set and is very simple to configure. You need to add the email address of the people with whom you want to share the report. You can also write messages to them. If you are sharing a report or a dashboard, you might get two slightly different options. If you share a dashboard, you will get an option like the one shown in Figure 29-2.

Figure 29-2. *Sharing dashboard in Power BI*

There are a few options to set:

- Allow recipients to share your dashboard
- Allow recipients to build content with the data associated with this dashboard
- Send email notifications to recipients

And at the top, you can enter the email of the people you share this dashboard with. For report sharing, the options are also similar, with a small difference (see Figure 29-3).

Figure 29-3. *Report sharing in Power BI*

By default, as you can see in Figure 29-3, the option called People in Your Organization with the Link Can View and Share is selected. This can be modified, but by clicking it, you have the options shown in Figure 29-4.

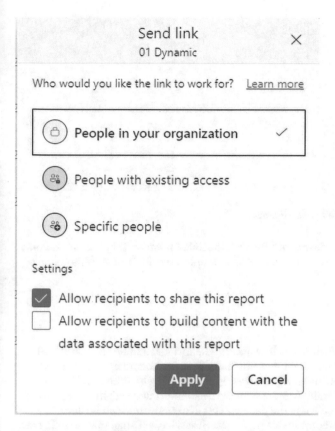

Figure 29-4. *Changing the settings of report sharing in Power BI*

You can choose whom to share the report with (the entire organization or specific people), and you can choose the access level of the audience to view, or plus reshare, or even plus build. There are also options to share in multiple ways—Copy link, Mail, Teams, and PowerPoint.

After configuring this, click the Share button. The recipient will immediately have access to the report. If you select Send Email Notification to Recipients, they will receive an email. Otherwise, they get a notification in Power BI. When users log in to the service (or in the mobile app for Power BI), they will find this dashboard or report in the Shared with Me section, which is in the Browse menu (see Figure 29-5).

Figure 29-5. *The Shared with Me section in the Power BI Service*

The recipient can also access the report or dashboard through the link. An important point here is that those with whom the report is shared need a Power BI Pro or PPU account to see the content (this is one of the limitations of this method of sharing).

Three Levels of Access

With dashboard (or report) sharing, users have three levels of access—Read, Read and Reshare, and Build. If you give them access without selecting the Allow Recipients to Share Your Dashboard option, this access is Read. If you choose the option mentioned previously, the access is Read and Reshare. To provide Build access, you need to select Allow Recipients to Build Content with the Data Associated with this Dashboard.

Build access provides the ability to connect live to the dataset. This live connection can be done through the Power BI Desktop, through a new report inside the Power BI service, or using Analyze in Excel. The live connection to a dataset in Power BI is a great step toward a multi-layer architecture for Power BI development.

Manage Permissions

Another way to set access is through Manage Permissions in the dashboard, report, or dataset. If you share a dashboard, by default, the report and the dataset will also be shared as read-only for users. Users can click the dashboard and go to the report; they can interact with the report quickly. However, they cannot edit the report (see Figure 29-6). Access to edit reports cannot be provided through this method.

Figure 29-6. *Restricting users from editing a report*

To manage permissions on every item (dashboards, reports, and datasets) individually, go to Manage Permissions in the More options of the object, as depicted in Figure 29-7.

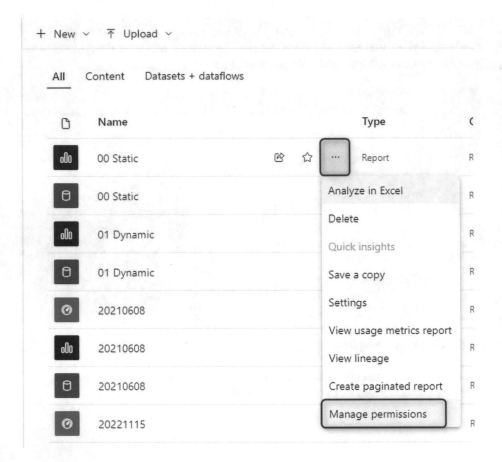

Figure 29-7. Managing permissions on a Power BI report, dashboard, or dataset

Manage Permissions will show you a detailed access list regarding the dashboard, reports, and datasets. You will see related reports and datasets on the left side of the Manage Permissions section (see Figure 29-8). You can click the report.

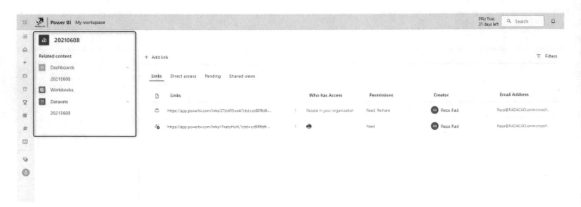

Figure 29-8. Related content in the Manage Permissions setting

Access can be seen through links or direct access (directly authorized through Manage Permissions). You will see the permission specified for that object by clicking a report or dataset. And you can change it. For example, the `reza@radacad.com` user has access as Read to the report in Figure 29-9 (because I shared this dashboard with him, the report sharing happened automatically after that). You can remove that access by clicking more options.

Figure 29-9. *Changing access levels through Manage Permissions*

You will see the Remove Access window, which asks whether you want to remove access to some of the related content (see Figure 29-10).

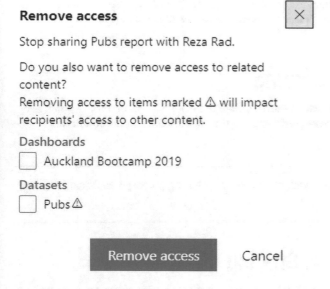

Figure 29-10. *Removing access to the related items in Power BI*

If you remove access to other items, you should be careful because that item might be used in multiple other objects. For example, if you remove access to the dataset, that dataset might be used in multiple reports.

If you shared a dashboard with a user but removed access to the report or dataset, the user will see the error message for tiles coming from that report when logged in and accessing the dashboard (see Figure 29-11). Users cannot drill into the report because they don't have access.

Figure 29-11. *A dashboard shared with a user, but with access to the report removed*

Dashboard or report sharing, like many other Power BI methods, is a paid feature. The account sharing the content should be a Power BI Pro account (Or PPU), and people using the shared content should be part of the paid account Power BI Pro account or PPU. Free users cannot leverage content shared with this method

Advantages of Dashboard Sharing

Dashboard (or report) sharing is the most basic way to share content in Power BI. This method is quick and easy to set up. The ability to share information very quickly makes this method the most common way to share for testing.

If you created Power BI content and want to share it with others easily for testing purposes, dashboard sharing is a good option.

Disadvantages of Dashboard Sharing

Dashboard sharing is simple; however, it has many drawbacks, which make it hard to use in production. I do not recommend using this method to share Power BI content with users in a production environment because of the reasons explained in the next sections.

No Edit Access

With dashboard sharing, you cannot specify edit access. For end users, you never want to give edit access; however, if you are working with a team of developers and want to provide them with access to edit the content, you cannot do that with dashboard sharing. You have to use other sharing methods, which are explained in the next few chapters.

Share Objects One at a Time

You can only share one dashboard at a time. What if you wanted to share hundreds of dashboards? You must go to each dashboard and share items individually. Sharing every dashboard would add a lot of maintenance overhead to your work. The best method is to have the contents under a group and share it all with others at once.

Licensing for a Large User Base

If you have thousands of users, this method is expensive. A Power BI Premium capacity can be set at the workspace level, and then free Power BI users can consume the content using Power BI apps, which is a more cost-effective way to share content.

Summary

Dashboard or report sharing is straightforward. It has three access levels—Read, Read and Reshare, and Build. You can use this method efficiently for test scenarios. When you want to share a dashboard with a user for testing, dashboard sharing is a good option.

Dashboard sharing, however, has some disadvantages. There is no edit access. Also, if you want to share multiple items, you have to go to each dashboard and share them individually. Because of these two significant limitations, dashboard sharing is never used in the development or production environment of Power BI implementation. Other methods, which I explain in the next few chapters, address these limitations.

■ ■ ■

CHAPTER 30

Power BI Workspaces

Workspaces provide another way of sharing Power BI content with other people. The benefit of this sharing approach is that you can share content with a group of people and create a collaborative development environment, whereby everyone can access the content. This chapter explains how to share workspaces, the limitations and advantages of doing so, and how this method is different from dashboard sharing. By the end of this chapter, you will understand which scenarios are suitable for this method of sharing.

What Are Power BI Workspaces?

Workspaces are shared environments. You can have multiple Power BI content in a workspace. One workspace can have hundreds of dashboards, reports, and datasets. Certain objects in the Power BI ecosystem can only exist within the context of a workspace, such as dataflows and datamarts. You can add people (or Power BI accounts) to the workspace and allow them to edit or read the content. In other words, workspaces are like shared folders containing the Power BI content in your organization.

One account may be part of multiple workspaces (see Figure 30-1) or various accounts and have access to one workspace. Everyone has a workspace named My Workspace. This is similar to the My Documents folder on your machine. My Workspace should never be used to share content with others, except for testing, because it is your personal workspace.

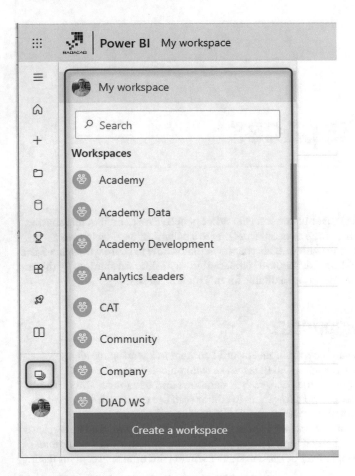

Figure 30-1. *Workspaces in the Power BI Service*

If you want to share content with others, your starting point is to create another folder, which in Power BI terminology, is called a workspace. Workspaces are also called App Workspaces and Organizational Workspaces, because you can create an app based on them and they are part of the organization's tenant.

Workspaces are best used as collaborative environments to share content between people on a team. Let's now look at how you can use workspaces.

Creating Workspaces

Creating workspaces is easy. You do so from the Power BI Service. Log in to the service and click Workspaces, as shown in Figure 30-2.

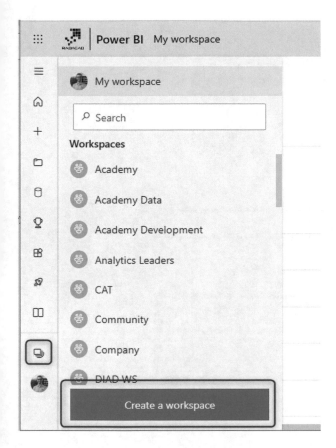

Figure 30-2. *Creating a Power BI workspace*

If you are already part of one or more workspaces, you'll see them in the list of workspaces. Click Create a Workspace. When you create a new workspace, you need to assign it a name (see Figure 30-3). The name of the workspace will be the name that others see when they join this workspace.

×

Create a workspace

Workspace image

⤒ Upload

🗑 Delete

Workspace name *

radacad sample workspace

Available

Description

Describe this workspace

Learn more about workspace settings

Advanced ∨

Figure 30-3. *Setting up general settings for a Power BI workspace*

The basic settings for the workspace include a name, a description, and an image. You are the workspace administrator (because you created it). You can use the Advanced section to set more detailed workspace settings, such as capacity settings.

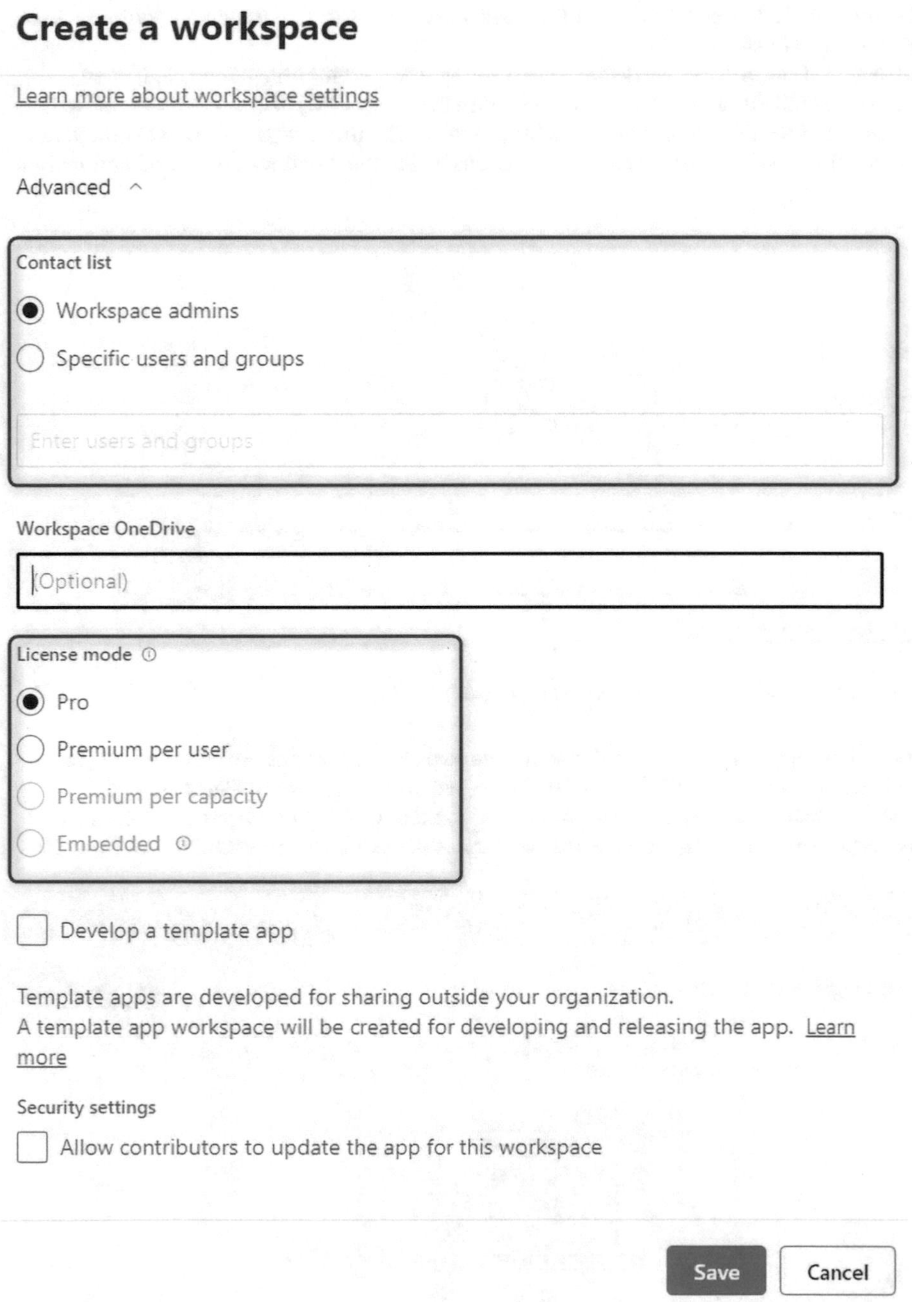

Create a workspace

Learn more about workspace settings

Advanced ⌃

Contact list

◉ Workspace admins

◯ Specific users and groups

Enter users and groups

Workspace OneDrive

(Optional)

License mode ⓘ

◉ Pro

◯ Premium per user

◯ Premium per capacity

◯ Embedded ⓘ

☐ Develop a template app

Template apps are developed for sharing outside your organization.
A template app workspace will be created for developing and releasing the app. Learn more

Security settings

☐ Allow contributors to update the app for this workspace

Save   Cancel

Figure 30-4. *Advanced settings for a Power BI workspace*

The Advanced settings include a contact list for the workspace. The workspace security settings will be set up later; this is just a contact list.

Another critical aspect of setting up a workspace is assigning it to a Premium workspace. If your organization purchased a Premium capacity or uses a Premium Per User (PPU) license, you can set up the Premium configuration in this section. Assigning a workspace to the Premium capacity enables you to use all the Premium functionalities (such as datamarts, AI functions inside the dataflow, computed entities, and so on). See Figure 30-5.

License mode ⓘ

○ Pro

◉ Premium per user

○ Premium per capacity

○ Embedded ⓘ

Default storage format

Small dataset storage format   ⌄

Learn more about dataset storage formats

Figure 30-5. *Premium capacity settings for a Power BI workspace*

If you want to use a OneDrive as a shared folder so the workspace users can share content (not just Power BI content, but any file), fill in the Workspace OneDrive text area, as shown in Figure 30-4.

After creating the workspace, you will be automatically navigated from My Workspace to your new workspace. However, as you can see in Figure 30-6, the workspace doesn't have any content yet.

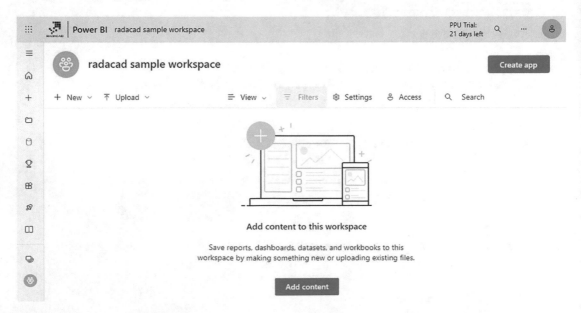

Figure 30-6. *A new workspace is created in the Power BI Service*

Adding Content to a Workspace

There are many Power BI objects that exist inside a workspace (see Figure 30-7). Some of those can be created directly from the service, such as reports, dataflows, dashboards, datasets, streaming datasets, datamarts, and paginated reports. Others can be published through other applications, such as the Power BI Desktop.

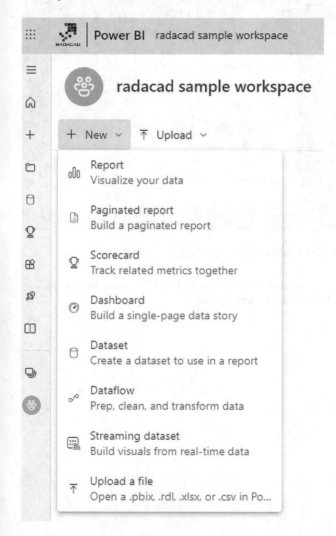

Figure 30-7. *Creating Power BI objects within the workspace*

When you open a Power BI file in the Power BI Desktop, you can click Publish, and if you are part of a workspace, you will see a popup window asking which workspace you want to publish the report to it. As an example, you could select the radacad sample workspace created here (see Figure 30-8).

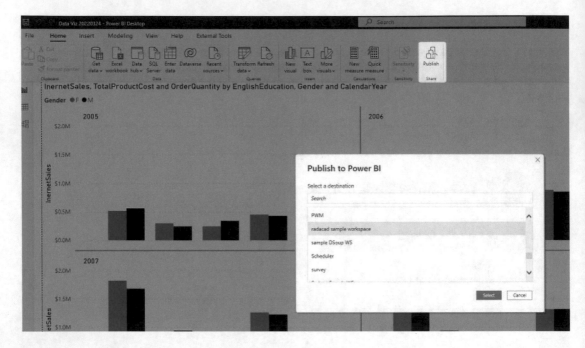

Figure 30-8. *Publish a Power BI file from the Power BI Desktop into a workspace*

After publishing the content to the workspace, you and anyone else who is part of that workspace will see that content. Figure 30-9 shows an example of content in a workspace.

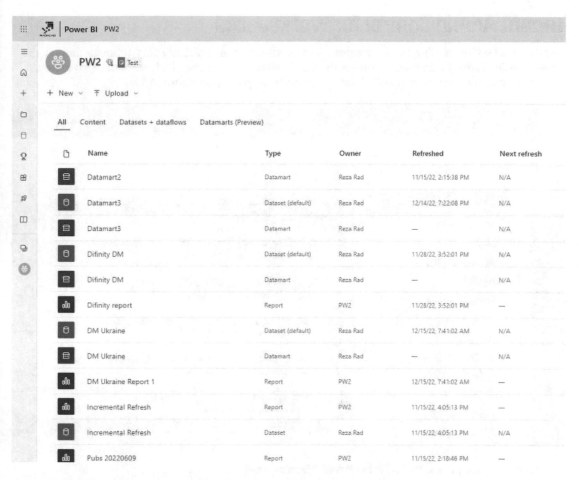

Figure 30-9. *Power BI workspace content*

Let's now talk about the access levels for the workspace users.

Four Levels of Workspace Access

With workspaces, you can provide four levels of access. Three provide edit access and one is read-only:

- **Viewer:** Can view the content in a read-only mode.

- **Contributor:** Can create, edit, publish, and delete content in the workspace. A contributor cannot modify users or publish an app.

- **Member:** Can publish and update an app. Can share or allow others to reshare items. Can add members or others with lower permissions. Members can also do everything that contributors can do.

- **Administrator:** Can delete and update the workspace. Can add and remove members (or even other admins). Administrators can also do everything that members can do.

Tenant Admin Control for Workspaces

The Power BI tenant administrator can control some settings for an organizational workspace through the Tenant Settings area. In the Tenant Settings, the administrator can control who is authorized to create a workspace and whether users can use a dataset across workspaces (see Figure 30-10).

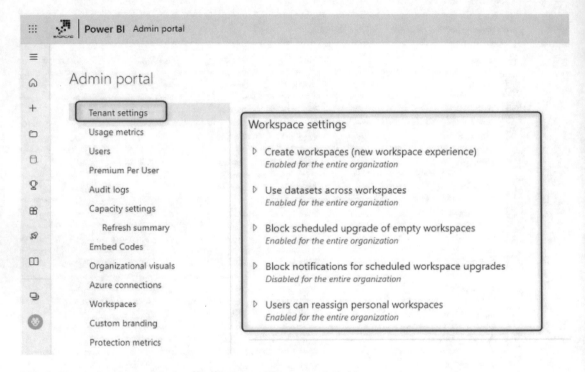

Figure 30-10. *Workspace settings for the Power BI tenant administrator*

The administrator can also control whether users can assign a personal workspace to a Premium capacity. This last option also allows the tenant administrator to set a location for personal workspaces throughout the organization, as shown in Figure 30-11.

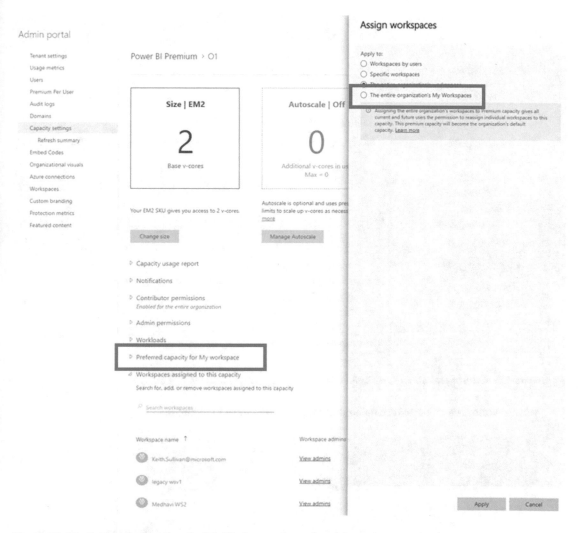

Figure 30-11. *Setting the location for My Workspace throughout the entire organization*
Source: powerbi.microsoft.com/en-us/blog/announcing-my-workspace-governance-improvement-pub-lic-preview/

Another important option for the tenant administrator is connecting to personal workspaces throughout the organization and gaining access to them. This is particularly helpful if the employee the workspace belongs to has left the company and the Power BI content has been left in their personal account without anyone else having access. This is illustrated in Figure 30-12.

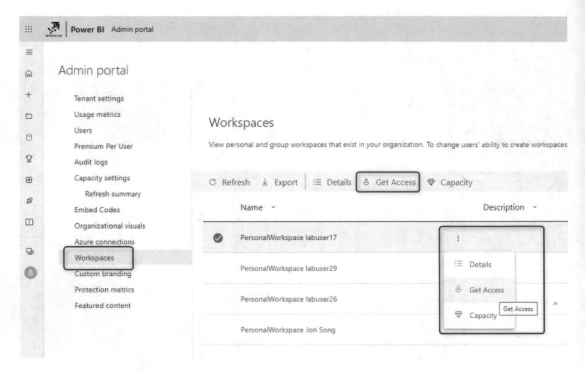

Figure 30-12. *Gaining access to personal workspaces throughout the Power BI tenant*

Administrators can also restore deleted workspaces, as shown in Figure 30-13.

Figure 30-13. *Restoring a Power BI workspace*

You can restore deleted workspaces only within 90 days after they were deleted. During this period, the restore can be done through the Admin Portal.

Advantages of Workspaces

Sharing multiple Contents with the team

You may have shared a dashboard with a couple of your colleagues in your organization, but after a few weeks, you need a new dashboard, and you share that dashboard with them. A couple of months later, another team member asks for access to a Power BI dataset to create a report and share it with others. Power BI workspaces enable you to share content (dashboards, reports, and datasets) with all group members. You don't need to share each dashboard with each user, because groups make it easy for you.

Sharing all types of objects

The dashboard only allows sharing the Power BI report, dashboard, and dataset. However, sharing through the workspace allows all the content to be shared. This includes but is not limited to dataflows, datasets, datamarts, dashboards, reports, metrics, paginated reports, and more.

Multiple workspaces

It is hectic when you are part of multiple teams, and each team has its own dashboards, reports, and datasets. Your Shared with Me section in Power BI could have hundreds of items, and finding content might become a problem. Power BI workspaces create a separate environment for all members of the group. You can easily switch between workspaces in Power BI.

Isolated user/group administration

When you share content with an individual in the organization, and that person leaves the company or is replaced by someone from another team, you have to remove sharing from a previous user account and assign it to the new user account. The best practice is to share content with groups. Workspace members can easily be managed by the administrator. Power BI workspaces can be shared with Office 365 groups. Once you use a group in Power BI, it is only an admin's task to add/remove members.

Best developer environment

You need an environment to share multiple Power BI content for a team of developers. Everyone needs to have edit access to the content provided by the team. A Power BI workspace is the perfect solution for a development environment. You can create a workspace as a development environment and then share it with other developer team members with edit access. Then you all have access to the same content in your development workspace.

A Power BI workspace is a perfect solution for a development environment.

Disadvantages of Workspaces

Workspaces do include some drawbacks you should consider.

Not suitable for end users

Workspaces are not suitable for sharing content with end users. You can give users of the workspace read-only access to the content. However, this is only half of the requirement. In an end-user sharing environment, one of the primary requirements is to have the development and user environment separated.

Assume that you created a workspace and shared it with the end users. If you suddenly make changes in the workspace while they are using it, their view of the workspace breaks and changes.

With one workspace, your development and user environment are the same.

You cannot use one workspace and share it between developers and users. Creating multiple workspaces also leads to another challenge. To overcome this challenge, you can use apps on top of the workspaces to share content with end users.

Complications of the workspace structure

Setting up a good workspace structure is a challenge. A workspace structure should cover the development, user needs, and deployment structure. This is more of a caution than a limitation. Use workspaces with care and make sure you have a good setup.

Power BI Pro or PPU

Creating Power BI workspaces, or even being part of them (even just to view them), requires a Pro or PPU license and is not part of a Power BI free user account. However, it is possible to create an app for the workspace from the Premium capacity and assign free Power BI users to it. This limitation is one of the main reasons this is not the most cost-effective option for sharing content with end users. See Figure 30-14.

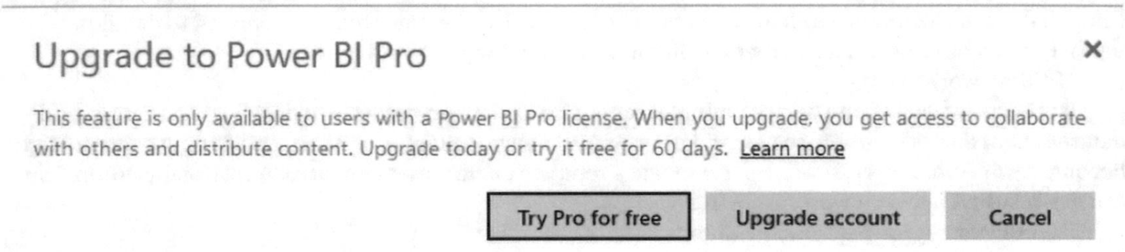

Upgrade to Power BI Pro   ✕

This feature is only available to users with a Power BI Pro license. When you upgrade, you get access to collaborate with others and distribute content. Upgrade today or try it free for 60 days. Learn more

> Try Pro for free   Upgrade account   Cancel

Figure 30-14. *The Power BI Pro option*

Summary

Power BI workspaces are a great way to share multiple Power BI content with users. If you have hundreds of dashboards, reports, and datasets, you can easily share them through a workspace with others.

Workspaces provide edit access and read-only access. Because of that, workspaces are a great way to create a collaborative development environment. Multiple developers can access the same content in a workspace with edit access.

Workspaces are better used in a development environment, not for an end-user environment. The main reason is that having one workspace for the dev or user environment makes it hard to develop. If a developer makes a change, the end user will be affected immediately. Managing multiple workspaces is also not an easy job.

CHAPTER 31

Power BI Apps

You've learned previously about some ways to share content in Power BI, such as using workspaces and dashboard sharing. This chapter explains everything about Power BI apps, a mechanism to share the content in Power BI in a way that includes security and governance. When Power BI apps are used with workspaces, you can build an ultimate sharing strategy in your organization.

Power BI Apps

Power BI apps differ from the mobile app for Power BI. Power BI apps share content with end users. You already learned about the limitations of dashboard sharing and workspaces. The Power BI App method provides an extensive approach to sharing content with end users. With Power BI apps, you can share content with end users without worrying about changing something in the development environment. Managing multiple environments is much easier with this approach. An app can be shared with a group of people or the entire organization.

In addition to separating the dev and user environments, apps come with another helpful point. Power BI apps can be shared with free users in the Power BI if the workspace in which the Power BI content is located is under a Premium capacity.

App Workspaces

To start creating an app, you'll need a workspace (see Figure 31-1). Workspaces in Power BI are called app workspaces because you can create an app on top of a workspace (they are also called organization workspaces). The content that you have in this workspace can be selected and shared with users. In the previous chapter, you learned how to create and manage workspaces.

© Reza Rad 2023
R. Rad, *Pro Power BI Architecture*, https://doi.org/10.1007/978-1-4842-9538-0_31

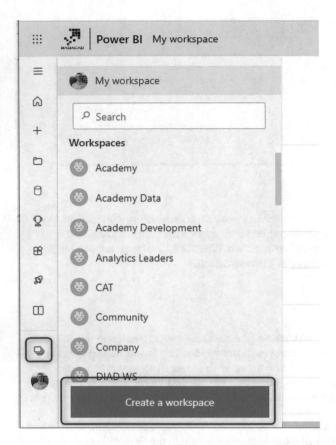

Figure 31-1. *Creating workspaces in Power BI*

An app workspace is like a shared folder with a group of people. Create a name for the app workspace. You can specify whether users can edit the workspace or have read-only access (there are four access levels). Note that this type of access is only for people you add to the workspace directly, not for the app's users. After creating the app workspace, you should first see a new workspace (folder) that is blank. You can publish the content to this workspace from the Power BI Desktop or create it from the Power BI Service.

Figure 31-2 shows an example of a workspace with some content in it.

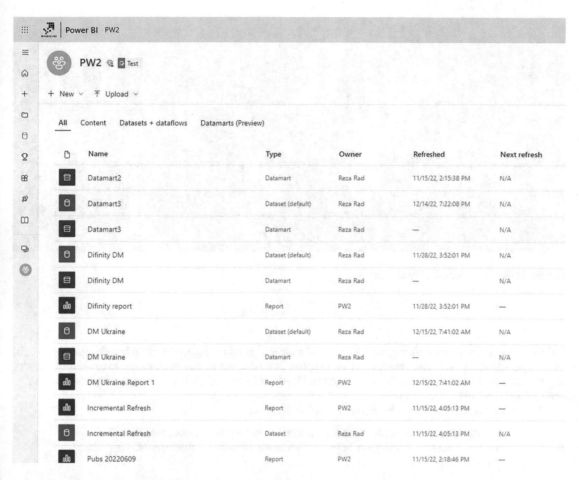

Figure 31-2. A sample Power BI workspace

Creating an App

The process of creating a Power BI app is also called publishing an app. To create the app, click the workspace in the Power BI Service, as shown in Figure 31-3.

Figure 31-3. *Creating a Power BI app*

Setup

There are three stages for creating the app. In the first stage, you do the general setup by adding details such as the app's name, description, logo, and theme color. Choosing the theme color can help users distinguish the environment when they switch between apps. (A Power BI user can be the user of multiple apps.) You can also set the contact information.

There are three settings for the app that require attention:

- Install this app automatically. I recommend selecting this option. However, the tenant administrator in your organization has to enable this feature first. I explain this shortly.

- Hide app navigation pane. An app can come with a navigation pane. The navigation pane is helpful when sharing multiple reports and dashboards through this app. If you are sharing only a single report, the navigation pane is better hidden.

- Allow users to make a copy of the reports in this app. If you have power users and business analysts, you might want to give them access to create copies of the report (but not change the reports in this app).

Once you set the configurations, you can go to the next step (see Figure 31-4).

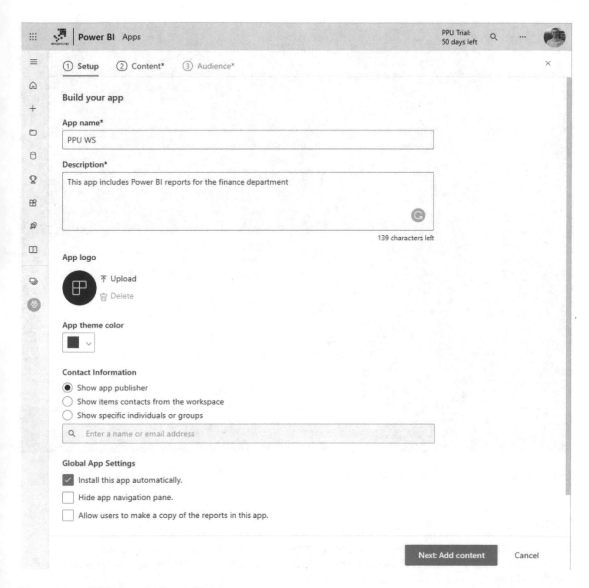

Figure 31-4. Setting up the Power BI App

Installing Apps Automatically

By default, the apps must be installed by the organization's users. This is an extra step that can be done automatically (which means that as soon as the app is created, it will be installed). The Power BI tenant administrator enables this automatic installation of the apps from the Tenant Settings area, as shown in Figure 31-5.

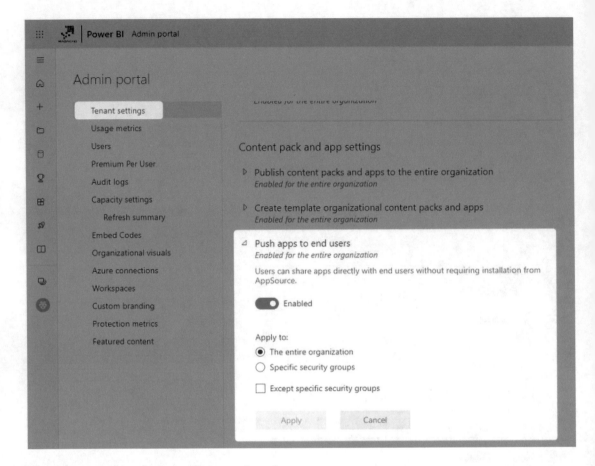

Figure 31-5. *Pushing the Power BI app to the end users*

Content

In the next tab, you will set the content for the app. This can be done by clicking Add Content (see Figure 31-6). If you want to share different content with different audiences, select all the content and add them here.

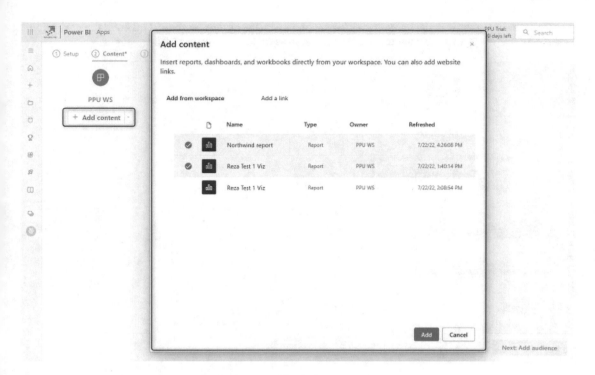

Figure 31-6. *Adding content to the Power BI app*

You can now build a navigation menu for your app. By default, the navigation only includes the content (reports and dashboard). You can build better navigation by adding custom links or sections (see Figure 31-7).

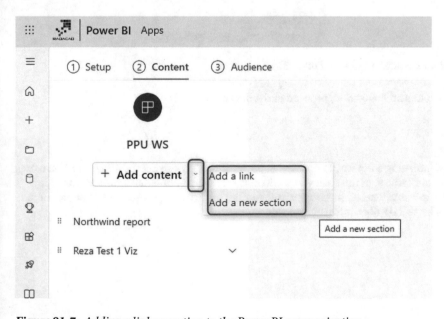

Figure 31-7. *Adding a link or section to the Power BI app navigation*

You can then organize the items under the sections, rename or reorder them, and build the navigation in the way you want your users to consume the content, as depicted in Figure 31-8.

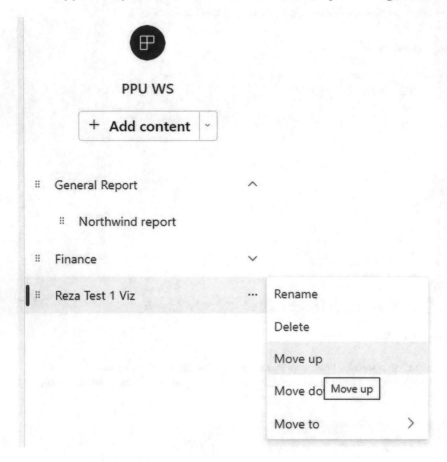

Figure 31-8. *Building custom navigation in the Power BI app*

After building the content and navigation, proceed to the next step.

Audience

The third and final stage of building a Power BI app is to set the audience. These are the app users. You can include different groups of audiences. In the past, you could only create one audience group per app. Now, you can have a group with access to part of the content and another group with access to another part of the content in the same app. Figure 31-9 illustrates this process.

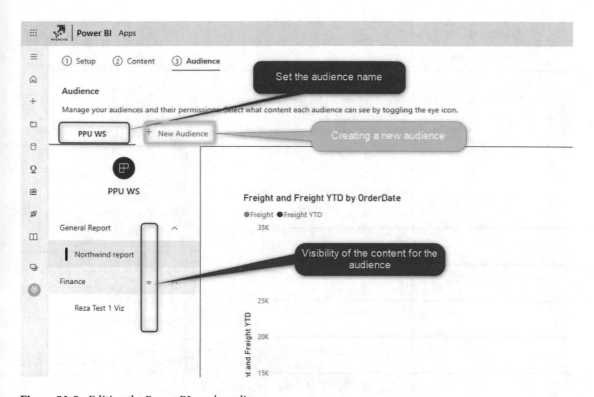

***Figure 31-9.** Editing the Power BI app's audience*

There will always be a default audience with the same name as the app. You can rename it by double-clicking the Audience tab.

For each audience, you can set the group of users who have access to it (see Figure 31-10). It is better to use Office 365 groups than the individual users. This enables you to manage the user list more easily outside the Power BI environment.

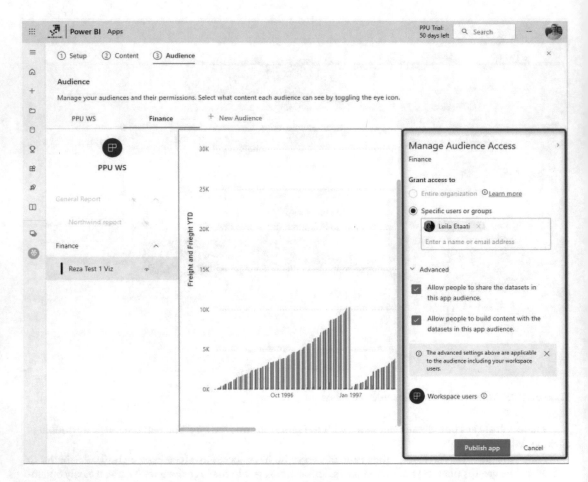

Figure 31-10. *Setting audience access to the Power BI app*

When you create the app, you can give the users access to reshare it or even build new content with the dataset available in the app (using a live connection). As you can see in Figure 31-10, I created a new Audience for Finance, allowed it to see only the finance section and report, and then authorized the users of this audience to reshare or build new content using the dataset of this app.

After publishing the app, users can access it immediately. They will either get the app installed automatically or need to install it themselves. You can also share the link with them to make it easier for them to access it, as demonstrated in Figure 31-11.

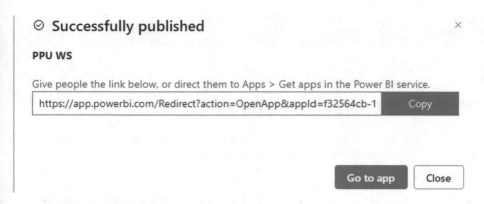

⊘ **Successfully published**   ✕

PPU WS

Give people the link below, or direct them to Apps > Get apps in the Power BI service.

https://app.powerbi.com/Redirect?action=OpenApp&appId=f32564cb-1   Copy

Go to app   Close

Figure 31-11. *The link to access the app*

Getting Apps

Users can go to their Power BI account page, click Apps, and then choose Get Apps. They will be able to see all the apps shared with them (see Figure 31-12).

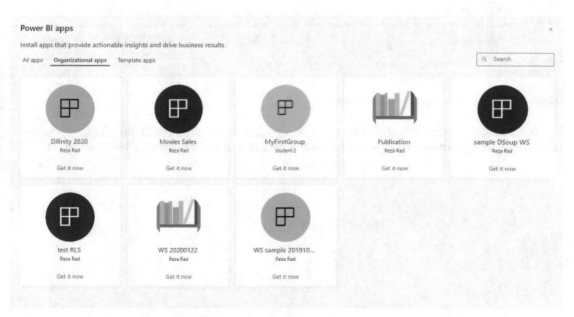

Figure 31-12. *Getting apps from the organization's tenant*

Users can simply install an app and use it right away. As you can see in Figure 31-13, users can have multiple apps.

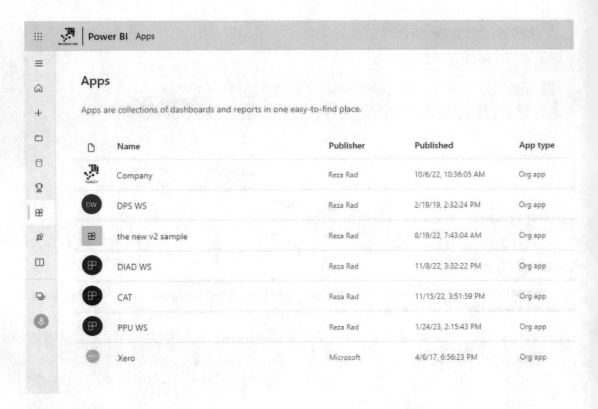

Figure 31-13. *Multiple apps can exist per user*

By clicking the app, users will be redirected to it and can explore its content. Depending on the access and the audience group the user is part of, they may have a different view of the app. See Figure 31-14.

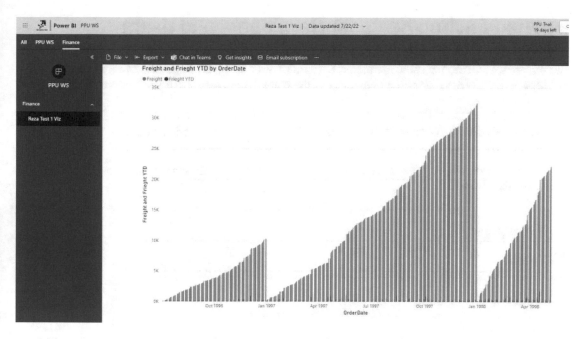

Figure 31-14. *End-user view of the Power BI app*

Making Changes to an App

You can apply any changes to the content in the workspace. The changes on the workspace will not affect users until you update the app. With the new update, the users will get the updated content. You can also unpublish an app (see Figure 31-15).

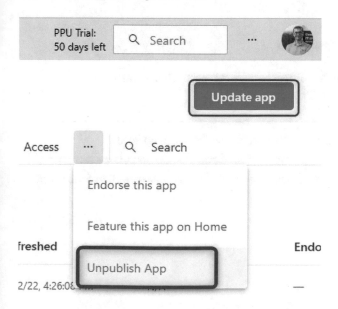

Figure 31-15. *Updating or unpublishing a Power BI app*

Isolated Environments for Developers and Users

One of the best advantages of using Power BI apps is having two separate environments—one for developers and one for users. The concept works merely because a Power BI app is always associated with a workspace. Workspaces act like developer environments, and the Power BI app serves as an end-user environment.

Workspaces are developer environments, and Power BI apps are end-user environments.

If you are a developer, you will have edit access to the workspace (through Contributor or Member roles). See Figure 31-16.

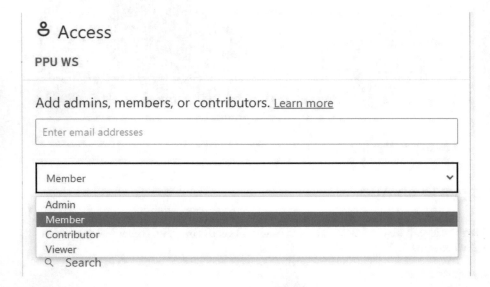

Figure 31-16. *Setting access for the workspace users*

All users who have edit access can change the content in the workspace. Their changes do not apply to the end-user environment until they update the app.

Changes in the workspace do not affect the end users' environment until the app is updated.

As a developer, you can make changes to the workspace, for example, you remove a chart from a report and then save it, as shown in Figure 31-17.

Figure 31-17. *Changes made to a workspace by a developer*

The end users will not be affected by this change. They will still see the full report, as shown in Figure 31-18.

Figure 31-18. *The full report remains visible to the end users*

To sync the developer and end-user environments, you need to update the app and apply the changes to the end-user side. Usually, developers in the workspace cannot do this. The access level of developers in the workspace is Contributor, which doesn't allow them to update the app. The Member is a user who can publish or update the app. This person is also called the deployment user. See `radacad.com/best-practice-for-power-bi-workspace-roles-setup` to learn more about workspace roles and how to set them up.

What About Data Refresh?

Data Refresh and access to up-to-date data is always a big issue for potential developers. You might wonder if you have to update the app so end users can get the updated data. The answer is that data will be updated if it is scheduled to refresh with a scheduling process determined at the dataset level or if it is Live Connection or DirectQuery. Regardless of the users or developers, the dataset refresh is a different process.

If you have set up your dataset to be refreshed, users will always have access to up-to-date data. You don't need to update the app for data changes. You just need to update the app for structural changes (adding, modifying, or removing tables, fields, relationships, and calculations) or visualization changes (adding, modifying, or removing visuals on the report). However, some structural changes in the dataset might cause the report in the app to fail (such as removing a field or a measure used in a report's visualization), as it depends on the existing dataset in the workspace.

Advantages of Power BI Apps

Separate environments for developers and end users

This method has two separate environments; an environment for developers to edit the Power BI content in a collaborative workspace and another environment for end users to consume the reports. End users are only able to view the reports, and developers can make changes.

Power BI apps are the best solution for isolated developer and end-user environments.

A cost-effective option for large userbases

If you have thousands of users and want to share Power BI content with them securely, sharing content with options that rely on per-user licensing is not cost-effective. A Power BI workspace can be assigned to a Premium workspace, and then if you create an app on top of that, the app's users can be free Power BI users. This is a big help for organizations with a large userbase. You can purchase a capacity, and as long as it can cover the load of the users over the Power BI content in the service, your free users can access it.

This option is one of the most common reasons why many organizations use Power BI apps combined with workspaces to share Power BI content.

Controlling multiple Power BI content sources

Similar to the workspace, the Power BI app allows you to share multiple dashboards, reports, and datasets simultaneously. Controlling multiple content sources means less maintenance overhead compared to dashboard sharing, which is one dashboard at a time.

External sharing

Another great benefit of Power BI apps is the ability to integrate them with Azure B2B services and provide external sharing. If you want to share Power BI content with people outside your company, you can do that with a combination of Azure B2B and the Power BI app.

Cons of Power BI Apps

Power BI apps do have an important limitation that you need to consider.

Changes to the dataset apply immediately

Power BI apps separate the developer and end-user environments, and the changes in a report in a workspace don't affect the end user until you update the app. However, this functionality doesn't work with the dataset in that way. The Power BI apps and workspaces share the same datasets, so any changes from a Scheduled Refresh or structural changes apply to both.

Summary

Power BI apps separate the development and user environments. They also provide a more cost-effective licensing option in some scenarios. Using Power BI apps, you can create a navigation menu for users with different audiences per app. These advantages make Power BI apps the most common method of sharing Power BI content.

CHAPTER 32

■ ■ ■

Publish to Web

All of the methods for sharing Power BI files in the Power BI Service (such as dashboard sharing, workspaces, apps, and so on) need paid Power BI subscriptions for consuming reports. Users need to be either Power BI Pro or free accounts under the Power BI premium capacity. The Publish to Web option is the only way to share Power BI content through the service for free. With this method, you can share Power BI content with users who don't have a Power BI account.

Publish to Web is an easy way to share public data. However, it has some disadvantages as well. In this chapter, you learn about this feature in more detail, and you learn how it is different from Power BI Embedded. I explain Publish to Web, and in another chapter, you'll learn about Power BI Embedded. In this chapter, you learn how easy it is to share your report with the public through a web page, which can be your blog post, an HTML page, or any other web page. I answer some frequently asked questions about this feature as well.

What Is Publish to Web?

Once you publish your Power BI report into a Power BI Service, you can share it with others by sharing it directly or using workspaces in Power BI. What if you want to share it with the public through the web? Let's say you want everyone to see the report and play with it (with all the interactive features in Power BI). In this case, you can use Publish to Web. Publish to Web allows you to create an embedded code for the Power BI report and use that code on the web page. This simple feature enables everyone to access the report. They won't be able to edit the report, but they will see the report, and the report will be fully interactive so they can highlight items, select slicers, and drill down.

It's very simple to use this feature. You must first deploy or publish the report into the Power BI website or service. Then click the report (not the dashboard). Once you open the report, click the File menu option, and under Embed Report, choose Publish to Web (see Figure 32-1).

© Reza Rad 2023
R. Rad, *Pro Power BI Architecture*, https://doi.org/10.1007/978-1-4842-9538-0_32

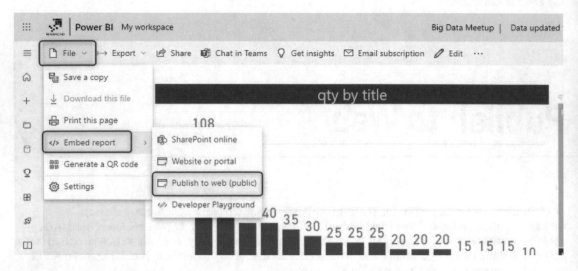

Figure 32-1. *Using Publish to Web from a Power BI report*

Then you will be informed about this feature in a message box that mentions this step will create a link and embed code for you to share with the world through a website or email. Click Create Embed Code, as shown in Figure 32-2.

✕

Embed in a public website

Get a link or embed code that you can include on a public website.

You may use the publish to web functionality to share content on a publicly available website. You may not use this functionality to share content internally, including through email, your internal network, or intranet site.

Publish a live version that will remain synchronized with the source report in Power BI. Any changes you make to the report will immediately be reflected in the published public version.

 Close

Figure 32-2. *Embedding in a public website*

Because this is all about sharing a report, you will be informed again to check the confidentiality of the data and make sure you are sharing content that is not harmful to the organization or someone when it is viewable to the public (see Figure 32-3).

Embed in a public website

⚠ You are about to create an embed code for this report. Once published, anyone on the internet will be able to access the report and the data it contains, and Microsoft may display the report on a public website or a public gallery.

Before publishing this report, ensure you have the right to share the data and visualizations publicly. Do not publish confidential or proprietary information, or an individual's personal data. If in doubt, check your organization's policies before publishing.

Publish   Close

Figure 32-3. *Confidentiality warning*

After clicking Publish, you will see the embed code plus a link to share through email. You can also choose the size of the screen for the embed code (see Figure 32-4).

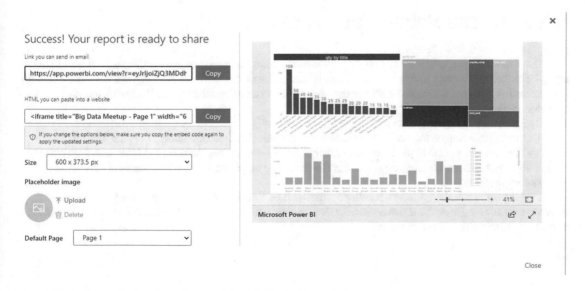

Figure 32-4. *The embed code and the public link for the Power BI report*

You can now browse the link to see the report in a browser, even if you open it in Incognito (or Private) mode, as illustrated in Figure 32-5.

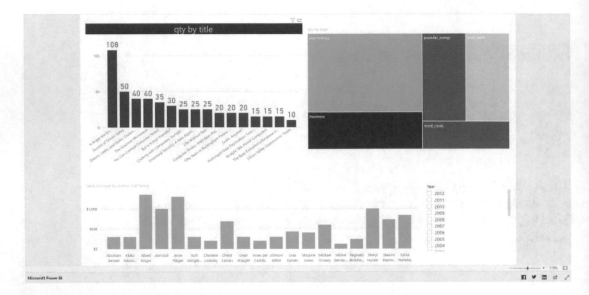

Figure 32-5. *Open the public link in a web browser*

To browse the report, you don't need to log in to the Power BI service. Users don't need anything except a browser to view this report. The report is fully interactive; users can highlight, select, and deselect items.

You can also add the embed code to your HTML page, blog post, or wherever you want users to see the report.

Security Issues with Publish to Web

Everyone Can See What You Share

The first thing you might think of is usually security. How can you manage security with this kind of setup? The short answer is that there is no security here. The report is shared through the web or email with everyone. So everyone who has the link or the embed code can access the report. They cannot edit it. But they can view it with no restrictions.

Users can share it with others

A report published on the web has a share section on the bottom-right side. Everyone can share this report with anyone else through all social media channels—Facebook, Twitter, and LinkedIn. This method of sharing is not secure. I recommend sharing the data only on your company or organization's website.

The report is public

This report is not shared only with those with the link, it is shared globally on the Internet. A search engine such as Google can find the report. All the reports with Publish to Web links are available. Figure 32-6 shows an example search result from Google.

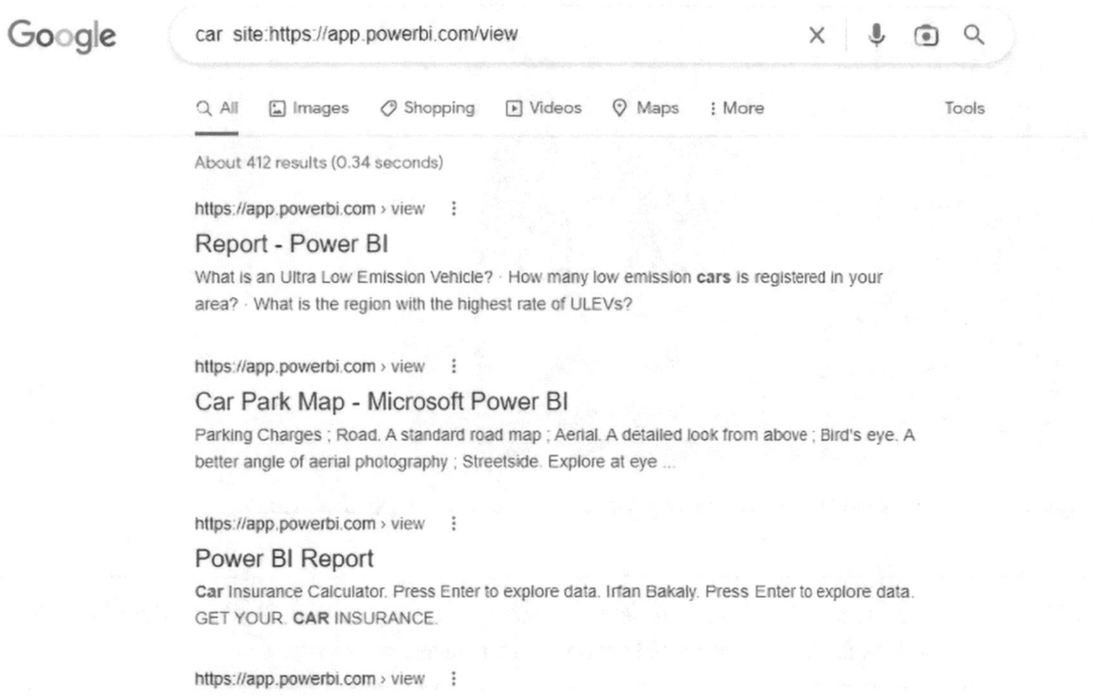

Google   car   site:https://app.powerbi.com/view   ✕   🎤   📷   🔍

🔍 All   🖾 Images   ⊘ Shopping   ▶ Videos   ⦿ Maps   ⋮ More   Tools

About 412 results (0.34 seconds)

https://app.powerbi.com › view   ⋮
Report - Power BI
What is an Ultra Low Emission Vehicle? · How many low emission **cars** is registered in your area? · What is the region with the highest rate of ULEVs?

https://app.powerbi.com › view   ⋮
Car Park Map - Microsoft Power BI
Parking Charges ; Road. A standard road map ; Aerial. A detailed look from above ; Bird's eye. A better angle of aerial photography ; Streetside. Explore at eye ...

https://app.powerbi.com › view   ⋮
Power BI Report
Car Insurance Calculator. Press Enter to explore data. Irfan Bakaly. Press Enter to explore data. GET YOUR. **CAR** INSURANCE.

https://app.powerbi.com › view   ⋮

Figure 32-6. *Searching for Power BI reports published publicly*

You must be sure that the report and its data don't reveal confidential information.

All report pages are visible

If you have a report with ten or more pages, it will be visible to browsers. You cannot limit which pages you want to show and which you don't. I recommend creating different reports if you want to restrict some pages and share them separately.

What if the report has row-level security applied?

If you have a report with row-level security applied to it, you can't create a Publish to Web link. Figure 32-7 shows an example of such a case.

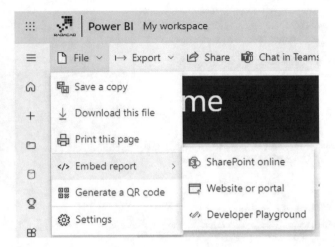

Figure 32-7. Publish to Web cannot be applied to row-level security enabled reports

---

Publish to Web is only recommended for public data sharing on your organization's website. There is no security option for Publish to Web; this method should not be used for confidential reports.

The link and embed code are synchronized with the report

If you make any changes to the report, all the changes will be synchronized because links and embed codes are simply references to this report. So people will always see the latest version of your report. If you also want to keep the report up-to-date, you can schedule it for data refresh.

Removing Access

If you want to revoke access to the report, you can do so quickly. Go to the Power BI service, and under Settings, click Manage Embed Codes (see Figure 32-8).

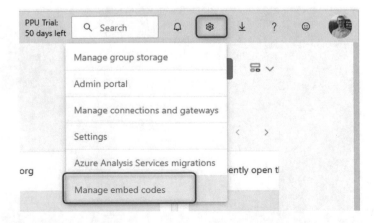

Figure 32-8. Finding all your embed codes in the Power BI Service

You will see the embed code and can delete it (see Figure 32-9). It is essential you be in the correct workspace because the list of public reports will show the reports only from that workspace.

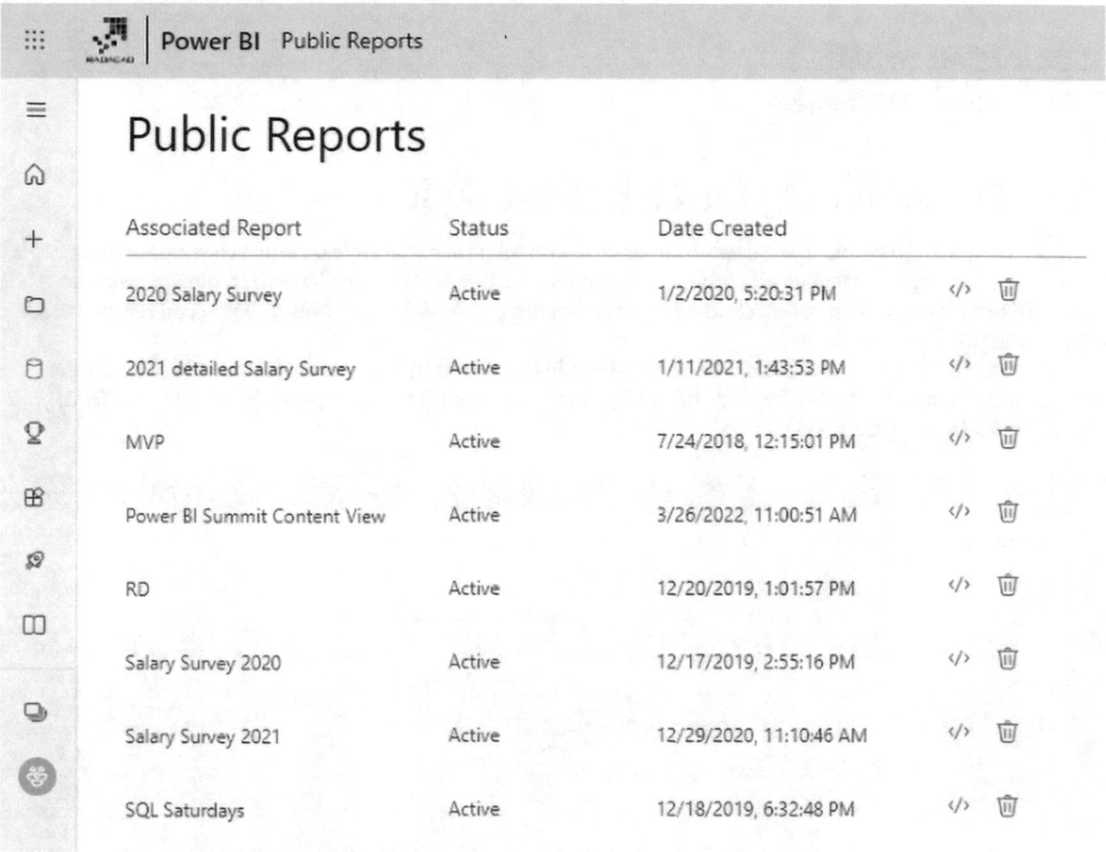

Associated Report	Status	Date Created		
2020 Salary Survey	Active	1/2/2020, 5:20:31 PM	</>	🗑
2021 detailed Salary Survey	Active	1/11/2021, 1:43:53 PM	</>	🗑
MVP	Active	7/24/2018, 12:15:01 PM	</>	🗑
Power BI Summit Content View	Active	3/26/2022, 11:00:51 AM	</>	🗑
RD	Active	12/20/2019, 1:01:57 PM	</>	🗑
Salary Survey 2020	Active	12/17/2019, 2:55:16 PM	</>	🗑
Salary Survey 2021	Active	12/29/2020, 11:10:46 AM	</>	🗑
SQL Saturdays	Active	12/18/2019, 6:32:48 PM	</>	🗑

Figure 32-9. Finding your embed codes and deleting them in the Power BI Service

Once you delete the embed code, no one can access the report from the web. You will see a notification message about this, as shown in Figure 32-10.

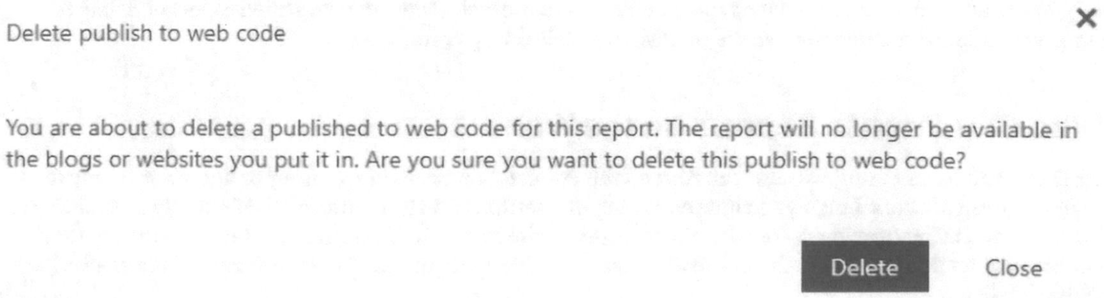

Delete publish to web code ✕

You are about to delete a published to web code for this report. The report will no longer be available in the blogs or websites you put it in. Are you sure you want to delete this publish to web code?

Delete   Close

Figure 32-10. Deleting a public report link

If you delete the embed code, the link and the embed code will show a message to the public web users that this content is not available.

This content is not available.
Learn more about Power BI.

Central Monitoring for all Embed Codes

Publish to Web might seem like a frustrating option with all its security holes. There is a need for an administration page to manage all embed codes across the Power BI tenant. There is a place where the Power BI tenant administrator can find all reports that are published to the web, and you can remove those from being published to the web.

To go to the Admin Portal, click the Setting icon in the Power BI Service, and then go to the Admin Portal. Click Embed Codes on the left side, and you will see all embed codes published by anyone from your organization (see Figure 32-11).

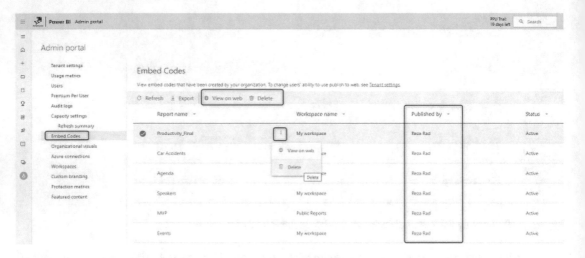

Figure 32-11. *Finding all the public reports in the Power BI tenant*

There are two options for each report published to the web—view the published report or delete it. Once you delete it, no one can use the published web link anymore.

Who Can Publish Reports on the Web?

The Power BI tenant administrator can turn off the Publish to Web feature entirely or authorize it only for a specific group of users. I highly recommend using this setting and either turning it off entirely or enabling it for a group of users from the BI or data analytics team who know all the security problems of this method. Do not turn on this feature for the entire organization. This configuration is in the Tenant Settings area (see Figure 32-12).

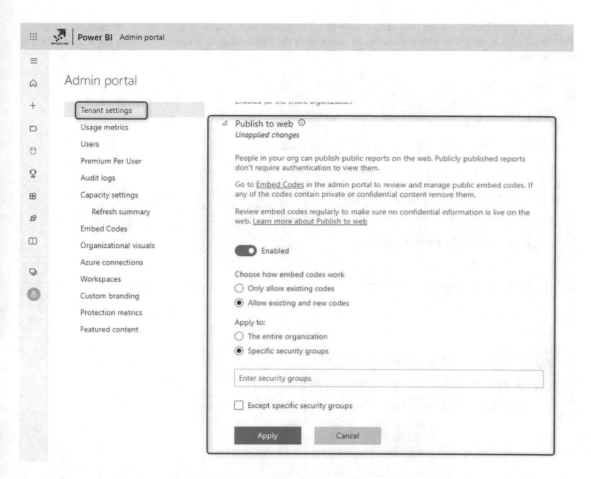

Figure 32-12. *Enabling or disabling Publish to Web in the Tenant Settings area*

Differences with Other Sharing Methods

You can share your dashboards and reports with people in your organization. This feature also gives you a link to the report. However, it is different from using the public link. Here are some differences between sharing dashboards and using a public link:

- Only those who have access to the dashboard will see the content. Sharing a dashboard link with the public won't show anything if they are not authorized to see it.

- Users need to have Power BI accounts.

- Power BI workspaces and apps are only for authorized groups of users, not for everyone.

- Power BI Embedded is different from Publish to Web.

Only those who have access to the dashboard will see the content

Once you share a report, you can choose who has access to it based on their Power BI accounts (see Figure 32-13). If they don't have a Power BI account or they don't have access to that content, they won't see the content.

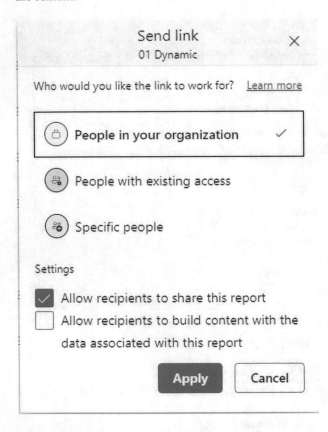

Figure 32-13. *Sharing content using dashboard (or report) sharing*

The dashboard link works only for authorized users

Despite having the dashboard link available, only authorized users can see the content when browsing the link. Otherwise, they will get a message that says they don't have permission to view this dashboard (see Figure 32-14).

Figure 32-14. *The message displayed to unauthorized users*

Power BI workspaces and apps are for authorized groups of users inside or outside of your organization, not for everyone

You can share dashboards, reports, and datasets with your organization's workspace. Users will have access to all the content or part of it (using the audience settings in the Power BI app). However, with Publish to Web, any users who have access to the page can see the report, regardless of whether they have a Power BI account (see Figure 32-15).

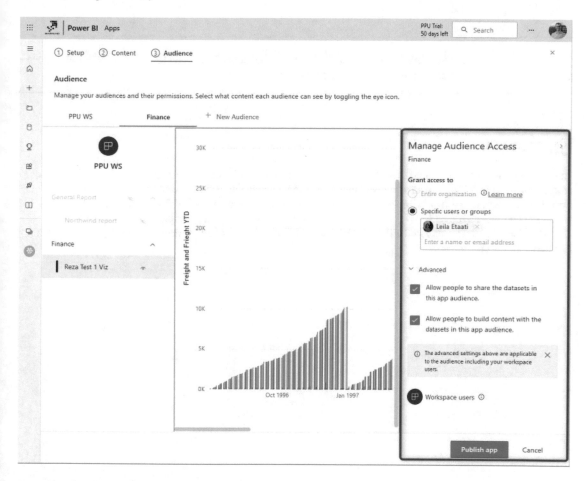

Figure 32-15. *Sharing content through Power BI apps*

Public access or organizational sharing

The difference between Publish to Web and the other sharing methods is about giving public access or sharing content through the organization:

- When you share dashboards or use the Power BI workspaces and apps, you share content with other users. These users should be Power BI users; they cannot access content anonymously. They must log in to the Power BI Service to access the content.

- With Publish to Web, anyone can access the report, even if they don't have a Power BI account. They don't need to log in. They can browse the page that contains Power BI embed code with no restrictions on viewing the report.

Power BI Embedded is different from Publish to Web

Power BI Embedded brings Power BI into applications. Yes, you can share your Power BI report through an application with API keys. You can share the report with application users, even if they don't have Power BI accounts. However, this is much more flexible. You can choose which reports you want to share with which users in the application. Power BI Embedded brings the Power BI experience into an application with security configuration enabled for users. Power BI Embedded is fully secured in a custom application, but the public reports are not.

Publish to Web is free but it's not a secure way of sharing, and it is for the public. Power BI Embedded is secure, paid service, and it's for specific people who you authorize.

Summary

In summary, Publish to Web is the only free way to share Power BI content. This method doesn't have any security bound to it. As soon as you publish a report to the web, anyone with that link can access the report and the data. This method of sharing is easy. However, it is not recommended for confidential data. This method is a reasonable option if you want to share public reports on your company's public website.

Publish to Web is entirely different from Power BI Embedded or Secure Embed; these methods should not be considered the same.

CHAPTER 33

Power BI Embedded

Power BI includes a very powerful method for sharing called Power BI Embedded. This method of sharing is powerful because you can share Power BI content in your custom application, and you can share it with your custom application users, regardless if they have Power BI accounts. In this chapter, you learn everything about Power BI Embedded, including but not limited to its scenarios and how to implement it.

Using Power BI Embedded

Power BI has strong and compelling sharing methods for organizations, such as workspaces and Power BI apps. However, there are scenarios where you may find a better sharing method. Consider using Power BI Embedded when you have scenarios like these:

- You want to share a Power BI report with users who do not have Power BI accounts, but your report needs to be shared securely so that only authorized users can see the content.

- You want to embed the Power BI report inside a custom application. This might be because your users are already using a custom application for other operational tasks, and having the Power BI report in the same application will give them a central point of work.

An example of these scenarios is an ISV company with customers from all other companies; their Office 365 tenant might be entirely different for every company. If the ISV company wants to share the Power BI report with all its clients, it first has to create Power BI accounts for each client in the tenant and then publish the Power BI report separately to each tenant. This process involves lots of repetitive work.

Power BI Embedded can really help this ISV company. They can embed Power BI reports in a custom ASP.NET application and then create users and passwords as part of the application. The username and password of the application are not Power BI users, of course. Everyone who has access to that page can consume the report.

There are a few things you need to know before choosing Power BI Embedded as your method of sharing:

- Licensing rules for Power BI Embedded are different. The page renders matter.

- Power BI Embedded doesn't have all the features of Power BI services (such as subscriptions, alerts, and so on).

- You need a web developer to handle embedding and any further changes.

© Reza Rad 2023
R. Rad, *Pro Power BI Architecture*, https://doi.org/10.1007/978-1-4842-9538-0_33

Power BI licensing is either per user (Free, Pro, and PPU) or capacity-based (Premium or Embedded). Power BI Embedded uses a capacity-based licensing, However, the capacity specification for entry nodes for the Embedded is very limited. It is important to choose a capacity that can cover the workload. Page renders can be a good indication of which licensing plan is appropriate.

When you use Power BI Embedded, you aren't using a Power BI Service. As a result, you will not have features such as usage metrics (per-user details) reports, alerts, subscriptions, and features that are specific to the service. You can obviously implement anything you want, but you need to have a good web developer on your team.

Power BI Embedded embeds a report into an application and needs a web developer to take care of this process. It is not just about the embedding itself; that may be a one-off process. When you embed the report into your application, all other requests come after that. You need to manage users and memberships for your web application. You may want to have a usage analysis of the report. You may want to have different levels of access to each report. Every extra feature comes as a request for the web developer to implement. It is possible to implement, but these all come at the cost of hiring a web developer.

Myths about Power BI Embedded

Power BI Embedded was recently enhanced. There are many myths about this method that need clarification:

- Power BI Embedded only works with Live Connection, not Import Data or Scheduled Refresh. This statement is a myth.

- Power BI Embedded does not support all data sources. This statement is a myth.

- You can only embed the Power BI report, not the dashboard or Q&A. This statement is a myth.

- Row-level security is not possible with Power BI Embedded. This statement is a myth.

Many of these statements were correct at the beginning phase of the Power BI Embedded (perhaps in 2015 or part of 2016). However, with recent updates and enhancements, you can do these things with Power BI Embedded. For your peace of mind, a Power BI team is only focused on embedded features, and they are working hard to bring more features to this technology regularly.

What Is Power BI Embedded?

After explaining these aspects of Power BI Embedded, it is now time to talk about what Embedded is. Power BI Embedded adds a report, dashboard, or dataset with Q&A to a custom application. This embedding is fully secure because it leverages the authentication keys and tokens. This way of embedding is not like Publish to Web. Publish to Web is not a secure method; however, Power BI Embedded is fully secure and customizable.

Embedded Playground

There is no place better than the Power BI Embedded Analytics Playground to familiarize yourself with the Embedded functionality and all its necessary codes. You can get to Playground from a Power BI report, as shown in Figure 33-1, or you can directly go to `playground.powerbi.com/`.

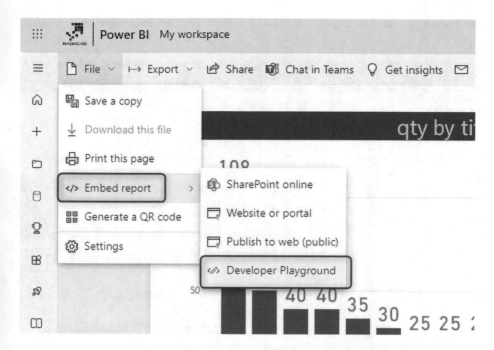

Figure 33-1. *Getting your report in the Power BI Embedded Playground*

If you navigate to the Developer Playground using the method shown in Figure 33-1, it will open the Playground with your report. You can then see what report in an embedded solution, as shown in Figure 33-2.

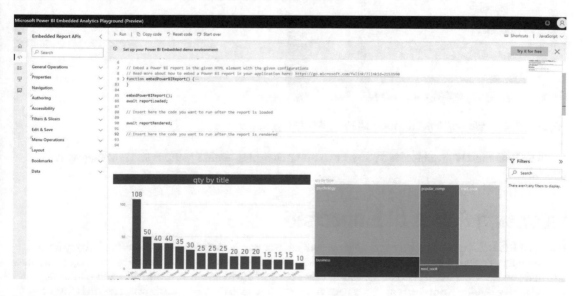

Figure 33-2. *The Power BI Embedded Playground*

The Playground is where you can also see other APIs and functions. Try them to see their code in action (see Figure 33-3).

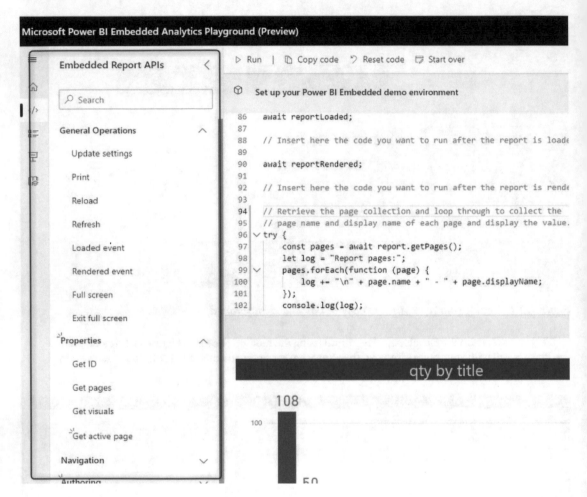

Figure 33-3. Trying APIs in the Power BI Embedded Playground

The Embedded Playground is a perfect way to start learning about functions and how they work in the code.

Licensing Power BI Embedded

Power BI Embedded is based on capacity sizes, and each capacity can cover some workload. Every time you open a page with a Power BI object, it is considered a page render. If you click a slicer, the page renders again; if you click a column chart and it causes other parts of the report to slice and dice, this counts as another page render. Knowing how many page renders you use in the peak hours of operation is important. The pricing list in Figure 33-4 is from azure.microsoft.com/en-us/pricing/details/power-bi-embedded/.

Node Type	Virtual Cores	Memory	Frontend / Backend Cores	Price
A1	1	3 GB RAM	0.5 / 0.5	$1.0081/hour
A2	2	5 GB RAM	1 / 1	$2.0081/hour
A3	4	10 GB RAM	2 / 2	$4.0242/hour
A4	8	25 GB RAM	4 / 4	$8.0565/hour
A5	16	50 GB RAM	8 / 8	$16.121/hour
A6	32	100 GB RAM	16 / 16	$32.2506/hour
A7	64	200 GB RAM	32 / 32	N/A
A8	128	400 GB RAM	64 / 64	N/A

Figure 33-4. *Power BI Embedded pricing*

The cost may look high; however, you get a different result for different scenarios. For a month of service with Power BI Embedded for about 300 page renders per hour (which an A1 should be enough), you pay about $700 USD, and 300 page renders should be enough for normal users of about 100 users. If you have 100 Pro users, on the other hand, you need to pay $1,000 USD. Power BI Embedded can be cheaper than Power BI Service in certain scenarios. However, for every scenario, the process needs to be considered separately.

Some SKUs Can Be Turned On and Off

A very helpful feature of Power BI Embedded is that it can be turned off and on with SKUs. There are two ways to get Power BI Embedded licensing:

- A SKUs (see Figure 33-4), which are part of Azure licensing
- EM SKUs, which are part of Office 365 licensing

A SKUs can be turned off when there is no operation. For example, the embedded capacity can be turned off when no one works after hours. As a result, the organization can save money (that is why you see hourly prices). Or if it is close to the end of the month, that is, peak days for the reporting, the SKU can be upgraded to a higher level and then downgraded to a lower level. This will ensure the reports' high performance and keep costs at a minimum.

To learn more about the differences between A and EM SKUs for Power BI Embedded, check out the licensing chapter earlier in this book.

Power BI Users or Custom Application Users

Power BI Embedded can work in two ways. You can use the users in your custom applications. These users might not have a Power BI account; they might not even have an Office 365 account. The other method is to leverage the Power BI accounts for the users and share content using Embedded. This latter method works similarly to the Secure Embed code.

Implementing Power BI Embedded

If you are not a developer and don't want to get into the coding part of Power BI Embedded, you can skip the rest of this chapter (or send it to your web developer). If you are a developer and want to learn how to use Power BI Embedded, keep reading. The following articles are all about implementing Power BI Embedded and using REST API step by step.

- **Part 1: Register your application:** The first step is to register your application. Any application that wants to interact with Azure should be registered and authorized through a process. (See radacad.com/integrate-power-bi-into-your-application-part-1-register-your-app.)

- **Part 2: Authenticate:** Every application that wants to interact with the Azure environment must undergo an authentication process. This authentication process passes a Client ID (and sometimes a Client Secret) to Azure and gets an authentication code. From this authentication code, an access token can be fetched. This access token should be involved in every request sent from your application to Power BI and Azure. Without this access token, your requests will fail. (See radacad.com/integrate-power-bi-into-your-application-part-2-authenticate.)

- **Part 3: Embed Content:** In this step, you learn about codes and the method to embed the content into your application after registration and authentication of the application. (See radacad.com/integrate-power-bi-into-your-application-part-3-embed-content.)

- **Part 4: Refresh Dataset:** The Power BI REST API is not just for embedding content or getting a list of dashboards and reports. It also has many functions to work with datasets, gateways, and data sources. One of the many exciting features of that is that you can quickly refresh a dataset from an application. You can refresh it as many times as you want, with any frequency you want. You can refresh your dataset after ETL runs through a console application. Or you can have a service application that kicks off a refresh every minute! There is no limitation on your data refresh anymore. (See radacad.com/integrate-power-bi-into-your-application-part-4-refresh-data-set.)

- **Part 5: Data Sources and Gateway Management:** The REST API in Power BI is powerful. In addition to embedding content in Power BI and refreshing datasets from API, it also gives you many functions to work with gateways and data sources. With this API, you can set up new data sources, clone datasets, check a data source's credentials, get a list of all data sources on a gateway, and do many other operations. In other words, Data source management can be fully automated with REST API. (See radacad.com/integrate-power-bi-into-your-application-part-5-data-source-management.)

- **Part 6: Real-time Streaming and Push Data:** In this article, I explain one of REST API's functionalities: pushing data to a streaming dataset. I've previously explained how to do real-time streaming using Azure Streaming Analytics and Power BI. However, this post explains real-time functionality just with the REST API. You don't need Azure services. (See radacad.com/integrate-power-bi-into-your-application-part-6-real-time-streaming-and-push-data.)

Summary

Power BI Embedded brings Power BI functionalities into your application. Imagine the analytical power of Power BI combined with your custom application. The result is revolutionary. You can leverage your users, interact with your web application's embedded object of Power BI, and implement many scenarios, including customized refresh and many other features. This method, however, works on a different licensing plan, and you need a web developer to enable it.

CHAPTER 34

■ ■ ■

Secure Embed

There is a method for sharing Power BI content called Secure Embed. This method of sharing is as simple as Publish to Web to implement, but it doesn't have the security issues of that method. You can securely publish Power BI reports through a custom web portal or application. This chapter explains Secure Embed in detail.

Why Another Embedding Method?

To understand why there is another method of sharing as embedded, you need some background information about the two other methods of sharing—Publish to Web and Power BI Embedded. Briefly speaking, Publish to Web (see Figure 34-1) is a method of sharing that can be implemented very simply, with just a few clicks, but has security issues and some limitations. Power BI Embedded (see Figure 34-2) is a secure method of sharing, but it needs a developer's touch and code lines to implement it. The Secure Embed method combines these two to achieve something secure but simple! Let's look at the pros and cons of each method first.

Publish to Web

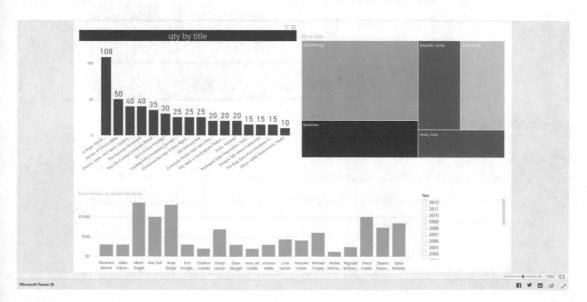

Figure 34-1. *Publish to Web*

R. Rad, *Pro Power BI Architecture*, https://doi.org/10.1007/978-1-4842-9538-0_34

Pros

- It can be embedded in any web page easily with just a few clicks.

Cons

- Everyone can see what you share. No security is available.

- All report pages are visible.

- Users can share the link and data with others.

- Row-level security is not supported.

Publish to Web is a very quick way to share, but it's not suitable for confidential data because it cannot be secured. Users won't even need Power BI accounts to access the content. They can see the content and even share it with others. Everyone with that link will have access to the data.

Power BI Embedded

Figure 34-2. *Power BI Embedded*

Pros

- You can share Power BI content securely with users.

- Users don't need to have Power BI accounts. It can work with Embedded licensing.

- Row-level security is supported.

Cons

- Implementation requires a web developer, because coding is involved in this method.

Power BI Embedded is a secure method of sharing that works perfectly for confidential data and when you have row-level security implemented. You can even share it with users who don't have Power BI accounts. However, the disadvantage of this method is the need for a web developer to take care of every change.

Secure Embed: Good Features from Both Worlds!

Now that you know the advantages and disadvantages of the previous two methods, you can see the need for a method that can simplify the process of Power BI Embedded and be secure enough for confidential data. That method is called Secure Embed. Using this method of sharing, the process of creating the embed code is as simple as doing it for the Publish to Web method. However, this method is secure, as users need to be authorized. They either need to have Power BI pro accounts or be part of an embedded licensing authorized by the person sharing the report. So with this method, you get good features from both methods! With Secure Embed, you can simply share Power BI content securely in a web portal or application. The next section explains how this method works.

Using Secure Embed

To use the Secure Embed method, go to a report in the Power BI Service. From the File menu, select Embed report, and then Website or Portal, as shown in Figure 34-3.

Secure Embed works only with reports in the Power BI Service, not with dashboards.

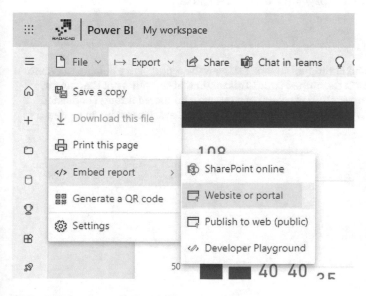

Figure 34-3. *Secure Embed in the Power BI Service*

As mentioned, this method makes creating the embed code very simple! With just a click, you get the embed code and the URL to share the reports on any platform you want (see Figure 34-4).

Securely embed this report in a website or portal ×

Here's a link you can use to embed this content.

```
https://app.powerbi.com/reportEmbed?reportId=69975d1e-7cde-419f-b185-096db835af05
```

HTML you can paste into a website

```
<iframe title="20210608" width="1140" height="541.25" src="https://app.powerbi.com/rep
```

Explore more embedding options in our Power BI embedded analytics playground   Close

Figure 34-4. *Getting the Secure Embed link from the Power BI Service*

There are two outputs for the Secure Embed code—the URL and the HTML embed code. Using the URL, you can directly share the reports with a link. You can share the link with any users you want. Using the HTML code, you can embed this report in web pages and custom web portals.

Who Can View the Report?

You've seen that sharing using this method is simple, but who can view the report? Is it available to everyone with the URL link or access to the page with the embed code? This method of sharing is not the same as Publish to Web. Users need a Power BI Pro (or PPU) account or a report to be shared through dedicated capacity licensing. If you send the URL to someone, they get a message that says, Please sign in to view this report, as depicted in Figure 34-5.

 Power BI

Please sign in to view this report

Sign-In

Figure 34-5. *Users of the Secure Embed code must sign in*

Reports shared through Secure Embed work with Power BI Pro (or PPU) user accounts of (users need to log in) or by adding the report under the embedded capacity.

This is not the whole story. If a user logs in, they still might not be authorized to see the report because it is not shared with them. If a user logs in through a Power BI Pro account but still doesn't have access to the report, they will see a message that says, To view this report, ask the author for access (see Figure 34-6).

Figure 34-6. *The author must grant access to certain users to view a report*

If users are accessing the report through Secure Embed using Power BI Pro accounts, the report should be shared with them by the report owner.

There are multiple ways to share accounts. The most straightforward way is via report sharing. To use report sharing, click the Share button on the report in the Power BI Service. You can also do this using Manage Permissions, as demonstrated in Figure 34-7.

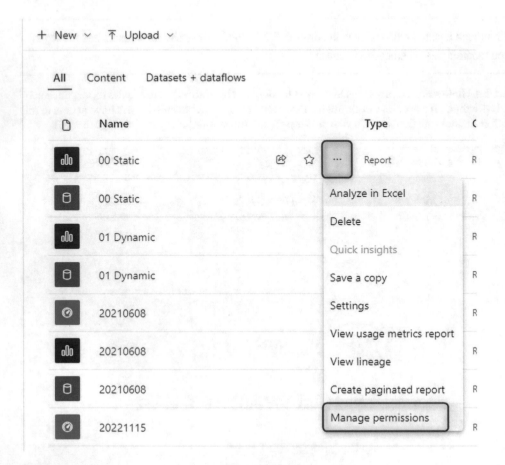

Figure 34-7. *Manage Permissions on the Power BI report*

This access can also be set up through workspaces or other sharing methods.

After you share the report, users can access it using Secure Embed. Figure 34-8 shows how this looks.

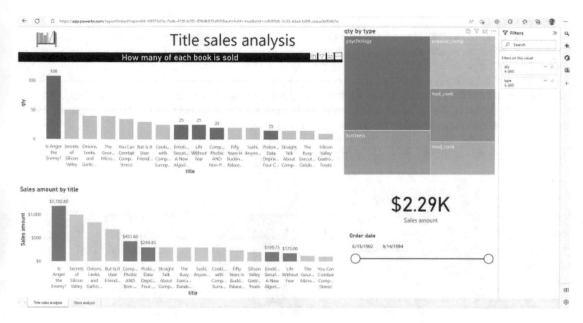

Figure 34-8. *A Secure Embed report opened in a web browser*

Users will have access to all the pages. At the time of writing this chapter, isolating access at the page level is impossible.[1] Access to the report means access to all pages in the report. This applies to all methods of sharing in Power BI.

Licensing Needs

This method of sharing is not free. You need to use one of these licensing paths:

- Using Power BI Pro or PPU (Premium per User)
- Using Power BI dedicated capacity (Premium or Embedded)

To use Power BI Pro or PPU, users need to have accounts, and then you can simply share the report with them. Another option is to use dedicated capacity. An important point here is that even if you have embedded licensing, the user has to log in to the page to see the Secure Embed content. This is different from Power BI Embedded, where you can use Power BI users or custom application users. A custom application user setting won't work with Secure Embed.

Advantages of Secure Embed

This section explains the advantages of the Secure Embed method.

Sharing with only a few clicks; no developer is needed

As you have seen in this chapter, I haven't written a single line of code. This method works by using the Secure Embed option. All you need to do is use the URL output of Secure Embed or embed the HTML code on a web page. Unlike Power BI Embedded (which needs a developer's touch), this method is very simple to implement.

---

[1] There is, however, a workaround. See radacad.com/page-level-security-workaround-in-power-bi

Secure sharing

Just by its name, Secure Embed, you can guess that it's secure. You also saw in this chapter, through an example, how the content is secured for those users who are authorized to see the content. Unlike Publish to Web, this method provides a secure method of sharing.

Row-level security is supported

Publish to Web doesn't support row-level security because there is no concept of the user logging in because no login is required. However, using Secure Embed, only authorized users will have access to the report, and as a result, row-level security is possible (see Figure 34-9).

Figure 34-9. *The Publish to Web does not support row-level security*

Limitations

Some limitations of Secure Embed are related to the content that can be shared. For example, ArcGIS Maps is not currently supported, as you can see in Figure 34-10.

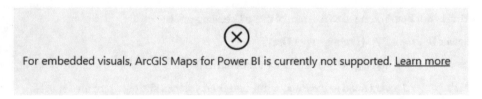

For embedded visuals, ArcGIS Maps for Power BI is currently not supported. Learn more

Figure 34-10. *ArcGIS Maps are not supported in Secure Embed*

Secure Embed, at the moment, doesn't support dashboards or paginated reports.

Another significant limitation of Secure Embed is that it won't work with custom applications' user setups. If you use the Secure Embed method, you must use Power BI user accounts. If you want to use a custom application's userbase, the better choice is Power BI Embedded.

Scenarios for Using this Method

This method provides a quick way to share data using an HTML embed code. If you are using SharePoint Online, there is a quick method to use for that (read the next chapter), but what about other web applications? What about SharePoint on-premises? This method can be a great option to securely share quickly through a web page.

Summary

Secure Embed is neither Publish to Web nor Power BI Embedded. It is combines features from both of these tools. Using Secure Embed, you can share your reports through a web portal with just a few clicks. However, unlike Publish to Web, Secure Embed is a secure method of sharing, because only authorized users have access to the data. As a result, this method also supports row-level security-enabled reports. However, there are scenarios where Power BI Embedded is a better option (for example, if you want to use the custom application's userbase).

■■■

CHAPTER 35

Embed in SharePoint Online and Teams

In this chapter, you learn about another method of sharing called Embed in SharePoint Online. Embedding in SharePoint Online is an excellent method for sharing Power BI content through a SharePoint portal. Because Power BI and Office 365 accounts are bound to each other, this method of sharing is prevalent for SharePoint users. You can use SharePoint as the portal. Power BI content can then be easily shared with Office 365 users through that portal.

How to Use Embed in SharePoint Online

To use this method, you must have a Power BI report published in the service. This method only works with Power BI reports (not dashboards). To share a report using this method, after logging into the service and opening a Power BI report, click the File menu. Under Embed Report, choose SharePoint Online (see Figure 35-1).

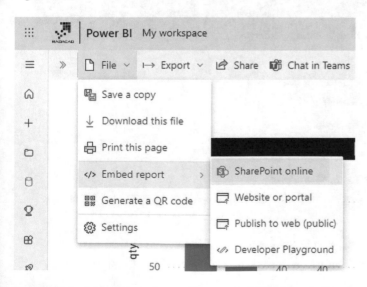

Figure 35-1. *Embedding a Power BI report in SharePoint Online*

The next step generates a link that can be used in SharePoint. Just copy the link from this step (see Figure 35-2).

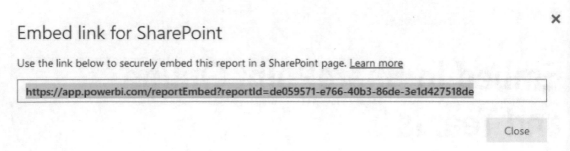

Figure 35-2. Link generated in SharePoint

The URL is needed in SharePoint Online for embedding the Power BI report. Log in to your SharePoint Online tenant. Go to the Pages section, as shown in Figure 35-3.

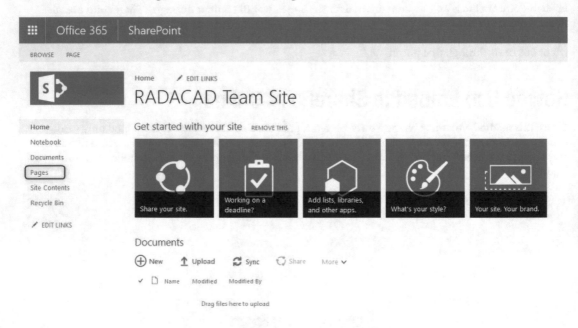

Figure 35-3. Navigating to the Pages section in SharePoint

Create a new site page (or edit an existing page), as demonstrated in Figure 35-4.

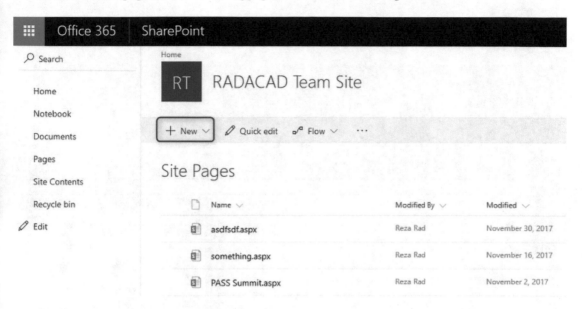

Figure 35-4. *Creating a new site page in SharePoint*

You can name this page something like "Power BI Embedded into SharePoint Online," then click Add Icon to add a new object. From the All Items list, select Power BI (see Figure 35-5).

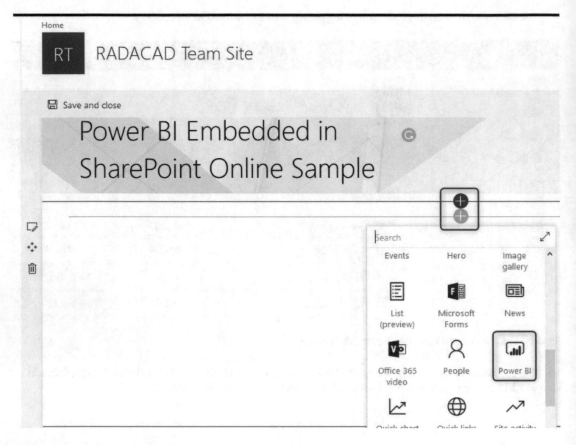

Figure 35-5. *Naming your new site and selecting Power BI*

The Power BI component is now inserted into your page. As shown in Figure 35-6, you can click Add Report. (At the time of writing this chapter, you can only embed reports, not dashboards, into SharePoint Online.)

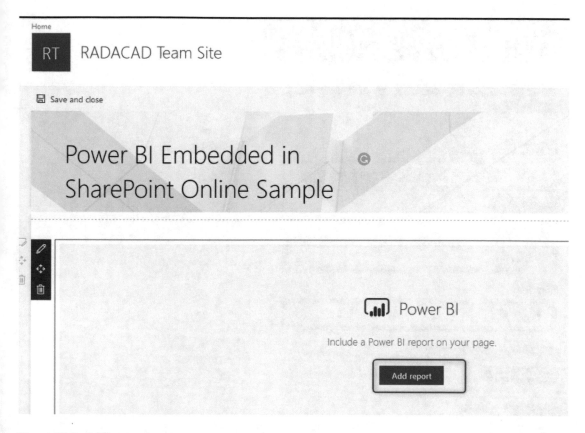

Figure 35-6. *Adding a report to your new team site*

You can now paste the embedded URL from the previous step for the Power BI report into this section and select the page (if the Power BI report has multiple pages), as shown in Figure 35-7.

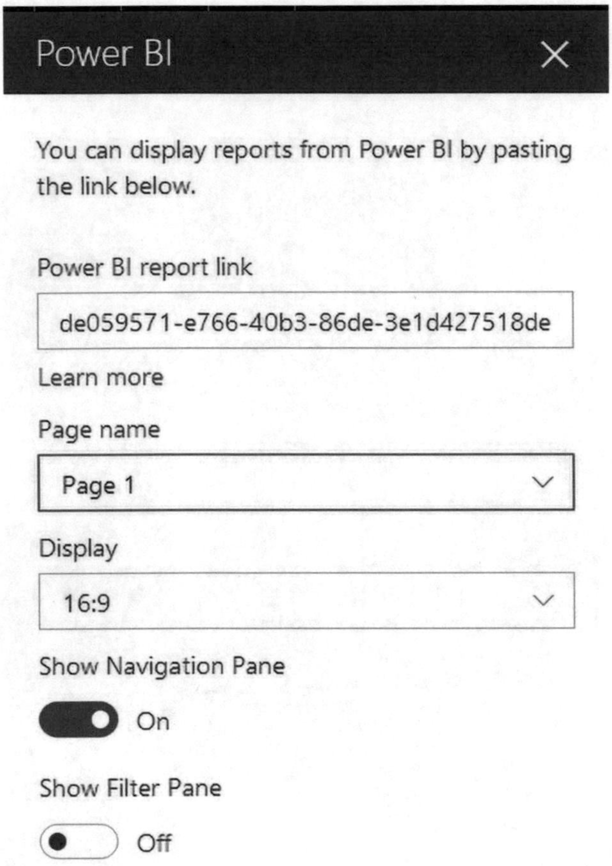

Power BI   ✕

You can display reports from Power BI by pasting
the link below.

Power BI report link

de059571-e766-40b3-86de-3e1d427518de

Learn more

Page name

Page 1   ⌄

Display

16:9   ⌄

Show Navigation Pane

On

Show Filter Pane

Off

Figure 35-7. Pasting in the embedded URL

As soon as you make these changes, you'll see the report preview on the page (see Figure 35-8).

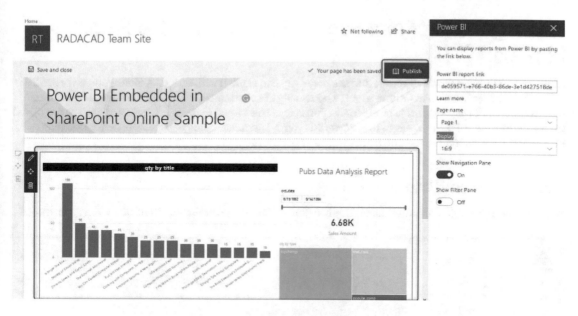

Figure 35-8. *The results generated by pasting in the embedded link*

You can now publish the page. Once the page is published, the Power BI embedded part will be part of it. The Power BI embedded in the SharePoint Online page will be interactive, like a standard Power BI report is (see Figure 35-9).

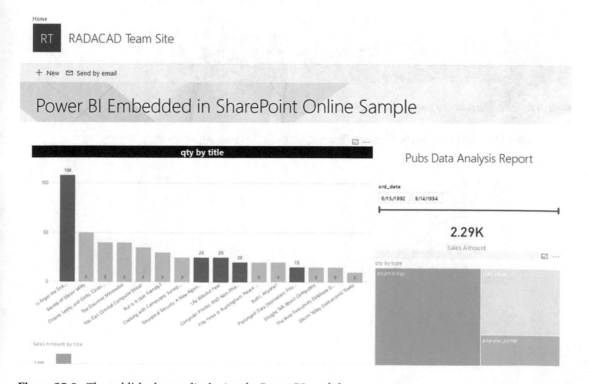

Figure 35-9. *The published page displaying the Power BI module*

Sharing a SharePoint Page with an Embedded Power BI Report

After embedding the Power BI report into the page, you can share it with others. A SharePoint page can be shared with other SharePoint Online users (who usually are also Office 365 users). However, one important note is that if a Power BI report is embedded in this page, users need to have Power BI accounts to see it, and their account should have access to that Power BI report. You must manage permission in two locations—from a SharePoint Online page and from the Power BI report.

Access to SharePoint

You can share the page with other users simply using the Share icon at the top-right side, as in Figure 35-10.

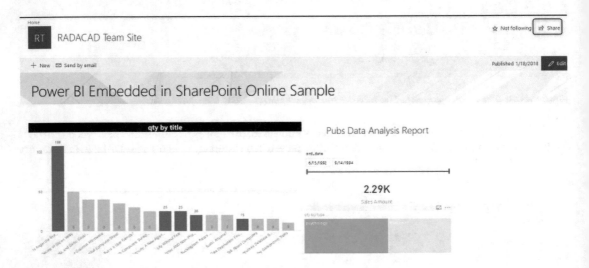

Figure 35-10. *Sharing the page with other users*

You can then add people from Office 365 accounts to the list (see Figure 35-11).

Figure 35-11. Adding people to your team site

If you take a closer look at Figure 35-11, you'll see that I shared it with three types of accounts:

- Power BI Pro account, which is the account named Reza Rad in the figure

- A Power BI free account

- An Office 365 account with no Power BI license

Power BI Permissions

Users also need to be permitted to access the Power BI report. You can use the Manage Permissions part of the dashboard to handle this, as shown in Figure 35-12.

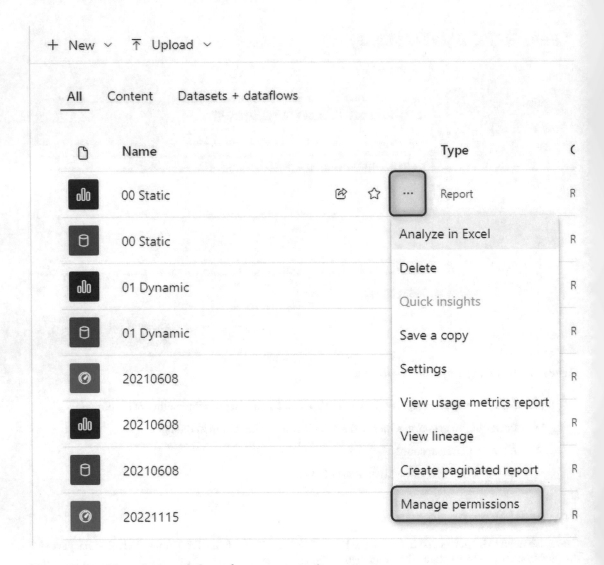

Figure 35-12. *Managing permissions of your new team site*

Choosing Manage Permissions shows you a detailed access list to the dashboard, reports, and datasets. You will see related reports and datasets on the left side of the Manage Permissions section (see Figure 35-13). You can click the report.

Figure 35-13. *A detailed access list displayed in Manage Permissions*

You will see the permission specified for that object by clicking a report or dataset. Now, let's see what each user will see when they log in to this page.

A Pro user, when the content is shared with them in the Power BI Service and the page is shared with them in SharePoint Online, will see the full page (see Figure 35-14).

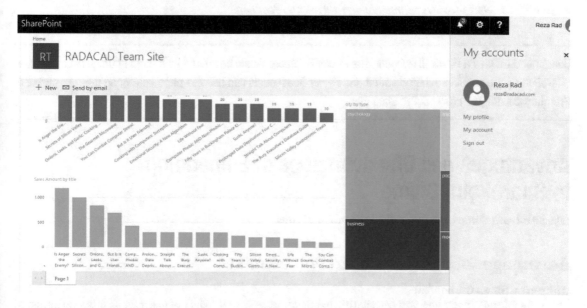

Figure 35-14. *A page that is fully accessible to a Pro user*

Other users, however, can't see the entire page. If the users don't have a Pro subscription, or if it is not part of a Power BI premium capacity, they can't see the content and will see an error, as shown in Figure 35-15.

Figure 35-15. *Non-pro users cannot access all elements of the page*

Users need to have a Power BI account. The Power BI report should be shared with them in the service, and the SharePoint page should be shared with them. Power BI accounts can use this page only when they are part of a Premium capacity or Power BI Pro accounts.

Advantages and Disadvantages of Embedding in SharePoint Online

Like all other methods, this method has its pros and cons.

Advantages of Embed in SharePoint Online

One portal for all the content

With SharePoint Online, you can share other documents as well. Why not use it for all other documents and the Power BI report? You can have one portal, which is the central sharing portal for your Office 365 tenant. Users usually love integrity.

Embedding is simple

Unlike with Power BI Embedded, embedding in SharePoint Online is easy. You just get the URL and embed it into a Power BI object in SharePoint Online. You don't need to write a single line of code for that purpose, but with Power BI Embedded, you need a developer.

Disadvantages of Embed in SharePoint Online

The Power BI Service is underutilized

One of the great aspects of Power BI components is the service. If you use SharePoint embedded, users will use that as the portal for reports. The Power BI Service has many exciting features that may not be well used in this scenario, such as alerts, feature dashboards, the dashboard itself, Q&A, and many other items. Users can still log in to the Power BI service and see the report, but the experience you created for them with SharePoint Online is not there.

Two places for managing permissions

At the time of writing this chapter, you need to manage permissions in the Power BI Service and in SharePoint Online. This takes time for maintenance and reconciliation to check whether the people who have access to the page are permitted to read the report.

Power BI and Teams

Power BI also integrates with Teams. Instead of starting data from the Power BI service, you can go to a Teams channel tab, add a Power BI item, select the report, and share it (see Figure 35-16).

Figure 35-16. *Adding a Power BI tab to Teams*

There is also a link to set the Manage Permissions from there (see Figure 35-17).

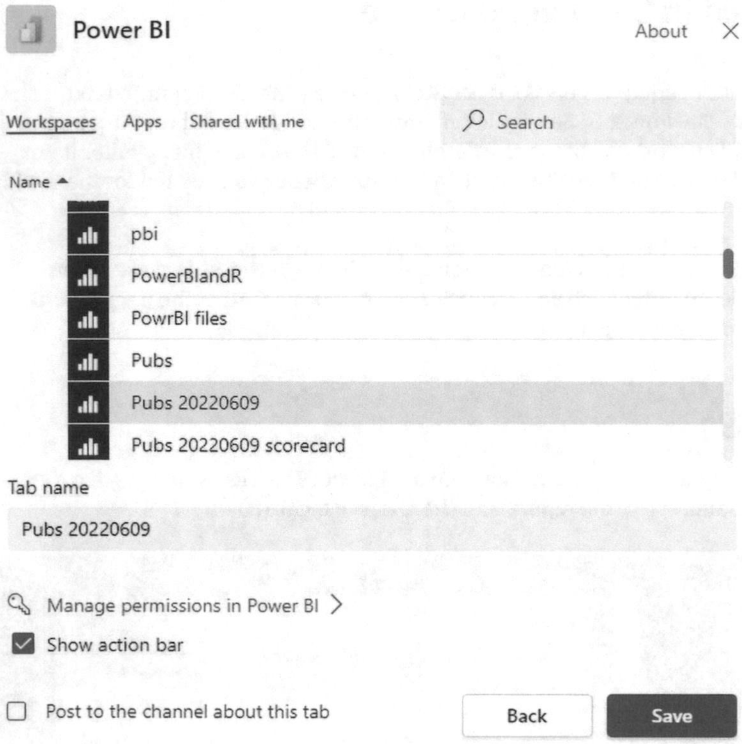

Figure 35-17. Embedding Power BI reports in Teams

Power BI and PowerPoint

Power BI can also be integrated and embedded into Microsoft PowerPoint. This process can be done by selecting the Insert tab and selecting Power BI. You can then paste the URL of the Power BI report (see Figure 35-18). All of these methods use the Secure Embed option.

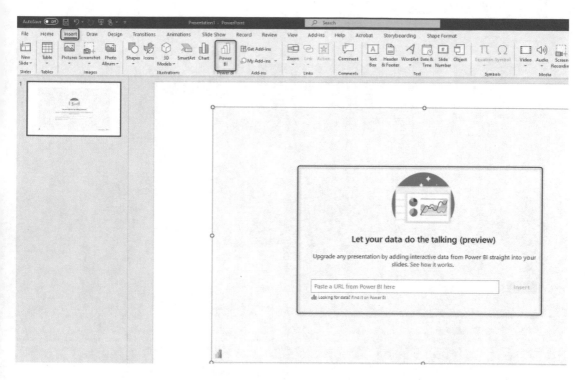

Figure 35-18. Embedding Power BI reports in PowerPoint

Summary

In summary, embedding in SharePoint Online is an easy way to add an interactive Power BI report to a SharePoint Online page. This method allows you to have a central SharePoint Portal for all your content and Power BI reports. Users need to be part of a paid Power BI subscription to use this feature. They will lose the Power BI service's functionalities because they are not available in SharePoint.

Power BI report also integrates well with Microsoft Teams and PowerPoint. The concept is similar; it uses Power BI user access to shared content.

■ ■ ■

CHAPTER 36

Comparison of Sharing Methods for Power BI

You have published your Power BI report and want to share it with others. You can share it using various methods—basic sharing, workspaces, apps, Publish to Web, Power BI Embedded, Secure Embed, and SharePoint Online. The wide range of sharing methods makes it confusing to choose the best one. It is very important to determine which method is best before sharing your content with users. In this chapter, you learn about all the different methods of sharing, the pros and cons of each, and scenarios in which to use each method. By the end of this chapter, you'll be able to choose the best sharing mechanism for sharing your Power BI reports.

Types of Sharing Methods

This chapter only covers the sharing methods that are interactive and cloud-based. It doesn't cover sharing a `*.pbix` file with others, which is a method of sharing, obviously, but not a proper sharing method. It doesn't cover exporting a Power BI report as a PDF and sharing it with others because that is not interactive. It also doesn't cover taking screenshots of a Power BI report and sharing it with others. Also, it doesn't cover sharing through on-premises solutions using the Power BI Report Server.

This chapter focuses on the cloud-based, interactive methods of sharing Power BI reports. It covers the following sharing methods:

- Basic sharing

- Workspaces

- Power BI apps

- The Publish to Web option

- Embed in SharePoint Online

- Power BI Embedded

- Secure Embed

© Reza Rad 2023
R. Rad, *Pro Power BI Architecture*, https://doi.org/10.1007/978-1-4842-9538-0_36

Basic Sharing for Dashboards and Reports

This is one of the most common ways to share Power BI content. However, it is not always the best way. Basic sharing is a very simple and easy-to-use method. You simply click the Share button in the dashboard or report and then share it with other users, as shown in Figure 36-1.

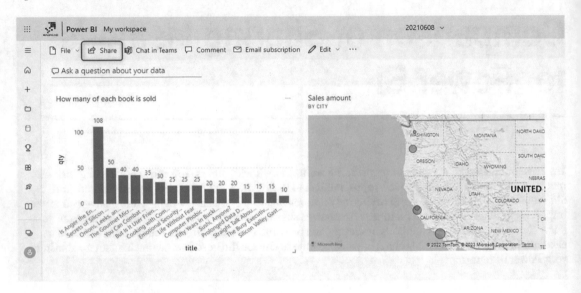

Figure 36-1. *Dashboard or report sharing*

This method of sharing gives users three levels of access—Read-only, Reshare, and Build.

By default, when you share a Power BI dashboard using this method, the report and the dataset are shared as well. However, you can go to Manage Permissions and set up permission for every item if you want, as depicted in Figure 36-2.

Figure 36-2. *Manage Permissions on the Power BI content*

Users can easily click the Shared with Me section of their profile, and they will see all the reports and dashboards shared with them (see Figure 36-3).

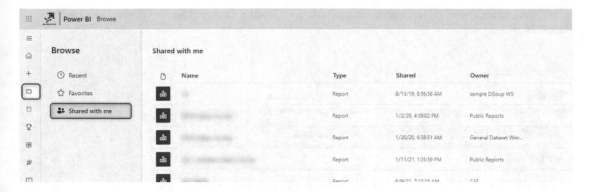

Figure 36-3. *Power BI reports that are shared with me*

This method of sharing has some pros and cons, discussed next.

Advantages of Dashboard Sharing

Dashboard sharing is the most basic way to share content in Power BI. This method is quick and easy to set up. You don't need to go through a lot of steps to set up dashboard sharing. The ability to share it very quickly makes this method the most common method of sharing for testing purposes.

If you create Power BI content and want to share it with others easily for testing purposes, dashboard sharing is a good option.

Disadvantages of Dashboard Sharing

Dashboard sharing is simple; however, it has many drawbacks, which make it unwise in a production environment. I do not recommend using this method to share Power BI content with users in a production environment because of the reasons mentioned next.

No Edit Access

With dashboard sharing, you cannot specify edit access. End users should never have edit access; however, if you are working with a team of developers and you want to provide them with access to edit the content, you cannot do that with dashboard sharing.

Share objects one at a time

You can only share one dashboard at a time. What if you wanted to share hundreds of dashboards? You must go to each dashboard and share items individually. Sharing every dashboard would add a lot of maintenance overhead to your work. The best method would be having all contents under a group and sharing them with others at once.

Workspaces

Workspaces are created to address the main two limitations of basic sharing—lack of edit access and not being able to share multiple objects. With a workspace, you can share as many items as you want in that workspace at once. You can also determine the access level of the workspace to be Edit or Read-Only (through four access levels). Workspaces, because of these two features, are heavily used as collaborative development environments.

There are four levels of workspace access—Admin, Member, Contributor, and Viewer—as shown in Figure 36-4.

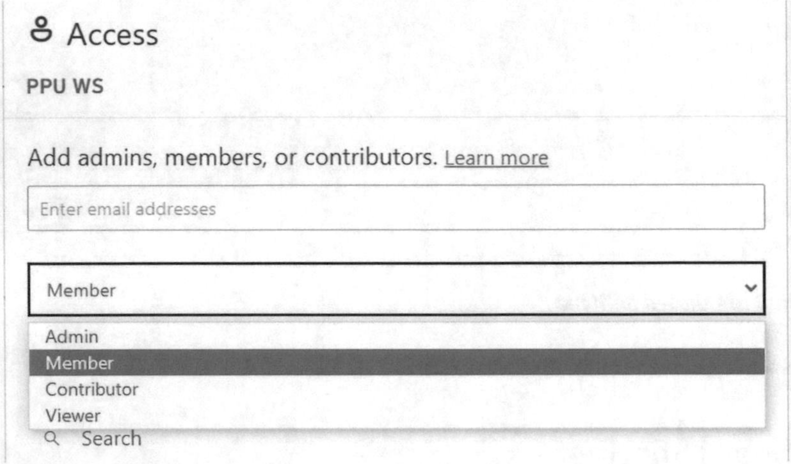

Figure 36-4. *Access levels for the users of the Power BI workspace*

Workspaces also have their advantages and disadvantages. Let's check these out.

Advantages of Workspaces

Sharing multiple datasets with the team

You may have shared a dashboard with a couple of your colleagues in your organization, but after a few weeks, a dashboard comes up, and you share that dashboard with them. A couple of months later, another team member asks for access to a Power BI dataset to create a report and share it with others. Power BI workspaces enable you to share content (dashboards, reports, and datasets) with all group members. You don't have to share each dashboard with each user; groups make it easy for you.

Sharing all types of objects

The dashboard only allows sharing of the Power BI report, dashboard, and dataset. However, sharing through the workspace allows all the content to be shared. This includes, but is not limited to, dataflows, datasets, datamarts, dashboards, reports, metrics, and paginated reports.

Multiple workspaces

It is hectic when you are part of multiple teams, and each team has its own dashboards, reports, and datasets. Your Shared with Me section in Power BI could have hundreds of items. Power BI workspaces create a separate environment for all members of the group. You can easily switch between workspaces in Power BI.

Isolated user/group administration

When you share content with an individual in the organization, and that person leaves the company or is replaced by someone from another team, you have to remove sharing from a previous user account and assign it to the new user account. The best practice is to share content with groups. Members of workspaces can then easily be managed by an administrator. Power BI workspaces can be shared with Office 365 groups. Once you use a group in Power BI, it is only the admin's task to add/remove members.

Best developer environment

You need an environment to share multiple Power BI content for a team of developers. Everyone needs to have edit access to the content provided by the team. Power BI workspaces are a perfect solution for the development environment. You can create a workspace as a development environment and then share it with other developer team members with edit access. Then you all have access to the same content in your development workspace.

Power BI workspaces are a perfect solution for development environments.

Disadvantages of Workspaces

Workspaces are useful, but there are some drawbacks.

Not suitable for end users

Workspaces are not suitable for sharing content with end users. You may wonder why that is. You can give users read-only access to the content. However, this is half of the requirement. In an end-user sharing environment, one of the primary requirements is to have the development and user environment separated.

Assume that you created a workspace and shared it with end users. If you suddenly make changes to the workspace while they are using it, their view breaks and changes.

With one workspace, your development and user environment are the same.

You cannot use one workspace to be shared between developers and users. Creating multiple workspaces also introduces another challenge. To overcome this challenge, you can use apps on top of the workspaces to share content with end users.

Complications of the workspace structure

Setting up a good workspace structure is a challenge. You need a workspace structure that covers the development, user needs, and deployment structure. This is more of a caution than a limitation. Use workspaces with care, and make sure you have a good setup.

Requires Power BI Pro or PPU (Premium Per User)

Creating Power BI workspaces, or even being part of one (even at the viewer access level), requires a Pro or PPU option and is not part of a Power BI free user account. However, it is possible to create an app for the workspace in a Premium capacity and assign free Power BI users to it. This limitation is one of the main reasons this is method not the most cost-effective option for sharing content with end users.

Power BI Apps

Workspaces are a great way to share content with users, but when it comes to having a development and user environment, managing multiple workspaces is not the best method. Power BI apps are best for multiple environment approaches. With Power BI apps, your development environment (the workspace) and user environment (the app) are isolated. Power BI apps can also be a cost-effective option for organizations with large userbases.

Creating an app for a workspace is very simple. Users can easily access it through the Apps section of their Power BI account, as shown in Figure 36-5.

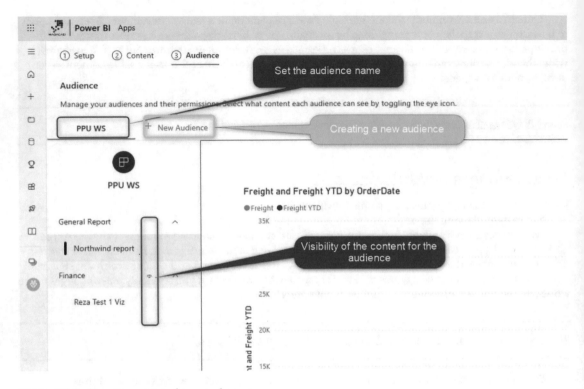

Figure 36-5. *Creating an app for a workspace*

Apps are great sharing methods for multiple environments and the best way to share with users in a production environment. However, apps also have their pros and cons, discussed next.

Advantages of Power BI Apps

Separate environments for the developer and end users

This method has two separate environments—an environment for developers to edit the Power BI content in a collaborative workspace and another environment for end users to consume the report. End users are only able to view the reports, and developers can make changes.

Power BI apps are the best solution when you need isolated developer and end user environments.

A cost-effective option for a large userbase

If you have thousands of users and want to share Power BI content with them securely, then sharing with options that rely on per-user licensing is not cost-effective. A Power BI workspace can be assigned to a Premium workspace, and then if you create an app on top of it, the app's users can be free Power BI users. This is a big help for organizations with large userbases. You can purchase a capacity, and as long as it can cover the load of the users over the Power BI content in the service, free users can use it.

This is one of the most common reasons that many organizations use Power BI apps combined with workspaces to share Power BI content.

Control over multiple Power BI data sources

Similar to workspaces, the Power BI app allows you to share multiple dashboards, reports, and datasets simultaneously. Controlling multiple sources means less maintenance overhead compared to dashboard sharing, which shares one dashboard at a time.

External sharing

Another great benefit of Power BI apps is the ability to integrate them with Azure B2B services and provide external sharing. If you want to share Power BI content with people outside your company, you can do that with a combination of Azure B2B and Power BI apps.

Cons of Power BI Apps

Power BI apps are one of the best and the most common methods of sharing in Power BI. There is a small thing that you need to be careful of, though.

Changes in the dataset are applied immediately

Power BI app separates developer and end-user environments, and the changes to a report in a workspace don't affect the end user until you update the app. However, this functionality doesn't work with the dataset in that way. The Power BI app and the workspace share the same datasets, so any changes to the schedule refresh or any structural changes will apply to both.

The Publish to Web Option

Sometimes, you don't need a secure way of sharing. You need an easy and free way of sharing, and your content is not confidential or sensitive. In that case, Publish to Web is your friend. This is the only free way to share data in Power BI, but be aware that this method is not secure.

The Publish to Web method gives you an embed code, which you can use on any web page to embed the Power BI report in it (see Figure 36-6).

Figure 36-6. *The Publish to Web option*

The embedded content is available to anyone who has access to that page. Publish to Web is a free way of sharing. If you think you might use this method, consider the following issues first.

Security Issues with Publish to Web

Everyone can see what you share

The first thing you might think of is usually security. How can you manage security with this method? The short answer is there is no security. The report is shared through the web or email with everyone. So everyone who has the link or the embed code can access the report. They cannot edit it. But they can view it without restriction.

Users can share the reports with others

A report published on the web has a share section on the bottom-right side. Everyone can share this report with anyone else through all social media channels—Facebook, Twitter, and LinkedIn. This method of sharing is not secure. I recommend sharing data this way only when you have a public report to place on your company or organization's website.

The report is public, and not only to those with the link

This report is not shared only with those with the link. It is shared globally on the Internet. That means a search engine such as Google can find the report. All reports with Publish to Web links are available in search results. You must be sure that the report doesn't reveal confidential information before using this method.

All report pages are visible

If you have a report with more than ten pages, all the pages will be visible to browsers. You cannot limit which pages you want to show and which you don't. I recommend creating different reports if you want to restrict some pages and share them separately.

What if the report has row-level security applied?

If you have a report with the row-level security applied to it, you can't create a Publish to Web link.

Publish to Web is only recommended for public data sharing on your organization website with the public. There is no security option for Publish to Web; this method should not be used for confidential reports.

Embed in SharePoint Online

If you are already using SharePoint Online as a portal for document management, consider using Embed in the SharePoint Online feature of Power BI reports. This method is secure, and you can share the report only with the Power BI users you want.

Power BI content can easily be embedded into a SharePoint Online page, as shown in Figure 36-7.

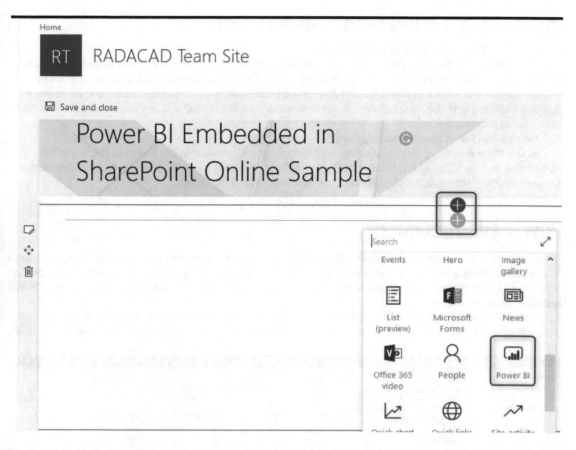

Figure 36-7. *Embedding Power BI content into a SharePoint Online page*

You manage security and sharing in two different places—from the SharePoint site, and in Power BI. This method also has its pros and cons.

Advantages of Embed in SharePoint Online

One portal for all content

With SharePoint online, you can share other documents as well. Why not use it for all other documents and the Power BI report? You can have one portal, which is the central sharing portal for your Office 365 tenant. Users usually love integrity.

Embedding is simple

Unlike Power BI Embedded, embedding in SharePoint Online is easy. You just get the URL and embed it into a Power BI object in SharePoint Online. You don't need to write a single line of code, but with Power BI Embedded, you need a developer.

Disadvantages of Embed in SharePoint Online

Power BI service golden plate is underutilized

One of the great aspects of Power BI components is the service. If you use SharePoint embedded, users will use it as the portal for reports. The Power BI Service has many exciting features that may not be well used in this scenario, such as alerts, feature dashboards, the dashboard itself, Q&A, and many other items. Users can still log in to the Power BI Service and see the report, but the experience you created for them with SharePoint Online is not there.

Two places for managing permissions

At the time of writing this chapter, you need to manage permissions in the Power BI Service and in SharePoint Online. This would take some time for maintenance and reconciliation to check whether those people who have access to the page are always permitted to read the report.

Power BI Embedded

Sometimes you want to embed the Power BI content into your custom application, and you want the content to be secured. In most cases, you want to leverage the custom user management of your current application rather than Power BI accounts. Power BI Embedded gives you all of these features. The only side effect is that you need a web developer.

Power BI Embedded uses an API called Power BI REST API, and it has many great features for interacting with Power BI content. Users can easily access reports through your application (see Figure 36-8).

Figure 36-8. *Accessing reports through an application via Power BI Embedded*

Pros and Cons of Power BI Embedded

With Power BI Embedded, you get a fully customizable solution. You can do whatever you want inside your application with Power BI content. You can embed reports, dashboards, tiles, and even Q&As. You can interact with those elements from the web page.

Power BI Embedded can work without the need for Power BI accounts. If you have a set of users without accounts or your users are not part of a single company, Power BI Embedded can be a great solution.

To implement Power BI Embedded, you need a web developer. It is not just about one-off embedding your first content; every change after that, or every new functionality you add to your application, needs a web developer's touch.

Another big advantage of Power BI Embedded is its ability to scale up or down on some SKU capacities and bring the costs down while keeping performance high.

Secure Embed

This method combines good aspects of Publish to Web and Power BI Embedded. Using Secure Embed (see Figure 36-9), you can share your reports through a web portal with just a few clicks. However, unlike Publish to Web, Secure Embed is a secure method of sharing, and only authorized users have access to the data. As a result, this method also supports row-level security-enabled reports.

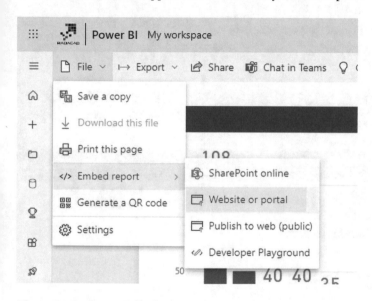

Figure 36-9. *Secure Embed*

Like all the other methods, this method also has its pros and cons.

Advantages of Secure Embed

Sharing with a few clicks, no developer is needed

You don't have to write a single line of code; it works by using the Secure Embed option. All you need to do is use the URL output of Secure Embed or embed the HTML code on the web page. Unlike Power BI Embedded (which needs a developer's touch), this method is very simple to implement.

Secure sharing

Since this method is called "Secure Embed," you probably guessed that it includes secure sharing. Content is available only to authorized users. Unlike Publish to Web, this is a secure method of sharing.

Row-level security is supported

The Publish to Web method doesn't support row-level security because there is no concept of the user logging in, because no login is required. However, using Secure Embed, only authorized users have access to the reports, and as a result, row-level security is possible.

Disadvantages and Limitations of Secure Embed

Power BI Embedded does limit the content that can be shared. For example, ArcGIS Maps is not currently supported. Secure Embed, at the moment, also doesn't support dashboards or paginated reports.

Another significant limitation of Secure Embed is that it doesn't work with user setups of custom applications. If you use the Secure Embed method, you must use the Power BI user accounts. If you want to use a custom application's userbase, your best bet is Power BI Embedded.

Summary

So far, you've learned what every method of sharing does; now you can see how they compare, all in one place. This is shown in Figure 36-10.

	Basic Sharing	Workspace	Power BI App	Publish to web	SharePoint Online	Power BI Embedded	Secure Embed
FREE				Yes			
No Power BI account needed				Yes		Yes	
Access Levels	Read	Read/Edit	Read	Read	Read	Read/Edit	Read
Secure	Yes	Yes	Yes		Yes	Yes	Yes
Dev/User Environment			Yes				
Sharing Multiple Items		Yes	Yes				
Extras						the need for Web Developer	

Figure 36-10. Comparing the Power BI sharing methods

Cheat Sheet for Choosing a Method

Basic sharing	A fast and quick method for sharing test reports and dashboards.
Workspaces	A great option for collaborative development environments between Power BI Developer teams.
Power BI apps	The best option to share reports with end users in a user environment that is isolated from the developer environment.
Publish to Web	The free method of sharing that is best for public datasets where the data is not confidential.
SharePoint Online	A good choice when SharePoint Online is the current portal for users in the organization.
Power BI Embedded	An option to bring Power BI content into your application, especially when user management can be done in the custom application.
Secure Embed	A great way to share simply and securely in SharePoint on-premises or a custom web application without the need for a web developer.

CHAPTER 37

Types of Power BI Users

Power BI users come in all different types. If you treat everyone equally, you will not have good Power BI adoption. You will likely spend too much on training and still gain poor adoption. This chapter explains the different types of users and the proper actions for each type.

The Different Types of Power BI Users

In the world of Power BI, there are different types of users in an organization. Some users develop the model, and others consume what is created. On bigger teams, there are more layers. Figure 37-1 shows the four types of Power BI users.

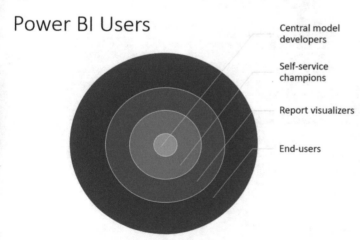

Figure 37-1. *Different categories of Power BI users*

These users are defined as follows:

- **End user**: Someone who browses the report (in the mobile app, web browser, or through an embedded web experience). This user might interact with the report by filtering, highlighting, drilling through it, and so on, but they never change the data or create a report.

R. Rad, *Pro Power BI Architecture*, https://doi.org/10.1007/978-1-4842-9538-0_37

- **Report visualizer**: This is a much smaller category than the end-user group. For this group, the reports that were built are not enough; they need to modify the visuals. This request might have come from their managers, or they prefer another way to view that data. This group does not change the data model or import new data tables. They might, however, add a few calculations added here and there to support their visualizations.

- **Self-service champions**: This is a smaller group than report visualizer group. This group does visualizations and brings new data into the model. They might have data sources that they want to integrate into the existing analysis, and they do some extra calculations based on that data too.

- **Central model developers**: This is the smallest group of Power BI users in every organization. This group builds data models (and reports) used by the rest of the organization (the end users). Their data models are often an important source for report visualizers and self-service champions.

Access Control

Depending on the user group, you should also have different types of access and different ways of sharing content. Figure 37-2 shows some suggestions.

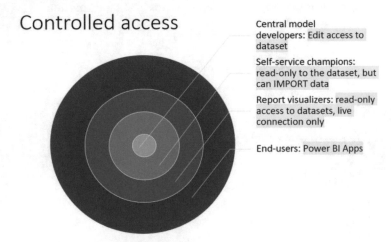

Figure 37-2. *Access control for Power BI user groups*

Giving an end user full edit rights to a data model and report can be problematic. Every user type requires a different level of access:

- **End users**: Access the model through Power BI apps or embedded with a read-only option in a web application. This ensures that these users can't change reports.

- **Report visualizers**: Have read-only access to the dataset. A report visualizer only needs a live connection to the data model to build visualizations. However, they can build their own reports. This level of access can be provided in different ways. Using Viewer access to the workspace or using apps are some methods for this purpose. These users do not have edit access to the dataset.

- **Self-service champions**: This group also has read-only access to the central dataset and models. They can import data from other sources, combine that data with this model, build a new model, and create their own reports. They can also create a chained dataset with a DirectQuery connection to the Power BI dataset.

- **Central model developers**: The only group with full edit access to the datasets and reports.

Training

Each group requires a different level of training because they are performing different functions, as shown in Figure 37-3.

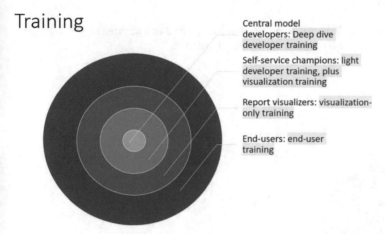

Figure 37-3. Each group's different levels of training

- **End users**: This is the quickest Power BI training option; a couple of hours of training is usually enough. This includes showing them how to navigate the app and drill through in reports or learn about drill down and up and some ways to get most of the existing Power BI reports. Most of the training relates to understanding the underlying data and how it is presented.

- **Report visualizers**: This group should be fully trained in visualization. Give this training as the module of Power BI for data analysts, which takes two days. Users learn how to create useful visualizations in Power BI. There isn't any point in training this group of users on data modeling.

- **Self-service champions**: Because this group wants to build its own data models, they must learn about modeling in Power BI in addition to visualization. Training takes longer and includes training for the Report Visualizer, as well as some parts of modeling, Power Query, and DAX. This can sometimes be close to a week of training, but consider splitting it into multiple sessions.

- **Central model developers**: For this group, you require the deepest dive Power BI training option. Deep dive training on Power Query, DAX, M scripting, modeling, and visualization is required. This group is likely to be the go-to resource for the self-service champions and report visualizers when they have questions. This group also requires a bit of architecture, administration, and governance training. This group requires multiple weeks of training, which needs to be split into multiple sessions.

Visit radacad.com/power-bi-training for a comprehensive agenda of a Power BI training, which covers all the agenda items mentioned here.

The Layers and User Categories Are Different in Each Organization

Each organization can have different layers. In small businesses, you often find two or three layers. The two layers can be the report developer and the end users, as shown in Figure 37-4.

Small businesses

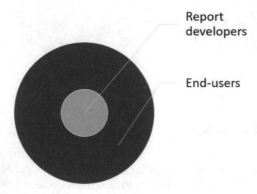

Report developers

End-users

Figure 37-4. Power BI users in small businesses

In larger organizations, you sometimes find layers within layers. The central developer layer can also be split into data transformation developers, data model developers, and core visualizer developers, as illustrated in Figure 37-5.

Layers within layers

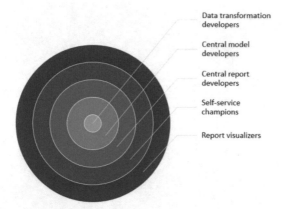

Data transformation
developers

Central model
developers

Central report
developers

Self-service
champions

Report visualizers

Figure 37-5. *Power BI users in a large organization*

You should explore the culture of the users in your organization and determine the structure of these layers.

Users Can Move Between Layers

Once a user is in a layer, it doesn't mean they will stay in that layer forever. Users change functions over time. You might have a report visualizer interested in doing some self-service stuff, so their job function changes. You should be ready to upskill users to ease the process of moving them to another layer.

Summary

It's important to understand the nature of the Power BI users in your organization and not mix these user groups. If you mix all these groups together and treat them all the same, you will likely end up with these problems, including:

- Spending too much training budget when it's not necessary

- Losing interest in downstream user layers

- Upstream users will likely start developing their own way of doing things

- The mix-up will hurt governance more than anything else

- Trust in Power BI will slowly vanish

- Power BI adoption may fail

■ ■ ■

CHAPTER 38

Best Practices for Setting Up Workspace Roles

Power BI workspaces have changed from the old days where there was Edit and View access only. You now have more options for roles in a workspace, and in my courses, I have found that many people choose the incorrect role without knowing what the role does. This chapter explains all the roles in the workspace and discusses the best way to set them up to create a secure workspace.

The Modern Power BI Workspace

There is an old version of Power BI workspace that a few people are still using. Microsoft started migrating those older workspaces (called workspace version 1) to the new version (workspace version 2), but you still might have some older versions in your environment. The older workspace version included Edit, View, and Admin access. It was easy to understand. In the new workspace (see Figure 38-1), there are four roles, as shown in Figure 38-2.

Figure 38-1. *Assigning roles in a Power BI workspace*

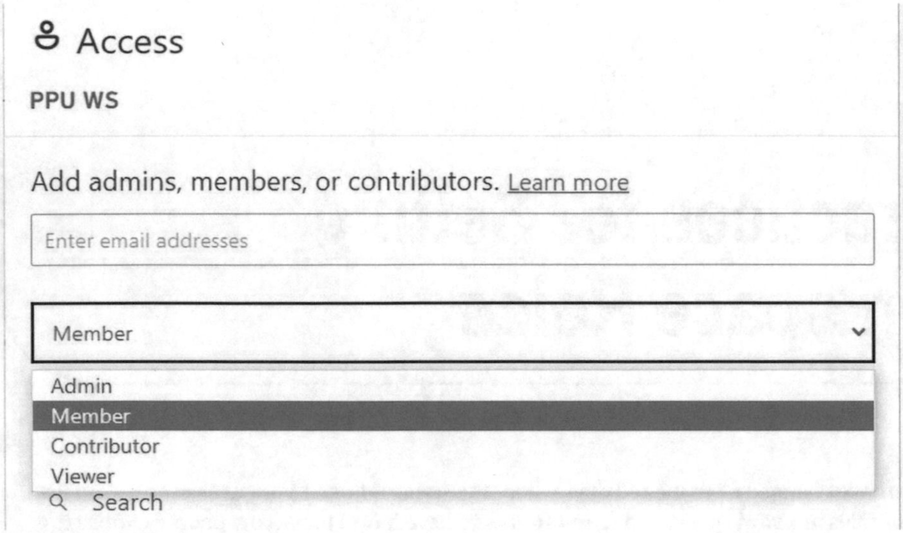

Figure 38-2. *Roles in the workspace*

Roles in the Workspace

This section looks at the roles and access levels in workspaces, beginning with Viewer.

Viewer

This role does what its name says in terms of viewer access. It authorizes the users to only view the report's content, dashboards, and workbooks (see Figure 38-3)_. The view role has read-only access to the content. They cannot access dataflows but can access the data stored in the dataflow.

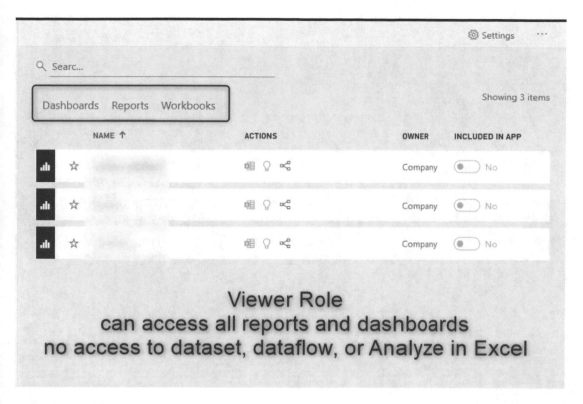

Figure 38-3. *The Viewer role*

If this role is also given build permission, the role can build content with Analyze in Excel or make a live connection to the dataset. I am not a big fan of this role. I explain why later in this chapter. There is a better option for people with this role.

Contributor

The Contributor role is for developers in the workspace. These people can access reports and dashboards, as well as datasets and dataflows. They can edit the content as well as delete it. They can publish a report to the workspace or remove it. The contributor role allows them to do all their development work in the workspace. See Figure 38-4.

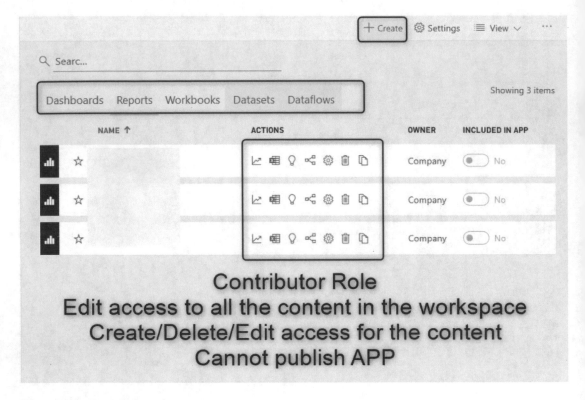

Figure 38-4. *Contributor role*

The Contributor role is the ideal role for Power BI developers. They can perform all of these actions:

- Publish a report to the workspace

- Edit the content in the workspace

- Delete the content in the workspace

- Access all workspace objects—reports, dashboards, workbooks, datasets, and dataflows

- Copy content, use Analyze in Excel, and more

This role should be assigned to all developers in the team. However, this role should not be confused with the next role: the Member role.

Member

The Member role has access to all the Contributor role's actions, plus has the ability to publish, unpublish, and update apps (see Figure 38-5). The Member role has the worst name of all the roles, and that is one of the reasons that many people don't understand it.

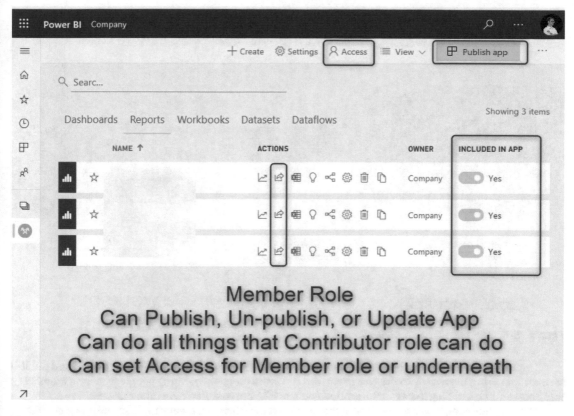

Figure 38-5. *The Member role*

Consider this role as the Deployment Role. This role can publish the content of a workspace as an App for the end-users.

The Member role has one of the most important actions in the workspace—pushing content from the DEV environment to the USER environment.

I have seen a lot of workspaces in which all the developers had Member access. The big problem with this is that any developer can publish apps to end users.

The separation of the Member and Contributor roles is one of the best advantages of the new workspace version. Check out my article at `radacad.com/workspace-v2-of-power-bi-what-are-advantages-vs-old-version` for more information about this. See Figure 38-6.

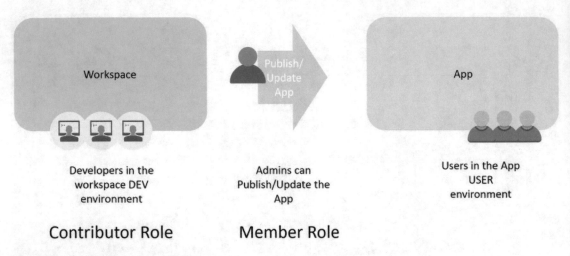

New Version of Workspace (V2): Developers CANNOT Publish/Update app mistakenly. Member Role can do that.

Figure 38-6. *Member versus Contributor role*

The last thing you want is for a developer from the DEV team to mistakenly push the button and publish content that is not user-ready to the end users. You can avoid that by separating people who have Member role access and restricting it only to the group of people who are your deployment managers.

There is, however, a tricky checkbox in the Advanced tab when you create a workspace that gives the Contributor role access to publish an app (see Figure 38-7). I strongly recommend *not* using this option. If you do this, you are making the Contributor and Member the same and going back to the old version of the workspace, where there is no control over who publishes content.

Security settings

☐ Allow contributors to update the app for this workspace

| Delete workspace | Save | Cancel |

Figure 38-7. *Do not select this option—being able to update an app should remain in the Member's domain only*

The Member role can also set access for roles in the workspace, as you can see in Figure 38-8.

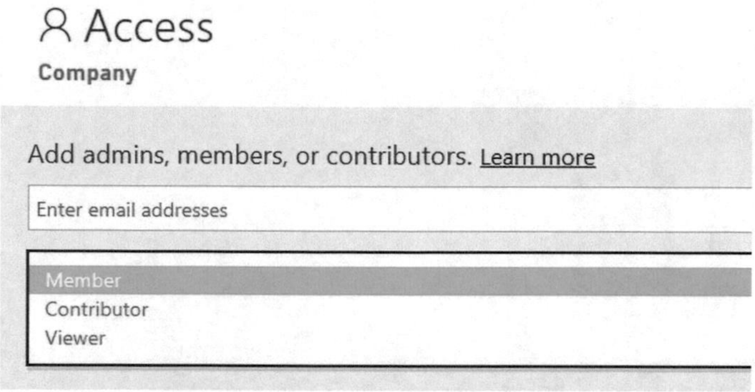

⅋ Access
Company

Add admins, members, or contributors. Learn more

Enter email addresses

Member
Contributor
Viewer

Figure 38-8. *Access levels from the Member role*

Another thing that the Member role can do is share reports and dashboards individually in the workspace (see Figure 38-9).

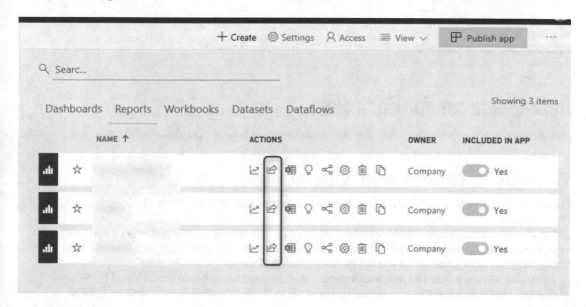

Figure 38-9. *Sharing content individually*

Admin

The Admin role has full access to the workspaces. In addition to doing all the Member's role actions, members of the Admin role can add or remove administrators to/from the workspace and can update or delete workspaces. See Figure 38-10.

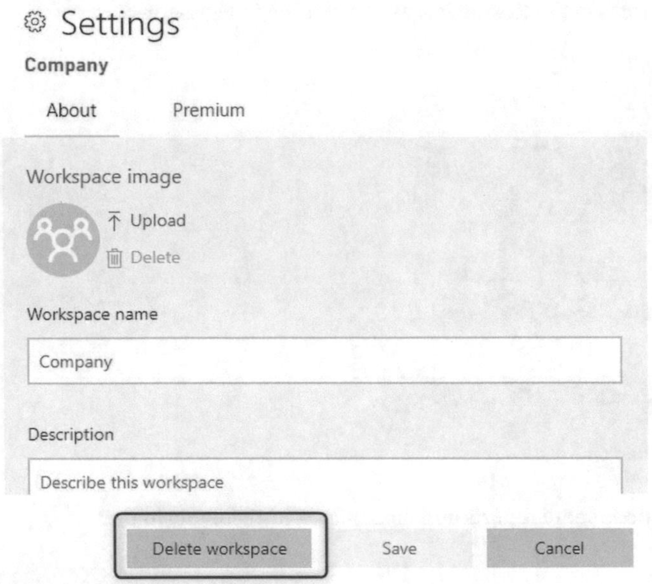

Figure 38-10. The Admin role

Best Practices for Each Role

Now that you are familiar with all the roles in the workspace, this section explains how to use them properly.

Viewer Role: Use Power BI Apps Instead

The Viewer role has read-only access to all content and cannot use Analyze in Excel.

End users

I have seen many organizations use the Viewer role to give access to their end users. This is a big mistake because you are giving users access to content in the developer environment. The DEV environment content is likely to be changed by any development team members.

Instead, use the Power BI apps, which create a good separation between the DEV and USER environments. Users have access to reliable content while the developers work on changes behind the scenes.

When you build a Power BI app, you can specify a navigation menu, design a great look and feel for your users, and give them the ability to slice and dice the data as they want. This is much better than Viewer access on the workspace. See Figure 38-11.

Figure 38-11. *The Publish app*

Test Users

Some organizations give Viewer access to test users. That way, the user can test the content before sending it to the end users using Power BI apps.

Although this might seem like a good use for the Viewer role, it's not. If you have 15 Power BI reports in the workspace, and out of those, only three are test-ready, you should only share those three reports. As you have already learned, the Member role can share reports and dashboards individually. Sharing items individually is a better way to give test users access than using the Viewer role. That way, you don't give users access to the entire DEV content, and users can focus only on the test materials.

Other organizations prefer to have a DEV workspace and a TEST workspace. If that is the case, Publish Power BI apps can be used for test users.

Contributor Role: Developers Only

Developers on your team should all have Contributor access to the workspace. There is no need to add them to the Member role. Reserve the Member role for the next group. Contributor access gives developers all the access they need. Developers can upload content, update it, change it, delete it, build new objects, and more.

Member Role: Deployment Group Only

On your team, there should be a deployment person or a group of deployment gatekeepers. This group of people ensures that the right content reaches the audience. They go through a process of checks to make sure the content is ready to publish to users. These people should have access to the Member role. They can publish content to the end users.

Admin Role: Admin Group

Don't assign the Admin role because you want to give someone a lot of access. Remember that even the Member role can give access to other Member-level or lower-level roles. For those reasons, there is little need for a person or a group of people to have the Admin role. Only give access to the group who needs to control the creation or deletion of the workspace or admin-level access.

Use Groups, Not Individual Accounts

The golden rule in security is to never use individual accounts. In the Power BI world, there are some places where you can, and others where you cannot, use security groups instead of individual accounts. Everywhere you can use a security group, make sure to use it instead of an individual account. Doing it this way makes access control even easier, because you can simply add and remove people from that security group.

Summary

Roles are not split into just View and Edit anymore. Figure 38-12 encapsulates the recommendations discussed in this chapter.

Role	Usage
Viewer	Don't use. Use Power BI App instead
Contributor	Developer Group only
Member	Deployment Group
Admin	The workspace admin

Figure 38-12. *Recommendations for the various roles*

■ ■ ■

CHAPTER 39

Build Access Level

I have often seen Power BI users with access to areas they shouldn't be able to access. In Power BI, you can share a report with a user for viewing only or give them access to view, build, and edit. These are all different levels of access. Build access is often confused with Edit access. This chapter explains the differences between these two access levels.

Build Access Example

One of the easiest ways to explain the difference between the Edit and Build access levels is through an example of building a Power BI report on top of an existing dataset. If you get data from a Power BI dataset, you are building a new report (or even a new dataset) on top of the existing dataset.

As shown in Figure 39-1, when using Get Data from a Power BI dataset, the user has access to some datasets.

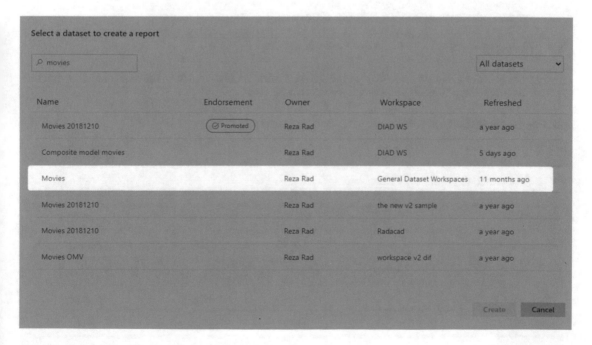

Figure 39-1. *Getting data from a Power BI dataset with Build access*

© Reza Rad 2023
R. Rad, *Pro Power BI Architecture*, https://doi.org/10.1007/978-1-4842-9538-0_39

The user profiled in Figure 39-1 sees all the datasets with movies in their name. The highlighted dataset, as an example, is shared with users who have View and Build access (see Figure 39-2).

Figure 39-2. *The user has Build access to the Power BI dataset*

If you remove Build access from this user, as shown in Figure 39-3, they lose access to that dataset when building a report or new content.

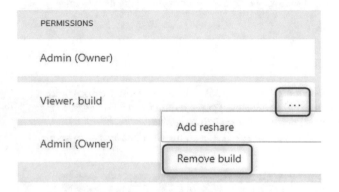

Figure 39-3. *Removing build access from a Power BI dataset*

As you can see in Figure 39-4's simple example, removing Build access from the dataset means that the user can no longer build any new content on top of that dataset.

Select a dataset to create a report

Name	Endorsement	Owner	Workspace	Refreshed
Movies 20181210	⊘ Promoted	Reza Rad	DIAD WS	a year ago
Composite model movies		Reza Rad	DIAD WS	5 days ago
Movies 20181210		Reza Rad	the new v2 sample	a year ago
Movies 20181210		Reza Rad	Radacad	a year ago
Movies OMV		Reza Rad	workspace v2 dif	a year ago

Figure 39-4. *Removing Build access will remove the dataset from the list of Get Data from the Power BI dataset*

Are Build and Edit the Same? A Row-Level Security Example

Now that you have been introduced to the Build access level, let's see if the Build and Edit access levels are the same. The short answer is no, they are not. The following row-level security example explains why.

Figure 39-5 shows a report on top of a dataset with RLS (row-level security) configuration defined.

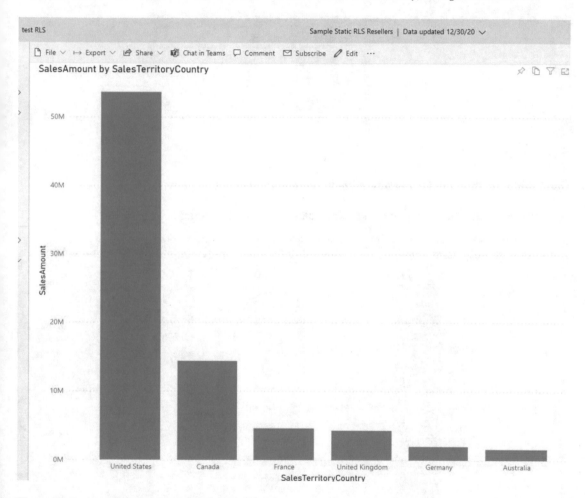

Figure 39-5. *A report on a dataset with RLS defined*

If I have a user with View and Build access to a dataset, the reports that the user can build depends on their access to the roles configured at the dataset level (see Figure 39-6).

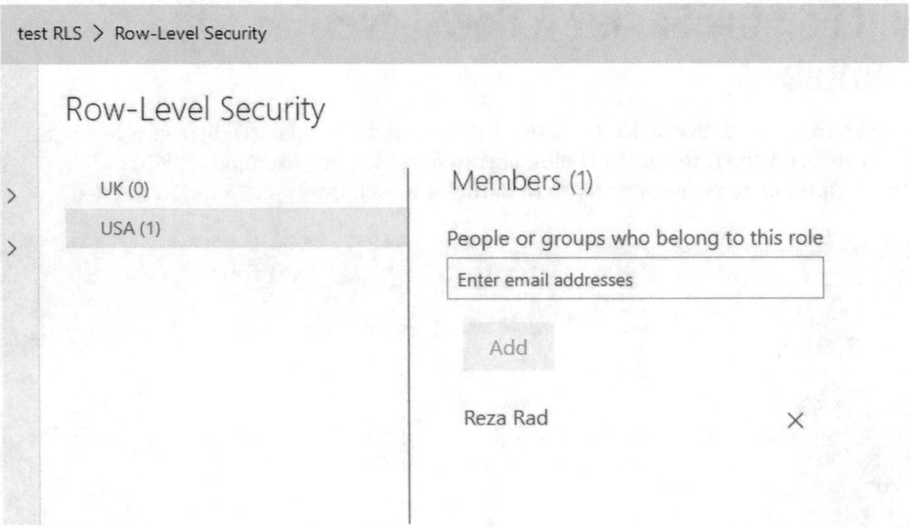

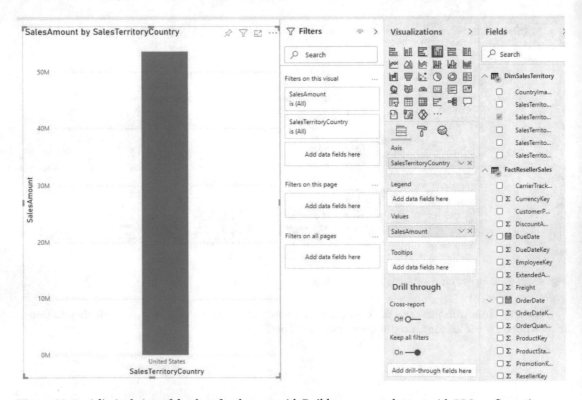

Figure 39-6. Row-level security configuration of the dataset

This user, if they build a report on top of that dataset, will see something like Figure 39-7.

Figure 39-7. A limited view of the data for the user with Build access on a dataset with RLS configuration

As you can see, the user can see only part of the data that they are allowed to see. If this user had Edit access to that dataset, all the data would be visible.

The difference between Build and Edit is not just on the RLS, it is also for editing the content. When a user has Edit access to a dataset, that user can change or delete the content. But the user with Build and View access can only build new content on top of that dataset and cannot change the original content.

This point is very important, because there are different types of users, and you should not give someone greater access than they need.

Providing Build But Not Edit Access

To give a user Edit access to a dataset, you can give them proper access to the workspace. Different methods provide Build and View access but not Edit access. Some of the most common methods are discussed next.

Manage Permissions: Add Build Access

On any given dataset, you can choose the Manage Permissions option (see Figure 39-8).

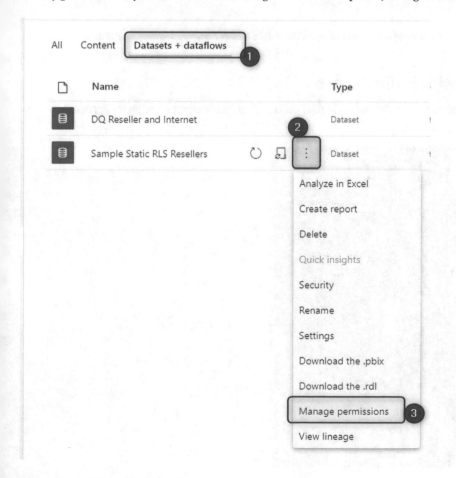

Figure 39-8. *Manage Permissions on the Power BI dataset*

From the Manage Permissions setting, you can add a user with the permissions of Build and View or add permission to an existing user in the list. You can also remove Build permission in the same place (see Figure 39-9).

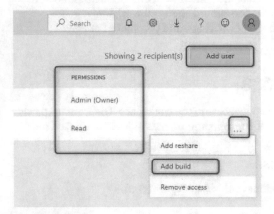

Figure 39-9. *Adding and removing Build access to a Power BI dataset through Managing Permissions*

Create an App with Build Access

Another common way to provide Build access to users is enabling access when creating an app, as shown in Figure 39-10.

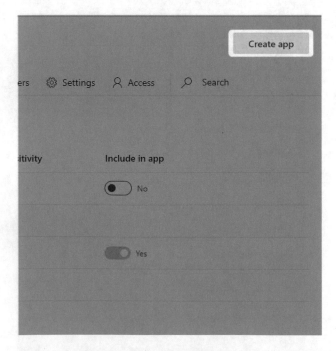

Figure 39-10. *Creating a Power BI app*

On the Audience tab of the App Creation wizard, you can choose whether the users can have Build permission, as shown in Figure 39-11.

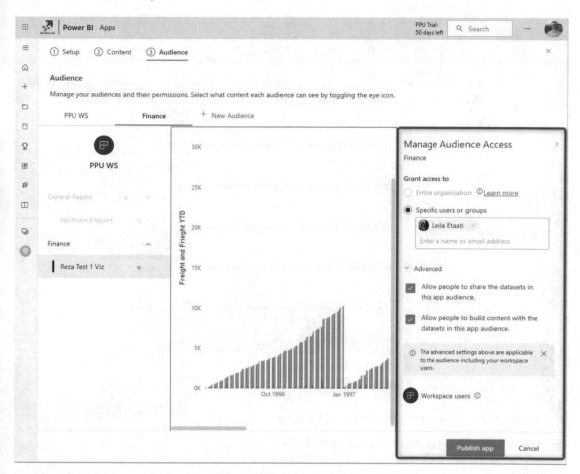

Figure 39-11. Enabling Build permission for Power BI app users

This will create Build access in the permissions area of the dataset (see Figure 39-12).

Figure 39-12. Build access is provided through the Power BI app

Providing access through the Power BI app is my recommendation. Because you can create different audiences in Power BI apps, set Build permission for an audience, and keep it unchecked for others, this is a perfect way to give Build permission, all of which you can see in Figure 39-13.

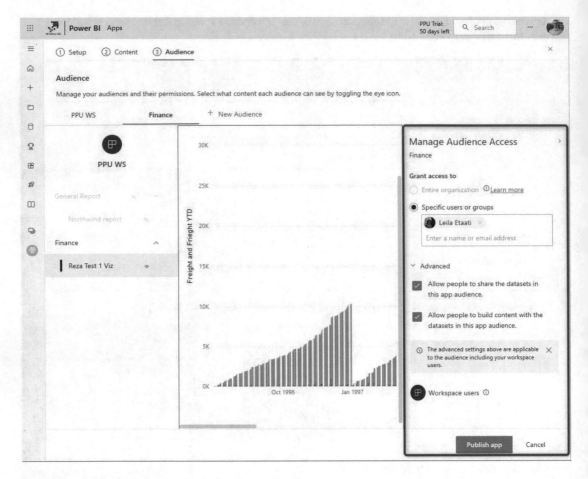

Figure 39-13. *Providing access through a Power BI app*

Who Should Have Build Access?

Report visualizers and self-service champions are among the users who need Build access to a dataset. Developers usually have Edit access, but other users who want to build content on top of an existing dataset require the Build access level.

Licensing

Users need a Pro license to run Build operations on Power BI datasets. Free Power BI users with Premium capacity can't build content unless they have a Pro license. (Note that the licensing options mentioned here could change in the future.)

Summary

In this chapter, you learned that the Build access provided alongside View differs from Edit access. A user with Edit access will see everything regardless of row-level security. But Build and View access respects the RLS configuration. Edit access also provides the ability to modify and delete content. You learned how to provide Build access but not Edit access. This is an important consideration for your Power BI sharing method.

■ ■ ■

CHAPTER 40

How to Organize Workspaces in a Power BI Environment

The question I often get during my Power BI architecture consulting sessions is "How should I organize my workspaces? Should I have one workspace with all the reports in it, or multiple workspaces? This chapter provides a guide on how to organize and set up workspaces in your organization.

In a nutshell, a *workspace* is an environment that hosts and shares Power BI content. This Power BI content includes but is not limited to datasets, dataflows, datamarts, reports, paginated reports, metrics, and dashboards.

Considering a Power BI Workspace as a Single Development-Sharing Unit

You can have multiple Power BI objects inside a workspace, but when you share the workspace, you share all of the objects. When I speak of sharing, I am referring to using one of the workspace sharing methods. By using Power BI apps, you can share a subset of the content, and using basic sharing, you can share an individual object. However, I don't recommend using basic sharing for content in the workspace (unless it is for testing reports). In the rest of this chapter, I do not consider that option for sharing workspace contents.

This means that the entire contents in your workspace can be shared with someone who has an access role in your workspace (the Administrator, Member, Contributor, or Viewer role) and a subset of that to the Power BI app users.

You cannot share part of a workspace's content with some users, and another part with other users. The Power BI workspace is one single sharing unit.

Separating Audiences Using Power BI Apps

You should consider a workspace as a single development-sharing unit because you can use one workspace for multiple groups of audiences. In a previous chapter, you learned how to create multiple audiences and share different content from the same workspace with a different group of users. However, developers are users with Edit access to the content, which is only for Admin, Member, or Contributor users. These access levels permit the user to access the entire contents of the workspace, not just part of it. So, the Power BI workspace is a single unit of sharing for developers or data analysts (see Figure 40-1).

R. Rad, *Pro Power BI Architecture*, https://doi.org/10.1007/978-1-4842-9538-0_40

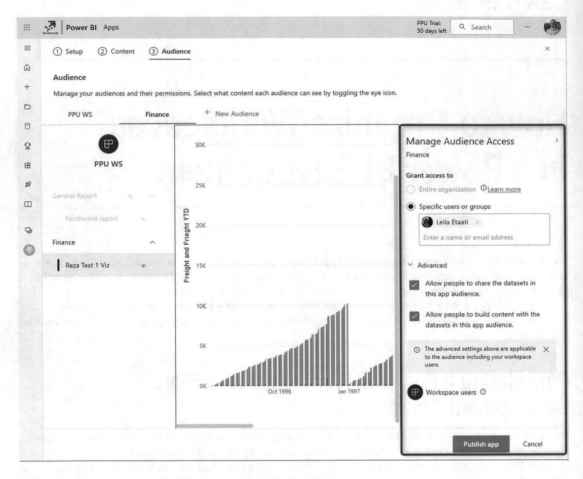

Figure 40-1. *The Power BI workspace is one unit of sharing for developers or data analysts*

Separating Developers with Multiple Workspaces

Based on this explanation, it is understandable that you will need separate workspaces for different groups of developers (or data analysts). Figure 40-2 shows two sets of reports that should be shared with two different audiences; they won't all be hosted in one workspace.

All the users will have the same view

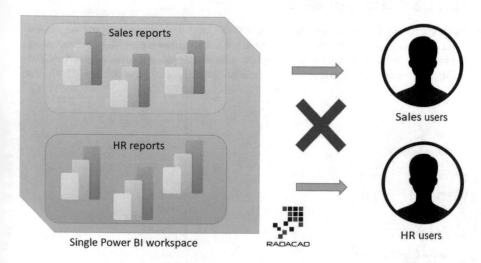

Figure 40-2. *Sharing the content of one workspace with a single group of analysts*

You need two different workspaces if you have two different sets of reports for two different groups of developers, as illustrated in Figure 40-3.

Separate workspaces for different audiences

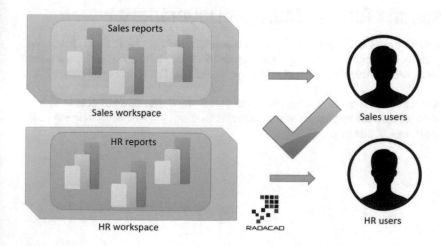

Figure 40-3. *Separating Power BI workspaces into different audiences*

Note that there is a difference between developers and end users. Developers need access to the workspace to edit the content, whereas end users use Power BI apps.

This means that if you have 12 groups of developers for 12 sets of different reports, you need 12 workspaces.

Split the Load, Use the Capacity

Another important reason for using separate workspaces is to split the load. This is normally the case when you use a dedicated capacity plan (Power BI Premium or Embedded). If you have a very high consumption rate report, you might want to keep it separate from other reports with low consumption rates and host it in a separate workspace. For each workspace, you can choose the dedicated capacity on which it will be hosted (see Figure 40-4).

Figure 40-4. *Capacity settings for a workspace*

Sharing Workspaces Among Multiple Developers

I've mentioned that one normal practice of having multiple workspaces is having one per developer group. This means, for example, having HR reports in the HR workspace and Sales reports in the Sales workspace. However, what if both of those reports use the Date table? Then you need that Date table to be accessible to both groups.

Having a shared workspace (see Figure 40-5) is an important part of the Power BI architecture. This technique reduces the redundancy in the implementation, increases consistency, and helps in the overall development process of the Power BI content.

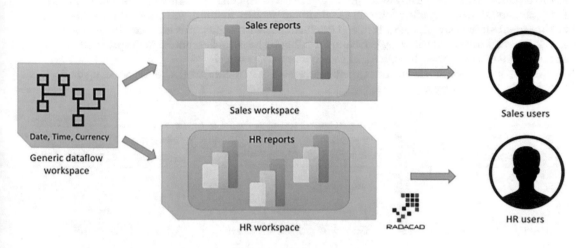

Figure 40-5. *Sharing Power BI workspaces to reduce redundancy*

Layers of Shared Workspaces

Shared workspaces can have more than just dataflows; they can have datasets too. You can also have layers of shared workspaces. For example, the Date table is likely used by many workspaces. On the other hand, something like the Account table might be only needed in a handful of workspaces (see Figure 40-6).

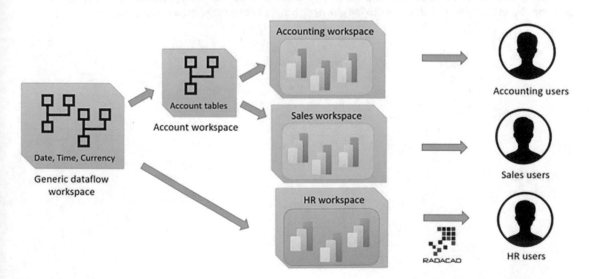

Figure 40-6. *Layers of Power BI shared workspaces are often needed*

Separating the Environments

Another good use case for having multiple workspaces is to separate environments. For a proper Power BI implementation (or any other software development implementation), you need to have a different environment for the Development, Test, and Production environments. This has many benefits to the development process and will bring trust into the adoption because the content in the production environment will be passed through multiple checks and validations.

Figure 40-7 shows the deployment pipeline in Power BI Premium, which helps you set up deployment between the environments.

Figure 40-7. *Deployment pipeline to manage DEV, TEST, and PROD environments*

Even if you do not have the Premium license, you can still use the concept of the DEV, TEST, and PROD environments and PowerShell scripts to handle deployment between them (see Figure 40-8).

Separating environments

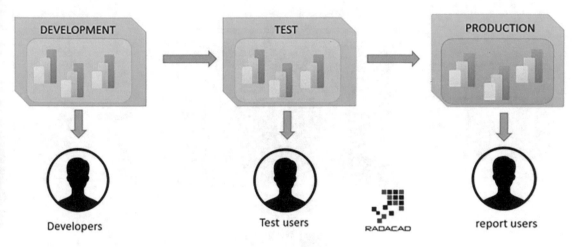

Figure 40-8. *Separating DEV, TEST, and PROD environments in Power BI workspaces*

Workspaces as development layers

Having the DEV, TEST, and PROD environments is not the only workspace structure that helps the development of Power BI solutions. There are some other development practices that you can use by separating workspaces including staging dataflows.

Staging dataflows

One of the key points of any data integration system is to reduce the number of reads from the source's operational system. In the traditional data integration architecture, this reduction is done by creating a new database called a *staging database*. The purpose of the staging database is to load data as is from the data source into the staging database on a regular schedule.

The rest of the data integration will then use the staging database as the source for further transformation and will convert it into the dimensional model structure.

I recommended that you follow the same approach using dataflows. Create a set of dataflows that are responsible for loading data as is from the source system (and only for the tables you need). The result is then stored in the storage structure of the dataflow (either in Azure Data Lake Storage or in a dataverse). This change ensures that the read operation from the source system is minimal.

Next, you can create other dataflows that source their data from staging dataflows. The benefits of this approach include:

- Reduce the number of read operations from the source system and reduce the load on the source system as a result.

- Reduce the load on data gateways if an on-premises data source is used.

- Have an intermediate copy of the data for reconciliation purposes, in case the source system data changes.

- Make the transformation dataflows source-independent.

Figure 40-9 illustrates staging dataflows and staging storage, and it shows the data being accessed from the data source by the staging dataflow. Entities are stored in cadavers or in Azure Data Lake Storage. The entities are then transformed along with other dataflows, which are sent out as queries.

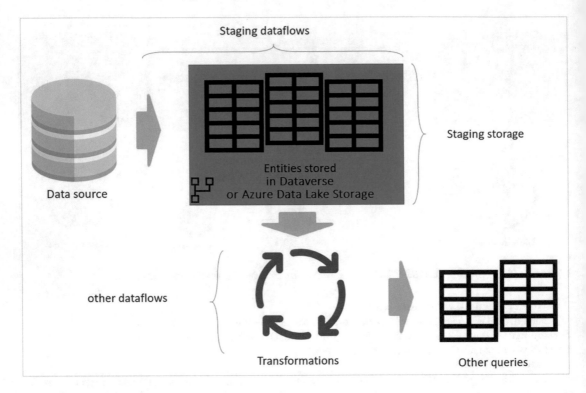

Figure 40-9. *Staging dataflows*

Transformation dataflows

When you've separated your transformation dataflows from the staging dataflows, the transformation will be independent from the source. This separation helps if you're migrating the source system to a new system. All you need to do in that case is change the staging dataflows. The transformation dataflows are likely to work without any problems, because they're sourced only from the staging dataflows.

This separation also helps when the source system connection is slow. The transformation dataflow won't need to wait for a long time to get records coming through a slow connection from the source system. The staging dataflow has already done that part, and the data will be ready for the transformation layer. See Figure 40-10.

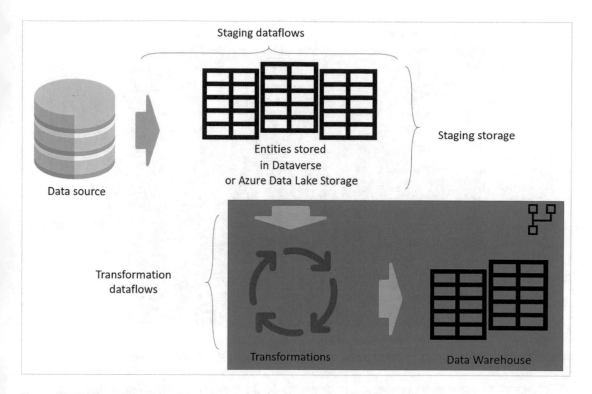

Figure 40-10. Separating transformation dataflows from staging dataflows

Layered architecture

A layered architecture is an architecture in which you perform actions in separate layers. The staging and transformation dataflows can be two layers of a multi-layered dataflow architecture. Trying to do actions in layers ensures the minimum maintenance required. When you want to change something, you just need to change it in the layer in which it's located. The other layers should continue to work fine.

Figure 40-11 shows a multi-layered architecture for dataflows in which their entities are then used in Power BI datasets.

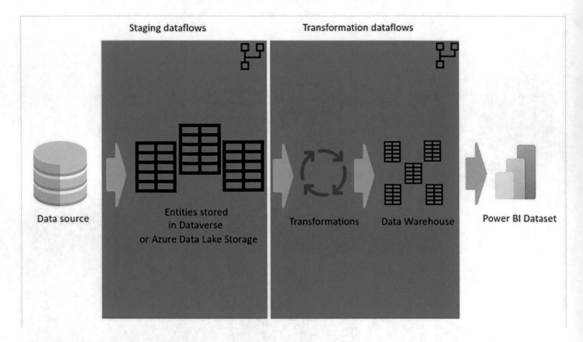

Figure 40-11. *Multiple layers of development workspaces for Power BI implementation*

Figure 40-11 shows multiple workspaces for staging dataflows and transformations. In real-world scenarios, there can be more than these two layers, depending on the complexity of the implementation.

Summary

To summarize, there are many important factors when organizing a workspace structure. You need to have separate workspaces based on the analysts' groups and then sometimes based on the audience. It is recommended to have DEV, TEST, and PROD layers through workspaces. You must consider using shared workspaces, which reduce redundancy and increase consistency. You can also split the load on the reports using multiple Power BI workspaces.

As you can see, there is a lot to think about when you design the workspace structure. This design will be different from organization to organization. I usually go through many of these processes in my architecture advisory gigs, so I thought it is better to explain some of them here, to help you too.

CHAPTER 41

■ ■ ■

Content Certification and Endorsement

Governance is an important aspect of every application and system. Your Power BI solution architecture needs good rules and processes set up for governance to ensure the content is trustworthy. In Power BI, the content can be endorsed and certified so that it conveys a level of trustworthiness to users. This chapter explains content certification and endorsement and how to use them.

The Importance of Endorsement

When your organization first begins using Power BI, there may not be a lot of data. But after a while, when the amount of Power BI content (reports, datasets, dataflows, and apps) increases throughout the organization, the need for better governance arises.

If a user faces multiple Power BI objects that present similar information, how does the user know which of these is more accurate? If users can't distinguish the trustworthiness of the content, they might present content that is not correct. Once it's revealed that the information was inaccurate, the trust of the organization in the entire Power BI adoption may collapse. A successful Power BI adoption requires trustworthy Power BI content.

Power BI content endorsement is a labeling system that shows the level of trustworthiness of each piece of content. This system itself is not complicated; it is just labeling. However, it uses an infrastructure for testing and checking reports and certifying them, which helps the entire Power BI trustworthiness and adoption process as a result.

Levels of Endorsement

The levels of endorsement for the Power BI content follow the principles of the Gold, Silver, and Bronze approach, which is a three-layer approach to determine trustworthiness of content. Gold is the most trusted and Bronze is the least. In the Power BI content endorsement, however, there are different names for it. Power BI content that has the highest level of endorsement is called Certified. The next level down is Promoted, and the last level has no endorsement. By default, Power BI content has no endorsement, which means it is at the lowest level of trustworthiness. See Figure 41-1.

© Reza Rad 2023
R. Rad, *Pro Power BI Architecture*, https://doi.org/10.1007/978-1-4842-9538-0_41

Figure 41-1. *Levels of certifications*

The labels don't really mean anything. These simply label the content. You have to come up with standards and define what exactly these mean. For example, here are some suggestions:

- The Power BI content developed by business analysts in different teams and departments across the organizations, with the data pulled into Power BI from all kinds of data sources, without any peer-review of the quality of the data source or the data quality itself, is considered having no endorsement (or you can call it Bronze-level content).

- Suppose the Power BI content is peer-reviewed by a second team (such as the BI or Data Insight team), and the quality of the data sources is verified. In that case, this is Promoted content, which is the next level up in trustworthiness (or you can call it Silver-level content).

- When the Power BI content is developed by the Data Insight or BI team, or a data analyst competent enough in the technology and understands the business requirements well. If the data sources have been all tested and the quality of the data source and the way in which they are pulled from is fully trusted (such as a data warehouse), and if the measures and reports are all tested and produce high-quality output, then the content can be considered Certified (this is the highest level of trustworthiness, which can be also called Gold-level content).

The endorsement levels should be clearly defined, detailed, and placed on a wiki page or an internal SharePoint site that is easily accessible (the wiki page or the SharePoint site can be linked to the Power BI environments using the Get Help links setup in the Power BI Admin Portal). This will help all the users know what to expect from each level of endorsement. If they see content that has no endorsement, they know what to expect.

What Kinds of Content Can Be Endorsed?

At the time of writing this chapter, four types of content can be endorsed in the Power BI service environments. These are as follows:

- Power BI datasets

- Power BI dataflows

- Power BI reports

- Power BI apps

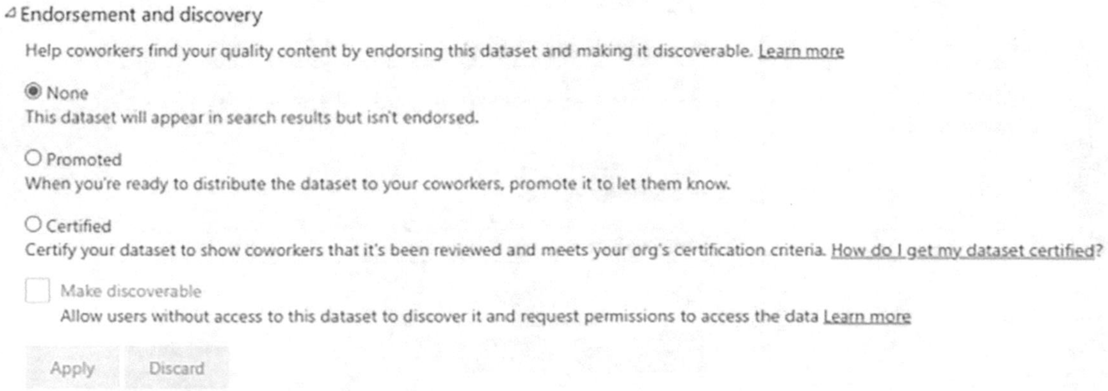

◁ Endorsement and discovery

Help coworkers find your quality content by endorsing this dataset and making it discoverable. Learn more

⦿ None
This dataset will appear in search results but isn't endorsed.

○ Promoted
When you're ready to distribute the dataset to your coworkers, promote it to let them know.

○ Certified
Certify your dataset to show coworkers that it's been reviewed and meets your org's certification criteria. How do I get my dataset certified?

☐ Make discoverable
Allow users without access to this dataset to discover it and request permissions to access the data Learn more

Apply   Discard

Figure 41-2. *Certifying contents in Power BI*

Who Can Endorse It?

It is important to understand who can endorse content and move it across the level of trustworthiness. It is not recommended to have this functionality open to everyone, because everyone will start certifying their content. You need to set up a specific team and define a specific procedure that the team follows in order to determine if the content is certified-worthy, promoted-worthy, or neither (see Figure 41-3).

Figure 41-3. Assigning a specific security group for certifying content

Once they do the test and pass the check, the content can be promoted or certified (see Figure 41-4). This team will then take responsibility for their test because the content is shown as certified under their name.

Figure 41-4. The user view of an endorsed report

The Power BI tenant administrator can choose who can certify the contents in the Power BI environment. It is always best to work with Active Directory (or Office 365) groups rather than individual users so that if users are added or removed from the team, it will be easier to manage them in the Office 365 group.

Dataset Discoverability

As part of certifying datasets, you can check the box to make them discoverable (see Figure 41-5). Ideally, you want the most trusted datasets to be discoverable throughout the organization so that power users can use that contents to build reports with a live connection to the Power BI dataset. This is an important governance step that will increase the adoption of shared datasets in your organization.

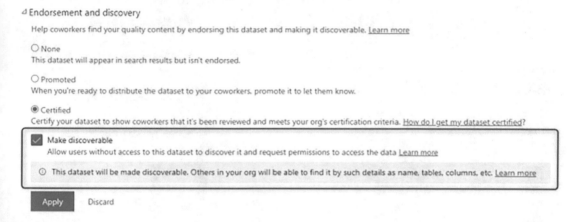

Figure 41-5. *Making a Power BI dataset discoverable*

An Example of an Endorsement and Content Certification

To certify content, go to the Power BI Service and choose the Setting area (see Figure 41-6). Then certify it.

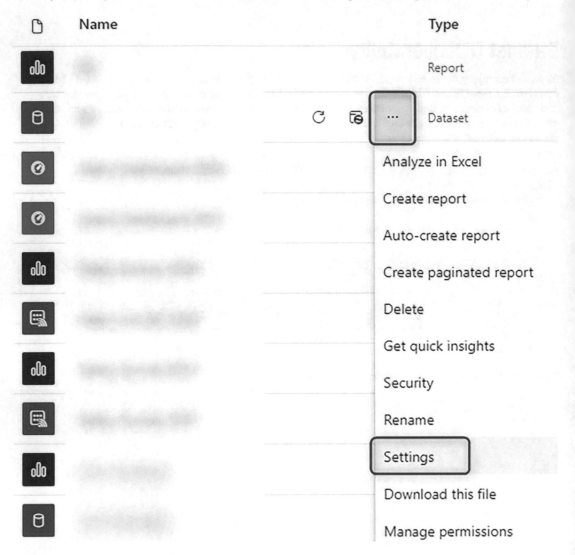

Figure 41-6. *Settings an object in the Power BI service*

Once you're in the settings, you can choose the appropriate endorsement (depending on your access level), as shown in Figure 41-7.

◿ Endorsement and discovery

Help coworkers find your quality content by endorsing this dataset and making it discoverable. Learn more

◉ None
This dataset will appear in search results but isn't endorsed.

○ Promoted
When you're ready to distribute the dataset to your coworkers, promote it to let them know.

○ Certified
Certify your dataset to show coworkers that it's been reviewed and meets your org's certification criteria. How do I get my dataset certified?

☐ Make discoverable
　　Allow users without access to this dataset to discover it and request permissions to access the data Learn more

Apply　　Discard

Figure 41-7. *Endorsement setup*

The content user can see if it is certified or not. Figure 41-8 shows the view of the content from the Power BI Desktop developer's point of view.

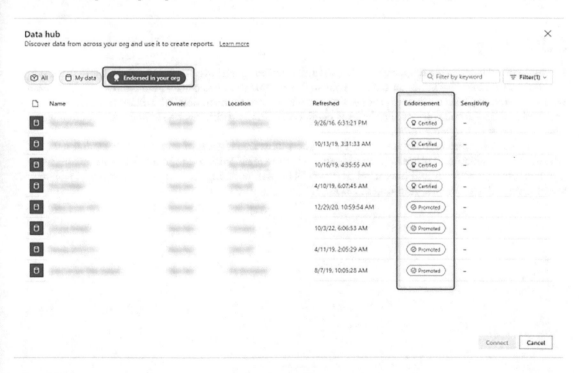

Figure 41-8. *The endorsed content's view from the Power BI Desktop*

Figure 41-9 shows the content from the end user's point of view.

Figure 41-9. *The endorsed content view from the Power BI Service*

Summary

As you learned in this chapter, a certification or endorsement is nothing but a simple labeling system. It is the *process* that makes it important. If everyone in the organization can certify their content, endorsement would be meaningless. If a process isn't defined that clearly explains in detail the difference between certified and promoted content and the tests needed to gain a certification level, then endorsement won't help the Power BI implementation.

Endorsement and certification of the Power BI content are features whereby the *process* defined within the organization is more important than the feature itself. With the right process, you can define a good governance strategy and have a better Power BI implementation, and, as a result, Power BI will be successfully adopted across your organization.

CHAPTER 42

Deployment Pipelines

All software applications need multiple environments. Separating the user's environment from the developer's environment comes with many benefits. Power BI is no exception. Having separate environments for different types of users can be helpful in many aspects. This chapter explains how Power BI handles this separation using deployment pipelines.

Why Multiple Environments?

Before discussing the deployment pipelines, it is important to understand why you need multiple environments in a Power BI implementation. The best way to understand it is to go through a sample scenario.

Jack is a Power BI developer who is part of the data analytics team in his organization. The data analytics team created a workspace for Sales reports, and they asked Jack to publish his reports, datasets, and dataflows to that workspace. Others in the data analytics team also have edit access to that workspace. Some test users use the same workspace to check the reports and the results. The end users connect to this environment through the same workspace. The structure is shown in Figure 42-1.

© Reza Rad 2023
R. Rad, *Pro Power BI Architecture*, https://doi.org/10.1007/978-1-4842-9538-0_42

End-user, Developer and Test environments are combined

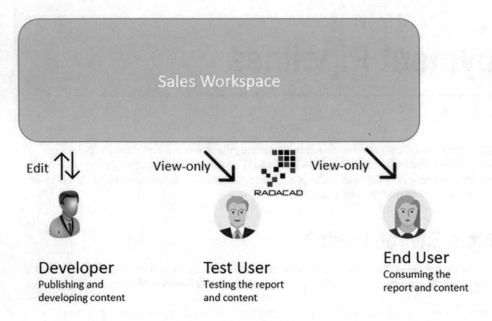

Figure 42-1. *Sample Power BI Implementation with all the environments combined*

The big problem with this structure is that as soon as the development team applies a change, the test user and the end user are impacted, even if the change is not final. This might lead to frustrating experiences for the end users, resulting in losing their trust in the reports. To separate the end-user experience, the analytics team can use a Power BI app instead.

To use an app, the data analytics team creates a workspace for Sales reports, and they ask Jack to publish his reports, datasets, and dataflows to that workspace. Others on the data analytics team also have edit access to that workspace. Test users use the same workspace to check for reports and results. The end users connect to this environment through an app. This structure is shown in Figure 42-2.

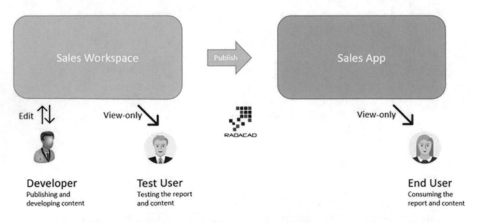

Figure 42-2. *Sample Power BI implementation with a separate end-user environment*

This environment uses one workspace to share between the developers (Jack and the data analytics team) and the test users. It then uses an app on top of that workspace for end users. In this scenario, the developers and end users are separated, but the developer is not separated from the test users. What if the developer is trying some features and is not ready for testing? At the same time, users are testing the content, getting different output, and becoming confused.

You can separate the developer and test environments by using another workspace. Figure 42-3 shows this new structure.

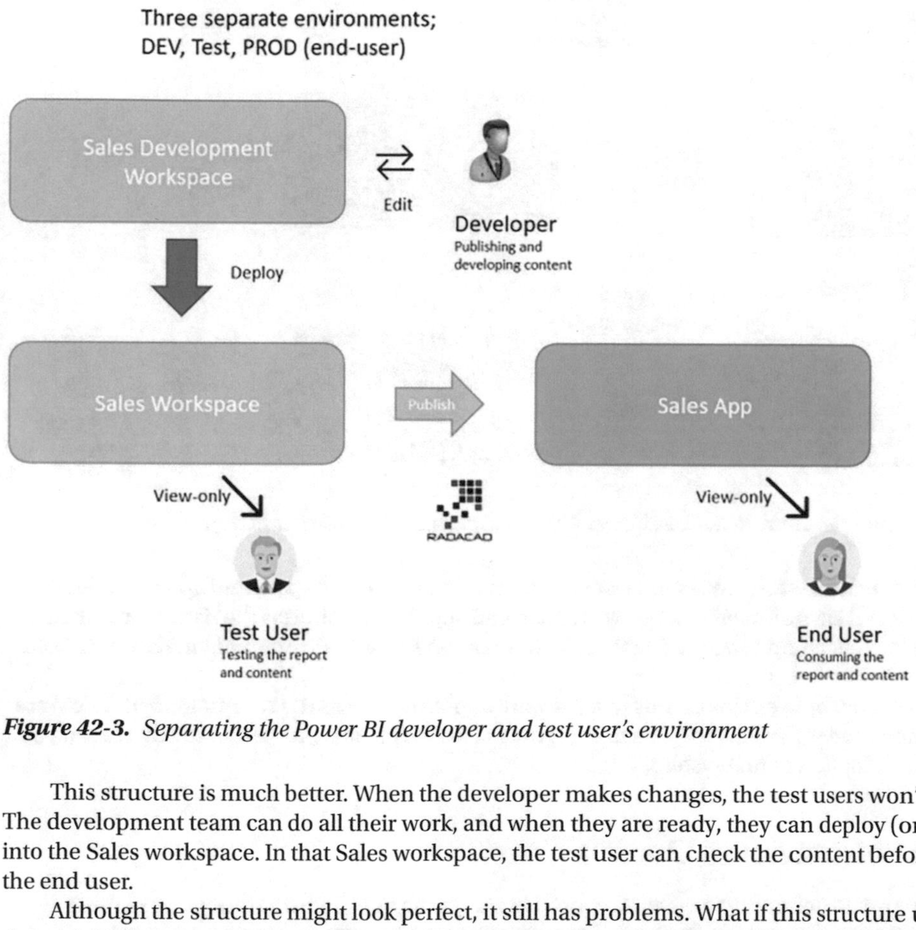

Figure 42-3. *Separating the Power BI developer and test user's environment*

This structure is much better. When the developer makes changes, the test users won't be impacted. The development team can do all their work, and when they are ready, they can deploy (or copy) the content into the Sales workspace. In that Sales workspace, the test user can check the content before publishing it to the end user.

Although the structure might look perfect, it still has problems. What if this structure uses a shared dataset? In that case, the reports that are shown in the Sales app are connected to the dataset, which is in the workspace, and when the dataset is updated, the reports may show the new results (which might not be correct because the test users haven't tested it yet). So, the environment can change to something like Figure 42-4 shows.

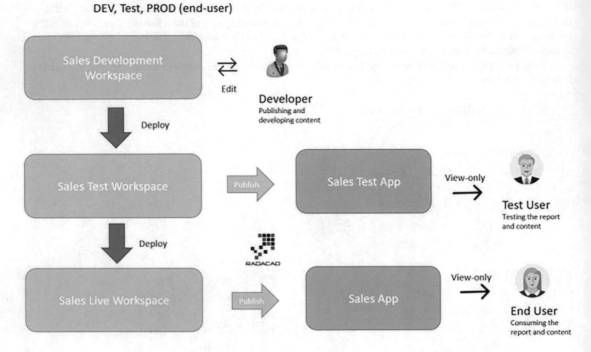

Figure 42-4. Three separate environments in Power BI with separate workspaces and apps

The structure in Figure 42-4 separates the test environment using its workspace and app and then the live (or Production/Prod) environment with its workspace and app. This minimizes the risk of unwanted changes appearing in other environments. These levels of isolation for each environment make them easier to change.

This is why having multiple environments in a software application system is recommended. There are different types of users, and separating their environments makes the change process more reliable and, as a result, leads to better adoption of that system.

How Many Environments Do You Need?

When I explain the structure of multiple environments, I often get the question, do I always need three environments? The answer depends on your solution architecture. Sometimes you may need more, sometimes fewer. Sometimes you may be fine with only two environments—Dev and Live—where the workspace of Live is used for test users. Sometimes you may need four or five environments, depending on roles and levels of test users in your organization.

You must carefully choose the right environment setup based on the Power BI solution architecture, the use of shared components such as dataflows, datasets, and datamarts, the culture of users in your organization, the self-service use of content, and many other factors.

What Is a Deployment Pipeline?

Now that you understand why you need multiple environments, it is the right time to discuss deployment pipelines in Power BI.

When you set up multiple environments, you need a mechanism to determine which environment is which (they may not always be called TEST, DEV, PROD, and so on). You also need a process for copying the content from one environment to another (for example, from DEV to TEST). You also need a process to compare the content in one environment with another, look for changes, and deploy any changes. (For example, comparing the TEST and LIVE environments to see which reports have changed.) You may need to change some connections during this process (for example, connect the TEST dataset to the test data source and the LIVE dataset to the live data source). Many more requirements come with having multiple environments. In other words, you need a tool for managing the deployment between multiple environments. This is where the deployment pipeline comes in (see Figure 42-5).

Figure 42-5. *Deployment pipelines in Power BI for managing multiple environments*
Source: learn.microsoft.com/en-us/power-bi/create-reports/deployment-pipelines-compare

Deployment pipelines in Power BI are components of the Power BI Service, and they enable you to manage multiple environments, define each environment, assign workspaces to the environments, compare the contents of two environments, deploy the changes, view histories of deployment, roll back the changes if needed, change the connections through the deployment process, and more. See Figure 42-6.

Figure 42-6. *Deployment pipelines in Power BI*

If you manage multiple environments in Power BI, deployment pipelines are a big help. This is a tool for the deployment team (which usually is a smaller section of the data analytics team in the organization). Deployment pipelines are not an end-user feature; they impact how the end user adopts Power BI in the organization.

Deployment pipelines are a Premium function in Power BI. This means you need workspaces to be part of a Premium capacity or Premium Per User accounts to use them.

How Does a Deployment Pipeline Work?

Let's now dive into the experience of deployment pipelines in Power BI and see how they work.

Creating Deployment Pipelines

To create a deployment pipeline, you must first log in to the Power BI Service and create a pipeline (see Figure 42-7).

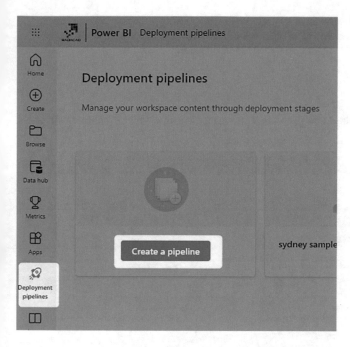

Figure 42-7. *Creating Power BI deployment pipelines*

Add a name and description for the pipeline. The next step is to assign workspaces to each environment.

Assigning a Workspace

A deployment pipeline in Power BI only comes with an option for three environments. You can assign workspaces to these environments by selecting them in the drop-down (see Figure 42-8).

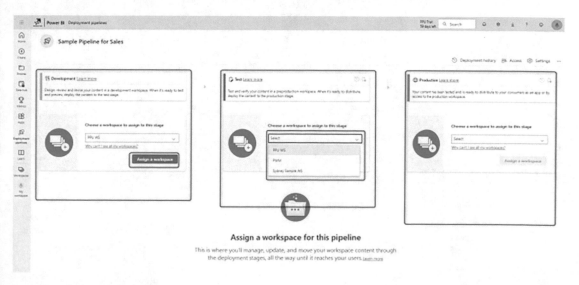

Figure 42-8. *Assigning workspaces to the deployment pipelines in Power BI*

If you don't see the workspace in the drop-down, it might be because you don't have a Premium workspace created yet, or maybe the workspace is already assigned in another deployment pipeline. Remember that one workspace can be used only in one deployment pipeline.

Comparing Content

Once the workspaces are assigned, the deployment pipeline summarizes the content in each environment (see Figure 42-9).

Figure 42-9. *The deployment pipeline shows the summary of the content in each environment*

You can then compare two of the environments using the Compare action. The Compare process gives you detailed output as to which content items need adding or updating, among other things (see Figure 42-10).

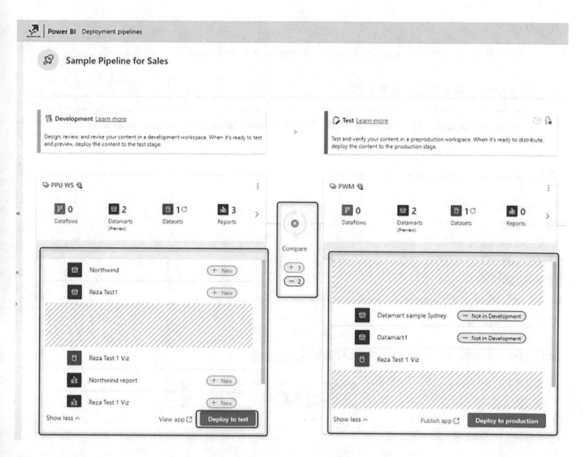

Figure 42-10. *Comparing content between two environments using the Power BI deployment pipeline*

After the comparison, you can choose to deploy. You can deploy to the test if you have compared the development with test environment. If you have compared the test with production, you can deploy it to production.

Deploy

The deploy process is simple to use. You can see the outcome as well, as shown in Figure 42-11.

Figure 42-11. *Deploy Power BI content*

If you want only a few items deployed, select them before clicking the Deploy button, as shown in Figure 42-12.

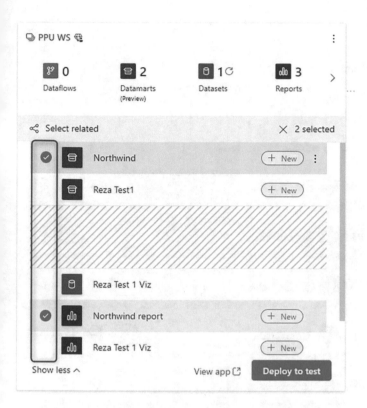

Figure 42-12. *Selecting content before deployment*

Once the deployment is done, you will get a report of the outcome. You can also compare the two environments after the deployment to see if the changes were applied.

It is important to keep in mind that the deployment will overwrite the destination content (if it exists in the destination).

Deployment History

One of the most important things in the deployment process is the ability to see the history of deployments and roll them back if needed. Fortunately, this feature exists as part of the deployment pipeline in Power BI (see Figure 42-13).

Figure 42-13. *Deployment history*
Source: learn.microsoft.com/en-us/power-bi/create-reports/deployment-pipelines-history

The history also has a detailed result that can be helpful for detailed checks.

Rules and Connections

If you want to set up different connection configurations for each environment, you can do that using deployment rules. For example, you can change the connection from the dataset to the data source when you deploy it from one environment to another. This function works even better when you use Power Query parameters.

Automate the Deployment

A user manually triggers deployment pipelines. However, you can automate that process using the Power BI REST API.

What If There Is No Premium License?

Deployment pipelines are a Premium feature in Power BI. If you don't have Premium licensing and still want to use this feature, you must implement it on your own. Fortunately, the REST API for Power BI can greatly help. You can use that to get the content of one workspace and then compare it with another. You can use the same REST API to download the content from one workspace and then upload it to the destination workspace. You can also change the connection details of content when publishing it. In short, it is possible to build a functionality like the deployment pipelines using PowerShell scripts and REST API calls. Still, it would take some time, and you would need to maintain the script, as the REST API functions might change. It is, however, a method that doesn't require Premium licensing.

Summary

Having multiple environments in a Power BI implementation is a very important aspect that helps the adoption of Power BI in your organization. You can create separate environments and manage the deployment process between these environments using deployment pipelines in Power BI. Deployment pipelines are a Premium function in Power BI. Still, they provide many great features, making them a very helpful tool for deployment.

Deployment pipelines in Power BI are only part of the big deployment strategy. Other technologies can be used with deployment pipelines, such as Azure DevOps and GitHub Actions, and combining the Power BI deployment pipelines (using their REST API) with those technologies gives you a more comprehensive pipeline solution.

CHAPTER 43

■ ■ ■

Data-Level Security

Power BI supports data security at the dataset level. This means everyone can see the data they are authorized to see. There are different levels of authorization in Power BI, including row-level security, column-level security, and object-level security. These levels help Power BI developers create one dataset and give users different views of the data from the same report. This chapter explains each of those methods and provides guidance on how to use them.

Introduction

If you want to create one piece of content and give users different views of it, data-level security is what you need. There are four levels of data-level security, as follows:

- Row-level security
- Column-level security
- Object-level security
- Page-level security

Among these four options, at the time of writing this chapter, the last one (page-level security) is not yet supported in Power BI. However, this chapter explains some workarounds for it.

Row-Level Security

Row-level security is perhaps the most common type of when discussing security data in the Power BI world. Let's understand it by looking at an example.

Jack built a Power BI report for the sales department. However, his organization has five different sales branches, one in each country. Each country's sales manager should see only their country's data, not others. (For example, Diana, the sales manager in the United States, should only see the U.S. data.) Everything else about the report and the layout and calculations is the same.

In such a scenario, your first solution might be to create five copies of the same report and filters in each report for each country, then share the report of each country with the sales managers of that country. This is not a good solution because you will have five reports to manage. Every change means you must create five copies or apply the change in five reports. This is not a maintainable solution. What if there were 20 countries? You can imagine the hardship of maintaining that many copied reports.

Suppose the data is stored in a table like the one shown in Figure 43-1. There is a column for Country, and the country values are in each table row.

© Reza Rad 2023
R. Rad, *Pro Power BI Architecture*, https://doi.org/10.1007/978-1-4842-9538-0_43

User	Country
Diana	USA
Mike	UK

Figure 43-1. Sample data for row-level security

The right way to implement this is to apply a security filter on the data and assign that security filter to the users. In that case, when users log in to the Power BI report, they can only see their own data and no one else's. You don't need copies of the report because everyone sees the data based on the security filter applied for their users. Because this type of security is applied at the data row level, it is called row-level security, sometimes RLS for short.

Row-level security is applied at the dataset level. That means even if you have reports with a live connection to the dataset, they will still follow the settings applied for each user. Maintaining a row-level security solution is simple because you only need to configure the security rules rather than have multiple copies of the same table.

Now that you know what row-level security is, let's look at how it is implemented.

Static Row-Level Security

Static row-level security is the simplest way to implement RLS. The following section details an example of how static RLS can be implemented.

For this example, I use the AdventureWorksDW Excel sample data source. You can download it from radacad.com/files/AdventureWorksDW2012.xlsx. There is a DimSalesTerritory table in this dataset with country details, as shown in Figure 43-2. This example applies security filters to this table.

SalesTerritoryKey	SalesTerritoryAlternateKey	SalesTerritoryRegion	SalesTerritoryCountry	SalesTerritoryGroup	CountryImage
1		1 Northwest	United States	North America	C:\Users\Reza\Dropbox\Speaking\TechDays Hong Kong 2014\Power View and Po
2		2 Northeast	United States	North America	C:\Users\Reza\Dropbox\Speaking\TechDays Hong Kong 2014\Power View and Po
3		3 Central	United States	North America	C:\Users\Reza\Dropbox\Speaking\TechDays Hong Kong 2014\Power View and Po
4		4 Southwest	United States	North America	C:\Users\Reza\Dropbox\Speaking\TechDays Hong Kong 2014\Power View and Po
5		5 Southeast	United States	North America	C:\Users\Reza\Dropbox\Speaking\TechDays Hong Kong 2014\Power View and Po
6		6 Canada	Canada	North America	C:\Users\Reza\Dropbox\Speaking\TechDays Hong Kong 2014\Power View and Po
7		7 France	France	Europe	C:\Users\Reza\Dropbox\Speaking\TechDays Hong Kong 2014\Power View and Po
8		8 Germany	Germany	Europe	C:\Users\Reza\Dropbox\Speaking\TechDays Hong Kong 2014\Power View and Po
9		9 Australia	Australia	Pacific	C:\Users\Reza\Dropbox\Speaking\TechDays Hong Kong 2014\Power View and Po
10		10 United Kingdom	United Kingdom	Europe	C:\Users\Reza\Dropbox\Speaking\TechDays Hong Kong 2014\Power View and Po
11		0 NA	NA	NA	

Figure 43-2. Sample data source for establishing static row-level security

Creating a Sample Report

Let's start by creating a sample Power BI Desktop report from the AdventureWorks Excel file. This example uses DimSalesTerritory and FactResellerSales (see Figure 43-3).

☐ ▦ DimSalesReason

☑ ▦ DimSalesTerritory

☐ ▦ DimScenario

☐ ▦ FactAdditionalInternationalProductDescription

☐ ▦ FactCallCenter

☐ ▦ FactCurrencyRate

☐ ▦ FactFinance

☐ ▦ FactInternetSales

☐ ▦ FactInternetSalesReason

☐ ▦ FactProductInventory

☑ ▦ FactResellerSales

☐ ▦ FactSalesQuota

Figure 43-3. Creating a sample Power BI Desktop report

Without making any changes to the Power Query Editor, load the report and build a simple column chart using Sales Amount (from FactResellerSales) and Country (from DimSalesTerritory). The chart shows sales by country, which can be used to create row-level security on geo-location information. Now add one card visualization for the total sales amount. Figure 43-4 shows the layout of this sample report.

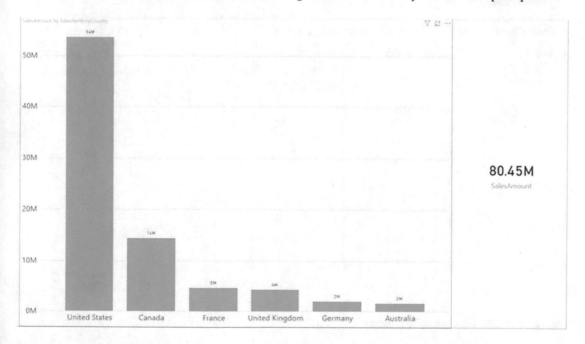

Figure 43-4. Layout of the sample report

In this view, the total reseller sales amount is $80M, and you have sales values for Australia, Canada, France, Germany, the UK, and the United States. Next, you see how to create some roles.

Creating Roles

The goal is to build roles for the sales managers in Australia and Canada. They should each only see their group in the dataset. To create roles, go to the Modeling tab on the Power BI Desktop (see Figure 43-5). You will see a section named Security.

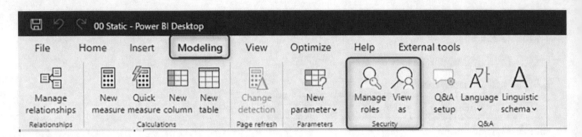

Figure 43-5. *Creating roles in the Modeling tab*

Click Manage Roles to create a new role. You will see the Manage Roles window, which has three panes, as shown in Figure 43-6.

Figure 43-6. *The Manage Roles window*

You can create or delete roles in the number one pane. You can see tables in your model in the number two pane. Then you can write your DAX filtering expression in the number three pane, or you can use the user-interface profited to define the filters.

Create a role and name it Australia Sales Manager. You will see two tables in the Tables section—FactResellerSales and DimSalesTerritory. Click Add to add the rule you want to the SalesTerritoryCountry column (see Figure 43-7).

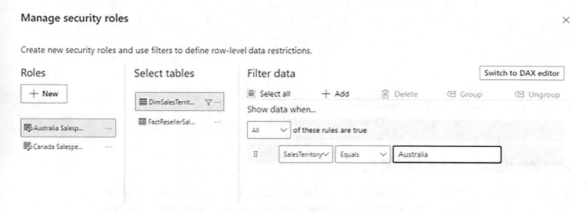

Figure 43-7. Creating a role for the Australian sales manager

You can also switch to the DAX Editor and see the DAX expression (see Figure 43-8).

Figure 43-8. Switching to the DAX Editor

Now create another role. Call it Canada Sales Manager, use the SalesTerritoryGroup filter this time, and change the value to Canada, as shown in Figure 43-9.

Figure 43-9. *Creating the Canadian sales manager role*

Testing Roles on the Desktop

Now that you have created two sample roles, you can test them. You can test them using the Power BI Desktop with the View As Roles menu option. This option allows you to view the report exactly as the user will see it. You can even combine multiple roles and see a consolidated view of a person who has multiple roles. Go to the Modeling tab and choose the View As Role option (see Figure 43-10).

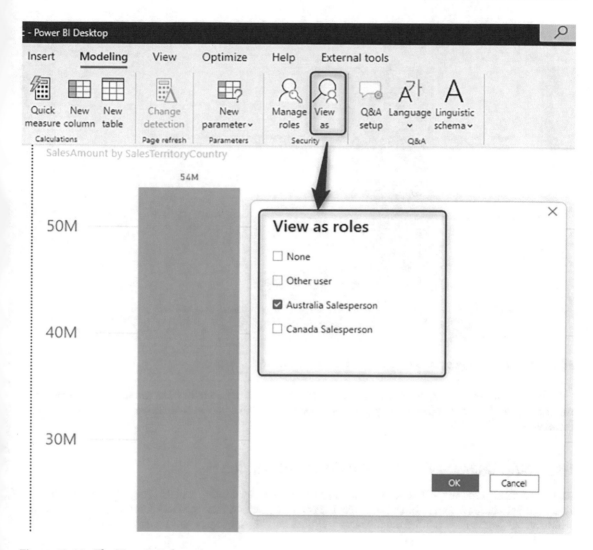

Figure 43-10. *The View As Role option*

Choose the Australian and Canadian sales managers and click OK. You will see sales for Australia and Canada only, with a total of $15.97M; you'll also see only the Australia and Canada countries. See Figure 43-11.

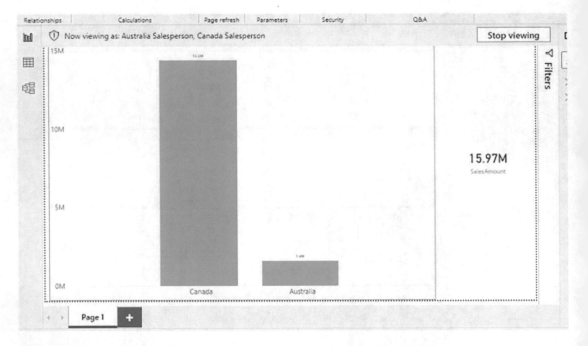

Figure 43-11. *Displaying sales data for Australia and Canada*

At the top of the report, there is a highlighted information line indicating that the view is showing the Australian and Canadian sales managers. If you click Stop Viewing, you will see the report in normal view (total view).

Assigning Users to Roles in the Power BI Service

Roles should be assigned to Power BI users (or accounts, in other words), and this should be done in the Power BI Service. Save and publish the report in Power BI. I named this report 00 Static. You can name it whatever you want. After publishing the report, choose Security for the dataset (see Figure 43-12).

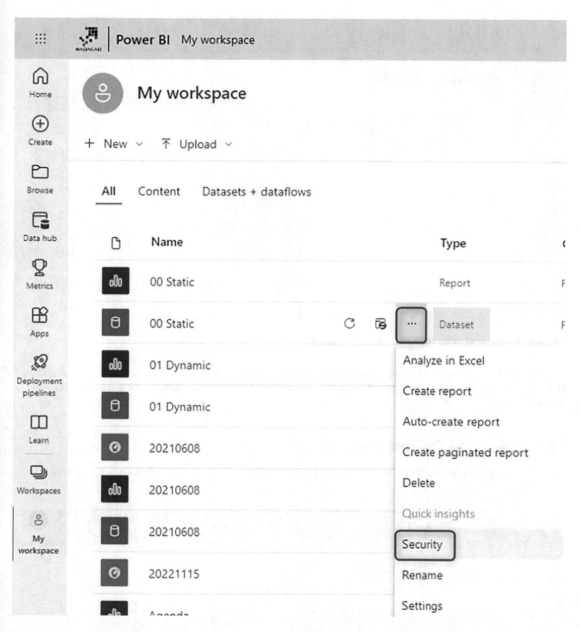

Figure 43-12. *Saving and publishing the report in Power BI*

Here, you can see roles and assign them to Power BI accounts in your organization (see Figure 43-13).

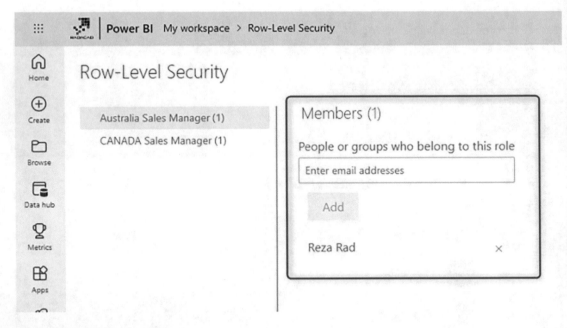

Figure 43-13. *Assigning roles to Power BI accounts*

You can set each user to more than one role, and the user will then have a consolidated view of both roles. For example, a user with Australia and Canada sales manager roles will see data from Australia and Canada.

Testing Roles in the Power BI Service

You can also test each role. Just click the ellipsis button beside the role and then choose Test as Role (see Figure 43-14).

Figure 43-14. *Testing a role*

The Test as Role option shows you the report in view mode for that role. You can change the role if you like. See Figure 43-15.

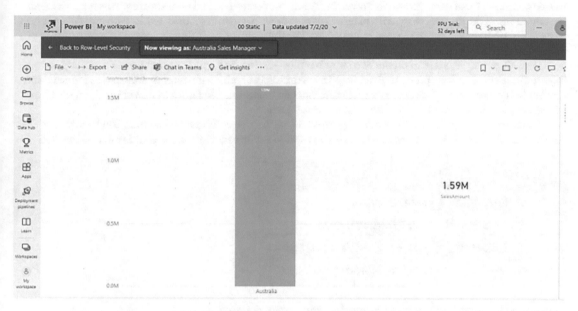

Figure 43-15. *Displaying a report in view mode*

Setting users in each role enables row-level security. If the user logs in with their account, they will only see data for their roles.

Republishing Won't Hurt

As mentioned in the first paragraph of this chapter, the great thing about this new feature is that RLS is part of the Power BI model. If you publish your Power BI model repeatedly with changes, you won't lose web configuration. You also won't lose users assigned to each role if you don't change the role names.

You've learned about a specific type of row-level security called static row-level security. It is called static because the filter values are statically determined in DAX expressions. Maintenance costs are very high if you want to apply such a filter to thousands of roles. In an ideal world, you want to apply security automatically based on users' login.

Dynamic Row-Level Security

Although static RLS is simple to set up, it is hard to maintain when there are many roles. Dynamic row-level security makes maintenance of the RLS much simpler. However, it requires more steps to set up. The following section is an example of dynamic RLS.

Sample Data

In this example, I use data entered in Power BI. There aren't any external data sources. This doesn't mean that dynamic security can't work with external data sources. Dynamic security works with any data sources as long as you have related data rows in the tables. For the simplicity of this example, it uses data sources inside Power BI.

For this example, you can create two simple tables—Sales Rep and Transactions. Sales Rep has information about sales representatives, and Transactions contains information about sales transactions. Each sales transaction is handled by a sales rep. You can create sample tables in Power BI. Open the Power BI Desktop, and, from the Data section, choose Enter Data.

Create a table like the one shown in Figure 43-16, with three columns of data in it. You have to use usernames similar to Power BI accounts that you want to set up security for. Name this table Sales Rep.

ID	Name	Email
1	Reza Rad	reza-zb\reza_
2	Leila Etaati	leila@radacad.com
3	Jack Horlock	jack.horlock@radacad.com
4	xyz	student2@radacad.com

Figure 43-16. Sample data used to establish dynamic row-level security

Create another table for transactions using the structure shown in Figure 43-17 and name it Transactions.

Date	Sales Rep	Sales Amount
Sunday, January 1, 2017	1	$100
Wednesday, February 1, 2017	2	$300
Wednesday, March 1, 2017	1	$50
Monday, February 12, 2018	3	$1,000,000

Figure 43-17. Sample transactions table

As you can see in Figure 43-17, each sales transaction is handled by a sales rep. Again I mention that these tables are added to Power BI for the simplicity of this example. Tables can come from everywhere.

Load the tables into Power BI; you don't need to do anything with Power Query at this stage. Go to the Relationship tab and verify the relationship between Sales Rep (ID) and Transactions (Sales Rep) to be as shown in Figure 43-18.

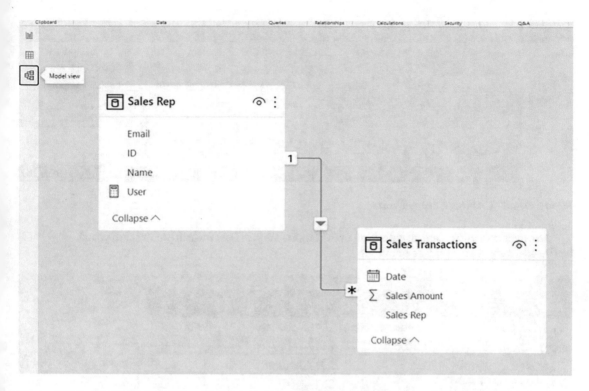

Figure 43-18. *Verifying the relationship between Sales Rep (ID) and Transactions (Sales Rep)*

Sample Report

This example uses basic table visualization. The table visualization shows the Date, Sales Amount (from Transactions), and Name (from Sales Rep), as shown in Figure 43-19.

Name	Email	Year	Month	Day	Sales Amount
Jack Horlock	jack.horlock@radacad.com	2018	February	12	$1,000,000
Leila Etaati	leila@radacad.com	2017	February	1	$300
Reza Rad	reza-zb\reza_	2017	January	1	$100
Reza Rad	reza-zb\reza_	2017	March	1	$50
Total					**$1,000,450**

Figure 43-19. *Sample report data*

The main reason for this visualization is to simply show that each user will see only their data rows from all tables. I also add a measure for USERPRINCIPALNAME() in DAX to see the user logged in from my report. So in the Data tab, create a new measure (see Figure 43-20) and name it User, with a value of USERNAME().

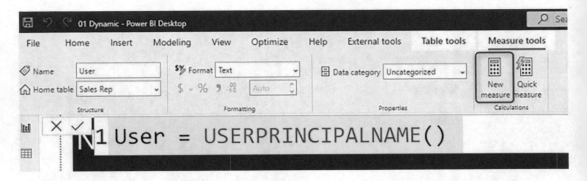

Figure 43-20. *Creating a new measure*

Now you can add a Card visualization to the report. Add the User measure to the card visual. Figure 43-21 shows the report's final view.

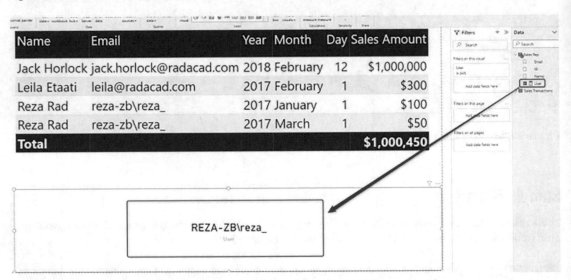

Figure 43-21. *A card visualization with the user measure*

The UserName() and UserPrincipalName() DAX Functions

The USERNAME() function in DAX returns the username of the logged-in user. However, there is a small trick to it. If you don't set up row-level security on your report, the USERNAME() function will return the user ID. To understand what I mean, publish your report to Power BI and browse it.

The UserPrincipalName() function in DAX works similarly to the UserName() function, with the difference that it always returns the username (not the unique identifier). Basically, UserPrincipalName() is a better function for testing, but it works the same in a production environment. Now you'll set up row-level security and assign users to it to see how it works. See Figure 43-22.

Figure 43-22. *Setting up row-level security and assigning users*

Row-Level Security in the Power BI Desktop

This example uses the row-level security technique to filter each role based on the username with the DAX username() function. To create security, go to the Modeling tab and choose Manage Roles. Create a role and name it Sales Rep. Then define a filter on the Sales Rep table, as shown in Figure 43-23.

```
[Username] = USERPRINCIPALNAME()
```

Figure 43-23. *Filtering roles based on username*

This filter simply indicates that the logged-in user will only see their records in the whole dataset. As you might remember, the username field in the Sales Rep table is defined as the usernames of the Power BI accounts. The Transactions table is also related to this table and is based on Sales Rep ID. So filtering one table will affect others. As a result, this single-line filter will enable dynamic row-level security in the whole Power BI solution.

Assigning Users to Power BI Security

Now save and publish your solution to Power BI. In the Power BI Service, go to the Security setting of the dataset you just published (I called mine 01 Dynamic), as shown in Figure 43-24.

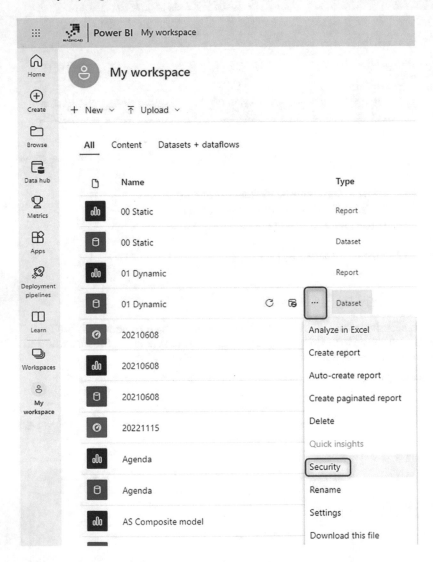

Figure 43-24. *Security setting for the published dataset*

In the Security tab, add all the users to the Sales Rep role (see Figure 43-25).

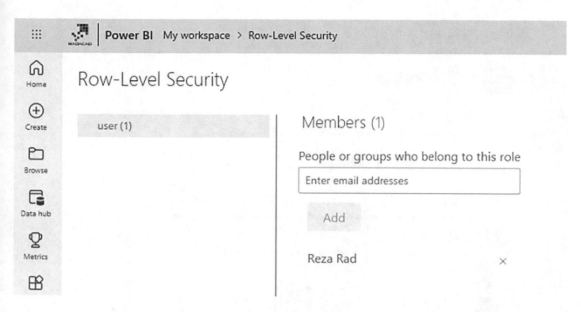

Figure 43-25. *Adding all the users to the Sales Rep role*

Adding a user here doesn't mean that they will see data in the report. Remember that this security is dynamic, which means that they will see their data rows only if the underlying dataset has a record for their username, and they will only see data rows related to their username, not others.

If you refresh the report in Power BI, you will see actual usernames, as shown in Figure 43-26.

Figure 43-26. *Actual usernames displayed after refreshing the report*

Sharing the Report or Dashboard

Other users should have access to the dashboard and report to see them. You can share the report using any method that gives the user a read-only view. In Figure 43-27, I used the individual report-sharing option.

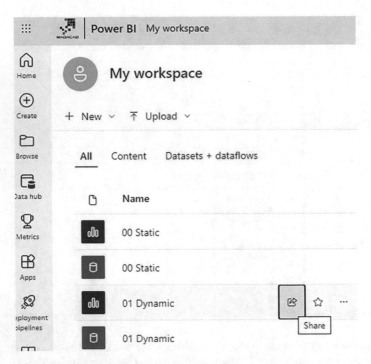

Figure 43-27. *Granting users access using the individual report-sharing option*

Now you can share it with other users (see Figure 43-28).

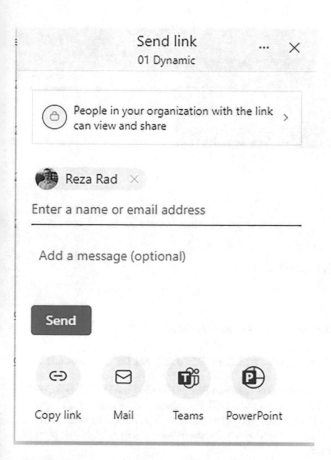

Figure 43-28. *Sharing the report with other users*

Testing the Security

If other users open the report, and if their usernames match one of the entries in the Sales Rep table, they will see their names and data rows in the report (see Figure 43-29).

Figure 43-29. *Users granted access can view data rows related to them in the report*

As you can see, my account only sees my transactions in the Sales Rep and Sales Transactions tables. Other users will have a different view.

You have seen how easy it is to use dynamic row-level security in Power BI using the DAX USERNAME() or UserPrincipalName() functions. Users can see their view of the world. However, you must ensure that your Power BI model's relationship is set up properly. Otherwise, people might see other table data when there is no relationship between their profile table and those tables. Dynamic row-level security is highly dependent on your data model, so keep your data model right.

To set up dynamic row-level security, you must set up your data model properly. Here are some details about that: radacad.com/what-do-you-need-to-implement-dynamic-row-level-security-in-power-bi.

Dynamic Row-Level Security Patterns

Dynamic row-level security can get complicated because the way that tables are related makes a big difference in how the filter propagates through the model. The following are examples of dynamic RLS patterns:

- Dynamic Row-level security with manager-level access in Power BI (radacad.com/dynamic-row-level-security-with-manager-level-access-in-power-bi)

- Dynamic row-level security with profiles and users in Power BI : Many-to-many relationship (radacad.com/dynamic-row-level-security-with-profiles-and-users-in-power-bi)

- Dynamic row-level security with organizational hierarchy Power BI (radacad.com/dynamic-row-level-security-with-organizational-hierarchy-power-bi)

- Dynamic row-level security in Power BI with organizational hierarchy and multiple positions in many-to-many relationship: Part 1 (radacad.com/dynamic-row-level-security-in-power-bi-with-organizational-hierarchy-and-multiple-positions-in-many-to-many-relationship-part-1)

- Dynamic row-level security in Power BI with organizational hierarchy and multiple positions in many-to-many relationship: Part 2 (radacad.com/dynamic-row-level-security-in-power-bi-with-organizational-hierarchy-and-multiple-positions-in-many-to-many-relationship-part-2)

For more information about row-level security, I suggest reading my book at www.amazon.com/Row-Level-Security-Power-BI-different/dp/1651119287.

Column-Level Security

What if you wanted to control access to a whole column? Say that the Sales team cannot see the Profit column but can see the Sales column in the same table. This is called column-level security.

Although column-level security is supported in Power BI, the implementation of that is not yet supported in the Power BI Desktop. This means it has to be done using another tool, called Tabular Editor, Visual Studio, or any other tool that can connect to the Power BI dataset and apply changes to it. Figure 43-30 shows an example of implementing it using the Tabular Editor.

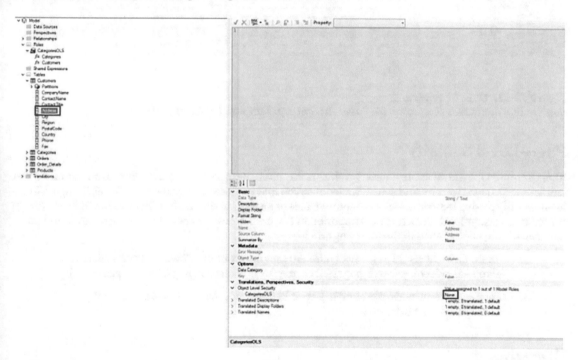

Figure 43-30. *Column-level security*
Source: learn.microsoft.com/en-us/power-bi/enterprise/service-admin-ols

Object-Level Security

What if you wanted access to a whole table to be controlled? Consider some users seeing the Sales table and others not. This is called object-level security, and similar to column-level security, it has to be implemented using another tool.

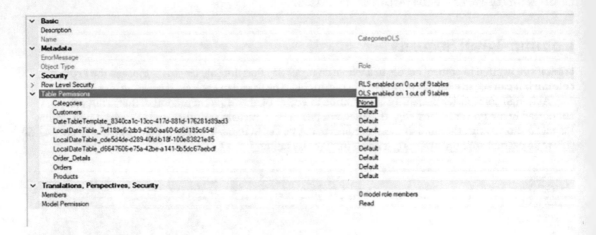

Figure 43-31. *Object-level security*
Source: *learn.microsoft.com/en-us/power-bi/enterprise/service-admin-ols*

Page-Level Security

RLS, CLS, and OLS are set at the dataset level. This means all the reports connected live to the shared dataset will follow the security rules and setup. Sometimes, you may need security at the visual level, though. Visual-level security means that some users see some visuals or pages, and others see others. At the time of writing this chapter, visual-level security is not supported in Power BI. However, there are a few workarounds you can use, which are explained in the following articles:

- Share different visual pages with different security groups in Power BI (radacad.com/
  share-different-visual-pages-with-different-security-groups-in-power-bi)

- Page-level security workaround in Power BI (radacad.com/page-level-security-
  workaround-in-power-bi)

Summary

There are different levels of data-related security in Power BI. Row-level security involves filtering rows of data for some users. Column-level security and object-level security are about controlling access to particular columns or tables, respectively. When data-level security is applied to a dataset, all the reports connected to it will follow its security rules. Row-level security can be static or dynamic. Dynamic row-level security is the preferred method for most situations because it is easier to maintain. However, it can come with some complexities of design. This chapter explained data-level security and row-level security.

■ ■ ■

CHAPTER 44

Power BI Helper

Microsoft has developed built-in tools for Power BI development—the Power BI Desktop, the Power BI Report Builder, the Power BI Gateway, and the Power BI Service for hosting the reports. Although these tools help you develop a Power BI solution, there are certain aspects of the process that can be further enhanced by using third-party tools. The Power BI community has a wide range of tools that can help with different aspects of Power BI. At RADACAD, we developed a free tool named Power BI Helper. This tool assists with many aspects of Power BI implementation, from the report's development to maintenance and performance tuning, to administration, documentation, and file cleanup. Knowing how to use this tool from the Power BI architecture perspective is helpful.

Documenting a Power BI File and Report

This section explains how to document everything in a Power BI file in a few clicks. The document output will contain all the DAX code (measures, columns, and tables) with the expressions, the tables with the Power Query scripts, information about visualization such as how many pages, bookmarks, and visuals are in each page, and even which tables and columns are used in visualization. All in just a few clicks.

Download and Install Power BI Helper for Free

If you haven't done so already, download and install Power BI Helper. It is a free application and it can help you do many useful things related to the development of the Power BI reports as well as the documentation process. You can download it from `powerbihelper.org/`.

Open Power BI Helper as an External Tool

After the install, while you have the Power BI file open in the Power BI Desktop, go to the External Tools tab and click Power BI Helper to open it, as shown in Figure 44-1. (Alternatively you can open it from Start and then from the programs on your Windows machine.)

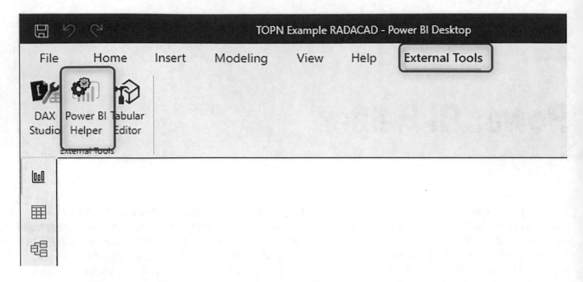

Figure 44-1. *Opening Power BI Helper from the Power BI Desktop*

Connect to Model

Once Power BI Helper is open, click Connect to Model, as shown in Figure 44-2. (Make sure that the Power BI file is already open in the Power BI Desktop.)

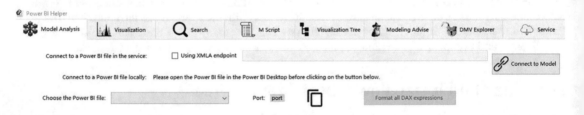

Figure 44-2. *Connecting to the model from Power BI Helper*

This option will detect all instances of Power BI files open in your desktop and will list them in a drop-down, as shown in Figure 44-3. You can choose the one you want to document.

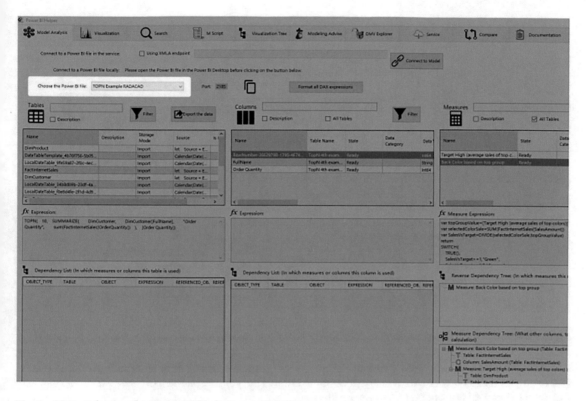

Figure 44-3. *Selecting the Power BI file in Power BI Helper*

If you have only one Power BI file open, the drop-down will show just that one. The rest of the page shows information about the model. It displays information such as the tables, columns, and measures with their expressions and expression trees.

Visualization Information

Power BI Helper should automatically find all the visualization information of the selected model. It shows you this information in the Visualization tab (see Figure 44-4).

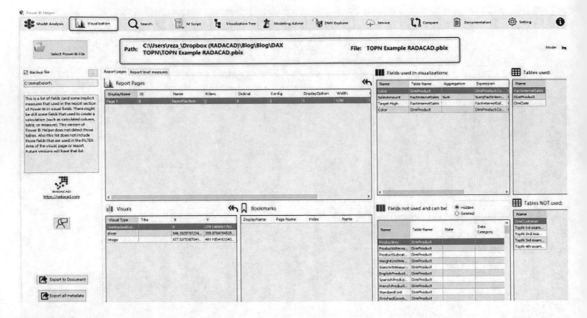

Figure 44-4. *Power BI Helper automatically shows the visualization information after selecting the model*

There are a few cases where Power BI Helper doesn't show the visualization information automatically (for example, if the Power BI file was just generated and has not yet been saved). In those cases, you can use the Select Power BI File option to choose the file.

Documentation

After that, you are just a click away from the documentation (this is in fact the second click after opening Power BI Helper). In the Documentation tab, click the Create Power BI document, as demonstrated in Figure 44-5.

Figure 44-5. *Generating the Power BI file*

Choose the location for the file (which is of HTML type), as shown in Figure 44-6.

Figure 44-6. *Saving the Power BI file documentation*

And that's it, you can now open the documentation.

What Is Included in the Documentation?

The documentation includes a large amount of information. Here is just some of the information available in the output document:

- Filename, path, and date of documentation

- All visualization pages and their details

- All visuals on every page with their details

- All the bookmarks and the pages the bookmarks are bound to

- All the columns and measures used in Power BI visuals

- All the tables used in Power BI visuals

- All the columns, tables, and measures not used in Power BI visuals (good source to clean up, although Power BI Helper can do that for you in a few clicks)

- All the tables in the model with their details. If they are calculated tables, their DAX expressions will be there too

- All the measures with their DAX expressions, and two tables of dependency tree and reverse dependency tree (useful for detecting where the measure is used, or what other fields/tables/measures used in the expression of this measure)

- All the relationships and their details

- All the roles (defined for row-level security) and their expressions

- Report-level measures if there are any

Configurations

As you have seen, creating the documentation is easy. If you want to configure the output document, you can do that from the Documentation tab, in two main sections—Style and Options.

Configure the Style of the Documentation

The Style configuration (see Figure 44-7) determines the fonts, colors, size of tables, headings, and other parts of the generated document.

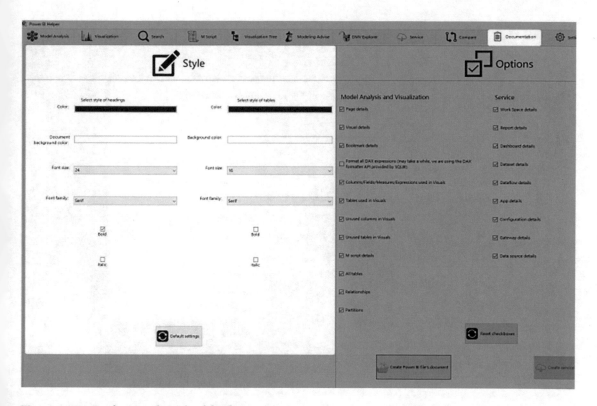

Figure 44-7. *Configuring the style of the documentation*

Sections and Information to Document

You can choose what information you want to document from the Power BI files. I recommend keeping them all selected for the full documentation, as shown in Figure 44-8.

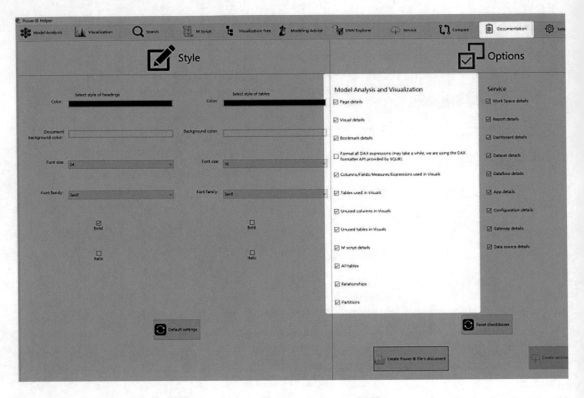

Figure 44-8. Choosing the information to document from a Power BI file

You can format all the DAX expressions before documentation, and this option uses the beautiful DAX formatter service from our friends at SQLBI (see www.sqlbi.com). If you use it, remember that every measure's expression will be sent to an API and the result of that will come back, so if you have too many DAX expressions, this will slow down the documentation process.

Exporting the Data in a Power BI Table

If you want to export the data in a Power BI table, you have options such as copy and paste, or you can put it in a visual and export it. However, there is an easier way. You can use Power BI Helper to export the table in a few clicks. The following sections explain how it is possible. First, open Power BI Helper from the Power BI Desktop.

Connect to Model

Once Power BI Helper is open, click Connect to Model. (Make sure that the Power BI file is already open in the Power BI Desktop.)

This option will detect all the Power BI files open on the desktop and will list them in a drop-down. You can choose the one you want to document (see Figure 44-9).

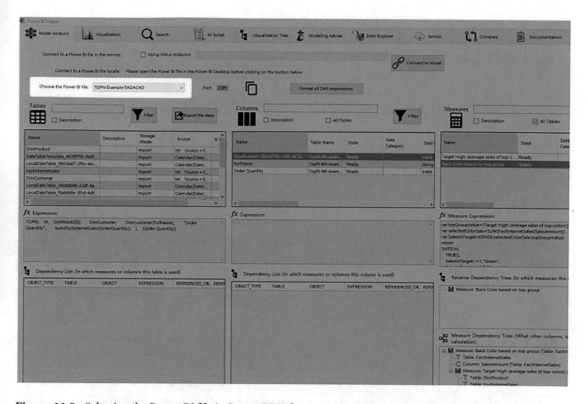

Figure 44-9. *Selecting the Power BI file in Power BI Helper*

If you have only one Power BI file open, the drop-down will show just that one. The rest of the page shows information about the model. It lists information such as the tables, columns, and measures with their expressions and expression trees.

Export the Data

In the same Model Analysis tab, select any table you want from the list of tables, and then click Export the Data, as shown in Figure 44-10.

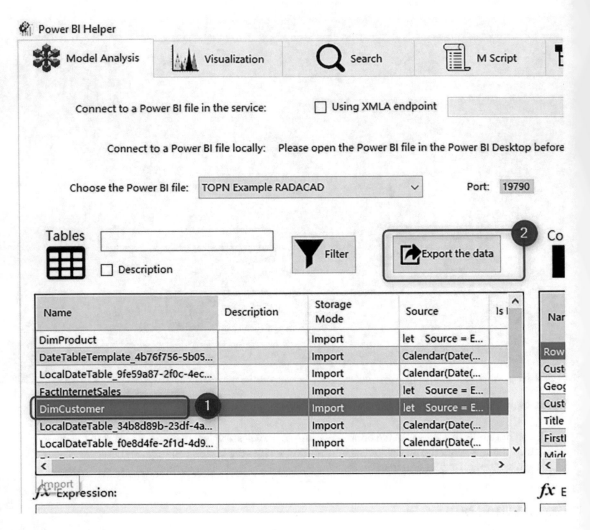

Figure 44-10. *Exporting data from a Power BI table*

This will export the data as a CSV file to the location you choose, as illustrated in Figure 44-11.

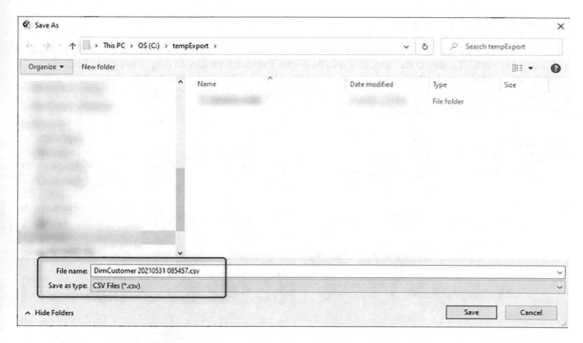

Figure 44-11. *Exporting table data as a CSV file*

Figure 44-12 shows example CSV output.

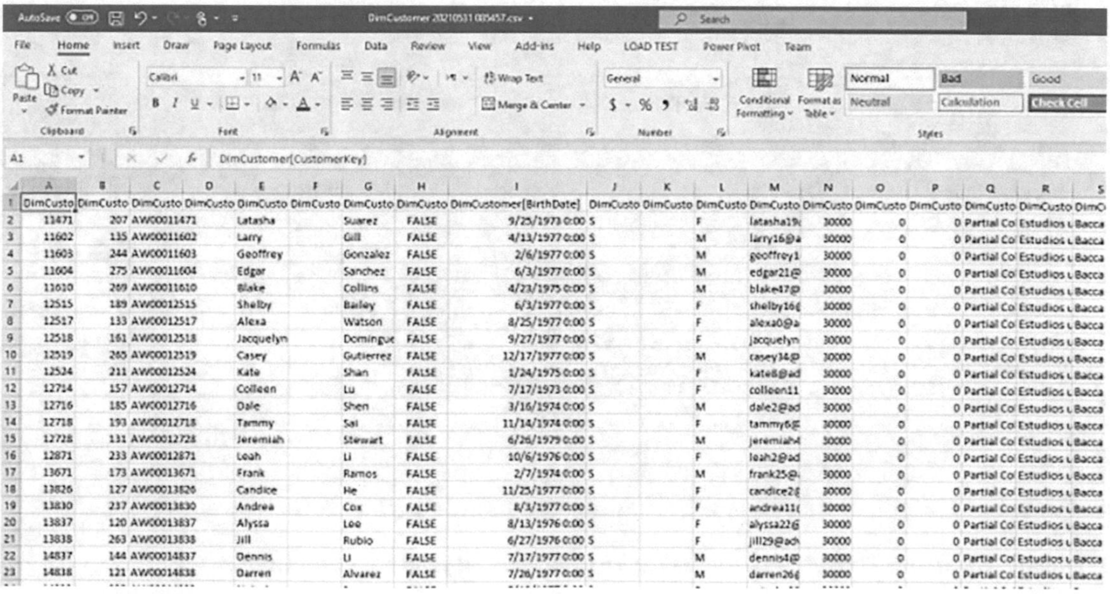

Figure 44-12. *A Power BI table exported to a CSV file*

Any Size, Any Table Type

When you use this method, you don't get any of the hassles you get with copy and paste. It's all very simple and easy to export. The size of the data in the table doesn't matter (it will take longer of course for bigger tables). Power BI Helper exports data of any size and works with DAX calculated tables, Power Query generated tables, and even automatically generated hidden tables by Power BI such as the default date tables. You can export them all. See Figure 44-13.

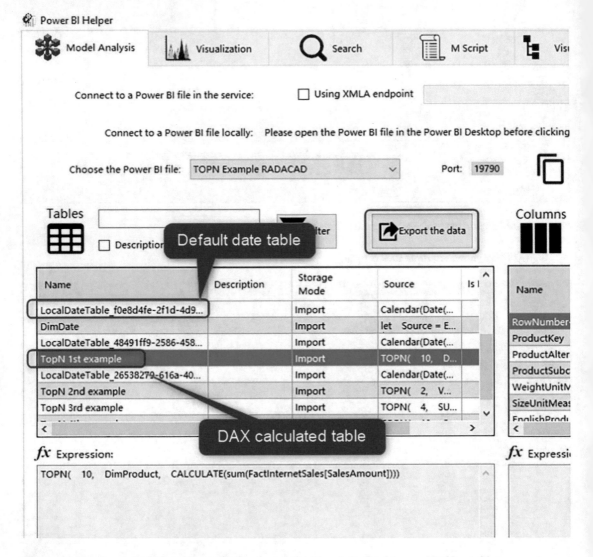

Figure 44-13. *Power BI Helper exports DAX calculated tables, default tables, and hidden tables*

Consider Using Analyze in Excel

Before I leave you to use this feature, I want to mention something. If the purpose of exporting the data is to analyze it further in Excel, then I strongly suggest you use Analyze in Excel instead of Export. Read the chapter about Analyze in Excel in this book to learn more about it.

Reducing the Size of Power BI File

One of the performance considerations of Power BI files is reducing the size as much as possible. This helps with development speed, because smaller files load faster in the Power BI Desktop. One way to reduce the size significantly is to determine which columns are consuming the most size and remove them. This section explains how you can easily do that using Power BI Helper.

Once Power BI Helper is open, click Connect to Model. (Make sure that the Power BI file is already open in the Power BI Desktop.)

This option will detect all the instances of Power BI files open in the desktop and will list them in a drop-down. Choose the one you want to review (see Figure 44-14).

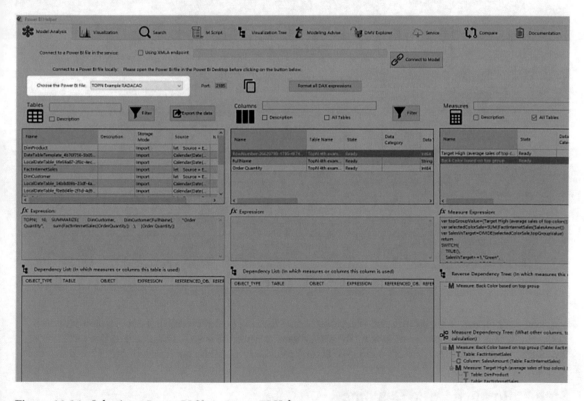

Figure 44-14. *Selecting a Power BI file in Power BI Helper*

If you have only one Power BI file open, the drop-down will show just that one. The rest of the page shows information about the model. It includes information such as the tables, columns, and measures with their expressions and expression trees.

Steps to Reduce File Size

My sample Power BI file is 72MB, as shown in Figure 44-15. I want to determine which columns are consuming the most space in this model.

Name	Date modified	Type	Size
Model.pbix	6/2/2021 8:48 AM	Microsoft.Microso...	73,230 KB

Figure 44-15. Power BI file size before tuning

When I open Power BI Helper and connect to that model, from the Modeling Advise tab, I can see how big each column is when it is in the Power BI model (see Figure 44-16).

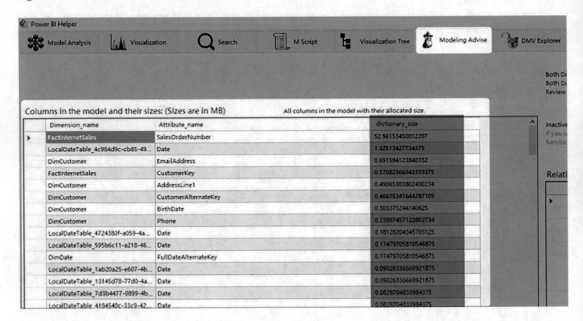

Figure 44-16. Checking the memory space consumed for each column in a Power BI file

The `dictionary_size` column is in megabytes, and it is the size of the column when expanded in memory. This might not be necessarily the size of the file when it's stored. For example, the `SalesOrderNumber` column doesn't use 52MB of the 72MB size of the file, but it is definitely a big part of it.

Step 1: Remove Large Columns

Once you identify columns that are using lots of space and you know you don't need them, you can go to the file in the Power BI Desktop and remove them, as demonstrated in Figure 44-17.

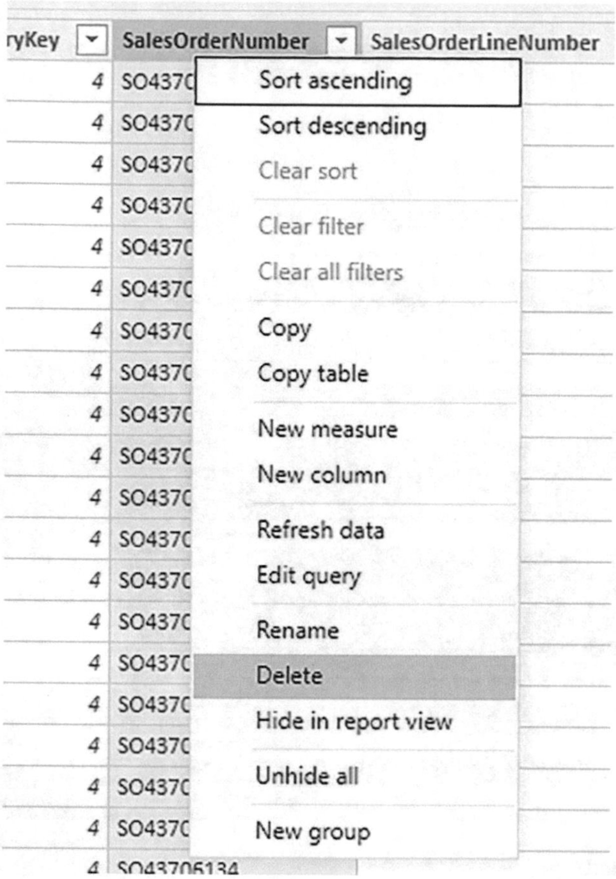

ryKey ▼	SalesOrderNumber ▼	SalesOrderLineNumber
4	SO4370	Sort ascending
4	SO4370	Sort descending
4	SO4370	Clear sort
4	SO4370	
4	SO4370	Clear filter
4	SO4370	Clear all filters
4	SO4370	Copy
4	SO4370	Copy table
4	SO4370	New measure
4	SO4370	New column
4	SO4370	
4	SO4370	Refresh data
4	SO4370	Edit query
4	SO4370	Rename
4	SO4370	Delete
4	SO4370	Hide in report view
4	SO4370	
4	SO4370	Unhide all
4	SO4370	New group
4	SO43705134	

Figure 44-17. Removing columns that are consuming a lot of space and are not useful for analysis

Step 2: Turning Off the Auto Date/Time

In the Modeling Advise report, you can also see evidence of having a default date table in Power BI (see Figure 44-18).

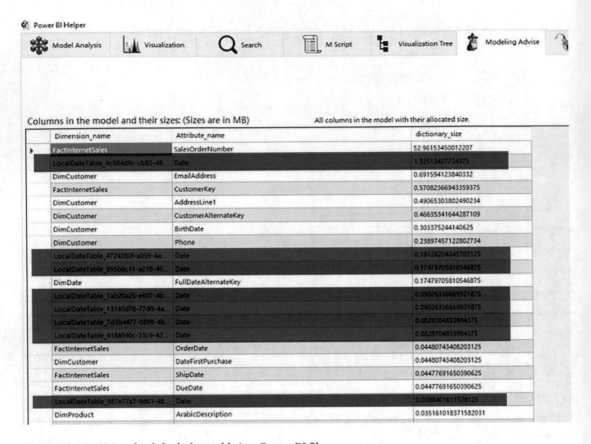

Figure 44-18. Using the default date table in a Power BI file

The default date table can be helpful. However, if you have too many date fields in your data model, and the range of dates is very wide, the ideal is to have a custom date table and disable the default date tables. Read my article at radacad.com/power-bi-date-dimension-default-or-custom-is-it-confusing to understand why.

You can go to the Power BI Desktop and choose File ➤ Options, Options. Uncheck the Auto Date/Time setting under Time Intelligence, as shown in Figure 44-19.

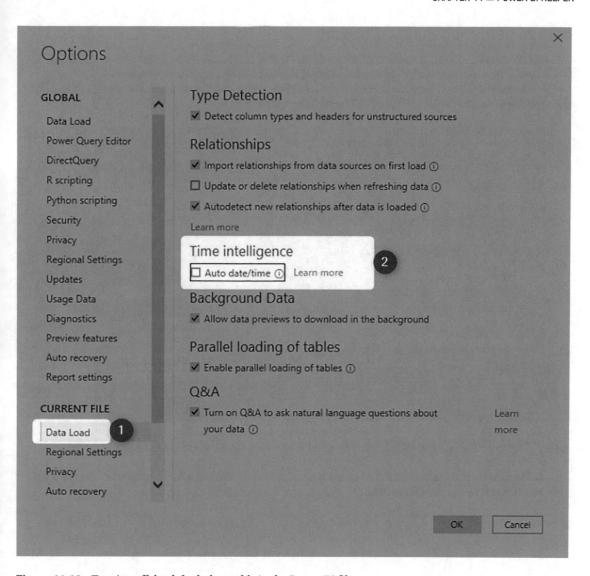

Figure 44-19. *Turning off the default date table in the Power BI file*

After making these changes and saving the file, the model size is reduced by 30 percent, as you can see in Figure 44-20.

🔲 Model.pbix	6/2/2021 8:48 AM	Microsoft.Microso...	73,230 KB
☐🔲 Model after change.pbix	6/2/2021 9:36 AM	Microsoft.Microso...	49,873 KB

Figure 44-20. *Power BI file size is reduced more than 30 percent after tuning*

Step 3: Removing Unused Columns

In a lot of Power BI reports, it might not be easy to determine which columns are not used in the file. You would have to consider visualizations, relationships, filters, and even in other calculations.

Power BI Helper can help you identify which columns are not used anywhere. You can check that by going to the Visualization tab in Power BI Helper (see Figure 44-21).

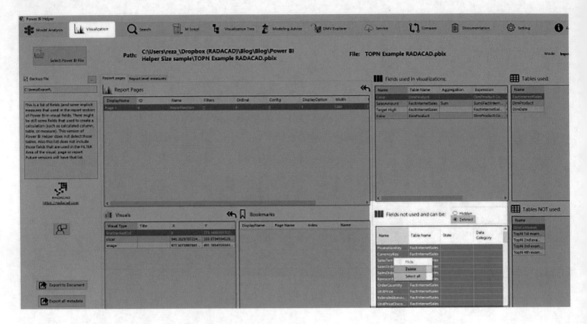

Figure 44-21. *Deleting the columns not used in visualizations or in other calculations*

This option simply deletes all the columns that are not needed. Figure 44-22 shows that the file was reduced in size by more than 80 percent.

Model after change.pbix	6/2/2021 9:52 AM	Microsoft.Microso...	49,079 KB
TOPN Example RADACAD.pbix	5/27/2021 11:34 AM	Microsoft.Microso...	2,543 KB
TOPN Example RADACAD after chang...	6/2/2021 9:55 AM	Microsoft.Microso...	656 KB

Figure 44-22. *Power BI file size reduced by more than 80 percent*

Documenting Power BI Tenant Objects

Previously I explained how you can document a single Power BI file. Another very common documentation requirement is to determine which objects and workspaces exist in the Power BI tenant and document them all. You might even want to download all the PBIX files from the service and keep them for versioning purposes. This section explains how you can do that in just a few clicks.

Service Tenant Settings in Power BI Helper

To use any of the Power BI Service features in Power BI Helper, you need to register Power BI Helper as an app under your tenant, which is explained next.

■ **Note**   Power BI Helper does *not* store any information from your tenant. The list of workspaces, datasets, dashboards, reports, dataflows, users—everything—is populated at runtime in the application. Nothing is stored on our servers or databases—not even your username, password, or application ID.

Register the App

Go to this URL in a web browser: dev.powerbi.com/apps. Sign in using your Power BI account (see Figure 44-23).

Figure 44-23. *Signing in to Power BI*

After logging in, go to the next step (see Figure 44-24).

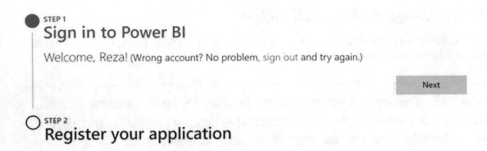

Figure 44-24. *Registering your application*

Apply the settings shown in Figure 44-25 in the Register Your Application dialog box.

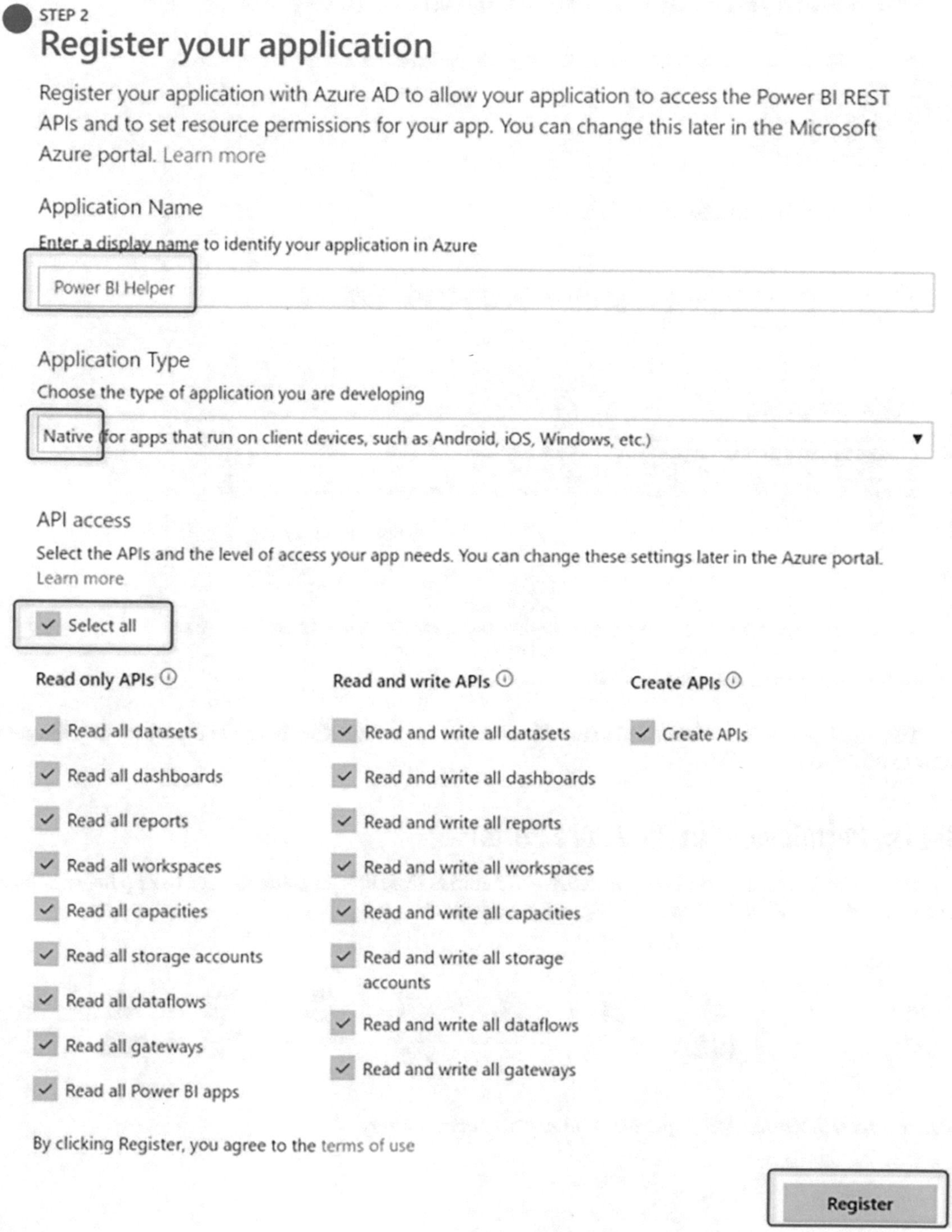

STEP 2
Register your application

Register your application with Azure AD to allow your application to access the Power BI REST APIs and to set resource permissions for your app. You can change this later in the Microsoft Azure portal. Learn more

Application Name

Enter a display name to identify your application in Azure

> Power BI Helper

Application Type

Choose the type of application you are developing

> Native (for apps that run on client devices, such as Android, iOS, Windows, etc.)   ▼

API access

Select the APIs and the level of access your app needs. You can change these settings later in the Azure portal. Learn more

☑ Select all

Read only APIs ⓘ

- ☑ Read all datasets
- ☑ Read all dashboards
- ☑ Read all reports
- ☑ Read all workspaces
- ☑ Read all capacities
- ☑ Read all storage accounts
- ☑ Read all dataflows
- ☑ Read all gateways
- ☑ Read all Power BI apps

Read and write APIs ⓘ

- ☑ Read and write all datasets
- ☑ Read and write all dashboards
- ☑ Read and write all reports
- ☑ Read and write all workspaces
- ☑ Read and write all capacities
- ☑ Read and write all storage accounts
- ☑ Read and write all dataflows
- ☑ Read and write all gateways

Create APIs ⓘ

- ☑ Create APIs

By clicking Register, you agree to the terms of use

Register

Figure 44-25. *Entering the desired settings in the Register Your Application dialog box*

After successfully registering the app, copy the Application ID (see Figure 44-26).

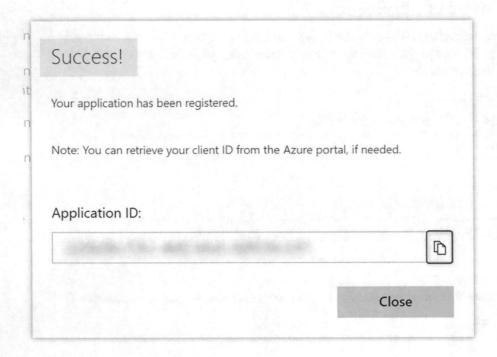

Success!

Your application has been registered.

Note: You can retrieve your client ID from the Azure portal, if needed.

Application ID:

Close

Figure 44-26. *Copying the application ID*

This Application ID will be added in the About tab of Power BI Helper later, but there are still a few more steps to do first.

Set Up Permissions in the Azure Portal

Log in to Azure Portal at `portal.azure.com`. Go to Azure Active Directory, and then go to App Registrations (see Figure 44-27). Find the Power BI Helper app and click it.

Azure services

Figure 44-27. *Locating App Registrations in Azure Active Directory*

Select the app, as shown in Figure 44-28, and continue.

Figure 44-28. *Selecting the Power BI Helper app*

Choose Request API Permissions and select Power BI Service, as shown in Figure 44-29.

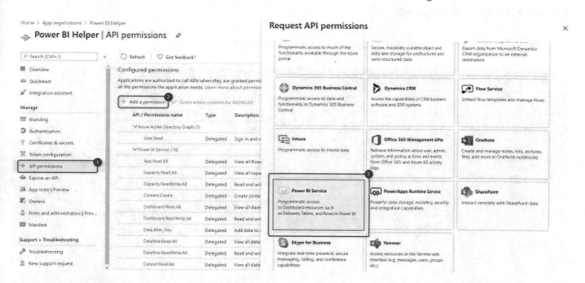

Figure 44-29. *Selecting Request API permissions*

Next, add all the requests, as shown in Figure 44-30.

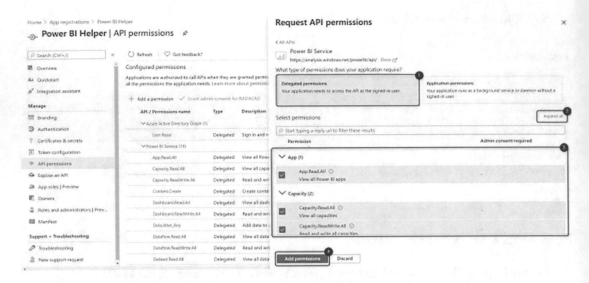

Figure 44-30. *Adding all requests*

Then choose Grant Admin Consent, as shown in Figure 44-31.

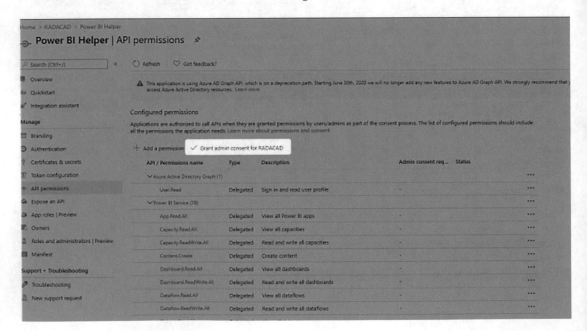

Figure 44-31. *Grant admin consent*

Go to authentication and enable LiveSDK, as shown in Figure 44-32.

Figure 44-32. *Enabling LiveSDK*

Add the Application ID to Power BI Helper

The last step is to add the Application ID to the Setting tab of Power BI Helper and then save it (see Figure 44-33).

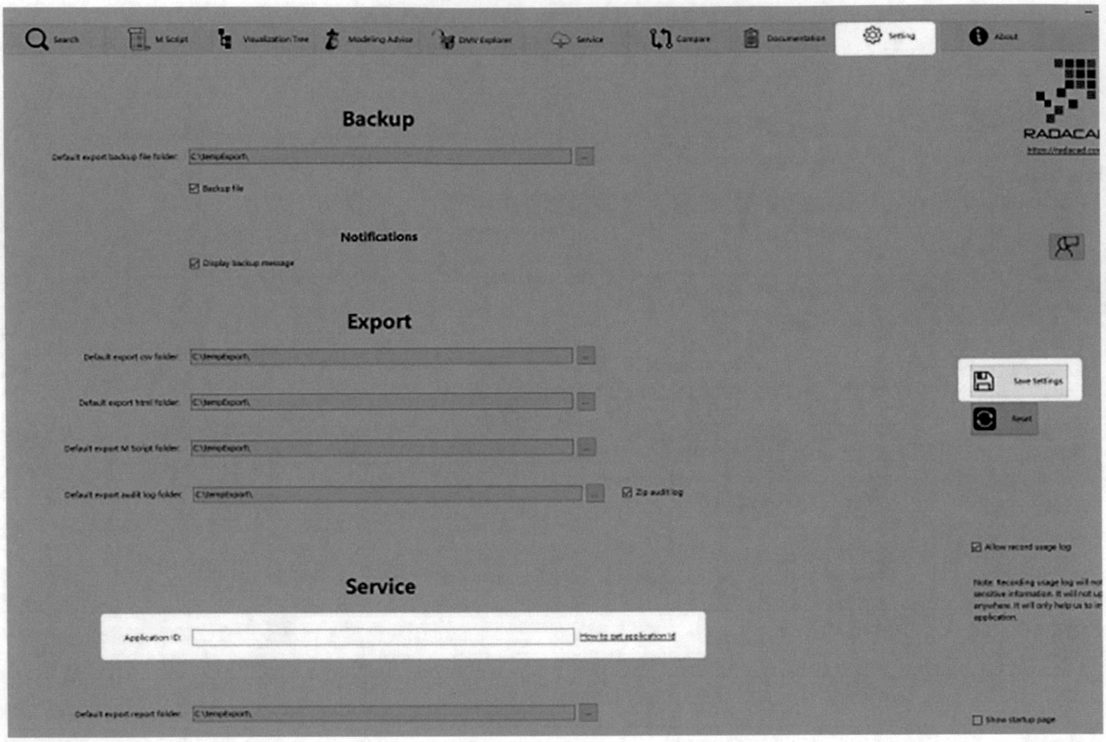

Figure 44-33. Adding the ApplicationID to the Setting tab of Power BI Helper

You can now use Power BI Helper's Service tab.

Scan Service Objects

After you register the app (this has to be done only once), you can log in with your Power BI account. As Figure 44-34 shows, go to the Service tab in Power BI Helper and log in. You should use the Power BI account that contains the objects you want to be document. (Power BI Helper can only see the objects that this Power BI account has access to. If you want all the content on the service, try the Power BI Administrator account.)

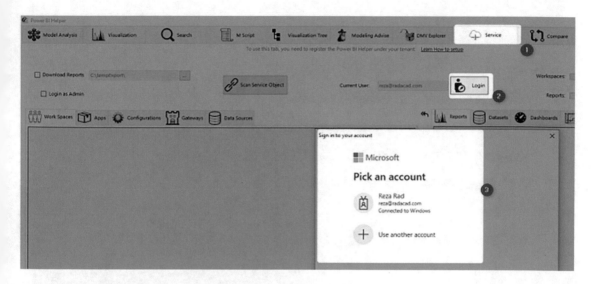

Figure 44-34. *Logging in to the service from Power BI Helper*

After logging in, you can choose if you want to download reports (and choose the folder to do so). You also need to check the box that says Login as Admin if you are using the Power BI Administrator account to log in. After that, you can choose Scan Service Object (see Figure 44-35).

Figure 44-35. *Service settings for Power BI Helper*

Scanning service objects might take some time; it depends on your Internet connection, whether you selected the Download Reports option, and the number of objects (reports, datasets, dataflows, and workspaces) you have on the Power BI tenant. After the process is done, you should see the objects listed in Power BI Helper.

In this tab of Power BI Helper, you can perform many operations on the objects. However, this chapter focuses on documentation. You can simply click Export to Document, or go to the Documentation tab and click Create Service Documentation (see Figure 44-36).

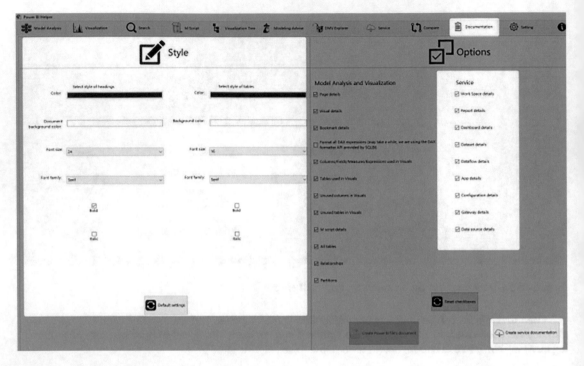

Figure 44-36. *Creating Power BI Service documentation*

Objects that are documented (at the time this chapter was written) include the following:

- Lists of workspaces
- Lists of reports
- Lists of dashboards
- Lists of datasets
- Lists of dataflows
- Lists of apps
- Configuration details
- Lists of gateways
- Lists of data sources

Configuring the Documentation's Output

As you have seen, creating the documentation takes just a few clicks. If you want to configure the output document, you can do that from the Documentation tab, in two main sections. The first is the Style section.

Configuring the Documentation's Style

As noted earlier in the chapter, the Style configuration determines the fonts, colors, size of tables, headings, and other parts of the generated document (see Figure 44-37).

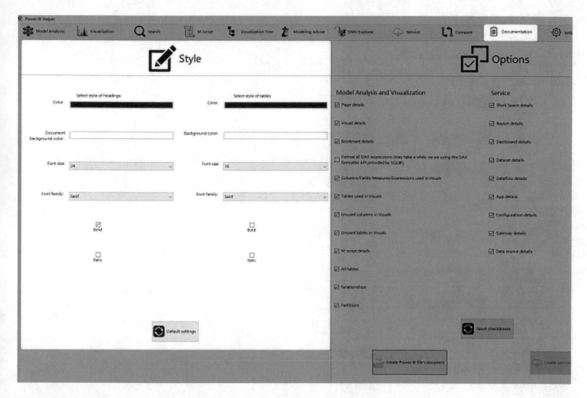

Figure 44-37. *Configuring the style of the documentation*

Sections and Information to Document

You can choose what information you want to document from the Power BI tenant (see Figure 44-38). I recommend keeping them all selected for the full documentation.

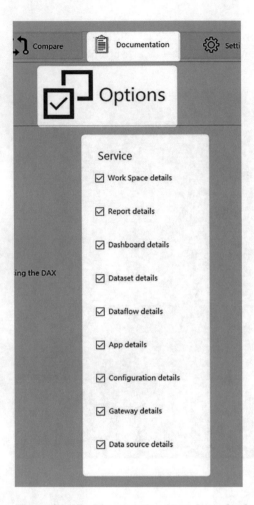

Figure 44-38. *Choosing the objects list to be documented from the Power BI Service*

Export the Information as CSV Files (Export Metadata)

I find it helpful to export this information as a CSV file for each object type. Power BI Helper can do that for you, simply by clicking the Export Metadata option (see Figure 44-39).

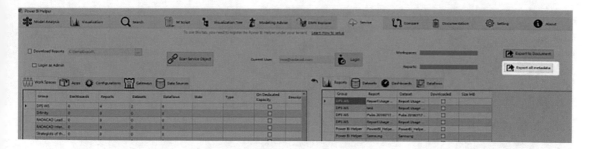

Figure 44-39. *Exporting a Power BI Service objects list as a CSV file*

Figure 44-40 illustrates the exported result.

Apps service export 20210604 104850.csv	6/4/2021 10:48 AM	Microsoft Excel C...	2 KB
Configurations service export 20210604 104850.csv	6/4/2021 10:48 AM	Microsoft Excel C...	1 KB
Dashboards service export 20210604 104850.csv	6/4/2021 10:48 AM	Microsoft Excel C...	1 KB
Dataflows service export 20210604 104850.csv	6/4/2021 10:48 AM	Microsoft Excel C...	8 KB
Datasets service export 20210604 104850.csv	6/4/2021 10:48 AM	Microsoft Excel C...	75 KB
DataSources service export 20210604 104850.csv	6/4/2021 10:48 AM	Microsoft Excel C...	6 KB
Gateways service export 20210604 104850.csv	6/4/2021 10:48 AM	Microsoft Excel C...	2 KB
Reports service export 20210604 104850.csv	6/4/2021 10:48 AM	Microsoft Excel C...	93 KB
WorkSpaces service export 20210604 104850.csv	6/4/2021 10:48 AM	Microsoft Excel C...	3 KB

Figure 44-40. *Exporting the Power BI Service metadata (document) as CSV files*

Exporting the Power BI Audit Log

This can be done in a few simple steps, without the need for code. Power BI-related activity can be often useful for determining the behavior of the users and for enhancing the adoption of Power BI. Getting the audit log isn't simple though. This section shows you an easy way (with no scripting required) to export the audit log of Power BI.

What Is the Power BI Audit Log?

The Audit log of Power BI lists all the Power BI-related activities done under your organization's tenant. You can get heaps of information from report usage, such as who opened the reports or dashboards, who shared them, who published them, who accessed them using Analyze in Excel, and much more. The Power BI Audit log includes (but is not limited to) a log of operations.

Difficulties Exporting the Audit Log

The Power BI Administrator can access the audit log in two ways. One is by going to the Office 365 admin center and exporting the log from there (see Figure 44-41).

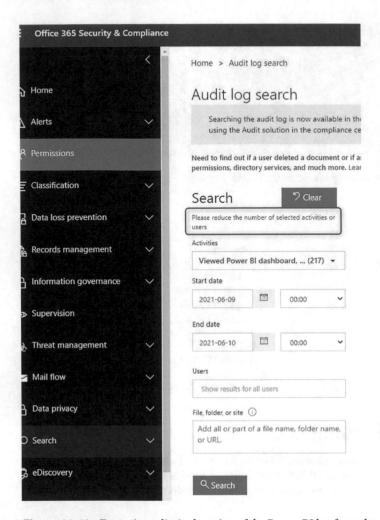

Figure 44-41. *Exporting a limited version of the Power BI log from the admin center of Office 365*

This method, however, only exports a limited result. As you see in Figure 44-41, you'll often get a message saying, "Please reduce the number of selected activities or users."

Another method is to use the PowerShell commands and scripts to export the log. The following section explains how to do this.

A Simple Way to Export the Audit Log Without Limitations

You don't need to write or run PowerShell scripts to export the audit log. All you need is the Power BI Helper tool.

Logging In

After you register the app, you can log in with your Power BI account. Go to the Service tab in Power BI Helper and log in. You should use the Power BI account that has either Power BI Administrator or Office 365 Administrator access to export the audit logs. You may also need to check the Login as Admin box (see Figure 44-42).

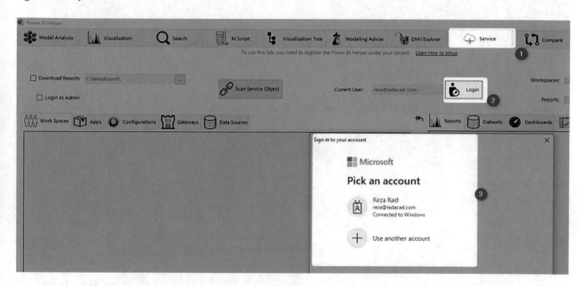

Figure 44-42. *Logging in to the service from Power BI Helper*

After logging in, go to the Export Audit Log section of the Service tab. From there, you can set the configuration of the period, set the export location, determine if you want the file to be zipped or not, and then export the log (see Figure 44-43).

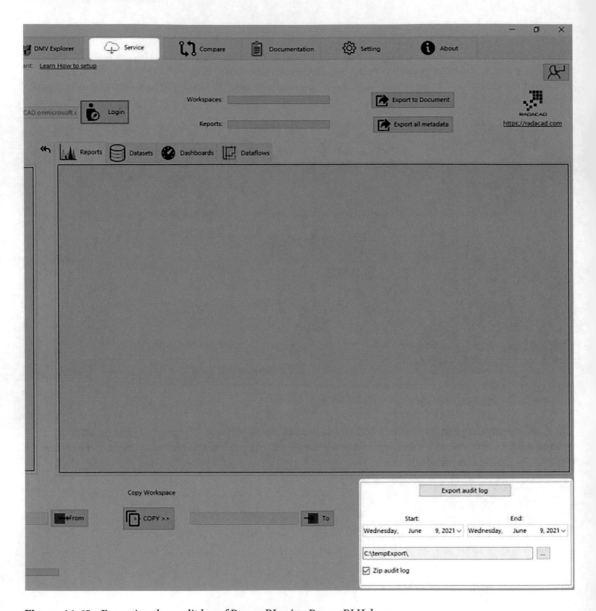

Figure 44-43. *Exporting the audit log of Power BI using Power BI Helper*

The settings for the export audit log are shown in Figure 44-44.

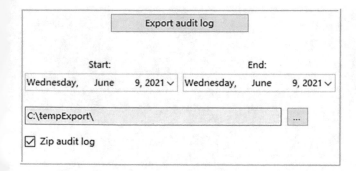

Figure 44-44. Exporting audit log settings in Power BI Helper

As shown in Figure 44-45, the audit log will be exported as CSV files (which can be zipped).

Name	Type	Compressed size	Password ...	Size	Ratio	Date modified
AuditLog 2021-05-10.csv	Microsoft Excel Comma S...	1 KB	No	2 KB	60%	6/9/2021 11:44 AM
AuditLog 2021-05-11.csv	Microsoft Excel Comma S...	2 KB	No	5 KB	77%	6/9/2021 11:44 AM
AuditLog 2021-05-12.csv	Microsoft Excel Comma S...	1 KB	No	2 KB	60%	6/9/2021 11:44 AM
AuditLog 2021-05-13.csv	Microsoft Excel Comma S...	1 KB	No	1 KB	42%	6/9/2021 11:44 AM
AuditLog 2021-05-14.csv	Microsoft Excel Comma S...	1 KB	No	1 KB	41%	6/9/2021 11:44 AM
AuditLog 2021-05-15.csv	Microsoft Excel Comma S...	1 KB	No	2 KB	60%	6/9/2021 11:44 AM
AuditLog 2021-05-16.csv	Microsoft Excel Comma S...	1 KB	No	2 KB	60%	6/9/2021 11:44 AM
AuditLog 2021-05-17.csv	Microsoft Excel Comma S...	1 KB	No	2 KB	60%	6/9/2021 11:44 AM
AuditLog 2021-05-18.csv	Microsoft Excel Comma S...	1 KB	No	1 KB	41%	6/9/2021 11:44 AM

Figure 44-45. Sample audit log exported as CSV files

Power BI File Cleanup in a Few Steps

If you have used a Power BI file for a while, you might have noticed that the model gets bigger and bigger. The file size increases and the number of pages, tables, fields also increase. You might get to a point where it becomes hard to determine which tables and fields are useful and which are not. You have to search for something to find it, and you have many duplicate calculations. This section explains how you can clean up the Power BI file by removing unused fields and measures simply and quickly.

Once Power BI Helper is open, click Connect to Model (Make sure that the Power BI file is already open in the Power BI Desktop.) Then, connect to the model from Power BI Helper.

This option will detect all the instances of Power BI files open in the desktop and will list them in a drop-down. Choose the one you want (see Figure 44-46).

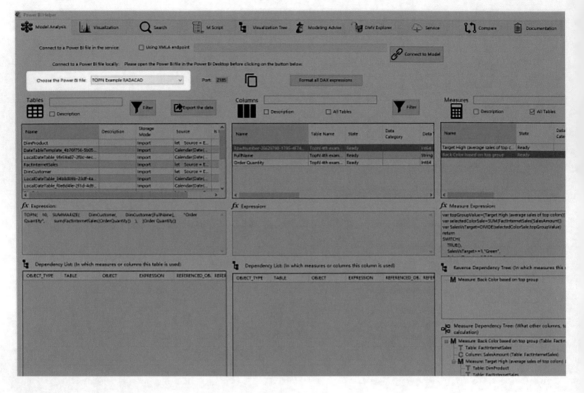

Figure 44-46. *Selecting the Power BI file in Power BI Helper*

If you have only one Power BI file open, the drop-down will show just that one. The rest of the page shows information about the model. It lists information such as the tables, columns, and measures with their expressions and expression trees.

Visualization Information

Power BI Helper automatically finds all the visualization information of the selected model and shows you the information in the Visualization tab (see Figure 44-47).

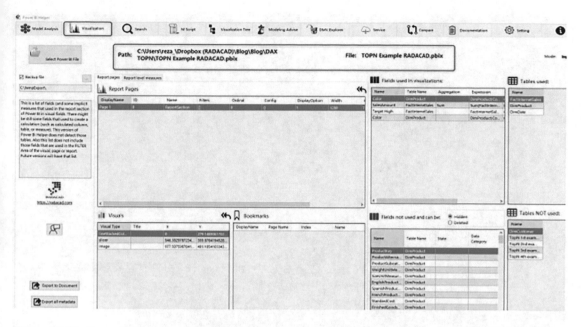

Figure 44-47. *Power BI Helper automatically shows the visualization information after selecting the model*

There are a few cases where Power BI Helper doesn't show the visualization information automatically (for example, if the Power BI file was just generated and has not yet been saved). In those cases, you can use the Select Power BI File option to choose the file.

Removing Unused Fields

If you find a field that's not used in any visual, filter, or other calculations, it is safe to remove this field. Power BI Helper can identify these fields even when they are DAX calculated columns or measures. Using the dependency tree of the measure, Power BI Helper will identify if the field is used in another calculation that is used in a visual or filter. You can see the fields that can be removed in Figure 44-48.

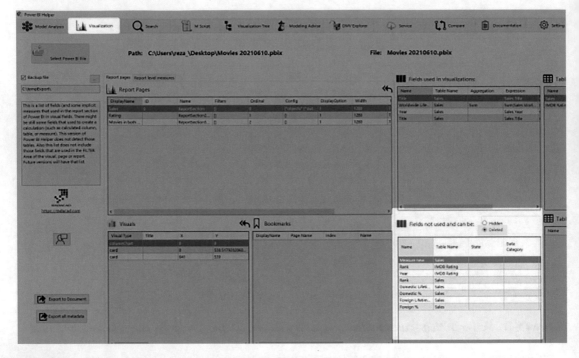

Figure 44-48. *Unused fields in Power BI detected using Power BI Helper*

As you can see in Figure 44-48's list, there is also a measure that is not used, and no other measures use this measure in any visuals or filters.

Figure 44-49 shows how you can remove them.

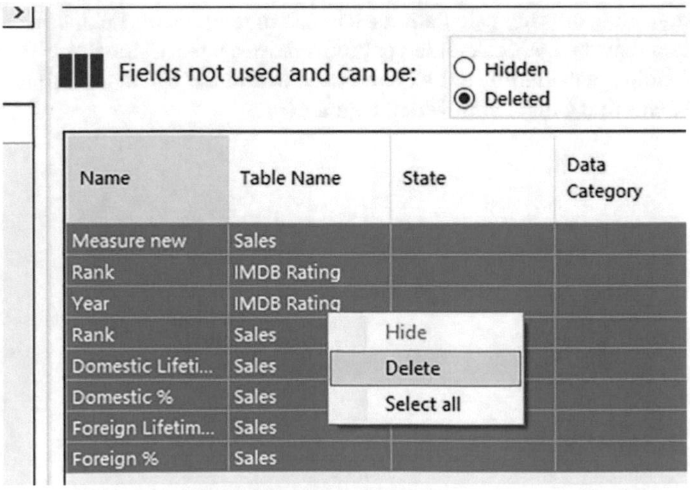

Figure 44-49. *Deleting unused fields in Power BI*

You can delete all the fields by using Select All and then Delete. Or you can delete them one by one.

Hiding Technical Fields

Technical fields are necessary for the model and cannot be deleted, but they are not used directly in visualizations. Examples of these fields include:

- Fields used in relationships
- Fields used to sort other columns
- Fields used to create a hierarchy

Technical columns are best hidden. You can see the fields to hide in Figure 44-50.

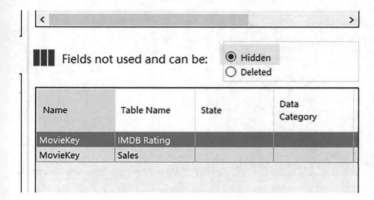

Figure 44-50. *Detecting fields in Power BI that can be hidden from the report view*

In this example, the fields are used in a relationship (that is why they don't appear in the list to be deleted). Hiding them is recommended if they are not used directly in visuals in Power BI.

Figure 44-51 shows how you can hide them.

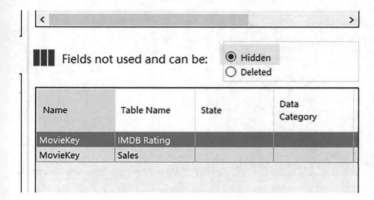

Figure 44-51. *Hiding Power BI fields in a few clicks using Power BI Helper*

Sample Output

The output will be saved in the same Power BI file that is open on the Power BI Desktop. You can see the result of the sample in Figure 44-52.

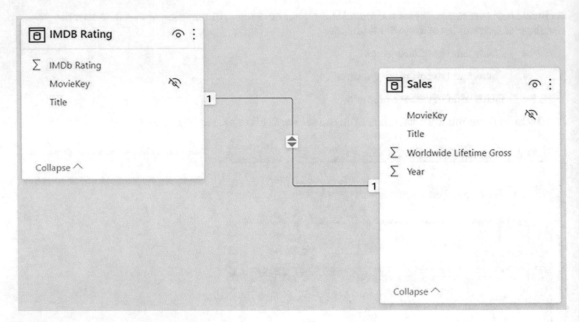

Figure 44-52. *Cleaned Power BI file*

Backup File

Power BI Helper, by default, keeps a version of the file before the changes are saved as a backup. This backup can be helpful if unwanted behavior is detected (see Figure 44-53).

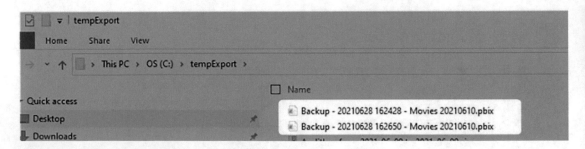

Figure 44-53. *Auto backup of Power BI file before changes*

You can customize the backup file's settings from the Setting tab of Power BI Helper (see Figure 44-54).

Figure 44-54. *Backup file settings in Power BI Helper*

Sample Scenarios

- If a field is directly used in a visual, it will not be removed or hidden

- If a measure is not used in visuals or other measures, it will be removed

- If a measure is not used directly in a visual, it will be hidden

Not Supported at Present

Fields and measures that are used across multiple files are not included in these actions (such as if another Power BI file uses the fields from this Power BI file).

Summary

For this last chapter of this book, I wanted to leave you with a useful tool, and that is why I included Power BI Helper. Power BI Helper is a free-to-use tool that helps with development, documentation, performance tuning, cleanup, and administration of your Power BI solution.

Index

Printed in the United States
by Baker & Taylor Publisher Services